THE GLOBALIZATION OF HEALTH CARE

The Globalization of Health Care

LEGAL AND ETHICAL ISSUES

Edited by I. Glenn Cohen

OXFORD
UNIVERSITY PRESS

OXFORD
UNIVERSITY PRESS

Oxford University Press is a department of the University of Oxford. It furthers the University's objective of excellence in research, scholarship, and education by publishing worldwide.

Oxford   New York
Auckland   Cape Town   Dar es Salaam   Hong Kong   Karachi   Kuala Lumpur   Madrid
Melbourne   Mexico City   Nairobi   New Delhi   Shanghai   Taipei   Toronto

With offices in
Argentina   Austria   Brazil   Chile   Czech Republic   France   Greece   Guatemala   Hungary
Italy   Japan   Poland   Portugal   Singapore   South Korea   Switzerland   Thailand
Turkey   Ukraine   Vietnam

Oxford is a registered trade mark of Oxford University Press in the UK and certain other countries.

Published in the United States of America by
Oxford University Press
198 Madison Avenue, New York, NY 10016

Library of Congress Cataloging-in-Publication Data
The globalization of health care : legal and ethical issues/edited by Glenn I. Cohen.
   p. cm.
   Includes bibliographical references and index.
   ISBN 978-0-19-991790-7 ((hardback) : alk. paper)
1. Medical care—Law and legislation. 2. Health services accessibility—Law and legislation.
3. Right to health—Moral and ethical aspects. 4. Health care reform. 5. Medical ethics.
I. Cohen, Glenn I.
K3601.G56 2013
344.04'1—dc23
                                                                                  2012022948

---

9 8 7 6 5 4 3 2 1

Printed in the United States of America on acid-free paper

Note to Readers
This publication is designed to provide accurate and authoritative information in regard to the subject matter covered. It is based upon sources believed to be accurate and reliable and is intended to be current as of the time it was written. It is sold with the understanding that the publisher is not engaged in rendering legal, accounting, or other professional services. If legal advice or other expert assistance is required, the services of a competent professional person should be sought. Also, to confirm that the information has not been affected or changed by recent developments, traditional legal research techniques should be used, including checking primary sources where appropriate.

(Based on the Declaration of Principles jointly adopted by a Committee of the American Bar Association and a Committee of Publishers and Associations.)

You may order this or any other Oxford University Press publication
by visiting the Oxford University Press website at www.oup.com

To Bert, Ginger, and Jon: Wherever you are on the globe, you are always close in my heart.

Contents

Acknowledgments

PUTTING THIS VOLUME together was a labor of love, and as in love the labor was shared. First and foremost, I would like to thank my students Katherine Kraschel and Allison Trzop who essentially acted as deputy editors, aiding me in substantively and technically editing half the book each. My assistant, Kaitlin Burroughs, helped with much of the administrative work that went into this volume. A larger number of research assistants aided me with the technical footnote editing of the chapters: Alex Anzalone, Joseph Brothers, Sean Driscoll, Mischa Feldstein, Sophie Kim, Keely O'Malley, Lisa Sullivan, and Beverly Vu. I thank Kathy Paras of the Harvard Law School Petrie-Flom Center for Health Law Policy, Biotechnology, and Bioethics and the members of the Harvard University Program on Ethics and Health for helping me organize the conference at Harvard Law School in May 2011 that prompted this book, as well as all the attendees and participants who helped shape its content. Finally, I am grateful to Harvard and the Petrie-Flom Center for their continued support of my work.

Introduction

*I. Glenn Cohen**

THE ERA OF health care globalization is upon us.

As the essays collected in this book show, that globalization has taken many forms with complex interactions: medical tourism[1]—the travel of patients from their home country to a foreign destination country in order to save on health care costs, receive coverage from their insurer, or access a service unavailable or illegal in their home country; medical migration—the "brain drain" of physicians and other health care practitioners, largely from the developing to the developed world; telemedicine—where the patients and providers stay put, but medical care is provided remotely; multi-regional clinical trials, where research on a promising drug or therapy is conducted in part in developing countries, even though the fruit of that research will in the short-term primarily benefit developed countries; the global intellectual property regime that both facilitates innovation and stymies access to drugs desperately needed in the world's poorest places; and the flow of tissues and information—for example the sharing of influenza vaccine strains during possible pandemics.

---

* Assistant Professor and Co-Director, Petrie-Flom Center for Health Law Policy, Biotechnology, and Bioethics, Harvard Law School. J.D., Harvard Law School. igcohen@law.harvard.edu.
[1] While I and many of the authors in this volume use the term "medical tourism" because it is the most common one being used, we do not intend to use the term pejoratively or suggest that the motivations of those engaging in the practice are frivolous in any way. The terms "medical travel" and "cross-border care" could just as easily be used, but we stick for the most part to the more common term.

The effects of this globalization of health care are massive, both in terms of profits to be made and of consequences for the lives of patients. To give but a few examples:

Although studies have come to widely different conclusions about the exact size of the current medical tourism trade, there is no doubt it is significant.[2] Offering one data point about just how significant the trade has become, Deloitte concluded that 750,000 U.S. patients traveled abroad in 2007 for inpatient and/or outpatient procedures, and predicted that the total number would rise to six million by 2010.[3] In one year alone, 952,000 California residents (roughly half of whom were Mexican immigrants) traveled to Mexico for medical care, dental care, or prescription drugs.[4] Looking more globally, in 2004, more than 150,000 foreigners sought medical treatment in India, and that number was projected to increase by 15 percent each year since then.[5] Also in 2004, Malaysian hospitals treated 130,000 foreign patients—a 25 percent rise from the previous year—and the most recent figures report that the country treated 578,403 foreign patients in 2011.[6] In 2005, Bumrungrad International Hospital in Bangkok, Thailand, alone saw 400,000 foreign patients.[7] The revenues generated by this trade are staggering: although these estimates are often contested, there have been claims that, in 2004, Cuba received $40 million from medical tourism, Malaysia $27.6 million, and Jordan $500 million; that medical tourism in India will generate $2.2 billion in revenues this year; and that Thailand projects it will earn $8 billion from medical tourism between 2010 and 2014.[8] This market is likely to expand significantly with the development of robust insurer-prompted medical tourism plans that each of four largest U.S.

---

[2] See, e.g., Nathan Cortez, *Embracing The New Geography of Health Care: A Novel Way to Cover Those Left out of Health Reform*, 84 S. Cal. L. Rev. 859, 878 (2011).

[3] By contrast, McKinsey & Company calculated in 2008 that only 5,000 to 10,000 U.S. patients per year were medical tourists. Tilman Ehrbeck et al., *Mapping the Market for Medical Travel*, McKinsey Q., May 2008, at 2, 3, 6. In part this discrepancy is due to undercounting by McKinsey because it excluded patients traveling in "contiguous geographies" such as from Canada to the United States or from the United States to Mexico. Cortez, *supra* note 2, at 878 n.119. That said, Deloitte has more recently downgraded its estimate to only 1.6 million U.S. medical tourists traveling per year in the foreseeable future. Tom Murphy, *Health Insurers Explore Savings in Overseas Care*, Associated Press, Aug. 23, 2009.

[4] Steven P. Wallace, Carolyn Mendez-Luck & Xóchitl Castañeda, *Heading South: Why Mexican Immigrants in California Seek Health Services in Mexico*, 47 Med. Care 662, 662 (2009) (using 2001 data).

[5] John Lancaster, *Surgeries, Side Trips for "Medical Tourists,"* Wash. Post, Oct. 21, 2004, at A1, *available at* http://www.washingtonpost.com/wp-dyn/articles/A49743-2004Oct20.html.

[6] Milica Z. Bookman & Karla K. Bookman, Medical Tourism in Developing Countries 3 (2007); Vasantha Ganesan, *Medical Tourism in the Pink of Health*, Bus. Times, Feb. 27, 2012, *available at* http://www.healthcareasia.org/2012/malaysia-medical-tourism-in-the-pink-of-health/.

[7] Arnold Milstein & Mark Smith, *America's New Refugees—Seeking Affordable Surgery Offshore*, 355 New Eng. J. Med. 1637, 1638 (2006).

[8] I. Glenn Cohen, *Protecting Patients with Passports: Medical Tourism and the Patient-Protective Argument*, 95 Iowa L. Rev. 1467, 1472 (2010) (citing Bookman & Bookman, *supra* note 6, at 3; Tourism Research and Marketing (TRAM), Medical Tourism: A Global Analysis 18 (2006); *Great Indian Hospitality Can Be Biz Too*, Economic Times (India), July 29, 2005, *available at* 2005 WLNR 11859886); Ozgur Tore, *Thailand Aims to be a World-Class Provider*, Focus on Travel News, Feb. 24, 2012, *available at* http://www.ftnnews.com/health-a-spa/15827-thailand-aims-to-be-a-world-class-health-provider.html.

insurer plans has introduced or is considering.[9] A new European Union Directive on governmental reimbursement for services provided in other Member States means that the European market for medical tourism is poised to continue growing as well.[10] Further, the importance of medical tourism to our thinking about the law and ethics of health care is only magnified when we expand our gaze to trades that are harder to quantify, such as cross-border travel to obtain abortions, assisted suicide, stem cell treatments, or reproductive technology services.[11]

The United States heavily depends on foreign-trained doctors to staff its health care system; as of 2005, a fifth of all doctors practicing in the United States were foreign trained.[12] This recruitment has had serious effects on the supply of doctors in the developing world. Between 1986 and 1995, for example, 61 percent of all graduates of the Ghana Medical School left their country for employment (54.9 percent to work in the United Kingdom, and 35.4 percent to work in the United States).[13] The effects of this migration on rich and poor nations are immense: a study estimated that roughly three million currently practicing health care professionals trained in less-developed countries had migrated to more-developed countries for work, and that it would have cost an average of $184,000 to train each of those professionals in more developed countries, such that poor countries lost $500 million in training costs and more developed countries saved roughly $552 billion.[14]

Like medical tourism, telemedicine also has the potential to radically reconfigure the geography of health care delivery. Telemedicine can usefully be divided into three categories of services based on the capital requirements needed to implement them successfully: image interpreted telemedicine services such as teleradiology, telepathology, and teleretinology; cybersurgery such as remote robotic surgery; and office-based telemedicine such as telepsychiatry and telecardiology.[15] Whereas the components needed by a U.S. hospital to engage in teleradiology can be purchased for under $150,000, the robotic surgical instrument needed for cybersurgery costs $1 million dollars with additional, harder-to-quantify expenses needed to pay for the remote network of technicians who operate and maintain the robotic instrument.[16] The costs for office-based telemedicine fall somewhere in between, with telepsychiatry services being fairly inexpensive and telecardiology much more costly to implement.[17] Telemedicine in the form of teleradiology already has a significant hold on the U.S. health care economy, with

---

[9]   Cohen, *supra* note 8, at 1486–88; Cortez, *supra* note 2, at 882–84.

[10] Directive 2011/24, of the European Parliament and of the Council of March 9, 2011 on the Application of Patients' Rights in Cross-Border Healthcare, 2011 O.J. (L 88) 45.

[11] *See, e.g.,* I. Glenn Cohen, *Circumvention Tourism*, 97 CORNELL L. REV 1309 (2012).

[12] Fitzhugh Mullan, *The Metrics of the Physician Brain Drain*, 353 NEW ENG. J. MED. 1810, 1811 (2005).

[13] David Sanders et al., *Public Health in Africa, in* GLOBAL PUBLIC HEALTH: A NEW ERA 135, 146 (Robert Beaglehole ed., 2003).

[14] BOOKMAN & BOOKMAN, *supra* note 6, at 106.

[15] Thomas R. McLean, *The Global Market for Health Care: Economics and Regulation*, 26 WIS. INT'L L.J. 591, 607 (2008).

[16] *Id.* at 607–608.

[17] *Id.* at 608.

a 2005 estimate suggesting that roughly half of all U.S. hospitals outsourced some of their radiology services.[18] India has thus far been the main beneficiary of this trade, with a diagnostic testing export market valued at $864 million dollars in 2005 and an estimated growth of 20 percent per annum since then.[19] As the costs of electronically coordinating service provision diminish over time, countries with low labor costs for health care professionals such as India are likely to provide a still larger share of tele-medical services to patients in the developed world, especially if health care costs in places such as the United States continue to rise.

As we turn to research and development, of the $39 billion that pharmaceutical companies spent on these activities in 2004, a full 21 percent was spent outside the United States.[20] By one estimate, in 2005 approximately 40 percent of all clinical trials were being run in the developing world, with projections that this number is rising such that 50 to 70 percent of all clinical trials will soon be run outside the United States.[21] When we examine who most needs access to these pharmaceuticals, a quite different picture emerges. In the developing world, huge populations continue to suffer from diseases that are readily preventable, including 611,000 deaths per year from measles, 1,778,000 from diarrhea, and 155,000 from syphilis.[22] Although neglected diseases account for 16.4 percent of the global disease burden, only 2 to 3 percent of global research and development expenditures go to research directed at those diseases, at least in part because just 1.5 percent of the 16.4 percent, or .25 percent, of the total global burden of disease, takes place in the *developed* world, where the pharmaceutical industry earns roughly 95 percent of its revenue.[23]

These numbers tell only part of the story, giving an account of what globalization theorists call "economic globalization," the movement of labor, capital, and industry that is associated with free trade.[24] As important for our purposes is the way this massive globalization of health care raises significant legal and ethical challenges, the main topic of this book. These challenges include:

- Does medical tourism offer a viable and ethical way to expand access to health care to domestic patients who would otherwise face cost barriers or waiting lists to access services? What effects does it have on the poor in the destination countries

---

[18] *Id.* at 611.

[19] *Id.*

[20] Nicolas P. Terry, *Under-Regulated Health Care Phenomena in a Flat World: Medical Tourism and Outsourcing*, 29 W. NEW ENG. L. REV. 421, 451 (2007).

[21] *See, e.g., id.* at 451; Abrahm Lustgarten, *Drug Testing Goes Offshore*, FORTUNE, Aug. 8, 2005, at 57, 57–61.

[22] William W. Fisher & Talha Syed, *Global Justice in Health Care: Developing Drugs for the Developing World*, 40 U.C. DAVIS L. REV. 581, 585–86 (2007).

[23] *Id.* at 612 (citing Bernard Pecoul et al., *Access to Essential Drugs in Poor Countries: A Lost Battle?*, 281 J. AM. MED. ASS'N 361, 364–65 (1999); Patrice Trouiller et al., *Drug Development for Neglected Diseases: A Deficient Market and a Public-Health Policy Failure*, 359 LANCET 2188, 2189 (2002)).

[24] *See, e.g.,* Mihaela Papa & David B. Wilkins, *Globalization, Lawyers, and India: Toward a Theoretical Synthesis of Globalization Studies and the Sociology of the Legal Profession*, 18 INT'L J. LEGAL PROF. 175 (2012).

where tourists receive care? How will the recent Obama health care reform in the United States and the European Directive in the European Union alter the existing industry and the legal and ethical issues it raises?

- Does medical tourism for services illegal at home—abortion, assisted suicide, reproductive technology—represent a problematic end run around domestic criminal prohibitions, or does it instead enable value pluralism and accommodate the needs of "medical exiles" without violating the laws of their home states? Should destination countries respect the legal prohibitions on access to services in the countries from which medical tourists come?

- Under what conditions can home country governments and institutions lawfully recruit physicians, nurses, and other health care professionals from developing countries that face chronic shortages of providers? Can these developing countries legally, ethically, and effectively use techniques such as long-term service contracts or restrictions on migration to avoid the decimating effects of this recruitment on their health care systems?

- Should the legal rules relating to licensure of physicians, the unauthorized practice of medicine, medical malpractice, and choice of law be altered to foster a robust telemedicine industry, and how would one go about doing so? Are arbitration or other dispute system designs appropriate ways to address patient and regulatory concerns regarding injuries incurred during the use of telemedicine?

- Can countries require pharmaceutical companies to register their trials and report negative results without the countries violating international trade law? Under what circumstances can unethical research practices conducted during pharmaceutical trials outside the United States be made actionable under U.S. law?

- Do World Health Organization (WHO) member states that share their influenza strains, enabling the creation of influenza vaccines, have a right to certain quantities of those vaccines? In what ways should the global intellectual property regime governing pharmaceuticals be altered to conform with principles of justice? More generally, under what circumstances are health inequities between countries unjust, and when do those inequities imply duties of assistance from other countries?

This book has as its audience not only academics of as many different stripes as our extremely international and interdisciplinary authors (from law, medicine, public health, business, history, geography, and philosophy), but also those in these globalizing industries and the policy makers who must deal with the consequences of these developments. That diversity in audience presented a significant challenge in how to organize the book: would it be better to do so by the various health care market sectors that are globalizing, or along more theoretical lines? I ultimately opted for the more market-sectoral division with Part V, the final part of the book, focused more squarely on governance and theory, as I set out in the next section of the Introduction.

However, I have always preferred having my cake and eating it too, so at the end of this Introduction I also briefly set out an alternative way of thinking about the contributions in this book, one more rooted in globalization theory.

I. The Structure of This Book and Its Contents

Part I of this book discusses the newest situs for health care globalization: medical tourism. The first six chapters in this part focus on medical tourism for services that are lawful in both the patient's home and destination country.

Three chapters, by Leigh Turner, Tom McLean, and a team led by Valorie Crooks, examine the risks and perception of risks associated with medical tourism. Turner's chapter reviews twenty-seven reported cases of medical tourists who died during or shortly after undergoing cosmetic surgery or bariatric surgery since 1993. He uses these in-depth case studies to suggest strategies that might improve patient safety, quality of care, disclosure of information, quality of advertising, and protection of patients in the global marketplace for health services. McLean's chapter looks at the legal remedies available to medical tourists in Europe when they experience an adverse event such as those in Turner's case studies. He examines the existing EU jurisdictional rules as applied to medical tourism, and discusses ways that health care service providers can avoid being sued in the domicile of their patients and the ways in which patients can choose providers to try and avoid that consequence. The media's depiction of medical tourism is quite different from the reality that Turner and McLean have uncovered, as Valerie Crooks and her team show in their chapter providing a media content analysis of Canadian print media depictions of medical tourism. They show how the lack of reliable information in these sources about the numbers and motivations of Canadians traveling abroad for care, and about how the public-health and resource-allocation effects of this practice domestically and abroad have hampered a balanced and informed public discussion of the ethical issues raised by medical tourism.

Nathan Cortez and Hilko Meyer examine the interplay among medical tourism, health insurance, and reimbursement for U.S. and EU patient populations respectively. Cortez examines whether, in the wake of President Obama's U.S. health insurance reform, cross-border health insurance plans might provide cost-effective alternatives to traditional domestic coverage. Meyer explains the fragmentation of health care delivery systems in the European Union, traces the history, and explains the content of the complex legal rules requiring EU Member States to reimburse citizens for health care received in other Member States under certain circumstances. He also offers a detailed analysis of the new 2011 European Directive on the matter and what it may mean for patients and providers.

In my chapter in the volume, I turn to the effect medical tourism has on access to health care in the destination country. I examine both the existing empirical evidence and developmental economic theorizing as to when medical tourism is likely to have negative effects. Drawing on the philosophical literature on global justice, I then discuss under what circumstances home countries bear obligations to prevent or remedy those negative effects.

The second half of Part I shifts to medical tourism for services that are illegal in the patient's home country, what I have elsewhere called "circumvention tourism."[25] Kimberly Mutcherson and Richard Storrow's chapters focus on "fertility tourism" (or "cross-border reproductive care") from opposite ends of the issue. Storrow examines the restrictive laws in some parts of Europe driving travel to other countries to access services, and shows how these laws reflect strong religiously and culturally inspired attitudes about responsible reproductive practices and parenting that the new reproductive technologies challenge. He examines the conflicting claims of nationalism and pluralism in this domain, and discusses how the legal doctrine of proportionality, as employed in the jurisprudence of the European Court of Human Rights, might act to lessen the demand for these services. Mutcherson examines the United States as a destination country for many of those seeking to avoid their home countries' restrictions on accessing reproductive technologies. She strongly argues against U.S. law or U.S. providers limiting access based on the country of citizenship of the patients, and instead presses that idea that travel to the United States for fertility services can be conceptualized as an opportunity to enhance freedom and protect the interests of would-be parents whose desires to parent could not be satisfied on their native soil.

Hazel Biggs and Caroline Jones compare the jurisprudence that has surrounded travel for reproductive technology services with that pertaining to travel for assisted suicide. Focusing on the legal treatment of the more than 150 British citizens who have gone to Switzerland to receive assistance in ending their lives, they show that although statutes, the common law, and prosecutorial policy are couched in terms of safeguarding the interests of vulnerable persons and groups, scant attention is paid to defining who genuinely is vulnerable, resulting in harm and injustice.

Finally, Aaron Levine and Leslie Wolf's chapter focuses on travel to access experimental stem cell therapies that may not be available or legal in the patient's home country, so-called "stem cell tourism." They discuss the roles that physicians should and do play in patients' decisions about unproven therapies, the professional guidelines for physicians regarding medical and stem cell tourism, and the legal obligations physicians have under U.S. law toward patients considering an unproven stem cell therapy. They use interviews with ten patients who engaged in stem cell tourism to describe how some patients interact with their physicians regarding unproven stem cell treatments and to assess preliminarily how well physicians are complying with these professional responsibilities.

Part II of the book focuses on medical migration, the movement of physicians and other health care providers across borders, usually from the developing to the developed worlds. In their chapter, Vivien Runnels, Corrine Packer, and Ronald Labonté

---

[25] *See generally* Cohen, *supra* note 11.

provide a multilevel framework for understanding recruitment of foreign health care professionals, consisting of the global or macro-level; the national, single country or meso-level; and the organizational and authority or micro-level. They show how this framework can help build more effective and ethical recruitment policies, and give a detailed analysis of the role of recruiters in Canada. Till Bärnighausen and Nir Eyal's chapter examines the ethics of one promising policy tool for reducing medical migration: the conditioning of medical school scholarships on a long-term commitment to work in underserved areas after graduation. Allyn Taylor and Ibadat Dhillon's chapter focuses on the role that international organizations can play, by giving a detailed account of the negotiations giving rise to the May 2010 adoption by the World Health Assembly (WHA) of the WHO Global Code of Practice on the International Recruitment of Health Personnel. Their chapter also explains the workings of the Code, its benefits and drawbacks, and what lessons about global health governance can be gleaned from the process that gave rise to it.

Part III of the book focuses on issues raised by the globalization of research and development. Trudo Lemmens and Candice Telfer argue that access to information about clinical trials and the safety and effectiveness of drugs and medical devices should be recognized as a fundamental component of the right to health, and that this link should be used to promote the establishment of solid knowledge-creation systems based on transparent data. They show how an international registry can be formed without violating existing international trade or intellectual property agreements. In her chapter, Bethany Spielman uses the Kano, Nigeria, pediatric trials of the oral antibiotic Trovan and the litigation it produced to examine the remedies available to individuals suing U.S.-based multinational corporations and the foreign states that host their clinical drug trials. She focuses on litigation under the Alien Tort Statute, an issue that is currently receiving some attention from the U.S. Supreme Court. Robert Gatter's chapter focuses on the politics and regulation of sharing influenza vaccine strains. He begins by describing the 2007 controversy that ensued when Indonesia (a world leader in the transmission of novel animal flu strains from animals to humans) briefly stopped sharing its flu strains with the WHO until the WHO agreed to organize intergovernmental negotiations on assuring that all member states that share their virus strains also receive the benefits of the network. He then explains the WHA's May 2011 "Pandemic Influenza Preparedness Framework for the Sharing of Influenza Viruses and Access to Vaccines and Other Benefits," which emerged from this controversy, and the benefits and drawbacks of its approach to ensuring equity in vaccine sharing. Cynthia Ho's chapter focuses on the way academic writing and policy analysis has missed something important in its articulation of the way patent law impedes making low-cost generic versions of essential medicines desperately needed in the developing world. Ho shows how the sort of regulations pertaining to data exclusivity and patent linkage that are rapidly being adopted in the developing world stand in the way of access to essential medicines. She also puts forth several solutions that may serve to minimize the harm likely to occur in developing countries that are forced to adopt regulatory regimes of these kinds. Finally, in their cChapter, Kevin Outterson, Thomas

Pogge, and Aidan Hollis turn their attention to the growing threat posed by antibiotic resistance. They show how such resistance distorts markets for innovative antibiotics in unusual and counterintuitive ways, giving major stakeholders economic incentives to waste these precious resources because insurance reimbursement rewards companies primarily for the sale of antibiotics, in a way that undermines public health goals. They instead pursue a regime of "de-linkage," in which product sales revenues are not the sole source of R&D cost recovery and profits, but are supplemented or replaced by other mechanisms such as prizes. In particular, they explain how proposals to create a Health Impact Fund that rewards companies for the health impacts of their drugs can be used to effectively coordinate global use of antibiotics in a way that manages the threat of resistance.

In Part IV of the book, chapters by Gil Siegal and by Deth Sao, Amar Gupta, and David Gantz focus on the movement of information across borders and telemedicine. Siegal's chapter examines globalization's effects on modern IT-driven health care, comprising not only telemedicine but also electronic medical records and medical databases. He explains the driving forces behind this phenomenon and the U.S., European, and international responses to e-health and telemedicine, which reveal the possibility of enhancing the globalization of affordable high-quality health care via a stronger commitment to IT exploitation. He offers an in-depth analysis of the legal regulation of these fields, focusing on licensure and liability, and shows how policy makers might bring together domestic and international regulatory efforts to better disseminate and use these technologies. Sao, Gupta, and Gantz's chapter begins by showing how, in the United States, existing state legal and regulatory regimes inhibit the full realization of telemedicine's benefits by subjecting interstate telemedicine providers to differing standards and requirements and by creating legal uncertainty in the event of cross-border disputes. They next demonstrate how a combination of public and private approaches can redress these shortcomings, focusing on a national regime for telemedicine with built-in public and private dispute resolution mechanisms. Finally, they turn to how the same proposals might be adopted on a global scale.

Part V of this book focuses more broadly on the theoretical and governance challenges posed by health care globalization. Jennifer Prah Ruger's chapter presents Shared Health Governance as a theory of global health governance, rooted in the political theory of Provincial Globalism, which asserts a general duty to reduce shortfall inequalities in, and address threats to, central health capabilities (premature mortality and escapable morbidity), and stipulates shared global and domestic responsibilities for doing so. She shows how Shared Health Governance advantageously allocates responsibility based on the specific duties and effectiveness of different actors, respects self-determination by groups and individuals, seeks voluntary commitments, and rests on internalizing the public moral norms it promotes as shared authoritative standards. Rooting his theorizing in the works of Friedrich Engels and Rudolf Virchow in the mid-1800s, Daniel Goldberg seeks to provide a historically informed theoretical account of global health inequality. He shows how laws and policies act as social determinants of health, shaping health and its distribution, both horizontally within individual polities and vertically across the international political order. After defending a claim that the developed world bears a much larger share of responsibility for laws, policies, and governance structures that create or intensify deleterious socioeconomic conditions, he uses Madison Powers and Ruth Faden's model of social justice as an ethical framework for conceptualizing global health priorities. Finally, Pavlos Eleftheriadis' chapter reaches deeply into philosophical thinking to answer the question: what kind of right is the international right to health care that is put forth in legal documents such as the International Covenant on Economic, Social, and Cultural Rights of 1966? He argues that it is a mistake to view the international right to health as reflecting a single moral principle, and instead argues that it is better understood as encompassing at least two principles: first, a moral duty to respect the sanctity of life—by avoiding injury or risk to others or by giving aid to those in need—which is based on the existence of special relationships or proximity. Second, he concludes there is also a basic political right to health care against one's own government, whenever such a government exercises jurisdiction over persons and territory. The content of the right, he claims, is the setting up of an effective health system—parallel, perhaps, to a general system of civil and criminal justice—enabling individuals to live without fear of violence or exploitation.

II. Globalization Theory

Although I have organized the book primarily by the portion of the health care market being globalized, it is also revealing to approach the relationship of the essays to one another from a more theoretical perspective. The term "globalization" is often used as a stand-in for a quite disparate set of ideas, but, as Scheuerman and others have suggested, two of its core ideas are *deterritorialization*—in which more and more important social practices occur in ways that are separate from the geographical location of the participants—and the growth of social *interconnectedness*—the way in which distant events and forces impact local and regional activities and choices.[26]

The essays in this volume can be thought of as clustered around these two seminal ideas. For example, the chapters by Storrow, Mutcherson, and Biggs and Jones show nations wrestling with the ability of their citizens to use travel to avoid domestic prohibitions on reproductive technology and assisted suicide and facing the question of whether to deterritorialize their prescriptive laws such that it follows their citizens outside of the home country. McLean's chapter evinces the way domestic civil procedural systems are struggling with how deterritorialized they ought to be in their assertions of tort jurisdiction. Cortez's and Meyer's chapters show the potential for,

---

[26] *See* William Scheuerman, *Globalization*, THE STANFORD ENCYCLOPEDIA OF PHILOSOPHY (Edward N. Zalta ed., 2010), http://plato.stanford.edu/archives/sum2010/entries/globalization/; Jan Aart Scholte, *Beyond the Buzzword: Towards a Critical Theory of Globalization*, *in* GLOBALIZATION: THEORY AND PRACTICE 43, 45–49 (Eleonore Kofman & Gillians Youngs eds., 1996); JOHN TOMLINSON, GLOBALIZATION AND CULTURE 9 (1999).

and challenges of, insurance markets not tied to geography. Siegal, Sao, Gupta, and Gantz's contributions examine the ways in which existing regulatory structures in the United States seem to inhibit more robust deterritorialization of telemedicine. Taylor and Dhillon; Runnels, Packer, and Labonté; and Ruger's chapters examine the ways in which deterritorialization requires moving to globalized governance structures, both in health-worker migration and more generally.

Interconnectedness raises both a descriptive question of how to map the new relations among people in different (sometimes distant) nation states, and the normative question of how their duties and rights should be conceptualized. Both strands are reflected in my chapter's attempt to examine the effects that medical tourism is having on access to health care in destination countries and to use global justice theories to determine what duties home countries bear to destination countries in this regard. In a similar vein, Gatter's chapter examines the attempts of have-not countries such as Indonesia to prompt global governance initiatives to ensure they get their fair share in the pandemic vaccine production process. The chapters by Taylor and Dhillon; Runnels, Packer, and Labonté; and Bärnighausen and Eyal document interconnectedness in the effects medical migration is having on both sending and receiving countries, and examine both multilateral solutions and what steps home country institutions may ethically take to reduce negative effects without unfairly impinging on the rights of health care professionals. Lemmens and Telfer show how legal obligations in international trade and intellectual property need not block more interconnected knowledge-creation systems, whereas Spielman documents the dark side of interconnectedness in nonconsensual experimentation. Outterson, Pogge, and Hollis show how the existing intellectual property regimes exacerbate the public health threat of antibiotic resistance and what might be done to avoid it by improving interconnectedness through the Health Impact Fund's reward structure. Ho's chapter shows how increased *doctrinal* interconnectedness through the adoption of patent-linkage and data-exclusivity rules in the developing world threaten access to essential medicine. Goldberg's and Eleftheriadis's chapters take on the interconnectedness at a more theoretical level, with Goldberg pressing the way in which recognition of the social determinants of health helps us see developed nations' role in creating and maintaining health inequalities and Eleftheriadis struggling to give normatively defensible content to an international right to health.

Still another way of thinking about the book's contributions is by distinguishing chapters focused on global governance (e.g., Ruger, Taylor and Dhillon, Gatter), from those focused on duties and rights in a globalized world (e.g., Goldberg, Eleftheriadis, my own chapter), from those focused on nation states' attempts to resist or at least gatekeep the forces of globalization (e.g., McLean; Meyer; Bärnighausen and Eyal; Mutcherson; Sao, Gupta, and Gantz).[27]

---

[27] For some excellent reflections on this phenomenon as to the globalization of the *legal* market, *see, e.g.*, Papa and Wilkins, *supra* note 24; Sida Liu, *Globalization as Boundary-Blurring: International and Local Law Firms in China's Corporate Law Market*, 42 LAW & SOC'Y REV. 771 (2008).

There are, of course, many other ways that the themes and policy proposals of this book could be brought together. John Berger once wrote: "never again will a single story be told as though it's the only one."[28] Much the same is true of the organization of this volume, and we are almost ready for that story to begin. However one thinks about the contributions in this volume, it is clear that globalization is the most significant development for health care in this new century and that the contributions in this volume have an important role in explaining that development and charting its future course.

I. Glenn Cohen, Cambridge, MA, 2013.

---

[28]   JOHN BERGER, G: A NOVEL 129 (1972).

Medical Tourism

FOR SERVICES LEGAL IN THE PATIENT'S HOME COUNTRY

PATIENT MORTALITY IN MEDICAL TOURISM

Examining News Media Reports of Deaths Following Travel for Cosmetic

Surgery or for Bariatric Surgery

Leigh Turner, PhD *

Introduction

Four years ago, while searching the Internet for articles about medical tourism and globalization of health care, I found a news report describing the death of Maria Morel, a woman from New Jersey who had traveled to the Dominican Republic for what the reporter described as a tummy tuck procedure and liposuction.[1] The article indicated that Morel experienced respiratory problems following her operation and died six days later. I later found an article that described the deaths of three American women who

---

* Associate Professor, Center for Bioethics and School of Public Health University of Minnesota. This chapter is an expanded and revised version of an article published in 2012 by Developing World Bioethics. I would like to thank the publisher of Developing World Bioethics, John Wiley and Sons, for permission to use material from that article in this chapter. In addition, I wish to thank Jeremy Snyder and Valorie Crooks for feedback they provided in response to draft versions of that journal article. This chapter is dependent upon news media reportage by many journalists. I want to acknowledge their effort to document deaths of medical tourists and emphasize the extent to which my case summaries depend upon their investigative reporting. In particular, I wish to highlight my debt to Sandra Dibble's coverage of mortality in U.S. medical tourists seeking cosmetic surgery in Mexico. Alone and also with her colleagues at *The San Diego Union-Tribune*, Dibble's publications raise troubling questions about the quality of medical care some U.S. citizens have received at clinics in Tijuana, Mexico. Finally, I would like to thank I. Glenn Cohen both for inviting me to contribute a chapter to this volume and for the opportunity to speak at the May 2011 "Globalization of Health Care" conference held at Harvard Law School.

[1] Victoria Corderi, *Plastic Surgery Tourism? Dangers of Going under the Knife on the Cheap.* MSNBC.COM (Mar. 18, 2005), http://www.msnbc.msn.com/id/7222253/ns/dateline_nbc/.

traveled to Mexico for cosmetic surgery, experienced complications during or follow-ing their operations, and died after being transported to medical centers in San Diego, California.[2] I found these articles thought-provoking and troubling. The journalists provided disturbing accounts of the quality of care these women received at the inter-national clinics they visited, suggesting that the women's deaths might have resulted from poor quality care, inadequate medical facilities, and inadequate responses to life-threatening medical emergencies. After discovering these two news media accounts, I decided to see whether I could locate additional news reports of deaths of individuals who had traveled abroad for cosmetic surgery or bariatric surgery. Not all researchers studying medical tourism would support such an approach. Some scholars find news media coverage of medical tourism too often sensationalistic and dominated by such topics as patients going abroad to purchase kidneys and couples traveling to India for commercial surrogacy. Acknowledging the need for caution, I am concerned that in their efforts to distinguish scholarly research from the work of journalists, academic researchers risk dismissing important findings first described by reporters. News media coverage of medical tourism must be examined in a critical manner. Such an approach differs from reflexively dismissing news reports as "sensationalistic" and "anecdotal." To focus my search I decided that I must place some constraints upon the process of finding and analyzing news media reports.

First, hoping to obtain basic demographic data, I decided to eliminate from my anal-ysis news reports that mentioned deaths of medical travelers but provided little infor-mation about such details as individuals' ages, their gender, the countries from which they departed, the nations to which they traveled for surgery, and when they died. This decision resulted in exclusion from analysis of several news reports that contained few details concerning deaths of individuals who had traveled to international medical facilities for cosmetic surgery or bariatric surgery.

Second, I restricted my searches to several English-language databases. Though in one case I was able to supplement an English-language report with several news reports written in Spanish and published by media sources in Mexico, four English-language databases were my primary resource for conducting searches. In the future, more comprehensive studies of news media coverage of mortality in travel for cosmetic surgery and bariatric surgery will likely benefit from researchers conducting searches in languages other than English and drawing upon additional research databases.

Third, I excluded from my analysis reports of individuals who experienced postop-erative complications but did not die after traveling abroad and undergoing cosmetic surgery or bariatric surgery. This decision meant that reports of patients who trav-eled abroad for cosmetic surgery or bariatric surgery and then experienced infections or strokes, or suffered permanent loss of consciousness, are not included in my

---

[2]   Cheryl Clark & Sandra Dibble, *When Cosmetic Surgery in Baja Goes Bad; Deaths Raise Questions about Risks at Clinics*, San Diego Union-Trib., July 14, 1996.

analysis.[3] It is possible that numerous patients reported to have had severe postoperative complications did not survive these threats to health. However, cases were excluded from analysis if I was unable to confirm mortality rather than morbidity as an outcome following surgery. There are several reasons I chose to focus upon mortality rather than morbidity. Reports of complications following travel for cosmetic surgery or bariatric surgery have already appeared in peer-reviewed medical journals.[4] In contrast, to date scholarship does not appear to have identified cases of mortality related to international travel for cosmetic surgery and bariatric surgery. In addition, although complications following travel for cosmetic surgery or bariatric surgery have potentially significant implications for patients and public health systems, in many instances physicians are able to address, at least to some extent, the postoperative complications described in these case reports. Reports in peer-reviewed medical journals describe postoperative care in which infections are treated, and in some instances reconstructive surgery is performed in an effort to treat injuries and scarring resulting from surgery and postoperative complications. In contrast, patients who die during surgery or in the postoperative period following cosmetic surgery or bariatric surgery suffer the ultimate loss. Furthermore, they die after undergoing elective procedures that did not have to be performed and that patients would not have chosen had they known what fate would befall them. I should note that while I searched for reports of mortality in medical travel for cosmetic surgery and bariatric surgery I found many news reports that described patients with significant postoperative complications after traveling abroad for cosmetic surgery or bariatric surgery. Had my analysis of news media sources included reports of both mortality and morbidity, the list of cases would have expanded dramatically. Newspapers in Australia, England, New Zealand, the United States, and elsewhere describe many cases in which individuals from these countries went abroad for cosmetic surgery or bariatric surgery and returned home with postoperative complications. Some of these narratives might reflect prejudicial

3   Vivian Tse, *Swedish Woman in Coma after Botched Breast Op*, THE LOCAL, Nov. 17, 2010, http://www.thelocal.se/30272/20101117/; Jennifer Kraus, *Common Operation across Border Goes Horribly Wrong*, NEWSCHANNEL5.COM, May 15 2010, http://www.newschannel5.com/Global/story.asp?S=12487185; Jennifer Kraus, *Medical Tourism Patient Fights for Life Again*, NEWSCHANNEL5.COM, July 22, 2010, http://www.newschannel5.com/global/story.asp?s=12856281; Andrew Horansky, *Texas Woman Nearly Dies after Surgery in Mexico*, KVUE.COM ABC, Feb. 17, 2011, http://www.kvue.com/news/Texas-woman-nearly-dies-after-surgery-in-Mexico-116368509.html.

4   *Nontuberculous Mycobacterial Infections after Cosmetic Surgery—Santo Domingo, Dominican Republic, 2003–2004*, 53 MORBIDITY MORTALITY WKLY. REP. 509 (2004); Martin Newman et al., *Mycobacteria Abscessus Outbreak in U.S.Patients Linked to Offshore Surgicenter*, 55 ANNALS OF PLASTIC SURGERY 107 (2005); Martin Newman et al., *Outbreak of Atypical Mycobacteria Infections in U.S. Patients Traveling Abroad for Cosmetic Surgery*, 115 PLASTIC & RECONSTRUCTIVE SURGERY 964 (2005); Jeremy Birch et al., *The Complications of "Cosmetic Tourism"—An Avoidable Burden on the NHS*, 60 J. PLASTIC RECONSTRUCTIVE & AESTHETIC SURGERY 1075 (2007); Alexander Handschin et al., *Pulmonary Embolism after Plastic Surgery Tourism*, 13 CLINICAL & APPLIED THROMBOSIS/HEMOSTASIS 340 (2007); Daniel Birch et al., *Medical Tourism in Bariatric Surgery*, 199 AM. J. SURGERY 604 (2010); Jeremy Snyder & Valorie Crooks, *Medical Tourism and Bariatric Surgery: More Moral Challenges*, 10 AM. J. BIOETHICS 28 (2010); E. Yoko Furuya et al., *Outbreak of Mycobacterium Abscessus Wound Infections among "Lipotourists" from the United States Who Underwent Abdominoplasty in the Dominican Republic*, 46 CLINICAL INFECTIOUS DISEASES 1181 (2008).

attitudes toward health care facilities based in such countries as India, Mexico, and Thailand. It is also possible that they competently and accurately report postoperative complications resulting from engaging in medical tourism.

Fourth, though I could have expanded my search to include reports of morbidity and mortality in all types of medical tourism, I chose to restrict my search to accounts of deaths of individuals undergoing cosmetic surgery or bariatric surgery. This decision meant that I did not seek articles describing morbidity and mortality in medical tourists undergoing such procedures as stem cell injections, treatments for cancer, "liberation therapy" for multiple sclerosis, or organ transplantation despite reports of patients who have suffered morbidity or mortality after traveling for such procedures.[5] Rather than pursue the overwhelming task of trying to identify reports of mortality associated with all types of medical tourism, I decided to limit my search to reports of mortality in patients traveling abroad for cosmetic surgery or bariatric surgery. Though for practical reasons I have limited the scope of my study, the research methods identified in this article could be used to investigate news media reportage of both mortality and morbidity in all modes of medical tourism. For example, news media reports can clearly be used to investigate cases where patients have died after traveling abroad for "liberation surgery" or stem cell injections.[6]

I. Databases and Search Terms

I conducted searches using ProQuest Newsstand, Google News, Google News Archive, and Google. In addition, I used Google Alerts to send to my e-mail account updates related to deaths of patients who had traveled abroad for cosmetic surgery or bariatric surgery. Search terms combined the general concepts of "medical tourist," "cosmetic

---

[5] Sheena Chew et al., *Olfactory Ensheating Glia Injections in Beijing: Misleading Patients with ALS*. 8 AMYOTROPHIC LATERAL SCLEROSIS 314 (2007); Bruce Dobkin et al., *Cellular Transplants in China: Observational Study from the Largest Human Experiment in Chronic Spinal Cord Injury*, 20 NEUROREHABIL NEURAL REPAIR 5 (2006); Ninette Amariglio et al., *Donor-Derived Brain Tumor following Neural Stem Cell Transplantation in an Ataxia Telangiectasia Patient*, 6 PLoS MED. e1000029 (2009); Cynthia B. Cohen & Peter J. Cohen, *International Stem Cell Tourism and the Need for Effective Regulation. Part I: Stem Cell Tourism in Russia and India: Clinical Research, Innovative Treatment, or Unproven Hype?* 20 KENNEDY INST. ETHICS J. 27 (2010); Jodie Burton et al., *Complications in MS Patients after CCSVI Procedures Abroad (Calgary, AB)*, 38 CAN. J. NEUROLOGICAL SCI. 741 (2011); Caroline Alphonso, *Death of MS Patient Fuels Debate over New Treatment*, GLOBE & MAIL, Nov. 19, 2010; Sean Kennedy et al., *Outcomes of Overseas Commercial Kidney Transplantation: An Australian Perspective*, 182 MED. J. AUSTL. 224 (2005); Muna Canales et al., *Transplant Tourism: Outcomes of United States Residents Who Undergo Kidney Transplantation Overseas*, 82 TRANSPLANTATION 1658 (2006); G.V. Ramesh Prasad et al., *Outcomes of Commercial Renal Transplantation: A Canadian Experience*, 82 TRANSPLANTATION 1130 (2006).

[6] Alphonso, *supra* note 5; Joanna Smith, *Fate of MS Patients Abroad Brings New Dilemma for Doctors*, TORONTO STAR, Nov. 19, 2010, http://www.thestar.com/article/894082--fate-of-ms-patients-abroad-brings-new-dilemma-for-doctors; Matt McClure, *Woman with MS Dies after Treatment; Suffered Massive Hemorrhage Following Operation in California*, WINNIPEG FREE PRESS, Sept. 7, 2011, http://www.winnipegfreepress.com/canada/Woman-with-MS-dies-after-treatment--125269119.html.

TABLE 1.1

Search Terms Used To Find News Reports

death medical tourism, death medical tourist, medical tourist dead, medical tourist died, medical tourist investigation, medical tourist death investigation, medical tourist charges, medical tourist police, death cosmetic surgery tourism, death cosmetic surgery tourist, death lipotourism, death lipotourist, death lipo tourist, death lipo tourism, dead facelift medical tourist, died facelift medical tourist, died medical tourist pectoral implants, dead medical tourist pectoral implants, dead medical tourist breast implants, died medical tourist breast implants, died medical tourist breast augmentation, died medical tourist breast augmentation, death medical tourist lap band, death medical tourist bariatric surgery, and death medical tourist gastric bypass.

surgery tourist," and "bariatric surgery tourist" with "death." TABLE 1.1 contains a list of the specific terms that I used when searching databases.

Despite my effort to select and use appropriate search terms, searches generated many articles describing deaths of tourists by car and motorcycle crashes, electrocution, fires and explosions, drowning, falls, and other accidents. I discarded these articles and selected for analysis only those publications describing deaths of individuals who were reported to have died during or shortly after undergoing cosmetic surgery or bariatric surgery. Searches proceeded in an iterative manner. Once I identified an article that provided an account of someone who had traveled abroad for cosmetic surgery or bariatric surgery and died during or after his or her operation, I then used that person's name as a search phrase. In some instances that step generated additional articles for review. In the case of more recent deaths, some searches revealed Facebook memorial walls and Internet posts by family members and friends. For reasons related both to research methods and research ethics, in this chapter I restrict my analysis to news media reports that are in the public domain and were intended for public consumption.

II. News Media Accounts of Deaths of Medical Tourists Undergoing Cosmetic Surgery or Bariatric Surgery

To summarize information retrieved from news media reports I provide brief descriptions of twenty-seven reported cases of mortality in individuals who traveled abroad and underwent cosmetic surgery or bariatric surgery at international medical facilities. When identifying medical procedures I chose to retain phrases reporters used when describing medical procedures. For example, several articles describe patients undergoing "tummy tucks." The standard clinical term for this procedure is "abdominoplasty." In an effort to retain language used in news media reports, I decided that I would not convert popular terms for procedures to their clinical labels.

Because the names of these individuals are disclosed in news media reports and therefore in the public domain, I have decided to identify them by name as well as by patient number. Cases are reported in chronological order and extend from 1993 to 2011.

Bertha Garcia, Patient One, traveled from Murrieta, California, United States to Tijuana, Mexico and underwent plastic surgery in 1993.[7] The surgery took place at a clinic, Villa of Youth, part of a larger complex known as the Villa Floresta Hospital Medical Center. According to Cheryl Clark and Sandra Dibble, two *San Diego Union-Tribune* reporters who investigated Garcia's death, Villa of Youth runs promotional events at hotels and restaurants in the United States. The clinic promotes "a 12-day vacation that will change your life forever."[8] Following surgery, Garcia went into cardiac arrest in the recovery room. She subsequently was transported to Sharp Chula Vista Medical Center in San Diego. Life support was discontinued two weeks after she was hospitalized in San Diego. Garcia died fourteen days following discontinuation of life support. A physician who treated Garcia in the San Diego emergency room where she was first cared for attributed her medical emergency to the injection of an "inappropriate medication."

Esperanza Pastrana, Patient Two, traveled from California, United States to a clinic in Tijuana, Mexico March 27, 1996.[9] At Unidad Medica Quirurgica de la Salud, she underwent a "tummy tuck" procedure. Pastrana experienced respiratory distress during or after surgery and was transported to Kaiser Permanente Medical Center in San Diego. Life support was discontinued days after her arrival, and she died within a week of having surgery.

Alice Marie Porter, Patient Three, traveled from Northridge, California, United States to Tijuana, Mexico on April 9, 1996.[10] She underwent liposuction and vaginal reconstruction at the Villa of Youth, the same clinic where Bertha Garcia had surgery. Following surgery, clinic staff members found Porter unconscious and not breathing. Porter was transported to Kaiser Permanente Medical Center, the same medical facility to which Pastrana was taken, diagnosed as being comatose, and admitted to the hospital's intensive care unit. Ventilator support was discontinued eight days after Porter's surgery, and she died three days later.

Carmen Mendoza, Patient Four, twice traveled from San Diego, California, United States and underwent breast implantation procedures at The MedCare Clinic in Tijuana, Mexico.[11] Surgery was performed by Dr. Silvia Garcia. Mendoza's incisions became infected following her first surgical procedure; her implants were then removed. Mendoza returned to the clinic for a second breast implant procedure in October 1996. There, she experienced a complication and died a short time following the operation. The physicians who own The MedCare Clinic claimed that the surgeon

7   Clark & Dibble, *supra* note 2.
8   *Id.*
9   *Id.*
10   *Id.*
11   Sandra Dibble, *Death after Operation Stirs Probe; Tijuana Plastic Surgeon's Credentials Questioned*, SAN DIEGO UNION-TRIB., Oct. 20, 1996.

and anesthesiologist were not members of their clinical practice and had rented the operating room for Mendoza's operation. Family members contacted Baja California state prosecutors and requested that charges be brought against both the surgeon and the anesthesiologist. I was unable to locate reports documenting the outcome of this investigation. In conversation with Sandra Dibble, the reporter investigating Mendoza's death, a Baja California prosecutor indicated that his office was investigating two additional deaths and seven to eight cases of injuries suffered by individuals who underwent cosmetic surgery at Tijuana clinics.[12]

Rosanna Pena de Encarnacion, Patient Five, traveled from New York, United States to Santo Domingo, Dominican Republic and underwent liposuction at The Fine Arts Medical Center on June 20, 1998.[13] Her surgeon was Dr. Frank Contreras. Fat removed during the liposuction procedure was subsequently injected into her buttocks. Pena de Encarnacion died at the clinic. The surgeon was charged with involuntary manslaughter, and a Dominican Republic court issued an order to suspend his medical license. I was unable to determine how this case was resolved.

Dhelmalyz Rios Rivera, Patient Six, traveled from Puerto Rico to Santo Domingo, Dominican Republic and underwent liposuction at The Fine Arts Medical Center in August 1998.[14] Fat removed during the liposuction procedure was then injected into her calves. Her surgeon was Dr. Edgar Contreras. Rios Rivera experienced complications following surgery, was flown back to Puerto Rico, and was subsequently admitted to intensive care. After being diagnosed with septic shock, below-the-knee amputations of both her legs were performed in an attempt to treat her life-threatening condition. Rios Rivera died approximately two weeks following admission to intensive care. A local pathologist stated that she died of blood poisoning and an embolism.[15] The surgeon was arrested, held for two days, and then released. In addition, the Dominican Republic Director of Health launched an inquiry into possible medical negligence. It appears that no additional legal action was taken.

Migdalia Cordero Cabrera, Patient Seven, traveled from San Juan, Puerto Rico to Santo Domingo, Dominican Republic and had a breast reduction operation on September 2, 1998.[16] Cabrera had to be hospitalized for an infection following the procedure. Two weeks after the operation Cabrera died. An investigation was initiated by Puerto Rican prosecutors. There are no publicly accessible reports documenting how the investigation was resolved. I was unable to find any reports of an investigation initiated by legal authorities or health care professionals in the Dominican Republic.

Ana Victoria Ariza, Patient Eight, traveled from Illinois, United States to Guadalajara, Mexico for liposuction in 2001.[17] Surgery was performed at a private clinic. Ariza

---

[12] *Id.*

[13] Karl Ross, *Quest for Physical Perfection Becomes Sad, Cautionary Tale.* WASH. POST, Sept. 12, 1998.

[14] *Id.*

[15] Michelle Faul, *Death after Plastic Surgery Prompts Probe of Surgeons*, SAN ANTONIO-EXPRESS NEWS, Sept. 4, 1998.

[16] Wire services, *Plastic Surgery Deaths Raise Serious Questions*, ORLANDO SENTINEL, Sept. 18, 1998.

[17] *Woman Dies during Liposuction Surgery*, GUADALAJARA REP., Mar. 16, 2001.

reportedly had an adverse reaction, experienced respiratory problems, and died following administration of an anaesthetic agent.

Heriberta X, Patient Nine, traveled from San Diego, California, United States to Tijuana, Mexico for liposuction and a "tummy tuck" operation in 2002.[18] (Her last name is not noted because her daughters requested that a surname not be used in news media coverage.) Surgery was performed by Dr. Manuel Guitierrez Romero. The patient returned home following the procedure but began feeling ill. She returned to Tijuana and sought treatment for an infection. She died—reportedly of a pulmonary embolism and cardiac arrest—while undergoing a second surgical procedure. There is no record of an investigation into her death.

Maria Morel, Patient 10, traveled from New Jersey, United States. to Santo Domingo, Dominican Republic in November 2004.[19] There, at The Fine Arts Medical Center (or Centro de Bellas Artes), she underwent liposuction and a "tummy tuck" procedure. Surgery was performed by Dr. Edgar Contreras.[20] A week after surgery Morel died, reportededly of a blood clot in her lungs. At the request of Morel's family, the Santo Domingo attorney general initiated an investigation, but there is no record of its outcome. Following Morel's death, reporters from MSNBC travelled to the Dominican Republic and investigated Dr. Contreras's credentials. They found that his license to practice medicine in the Dominican Republic had been suspended in 1999. The suspension remained in effect at the time of Morel's death.[21]

An unidentified Austrian woman, Patient Eleven, traveled from Austria and underwent liposuction surgery in western Hungary on January 4, 2005.[22] The patient died a day after surgery. A police investigation was initiated in Hungary, but there is no account of how it concluded.

Kay Cregan, Patient Twelve, traveled from Croom, Ireland to New York, United States in March 2005.[23] On March 14, 2005, she had a face-lift, eyelid surgery, chin augmentation, nasal reconstruction, and surgery to her neck and lips. Surgery was performed by Dr. Michael Sachs at the operating room in his office. Dr. Sach's marketed cosmetic surgery procedures through his Web site, www.MichaelevanSachs.com. There, his practice, which consisted of an unaccredited operating room and recovery room, was promoted as The Sach's Institute for Facial Plastic and Reconstructive Surgery.[24] The morning following surgery Cregan collapsed in the recovery room and

[18] B. Hitt, *CBS13 Investigates: Surgery South of the Border*, Nov. 3, 2008, http://www.lapbandsurgery.com/email/cbs13/.

[19] Marjory Sherman & Yadira Betances, *The Price of Perfection*, EAGLE-TRIB., Nov. 21, 2004, http://lopeztallaj.com/enlosmedios/publicaciones/paginasexternas/eagletribune/eagletribune.htm; Corderi, *supra* note 1.

[20] Corderi, *supra* note 1.

[21] *Id.*

[22] *Hungarian Police Probe Death of Austrian Patient Who Died after Liposuction*, ASSOCIATED PRESS, Feb. 1, 2005.

[23] Sean O'Driscoll, *Cosmetic Surgery Was "Significant" in NY Death*, IRISH TIMES, May 26, 2005; Warren St. John, *The Irish Patient and Dr. Lawsuit*, N.Y. TIMES, Apr. 24, 2005; John Eligon & Colin Moynihan, *Verdict after Fatal Plastic Surgery Surprises a Victim's Family*, N.Y. TIMES, Apr. 30, 2010.

[24] St. John, *supra* note 23.

went into cardiac arrest. Attempts to resuscitate her were unsuccessful, and she was transported by ambulance to St. Luke's-Roosevelt Hospital Center. She was removed from life support and died March 17, 2005. At the time of Cregan's death Dr. Sachs had settled thirty-three malpractice lawsuits over the last decade of his practice.[25] Dr. Sachs surrendered his medical license following an investigation by the New York State Department of Health's Office of Professional Medical Conduct. In 2010 Dr. Sachs paid $2.1 million to settle the malpractice suit resulting from the death of Cregan. The suit against Susan Alonzo-Francisco, a nurse at Dr. Sachs' clinic, resulted in a $1 million settlement.[26]

Stella Obasanjo, Patient Thirteen, wife of Olusegun Obasanjo, then-president of Nigeria, traveled from Nigeria to Marbella, Spain and underwent liposuction at The Molding Clinic in October 2005.[27] Following significant blood loss during surgery Obasanjo was transported from the clinic to a nearby hospital emergency room. Obasanjo was declared dead upon arrival at the hospital. According to the verdict delivered by the Spanish court, Obasanjo died as a result of blood loss after the canella used to perform liposuction punctured her liver and colon. The physician was sentenced to one-year imprisonment for manslaughter, fined 120,000 Euros, and had his medical license suspended for three years.[28]

Patricia Jenkins-Lyons, Patient Fourteen, traveled from Bristol, England to Lanarca, Cyprus in November 2005.[29] There, on November 17, 2005, she had a face-lift at the Andreas Skarparis Clinic. Following surgery Jenkins-Lyons experienced complications as well as symptoms of dizziness and breathlessness. She was transferred to Lanarca General Hospital, went into cardiac arrest, and died there November 19, 2005. After four years, police in England ended their investigation due to their inability to obtain medical documents from Cyprus. An English Home Office forensic pathologist tasked with conducting a postmortem was unable to perform standard toxicity tests because Jenkins-Lyons's body was embalmed in Cyprus before being returned to England. In his report to the coroner's inquest, the pathologist reported that his investigation revealed that Jenkins-Lyons's cause of death was likely a pulmonary embolism.[30]

Jude Jarvis, Patient Fifteen, traveled from Rhode Island, United States to Mumbai, India on May 6, 2006.[31] On June 9, 2006, Jarvis underwent a breast reduction and

[25] Richard Oakley, *Dying to Be beautiful*, SUNDAY TIMES, Mar. 27, 2005.

[26] Eligon & Moynihan, *supra* note 23.

[27] Jeremy Laurance, *Nigerian President's Wife Dies after Plastic Surgery Operation in Spain*, INDEPENDENT, Oct. 25, 2005; Giles Tremlett, *Spanish Look into Death of Nigerian First Lady after Cosmetic Surgery*, GUARDIAN, Oct. 25, 2005; Jonathan Clayton & Edward Owen, *President's Wife Died in Coma after Surgery "for Slimming,"* TIMES, Oct. 25, 2005.

[28] *Stella Obasanjo's Killer Doctor Jailed*, VANGUARD, Sept. 22, 2009.

[29] *Bristol Woman Died after Facelift*, BRISTOL EVENING POST, Nov. 14, 2008; *Woman Died after Facelift in Cyprus*, W. DAILY NEWS, Nov. 14, 2008; *Receptionist Died after Having a Facelift*, TELEGRAPH, Nov. 13, 2008.

[30] *Woman Died after Facelift in Cyprus*, *supra* note 29.

[31] Tom Mooney, *Cosmetic Surgery Overseas Ends in Death for R.I. Woman*, PROVIDENCE J., May 19, 2006; Jennifer Wolff, *Passport to Cheaper Health Care?*, GOOD HOUSEKEEPING, Sept. 1, 2007.

tummy tuck procedure at Wockhardt Hospital. She died four days after the operation. A family member reported that Jarvis's physicians attributed her death to a blood clot that reached her lungs and caused a pulmonary embolism. There appears to have been no investigation following Jarvis's death.

Nancy Rudolf, Patient Sixteen, traveled from Roseburg, Oregon, United States to Curitiba, Brazil in July 2006.[32] There Rudolf underwent duodenal switch surgery. The procedure was performed by Dr. Joao Marchesini. Three days following surgery Rudolf died. In news media coverage a family member attributed the cause of death to a pulmonary embolism. There are no reports of an investigation following her death.

Annisha Murray, Patient Seventeen, traveled from Florida, United States to Ensenada, Mexico for gastric bypass surgery on May 31, 2007.[33] Her surgeon was Dr. Alejandro Aguirre Wallace. Murray left Mexico five days after her operation and returned to Florida. Fewer than twenty-four hours following her return home Murray's fiancée found her in respiratory distress. Murray died June 9, 2007. The Palm Beach County Medical Examiner's Office concluded that she died of peritonitis. There are no reports of an investigation in Mexico.

An unidentified forty-two-year-old woman, Patient Eighteen, traveled from Wellington, New Zealand to Kuala Lumpur, Malaysia for lap band surgery in June 2007.[34] Her trip was organized by Gorgeous Getaways, an Australian medical tourism company. Two weeks after surgery, while recovering at a Malaysian resort, the patient is reported to have collapsed and died. Family members requested an investigation by the local coroner; but lack of access to medical records hampered the investigation.

Pierre Christian Lawlor, Patient Nineteen, traveled from Dublin, Ireland to Bogota, Colombia for liposuction and cosmetic surgery on his face. Surgery took place on September 3, 2007.[35] The procedure was performed at Centro Colomblade Cirugia Plastica. Lawlor is reported to have died on the operating table after experiencing heart failure. Lawlor's spouse noted the possibility that the patient had consumed cocaine and alcohol the day before surgery. The Irish state pathologist indicated that the death should be classified as "per operative," and the Dublin County Coroner concluded that the death was "caused by cardiac failure related to prolonged surgery." These decisions had no practical effect because the treating physician was based in Colombia and outside the jurisdiction of the Dublin County Coroner's Office.

---

[32] Wolff, *supra* note 31.

[33] Ana Ceron, 8 *Days after Surgery in Mexico, Bride's Dreams Die With Her,* PALM BEACH POST, July 15, 2007; Ana Ceron & Jeremy Schwartz, *Infection Killed Woman Who Got Gastric Bypass in Mexico,* PALM BEACH POST, Aug. 30, 2007.

[34] Kevin Meade, *Death Raises Warning on Overseas Surgery,* AUSTRALIAN, Oct. 29, 2007; *Woman Dies after Trip for Stomach Op,* SUNDAY STAR TIMES, Oct. 27, 2007.

[35] Steven Carroll, *Coroner Warns on Dangers of Cosmetic Surgery,* IRISH TIMES, July 2, 2008; *Family Granted Leave to Seek to Quash Inquest Verdict on Son's Death,* IRISH TIMES, Aug. 28, 2008; Conor Feehan, *Family's Fight for Son Who Died after Plastic Surgery,* HERALD, Aug. 30, 2008. Tim Healy, *A Fresh Inquest Has Been Ordered into the Death of a Dublin Man Who Died while Undergoing Cosmetic Surgery in Colombia,* IRISH INDEP., May 21, 2010.

Lorena Ramirez, Patient Twenty, traveled from the United States to Guadalajara, Mexico for breast reduction surgery in July 2007.[36] The surgeon, Dr. Agustin Huerta, reportedly performed a full mastectomy and then inserted breast implants. Ramirez's incisions opened and became infected after surgery, and she spent over a month in hospital. She is reported to have died of a heart attack in October 2007. News reports state that the physician had a medical degree but no training in plastic surgery procedures. According to news reports, the physician was arrested and charged with fraud, medical irresponsibility, severe damages, and professional usurpation. At the time of his arrest forty-three patients had filed complaints against him. Dr. Huerta was jailed for one year.[37]

Silvia Anguiano Connalley, Patient Twenty-One, traveled from San Diego, California, United States to Tijuana, Mexico for liposuction and a breast lift in July 2008.[38] Her operation was performed at the Clinica de Cirugia Cosmetica Integral (Comprehensive Cosmetic Surgery Clinic), a facility located within the Tijuana Grand Hotel. Connalley experienced heart failure during surgery and died at the clinic July 8, 2008. Family members filed a complaint with the state attorney general. It is unclear how the investigation concluded.

Patrice Lachon Clark, Patient Twenty-Two traveled from Houston, Texas, United States to David, Panama for liposuction in June 2009.[39] Clark traveled there with a group of other U.S. patients. Surgery was performed by Dr. Paul Alegria at Hospital Chiriqui, a private facility. Clark reportedly had surgery June 21, 2009, was transferred to a recovery room, and then died after suffering respiratory failure. Family members requested a medical forensic investigation. An autopsy was reportedly scheduled. There is no record of how the investigation concluded.

Brigitta C., Patient Twenty-Three, traveled from Mattersburg, Austria to Hungary for liposuction in January 2009.[40] The patient experienced severe pain following the operation and died January 12, 2009. The Austrian Municipal Prosecutor's Office in Eisenstadt ordered an investigation of the case, but its outcome is unknown.

F.S., Patient Twenty-Four, traveled from Belarus and underwent a breast enlargement procedure at a private clinic in Dubai, U.A.E. in 2010.[41] Two days after undergoing

---

[36] Associated Press, *Mexican Doctor Charged with Posing as Plastic Surgeon, Botching Dozens of Operations*, INT. HERALD TRIB., Dec. 28, 2007; Jessica Bernstein-Wax, *Scam Artists Taint Medical Care in Mexico; Unqualified Doctors Performing Plastic Surgery Are a Risk to Patients, and to the Nation's Campaign to Attract U.S. Citizens*, L.A. TIMES, Jan. 6, 2008.

[37] J. Zamora, *Pide Respeto el Doctor Agustin Marcos Huerta Navarro*, EL OCCIDENTAL, Jan 31, 2009.

[38] *Death and Funeral Notices*, SAN DIEGO-UNION TRIB., July 20, 2008; *Dies Woman during Plastic Surgery in Tijuana*, QUE PASA BAJA, July 11, 2008, http://quepasabaja.com/?p=552.; Rafael Morales, *Investigan Muerte de una Dama*, EL-MEXICANO, July 9, 2008; *Fallecio en una Cirugia Estetica*, EL-MEXICANO, July 10, 2008.

[39] Jose Vasquez, *American "Medical Tourist" Women Dies in David after Undergoing Liposuction*, BOQUETE TIMES NEWSPAPER, June 22, 2009.

[40] *Austrian Dies after Liposuction in Hungary*, CABOODLE.HU- HUNGARIAN PORTAL, Jan. 30, 2009, http://www.caboodle.hu/nc/news/news_archive/single_page/article/11/austrian_die/?cHash=7f191cec8d.

[41] Bassam Za'za, *Woman Dies of Organ Failure after Breast Enlargement Operation*, GULF NEWS, Mar. 2, 2010; Bassam Za'za, *Doctor, Cosmetician Held Liable for Woman's Death from Botched Surgery in Dubai*, GULF NEWS, Mar. 29, 2010.

the procedure the patient experienced complications, was admitted for treatment at two private medical facilities, and then died. Cause of death was reportedly attributed by the court to a "bacterial contamination" and a "wrong injection." The private clinic was ordered closed by the Dubai Misdemeanors Court, and the treating physician was convicted for unlawfully operating on the patient and accidentally causing her death. The physician was sentenced to a fine and one year in jail. However, sentencing occurred after the accused physician had already left the country. Media coverage of the court ruling suggests that at the time of the operation, the physician was practicing in Dubai without having a medical license provided by Dubai health authorities. A cosmetic specialist involved in managing the cosmetic surgery clinic received a two-month suspended imprisonment and a fine.

Marie de Lourdes Trinidad Mendivil, Patient Twenty-Five, traveled from Chula Vista, California, United States to Tijuana, Mexico and underwent liposuction in May 2010.[42] The procedure was performed May 22, 2010 by Dr. Louis May Villanueva at The Millennium Cosmetic & Laser Institute. Shortly after the operation concluded Mendivil experienced heart failure; efforts to revive her were unsuccessful. Following Mendivil's death, Baja California health inspectors temporarily closed the clinic, but the facility has since reopened. The Baja California Attorney General's Office opened an investigation into the case, and in July 2011 Dr. Villanueva was charged with manslaughter, arrested, and taken to a state penitentiary in Mexico.[43] At present there is no record of findings from the investigation or a court decision.

Cheronna Marie Williams, Patient Twenty-Six, traveled from Chula Vista, California, United States to Tijuana, Mexico for lap band surgery in May 2011.[44] The operation was performed May 26, 2011 by Dr. Pedro Kuri at Hospital Angeles. Following surgery, Williams reportedly suffered a cardiac arrest and died. Significant hemorrhaging is reported to have occurred before her cardiac arrest. Williams's family registered a complaint with the Baja California Attorney General's Office, which initiated an investigation. I was unable to locate any information concerning its outcome.

Gaetano Gambino, Patient Twenty-Seven, flew from Taylorville, Illinois to Curibita, Brazil for duodenal switch surgery.[45] Gambino's father, a brother, and a sister-in-law had all previously undergone bariatric surgery performed by Dr. Joao Batista Marchesini. Gaetano Gambino died in Curibita on September 25, 2011, less than two weeks after undergoing surgery. Gambino reportedly had a pulmonary embolism and additional

---

[42] Keith Darce & Sandra Dibble, *Officials in Baja Close Clinic Where U.S. Woman Died*, SAN-DIEGO UNION-TRIB., May 29, 2010; *Doctor Claims He Was Not at Fault in Woman's Liposuction Death*, 10NEWS. COM, May 25, 2010, http://www.10news.com/news/23677779/detail.html; *Doctor's Credentials Questioned after Woman's Liposuction Death*, 10 NEWS.COM, May 25, 2010, http://www.10news.com/news/23676557/detail.html.

[43] Sandra Dibble, *TJ Physician Detained in Liposuction Death*, SIGN ON SAN DIEGO, July 1, 2011.

[44] Sandra Dibble, *Family Seeks Answers after Woman's Lap-Band Death*, SAN DIEGO UNION-TRIB., June 9, 2011, http://www.signonsandiego.com/news/2011/jun/09/family-seeks-answers-after-womans-lap-band-death/.

[45] Dean Olsen, *Hope for Weight Loss Sent Man to Brazil for Surgery—and Death*, ST. J. REG., Nov. 27, 2011, http://www.sj-r.com/top-stories/x301774663/Hope-for-weight-loss-sent-restaurateur-to-Brazil-for-su rgery-and-death?zc_p=0.

postoperative complications prior to his death. When contacted by a reporter at the Springfield, Illinois *State-Journal Register*, Dr. Marchesini declined to participate in a telephone interview and stated that Brazilian laws prevented him from discussing Gambino's death.[46] The anticipated cost of Gambino's bariatric surgery procedure was $8000. In total, counting travel expenses and bills resulting from treatment for Gambino's postoperative complications, the family paid approximately ten times that amount. There are no reports of an investigation in Brazil.

Table 1.2 provides a summary of information extracted from news media accounts of deaths of twenty-seven individuals who left their local communities and traveled abroad for cosmetic surgery or bariatric surgery. Columns identify the reported age of the individuals at time of death, gender, identified surgical procedures, departure nation (country from which individual left for medical care), destination nation (country in which surgery was performed), and year of death.

III. Overview of Reported Deaths

Of the twenty-seven reported deaths, twenty-five of the individuals were women. The youngest person reported to have died was twenty-one, and the eldest was sixty-five. Eleven individuals died after receiving health care in Mexico. Of the eleven reported deaths in Mexico, eight occurred in Tijuana. Of the remaining patients, four died after receiving care in the Dominican Republic, two died after having liposuction in Hungary, two died after having duodenal switch surgery in Brazil, and single deaths were reported to have occurred in Colombia, Cyprus, India, Malaysia, Panama, Spain, the United Arab Emirates (Dubai), and the United States. Identified surgical interventions included thirteen liposuction procedures, four tummy tucks, three breast implants/breast lifts, three breast reductions, two facelifts, two injections of fat into buttocks or calves, two lap bands, one gastric bypass, two gastric reduction duodenal switch procedures, one vaginal surgery with the specific type of procedure unspecified, one facial surgery with the specific type of surgery unstated, one plastic surgery with the specific procedure unspecified, and one patient reported as having surgery to her nose, chin, lips, and eyelids. There were more surgical procedures than there were individuals because nine patients underwent more than one surgical procedure.

Law enforcement officials including state pathologists, state attorney generals, local public prosecutors, and local police were reportedly contacted in fourteen of twenty-seven cases. In most of the reported cases it was not possible to locate additional information concerning outcomes of investigations by law enforcement authorities. It is possible that most investigations did not result in meaningful findings concerning how medical complications occurred and whether negligent medical care played a role in causing deaths of patients. Investigations might have generated results that

---

[46] *Id.*

TABLE 1.2

Chronological Summary of Cases

Patient	Age	Gender	Procedure	Departure Nation	Destination Nation	Year of Death
Patient 1	65	F	Plastic surgery	California, U.S.	Tijuana, Mexico	1993
Patient 2	38	F	Tummy tuck	California, U.S.	Tijuana, Mexico	1996
Patient 3	57	F	Liposuction, vaginal reconstruction	California, U.S.	Tijuana, Mexico	1996
Patient 4	23	F	Breast implants	California, U.S.	Tijuana, Mexico	1996
Patient 5	36	F	Liposuction, fat injected into buttocks	New York, U.S.	Dominican Republic	1998
Patient 6	26	F	Liposuction, fat injected into calves	Puerto Rico	Dominican Republic	1998
Patient 7	26	F	Breast reduction surgery	Puerto Rico	Dominican Republic	1998
Patient 8	37	F	Liposuction	Illinois, U.S.	Guadalajara, Mexico	2001
Patient 9	X	F	"Tummy tuck," liposuction	California, U.S.	Tijuana, Mexico	2002
Patient 10	43	F	"Tummy tuck," liposuction	Newark, New Jersey, U.S.	Dominican Republic	2004
Patient 11	31	F	Liposuction	Austria	Hungary	2005
Patient 12	42	F	Facelift, surgery on nose, eyelids, chin, lips	Ireland	Manhattan, New York	2005

Patient	Age	Sex	Surgery	Home	Destination	Year
Patient 13	59	F	Liposuction	Nigeria	Marbella, Spain	2005
Patient 14	62	F	Facelift	England	Lanarca, Cyprus	2005
Patient 15	35	F	Tummy tuck, breast reduction	Rhode Island, U.S.	Mumbai, India	2006
Patient 16	44	F	Gastric reduction duodenal switch surgery	Roseburg, Oregon, U.S.	Curitiba, Brazil	2006
Patient 17	21	F	Gastric bypass surgery	Palm Beach, Florida	Ensenada, Mexico	2007
Patient 18	42	F	Lap band surgery	Wellington, New Zealand	Kuala, Lumpur, Malaysia	2007
Patient 19	33	M	Liposuction, facial surgery	Dublin, Ireland	Bogota, Colombia	2007
Patient 20	39	F	Breast reduction	U.S.	Guadalajara, Mexico	2007
Patient 21	55	F	Liposuction, breast lift	California, U.S.	Tijuana, Mexico	2008
Patient 22	30	F	Liposuction	Houston, U.S.	David, Panama	2009
Patient 23	57	F	Liposuction	Austria	Hungary	2009
Patient 24	24	F	Breast implants	Belarus	Dubai	2010
Patient 25	48	F	Liposuction	California, U.S.	Tijuana, Mexico	2010
Patient 26	33	F	Lap band surgery	California, U.S.	Tijuana, Mexico	2011
Patient 27	46	M	Duodenal switch surgery	Illinois, USA	Curibita, Brazil	2011

were not reported. It is also possible that results of investigations were reported but were not captured by my repeated efforts to find them. Of reported outcomes, in three cases physicians settled lawsuits, spent time in jail, surrendered their license to practice medicine, and/or paid fines. In one court decision the treating physician was sentenced to jail and fined but left the country prior to sentencing. One investigation is presently under way; the physician is charged with manslaughter and is in a state penitentiary awaiting trial. Though family members requested investigations in nearly half of all cases, I was unable to establish how many of these requests resulted in thorough investigations of how patients died following cosmetic surgery or bariatric surgery.

IV. Protecting Medical Tourists from Risk of Harm

The twenty-seven case reports that I document suggest numerous points to consider when exploring how to protect medical tourists from risk of harm or death while undergoing cosmetic surgery or bariatric surgery. These practical considerations are proposed as recommendations based upon my review of news accounts of deaths of medical tourists and review of numerous peer-reviewed publications describing postoperative complications in patients who traveled abroad for cosmetic surgery or bariatric surgery, as well as contemporary scholarship examining deaths and postoperative complications in individuals having cosmetic surgery or bariatric surgery at domestic facilities. These accounts of medical tourism ending in deaths of patients deserve serious consideration. In particular, they should direct attention toward what steps might be taken to minimize risks to medical tourists, promote quality of care and patient safety in medical tourism, and ensure that individuals are aware of both risks and benefits when considering whether to travel abroad for care.

First, it is important to note that twenty-five of the twenty-seven deaths of individuals traveling abroad for cosmetic surgery or bariatric surgery were women. This finding corresponds with contemporary surveys tracking cosmetic surgery procedures within the United States. According to the American Society for Aesthetic Plastic Surgery, in 2009 over 90 percent of cosmetic surgery procedures in the United States were performed on women.[47] If state and federal health agencies, patients' rights associations, and other organizations are interested in promoting public awareness of risks of undergoing cosmetic surgery both domestically and at international health care facilities, it is important to ensure that such messages are directed at women. Web sites, billboards, television and radio programs, magazine advertisements, and other media are all used to market to women cosmetic surgery and bariatric surgery performed in both domestic and international settings. These forms of communication can also be used to help women better understand risks associated with cosmetic surgery and bariatric surgery.

---

[47] Am. Soc'y for Aesthetic Plastic Surgery, Cosmetic Surgery National Data Bank Statistics (2009), http://www.surgery.org/sites/default/files/2009stats.pdf.

Many of the news media reports that I reviewed indicate that cost savings were a significant reason women traveled to Mexico, the Dominican Republic, and elsewhere for surgery. One report for example, describes a young woman using cash, twelve postdated checks, and three credit cards to purchase her weight loss surgery in Mexico.[48] Though additional sources of evidence are needed to buttress the case for this claim, and I acknowledge that medical tourism is motivated by many factors, if public health officials in various countries are concerned about the quality of care offered by some international medical facilities it might be prudent to place particular emphasis upon targeting to low- and middle-income women public safety messages about risks of cosmetic surgery and bariatric surgery procedures. This point requires qualification. One patient death described in this analysis involved the spouse of a head of state. Stella Obasanjo had considerable financial resources at her disposal, and she died after having liposuction at a medical facility most women could never afford. Acknowledging exceptions, limited financial means and the prospect of cost savings seem to drive some individuals to international hospitals and clinics. This knowledge can be used to develop targeted messages about health risks associated with undergoing cosmetic and bariatric surgery procedures at international medical facilities.

Second, many of the deaths described in news media reports appear to have occurred outside hospital settings. For example, one article describes the death of a woman who had surgery at a three-bed clinic.[49] Several studies of cosmetic surgery procedures performed in the United States report that there is an estimated tenfold increase in adverse incidents and deaths when cosmetic surgery procedures are performed in office settings rather than in ambulatory surgery centers.[50] Perhaps both domestic and international deaths associated with undergoing cosmetic surgery and bariatric surgery could be reduced by mandating that all but minimal-risk cosmetic surgery procedures, and all bariatric surgery procedures, be performed in hospitals and ambulatory medical centers rather than in small clinics and physicians' offices. Immediate access to intensive care units and other specialized health services combined with better access to appropriately trained health care specialists would increase the likelihood that patients with potential life-threatening medical emergencies have access to optimal medical care. Performing surgical procedures in clinics that lack such resources might be a factor when individuals undergoing cosmetic surgery or bariatric surgery experience respiratory distress or cardiac arrest and do not survive these episodes. Eight deaths are reported to have occurred at clinics in Tijuana. Additional studies are needed to see whether particular features of cosmetic surgery clinics there might put patients at risk of morbidity and mortality. The four deaths in the Dominican Republic,

---

[48] Ceron, *supra* note 33; Ceron & Schwartz, *supra* note 33.

[49] Dibble, *Death after Operation, supra* note 11.

[50] Madelyn Quattrone, *Is the Physician Office the Wild, Wild West of Health Care?*, 23 J. Ambulatory Care Mgmt. 64 (2000); Hector Vila et al, *Comparative Outcomes Analysis of Procedures Performed in Physician Offices and Ambulatory Surgery Centers*, 138 Archives Surgery 991 (2003); J. Bauer Horton et al, *Patient Safety in the Office-Based Setting*, 117 Plastic & Reconstructive Surgery 61e (2006).

combined with reports of an outbreak of infections in U.S. patients who underwent cosmetic surgery in the Dominican Republic, also suggests the importance of examining practice environments and regulation of health professionals in this setting.[51]

Third, in many countries physicians who are not trained as board-certified plastic surgeons routinely perform cosmetic surgery procedures. The news media reports describing deaths of cosmetic surgery tourists provide little insight into whether the physicians involved in these cases were board-certified in plastic surgery or had equivalent professional credentials. Further study of the deaths described in this chapter might provide additional insight into the training and credentials of surgeons and anesthesiologists involved in performing surgery and providing postoperative care. Although such information is presently unavailable, it is nonetheless important to note that domestic and international cases of deaths occurring during or shortly after cosmetic surgery reveal the importance of ensuring that cosmetic surgery is performed according to demanding standards of practice.[52] The same exacting standards must be applied to performance of bariatric surgery and postoperative management of patients who undergo bariatric surgery. Morbidity and mortality rates in cosmetic surgery and bariatric surgery at both domestic and international health care facilities likely could be reduced by restricting the types of physicians permitted to perform most cosmetic surgery and bariatric surgery procedures. Such a move would doubtless be challenged by non–board-certified physicians performing these procedures. However, patient safety and improved quality of care should take precedence over the financial interests of physicians involved in performing complex procedures for which they lack adequate training.

Next, of the twenty-seven reported deaths, four fatalities occurred in the Dominican Republic. Two of these deaths involved individuals traveling from the United States, and two deaths involved persons from Puerto Rico. According to the U.S. State Department Website, "The U.S. Embassy in Santo Domingo and the CDC are aware of several cases in which U.S. citizens experienced serious complications or died following elective cosmetic surgery in the Dominican Republic."[53] Though I did not find news media reports of U.S. citizens dying during or after having cosmetic surgery in Peru, the U.S. Department of State Web site for Peru states, "Over the last few years, at least five American citizen visitors have died during liposuction operations in Peru. Others have suffered from serious complications including coma. While some of these deaths or complications occurred in ill-equipped, makeshift clinics, travelers are urged to carefully assess the risks of having this type of surgery performed overseas, even when opting for a treatment at one of the better-known clinics."[54]

---

[51] Furuya et al., *supra* note 4.

[52] ALEX GOODWIN ET AL., NAT'L CONFIDENTIAL ENQUIRY INTO PATIENT OUTCOME & DEATH, ON THE FACE OF IT: A REVIEW OF THE ORGANIZATIONAL STRUCTURES SURROUNDING THE PRACTICE OF COSMETIC SURGERY (2010), http://www.ncepod.org.uk/2010cs.htm.

[53] U.S. Department of State, *Dominican Republic Country Specific Information*, TRAVEL.STATE.GOV (APR. 12, 2011), http://travel.state.gov/travel/cis_pa_tw/cis/cis_1103.html.

[54] U.S. Department of State, *Peru Country Specific Information*, TRAVEL.STATE.GOV (Nov. 15, 2011), http://travel.state.gov/travel/cis_pa_tw/cis/cis_998.html.

If consular and embassy officials are familiar with cases in which citizens from their countries experience significant surgical complications that prompt questions about quality of care and patient safety at international medical facilities, it is important that they document and publicize this phenomenon. If the cases I review are part of a trend noticed by embassy employees in particular countries then these authorities could play an important role in protecting medical tourists by better documenting and disclosing these cases. Furthermore, if officials staffing embassies located in destinations for medical tourism are encountering increased numbers of citizens harmed while traveling abroad for medical care, it is not evident that public awareness is *significantly* increased by posting information to the Web site of either the U.S. Department of State or the Centers for Disease Control and Prevention. The CDC's "Health Information for International Travel 2010," or "Yellow Book" as it is more commonly known, mentions variations in international quality of care and regulation of medical facilities and provides practical advice for individuals considering traveling abroad for health care.[55] However, it is unclear whether most prospective medical tourists are familiar with this book or consult the U.S. Department of State Web site. If government agencies in the United States and elsewhere have reasonable grounds for concern about the quality of care their citizens risk encountering when traveling to particular health care destinations, they should reassess how to publicize this information. Improved efforts to promote public awareness about potential risks to health when traveling abroad for cosmetic surgery, bariatric surgery, and other procedures might help prospective medical tourists make more informed decisions about where to have surgery. Of course, without better tracking of clinical outcomes, there will be little reliable information available to communicate and only limited prospects for evidence-based, informed public debate about individual and public implications of medical tourism.

Fifth, drawing upon the news media reports that I identify and summarize, it is not possible to reach definitive conclusions about the quality of information provided to the twenty-seven individuals reported to have died after traveling abroad for medical care. The news reports prompt questions about whether risks associated with undergoing particular procedures were adequately disclosed, and the extent to which patient decision making was informed. However, they do not provide direct insight into what information individuals received before deciding to have surgery. Several recent publications raise troubling questions about the quality of information provided by Web sites of medical tourism companies and destination medical facilities.[56] These articles suggest that when prospective medical tourists turn to Web sites for information about risks and benefits of medical tourism they are likely to encounter information that

---

[55]   *CDC Health Information for International Travel*, CTRS. FOR DISEASE CONTROL & PREVENTION (2010), http://wwwnc.cdc.gov/travel/content/yellowbook/home-2010.aspx.

[56]   Reza Nassab et al., *Cosmetic Tourism: Public Opinion and Analysis of Information and Content Available on the Internet*, 30 AESTHETIC SURGERY J. 465 (2010); Alicia Mason & Kevin Wright, *Framing Medical Tourism: An Examination of Appeal, Risk, Convalescence, Accreditation, and Interactivity in Medical Tourism Web Sites*, 16 J. HEALTH COMM.163 (2010); Elisa Sobo et al., *Selling Medical Travel to U.S. Patient-Consumers: The Cultural Appeal of Website Marketing Messages*, 18 ANTHROPOLOGY & MED. 119 (2010).

emphasizes benefits of medical procedures and fails to adequately disclose risks associ-ated with surgery.[57] Reports of postoperative complications experienced by medical tour-ists as well as accounts of deaths reveal the importance of disclosing procedure-related risks. It is possible that some medical tourists are making decisions based upon selec-tive information about risks and benefits of undergoing cosmetic and bariatric surgery procedures. Government agencies responsible for promoting standards in advertising could play a role in more rigorously addressing marketing claims found on Web sites of medical tourism facilitators and destination hospitals and clinics. Though domestic government agencies lack capacity to unilaterally regulate Web sites and other promo-tional materials outside their domestic legal jurisdictions, they nonetheless could alert citizens if international medical tourism companies and destination health care facili-ties are failing to disclose risks and making misleading claims about benefits of surgical procedures, patient safety, and quality of care. In addition, they could work in bilateral fashion with their regulatory counterparts in other countries, share information about particularly egregious instances of misleading advertising, and attempt to improve the quality of information provided to patients by international hospitals, clinics, and medical tourism companies. Timely, effective, and targeted responses by government regulatory bodies to the marketing of health care at international medical facilities might increase the likelihood that prospective medical tourists have better access to information required for them to make informed choices when deciding whether to have particular procedures.[58]

Sixth, reports of complications and deaths related to cosmetic surgery and bariatric surgery in both domestic and international settings indicate the need to promote a pub-lic conversation about the routinization and normalization of such procedures as lipo-suction, breast augmentation, and lap band surgery.[59] Though widely performed, these procedures can result in surgical complications and even deaths of patients. Better tracking of patient outcomes in both domestic and international medical facilities might lead to evidence-based calls for more restrictive use of particular surgical techniques. Practices of informed consent ensure that risks and benefits are disclosed to prospec-tive patients. However, prior to information disclosure and patient decision making it is important to ask whether patients should be exposed to some risks. Rather than ask-ing whether patients face greater risks when having cosmetic surgery at international facilities instead of local medical centers, I suggest that it is time for a broader public debate about risks patients face when undergoing various cosmetic surgery procedures in both domestic and international settings. Such a conversation will be hampered by

---

[57] Kali Penney et al., *Risk Communication and Informed Consent in the Medical Tourism Industry: A Thematic Content Analysis of Canadian Broker Websites*, 12 BMC MED. ETHICS 17 (2011); Neil Lunt & Percivil Carrera, *Systematic Review of Web Sites for Prospective Medical Tourists*, 66 TOURISM REV. 57 (2011).

[58] Jo Gilmartin, *Contemporary Cosmetic Surgery: The Potential Risks and Relevance for Practice*, 20 J. CLINICAL NURSING 1801 (2010).

[59] Brett Coldiron, *Office Surgery Incidents: What Seven Years of Florida Data Show Us*, 34 DERMATOLOGIC SURGERY 285 (2008).

significant gaps in current statistics concerning complications from cosmetic surgery and bariatric surgery. Datasets are severely lacking when board-certified plastic surgeons and bariatric surgeons report complications to their professional societies while physicians who lack such training and work in private facilities with little external oversight do not disclose morbidity and mortality data. If data from both domestic and international physicians who are not board-certified in plastic surgery or cosmetic surgery were collected, it is possible that many surgical procedures would be revealed to be considerably riskier to patients than at present they are assumed to be.

Finally, news reports of the deaths of medical tourists at facilities in Mexico combined with the absence of reports of medical travel-related mortality from many well-known destinations for medical tourists suggests the importance of developing effective strategies for tracking flows of medical travelers, documenting what procedures they undergo, identifying what types of facilities they visit, verifying the qualifications of treating physicians, and evaluating the safety of particular practice environments. Though news media reports do not provide insight into the relative risk of traveling to particular health care destinations, I was struck by how many deaths are reported to have occurred in Mexico and the absence of reports of deaths of medical travelers in such countries as Singapore and Thailand. This finding might be a product of the search strategies I utilized, the databases I used, or other factors. However, it is also plausible that specific features of small-scale, private, for-profit clinics along the Mexican side of the U.S.–Mexico border leave their clients particularly vulnerable to surgical complications. The four deaths in the Dominican Republic, three of which occurred in a single medical facility, and two deaths at a single physician's practice in Brazil also suggest the need for paying particular attention to these destinations. If cases of morbidity and mortality are clustered at several international medical destinations, perhaps it is possible to develop "channels" or "gates" that will help protect medical travelers and increase the prospect that they seek care at facilities recognized for promoting patient safety.[60] Individual patients, health insurance companies, and medical tourism facilitators can all benefit from increased access to evidence that will help direct patients toward health care facilities with exemplary records of patients safety and away from hospitals and clinics where quality of care is in question. Steering medical tourists toward particular international medical facilities and away from specific hospitals and clinics might reduce the incidence of morbidity and mortality in medical tourists. Rigorous empirical research is needed to address this issue.

V. Importance of Documenting Clinical Outcomes in Medical Travel

Despite sustained public and academic interest in medical tourism, there is only limited academic analysis of clinical outcomes for medical tourists.[61] Proponents of

---

[60] I. Glenn Cohen, *Protecting Patients with Passports: Medical Tourism and the Patient-Protective Argument*, 95 IOWA L. REV. 1467 (2010).

[61] Neil Lunt & Percivil Carrera, *Medical Tourism: Assessing the Evidence on Treatment Abroad*, 66 MATURITAS 27 (2010).

medical tourism emphasize cost savings, high quality of care at international facilities, expedited access to treatment, choice in health services, and other benefits.[62] In contrast, critics express concerns that medical tourists enter a poorly regulated global marketplace; are at risk of receiving inadequate preoperative counseling, substandard medical care, and poorly coordinated postoperative treatment; and exacerbate health inequities in the countries they visit.[63] Both proponents and critics of medical tourists have only a limited body of case reports, surveys, and other studies to bolster their claims. Very little comparative research is available to compare the quality of care medical tourists receive at international facilities against clinical data from comparable domestic facilities.

One reason it is difficult to make informed, evidence-based judgments about quality of care and patient safety in medical tourism is the lack of systematic, rigorous, comparative data. There are no databases tracking global flows of patients and documenting clinical outcomes in individuals who leave their local communities and arrange care at international facilities. The total number of individuals who travel abroad every year for medical procedures is unknown. Likewise, there are no reliable data concerning morbidity and mortality rates in medical tourism. Lack of credible data at the global level of analysis persists when trying to "dig down" and examine morbidity and mortality rates in medical travelers from such countries as Australia, Canada, and the United States. For example, despite repeated assertions about the annual number of U.S. residents traveling to medical facilities outside the United States, there is no registry tracking how many U.S. citizens leave the country for care, why they go abroad for treatment, where they receive care, what kind of medical interventions they seek, and what happens to them as a result of obtaining health care outside the United States. According to one widely cited report produced by Deloitte, in 2007 approximately 750,000 U.S. residents sought health care outside the United States, and an estimated 648,000 traveled abroad in 2009.[64] In contrast, drawing upon data from the U.S. Bureau of Economic Analysis and U.S. International Trade Administration as well as survey data, Johnson and Garman estimate that between 50,000 to 121,000 U.S. residents sought medical care outside the United States in 2007.[65] As these varying estimates reveal, there is considerable disagreement concerning how many U.S. residents seek health care outside the United States every year. The situation is the same in Australia, Canada, and elsewhere. Speculative claims abound concerning the number of individuals traveling abroad for care. Rigorous quantification of medical tourism

[62] DEVON HERRICK, MEDICAL TOURISM: GLOBAL COMPETITION IN HEALTH CARE, NCPA REPORT NO. 304 (2007), http://www.ncpa.org/pdfs/st304.pdf; Aaditya Mattoo & Randeep Rathindran, *How Health Insurance Inhibits Trade in Health Care*, 25 HEALTH AFF. 358 (2006).

[63] Andrea Whittaker, *Pleasure and Pain: Medical Travel in Asia*, 3 GLOBAL PUB. HEALTH 271 (2008).

[64] DELOITTE CENTER FOR HEALTH SOLUTIONS, MEDICAL TOURISM: UPDATE AND IMPLICATIONS—2009 REPORT (2009).

[65] Tricia Johnson & Andrew Garman, *Impact of Medical Travel on Imports and Exports of Medical Services*, 98 HEALTH POL'Y 171 (2010); Brandon Alleman et al., *Medical Tourism Services Available to Residents of the United States*, 26 J. GEN. INTERNAL MED. 492 (2010).

is scarce, and it appears that numbers are mobilized to market medical tourism and make it seem more commonplace than it truly is.

Most health-related databases are built for the intended purpose of collecting data related to provision of domestic medical care. They are not designed to track patients across national borders. Designing new databases or expanding existing ones capable of monitoring medical tourists is extremely difficult because the global marketplace for health services is decentralized, legislation governing health care facilities and health care professionals typically is domestic in scope rather than transnational, and many procedures purchased by medical tourists are performed in private, for-profit health care facilities that do not disclose to domestic databases basic information concerning infection rates, postoperative complications, and medical errors. Medical tourists typically make individual arrangements with destination medical facilities or plan their trips with the assistance of medical tourism facilitators.[66] They do not organize trips with the aid of some centralized transnational body or report their travel plans to domestic government agencies. Some cross-border medical care involves government participation, such as when provincial health systems in Canada make arrangements for Canadian citizens to receive care at select facilities in the United States. However, it appears that most medical travel is based upon individual decisions to pay out-of-pocket for care at international medical facilities. As a result, building databases that track medical tourists and their clinical outcomes is going to be very challenging.

Given the absence of databases tracking movement of patients and documenting clinical outcomes in medical tourism, there is at present no credible basis for making three types of empirical claims. First, it is not possible to make accurate statements concerning how many individuals leave their local community and travel abroad for medical care. Second, there is no basis for making evidence-based assertions about how many medical tourists experience clinical benefits and how many experience surgical complications, infections, and other treatment-related health problems. Third, because there are no databases tracking how many individuals participate in medical tourism and how many of these persons experience benefits or harms as a result of traveling abroad for care, there is considerable uncertainty concerning whether individuals traveling to particular locations are at greater risk of experiencing complications from treatment when they travel for care instead of visiting domestic medical facilities. Case reports establish that some medical tourists have experienced serious postoperative complications at international hospitals and clinics. However, it is important to understand that postoperative infections, medical errors, and negligent medical care also occur at domestic health care facilities.

Although I acknowledge that clinical registries and systematic comparative outcomes data in medical tourism do not exist and recognizing that reliable quantitative

---

[66] Neil Lunt et al., *Nip, Tuck and Click: Medical Tourism and the Emergence of Web-Based Health Information*, 4 OPEN MED. INFORMATICS J. 1 (2010).

studies are needed to make judgments about relative patient safety and quality of care when comparing outcomes in medical tourism to the quality of care individuals should expect to receive at domestic health care facilities, analysis of news media articles describing the reported deaths of twenty-seven medical tourists reveals the importance of better documenting clinical outcomes in medical tourism. This analysis, though it documents reported deaths of medical tourists, should not be used to claim that domestic medical care is "safe" and medical tourism is "unsafe." Indeed, during my research I was struck by the number of reports I found that described patients who experienced serious complications or died after undergoing cosmetic surgery in domestic health care facilities. It appears that quality of care, patient safety, and adequate review and regulation of medical devices used in cosmetic surgery is problematic in many settings.

Noting the need for more systematic efforts to track clinical outcomes in medical tourism, I hope this study provides a meaningful complement to peer-reviewed publications that describe medical complications in cosmetic surgery travelers and individuals who have gone abroad for cosmetic surgery but provide no case reports of patients who died during surgery or shortly after receiving treatment. If these news media accounts are accurate, then peer-reviewed publications are failing to identify, document, and analyze deaths of patients who have traveled abroad for cosmetic surgery and bariatric surgery. By describing these cases I hope to promote increased interest in tracking medical tourists, studying clinical outcomes in medical tourism, and addressing in an empirically informed manner the many ethical, clinical, legal, and social issues generated by the emergence of a global marketplace in health services.

VI. Challenges in Using News Media Reports

Numerous challenges are associated with attempting to analyze news media accounts of deaths of medical tourists. First, if journalists crafting these narratives make errors when crafting their accounts, some of these mistakes could be reproduced in the information I extracted, recorded, and categorized. Journalists have only a limited time to prepare news stories; the pressure to meet deadlines, along with other factors, can lead to inaccurate reportage.

Second, after searching for news media reports I was in some cases able to supplement news media accounts by finding obituaries, Web-based posts written by individuals claiming to be family members of deceased individuals, contributions to cosmetic surgery discussion boards, and, in one case, detailed court records. In most instances, I was unable to locate additional sources corroborating claims made in news media accounts. In short, I acknowledge that there are identifiable disadvantages to using news media accounts when attempting to track deaths of medical tourists. In the next phase of research I will address some of these constraints by contacting family members and friends of the individuals identified in these news reports. Interviews with them might generate insights unavailable in the newspaper reports I analyze, and confirm whether various details in news reports are accurate.

VII. Search Terms, Databases, Sources Contained in Databases, and Bias

Decisions concerning choice of search terms inform what articles are found in databases. Though I entered many different search terms into the databases I used, it is possible that my use of search terms introduced bias into the search process and influenced the particular types of news media reports that I found. In addition, decisions to search particular databases presumably had an impact upon what reports I found. Use of languages other than English as well as use of other search terms and databases might lead to identification of additional case reports of mortality in travel for cosmetic surgery and bariatric surgery.

By conducting searches using ProQuest NewsStand, Google, Google News, and Google News Archive, I attempted to take a "wide angle" approach to locating reports of mortality in international travel for cosmetic surgery and bariatric surgery. However, use of these databases likely introduced bias into my findings. For example, at present ProQuest NewsStand includes 1394 news sources from all over the world.[67] The database contains such major U.S. news media sources as *The New York Times*, *Los Angeles Times*, *Wall Street Journal*, and *Washington Post*. It also contains articles from such "international" newspapers as *The Guardian*, *The Globe and Mail*, *The Hindu*, *Jerusalem Post*, and *South China Morning Post*. Though the database contains news sources from around the world, review of newspapers listed in the database indicates that it has more news sources from the United States than from other countries. Although I did not deliberately seek to find reports of patients who originated in particular countries and traveled to specific destinations, my choice of English language databases combined with the many U.S. news sources in the ProQuest NewsStand database likely contributed to the number of reports I found that described mortality in medical tourists from the United States. It is possible that searches of databases containing more newspaper articles from news media sources based in countries other than the United States might find additional reports of mortality in medical tourists originating from countries other than the United States.

I did not deliberately seek to find reports of deaths of medical tourists in particular medical tourism destinations. Though I did not focus on Mexico as a destination for medical tourists, my searches identified numerous reports of medical tourists from the United States who died during or after having cosmetic surgery or bariatric surgery in Mexico. Indeed, I am struck by the number of reports of deaths following cosmetic

---

67 PROQUEST NEWSPAPERS, http://proquest.umi.com.ezp1.lib.umn.edu/pqdweb?RQT=317&TS=13217597 44&clientId=2256&SQ=*&PageNum=1&link=1.

surgery in Mexico. Sandra Dibble, a reporter for *The San Diego Union-Tribune* has for many years alone and with her colleagues published articles about Californians who traveled to hospitals and clinics in Mexico and either died during or after surgery or returned to the United States with postoperative complications. Numerous articles by Dibble are used as sources for cases described in this article. What I am unable to determine is whether news media coverage of morbidity and mortality in medical tourism is connected to the actual incidence of morbidity and mortality at particular international medical facilities. It is conceivable that Dibble has recognized a significant health news story; understands that many residents of California travel to Mexico for cosmetic surgery, dental care, and other procedures; and provides detailed coverage of cases where U.S. citizens experience postoperative complications or die after having surgery at clinics in Mexico. It is also possible that journalists based in other settings are unaware of incidents involving medical tourism and mortality at medical facilities in countries other than Mexico, decide not to write about such cases, are aware of reports of mortality in medical tourists but select other stories to cover, or are assigned by editors and producers to other stories.

Use of particular databases, choice of search terms, and sources captured by these databases presumably all have an effect upon the news media reports that I have identified. Given the number of reports describing mortality associated with surgery performed at medical facilities in Mexico there is reason to be concerned about the quality of care provided to some medical tourists at particular medical facilities in Mexico. However, databases to identify news media reports cannot be used to establish with certainty whether some destinations for medical tourism are riskier and offer lower-quality care than other international hospitals and clinics. What analysis of news media reports can do is demonstrate the importance of developing rigorous tools to assess clinical outcomes in medical tourism for cosmetic surgery and other procedures.

VIII. Correlation is not Causation

My summary of news reports of deaths of medical tourists might lead some readers to assume that medical errors, poor quality of care, or specific actions performed by treating physicians must have caused the patients to die during or shortly after surgery. To the contrary, although the news reports I located generate serious concerns about the quality of care some medical tourists receive when they go abroad for surgery, news media accounts do not provide a basis for establishing causality and legal responsibility and cannot be used to make claims about medical negligence or professional standards of care. Determinations of medical negligence are achieved through established legal procedures and rules of evidence. According to news media accounts, in four instances physicians were deemed to have contributed to the deaths of patients. In a fifth case a physician was charged with manslaughter, but a verdict has not yet been delivered. Whatever the merits of drawing upon news media accounts, these narratives identify correlations between surgical procedures and deaths and prompt questions about quality of care, medical professionalism, and adequacy of treating facilities. However, they do not establish causation or culpability. With the exception of the four instances that resulted in successful legal action against treating physicians, causality, the role of treating health care providers, and the extent to which the health care environment exposed patients to risk or helped shield them from harm remain unknown.

Many of the news reports offered sharp criticisms of the care patients received. Although these accounts prompt legitimate concerns about quality of care and treatment of cosmetic surgery travelers, they do not lead to definitive conclusions about conditions in clinics, patient selection and screening criteria used prior to performing surgery, surgical technique, or postoperative care. It is conceivable that some patients had underlying medical conditions and these previously unknown health problems played a deciding role in the deaths of these individuals. In addition, it is possible that adverse events occurred but treatment received by the medical tourists fell within what reasonable, prudent health care professionals would regard as an adequate standard of care. In short, it is important to exercise caution when considering these news accounts. With this caveat noted, if these news reports are accurate, they document twenty-seven deaths that are nowhere acknowledged or addressed in peer-reviewed scholarship concerning medical tourism. Although I recognize the need for caution in interpreting these news media reports, these twenty-seven cases prompt legitimate questions concerning whether steps could have been taken to better protect these individuals from harm and reduce risk of a fatal outcome following elective surgical procedures.

IX. Case Reports do not Establish Relative Risk

Just as it is important to avoid the error of confusing correlation with causation, it also is important to note that analysis of reports of deaths of medical tourism cannot be used to support the claim that medical tourism poses greater risks to patients than obtaining care at domestic health care facilities. While searching for articles describing deaths of medical tourists I found numerous news media reports summarizing deaths of individuals who had undergone liposuction, breast augmentation, and other cosmetic surgery procedures in their home states within the United States as well as in Australia and Canada.[68] Accurate datasets providing information about clinical

---

[68] Elizabeth Fernandez & Lance Williams, *If Liposuction Were a Drug, It Would Have Been Pulled from the Market*, S.F. CHRON. Sept. 13, 1998; Elizabeth Fernandez, *When the Desire to Be Thin Is Last Wish on Earth*, S.F. CHRON. Sept. 14, 1998; Sue Hewitt, *Cosmetic Surgery Death Probe*, HERALD SUN, Jan. 28, 2007; Christie Blatchford, *Prosecution Portrays Stunning Failures in Lipo Death*, GLOBE & MAIL, July 22, 2010; Rob Cribb, *Lipo Death Spurs Look at Hazy Rules*, TORONTO STAR, July 24, 2010; Jmaiek Omarnicki, *Inquiry Opens on Plastic Surgery Death*, CALGARY HERALD, Jan. 19, 2011; Dan Lett, *The Search for Integrity in the Cosmetic Surgery Market*, 178 CANADIAN MED. ASS'N J. 274 (2008).

outcomes in patients undergoing care at domestic health care facilities and in individuals obtaining medical care at international sites are needed to make credible assertions about whether relative risk of morbidity and mortality is increased by leaving particular social contexts and traveling to specific international clinics and hospitals. Again, with this caveat noted, without providing insight into relative risks these case reports suggest that prospective medical tourists need to be aware that elective cosmetic surgery procedures and bariatric surgery procedures at international medical facilities have resulted in both morbidity and mortality. The case reports also give credence to the concept of developing strategies intended to minimize risks individuals face when they travel abroad for medical care.

Conclusion

Drawing upon news media accounts, I review twenty-seven reported cases of medical tourists who died during or shortly after undergoing cosmetic surgery or bariatric surgery. Eleven of these individuals died after having cosmetic surgery or bariatric surgery in Mexico, and four died after undergoing cosmetic surgery in the Dominican Republic. An additional two deaths occurred at a single physician's practice in Brazil. In short, of the twenty-seven reported deaths, seventeen of them can be connected to health care facilities in three countries. In four of the twenty-seven cases, physicians were fined, sued, or jailed. In a fifth case, the physician is charged with manslaughter and awaits trial. In the remaining cases it is not possible to make assertions about medical negligence or malpractice. If these news media reports are accurate, they should be considered in conjunction with case reports in medical tourism of postoperative complications.

Though it is not possible to claim on the basis of these news media accounts that medical travelers are at greater risk when obtaining medical care abroad than they are at domestic health care facilities, it is possible to assert that if these reports are credible, since 1993 at least twenty-seven medical tourists are reported to have died during or after undergoing elective cosmetic surgery or bariatric surgery. These deaths should prompt reflection upon what strategies might improve patient safety, quality of care, disclosure of information, quality of advertising, and protection of patients in the global marketplace for health services. In addition, reports of these deaths in news media but not in scholarly publications should prompt questions about whether current peer-reviewed scholarship addressing clinical outcomes in medical tourism is underreporting patient mortality.

Whether individuals die after undergoing cosmetic surgery or bariatric surgery in domestic health facilities or in international hospitals and clinics, it is important to ask whether patients are being adequately protected and what might be done to reduce the likelihood of additional cases of postoperative complications and deaths. Both cosmetic surgery and bariatric surgery are sometimes assumed to involve "minor" procedures that do not generate concerns about patient safety. To the contrary, both morbidity and mortality can result from these procedures. Individuals considering cosmetic surgery or bariatric surgery must be aware of the possibility of risks to health and complications from surgery in both domestic and international health care facilities. Current marketing of cosmetic surgery by both domestic clinics and international facilities could play a role in leading prospective medical tourists to underestimate risks of surgical procedures and overestimate anticipated benefits.

In the existing body of peer-reviewed scholarship addressing travel for cosmetic surgery and bariatric surgery travel there are to the best of my knowledge no reports of deaths of patients at international medical facilities. Rather, case reports are limited to instances of patients returning to their local communities with postoperative complications. This analysis of twenty-seven news media reports of travel for cosmetic surgery and bariatric surgery suggests that accounts of post-operative morbidity must be supplemented by reports of patient deaths. Patients in both local and international settings could be better protected from risk of injury and death if cosmetic surgery and bariatric surgery were subjected to far more stringent regulatory oversight. In addition, reports of deaths of cosmetic surgery patients and bariatric surgery patients are relevant to larger public conversations about whether surgical techniques that have become routinized and normalized need to be subjected to public debate and better government scrutiny. Deaths of patients undergoing elective surgical procedures, whether they occur in domestic facilities or international hospitals and clinics, should prompt us to ask how they could have been avoided.

The news reports that I review indicate the importance of establishing effective measures for tracking clinical outcomes in medical tourism. In addition, they raise the possibility that there is a serious gap in contemporary scholarship addressing medical tourism for cosmetic surgery and bariatric surgery. The emergence of a global marketplace in health services has not been accompanied by the development of transnational regulatory bodies tasked with monitoring and regulating medical tourism. At present, clinical databases and health researchers are not systematically tracking global flows of medical tourists and documenting clinical outcomes. More rigorous analysis of the consequences of medical tourism for individual patients, public health, and health systems would make a significant contribution to normative analysis of medical tourism. Critics of my effort to use news media reports will argue that news accounts of deaths of medical tourists consist of nothing more than unsubstantiated anecdotes or exercises in sensationalistic journalism. I am aware of the disadvantages associated with using news media reports to document deaths of medical tourists. Acknowledging the caution with which findings drawn from news reports must be used, I suggest that the risks of using these reports are outweighed by the risk of dismissing news reports of deaths of medical tourists. Calling news media reports "sensationalistic" and ignoring narratives by journalists could lead to underestimation of risks associated with participating in medical tourism for cosmetic surgery and bariatric surgery.

Whatever the advantages and disadvantages of using news reports describing deaths of medical tourists, this approach suggests the value of using both normative analyses and empirical research methods to address such topics as quality of information disclosure, adequacy of patient consent, safety of particular surgical procedures, and quality of postoperative care in medical travel. If "what isn't counted doesn't count," as some health researchers state, then there is an obvious need to begin "counting" medical tourists and clinical outcomes to better understand what is happening in the global marketplace for health services.

2

JURISDICTION 101 FOR MEDICAL TOURISM

PURCHASES MADE IN EUROPE

*Thomas R. McLean**

Introduction

In the European Union, receiving proper medical care is considered a virtual right.[1] To secure this right without having to wait in a queue, and for other reasons,[2] 4 percent of Europeans make cross-border health care purchases.[3] Given human nature, few purchasers of cross-board health care contemplate jurisdiction prior to making their purchase. Yet, should a patient purchasing overseas health care services experience an adverse outcome at the hands of a foreign medical tourism vendor (MTV) (i.e., a health care provider or facilitator), jurisdiction is a key component in determining whether that purchaser will receive compensation for his or her injury.

Given the present rate of cross-border travel to purchase health care services in the European Union, it can be estimated that each year perhaps as many as 100,000 EU

---

* MD, JD, FACS, ESQ. CEO, Third Millennium Consultants, LLC, Shawnee KS, (tmclean@isp.com). I am indebted to my friend and colleague Mr. Laurence Vick, with Michelmore, LLP, (a United Kingdom law firm), for his assistance in the translation of EU jurisdictional concepts into U.S. jurisdictional concepts.

[1] Treaty on European Union (Maastricht Treaty) art. 95, Feb. 7, 1992, 31 I.L.M. 253, *available at* http://eur-lex.europa.eu/en/treaties/dat/11992M/htm/11992M.html.

[2] David Charter, *Patients to Beat NHS Queues in EU Plan for Open Health Market*, THE TIMES AND SUNDAY TIMES, Dec. 18, 2007, *available at* http://www.timesonline.co.uk/tol/life_and_style/health/article3065786.ece.

[3] Press Release, European Parliament, An EU Citizen's Right to Get Medical Treatment in Another Member State (Oct. 27, 2010), *available at* http://www.europarl.europa.eu/en/pressroom/content/20101025IPR90069/.

medical tourists may seek compensation from their MTVs.[4] Accordingly, the purpose of this chapter is to provide medical tourists and their attorneys with a background in the EU's jurisdiction laws. The principles underlying modern EU jurisdiction were first articulated in 1968 in the Brussels Convention[5] and were initially only applicable to a few European countries. In the ensuing forty years, the Brussels Convention has undergone only a few minor modifications while its application has been extended to all EU Member States and certain "Third States"[6] by several treaties. However, as these subsequent treaties have almost identical wording, herein the Brussels Convention and its progeny will be simply referred to as "the Brussels Convention."[7]

In general, under the Brussels Convention, jurisdiction is not an issue when a patient and an MTV are domiciled in the same country. Should the patient and the MTV be domiciled in different EU Member States, then the Brussels Convention gives the country where the MTV is domiciled jurisdiction over medical tourism transactions.[8] However, the Brussels Convention's general jurisdiction rules are subjected to

---

[4] In the European Union, with its population of 500 billion people, 4 percent of the population made cross-border health care purchases in 2007. *EU27 Population 501 million at January 1, 2010*, EUSTAT (July 27, 2010); Press Release, An EU Citizen's Right, *supra* note 3. When these health care purchases require that the patient be hospitalized, 10 percent of such purchases will result in an adverse outcome. European Council, *Council Recommendation on Patient Safety, including the Prevention and Control of Healthcare Associated Infections* (June 9, 2009), http://www.consilium.europa.eu/uedocs/cms_data/docs/pressdata/en/lsa/108381.pdf. Using a standard figure of 5 percent for translating the number of adverse events experienced by patients into the number of medical malpractice lawsuits filed by plaintiffs, then perhaps as many as 100,000 medical tourists who purchased cross-border health care services in the European Union will seek compensation for their adverse events each year. R.A. Brennan et al., *Incidence of Adverse Events and Negligence in Hospitalized Patients: Results of the Harvard Medical Practice Study*, 324 NEW ENG. J. OF MED. 370 (1991). This figure can, and should be adjusted, if hard-to-obtain data become available. This figure of 100,000 lawsuits/year should be increased if data for American or Asian medical tourism purchases in Europe is obtained. On the other hand, this figure of 100,000 lawsuits/year should be decreased if data can be obtained that includes the precise demographics for medical tourism purchases, because many of these purchases (*e.g.*, dental procedures) do not require hospitalization. Finally, this 100,000 lawsuits/year figure assumes EU citizens file lawsuits after an adverse event similar to the rate that U.S. citizens would seek compensation. This may or may not be true.

[5] *See* Brussels Convention on Jurisdiction and the Enforcement of Judgments in Civil and Commercial Matters, Sept. 27, 1968, 29 I.L.M. 1413, *available at* http://curia.europa.eu/common/recdoc/convention/en/c-textes/brux-idx.htm.

[6] European Commission, Fifth Framework Programme, *available at* http://cordis.europa.eu/fp5/src/3rdcountries.htm. The reference to "Third States" is a term of art used to refer to those countries that have various commitments to the EU, but are neither de jure Member States or countries that are in the formal process of becoming de jure Member States. *Id.* A detailed discussion of EU membership and commitment status is beyond the scope of this chapter.

[7] Brussels I Regulation, officially the Council Regulation (EC) No 44/2001, Dec. 22, 2000, [2001] O.J. L 012, *available at* http://eur-lex.europa.eu/LexUriServ/LexUriServ.do?uri=CONSLEG:2001R0044:20090408:EN:PDF. Lugano Convention, Sept. 16, 1988, 28 I.L.M. 620, *available at* http://curia.europa.eu/common/recdoc/convention/en/c-textes/_lug-textes.htm. The original Brussels Convention plus these two treaties are often referred to as the "Brussels Regime"; herein these treaties will be collectively referred to as the "Brussels Convention." Note that although the wording found in these treaties is virtually identical; the specific treaty's article-numbering system varies from treaty to treaty. Accordingly, the article citations used in this chapter refer to those found in the most recent treaty.

[8] Jackson v. Owusu, 2005 E.C.R. I-1383.

modification by: (1) MTV's willingness to make a voluntarily appearance in a court where the patient is domiciled;[9] (2) locus of the contract's performance;[10] (3) arbitration[11] and forum-shifting jurisdictional clauses;[12] and (4) a patient's demonstration that he or she is a consumer.[13]

Of the factors that will shift jurisdiction away from a MTV's domicile, the most interesting is consumer status. In the European Union, a consumer transaction arises when someone purchases a good or service outside of his or her personal expertise. Additionally, if after receiving a special invitation, a consumer makes a cross-border purchase, then the courts where the consumer is domiciled have jurisdiction over that transaction. What constitutes a special initiation to a consumer is determined by a fact-sensitive inquiry, but consumer status may be created by the contents found within the vendor's advertisements. Consumer status also impacts how jurisdictional clauses are interpreted. Unless a consumer contract is fair, its jurisdictional clause will not be enforced. So, unless medical tourism services are purchased by a health care professional, they will likely be deemed as consumer transactions, and MTVs may inadvertently lose control of their "home court" jurisdictional advantage if they are careless in drafting their contracts or advertisement.

Finally, regardless of which EU Member States adjudicate a medical tourism dispute, enforcement is the rule. This is because the Brussels Convention establishes for EU Member States an exequatur procedure for the immediate recognition and enforcement of foreign judgments. As the grounds for nonenforcement of a foreign judgment are limited, consideration is even afoot to abolishes the need for exequatur altogether. Thus, foreign judgments and awards should be taken seriously.

This chapter will review all of these concepts. Part I briefly examines Europeans' right to medical tourism services under the Treaty of Maastricht.[14] Part II then examines the easy situation where the medical tourist and vendor(s) are both domiciled in the same country, as well as the general rule for determining diversity jurisdiction when the parties to a dispute are domiciled in different EU countries. Next, Part III examines the numerous loopholes to the general rule for determining diversity jurisdiction. Finally, Part IV examines the ability of a plaintiff to have a judgment or award enforced when diversity jurisdiction is present. This chapter concludes that after an adverse medical outcome, unwary medical tourists and MTVs may find that they have accepted more liability than they have realized.

I. Medical Tourism as a "Right"

The Treaty of Maastricht, which created the European Union in 1992, grants EU citizens a basic right to health care services, and stipulates that these services are to be covered

---

[9] Brussels Convention, *supra* note 7, at art. 24.
[10] *Id.* at art. 5.
[11] *Id.* at art. 1.
[12] *Id.* at art. 7.
[13] *Id.* at art. 15.
[14] Maastricht Treaty, *supra* note 1.

by the citizen's national health care service.[15] However, this right to national health care benefits is not absolute because Article 95 of the Treaty prohibits EU Member States from adopting rules or regulations that would constrain the fiscal policies of other EU Member States.[16] An example of such a constraint would be one Member State's open-ended demand for reimbursement for services rendered to another Member State's citizens.

The leading case that examines the limitations imposed by Article 95 on EU medical tourism (or patient mobility—as it is known in Europe) is *Watts v. Bedford Primary Care Trust*.[17] At the time of this case, the United Kingdom's health care policy required the National Health Service (NHS) to cover the cost of hip replacements within twelve months of a request being filed for this procedure.[18] After the NHS repeatedly stonewalled Mrs. Watts's request for coverage for her elective hip replacement, she filed a lawsuit to obtain pre-authorization to purchase her hip replacement from an overseas MTV.[19]

When the European Court of Justice (ECJ) heard *Watts*, it was aware that the EU Member States' national health care systems had to make certain trade-offs to keep their systems operational. In particular, the ECJ recognized that the EU Member States cannot afford to provide all medical services demanded by their citizens. Given a finite capacity to cover the cost of health care, "persons requiring...medical treatment[s] will not always be able to obtain that treatment within acceptable time–limits within their national systems."[20] For such patients the European Union established the S2 (formerly E112) system for purchasing covered health care from other Member States.[21]

Under the S2 system, medical tourism services purchased abroad will be covered by the patient's national health care service if the patient obtains pre-authorization to purchase the needed medical care. However, *Watts* then added that a national health care system cannot refuse to grant S2 preauthorization if:

(1) the treatment must be among the benefits insured in the competent Member State and (2) the treatment required cannot be provided "within the time normally necessary for obtaining the treatment in question in the Member State of residence, taking account of his current state of health and the probable course of his disease."[22]

Accordingly, in *Watts*, the court found that because the NHS failed to provide a valid justification for denying Mrs. Watts with S2 preauthorization, Mrs. Watts was entitled to receive pre-authorization and reimbursement for her hip replacement.

---

[15] *Id*. at art. 95(3).

[16] *Id*. at art. 95(2).

[17] Case C-372/04, Watts v. Bedford Primary Care Trust, 2006 E.C.R. I-4325.

[18] *Id*. at point 20.

[19] *Id*. at points 10–14.

[20] *Id*. at point 20.

[21] Anglo Info, *Healthcare Abroad—Europe, available at* http://london.angloinfo.com/countries/uk/euhealth.asp.

[22] *Watts*, 2006 E.C.R. I-4325 at point 30 (citing Maastrict Treaty, *supra* note 1, at art. 22(2)).

In subsequent years, *Watts* has been modified by several cases and proposed directives. In *Aikaterini Stamatelaki v. NPDD Organismos Asfaliseo*[23] the ECJ weighed the rights of a Greek patient to obtain reimbursement for medical tourism services purchased from a British MTV. Although *Stamatelaki* recognized that EU Member States' regulations (especially the need for precertification) are to be respected,[24] in general, such national regulations may not impair the ability of foreign MTVs to compete against national providers.[25] According to the ECJ, although national regulations that discriminate against foreign MTV are not per se verboten, such regulations must be supported with a valid justification[26] that is no more burdensome than is necessary.[27] *Stamatelaki* was subsequently remanded for further development.

An example of what the Court considered to be an unnecessarily burdensome restriction on foreign MTVs was provided by *Procureur du Roi v. Ioannis Doulamis*.[28] In this case, a dentist advertised his services in an overseas telephone book.[29] The relevant national law, however, flatly prohibited dentists from advertising their services. In *Procureur du Roi*, the ECJ recognized that EU Member States could potentially justify regulations that protected their citizens from unscrupulous overseas health care providers. On the other hand, the trust between a patient and a health care provider is "based initially on the reputation of the professional or the healthcare establishment and, in general, the more treatment the patient receives, the more that trust is strengthened."[30] To gain this initial trust, patients require some information, even if that information is found in an advertisement. Accordingly, the court ruled that a flat prohibition against MTVs advertising their services was unnecessarily restrictive.[31]

In 2008, the European Commission adopted a proposed directive to clarify the rules for internal medical travel. In the final iteration of this proposed directive, which was adopted as a formal directive in 2011,[32] two key changes were made to the S2 system.[33] First, because pre-authorization for "cross-border non-hospital care represents an obstacle to the free movement of health services that is not justified," such authorization was abolished. Accordingly, under the new directive pre-authorization for medical tourism purchases would only be necessary if the needed treatment

---

[23] Case C-444/05, Aikaterini Stamatelaki v N.P.D.D. Organismos Asfaliseo, 2007 E.C.R. I-3185.

[24] *Id.* at point 22.

[25] *Id.* at point 45 (citing Maastricht Treaty, *supra* note 1, at art. 49).

[26] *Id.* at point 50.

[27] *Id.* at point 60.

[28] Case C-446/05, Procureur du Roi v. Ioannis Doulamis, 2008 E.C.R. I-1377.

[29] *Id.* at point 27.

[30] *Id.* at point 94.

[31] *Id.* at point 98.

[32] *The EU Directive on Cross Border Healthcare…Where Are We Now?*, INT'L. MED. TRAVEL J. (2010), *available at* http://www.imtjonline.com/articles/2010/eu-directive-on-cross-border-healthcare-30077.

[33] *Id.*

required hospitalization.[34] On one level, jettisoning pre-authorization for nonhospitalized care makes sense and could facilitate medical tourism among the EU Member States. Unfortunately, there is no generally accepted definition for what care requires hospitalization.

Second, the new EU directive expands the traditional pool of justifications for denying pre-authorization. In addition to denying pre-authorization for hospital care because the patient's national health care service can provide the requested service within a reasonable time, the new directive would also allow pre-authorization to be denied if there was a concern that the returning medical tourist might create a public safety risk, or there was a concern for the competency of the foreign MTV who was to provide the requested service.[35] Although these two new justifications for the denial of S2 preauthorization creates a slippery slope with respect to their application, that is not our concern.

What is important to recognize here is that *Watts* and its progeny are likely to expand the European Union's internal market for medical tourism services,[36] and hence increase the number of potential cases of overseas iatrogenic injury (that is, injury caused by medical care). Of course, whether the iatrogenically injured medical tourist can recover damages from a foreign MTV, in turn, depends on jurisdiction.

II. The Easy Case and the General Rule

Few jurisdictional issues arise when Europeans purchase health care services from a domestic vendor. The domestic courts will have jurisdiction over both parties, and many, if not all, practical issues (such as service of process and extradition[37]) are moot. So, when the patient and provider are from the same EU Member State, the provider's professional liability risk(s) will be determined by the nature of the service provided and the laws (both procedural and substantive) of the country where the parties reside. Accordingly, although it may not be possible to precisely calculate a vendor's risk for having to provide compensation for an iatrogenic injury, the risk is generally recognized by both the patient and health care provider.

On the other hand, when patients make cross-border health care purchases in the European Union, the situation becomes more complex. Under international conditions, EU MTVs may perceive their professional liability risk to be less than when they provide health care to a domestic patient. This is because the international patient

---

[34] *Id.; cf.* Martin Banks, *New EU Healthcare Rules "Will Not Promote Medical Tourism" Says Parliament's Rapporteur,* THE PARLIAMENT, Jan. 18, 2011 (questioning whether the proposed directive will in fact stimulate internal EU medical travel), *available at* http://www.theparliament.com/latest-news/ article/newsarticle/new-eu-healthcare-rules-will-not-promote-medical-tourism-says-parl iaments-rapporteur.

[35] *The EU* Directive, *supra* note 32.

[36] *Id.*

[37] Thomas R. McLean, *The Global Market for Health Care: Economics and Regulation,* 26 WIS. INT'L L.J. 591 (2008).

would be inconvenienced by having to return to the MTV's country to prosecute a legal action.[38] To a degree, this perception is correct, but it may provide false security.

To begin our analysis of cross-border jurisdiction, assume that both the patient and MTV are domiciled in different EU Member States. This is important because the scope of the Brussels Convention is applicable only to EU members. If either the patient or the MTV reside outside the European Union other jurisdictional treaties may come into play. In general, under the Brussels Convention, when parties to a transaction are domiciled in different countries, jurisdiction belongs to the country where the defendant (i.e., the MTV) is domiciled. Two points must be understood to appreciate the subtlety of this rule. First, jurisdiction turns on the defendant's domicile, not the defendant's citizenship. Second, where a defendant is domiciled is determined by the law of the country where the defendant is found.[39] Accordingly, under the Brussels Convention's general rule, Belgium would have jurisdiction over an Italian citizen who resides in Liege and provides medical services to a citizen of Sweden who is domiciled in London.

Domiciliary determination, in turn, provides fodder for litigation.[40] The reason for litigating domicile is that the European Union finds forum shopping (choosing a court in order to get a more favorable reception to one's legal claims) distasteful. Accordingly, in the European Union the court that is first seized with a case must decide whether it has jurisdiction,[41] and if it does have jurisdiction then that court cannot transfer the case away.[42]

In *Owusu v. Jackson*,[43] a complex tort case where the locus of injury occurred in Jamaica,[44] the UK trial court ruled that it had jurisdiction to hear the case because one of the many defendants was domiciled in the United Kingdom. The plaintiff appealed this decision, arguing that Jamaica was a more appropriate venue because it was the site of the injury and all of the relevant evidence was located there. The *Owusu* court realized that if it allowed the case under review to be transferred to Jamaica, such a holding would: (1) foster judicial uncertainty; (2) promote distrust among legal systems of the Member States; and thereby (3) undermine the development of the European Union's internal market.[45] Accordingly, the ECJ took the position in *Owusu* that the Brussels Convention did not contemplate the use of the doctrine of *forum non conveniens* (a discretionary doctrine that dismisses a case due to the forum chosen being deemed inconvenient or unjust).

---

[38] *Id.*

[39] Brussels Convention, *supra* note 7, at art. 2.

[40] THALIA KRUGER CIVIL JURISDICTION RULES OF THE EU AND THEIR IMPACT ON THIRD STATES (2008).

[41] Case C-116/02, Continental Bank Gasser GmbH v. MISAT, 2003 E.C.R. I-14693.

[42] Brussels Convention, *supra* note 7, at art. 2; Case C-281/02, Owusu v. Jackson, 2005 E.C.R. I-1383; *cf.* Choudhary v. Bhatter, [2009] E.W.C.A. (Civ) 1176 (Eng.) (a case of complex facts that allowed the use of *forum non conveniens* to shift venue to another location).

[43] *Owusu*, 2005 E.C.R. I-1383.

[44] *Id.* at points 3–5.

[45] Rt. Hon. Sir Anthony Clarke, *The Differing Approach to Commercial Litigation in the ECJ and the Courts of England and Wales*, Feb. 23, 2006, *available at* http://www.judiciary.gov.uk/media/speeches/2006/speech-mor-23022006.

III. The Loopholes

A. VOLUNTARILY APPEARANCES

Notwithstanding *Owusu's* preference to lock in jurisdiction to where at least one defendant can be found, jurisdiction under the Brussels Convention may be shifted to another forum by several mechanisms. First, the Brussels Convention allows for defendants to make voluntary appearances before foreign magistrates.[46] This, of course, begs the question why an attorney would allow the client to do something that seems foolish. The reason a defendant would want to make a voluntary appearance has to do with how the Brussels Convention treats default judgments. As a general rule, a foreign default judgment will be recognized and enforced by the country where the defendant is domiciled *if* the defendant was served with "due form" *and* given sufficient time to prepare a defense.[47] The European concept of "due form," like the American concept of "due process," is a term of art. In general, however, the element of due form will be satisfied with respect to service of process if a number of predetermined documents are delivered to, and accepted by, the defendant.

Early on, in *Isabelle Lancray v. Peters und Sickert KG,*[48] the ECJ examined whether due form required that a translated copy of a complaint be served on a defendant. The Court began its opinion by observing that the Brussels Convention does not dictate the procedure required for service of process. Rather, under the Brussels Convention, service of process is to be in accordance with the "conventions and agreements concluded between the Contracting States,"[49] and curing any service of process defect is to be in accordance with the laws from the rendering member state as these laws are reconciled with any relevant international convention.[50] Although the *Lancray* court never explicitly held that a translated copy of the complaint was a due form requirement, the case was so interpreted for many years.

In 2006, *Lancray* was overturned by *Heidland Werres Diederichs v. Flexiquip Hydraulics Ltd.*[51] In reaching its opinion in *Diederichs*, the ECJ made two key observations. The first, under the Hague Service Convention (HSC) of 1965,[52] which is the convention usually used to provide international service of process, there is nothing that mandates that a translated copy of the complaint be served on a defendant.[53] Second, for EU Member States, the HSC was superseded by European Union Council Regulation (CR) 1348/2000. In relevant part, this CR states that the complaint served on the

---

[46]   Brussels Convention, *supra* note 7, at art. 24.

[47]   Case C-305/88, Lancray v. Sickert, 1990 E.C.R. I-2725 (citing Brussels Convention, *supra* note 7, at art. 27(2)). Both elements must be present.

[48]   *Id.*

[49]   *Id.* at point 27.

[50]   *Id.* at point 29.

[51]   Heidland Werres Diederichs v. Flexiquip Hydraulics Ltd., [2006] N.I.Q.B. 100 (Ir.).

[52]   Hague Service Convention, Nov. 15 1965, 26 I.L.M.1339, [hereinafter HC], *available at* /http://www.hcch.net/index_en.php?act=conventions.text&cid=17.

[53]   *Diederichs* at point 37 (citing HC, *supra* note 52, at art. 5).

defendant must either be in the official language of the Member State or a language that the defendant understands.[54] In addition, when the complaint is written in a language that is nonconforming with CR 1348/2000, due form for service of process will still be satisfied if the defendant accepts service after being informed that he or she may refuse to accept the service.[55]

So when should a defendant make a voluntary appearance before a foreign tribunal? The answer is when the defendant has reason to believe that the service of process is defective (i.e., without due form). Like the situation in the United States where a defendant makes a limited appearance before a tribunal to challenge its claim of jurisdiction,[56] a voluntary appearance allows an EU defendant the opportunity to challenge a foreign court's claim to have jurisdiction. If the court lacks jurisdiction, the case can be dismissed. Alternatively, a voluntary appearance is to be preferred to not making an appearance and receiving a default judgment (which will likely be enforced).

B. THE LOCUS OF THE MEDICAL TOURISM CONTRACT'S PERFORMANCE

Contracts are often performed at a location that is different from the location where the contract was executed. Under Article 5(1) of the Brussels Convention, jurisdiction belongs to the place of the obligation's performance, not where the contract was executed. However, legal opinions concerning the application of Article 5(1)'s "subordinate" jurisdiction often reach divergent conclusion.[57] Early on, the European Union's desire for legal certainty with respect to jurisdiction resulted in the ECJ opining that Article 5(1) jurisdiction "should be interpreted in such a way as to enable a normally well-informed defendant reasonably to foresee before which courts, other than those of the State in which he is domiciled, he may be sued."[58]

So, to provide guidance for individuals who are domiciled in one EU Member State, but deliver goods to, or perform services in, another EU Member State, the ECJ created a two-pronged test for determining whether Article 5(1) jurisdiction applies. Such jurisdiction is appropriate when "both the nature of the contractual obligation forming the basis of the action and the place of performance by recourse to the applicable national law via the private international law of the forum."[59]

Arguably, this two-pronged test for the applicability of Article 5(1) jurisdiction fails to provide elucidation. Not surprisingly, in 2001 the Brussels Convention was amended in an attempt to simplify and clarify the application of Article 5(1) jurisdiction. With

---

[54] *Id.* (citing Council Regulation (EC) 1348/2000 art. 8, May 29, 2000).

[55] *Id.* at point 38.

[56] Agbemavor v. Keteku, 629 S.E.2d 337 (N.C. Ct. App. 2006).

[57] Claude Witz, *The Place of Performance of the Obligation to Pay the Price Art. 57 CISG*, 25 J. LAW & COMMERCE 225, 229–330 (2006), *available at* http://www.uncitral.org/pdf/english/CISG25/Witz.pdf.

[58] Case C-440/97, G.I.E. Groupe Concorde v. Master of the Vessel "Suhadiwarno Panjan," 1999 E.C.R. I-6307.

[59] Anastasia Vezyrtzi, *Jurisdiction and International Sales under the Brussels I Regulation: Does Forum Shopping Come to an End?*, COLUM. J. EUROPEAN L. ONLINE (June 2009), http://www.cjel.net/wp-content/uploads/2009/06/vezyrtzi1.pdf.

respect to the performance of a service in a foreign EU Member State, performance is deemed to occur at "the place ... where, under the contract, the services were provided or should have been provided."[60] At least one court has interpreted this new Article 5(1) (b) jurisdiction to apply to the "place of the main provision of services by the agent, as it appears from the provisions of the contract or, in the absence of such provisions, the actual performance of that contract or, where it cannot be established on that basis, the place where the agent is domiciled."[61]

These interpretations only modestly improve our understanding of Article 5 jurisdiction, and in some cases (such as with airlines), these new interpretations create uncertainty. For example, when an airline disadvantages a passenger, the passenger may bring litigation in either the country of arrival or departure, because contract performance occurs equally in both countries.[62] At first glance, the high physical nexus required for MTVs to deliver their services to patients would seem to preclude the application of Article 5 jurisdiction. This may not be correct.

Consider a situation where a patient uses the Internet to contact an overseas facilitator to arrange medical travel. Assume further that the patient purchases a medical travel package with a credit card, and the facilitator responds by e-mailing the patient the details, including the conformation numbers. In this hypothetical, where are the services rendered? Alternatively, consider a situation where a patient purchases medical tourism services from a multinational healthcare provider (MHP).[63] In particular, assume that an Irish patient is evaluated in the Dublin office of a MHP, undergoes a surgical procedure in Greece where the MHP can provide surgical services in the most cost effect manner, and receives her postoperative care at the Dublin office. Given the multiple points of care, where did this Irish patient receive her health care?

At issue in the first hypothetical is where in the physical world a cyberspace transaction is performed, and the issue in the second is which of the many sites of partial contract performance is the site of *the* contract performance. At present, there are no concrete answers to these questions.[64] So, a formal answer to how Article 5 jurisdiction will be imposed on EU internal medical tourism awaits an appropriate test case. In the course of ordinary business, however, sophisticated vendors often try to avoid these Article 5 issues by contractually assigning jurisdiction. Unfortunately, this method is also less than ideal.

---

[60] Brussels Convention, *supra* note 7, at art. 5(1)(b).

[61] Case C-19/09, Wood Floor Solutions Andreas Domberger GmbH v. Silva Trade SA, [2010] 1 W.L.R. 1900.

[62] Case C-204/08, Rehder v. Air Baltic Corporation, 2009 E.C.R. I-6073.

[63] With the recent economic downturn, the consolidation of the European health care market has resulted in a substantial increase in the number of MHPs. European Federation of Public Service Unions, *European Healthcare Services, Multinational Companies and a European Healthcare Market* (Sept. 2010), *available at* http://www.epsu.org/IMG/pdf/Final_report_EWC_health_care_2010_-_Jane_Lethbridge. pdf.

[64] Faye Fangfei Wang, *Obstacles and Solutions to Internet Jurisdiction: A Comparative Analysis of the EU and US laws*, 3(4) J. INT'L COMMERCIAL L. & TECH. 233, 236–37 (2008).

C. ARBITRATION AND JURISDICTION CLAUSES

This brings us to the next Brussels Convention jurisdictional loophole, which is created by the use of an arbitration clause. Article 1 of the Brussels Convention, which addresses the scope of the convention, states that the "Convention shall not apply to…arbitration."[65] Arbitration was intentionally excluded from the scope of the Brussels Convention because, by 1968 when the Brussels Convention was enacted, arbitration (and its enforcement) was already the subject of a number of other international accords,[66] and in particular the New York Convention.[67]

Yet, the relationship between the Brussels Convention and arbitration clauses is long and complicated.[68] For example, how arbitrators are selected and the remedies available through arbitration have been the subject of litigation in the European Union. Early on, the ECJ held that the way arbitrators are selected is a contract question, as the answer is arrived at independently of the procedures used in arbitration, and therefore not covered under the Brussels Convntion.[69] In another case, the ECJ held that when the remedy sought by one of the parties to a dispute is not available in arbitration (e.g., a protective order), the national courts have jurisdiction regardless of the existence or validity of an arbitration clause.[70]

An important case in this line, *Allianz v. West Tankers*[71] involved a maritime collision off the coast of Sicily. After settling the claim, the insurers filed a subrogation claim against West Tankers (the owner of the ship that collided with the jetty) in an Italian court.[72] West Tankers, in turn, filed a parallel action in an English court for a protective order to enforce the shipping contract's arbitration clause. Specifically, West Tankers sought to have the English court issue an order to the Italian court to stay its proceedings until the dispute could be arbitrated.[73] After the trial court granted the injunction, the case was then twice appealed.[74]

By characterizing this case as an "anti-suit injunction,"[75] the ECJ signaled how it viewed the crux of the matter: the sovereignty of EU Member States would be undermined if their national courts had to honor orders from the courts of other Member

---

[65] Brussels Convention, *supra* note 7, at art. (1)(4).

[66] Klára Svobodová, *Arbitration Exception in the Regulation Brussels I* (2009), *available at* http://www.law.muni.cz/sborniky/dp08/files/pdf/mezinaro/svobodova.pdf (citing P. Jenard, *Report on the Convention on Jurisdiction and the Recognition and Enforcement of Judgments in Civil and Commercial Matters*, O.J. C59, May 3, 1979).

[67] New York Convention, Convention on the Recognition and Enforcement of Foreign Arbitral Awards, June 10, 1958, 330 U.N.T.S. 4739.

[68] Svobodová, *supra* note 66.

[69] Case C-190/89, Rich v. Societá Italiana Impianti, 1991 E.C.R. I-3855, at points 4–7.

[70] Case C-391/95, Van Uden Maritime B.V. v. Komanditgesellschaft in Firma Deco Line, 1998 E.C.R. I-7091, at points 19–34.

[71] Case C-185/07, Allianz v. West Tankers, 2009 E.C.R. I-663.

[72] *Id.* at point 11.

[73] *Id.* at point 12.

[74] *Id.* at points 13–14.

[75] *Id.* at point 20.

States.[76] This was a position that the ECJ had no interest in advancing. Accordingly, the Court held that it was incompatible "for a court of a Member State to make an order to restrain a person from commencing or continuing proceedings before the courts of another Member State on the ground that such proceedings would be contrary to an arbitration agreement."[77] In dismissing the English court's order, the ECJ then added that whether this case should be referred for arbitration was a matter for the Italian court to decide.[78]

Since the *West Tanker* case was handed down, commentators have postulated that in disputes involving arbitration clauses, this case will encourage the use of "parallel proceedings as tactical step."[79] It is not hard to imagine how parallel proceedings could be used in medical tourism arbitration disputes. For example, an iatrogencially injured patient could file a lawsuit requesting that remedial medical care be provided in lieu of a monetary award. Depending on the specifics of the care sought, an arbitration panel may not be in a position to order such relief. This inability of the arbitration panel to provide the requested relief could then be used to justify a parallel proceeding. If such tactical strategy were to become the norm in medical tourism, the value of arbitration clauses to EU MTVs would be substantially reduced.[80]

Contracts with arbitration clauses frequently contain jurisdiction (i.e., a forum-shifting) clauses. Although arbitration and jurisdiction causes are often used in tandem, they serve different purposes. Arbitration clauses concern dispute resolution, whereas jurisdiction clauses concern where a dispute will be heard; thus jurisdiction clauses influence the choice of laws selected.

Under the Brussels Convention, parties to a contract may use a jurisdiction clause to override the default rules for jurisdiction determination.[81] Of course, such forum-shifting clauses have limits. In general, however, a jurisdiction clause will be valid if:

First, at least one of the parties to the agreement must be Community-domiciled. Second, the agreement must be: (a) in writing or evidenced in writing; or (b) in a form which accords with practices which the parties have established between themselves; or (c) in international trade or commerce, in a form which accords with a usage of which the parties are or ought to have been aware and which in such trade or commerce is widely known to, and regularly observed by, parties to contracts of the type involved in the particular trade or commerce concerned.[82]

---

[76] *Anti-Suit Injunctions No Longer an Efficient Tool for Arbitration in the EU: Allianz SpA, Generali Assicurazioni Generali SpA v. West Tankers Inc*, MALLESONS STEPHEN JAQUES (June 2009), www.ashurst.com/doc.aspx?id_Content=4257.

[77] *West Tankers*, 2009 E.C.R. I-663, at point 35.

[78] *Id.* at point 33.

[79] *The European Court of Justice Decision in* West Tanker—*European Arbitration Holed beneath the Waterline?*, ASHURST (Feb. 2009), http://www.ashurst.com/listing.aspx?id_content=26&id_queryContent= 1377&id_ContentType=13.

[80] MALLESONS, *supra* note 76.

[81] Brussels Convention, *supra* note 7, at art. 23.

[82] *Issue 107—Brussels I Regulation Article 23 Cases*, FIN. MKTS. LAW COMM. 8 (2008), www.fmlc.org/Documents/Issue107assessment.pdf. As used here, community-domicile contemplates that at least

More generally, for a jurisdictional clause to be valid, a court must find that the "clause conferring jurisdiction upon [a country] was in fact the subject of consensus between the parties which must be clearly and precisely demonstrated."[83] In the European Union, a valid jurisdiction clause has certain advantages. Jurisdiction clauses can be used to avoid jurisdictional ambiguities, such as when a party is domiciled in one EU Member State but delivers services to another EU Member State (i.e., to invoke or clarify Article 5(1)(b) jurisdiction). Jurisdictional clauses are also not likely to provide fodder for the initiation of a parallel proceeding in another venue. Unfortunately for MTVs, the Achilles' heel of jurisdictional clauses is that such clauses are only applicable to non-consumer transactions.[84]

D. PATIENTS AS CONSUMERS

Indeed, under the Brussels Convention consumer transactions are accorded their own jurisdictional loophole. In the European Union, consumers are entitled to certain rights.[85] For the purposes of jurisdiction, a consumer is someone who purchases a good or service outside of his or her professional expertise.[86] Accordingly, unless a medical tourism purchase is made by a health care professional, who provides that service as part of his or her daily work, the purchase of overseas medical services are very likely to be considered a consumer transaction, and consumer transactions carry two key benefits.

The first benefit of consumer status in commercial transaction is protected-bases jurisdiction (PBJ). Subject to certain restrictions, PBJ allows consumers to bring lawsuits to recover damages against vendors in the country where they are domiciled.[87] In particular, for noninstallment contracts, PBJ is available to consumers if either the contract for services was formed where the consumer is domiciled or if the consumer is enticed (i.e., receive a "specific invitation") to travel to the vendor's country to form the contract.[88] Conversely, if a European medical tourist voluntarily travels to a second

---

one codefendant is domiciled in the country that is assigned jurisdiction under the contract. Brussels Convention, *supra* note 7, at art. 6(1).

[83] Case C-307/06, O'Connor v. Masterwood Ltd., [2009] I.E.S.C. 49, 14 (quoting Case C-106/95, M.S.G. v. Gravières Rhénanes, 1997 E.C.R. I-911, at point 14).

[84] *Infra*, next section.

[85] *See, e.g.*, Directive 1999/44/EC of the Eurpean Parliament on Certain Aspects of the Sale of Consumer Goods and Associated Guarantees, 1999 O.J. L171.

[86] Brussels Convention, *supra* note 7, at art. 15. *See also* Youseph Farah, *Jurisdictional Rules Applicable to Electronic Consumer Contracts* (Apr. 2006), http://www.bileta.ac.uk/Document%20Library/1/Jurisdiction%20over%20disputes%20relating%20to%20electronic%20consumer%20contracts%20under%20Brussels%20I.pdf (a consumer contract arises when "an individual, not acting in the course of business, whereby he acquires goods or services for his own private consumption, from a supplier acting in the course of a business").

[87] Brussels Convention, *supra* note 7, at art. 16. Because PBJ is intended to protect the weaker party in a transaction, *id.* at art. 15, the application of PBJ cannot be waived by agreement; unless the agreement satisfies certain requirements. *Id.* at art. 17; *see infra*, next section.

[88] Brussels Convention, *supra* note 7, at art. 13(3). PBJ is available for noninstallment contracts if contract formation occurred in "(a) in the State of the consumer's domicile the conclusion of the contract was preceded by a specific invitation addressed to him or by advertising; and (b) the consumer took in

EU Member State, PBJ will not be available to the medical tourist in the event of an adverse outcome.[89]

Importantly, a special invitation can be created by advertisement. Demonstration of a special invitation that entices a consumer to cross a border to purchase goods or services requires a fact-based inquiry that, at least from a U.S. attorney's perspective, resembles minimum contact analysis.[90] In *Gabriel v. Schlank & Schick GmbH*[91] the ECJ applied such an inquiry to a foreign vendor's advertising campaign. After receiving a vendor's letter stating that the consumer had won a lottery and that purchase of certain goods was a condition precedent to receiving the lottery's winnings,[92] the consumer traveled to the vendor's country and made the required purchase. In granting the consumer PBJ, the *Gabriel* court observed:

> concepts of "advertising" and "specific invitation addressed" . . . cover[s] all forms of advertising carried out in the Contracting State in which the consumer is domiciled, whether disseminated generally by the press, radio, television, cinema or any other medium, or addressed directly, for example by means of catalogues sent specifically to that State, as well as commercial offers made to the consumer in person.[93]

Again, although the ECJ has yet to consider a consumer medical tourist transaction case, imagining such a case is not difficult. Consider an EU facilitator's Internet advertisement that is published in another Member State's health care market that "guarantees [a] fabulous vacation during your treatment so that you can get maximum benefit from your trip."[94] It would not be unreasonable to believe that such an advertisement would entice a consumer-patient to cross a border to purchase health care. Accordingly, if this advertisement were to be deemed to have been specifically directed at a particular country's health care market (e.g., using the country-specific URL), then this Internet advertisement may also be deemed to have created a special invitation that could serve as the basis for asserting PBJ.

---

that State the steps necessary for the conclusion of the contract." Farah, *supra* note 86. The requirement that consumer status turns on where a contract was formed has become a hot topic in the age of e-commerce. *Id.*

[89] KRUGER, *supra* note 40.

[90] *Compare* Case C-96/00, Gabriel v. Schlank & Schick GmbH, 2002 E.C.R. I-6367, *with* Case C-27/02, Engler v. Janus Versand GmbH, 2005 E.C.R. I-481 (what constitute a "specific invitation" is determined by a fact-sensitive inquiry).

[91] *Gabriel*, 2002 E.C.R. I-6367.

[92] In essence, the vendor in this case was using the "Nigerian letter" scam (i.e., a 419 scam) to entice consumers to make purchases. *See* MISHA GLENNY, MCMAFIA (Vintage 2009).

[93] *Gabriel*, 2002 E.C.R. I-6367, at point 44.

[94] *Complex Medica & Dental Travel Agency: Dentists in Krakow, Poland*, Dental Travel Agency (Apr. 26, 2009), http://www.treatmentabroad.net/cosmetic-dentistry-abroad/poland/dental-travel-agency/. A year and a half after this advertisement was placed on the Internetm the same MTV had toned down its advertising claims; *see Dental Holiday Abroad*, Dentists in Poland (Dec. 03, 2012), http://www.dentistsinpoland.com/eng/dental_holiday/day/2012-12-03.

The second benefit of consumer status in medical tourism transaction concerns the use of jurisdictional clauses. Under EU law, a "consumer is in a weak position vis-à-vis the seller or supplier, as regards both his bargaining power and his level of knowledge."[95] Therefore, the European Union considers a contract to be nonbinding on a consumer if it is unfair.[96] More specifically, an unfair contract clause is nonbinding on a consumer "if has not been individually negotiated shall be regarded as unfair if, contrary to the requirement of good faith, it causes a significant imbalance in the parties' rights and obligations arising under the contract."[97]

In addition, "a term shall always be regarded as not individually negotiated where it has been drafted in advance and the consumer has therefore not been able to influence the substance of the term, particularly in the context of a pre-formulated standard contract."[98] Consequently, these rules suggest that the typical MTV contract, which uses boilerplate language (e.g., jurisdiction clauses), will be nonbinding on EU medical tourists.

In late 2010, a case that involved the enforceability of a jurisdictional clause in a consumer contract was handed down. In *VB Pénzügyi Lízing Zrt. v. Ferenc Schneider*,[99] VB Pénzügyi loaned Schneider money to purchase a car.[100] When Schneider fell behind on his contractual obligations, VB Pénzügyi filed a lawsuit to recover the money it was owed.[101] Invoking the jurisdictional clause in its contract with Schneider, VB Pénzügyi filed the lawsuit in a Hungarian court rather than filing the lawsuit in the country where Schneider was domiciled (and where the courts would have PBJ over Schneider's consumer transactions).[102] Schneider, in turn, challenged the jurisdiction of the Hungarian trial court.

In analyzing this case, the *VB Pénzügyi* court began its opinion with the observation that because of the intrinsic contractual imbalances in consumer contracts, courts must, on their own initiative, review consumer contracts for their fairness.[103] When the *VB Pénzügyi* court failed to find evidence that the trial court had reviewed the contract for fairness (including its jurisdictional clause's requirement for the defendant to have to travel far from his home to litigate this case),[104] *VB Pénzügyi* remanded the case for further development.[105] *VB Pénzügyi* thus raises a cautionary note for medical tourism

---

[95] Case C-137/08, V.B. Pénzügyi Lízing Zrt. V. Ferenc Schneider, 2010 E.C.R. I-0000, at point 46.

[96] Brussels Convention, *supra* note 7, at art. 6(1). What is unfair in a consumer contract is spelled out in the laws of the individual member states. *See, e.g., The Unfair Terms in Consumer Contracts Regulations*, The National Archives (1999), http://www.legislation.gov.uk/uksi/1999/2083/contents/made (listing the UK's unfair consumer practices).

[97] Council Directive 93/13/EEC of Apr. 5, 1993, Article 3(1).

[98] *Id.* at Article 3(1).

[99] *V.B. Pénzügyi*, 2010 E.C.R. I-0000.

[100] *Id.* at point 14.

[101] *Id.* at point 15.

[102] *Id.* at point 16.

[103] *Id.* at points 46–51.

[104] *Id.* at points 52–56.

[105] *Id.* at points 56–57.

vendors who are relying on the jurisdictional clause in an adhesion contract. MTVs who wish to use such jurisdictional clauses should plan on being able to demonstrate that the clause was a specifically negotiated point in the contract's formation (e.g., the patient-consumer initialed the clause) or that the patient received some benefit (e.g., a discounted price).

E. A FINAL "LOOPHOLE"

The final loophole is a technicality: the Brussels Convention is formally applicable only when both parties are domiciled in the European Union.[106] That is, the scope of the Brussels Convention does not necessarily cover parties who are domiciled in "Third States," states that are neither de jure EU Member States or in the process of being admitted to the European Union.[107] In actual practice, however, the scope of the Brussels Convention may reach individuals domiciled in Third States in a number of situations including consumer transactions when the defendant voluntarily appears before an EU court, *lis pendens* matters, and exequatur proceedings.[108] More generally, because EU courts have jurisdiction to hear disputes arising from services rendered within their borders, EU courts are competent to hear professional negligence cases against European MTVs that are brought by non-Europeans.[109]

Therefore, as a general rule, American or Asian medical tourists who are injured by an EU MTV may return to the country where the purchase was made to file a lawsuit for compensation. Although this road to compensation will create hardship for injured American or Asian medical tourists, at least the road is open. In contrast the alternative road involving the American or Asian courts may not be a viable road for the iatrogenically injured medical tourist to recover damages against an EU MTV because the American or Asian courts may not have jurisdiction over the EU MTV.[110]

IV. Recognition and Enforcement

A. EXEQUATUR

In the European Union, an exequatur proceeding is used to enforce foreign judgments. The first step to enforce a foreign judgment in the European Union is recognition, which occurs virtually automatically when the judgment to be enforced is handed down

---

[106] KRUGER, *supra* note 40.

[107] *See supra* note 6.

[108] Radka Chlebcová, *The Impact of Civil Jurisdiction Rules on Third States (Article 4)* (Jan. 1, 2011), http://www.law.muni.cz/sborniky/dp08/files/pdf/mezinaro/chlebcova.pdf

[109] Consideration also needs to be given to international agreements, which many be binding on the rendering and referring countries. Further discussion of such agreements is beyond the scope of this chapter.

[110] A detailed discussion of the jurisdiction of the courts in the United States or in Asia over EU MTVs is beyond the scope of this chapter.

by a court located in another EU Member State.[111] No special procedure is required.[112] Indeed, the grounds for nonrecognition are so limited[113] that "declarations of enforceability . . . are rarely refused."[114]

The second step of an exequatur proceeding involves the formal decision of an EU court to order the enforcement of the foreign judgment or award. Under Article 27 of the Brussels Convention, the three basic grounds for nonenforcement of a foreign judgment from another EU Member State are: (1) the judgment is an invalid default judgment; (2) the judgment would create a conflict with existing laws or judgments within the enforcing country; or (3) the judgment is against the enforcing country's public policy.

Enforcement actions concerning conflicts in the law or public policy have been reported,[115] but they are uncommon. However, once again it is not hard to imagine a set of circumstances where an EU court would not enforce a foreign court's default judgment concerning the rendering of defective medical tourism services because to do so would go against the rendering country's prior legal opinions or public policy. For example, it seems unlikely that an Italian court would be willing to enforce a monetary award granted by a UK court to an Italian patient who experienced an adverse outcome after traveling to Bristol to obtain an abortion.

On the other hand, EU courts are likely to enforce valid default judgments against MTVs, as these judgments are unlikely to create conflicts of law or public policy. In fact, in *Apostolides v. Orams*,[116] the ECJ demonstrated its willingness to order the enforcement of a default judgment under extreme conditions. In 2002, the Orams purchased a Cyprus villa that was located on a part of the island that had been occupied by a non-EU Member State (Turkey) since 1974.[117] Two years later, Apostolides filed a lawsuit in a Cyprus court challenging the Orams's title to the land and seeking to demolish the villa.[118] After receiving a potentially defective service of process, the Orams's attorney failed to make a timely appearance. Accordingly, a default judgment was entered against the Orams.[119] The following year, Apostolides initiated an exequatur proceeding in a UK court to enforce the default judgment.[120] The Orams responded by appealing the default judgment.

---

[111] Brussels Convention, *supra* note 7, at art. 34.

[112] *Id.*

[113] *Id.* at art. 35.

[114] Andrew Dickinson, *Brussels I Review—The Abolition of Exequatur?*, CONFLICTS OF LAW.NET (June 8, 2009), http://conflictoflaws.net/2009/brussels-i-review-the-abolition-of-exequatur.

[115] Case C-394/07, Gambazzi v. Daimler Chrysler, 2009 E.C.R. I-2563. This case involved a default judgment from an English court wherein an Italian attorney was disbarred. The ECJ recommended that sanction be enforced throughout Europe. The Italian court in Milan declined to enforce the disbarment as it was against Italian public policy. *Id.*

[116] Case C-420/07, Apostolides v. Orams, 2009 E.C.R. I-3571.

[117] *Id.* at points 18–19.

[118] *Id.* at point 21.

[119] *Id.* at points 22–25.

[120] *Id.* at points 28–29.

The ECJ took notice that the elements required to set aside a default judgment—that the defendant was not served with "due form" or given sufficient time to prepare a defense[121]—were not an issue in this case. By hiring an attorney, the Orams waived any argument they had with respect to the due form of the services of process or that they had inadequate time to prepare a defense. That is, although the Court was aware that the Orams may not have been served with due form, the Court concluded that because the Orams had taken steps to challenge the service of process, they had adequate time to prepare a defense, and due form with respect to service of process was not an issue.[122] As the default judgment was valid, the ECJ also ruled that the actual impossibility of its judgment being enforced in Turkish-occupied Cyprus was not an issue.[123] In short, the *Apostolides* opinion means that the European Union will enforce a valid default judgment to the extent that it can be, thereby creating a strong incentive for defendants to make timely voluntary appearances when they believe due form was not provided during service of process.

B. PUTTING THE PUZZLE PIECES TOGETHER

Although not formally reported, there is one actual case of alleged MTV negligence that illustrates many of the points discussed herein.[124] A British woman traveled to Belgium to undergo an eye operation that was performed by an Italian surgeon.[125] Postoperatively, the patient sustained facial nerve damage and required a second operation.[126] Subsequently, when the patient sought compensation, the patient's attorney filed a lawsuit in a UK court.[127] Factors used by the United Kingdom to justify its assertion of PBJ in this case included the fact that the patient was a consumer[128] and that she had received a special invitation (i.e., the clinic had targeted UK customers with a UK-based Web address and used media-based advertising directed at the UK market).[129]

It is unclear from the case report whether the Belgium clinic's contract contained a jurisdiction clause. However, Vick, the attorney for the plaintiff in this case, opined that "[i]f a clinic has successfully incorporated a jurisdiction clause then that will become a factor against us that would weaken our argument for getting jurisdiction here. However, the clinic is going to have to prove that the jurisdiction clause is binding."[130] Thus, it seems likely that if a jurisdictional clause were present, Vick would use *VB Pénzügyi* to challenge its validity.

---

[121] Case C-305/88, Lancray v. Sickert, 1990 E.C.R. I-2725 (citing Brussels Convention, *supra* note 7, at art. 27(2)).

[122] *Orams*, 2009 E.C.R. I-3571 at points 77–80.

[123] *Id.* at point 82(3).

[124] Caroline Ratner, *Medical Tourism and the Law: Could Your Clinic Be Sued in a UK Court?*, INT'L MED. TRAVEL J. (2010), http://www.imtjonline.com/articles/2010/medical-tourism-negligence-30043/.

[125] *Id.*

[126] *Id.*

[127] *Id.*

[128] Personal written communication with Laurence Vick, attorney for the plaintiff, Jan. 2010.

[129] Ratner, *supra* note 124.

[130] *Id.*

The clinic's position in this case was that jurisdiction belonged to the Belgium courts, regardless of whether the basis for that jurisdiction was predicated on the general default rule for diversity jurisdiction (i.e., the defendant's domicile) or a jurisdiction clause. Although the clinic hired an attorney, who had several conversations with Vick, the clinic failed to make a timely appearance in the UK court.[131] Therefore, a default judgment was entered against the clinic. As the facts in this case are analogous to those in *Apostolides*, it is likely that Vick will not have any difficulty obtaining an order to enforce the default judgment against the clinic from a Belgium court.

Conclusion

Most medical tourism purchase result in a positive outcome for the patient and the MTV. For this situation, neither party ever needs to contemplate jurisdiction. Yet, for the iatrogenically injured patients, the ability to obtain jurisdiction over an EU MTV is critical if the patient is going to receive compensation. Conversely, all medical tourists should assume that EU MTVs will attempt by any legal means available to limit their liability.

Thus, both European Union MTVs and patients should be aware of the general default rule for determining diversity jurisdiction (i.e., jurisdiction belonging to the courts where the defendant is domiciled). MTVs should exercise care in using contractual mechanisms (e.g., jurisdiction and arbitration clauses) to modify the default rule for diversity jurisdiction. Failure to do so may embroil the MTV in unanticipated litigation in a foreign court. MTVs also need to be mindful that the courts are likely to view almost all medical tourists as consumers, a status that will grant an iatrogenically injured patient with protected-bases jurisdiction (if they are enticed by advertisement to purchase health care services) and will potentially undermine the enforceability of the vendor's jurisdictional clauses. For the patients who purchase overseas medical tourism service, they must realize that jurisdiction matters if they should seek compensation for an iatrogenic injury. In short, EU medical tourists should carefully read any contract they sign and ask appropriate questions.

---

[131] *Id.*

3

CANADIAN PRINT NEWS MEDIA COVERAGE OF

MEDICAL TOURISM

Examining Key Themes and Ethical Gaps

Valorie A. Crooks,* Jeremy Snyder,† Leigh Turner,§ Krystyna Adams,**

*Rory Johnston,‡ and Victoria Casey§§^*

Introduction

Medical tourism is the term used to describe patients intentionally traveling abroad to privately access medical care.[1] The global phenomenon of patients leaving their home countries to obtain nonemergency surgical procedures and other medical interventions is gaining popularity as a result of the increasing affordability of travel, services or high quality care available elsewhere, and overall affordability of medical services.[2] The rise of

---

^ This research was funded by a Catalyst Grant awarded by the Canadian Institutes of Health Research.
* Department of Geography, Simon Fraser University.
† Faculty of Health Sciences, Simon Fraser University.
§ Center for Bioethics, University of Minnesota.
** Faculty of Health Sciences, Simon Fraser University.
† Department of Geography, Simon Fraser University.
§§ Department of Geography, Simon Fraser University.

[1] Valorie A. Crooks et al., *What Is Known about the Patient's Experience of Medical Tourism? A Scoping Review*, 10 BMC HEALTH SERVS. RES. 266 (2010). Although this care is sought privately, in some cases patients may seek reimbursement for the incurred expenses from public or private health insurance. We expand upon this point later on as it relates to the use of medical tourism services by Canadian patients.

[2] Laura Hopkins et al., *Medical Tourism Today: What Is the State of Existing Knowledge?*, 31 J. PUB. HEALTH POL'Y 185 (2010); Rory Johnston et al., *An Industry Perspective on Canadian Patients' Involvement in Medical Tourism: Implications for Public Health*, 11 BMC PUB. HEALTH 416 (2011).

the highly privatized medical tourism industry in lesser-developed countries in particular, which is where growth is thought to be most rapid, is attributable to many developments. Low labor and living costs, the availability of inexpensive pharmaceuticals, and the low cost or absence of malpractice insurance are particularly important factors in establishing numerous emerging economies as destinations for medical tourists.[3]

Despite impressive growth and considerable support for promoting trade in health services and developing a global health services marketplace, the medical tourism industry is the subject of considerable criticism.[4] Contemporary critical analysis examines numerous ethical issues associated with medical tourism. Six ethical concerns are consistently identified in this literature. First, there is concern that achieving informed consent is compromised through the practice of medical tourism due to the limited contact between provider and patient prior to delivering care, the pressure to receive care once the patient has already traveled a long distance to access it, and the financial conflicts of interest that could lead medical tourism facilitators and destination hospitals to minimize risks and emphasize benefits of purchasing particular medical interventions.[5] Second, in cases where medical attention is required in patients' home countries upon returning from private care abroad, there is concern that the need for follow-up treatment places an unfair burden on public health care resources.[6] Third, concerns regarding fairness emerge when patients from countries with public health care systems "queue jump" to obtain care privately abroad and also in cases where their nondomestic care is reimbursed by the domestic system.[7] Fourth, further concerns over fairness and public health emerge in relation to the potential for medical tourism to expose populations to increased collective risk of infection when patients return from medical care abroad.[8] Fifth, numerous concerns exist regarding

---

[3] Hopkins et al., *supra* note 2; Johnston at al., *supra* note 2; Marc Lautier, *Export of Health Services from Developing Countries: The Case of Tunisia*, 67 Soc. Sci. & Med. 101 (2008); Neil Lunt et al., *Medical Tourism: Treatments, Markets, and Health System Implications: A Scoping Review* (2011), http://www.oecd.org/dataoecd/51/11/48723982.pdf; Andrea Whittaker, *Pleasure and Pain: Medical Travel in Asia*, 3 Global Pub. Health 271 (2008).

[4] Rory Johnston et al., *What Is Known about the Effects of Medical Tourism in Destination and Departure Countries? A Scoping Review*, 9 Int'l J. Equity Health 24 (2010); Amit Sen Gupta, *Medical Tourism in India: Winners and Losers*, 5 Indian J. Med. Ethics 4 (2008); Leigh Turner, *"First World Health Care at Third World Prices": Globalization, Bioethics and Medical Tourism*, 2 Biosocieties 303 (2007); Leigh Turner, *Quality in Health Care and Globalization of Health Services: Accreditation and Regulatory Oversight of Medical Tourism Companies*, 23 Int'l J. Quality Health Care 1 (2011).

[5] Kali Penney et al., *Risk Communication and Informed Consent in the Medical Tourism Industry: A Thematic Content Analysis of Canadian Broker Websites*, 12 BMC Med. Ethics (2011); Turner, *"First World Health Care"*, *supra* note 4; Roy G. Spece, *Medical Tourism: Protecting Patients from Conflicts of Interest in Broker's Fees Paid by Foreign Providers*, 6 J. Health & Biomed. L. 1 (2010).

[6] Daniel W. Birch et al., *Medical Tourism in Bariatric Surgery*, 199 Am. J. Surgery 604 (2010); Ian K. Cheung & Anthony Wilson, *Arthroplasty Tourism*, 187 Med. J. Austl. 666 (2007); Johnston et al., *supra* note 2; Jeremy Snyder et al., *The "Patient's Physician One-Step Removed": The Evolving Roles of Medical Tourism Facilitators*, 37 J. Med. Ethics 530 (2011).

[7] Annette de Arellano, *Patients without Borders: The Emergence of Medical Tourism*, 37 Int'l J. Health Servs. 193 (2007); Snyder et al., *supra* note 6.

[8] Heng Leng Chee, *Medical Tourism in Malaysia: International Movement of Healthcare Consumers and the Commodification of Healthcare* (Asia Res. Inst., Working Paper No. 83, 2007); Johnston et al., *supra* note 2.

the potential for medical tourism to divert resources away from local populations in destination countries, including through straining public health care systems, taxing health human resources supplies, and promoting advanced biomedical technologies and medical specialization rather than directing public resources toward primary health care and public health systems.[9] Six, related to this is concern that the needs of international patients are prioritized over the needs of local citizens, including through the "crowding out" of local patients.[10]

Media coverage, along with the growing online presence of facilitators (i.e., agents who specialize in making arrangements for international patients) and destination hospitals, has increased the visibility of the medical tourism industry and played a critical role in providing information to potential medical tourists regarding procedures, costs, and destinations.[11] Illustrating this visibility, medical tourism garners significant attention in Canadian news media outlets. News reports describing experiences of Canadian medical tourists also provide information concerning medical tourism companies and international health care destinations.[12] In this chapter we examine Canadian print news media coverage of medical tourism. Many researchers argue that media messages increasingly are an important source of health information for patients as a result of the introduction of the "Internet age" of knowledge transfer and dissemination.[13] This development coincides with patients' increasing desires to have more control over health-related decisions, leading them to seek information from sources such as the print media to inform them of their options.[14] Certainly, patients are but one of the knowledge user groups for print media about medical tourism.

Our aim in this chapter is to analyze Canadian print news media coverage of medical tourism and determine if and how the six main domains of ethical concern associated with the global health services practice of medical tourism as identified above are incorporated into or reflected in the main themes of this dialogue. We first provide an overview of media analysis and the strategy we used to identify print news media articles. Following this, we offer a discussion of the main message points, or themes, identified as a result of a content analysis conducted on the articles we reviewed. We subsequently consider if and how the ethical issues associated with medical tourism

---

[9] Hopkins et al., *supra* note 2; Johnston et al., *supra* note 4; Lunt et al., *supra* note 3; Glenn Cohen discusses this issue in much more depth in Chapter 6 in this book.

[10] Melisa Martínez Álvarez et al., *The Potential for Bi-Lateral Agreements in Medical Tourism: A Qualitative Study of Stakeholder Perspectives from the UK and India*, 7 GLOBALIZATION AND HEALTH (2011); Chantal Blouin, *Trade Policy & Health: From Conflicting Interests to Policy Coherence*, 85 BULL. OF THE WHO (2007); Turner, *"First World Health Care"*, *supra* note 4.

[11] Crooks et al., *supra* note 1; Johnston et al., *supra* note 2; Neil Lunt et al., *Nip, Tuck and Click: Medical Tourism and the Emergence of Web-Based Health Information*. 4 OPEN MED. INFORM. J. 1 (2010).

[12] Johnston et al., *supra* note 2; Jeremy Snyder et al., *What Do We Know about Canadian Involvement in Medical Tourism? A Scoping Review*, 5 OPEN MED. (2011).

[13] Tomas Mainil et al., *The Discourse of Medical Tourism in the Media*, 66 TOURISM REV. 31 (2011); CLIVE SEALE, MEDIA AND HEALTH (2002).

[14] Mainil et al., *supra* note 13.

are factored into Canadian news media coverage of this global health services practice. We conclude our analysis by considering the implications of our findings for future Canadian media coverage of medical tourism.

I. Media Analysis Strategy

There are many different types of media analysis, all of which commonly involve examining the content of media sources to discover how coverage of political, economic, social, and cultural developments contribute to our understanding of particular issues.[15] In this analysis we use content analysis to examine how Canadian print news media "frame" or describe medical tourism. In content analysis, the constituent parts of texts are counted, coded, analyzed, and assessed according to frequency rates and potential significance, often by theme.[16]

Although print media sources are included in several scholarly reviews of medical tourism,[17] to date there is little dedicated analysis of newspaper articles covering medical tourism. However, several analyses of related sources, such as Web sites and promotional pamphlets,[18] do exist. These publications suggest that there is considerable interest in understanding the nature, focus, and scope of print messages associated with medical tourism.

For our content analysis, we reviewed a two-year period (July 2008–July 2010) of Canadian print news sources. With the guidance of a reference librarian we devised a comprehensive strategy that involved searching four media databases (GoogleNews, Canada.com, LexisNexis, and Canadian Newsstand) and five media Web sites (CBC News, CTV News, Global News, The Globe and Mail, and The National Post) using four keywords (*health tourism, medical tourism, medical travel,* and *health travel*). Seventy-eight unique articles were identified. Two reviewers read each article to determine whether it should be included in the media analysis and to identify, extract, and summarize key information. Articles were excluded from our analysis if reviewers determined that medical tourism was not the main focus, that the majority of the content was duplicated from another article (which can happen when text from press releases is copied into articles), or if we were unable to obtain a full copy. Through this process, nineteen articles were excluded. The fifty-nine included articles were gathered from twenty-four Canadian print media sources. Five of these sources were national in scope, six were provincial or territorial, and the remainder were local.

---

[15] CENTER FOR STRATEGIC AND INTERNATIONAL STUDIES, *Media Analysis*, http://csis.org/category/topics/global-trends-and-forecasting/media-analysis (last visited Aug. 20, 2011).

[16] ANDERS HANSEN ET AL., MASS COMMUNICATION RESEARCH METHODS, 91–129 (Anders Hansen ed., 1998).

[17] *E.g.,* Crooks et al., *supra* note 1; Johnston et al., *supra* note 4; Snyder et al., *supra* note 12.

[18] *E.g.,* Valorie A. Crooks et al., *Promoting Medical Tourism to India: Messages, Images, and the Marketing of International Patient Travel,* 72 SOC. SCI. & MED. 726 (2011); Lunt et al., *supra* note 11; Penney et al., *supra* note 5.

Standard information was extracted from each included article and entered by each reviewer into a shared spreadsheet. This information spanned five categories, each of which comprised unique columns in the spreadsheet: (1) bibliographic information, (2) overview, (3) portrayal, (4) binary indicators, and (5) conclusion. Bibliographic columns recorded details related to the source. Overview columns recorded information on the core issues covered in the source, any reference to firsthand sources of information (such as interviewees), and up to three keywords. For the portrayal columns, reviewers were asked to respond to two questions: how is medical tourism portrayed (an economic, resource, patient care, or waiting list issue), and what position does the article take toward medical tourism (positive, neutral, or negative)? Binary indicator columns recorded yes/no responses to eight questions: does the article mention patient safety risks; does the article discuss positive impacts for Canada; does the article mention negative impacts for Canada; does the article mention cost savings for patients; does the article mention specific facilitation companies; does the article mention specific destination countries; does the article have an overt tourism focus; and does the article have an overt health focus? Finally, for the conclusion category, each reviewer was asked to summarize up to two main concluding points from the source.

Our content analysis involved generating quantitative counts of all binary indicators and the two portrayal columns. In instances where there was a discrepancy between what the two separate reviewers recorded for the binary indicators and portrayal categories, of which there were thirty-five in total, a third reviewer was used. For the other categories of extracted information, broad themes were identified to characterize the breadth of what was recorded in the spreadsheet. Particular issues were assigned to these broad themes, and quantitative counts were generated to characterize their frequency. Two investigators oversaw this process in order to strengthen the interpretation of these themes and the assignment of numeric values to represent the frequency of each associated issue.

II. Media Analysis Findings

As noted above, fifty-nine articles were included in our media analysis.[19] Twenty-nine exhibited a neutral position on medical tourism, twenty-one expressed a positive position, seven took a negative position, and two took no discernable position. Six articles had an overt tourism focus, whereas the remaining fifty-three had an overt health focus. Thirty-one of the sources made at least passing reference to the potential positive impacts of medical tourism for Canada, whereas nineteen made reference to potential negative impacts. All but two sources made reference to specific medical tourism destination countries. The countries referred to included: Canada, India, Thailand, Singapore, South Korea, the United States, Mexico, Hungary, Serbia, Poland, Australia, South Africa, and Spain. Many articles mentioned numerous issues related

---

[19] Due to space constraints, a list of included articles is not provided here. Such a list can be obtained by contacting the authors directly.

to medical tourism. As we focused upon the main themes or narrative frames found in articles, medical tourism was characterized as an economic issue by thirty-six sources, a patient care issue by eleven, a wait list issue by twelve, a system availability or resource issue by five, a patient care and safety issue by five, and an ethical issue by one. As can be understood by this summary, some articles had more than one dominant characterization of medical tourism.

We identified five broad themes in the Canadian print media articles that we examined. These themes are: (1) Canadian patient motivations; (2) Canadian health system reform; (3) Canada as a destination for medical tourists; (4) business dimensions; and (5) industry limitations. In the remainder of this section of the chapter we review each of these themes. Consistent with a content analysis approach, wherever possible we indicate the number of sources reporting on a particular issue. Quantitative information (i.e., how many sources addressed particular topics) is provided in brackets using the "n = x" format.

A. CANADIAN PATIENT MOTIVATIONS

Our analysis reveals that Canadian print news media articles identify various factors used to explain why Canadian patients go abroad for private medical care. The affordability of international medical travel due to the competitiveness of airline and hotel pricing and the quoted rates of procedures in destinations is one such motivating factor (n = 11). There was, however, some mention in the sources that care costs in the medical tourism industry might be unaffordable for some Canadian patients (n = 4). News media reports also noted that some patients who want to access more luxurious facilities than what are available domestically are drawn into medical tourism out of a desire to access "luxury care" elsewhere and have little concern for costs or affordability (e.g., recovering in high-end resorts, being treated at private hospitals with greater patient-to-staff ratios) (n = 2). Interestingly, although affordability of medical care is often discussed in the academic literature as a factor motivating patients to seek care abroad,[20] procedure availability was the most commonly discussed motivating factor in our media review (n = 12). Specifically, gaining access to procedures not available domestically due either to wait times or lack of capacity (due to rationing, illegality, or lack of trained professionals) were cited as reasons Canadian patients might consider going to another country for medical care.

B. CANADIAN HEALTH SYSTEM REFORMS

The Canadian public health care system[21] was often mentioned and criticized in the sources reviewed. A key theme of this discussion pertained to the perceived need for

---

[20] Crooks et al., *supra* note 1; Hopkins et al., *supra* note 2; Lunt et al., *supra* note 3.

[21] Although here we refer to "health system" in the singular, it is important to note that each Canadian province and territory operates its own health system in accordance with the Canada Health Act. Much health care funding is transferred from the federal government to the provinces and territories where decisions are made provincially/territorially and sometimes even regionally about where and how these funds will be spent.

health system reform. The practice of Canadians going abroad for private medical care paid out-of-pocket through the medical tourism industry was, in some articles, portrayed as symptomatic of health system challenges. Although there was recognition of the need to address these challenges through domestic reform, the presence of the medical tourism industry was thought to offer the option of the public system sending Canadians elsewhere for medical care as a way of addressing certain system limitations.[22] More specifically, health reforms that enable Canadian patients to travel abroad for medical care through the public system were viewed as a way to overcome challenges posed by wait lists (n = 6) and larger system inefficiencies (n = 10). However, concerns were raised about this idea. Specific concerns were namely the issues of determining what costs the public health system should cover if patients are required to go abroad for care or do so as a result of constrained choices in the domestic system (n = 6) and of determining how follow-up care will be provided domestically (n = 2).

C. CANADA AS A DESTINATION FOR MEDICAL TOURISTS

The possibility of establishing a domestic medical tourism industry received some attention in the sources reviewed. Much of this attention was prompted by an announcement from British Columbia's Minister of Health indicating that he wanted to make the province a destination for international patients, including through offering care by using resources in the public health care system[23] and creating new opportunities for private care.[24] However, his announcement provided little insight into how this

---

[22] The Canada Health Act requires that public health care be portable across provincial and territorial jurisdictions, meaning that one can access publicly provided care outside of one's home region but within Canada without cost (see http://laws-lois.justice.gc.ca/eng/acts/C-6/page-1.html). This portability can be extended to nondomestic care, but only in very limited circumstances. There are some established cross-border care arrangements with clinics in the United States where specific treatments in these facilities are covered through the public system. Patients can also go abroad outside of these established arrangements and have this care reimbursed if they can demonstrate that medically necessary care is not available at all or in a timely fashion in their region and that irrevocable tissue damage or other negative health outcomes are imminent. Permission to do this must be sought through the provincial or territorial health plan prior to going abroad. Typically, payment is made out-of-pocket, and reimbursement will be arranged only upon return to Canada; for an extended discussion of the use of medical tourism by Canadian patients to overcome health system limitations, see Jeremy Snyder et al., *Perceptions of the Ethics of Medical Tourism: Comparing Patient and Academic Perspectives*, doi: 10.1093/phe/phr034 PUBLIC HEALTH ETHICS (in press).

[23] The Canadian health care system, known as Medicare, is run using a single-payer model for medically necessary, non-extended hospital or physician-based health care.] As per the Canada Health Act, all Canadians are entitled to access this care through the public system with no direct payment. With some exceptions, it is not possible to privately purchase the care covered by Medicare within Canada as the Canadian system does not support a two-tier model.

[24] E.g., The Canadian Press, *BC to Market Health Tourism*, CBC (Mar. 9, 2010), http://www.cbc.ca/news/canada/british-columbia/story/2010/03/09/bc-health-tourism-falcon-dix.html; The Canadian Press, *B.C. Hospitals to Vie for Patients under New Bill*, CBC (Apr. 12, 2010), http://www.cbc.ca/news/canada/british-columbia/story/2010/04/11/bc-hospital-reform.html; The Canadian Press, *B.C. Mulls High-End Health Centres for Foreigners*, CTV (Mar. 10, 2010), http://bc.ctvnews.ca/b-c-mulls-high-end-health-centres-for-foreigners-1.490577.

plan was to be enacted. As a result, reviewed sources contained considerable speculation regarding the potential impacts of a domestic or Canadian medical tourism
industry. It was most commonly asserted that a domestic medical tourism industry
could be used to generate revenues that could be reinvested into the public health care
system (n = 18). Concerns were raised, however, over the fact that offering services to
international patients using public health care would make for a poor use of resources
(n = 2), create a two-tier system (n = 5), and could result in prioritizing care for international patients over Canadian citizens (n = 5). More positive accounts of establishing a
domestic Canadian medical tourism industry claimed that such an industry could fix
some existing inefficiencies associated with the Canadian system such as wait lists,
underutilization of available operating room time, and physician billing requirements
(n = 11). Apathy toward system change (n = 1) and lack of the necessary legal and regulatory environment to enable the provision of care for international patients (n = 5)
were described as posing barriers to establishing a domestic medical tourism industry
and realizing its potential benefits.

D. BUSINESS DIMENSIONS

Various aspects of the business side of the medical tourism industry were addressed in
the sources included in our media review. Consistent with the academic literature,[25] the
permeability of borders and globalization of health care were described as enabling the
development and spread of the industry (n = 4). Several articles in our sample noted
that facilitators play an important role in this global industry, and that the industry
has enabled the creation of this new "professional" group (n = 6). Overall, the industry
was commonly portrayed as being competitive, with destinations vying over patients
(n = 7) and facilities needing to craft marketing campaigns to attract customers (n = 9).
Destination nations were thought to benefit from the establishment of the industry
through job creation (n = 2) and enhanced use of tourist facilities (n = 4). Meanwhile,
there was some limited recognition that the industry can create or exacerbate inequities through the establishment of health clinics that exclusively treat international
patients versus local citizens (n = 2).

E. INDUSTRY LIMITATIONS

A number of limitations of the global health services practice of medical tourism were
noted by the sources reviewed in our media analysis. The most commonly discussed
limitation pertained to the lack of industry standards and regulations in destination countries (n = 12). Such discussion included references to there being no transnational or national regulatory bodies for the industry, a lack of professionalization
among facilitators, a lack of centralization for the industry, and a general concern that
patients interested in medical tourism would not be able to adequately interpret these

---

[25] Hopkins et al., *supra* note 2; Johnston et al., *supra* note 4; Lunt et al., *supra* note 3.

issues and the impacts they may have on care quality. Another industry limitation considered by the sources is that of cost, in that the costs of care and travel abroad may be prohibitively high, particularly in cases where patients cannot obtain reimbursement through the Canadian public Medicare system (n = 4). Other limitations mentioned include the potential for medical tourism to create or exacerbate rural-to-urban brain drain in destination countries (n = 2), to erode the duty to care for one's own citizens (n = 2), and to create follow-up care costs in Canada's public health care system due to individual patients' decisions to go abroad for private medical care (n = 2).

III. Considering the Ethical Gaps

We stated at the outset of the chapter that our purpose is to determine whether the six main domains of ethical concern associated with the emergence of a global marketplace in health services are addressed in Canadian print news media coverage of medical tourism. To reiterate, these domains pertain to: (1) information disclosure and informed consent; (2) potential for unfair burden on public resources in patients' home countries; (3) fairness regarding queue jumping; (4) risks to public health; (5) potential for diversion of public resources in destination countries; and (6) prioritization of needs of international patients over local citizens. The five main themes identified in our media analysis touched most explicitly on four of these six domains of ethical concern, with little consideration being given to the domains of informed consent and the risks to public health associated with disease transmission occurring as a result of participation in medical tourism.[26] Though moral issues were addressed in the print news media sources, even in news reports where explicit reference was made to one or more of the domains of ethical concern, discussion of the specific issue was rarely framed using an ethics lens. Rather, news reports mentioned "risks" and raised questions about patient safety in medical tourism without using explicitly ethical terms and concepts such as informed consent, fairness, and health equity. Though the language of risk and patient safety provides a vocabulary for examining ethical issues, the focus of many articles on the journeys of individual medical tourists rather than broader concerns related to public health and the fair allocation of resources means that Canadian print news media coverage of medical tourism has numerous gaps. In this section we identify gaps in Canadian news media coverage of ethical dimensions of medical tourism.

---

[26] It is worth noting that two important issues related to medical tourism have received significant media coverage following the period of our media review. The first pertains to the spread of New Delhi metallo-beta-lactamase (NDM-1) by some international patients, including Canadians, treated in India. Coverage of this issue has included explicit consideration of the public health implications of medical tourism. The second pertains to the use of chronic cerebrospinal venous insufficiency (CCSVI) therapy to treat multiple sclerosis, which is a treatment that is not available in Canada. Coverage of this issue has included some explicit consideration regarding informed consent in the medical tourism industry.

As we noted in the previous section, some reviewed news media sources identified ethical concerns about medical tourism's impact on fair access to medical care within Canadian provincial health systems. This examination of fair access within the domestic Canadian context was commonly expressed in terms of suggesting that medical tourism allows patients to queue jump and access care abroad more quickly than is available domestically. The ethical concern here is that medical tourism rations these resources according to the ability to pay rather than medical necessity. More specifically, access to health care on the basis of personal wealth rather than need prompts concerns that medical tourism promotes inequitable access to care. A related but less visible concern in these media pieces is medical tourism's impact on global health equity. In the academic literature examining the ethical dimensions of medical tourism, many researchers note the possibility that medical tourism has the potential to negatively impact access to care within the public health systems of destination countries by diverting resources from public health systems into the private sphere.[27] It is possible that when Canadian patients choose to exit the local health system they contribute to health inequities in both domestic and global contexts. Where equity and resource allocation issues were noted, the news media reports we reviewed typically focused on domestic equity impacts of medical tourism. In contrast, there was little mention of global health equity and the effects of medical tourism within the countries attracting international patients.

The media sources we reviewed tended to focus on price savings and wait times as principal motivators for Canadian medical tourists rather than local (un)availability of procedures. The narrative frame related to cost savings as a driver of medical tourism resembles the popular U.S. narrative that medical tourism is driven by uninsured and underinsured individuals searching for affordable medical care that is paid for as an out-of-pocket expense. In many respects, this narrative frame displays a lack of understanding of why Canadians engage in medical tourism. Because Canada has a provincially or territorially administered system of publicly funded, universal health care, the country does not have the large population of uninsured and underinsured individuals found in the United States. We suspect that this narrative frame appears in Canadian print news media because Canadian newspapers sometimes republish articles that appear in U.S. publications. In contrast, news media accounts of medical tourism initiated as a result of wait times for treatment in Canada appear to better capture one reason some Canadians decide to participate in medical tourism. Given the delays for various types of surgical and diagnostic procedures, particularly in Canada, it is unsurprising that journalists link treatment delays to patients' decisions to engage in medical tourism. We realize, however, that some discussion of cost savings in Canadian news media accounts is understandable because patients who decide to avoid wait times by engaging in medical tourism must typically pay out-of-pocket for their medical treatment. In addition because dental care and some other procedure

---

[27] Rupa Chanda, *Trade in Health Services*, 80 BULL. OF THE WHO 158 (2002); *see also* Chapter 6 in this book.

categories are not covered by Medicare, patients lacking private insurance for such care may be sensitive to the potential for cost savings. Cost of treatment could play a factor as Canadians make decisions about where they can obtain affordable medical care.

We identified sparse coverage of two of the key ethical concerns raised in the academic literature on medical tourism. First, informed consent is a core ethical component of medical care and biomedical research. Numerous studies reveal that some medical tourists lack information on the risks entailed by this practice, qualifications of doctors and facilitators, payment structures for facilitators and doctors, and medical malpractice coverage.[28] News media narratives describing patients' experiences inadequately convey the array of issues that those considering engaging in medical tourism must consider, including the lack of regulatory protections for patients, the lack of standards for accreditation of various practitioners, and the problems with assessing the claims of industry members online.[29] The news media sources that we reviewed also paid little attention to the quality of information provided to medical tourists and the extent to which medical tourists make truly informed choices before being treated at international medical facilities. Information quality holds direct implications for the abilities of medical tourists to give informed consent.

Second, few of the media sources we reviewed noted ethical concerns around the domestic resource costs of medical tourism. These costs take the form of patients requiring standard follow-up care for procedures provided abroad and care for the complications of elective procedures. When patients choose to exit their provincial or territorial health system for necessary care, it often appears as though they reduce local resource demands by paying out-of-pocket for care that otherwise would have been provided by the publicly funded health care system. However, if medical tourists return home with complications, Canadian health care providers have a duty to provide medically necessary care. By going abroad for treatment and then undergoing treatment for complications, these patients may jump the queue and receive care ahead of other patients. In addition, providing follow-up care can generate costs equal or greater to that which would have been required had the patient not gone abroad.[30] Similarly, patients seeking elective or experimental procedures that are not provided within the public system can create new costs for the system as a result of their need for follow-up care and treatment of complications resulting from surgery abroad. These ethical issues are difficult to convey in the media; they are long-term effects that can take years to appear. In most Canadian provinces and territories there is little effort to measure costs associated with providing follow-up care to Canadians who have engaged in medical tourism.[31] By focusing on the personal narratives and journeys of patients, it appears that media analysis of medical tourism neglects important, long-term ethical concerns for the domestic system.

---

[28] Alicia Mason & Kevin B. Wright, *Framing Medical Tourism: An Examination of Appeal, Risk, Convalescence, Accreditation, and Interactivity in Medical Tourism Web Sites*, 16 J. HEALTH COMM. 163 (2011); Penney et al., *supra* note 5; Spece, *supra* note 5.

[29] Turner, *Quality in Health Care*, *supra* note 4.

[30] Birch et al., *supra* note 6.

[31] Snyder et al., *supra* note 12.

The Canadian news media accounts of medical tourism we reviewed addressed ethical issues related to quality of care and patient safety at international health care facilities. Numerous reports raised concerns about the quality of care medical tourists might encounter by traveling abroad for surgery and other medical procedures. Canadian news reports also raised reasonable concerns about whether going abroad for treatment enables Canadians with sufficient resources to jump the queue and gain faster access to treatment than those receiving care at domestic health care facilities. In contrast, the reviewed sources' consideration of medical tourism paid only limited attention to the quality of information provided to Canadians by medical tourism companies, international hospitals, and other organizations; public health threats related to medical tourism and transmission of infectious disease (health risks Canadians face when they go abroad to undergo medical procedures that are not approved for use within Canada); the need to provide postoperative care to Canadians who go abroad for treatment and the domestic health equity effects of medical tourism; and health equity effects of Canadians receiving care in countries with overwhelmed and underfunded public health care systems. Our media analysis suggests that news reports most commonly, and perhaps most effectively, describe journeys of particular medical tourists without engaging in these "deeper" issues. Although such narratives capture important features of medical tourism, they tend to pay little attention to the public health and health equity effects of medical tourism that have been highlighted in the ethics literature. Given the important role of news media in public debate, richer, more complex news media accounts of medical tourism could play a valuable role in promoting more robust public discussion of ethical issues related to participation of Canadians in medical tourism.

IV. Implications for Future Canadian Media Coverage of Medical Tourism

The news media reports we reviewed paid little attention to availability within Canada of particular medical procedures sought abroad by medical tourists. As a result, news reports neglected the distinct ethical issues raised by medical tourism driven by lack of access within Canada to novel medical interventions in particular.[32] For example, some Canadians engage in medical tourism to undergo experimental procedures that are not approved within Canada. This variety of medical tourism has repercussions for patient safety in that there can be few reliable assurances regarding care quality or health outcomes.[33] In addition, it raises challenging questions about local approval processes for new medical treatments within the context of a global trade in health services.

When Canadians engage in medical tourism to obtain access to emerging medical therapies, it is possible that such trips point to shortcomings with Canada's regulatory oversight of emerging technologies and medical devices. The same is likely true when patients from other countries leave their home nations to access such procedures abroad. It is also possible that an inability to gain access to particular medical interventions

---

[32] Snyder et al., *supra* note 6; Snyder et al., *supra* note 22.
[33] Crooks et al., *supra* note 1.

within Canada is a sign of a robust domestic system of regulatory oversight, meaning that some medical tourists who go abroad for experimental procedures may be at increased risk of exposure to medical interventions that are not justified by credible forms of evidence. Lack of local availability for approved procedures can reflect ethical issues such as problems with the equitable distribution of public medical resources within Canada. Patients may be faced with an ethical quandary over paying out-of-pocket for care that they see as necessary but that is not being provided by the public system in a fair and timely manner.[34] At a systemic level, all health systems must confront the tensions inherent in addressing the needs of patients in a time where national borders are increasingly porous and global trade in health services is expanding. Issues such as these need to be given attention in Canadian news media coverage of medical tourism in order to attune readers to some of the ethical dimensions of this global health services practice. The same is true for coverage of medical tourism in other countries.

Both health researchers and journalists within and beyond Canada experience serious challenges in adequately describing a health care phenomenon where basic data about its scope and effects are lacking.[35] This problem was manifested in the news media sources we reviewed. Many of the sources provided narratives of individual patients who had privately gone abroad for care. Journalists described the journeys of particular Canadians, but appear to have had difficulty addressing broader ethical and social dimensions of medical tourism. Further to this, news media coverage was often one-dimensional, with reporters focused upon risks assumed to be present when patients travel long distances to countries not normally associated with state-of-the-art medical care. Although medical tourism is an issue that deserves media coverage and public debate, the dearth of reliable information about the numbers and motivations of Canadians traveling abroad for care, public health and resource allocation effects of this practice domestically and abroad, and long-term trends risks hampering a balanced and informed public discussion of the ethical issues raised by medical tourism.

News media coverage of the proposal to turn the province of British Columbia into a medical tourism destination provides an example of the speculation that can occur in the absence of evidence-based public debate about this global health services practice. While media coverage speculated on the potential impacts of this proposal, the lack of detail of what this plan would entail and failure to provide any empirical data concerning how it would impact local access to care resulted in a missed opportunity for a more informed public debate about the ethical issues and policy challenges that would need to be addressed if British Columbia or any other Canadian province attempted to become a destination for medical tourists. Future media coverage could, alternatively, embrace such an opportunity. This holds true for any debatable, contested, or potentially even novel practice associated with medical tourism in all home and destination nations. Embracing such opportunities can facilitate increased awareness about the ethical concerns associated with medical tourism, which, among a number of other factors, we view as being beneficial to enabling potential medical tourists to make informed decisions.

---

[34] Snyder et al., *supra* note 22.

[35] Hopkins et al., *supra* note 2; Johnston et al., *supra* note 4; Lunt et al., *supra* note 3.

4

CROSS-BORDER HEALTH CARE AND THE HYDRAULICS OF HEALTH REFORM

Nathan Cortez*

Introduction

In retrospect, it seems obvious that patients would leave the United States for health care. Ours is by far the world's most expensive health care system, and has been for some time. In the years leading up to 2010, U.S. residents had to confront not only persistently rising costs, but also evaporating insurance coverage—forcing them to pay more for less. In response, some patients began exploring affordable alternatives outside the United States, particularly in developing economies in Asia and Latin America, where some hospitals can offer comparable care for a fraction of the U.S. price. Media fascination with so-called "medical tourism" grew as academics, policy makers, and the medical community openly marveled that our health care system could force patients to seek something as basic as medical care overseas. Almost inevitably, some U.S. employers and insurers, also suffocating under the weight of domestic prices, began evaluating whether foreign providers might provide a feasible, economical alternative. In the last decade, the medical tourism phenomenon has emerged—quite ironically—as both a symbol of our health care system's excesses as well as a potential solution.

Just as this foreign alternative emerged—what I have described elsewhere as our "foreign safety net"[1]—U.S. policy makers began to confront our health system's

---

* Assistant Professor, Southern Methodist University, Dedman School of Law. Section I of this chapter was adapted from Nathan Cortez, *Embracing the New Geography of Health Care: A Novel Way to Cover Those Left out of Health Reform*, 84 S. Cal. L. Rev. 859 (2011).
[1] Nathan Cortez, *Embracing the New Geography of Health Care: A Novel Way to Cover Those Left out of Health Reform*, 84 S. Cal. L. Rev. 859, 876–77 (2011).

problems internally. In 2010, Congress passed the Patient Protection and Affordable Care Act, the most significant health legislation since Congress created Medicare and Medicaid almost fifty years ago.[2] Although the Act aspires to achieve the holy trinity of health policy—lowering costs, improving quality, and expanding access[3]—by far its most significant contribution is to expand access to health insurance. The Act broadens eligibility for public insurance programs such as Medicaid and tries to transform the private insurance market into the competitive venue we have always coveted (and that always seems to elude us). As a result, the Congressional Budget Office (CBO) estimates that the Act will reduce the number of nonelderly uninsured by thirty-two million by 2019, from fifty-five million to twenty-three million.[4] A more recent report predicts that the Act will expand insurance coverage among the nonelderly by a smaller but still significant amount—twenty-eight million.[5] Either way, this is a major accomplishment for our health care system, long notorious among our peer countries for being easily the most expensive and least inclusive.

These domestic and international developments reveal the hydraulics of health care. Domestically, U.S. patients are being pushed out of our health care system. The number of uninsured has climbed virtually unabated since the 1980s, stretching further and further up the income ladder. And those lucky enough to retain coverage have been asked to pay higher premiums, bear a larger burden of cost-sharing and out-of-pocket expenses, and accept fewer benefits—again, being asked to pay more for less. Public programs such as Medicare and Medicaid have stretched to their breaking points, and Medicare now represents the single biggest threat to our national debt. Finally, we rely on a severely marbled, fragmented system of safety net providers that struggles to fill the gaps left by public and private insurance. The steady accretion of these pressures has made low-cost foreign providers a surprisingly feasible safety valve for some.

Meanwhile, hydraulic pressures from abroad have pulled U.S. patients away. Patients are being lured overseas by low-cost foreign providers promising care that meets or exceeds U.S. quality standards. A confluence of factors has made this possible. Foreign physicians and hospitals increasingly can meet U.S. quality standards. International standards for medical education, hospital accreditation, and related activities have converged, driven by market incentives. The principles and technologies of Western scientific medicine have spread. Countries have opened their health systems to foreign direct investment and joint ventures with hospitals and universities from Western countries. And the Internet has allowed the relatively nascent medical tourism industry to market

[2] Patient Protection and Affordable Care Act, H.R. 3590, 111th Cong. (2nd Sess. 2010), Pub. L. No. 111-148, *as amended* by the Health Care and Education Reconciliation Act of 2010, H.R. 4872, 111th Cong. (2nd Sess. 2010), Pub. L. No. 111-152 [hereinafter the "Affordable Care Act" or simply "the Act"].

[3] Nathan Cortez, *Patients without Borders: The Emerging Global Market for Patients and the Evolution of Modern Health Care*, 83 IND. L.J. 71, 95 n.228 (2008).

[4] Letter from Douglas W. Elmendorf, Director, Congressional Budget Office (CBO), to Rep. Nancy Pelosi (Mar. 20, 2010), at 9 tbl.4 (on file with author) [hereinafter "CBO Letter"].

[5] Matthew Buettgens & Mark Hall, *Who Will Be Uninsured after Health Insurance Reform?*, THE URBAN INSTITUTE, Mar. 10, 2011, at 1, *available at* http://www.rwjf.org/coverage/product.jsp?id=71998.

itself to patients who possess the requisite combination of medical and financial need to consider the drastic step of leaving their home country for health care.[6]

But a question lingers over medical tourism and cross-border health care: how will these domestic and international hydraulics interact after U.S. health reform? The Affordable Care Act is designed, above all, to alter incentives, many of which currently combine to make foreign providers an attractive alternative for some. Will the Act obviate the need to seek economical alternatives outside the United States? Will it actually make care "affordable," as its title suggests? Or will foreign providers remain a safety valve for the world's most expensive health care system? What niche will foreign providers fill in post-reform America? The parties that currently rely on low-cost foreign providers—patients, employers, and insurers—are caught in the hydraulics between domestic health reform and international competition for patients.

This chapter explores these hydraulics and predicts two distinct courses. First, foreign providers will remain an important outlet for U.S. patients who are not eligible for public insurance and cannot afford private insurance, even after the Affordable Care Act is fully implemented. Second, and perhaps more controversially, employers and insurers will continue to experiment with foreign providers—either by adding them to their provider networks or by creating true cross-border health plans—and these plans will be used to satisfy the new individual insurance mandate and possibly also to compete in the new state insurance exchanges created by the Affordable Care Act.

I evaluate first whether insurance plans that utilize foreign providers could satisfy the requirement to maintain "minimum essential coverage" under the new mandate. Because the Affordable Care Act defines "minimum essential coverage" so broadly, and by reference to existing coverage, I conclude that nothing in the Act would prohibit such a result.

Second, I evaluate whether plans that use foreign medical providers can offer "essential health benefits" and thus meet the requirements for "qualified health plans" to participate in the new state insurance exchanges beginning in 2014. Given the language of the Act, it seems that they could. Although several provisions might make it difficult for cross-border plans to qualify for the exchanges, several provisions also encourage states to innovate and maintain flexibility to cover their populations, which leaves open the chance that states would allow insurers to experiment with cross-border plans. For example, the Act might allow states to create pilot programs of limited geographic scope for the purpose of experimenting with cross-border provider networks.

To be clear, the Affordable Care Act neither refers to nor contemplates foreign providers. Nevertheless, its provisions will affect cross-border health care in profound ways. Of course, the U.S. Department of Health and Human Services (HHS) and other agencies, such as the Internal Revenue Service (IRS), will promulgate regulations implementing and interpreting the Act, the volume of which will dwarf the 950 pages of the Act itself. Thus, it is possible that these regulations will address cross-

---

[6] For an overview of these trends, see Nathan Cortez, *International Health Care Convergence: The Benefits and Burdens of Market-Driven Standardization*, 26 WISC. INT'L L.J. 646 (2009).

border health care phenomena such as medical tourism, or more likely, affect these phenomena indirectly without directly confronting them. One goal of this chapter is to help policy makers appreciate how their regulatory efforts might interact with various international hydraulics. And those interested in cross-border trends such as medical tourism can better appreciate the hydraulics of domestic health reform.

I. Our Foreign Safety Net: Searching for Care Beyond the Affordable Care Act

The Affordable Care Act is the most important health legislation since Congress created the Medicare and Medicaid programs in 1965.[7] Yet, despite its historical importance, the Act will not cover all the uninsured in the United States. Most of the millions of U.S. residents who will obtain new coverage under the Act will have to wait years for it. The Act is being implemented in distinct phases, the last and most important of which begins on January 1, 2014. On that date, eligibility for Medicaid greatly expands, turning it into a genuine health insurance program for the poor.[8] Also on that date, the major insurance market reforms take effect, including the state insurance exchanges and a medley of other programs intended to expand access to private, nongovernmental, and quasi-governmental insurance programs.

Nevertheless, until 2014, roughly fifty million U.S. residents will remain uninsured—what I call the "interim uninsured." And between 2014 and 2019, anywhere from twenty-one million to thirty-one million will remain uninsured—what I call the "residually uninsured." In this section, I describe how foreign providers can fill gaps in coverage for the interim uninsured, and after that, for the residually uninsured. I argue that foreign providers will remain a discrete and crucial part of the safety net for both populations.

A. THE INTERIM UNINSURED

In the immediate future, the uninsured population will remain just as massive and conspicuous as before March 21, 2010, the day President Obama signed the Affordable Care Act into law. Currently, fifty million U.S. residents have no health insurance—comprising almost one-fifth of the nonelderly population.[9] And when examined over a two-year period, a staggering one-third of the nonelderly population (eight-two million) lacks insurance at some point.[10] In addition to the fifty million interim uninsured, another twenty-five million are considered to be "underinsured," because their insurance plans require them to spend an excessive portion of their incomes on premiums and various cost-sharing obligations, such as deductibles and copayments.[11] Like the uninsured, the

---

[7] Social Security Act Amendments of 1965, Pub. L. No. 89-97, 79 Stat. 286 (1965).

[8] Cortez, *supra* note 1, at 869.

[9] CBO Letter, *supra* note 4, at 9 tbl.4.

[10] Timothy Stoltzfus Jost, *Our Broken Health Care System and How to Fix It: An Essay on Health Law and Policy*, 41 WAKE FOREST L. REV. 537, 540 (2006) (citing data for 2002 and 2003).

[11] Cathy Schoen et al., *How Many Are Underinsured? Trends among U.S. Adults, 2003 and 2007*, 27 HEALTH AFF. (WEB EXCLUSIVE ISSUE) W298 (2008), at W298–99.

number of underinsured has risen along with prices.[12] Taken as a whole, the uninsured and underinsured comprise almost *half* of the U.S. nonelderly population.[13]

The un- and underinsured can be hard to characterize aside from their defining trait—lacking adequate health insurance. If we just focus on the uninsured, we find they are demographically diverse,[14] spanning "every age, race, and citizenship status."[15] The uninsured are also economically diverse. Over one-fifth of the uninsured live in households that earn at least $50,000 annually, and almost one-tenth live in households that earn at least $75,000.[16] The vast majority of uninsured work, though many earn modest or even meager wages.[17] Adding the underinsured to this mix certainly amplifies the population's demographic and economic diversities.

Of course, the un- and underinsured are joined by the defining trait that they generally do not qualify for, are not offered, and/or cannot afford adequate health insurance. Many uninsured patients earn too much to qualify for Medicaid.[18] Many are too young to qualify for Medicare, which covers those age sixty-five and older.[19] And many simply cannot afford private insurance.[20] Not surprisingly, the un- and underinsured must rely on safety net providers, such as community health centers, free clinics, public hospitals, and emergency departments.[21] Foreign providers have emerged as perhaps the last alternative for patients who have fallen through the cracks in our health care system.

Perhaps not coincidentally, U.S. patients are becoming less reluctant to consider foreign providers as a low-cost alternative. In a 2006 survey, Arnold Milstein and Mark Smith found that between 10 to 35 percent of respondents who had an ailing family member would travel overseas for nonemergency surgery, depending on the magnitude of the cost-savings.[22] And in 2009, a Gallup poll of over five thousand adults

---

[12] *Id.* at W298.

[13] *Id.* at W301 (Exhibit 1).

[14] Jost, *supra* note 10, at 540–42; Nan Hunter, *Risk Governance and Deliberative Democracy in Health Care*, 97 GEO. L.J. 1, 58 (2008); I. Glenn Cohen, Protecting Patients with Passports: Medical Tourism and the Patient-Protective Argument, 95 IOWA L. REV. 1467, 1524 (2010).

[15] Cortez, *supra* note 1, at 865 (citing CARMEN DeNAVAS-WALT, BERNADETTE D. PROCTOR & JESSICA C. SMITH, U.S. CENSUS BUREAU, P30-238, INCOME, POVERTY, AND HEALTH INSURANCE COVERAGE IN THE UNITED STATES: 2009 21 tbl.7 (2010)).

[16] Cortez, *supra* note 1, at 866.

[17] Jost, *supra* note 10, at 541; DeNAVAS-WALT ET AL., *supra* note 15, at 21 tbl.7.

[18] Note that states currently set different Medicaid eligibility criteria, including very different income and resource limits, and that these criteria will continue to diverge until several Medicaid provisions in the Affordable Care Act take effect in 2014. *See* U.S. Dep't of Health & Human Serv., *Medicaid Income and Resource Guidelines* (2011), *available at* http://www.cms.hhs.gov/MedicaidEligibility/07_IncomeandResourceGuidelines.asp; Kaiser Family Foundation, *Income Thresholds for Jobless and Working Parents Applying for Medicaid by Annual Income as a Percent of Federal Poverty Level (FPL)* (2012), http://www.statehealthfacts.org/comparereport.jsp?rep=130&cat=4.

[19] 42 U.S.C. § 426(a)(1).

[20] SCHOEN ET AL., PAYING THE PRICE: HOW HEALTH INSURANCE PREMIUMS ARE EATING UP MIDDLE-CLASS INCOMES 3 fig.1 (Aug. 2009), The Commonwealth Fund, http://www.commonwealthfund.org.

[21] Cortez, *supra* note 1, at 872–76.

[22] Arnold Milstein & Mark Smith, *Will the Surgical World Become Flat?*, 26 HEALTH AFF. 137, 138–40 (2007).

showed that 29 percent would consider using foreign providers to treat a "major medical problem." The percentage willing to travel rose to 40 percent if they could obtain "equal quality and significantly cheaper cost"[23]—which today is not an unrealistic expectation.

These survey results lend some credibility to the anecdotal evidence suggesting that U.S. patients increasingly travel for health care. Of course, the precise number of medical tourists is difficult if not impossible to peg with any confidence, as no one systematically tracks medical tourists. Existing data are incomplete and unreliable.[24] The industry and foreign governments seem to inflate the number of medical tourists.[25] Reputable consulting firms cannot seem to agree on even ballpark estimates. McKinsey & Company estimated that only 5,000 to 10,000 United States patients travel for inpatient procedures annually.[26] In contrast, Deloitte estimated that 750,000 U.S. patients traveled in 2007, although this included both inpatient and outpatient procedures.[27] Deloitte infamously predicted that by 2010 the number of medical tourists would rise to five or six million, but has since shaved that estimate to only 1.6 million.[28] It is likely to be even less.[29] All these estimates are practically unverifiable. No government agency tracks the number of outbound medical tourists, and recipient hospitals and host nations are likely to either protect this information or embellish it.

Nevertheless, there seems to be wide consensus that more U.S. patients are discovering low-cost foreign providers, particularly for specialty and high-tech procedures that require inpatient care.[30] For years, U.S. patients have been pushed out of the U.S. health care system, and a nascent industry centered around low-cost foreign providers is emerging in response. Until 2014, this market will continue to cater to the interim uninsured.

B. THE RESIDUALLY UNINSURED

Beyond 2014, the cross-border market most likely will cater to the residually uninsured—who will remain uninsured even after the final wave of the Affordable Care Act takes effect. After this date, the uninsured population will decrease only gradually.

---

[23] Christopher Khoury, *Americans Consider Crossing Borders for Medical Care*, GALLUP (May 18, 2009), http://www.gallup.com/poll/118423/americans-consider-crossing-borders-medical-care.aspx.

[24] Cortez, *supra* note 1, at 877.

[25] *Id.* at 877–78; Ian Youngman, *How Many American Medical Tourists Are There?*, INT'L MED. TRAVEL J. (2009), http://www.imtjonline.com/articles/2009/how-many-americans-go-abroad-for-treatment-30016/; Ian Youngman, *Medical Tourism Statistics: Why McKinsey Has Got It Wrong*, INT'L MED. TRAVEL J. (2009), http://www.imtjonline.com/articles/2009/mckinsey-wrong-medical-travel/.

[26] Tilman Ehrbeck, Ceani Guevara & Paul D. Mango, *Mapping the Market for Medical Travel*, MCKINSEY Q., May 2008, at 2–3, 6.

[27] Deloitte, *Medical Tourism: Consumers in Search of Value* 4 (2008), http://www.deloitte.com/dtt/cda/doc/content/us_chs_MedicalTourismStudy(3).pdf.

[28] Tom Murphy, *Health Insurers Explore Savings in Overseas Care*, ASSOCIATED PRESS, Aug. 22, 2009, *available at* http://www.ktvb.com/news/health/64299307.html.

[29] Cortez, *supra* note 1, at 878 n.119; Youngman, *supra* note 25.

[30] Cortez, *supra* note 1, at 882.

In 2014 the number of uninsured is estimated to drop from fifty million to thirty-one million.[31] In 2015, it is predicted to drop further to twenty-six million, and between 2016 and 2019, it is expected to hover between twenty-one million and twenty-three million.[32]

Who will be the residually uninsured? Defining this population requires us first to understand who will gain coverage under the Affordable Care Act. Those who will gain coverage are primarily those who are *required* to maintain it pursuant to the new individual mandate.[33] Indeed, Congress designed the Act to make insurance more accessible to those who must maintain "minimum essential coverage" beginning in 2014.[34]

The newly insured will find coverage through different reforms in the Act. For example, an estimated twenty-four million will purchase individual health plans through the new state "health benefit exchanges,"[35] which Congress hopes will offer competitive plans to those who are not covered by their employers and who are not eligible for Medicaid or other public insurance.[36] At the same time, the Act expands eligibility for Medicaid and the state Children's Health Insurance Program (CHIP), which is expected to raise the number enrolled in these programs from thirty-five million to roughly fifty-six million by 2019.[37] Eligibility will reach those with incomes up to 133 percent of the federal poverty line,[38] eliminating the much lower income thresholds states currently use, as well as the non-income criteria that presently limit Medicaid to "children and some parents, pregnant women, those who are permanently and totally disabled, and the elderly."[39]

The effect of health reform on access to private, employer-sponsored insurance is much harder to predict. Employers are expected to cover six to seven million more employees over the next decade who otherwise would not be covered under previous law.[40] However, between eight and nine million employees are predicted to lose their employer-sponsored coverage after implementation, when their employers choose to pay fees in lieu of offering health insurance.[41] Further complicating matters, between one and two million employees who currently have insurance through their employers will instead purchase policies through the state exchanges.[42] Tallying these numbers, the expected net effect is that three million fewer employees will have employer-sponsored health insurance than is the case now.[43]

---

[31]   CBO Letter, *supra* note 4, at tbl.4.

[32]   *Id.*

[33]   Affordable Care Act § 1501.

[34]   Cortez, *supra* note 1, at 868.

[35]   CBO Letter, *supra* note 4, at 9 tbl.4.

[36]   Affordable Care Act §§ 1311–1324.

[37]   CBO Letter, *supra* note 4, at 9 tbl.4.

[38]   Affordable Care Act § 2001.

[39]   Kaiser Family Foundation, *Medicaid and the Uninsured* (Dec. 2009), http://www.kff.org/medicaid/upload/7993.pdf; Sidney Watson, *Commercialization of Medicaid*, 45 St. Louis U. L.J. 53, 57 (2001).

[40]   CBO Letter, *supra* note 4, at 10 tbl.4.

[41]   *Id.* at 10.

[42]   *Id.*

[43]   *Id.*

Yet, these predictions are just that, and they may deviate significantly upward or downward depending on the success of several new programs created by the Act. For example, the Affordable Care Act creates nonprofit insurance "cooperatives" to offer an alternative to private plans in the state insurance exchanges.[44] Policy makers hope these "Co-Ops" will force competing private plans to offer more generous benefits for lower prices. Similarly, the Act calls for the U.S. Office of Personnel Management to offer multi-state plans via private insurers in each state exchange.[45] Again, no one can predict whether these programs will achieve or even approximate their intended outcomes.

Outside these newly insured, who will constitute the remaining twenty-three million—the residually uninsured? Matthew Buettgens and Mark Hall asked what this population would look like if the Affordable Care Act were fully implemented in 2011.[46] They estimated that 40 percent of the twenty-three million uninsured would be eligible for Medicaid or CHIP but not enrolled, and that another 22 percent would be undocumented immigrants.

Focusing on nonelderly adults, Buettgens and Hall's model estimates that nineteen million would remain uninsured. Of this nineteen million, 37 percent would be eligible for Medicaid but not enrolled for one reason or another, mostly young singles without dependents. Twenty-five percent would be undocumented immigrants, more than half of whom would have incomes below 138 percent of the federal poverty level, which means Medicaid would cover their emergency care. Sixteen percent would not have access to "affordable" insurance as defined by the Act and would thus be exempt from the personal mandate. Eight percent would be eligible to participate in the state insurance exchanges with some federal subsidies. And the remaining 15 percent of the uninsured nonelderly would both be subject to the mandate and would have access to affordable coverage, but would not be eligible for subsidies in the state exchanges.[47]

Which of these groups might look for care overseas? Using the estimates above, nineteen million nonelderly will be residually uninsured. Of this population, roughly seven million would be eligible for Medicaid but not enrolled.[48] Under the Affordable Care Act, Medicaid covers those who earn below 138 percent of the federal poverty line, which itself depends on the household's size.[49] These seven million residents might eventually enroll in response to better outreach, or perhaps through automatic enrollment by hospitals that treat them and identify them as being eligible.[50] However, it is unlikely that this population would go to the trouble of seeking care overseas if they have not bothered to enroll in virtually free coverage back home. Moreover, even though foreign providers offer a substantial discount from domestic prices, it may still

[44] Affordable Care Act § 1322 (referring to Consumer-Oriented and Operated Plans, or "CO-OPs").
[45] Affordable Care Act §§ 1334, 10104(q).
[46] Buettgens & Hall, *supra* note 5.
[47] *Id.* at 1, 5, 10 tbl.4.
[48] *Id.* at 10 tbl.4 (taking 36.5 percent of 18,558,500).
[49] Affordable Care Act § 2001.
[50] Buettgens & Hall, *supra* note 5, at 6.

be prohibitively expensive for those earning less than 138 percent of the federal poverty line to pay for a plane ticket and lodging, not to mention the foreign provider's charges. The exception may be those uninsured who live close to the Mexico border, for whom travel expenses would not be significant, in addition to other regular visitors to Mexico. Even so, Buettgens and Hall estimate that the median income for these nonelderly Medicaid eligibles is only $3,008[51]—which seems far below what it would require to afford overseas care.

That leaves roughly twelve million of the nonelderly residuum that might consider utilizing foreign providers under certain circumstances. This population obviously earns significantly more than those eligible for Medicaid.

First, of this twelve million, roughly three million will be exempt from the individual mandate because they are not offered affordable insurance where they live and work.[52] To qualify for this exemption, premiums for the plans available must exceed 8 percent of the family's modified adjusted gross income. According to Buettgens and Hall, the median family income for this group is $31,000, and the average age is fifty-one.[53] This group captures some of the population that earns too much for Medicaid and is too young for Medicare, and therefore might utilize low-cost foreign providers under the right circumstances—although even this alternative might prove too expensive.

Second, another 1.4 million will qualify both for the affordability exemption and for subsidies in the state insurance exchanges.[54] Those eligible for subsidies have a modified adjusted gross income less than 400 percent of the federal poverty line. This group would not be required to purchase coverage under the mandate because their premium costs would still be too high, even with a subsidy. Buettgens and Hall estimate that this population is younger (a median of thirty-three years) and earns slightly more (a median family income of $36,000).[55] The subsidy may or may not encourage them to purchase insurance in the exchanges eventually. For those choosing to remain uninsured, foreign providers might fill the gap in coverage, particularly for invasive, nonemergency inpatient procedures.

The third group might represent the sweet spot for foreign providers. Approximately 2.8 million of the residually uninsured will earn too much to qualify for Medicaid or for federal subsidies in the exchanges.[56] Moreover, they will go uninsured although the insurance premiums they are offered do not exceed 8 percent of their modified adjusted gross income.[57] According to Buettgens and Hall, this population will consist mostly of higher income families with dependents. Most important for the present analysis, the average age is forty-three and the average income is over $66,000

---

51   *Id.* at 11 tbl.5.
52   *Id.* at 10 tbl.4 (taking 16.2 percent of 18,558,500).
53   *Id.* at 11 tbl.5.
54   *Id.* at 10 tbl.4 (taking 7.5 percent of 18,558,500).
55   *Id.* at 11 tbl.5.
56   *Id.* at 10 tbl.4 (taking 15.3 percent of 18,558,500).
57   *Id.*

annually.[58] Individuals in this group might remain uninsured for several reasons, and in a pinch, would be most likely to seek care overseas. They seem to be both price sensitive and possess the requisite resources to pay out-of-pocket for foreign travel and medical care. Moreover, 80 percent live in metropolitan statistical areas (MSAs),[59] which are more likely to have international airports than rural areas and thus be more convenient departure points.

Finally, a subgroup of the residually uninsured that deserves separate discussion is undocumented immigrants. Congress made clear that the Affordable Care Act did not cover immigrants who are not lawfully present.[60] For example, undocumented immigrants may not enroll in special state plans for low-income individuals not eligible for Medicaid.[61] They are not eligible to enroll in the plans offered by health care cooperatives.[62] They are not eligible for cost-sharing subsidies or premium tax credits to purchase private health insurance.[63] And even without federal subsidies or tax credits, they still may not purchase policies in the newly created exchanges.[64]

In contrast, immigrants who are "lawfully present" according to federal immigration statutes and regulations enjoy access to most (but not all) programmatic expansions under the Affordable Care Act.[65] Lawfully present immigrants must maintain coverage under the individual mandate.[66] They may purchase plans in the new state exchanges.[67] And they can use federally funded premium tax credits and cost-sharing subsidies to buy coverage.[68] The main distinction between lawfully present immigrants and U.S. citizens and nationals who are fully eligible is that lawfully present immigrants may have to wait years to become eligible for Medicaid. The Affordable Care Act did not liberalize the immigrant eligibility rules for Medicaid and related programs.[69] As a result, the Act requires lawfully present immigrants to maintain insurance coverage under the mandate, even though they may not be eligible for Medicaid for five or ten years, due in part to the vagaries of immigration law.[70] Thus, lawfully present immigrants

---

[58] *Id.* at 11 tbl.5.

[59] *Id.*

[60] Cortez, *supra* note 1, at 870–71.

[61] Affordable Care Act § 1331(e)(1)(B).

[62] Affordable Care Act § 1322.

[63] *See, e.g.*, Affordable Care Act § 1401 (limiting tax credits to those lawfully present); § 1402(e) (stating that no cost-sharing reductions shall apply to individuals not lawfully present); § 1412(d) (stating that "Nothing in this subtitle or the amendments made by this subtitle allows Federal payments, credits, or cost-sharing reductions for individuals who are not lawfully present in the United States.").

[64] Affordable Care Act § 1312(f)(3). Note that those not lawfully present are generally exempt from the individual mandate, *id.* at § 1501, although other immigrants are not. RUTH ELLEN WASEM, CONG. RESEARCH SERV., R40889, NONCITIZEN ELIGIBILITY AND VERIFICATION ISSUES IN THE HEALTH CARE REFORM LEGISLATION 3 TBL.1 (2010).

[65] Cortez, *supra* note 1, at 871.

[66] Affordable Care Act § 1501(b).

[67] Affordable Care Act §§ 1312(f)(3), 1411.

[68] Affordable Care Act §§ 1401, 1402(e)(2).

[69] Cortez, *supra* note 1, at 871.

[70] *Id.* at 871–72 (note that the Act tries to compensate for this gap in various ways, although these compensatory measures may not fully plug the hole for authorized immigrants).

might consider foreign providers in a pinch, although again, they are likely to have incomes too low to make this a reality, with the possible exception of border residents and regular visitors to Mexico.

Although immigrants probably represent the single largest demographic that will utilize foreign providers, immigrants in the United States access care in complex ways. Many immigrants in the United States are not offered private insurance because they work only part-time or in positions or sectors that historically do not cover employees.[71] Many immigrants may be reluctant to buy insurance because they are concerned about their immigration status. And some cannot buy insurance because it is simply too expensive.[72] It is increasingly common for immigrants living in the United States to be both undocumented and uninsured,[73] which seem to go hand in hand. As a result, immigrants typically demand safety net care more than others.[74] Immigrants also tend to reside in regions where health care providers and facilities are sparse and where providers in Mexico may be more accessible.[75]

For all these reasons, immigrants living in the United States increasingly rely on foreign providers, particularly those in Mexico, Costa Rica, and other Latin American countries.[76] Stephen Wallace, Carolyn Mendez-Luck, and Xóchitl Castañeda of UCLA estimate that 952,000 California residents—half of whom are Mexican immigrants—travel to Mexico for medical care, dental care, or prescription drugs each year.[77] Indeed, U.S. residents have long traveled to Mexico for these services, for a number of obvious reasons, such as price, geographic accessibility, language, and cultural comforts.[78]

Thus, there are very distinct populations in post-reform America that might consider using low-cost foreign providers. Yet, a lingering question is whether populations that are eligible for public or private insurance in the United States will "free ride" until they need care—that is, not purchase health insurance until they need it. The Affordable Care Act prohibits insurers from rejecting customers with preexisting medical conditions, requiring "guaranteed issue." Thus, instead of taking the dramatic step of traveling outside the United States for care, might these patients simply purchase insurance when an acute need for it arises? If insurers must take all comers, will not some rational patients wait until they need insurance to purchase it, knowing they cannot be denied?

---

[71] David C. Warner & Pablo G. Schneider, *Cross-Border Health Insurance: Options for Texas*, Policy Research Project on Cross-Border Health Insurance, Lyndon B. Johnson School of Public Affairs, University of Texas 7 (2004) (unpublished manuscript) (on file with author).

[72] *Id.* at 7.

[73] Marion E. Lewin & Raymond J. Baxter, *America's Health Care Safety Net: Revisiting the 2000 IOM Report*, 26 HEALTH AFF. 1490, 1491 (2007).

[74] INSTITUTE OF MEDICINE, AMERICA'S HEALTH CARE SAFETY NET: INTACT BUT ENDANGERED 49–51 (Marion Ein Lewin & Stuart Altman eds. 2000).

[75] *See generally* Warner & Schneider, *supra* note 71.

[76] Ian Youngman, *Where Do American Medical Tourists Go Abroad for Treatment?*, INT'L MED. TRAVEL J. (2009), http://www.imtjonline.com/articles/2009/where-do-americans-go-abroad/.

[77] Stephen P. Wallace, Carolyn A. Mendez-Luck, & Xóchitl Castañeda, *Heading South: Why Mexican Immigrants in California Seek Health Services in Mexico*, 47 MED. CARE 662 (2009).

[78] Cortez, *supra* note 1, at 881.

The main disincentive for doing precisely this is the individual mandate, which imposes a tax penalty on those who can purchase affordable coverage but choose not to. Although the tax penalties begin at quite modest amounts (just $95 in 2014), they rise quickly to $350 in 2015, and $695 in 2016.[79] Are these tax penalties sufficiently large to deter free riders? Buettgens and Hall estimate that 4.2 million will remain uninsured despite having an affordable option, and despite earning more than $36,000 per year.[80] Will free riding and contemplating the tax penalty become a new intermediate step before exploring overseas providers? It very well could. Nevertheless, those not covered by and not designed to benefit from the Affordable Care Act may continue to use foreign providers as a safety net.

II. Cross-Border Care Within the Affordable Care Act?

The most important U.S. health legislation in the last fifty years does not address or even contemplate medical tourism, foreign medical providers, cross-border insurance, or related emerging international phenomena. Only once has Congress addressed medical tourism directly, in a 2006 hearing held by the Senate Special Committee on Aging.[81] Yet the title of that hearing posed the operative question: "can medical tourism reduce health care costs?"[82]

Undoubtedly, it can for some. Those with desperate financial and medical need have found foreign providers to be a lifeline—a foreign safety net. But more recently, employers and insurers of all sizes have been enticed by the measurable cost-savings. Will health reform obviate the need for low-cost foreign providers? If not, what permutations will survive, and what niche will they fill?

The answer depends on how providers, insurers, and patients react to health reform. Congress designed the Affordable Care Act to alter incentives. Employers will have new financial incentives (and perhaps disincentives) to offer insurance to their employees. Insurers will have new incentives to compete for customers. Providers will have new incentives to offer quality care. States will have new incentives to experiment with programs that cover the previously uninsured. And individuals will have new incentives under the mandate to maintain minimum essential insurance coverage. Will these interlocking incentives reduce demand for low-cost foreign care? Or will cross-border plans find a place within the newly reformed landscape?

A. CROSS-BORDER HEALTH PLANS

Before exploring how cross-border health plans might fit within the Affordable Care Act, it is worth describing the various incarnations and how they operate. Employers and insurers of all sizes have experimented with outsourcing certain treatments. Some

---

79 Affordable Care Act § 1501 (amending Internal Revenue Code § 5000A(c)).
80 Buettgens & Hall, *supra* note 5, at 11 tbl.5.
81 The Globalization of Health Care: Can Medical Tourism Reduce Health Care Costs?: Hearing Before the Senate Special Committee on Aging, 109th Cong. (2006) [hereinafter "Senate Hearing"].
82 *Id.*

have added foreign facilities to their provider networks while others have created genuine cross-border plans that offer a range of services in multiple countries, with varying financial incentives to use them.[83]

For example, the four largest private health insurers in the United States have either created or are considering medical tourism programs.[84] Pilot programs have come and gone. Smaller employers and insurers generally have been more adventurous, perhaps because they feel cost pressures more intensely.[85] A well-known example is BlueCross BlueShield of South Carolina, which contracted to outsource certain surgeries to a hospital in Thailand.[86] Another prominent example is BasicPlus Health Insurance, which has contracted with around two hundred U.S. employers to offer a network of foreign providers through a medical tourism company.[87] United Group Programs was reported to have agreed to outsource surgeries for dozens of U.S. companies.[88] Blue Ridge Paper Products in North Carolina agreed to send its employees to India for surgery.[89] More recently, Hannaford Brothers, a New England grocery store chain, contracted with Aetna to outsource knee and hip surgeries to Singapore, though no employees have exercised this option yet.[90] Each of these examples generated its own cycle of media scrutiny and wonderment.

More quietly, other insurers have constructed genuine cross-border plans that cover a more balanced mix of domestic and foreign providers. The best examples are managed care plans offered in California by Health Net, Blue Shield, and SIMNSA, all of which encourage California residents to seek certain medical care in Mexico.[91] These plans are documented to cost 40 to 50 percent less than traditional plans that cover only providers in the United States.[92] Geographically, they are centered in border-accessible metropolitan areas such as San Diego and Los Angeles.

Finally, and perhaps more significantly long-term, many health insurers now offer "consumer-directed health plans" that ask patients to pay higher premiums and deductibles (and bear more cost-sharing obligations in general), on the rationale that patients

---

[83] Cortez, *supra* note 1, at 882.

[84] Murphy, *supra* note 28.

[85] Cortez, *supra* note 1, at 882.

[86] BlueCross BlueShield and BlueChoice HealthPlan Pioneer Global Healthcare Alternative (Feb. 8, 2007), http://www.bluechoicesc.com/news.aspx?article_id=21; Bruce Einhorn, *Medical Travel Is Going to Be Part of the Solution*, Bus. Week, Mar. 17, 2008, http://www.businessweek.com/globalbiz/content/mar2008/gb20080312_835774.htm.

[87] Press Release, Companion Global Healthcare, Inc., Insurance Company Includes Global Network Option in Limited Benefit Plans (June 4, 2008), *available at* http://www.companionglobalhealthcare.com/news.aspx?article=36.

[88] Joe Cochrane, *Why Patients Are Flocking Overseas for Operations*, Newsweek Int'l, Oct. 30, 2006, at 1.

[89] Senate Hearing, *supra* note 81 (Statement of Bonnie Blackley). Blue Ridge canceled its program after pressure from protests by the United Steelworkers Union. Saritha Rai, *Union Disrupts Plan to Send Ailing Workers to India for Cheaper Medical Care*, N.Y. Times, Oct. 11, 2006, at C6.

[90] Ian Youngman, *What Happened to Those 2008 Medical Tourism Forecasts?*, Int'l Med. Travel J. (2009), http://www.imtjonline.com/articles/2009/what-happened-to-those-2008-medical-tourism-forecasts-30002/.

[91] Cortez, *supra* note 1, at 883. David Warner and Pablo Schneider have published a comprehensive analysis of these plans. Warner & Schneider, *supra* note 71.

[92] Ly Tran, Note, *Sick and Tired of the Knox-Keene Act: The Equal Protection Right of Non-Mexican Californians to Enroll in Mexico-Based HMO Plans*, 14 Sw. J.L. & Trade Am. 357, 358 (2008); Sonya Geis, *California HMOs Send Some Enrollees to Mexico*, Wash. Post, Nov. 8, 2005, at A03.

will utilize care more judiciously when they have more "skin in the game."[93] These plans often require patients to spend more than $5,000–$10,000 out-of-pocket. As more patients use these plans, more may explore whether foreign providers can help them save money.[94] Dental insurance essentially forecasted this possibility—U.S. patients frequently travel for dental care in part because dental plans are generally structured as consumer-directed plans, requiring patients to bear higher cost-sharing burdens.[95] Indeed, foreign providers have emerged as an alternative for "dental care and cosmetic surgery because few have health insurance that covers those services."[96]

In summary, there are a range of insurance designs that utilize foreign providers, some of which cater to very different demographic populations. Will these plans survive after the Affordable Care Act is fully implemented? The answer partly depends on two subsidiary questions—whether cross-border plans can satisfy the individual mandate, and whether insurers can offer cross-border plans in the new state exchanges.

B. COULD CROSS-BORDER PLANS SATISFY THE INDIVIDUAL MANDATE?

Beginning in 2014, section 1501 of the Affordable Care Act requires the bulk of U.S. residents to maintain "minimum essential coverage."[97] Like other provisions in the Act, this individual mandate tries to alter incentives. Section 1501 creates new incentives (tax penalties) for covered persons to maintain minimum health insurance coverage. Although the penalties begin quite modestly (just $95 in 2014), they rise quickly to $350 in 2015, and $695 in 2016.[98] Could patients avoid these penalties and comply with the mandate by purchasing one of the cross-border plans describe above?

According to the bare language of the statute, yes. The Act defines "minimum essential coverage" vaguely by referring to the types of insurance plans that qualify, rather than by referring, for example, to a set of benefits that "minimum" coverage entails (the Act defines "essential health benefits" elsewhere and for other purposes).[99] Thus, by definition, government insurance offered via Medicare, Medicaid, CHIP, TRICARE, and the Veteran's Administration provide minimum essential coverage.[100] Also, employer-sponsored plans, plans in the individual exchanges, and grandfathered plans qualify as minimum essential coverage. Thus, the cross-border plans outlined above would generally qualify as "minimum essential coverage" under the language of the Act—although again, the voluminous regulations expected by implementing agencies such as HHS may promulgate requirements that complicate this conclusion.

---

[93] TIMOTHY STOLTZFUS JOST, HEALTH CARE AT RISK: A CRITIQUE OF THE CONSUMER-DRIVEN MOVEMENT 133–38 (2007).

[94] Murphy, *supra* note 28; Deloitte, *supra* note 27, at 4–5.

[95] Cortez, *supra* note 1, at 880; Murphy, *supra* note 28.

[96] Cortez, *supra* note 1, at 880 (citing Cohen, *supra* note 14, at 1480 n.45).

[97] Affordable Care Act § 1501(b).

[98] Affordable Care Act § 1501.

[99] Affordable Care Act § 1501(b).

[100] Affordable Care Act § 1501(b).

C. COULD CROSS-BORDER PLANS QUALIFY FOR THE EXCHANGES?

The Affordable Care Act requires states to establish American Health Benefits Exchanges, with the goal of creating a relatively well-defined alternative market for purchasing individual and small group insurance plans in each state.[101] Congress designed these exchanges to offer competitive plans to individuals and small business employees that are not offered or cannot afford insurance through their employers.[102] Traditionally, both the individual and small group markets have been criticized for being unaffordable and not particularly generous with benefits compared to the larger group markets.[103] The state exchanges are designed to address both these deficiencies, with the idea of liberating and stimulating the individual and small group markets.[104]

In general, plans offered in the exchanges must be "qualified health plans" that offer "essential health benefits."[105] Could a cross-border health plan be certified as a "qualified" plan? Could plans that use foreign medical providers offer "essential health benefits" as defined in the Act?

Before the Affordable Care Act, states largely determined what types of medical treatments insurance policies must cover, and under what conditions.[106] Taking advantage of this traditional authority to regulate health insurance, states have imposed thousands of mandated benefits.[107] But the Act now requires that plans offered in the state exchanges meet criteria for "qualified health plans" and offer a package of "essential health benefits"—which sets a different, federal baseline.[108] Although states may require plans offered in their exchanges to offer additional benefits, states must assume the cost of such additional requirements.[109]

Cross-border plans sold in the exchanges would have to offer "essential health benefits," which the Act defines as including several general categories of services, including ambulatory patient care, emergency care, hospitalization, maternity and newborn care, mental health care, substance abuse care, prescription drugs, rehabilitative services, laboratory services, preventative care, chronic disease management, and pediatric care.[110] It delegates responsibility to HHS to define further what "essential health benefits" entail, although it expects the scope of benefits to coincide roughly with those provided by most employer plans.[111] Again, nothing here expressly precludes or even contemplates cross-border plans.

---

[101] Affordable Care Act § 1311(b).

[102] Affordable Care Act § 1311(b).

[103] Roland McDevitt et al., *Group Insurance: A Better Deal for Most People than Individual Plans*, 29 HEALTH AFF. 156 (2010).

[104] Cortez, *supra* note 1, at 868.

[105] Affordable Care Act §§ 1301, 1302.

[106] Amy B. Monahan, *Initial Thoughts on Essential Health Benefits*, in N.Y.U. REV. EMPLOYEE BENEFITS & EXECUTIVE COMPENSATION, 2010, at ch. 1B, http://ssrn.com/abstract=1646723.

[107] Cohen, *supra* note 14, at 1544.

[108] Affordable Care Act §§ 1301, 1302.

[109] Affordable Care Act § 1311(d)(3).

[110] Affordable Care Act § 1302(b)(1).

[111] Affordable Care Act § 1302(b)(2).

However, each state exchange may choose whether to certify plans based on the state's determination that a plan "is in the interests of qualified individuals and qualified employers."[112] Thus, one could imagine states prohibiting cross-border plans from being sold in their exchanges based on negative media coverage or lobbying from local providers, which might be used to justify a finding that the plans are not in the "interests" of those who might want to buy such plans.

Notably, the Act exempts self-insured plans and "multiple employer welfare arrangements" used by many large employers from the requirement that they offer essential health benefits.[113] Thus, for example, one version of a multiple employer welfare arrangement is the cross-border plans offered by the Western Growers Association to seasonal migrant workers, which by virtue of the plans' design under ERISA would not be required to provide "essential health benefits," as defined in the Act. Moreover, plans sold outside the individual and small market exchanges are exempt from requirements governing exchange plans, but are still subject to state benefit requirements.[114]

Still, if insurers intend to offer cross-border plans in the state exchanges, they may have to wait for more concrete guidance from HHS. The following is a list of potential statutory (as opposed to regulatory) barriers for some of the cross-border plans described above.[115]

First, HHS must define through regulation what additional requirements to impose on plans as a condition of certifying them for the exchanges.[116] For example, would cross-border plans that heavily incentivized beneficiaries to seek certain care overseas "have the effect of discouraging the enrollment in such plan[s] by individuals with significant health needs"?[117] Would a cross-border plan be able to offer a "sufficient choice of providers" if it contracts with only one foreign hospital for certain expensive procedures?[118] Would cross-border plans targeted at low-income populations that are not eligible for Medicaid be able to include "essential community providers . . . that serve predominately low-income, medically-underserved individuals"?[119] Would cross-border plans have trouble gaining accreditation for clinical quality, consumer access, provider credentialing, and network adequacy and access?[120] Provider credentialing might be a problem for foreign providers, and network adequacy and access might be viewed with skepticism in a cross-border network.

These various requirements from the Affordable Care Act raise questions whether cross-border plans could operate in the exchanges. And these are only the bare bones

---

[112] Affordable Care Act § 1311(e)(1)(B).
[113] Affordable Care Act § 1301(b)(1)(B). MEWAs are a type of self-funded ERISA plan offered by groups of employers in a bona fide trade, industrial, or professional organization. 21 U.S.C. § 1002(40)(A).
[114] Affordable Care Act § 1312(d)(2). For an analysis of other, non-ACA sources of federal and state law that might serve as barriers to cross-border insurance plans, see Cohen, *supra* note 14, at 1557–59.
[115] *See* the description of cross-border plan designs in Section II.A *supra*.
[116] Affordable Care Act § 1311(c).
[117] Affordable Care Act § 1311(c)(1)(A).
[118] Affordable Care Act § 1311(c)(1)(B); Public Health Service Act § 2702(c).
[119] Affordable Care Act § 1311(c)(1)(C).
[120] Affordable Care Act § 1311(c)(1)(D).

requirements within the Act. Department regulations may impose more specific requirements that explicitly—or more likely, by implication—disqualify cross-border plans from the state exchanges.

A second potential barrier for cross-border plans is that the Affordable Care Act requires that exchange plans contract with hospitals and providers that meet patient safety and quality standards prescribed by HHS. For example, the Act allows qualified health plans to contract with hospitals with more than fifty beds only if the hospital uses patient safety evaluation systems under the Public Health Service Act and follows other discharge rules.[121] Providers contracting with qualified health plans in the exchanges must also implement quality improvement requirements issued by HHS.[122] Thus, cross-border exchange plans that integrated foreign hospitals and providers into their networks would have to ensure that the foreign facilities and practitioners could satisfy these potentially large and evolving quality requirements—something that might be difficult to do, and something that might dissuade foreign providers from participating. Again, provisions like this were not written with the idea of excluding foreign providers but might have the practical effect of doing so.

Yet, given these potential obstacles, there are at least as many provisions in the Affordable Care Act that might encourage cross-border plans in the exchanges. For example, exchange plans will be subject to a rating system that measures their relative quality and price,[123] and cross-border plans might score particularly well in contrast to plans that cover only domestic care. One could imagine the news headlines reporting that cross-border plans rated well above domestic-only plans in the exchanges.

A potential avenue for states to experiment with cross-border plans is by creating a so-called "subsidiary exchange" for border regions under section 1311(f)(2) of the Act. That section allows states to establish subsidiary exchanges for a "geographically distinct area," though it must be as large as a rating area under the Public Health Service Act.[124] Border states such as California and Texas might consider creating special subsidiary exchanges for their border regions and allowing cross-border plans to be sold only in these subsidiary exchanges. Health care needs can diverge significantly from region to region, and cross-border plans might make sense in border regions such as like McAllen, Texas, and at the same time not be particularly feasible in places such as Salt Lake City, Utah.

Another potential opening for cross-border plans is that the Act encourages state exchanges to reward quality care through market-based incentives.[125] Thus, states can reimburse exchange plans for improving patient outcomes, coordinating care, and managing chronic diseases well.[126] The Health Care and Education Reconciliation Act added to the Affordable Care Act a provision allowing market-based incentives for

---

[121] Affordable Care Act § 1311(h)(1)(A) (citing Public Health Service Act IX(C)).
[122] Affordable Care Act § 1311(h)(1)(B).
[123] Affordable Care Act § 1311(c)(3).
[124] Affordable Care Act § 1311(f)(2) (citing section 2701(a) of the Public Health Service Act).
[125] Affordable Care Act § 1311(g).
[126] Affordable Care Act § 1311(g)(1)(A).

programs that "reduce health and health care disparities."[127] Cross-border plans targeted to border populations and particularly Spanish-speaking individuals that might prefer providers in Mexico, for example, might qualify for such a program.

Finally, the Affordable Care Act also encourages states to design alternatives to the exchanges. For example, the Act allows states to craft programs for low-income individuals who earn too much to qualify for Medicaid.[128] These programs must consider differences in local access to care,[129] which might justify cross-border plans in border regions. To participate in such a program, the household must earn between 133 percent and 200 percent of the federal poverty line, and any immigrant participants must be lawfully present.[130] Beginning in 2017, states can also apply to HHS to waive the requirements governing exchanges, qualified health plans, and essential health benefits if the state can craft an alternative system that provides coverage and protection for state residents comparable to that provided by the Act.[131] Again, it is not hard to imagine cross-border plans as an option here.

The Act often casts these various programs as encouraging state "flexibility" and "innovation."[132] In that spirit, state programs encouraging cross-border plans for certain hard-to-insure populations would not lack for either.

Conclusion

The cross-border health care market emerged in response to hydraulic pressures on U.S. patients. The world's most expensive health care system has pushed patients out, while foreign providers eager to attract foreign clientele have pulled patients in.

The Affordable Care Act exerts its own hydraulic pressures, in the hopes of covering more patients domestically. Nevertheless, several populations may still use foreign providers after we implement the Act. Those left out of reform will continue to rely on foreign providers, although in all likelihood in smaller numbers than before health reform. But even those insured under the Act may be asked to consider insurance plans designed to take advantage of the striking cost savings foreign providers can offer. Such plans would probably satisfy the new requirement to maintain "minimum essential coverage," and would thus appeal to cost-sensitive employers and employees. Moreover, cross-border plans might seep into the new state exchanges, particularly through pilot programs in border states that make use of provisions encouraging states to innovate and maintain flexibility in covering their diverse populations.

The hydraulics continue.

---

[127] Affordable Care Act § 1311(g)(1)(E) (added by the Health Care and Education Reconciliation Act § 10104(g)).

[128] Affordable Care Act § 1331.

[129] Affordable Care Act § 1331(c)(2)(B).

[130] Affordable Care Act § 1331(e)(1)(B) (as amended by the Health Care and Education Reconciliation Act § 10104(o)(2)).

[131] Affordable Care Act § 1332.

[132] *See generally* Affordable Care Act §§ 1331, 1332.

5

CURRENT LEGISLATION ON CROSS-BORDER HEALTH CARE IN

THE EUROPEAN UNION

*Hilko J. Meyer**

Introduction

Compared to other countries of the world, and even to other Western industrialized countries, the majority of citizens in the European Union enjoy excellent, or at least relatively good, coverage of health care and health care costs. However, a closer look reveals a much more differentiated picture. Growing demand of an aging population for health care services and products, growing supply of innovative technology and pharmaceuticals, and increasing health awareness of patients lead to rising expenses for public health care while at the same time rising unemployment rates and increasing state debts reduce the ability of governments to strengthen or even stabilize the financial resources of national health care systems. The answer of European Union Member States is continuous health care reforms focused on cost-containment. The measures include a reduced scope of coverage of public health care, increased insurance rates and/or co-payments—and in some cases rationed care.

These developments should prompt European patients to seek medical care in another country. Additionally, it should lead some governments to consider concentrating on providing health care only for the most common diseases while sending patients abroad for specialized treatment as a means of cost containment. Therefore, it is all the more remarkable that according to EU sources only 1 to 4 percent of public health care budgets are spent on cross-border health care. Most of that sum is spent in border regions where common health care planning between Member States takes place. These numbers are somewhat hard to interpret in that there might also be a

---

* Professor of Law, Frankfurt University of Applied Sciences, Frankfurt am Main.

portion of medical tourism in the European Union that is paid for privately and there-fore does not appear in the statistics.

The main reason for the relatively low level of health tourism is the fragmenta-tion of the EU health care market into twenty-seven different national health care systems. Public health care in Europe is extremely different from country to country concerning finance, scope, access, and price. The systems can be broadly divided into tax-financed national health services (Beveridge system) and insurance contribution–based social security systems (Bismarck system). Today most national systems have elements of both historic models.[1] This convergence process is, however, not the result of a stringent approach of the European Union but of a search process reflecting the common principles of Member States as well as their frequently changing health care priorities.

The rights, freedoms, and principles set out in the Charter of Fundamental Rights of the European Union,[2] which was given the same legal value as the European Union Treaties by the Treaty of Lisbon,[3] include the following fundamental rights: "Everyone has the right of access to preventive health care and the right to benefit from medical treatment under the conditions established by national laws and practices. A high level of human health protection shall be ensured in the definition and implementation of all Union policies and activities."[4]

The central competencies of the European Union in the area of health care are lim-ited to special aspects of common safety concerns in public health matters[5] and to the coordination and support of the actions of the Member States.[6] Thus, Member States remain the main actors in this field:

> Union action shall respect the responsibilities of the Member States for the defi-nition of their health policy and for the organisation and delivery of health ser-vices and medical care. The responsibilities of the Member States shall include the management of health services and medical care and the allocation of the resources assigned to them.[7]

However, the principles of free movement of persons, products, services and capital as laid down as fundamental market freedoms in the founding Treaties of the European Union require free cross-border access to medical treatment for all patients living inside the European Union as well as free cross-border trade of health care products

---

[1] Jouke van der Zee & Madelon W. Krone, *Bismarck or Beveridge: A Beauty Contest between Dinosaurs*, 7 BMC HEALTH SERVICE RES. 94 (2007).
[2] Charter of Fundamental Rights of the European Union, 2000 O.J. (C364) 1 [hereinafter CFR].
[3] Consolidated Version of the Treaty on European Union, art. 6(1), 2008 O.J. (C115) 13 [hereinafter TEU].
[4] CFR art. 35.
[5] Consolidated Version of the Treaty on the Functioning of the European Union, art. 4(2)(k), 2008 O.J. (C 115) 47 [hereinafter TFEU].
[6] TFEU art. 6(a).
[7] TFEU art. 168(7).

and services between Member States. Thus, the European Union has a long history of central legislation on cross-border health care. The resulting conflicts between these principles of European law—national responsibility for organizing and funding health care and social security versus European internal market freedoms and secondary legislation—have led to numerous judgments of the European Court of Justice (ECJ), which have continually improved the rights of patients but have left several questions unanswered.

The first attempt of the European Commission to impose a codification of this case law as part of the "European Services Directive" failed in 2005, causing a severe crisis for the European integration process.[8] In December 2010 the main legislative bodies of the European Union, the Council, and the European Parliament agreed on a new proposal that is less ambitious but eliminates a number of obstacles for patients who seek treatment in an EU Member State other than their home country.[9] The Directive, which was finally adopted in February 2011 and published in April 2011, also clarifies patients' right to be reimbursed by the health care system of their home country after treatment in another Member State.[10] The Directive now must be implemented into national legislation by all twenty-seven Member States of the European Union within thirty months.

The rest of this chapter seeks to further elucidate the European experience with the globalization of health care and its attendant legal and ethical challenges. The next section briefly sets out the European Union's history in regulating medical tourism. The next four sections discuss the legislation on coordination of social security systems aimed at securing freedom of movement of migrant workers, the case law of the European Court of Justice on the freedom of provision of services in the healthcare sector, the codification of case law through the services Directive, and the new Directive on the application of patients' rights in cross-border healthcare

I. The Legislation on the Coordination of Social Security Systems

On January 1, 1959, only one year after the enforcement of the Treaty of Rome founding the European Economic Community, the Council Regulation Number Three concerning social security for migrant workers came into force.[11] This involved Council members merely transferring a signed but not ratified European Convention[12] between the six

---

[8] *See infra* Section IV.

[9] *See infra* Section V.

[10] Directive 2011/24/EU of the European Parliament and of the Council of March 9, 2011 on the Application of Patients' Rights in Cross-Border Healthcare, 2011 O.J. (L 88) 45 [hereinafter Patients' Rights Directive].

[11] Regulation (EEC) 3/1958 of September 25, 1958 Concerning Social Security for Migrant Workers, 1958 O.J. (30) 561 [hereinafter Regulation Number 3].

[12] The Convention was prepared under the Treaty Establishing the European Coal and Steel Community, Apr. 18, 1951, 261 U.N.T.S. 140, and intended to replace the bilateral agreements on migrant workers; *see* Rob Cornelissen, *50 Years of European Social Security Coordination*, 11 EUR. J. SOC. SEC. 9 (2009).

Member States (Belgium, France, Germany, Italy, Luxembourg, and the Netherlands) into European legislation. But this was more than a formal change of the legal basis. Establishing legislation under the EEC Treaty meant that traditional intergovernmental agreements were replaced by a statutory legislation procedure producing legally binding law controlled by an independent European court. Doing so not as a federal state but as a confederation of states was something very new at that point of time and laid the fundamentals of what can be described as the European version of "integration through law."[13] It would go far beyond the scope of this chapter to describe the consequences of this approach, but it is obvious that conflicts on competencies between individual Member States and the "supranational" community were an important element of European integration during the last fifty years.

Council Regulation Number Three was an early example of the so-called secondary European law, which consists of legal instruments based on the European Treaties (primary law) and includes regulations, directives, and decisions. According to Article 288 of the Treaty on the Functioning of the European Union (TFEU), a *regulation* shall have general application and shall be binding in its entirety and directly applicable in all Member States whereas a *directive* shall be also binding, as to the result to be achieved, upon each Member State to which it is addressed, but shall leave to the national authorities the choice of form and methods. According to Article 48 of the TFEU the European Parliament and the Council shall, acting in accordance with the ordinary legislative procedure,[14] adopt such measures in the field of social security as are necessary to provide freedom of movement for workers. To this end, they shall make arrangements to secure for employed and self-employed migrant workers and their dependents "aggregation, for the purpose of acquiring and retaining the right to benefit and of calculating the amount of benefit, of all periods taken into account under the laws of the several countries" and "payment of benefits to persons resident in the territories of Member States."[15]

It is crucial to understand that this provision does not transfer any direct competence concerning the structure of and/or the scope and amount of benefits provided by the social security system from the Member States to the European Union. Also under the Treaty of Lisbon the responsibility for the social security system, including the health care system, remains with the individual member country. Most Member States, referring to the "principle of territoriality" as part of their sovereign powers, have implemented territorial elements in defining the scope of their social security schemes, in determining the qualifying conditions, and in determining conditions for the calculation and payment of benefits.[16] The main provision in the field of health care is the exclusion of benefits during the time the person is abroad. In addition, benefit

---

[13] INTEGRATION THROUGH LAW: EUROPE AND THE AMERICAN FEDERAL EXPERIENCE (Mauro Cappelletti, Monica Seccombe & Joseph H. Weiler, eds. 1985).

[14] TFEU art. 294 provides that in the ordinary legislative procedure, acts are adopted on proposal of the Commission by the European Parliament and the Council of Ministers, the latter acting by a qualified majority. In 1958, regulations were adopted by the Council alone, acting unanimously.

[15] TFEU art. 48(1)(a) and (b).

[16] Rob Cornelissen, *The Principle of Territoriality and the Community Regulations on Social Security (Regulations 1408/71 and 574/72)*, 33 COMMON MARKET L. REV. (1996) 439, 469.

entitlement conditions differ in the extent to which the individual country builds into its benefits the need to have fulfilled contribution conditions and/or requirements about nationality, length of residence in the country, or the condition that a person should be present when claiming a benefit.[17] On the other hand, from the very beginning of the European integration it was obvious that the significant differences among the social security systems of the individual Member States would be serious obstacles to the free movement of workers (Article 45 of the TFEU), which is one of the basic "market freedoms" laid down in the Treaties from the beginning and considered to be part of the "foundations" of the Community.

The solution for this conflict provided by Article 48 of the TFEU is that measures on social security taken by the European Union may not be aimed at *harmonizing* the social security systems of Member States but at securing and promoting the freedom of movement of migrant workers by *coordinating* the relevant social security provisions of the individual states. The regulations adopted on this legal basis do not form a separate part of social security law but try to "rectify" the discriminatory effects of the principle of territoriality on migrant workers and the members of their families.[18]

This "coordinating social security law" consists of several regulations[19] that have been amended many times during the last fifty years, mostly in order to follow, and in some cases to counter, the rulings of the European Court of justice (ECJ).[20] The original basic principles of aggregation of periods, equal treatment, and export of benefits on applicable legislation and administrative cooperation remain unchanged, but the technical details, the procedures, and especially the scope of application of the rules have evolved significantly. Regulation 883/04 extended the personal scope of the coordination rules to all persons who are, or have been, subject to legislation of a Member State that is within the scope of the Regulation and the members of his/her family. In terms of sickness benefits, not only migrant workers but also tourists and students who fulfill these preconditions are covered by the provisions of the Regulation.

When it comes to *unplanned* cross-border health care the Regulation provides in Article 19 that a person insured in one Member State ("competent Member State") and staying in another Member State ("Member State of stay") shall be entitled to the benefits in kind that become necessary on medical grounds during the person's stay, taking into account the nature of the benefits and the expected length of the stay. "Benefits in kind" means benefits in kind provided for under the legislation of a

---

[17] Simon Roberts, *A Short History of Social Security Coordination, in* 50 Years of Social Security Coordination: Past—Present—Future 11 (Yves Jorens ed. 2010).

[18] Cornelissen, *supra* note 12, at 10.

[19] Regulation Number 3, *supra* note 11, was followed by Regulation (EEC) No. 1408/71 of the Council of June 14, 1971 on the Application of Social Security Schemes to Employed Persons and Their Families Moving within the Community, O.J. (L 149) 2 [hereinafter Regulation 1408/71] and finally by Regulation (EC) No. 883/2004 of the European Parliament and of the Council of April 29, 2004 on the Coordination of Social Security Systems, O.J. (L 166) 1 [hereinafter Regulation 883/2004], which came into force on May 1, 2010.

[20] Examples for both types of amendment can be found at Cornelissen, *supra* note 12, at 9.

Member State that are intended to supply, make available, pay directly, or reimburse the cost of medical care and products and services ancillary to that care. This includes long-term care benefits in kind. These benefits shall be provided on behalf of the competent institution by the institution of the place of stay, in accordance with the provisions of the legislation it applies, as though the persons concerned were insured under the said legislation. In order to simplify the procedures, the former application form system has been replaced by the European Health Insurance Card (EHIC). It entitles the holder to the benefits guaranteed by the Regulation (i.e., to the same treatment at the same cost as a national of that country). This follows the rule of equal treatment with nationals laid down in the TFEU.[21]

Concerning *planned* medical tourism, however, the rules are much more restrictive. According to Article 20(1) of the Regulation, persons travelling to another Member State with the purpose of receiving health care benefits in kind during the stay shall seek authorization from the competent institution before they travel abroad. In order to benefit from this provision, the document S2 (ex-form E112), must be obtained from the health insurance institution of the country of residence. The authorization shall only be accorded where the treatment in question is among the benefits provided for by the legislation in the Member State where the person concerned resides and where he/she cannot be given such treatment within a time limit that is medically justifiable, taking into account his/her current state of health and the probable course of his/her illness. This gives the competent institution extensive discretionary power to refuse where the treatment in question is not among the benefits provided for by its legislation.

These restrictive conditions were implemented as a reaction to the case law of the ECJ,[22] which, in the view of some Member States, tended to erode the "principle of territoriality" anchored in their national social security legislation.[23] In the Lisbon Treaty the Member States added another provision to Article 48 of the TFEU pointing in the same direction. Where a member of the Council declares that a draft legislative Act based on Article 48 TFEU would affect important aspects of its social security system, including its scope, cost, or financial structure, or would affect the financial balance of that system, it may request that the matter be referred to the European Council. In that case, the ordinary legislative procedure shall be suspended and replaced by a special procedure, starting with a discussion in the European Council where Member States are represented by their heads of state or government.[24]

Altogether, the European Union Regulations on social security have established a unique coordination system, which puts the right of European citizens to move, work, and reside freely within the Union into practice. However, the Regulations present

---

[21] TFEU art. 18 states that within the scope of application of the EU Treaties, and without prejudice to any special provisions contained therein, any discrimination on grounds of nationality shall be prohibited.

[22] Cornelissen, *supra* note 12, at 10.

[23] Cornelissen, *supra* note 16, at 439.

[24] TEU art. 10.

significant hurdles for those who want to have the choice between health care providers throughout the European Union while being covered by their national health care schemes.

II. The Case Law of the European Court of Justice on the Free Provision of Services in the Health Care Sector

The ECJ has played and continues to play a dominant role in the European integration process. The foundation for this role is constituted by the provisions of the Treaties, which give the Court the exclusive power to interpret the Treaties with binding effect for all public and private persons and bodies throughout the European Union. What gives the Court's decisions an enormous practical relevance is the provision that every court or tribunal of a Member State may, if it considers that a decision on the interpretation of the Treaties or the secondary law is necessary to enable it to give judgment, stop domestic legal proceedings and request the ECJ to give a ruling thereon.[25] Although this is not a formal legal remedy, the practice of national courts guarantees that the ECJ is concerned not only with cases put before it by Member States or the Commission but also with "ordinary" cases covering parties and objects of dispute from all areas of law.

Due to their self-conception of being the "motor of integration,"[26] the European judges made several landmark decisions. In the *Van Gend en Loos* decision of 1963[27] the ECJ took the novel view that a provision of the EEC Treaty can create individual rights if the provision meets specific conditions such as the clarity of the text and the unconditionality of the obligation. This means that private litigants have a right against their government to require it to adhere to international treaties, and thus they have legal standing to demand government compliance.[28] In the *Costa v. ENEL* decision of 1964 the Court ruled that European law has supremacy over national law not because national constitutional law allows it, but by European law's own nature as a supranational legal order.[29] In the *Simmenthal* decision of 1979, the Court declared that the supremacy doctrine also means that every national court, in a case within its jurisdiction, has to apply European law in its entirely, has to protect rights of individuals, and must accordingly set aside any provision of national law that may conflict

---

[25] TFEU art. 267.

[26] *Cf., e.g.*, Joseph H. Weiler, *The Court of Justice on Trial; A Review of Hjalte Rasmussen: On Law and Policy in the European Court of Justice*, 24 COMMON MARKET L. REV. 555 (1987); Donna Starr-Deelen & Bart Deelen, *The European Court of Justice as a Federator*, 26 PUBLIUS: J. FEDERALISM 81 (1996); Henri de Waele, *The Role of the European Court of Justice in the Integration Process: A Contemporary and Normative Assessment*, 6 HANSE L. REV. 3 (2010); Martin Hoepner, *Der Europäische Gerichtshof als Motor der Integration: Eine akteursbezogene Erklärung*, 21 BERLIN J. SOZIOL 203 (2011).

[27] Case 26/62, Van Gend en Loos v. Neth. Inland Revenue Inst., 1963 E.C.R. 1.

[28] KAREN J. ALTER, ESTABLISHING THE SUPREMACY OF EUROPEAN LAW: THE MAKING OF AN INTERNATIONAL RULE OF LAW IN EUROPE 18 (2001).

[29] Case 6/64, Costa v. ENEL, 1964 E.C.R. 585.

with European law.[30] In the decision *Luisi and Carbone* of 1984[31] the ECJ extended the freedom to provide services within the European Union as laid down in article 56 of the TFEU to the freedom to receive services.[32]

Although this case law had developed over a long period of time, most national governments were caught by surprise when the ECJ ruled in the *Kohll*[33] and *Decker*[34] cases in 1998. With these rulings the ECJ established a new track for individuals to demand reimbursement of planned cross-border health care from the social security system of their home country.

In the first case *Kohll*, a Luxembourg national, made a request to the *Union des Caisses de Maladie*, with which he was insured, asking for authorization for his daughter (a minor) to receive treatment from an orthodontist established in Trier (Germany). The request was rejected on the grounds that the proposed treatment was not urgent and that it could be provided in Luxembourg. Mr. Kohll appealed this decision, arguing that the Luxembourgian provisions relied on were contrary to European law. He went through all appeals until the Luxembourg Cour de Cassation considered that the argument raised a question concerning the interpretation of Community law and referred the case to the ECJ for a preliminary ruling.

On April 28, 1998, the ECJ ruled that the fact that national rules fall within the sphere of social security cannot exclude the application of the Treaty rules on free movement of goods and services. The ECJ held that although EU law does not detract from the powers of the Member States to organize their social security systems, they must nevertheless comply with EU law when exercising those powers. The coordination system of Regulation 1408/71 is based on the free movement of workers; therefore it is not intended to regulate, and hence does not in any way prevent the reimbursement by Member States, at the tariffs in force in the competent State, of the cost of medical products purchased in another Member State, even without prior authorization. Therefore, the ECJ concluded that Articles 56 and 57 of the TFEU preclude national rules under which reimbursement is subject to authorization by the insured person's social security institution. The ECJ then pointed out that as such rules deter insured persons from approaching providers of medical services established in another Member State they constitute, for providers and their patients, a barrier to freedom to provide services. Finally the ECJ held that these national rules are not justified by the risk of seriously undermining the financial balance of the social security system, because medical tourism has no significant effect on the financing of the social security system. The Court also rejected the argument that the national rules were justified by different professional standards prevailing in other Member States. Referring to several European directives, coordinating or harmonizing the conditions for taking up

---

[30] Case 70/77, Simmenthal v. State Fin. Admin., 1978 E.C.R. 1453.
[31] Joined Cases 286/82 and 26/83, Luisi and Carbone v. Ministero del Tesoro, 1984 E.C.R. 377.
[32] So-called "passive" freedom to provide services.
[33] Case C-158/96, Kohll v. Union des Caisses de Maladie, 1998 E.C.R. I-01931.
[34] Case C-120/95 Decker v. Caisse de Maladie des Employés Privés, 1998 E.C.R. I-01831.

and pursuing the professions of doctor and dentist, the Court decided that doctors and dentists established in other Member States must be afforded all guarantees equivalent to those accorded to doctors and dentists established on national territory, for the purposes of freedom to provide services.[35]

The news of these rulings landed like a bombshell on the capitals of the Member States. The European Commission and consumerist associations welcomed the new freedom of patient mobility, whereas representatives of governments and social security organizations warned against the erosion of the territoriality principle and the national sovereignty regarding social security. Nevertheless, some weeks later, after an in-depth analysis of the decisions, most governments gave an "all clear" signal stating that their social security system was not affected by these rulings. They argued that in Luxembourg an insurance system with maximum reimbursement rates prevailed, whereas in countries such as Germany and the Netherlands benefits were provided in-kind and on the basis of contracts between sick-funds and health care providers. These countries, and the United Kingdom and Sweden with their state-run National Health Systems, did not even have mechanisms for subsequent refund of treatment expenses. In addition, a number of governments argued that hospital services did not constitute an economic activity within the meaning of Article 57 of the TFEU, particularly when they are provided in-kind and free of charge under the relevant sickness insurance scheme. The German government considered that the structural principles governing the provision of medical care are inherent in the organization of the social security systems and do not come within the sphere of the fundamental economic freedoms guaranteed by the Treaty, because the persons concerned are unable to decide for themselves the content, type, and extent of a service, or the price they will pay.[36] Because this was an integral component of their social security system these governments believed ECJ would have no right to implement a path to reimbursement in those systems.

Nonetheless, the ECJ adopted the opposite position. In a series of decisions, the Court ruled that public funding of hospital medical treatment does not remove such treatment from the sphere of services within the meaning of Article 57 of the TFEU. Even if such treatment is financed directly by the sickness insurance funds on the basis of contractual agreements between them and the providers of health treatment and preset scales of fees, it falls within the scope of the TFEU. The ECJ argued that Article 57 does not require that the service be paid for by those for whom it is performed and that the payments made by the medical insurance funds, albeit set at a flat rate, are indeed the consideration for the hospital services, and unquestionably represent remuneration for the hospital that receives them and that is engaged in an activity of an economic character.[37]

---

[35] *Cf.* Directive 2005/36/EC of the European Parliament and of the Council of September 7, 2005 on the Recognition of Professional Qualifications, 2005 O.J. (L 255) 22.

[36] *Cf.* the statements of governments in the case C-157/99 Geraets-Smits and Peerbooms v. Stichting, 2001 E.C.R. I-05473, 50, 51.

[37] *Garaets-Smits*, 2001 E.C.R. I-05473 at 56–58.

The Court, however, drew a distinction between nonhospital and hospital treatment. In case of nonhospital treatment a prior authorization requirement would not be justifiable,[38] but the same is not true for hospital treatment because of the need to maintain an adequate, balanced, and permanent supply of hospital care on national territory and to ensure the financial stability of the sickness insurance system. However, that applies only in so far as authorization cannot be refused on the ground that it is not "normal" in the patient's home country, that is, where it appears that the treatment concerned is sufficiently tried and tested by international medical science. Furthermore, an authorization may be refused on the ground of lack of medical necessity only if the same or equally effective treatment can be obtained without undue delay at an establishment having a contractual arrangement with the insured person's sickness insurance fund.[39]

In terms of restricting the competencies of Member States in the field of their social security systems, the case law of the ECJ reached a peak when it had to decide the famous case of Yvonne Watts.[40] The case involved an elderly British patient who, after waiting for a hip surgery for several months, asked the National Health Service (NHS) for authorization under Article 22 of Regulation 1408/71[41] to go abroad for medical treatment. Her request was refused several times on the ground that she could receive treatment in a local hospital "within the government's NHS Plan targets" and therefore "without undue delay." Before the application for judicial review of that refusal decision was decided by the Administrative Court, Watts underwent a hip replacement operation in Abbeville (France). She paid the fees for that surgery, equivalent to GBP 3900, and claimed reimbursement from the NHS when she came back. After the Administrative Court dismissed Mrs. Watts's application for treatment abroad and reimbursement, the Court of Appeal (England and Wales) decided to stay the proceedings and to refer several questions to the ECJ. The questions concerned not only the interpretation of the primary and secondary law of social security and the previous decisions of the ECJ, but also focused on the underlying question of European versus national competencies. Question 7 of the Court of Appeal reads as follows:

> Are art 49 EC[42] and art 22 of Regulation No 1408/71[43] to be interpreted as imposing an obligation on Member States to fund hospital treatment in other Member States without reference to budgetary constraints and, if so, are these requirements compatible with the Member States' responsibility for the organisation and delivery of health services and medical care, as recognised under art 152(5) EC?[44]

---

[38] Case C-385/99, Müller-Fauré and van Riet v. Onderlinge, 2003 E.C.R. I-4509, 93, 95.

[39] *Garaets-Smits*, 2001 E.C.R. I-05473 at 108.

[40] Case C-372/04, Watts v. Bedford Primary Care Trust and Sec'y of State for Health, 2006 E.C.R. I-o 4325.

[41] *Supra* note 12. This authorization procedure is named the "E 112 scheme" after the harmonized application form. It has been replaced by the "S1 scheme," Regulation 883/2004, *supra* note 19, art 20.

[42] Now TFEU art. 56.

[43] Now transformed to art. 19-21 of Regulation 883/2004, *supra* note 19.

[44] Now transformed to TFEU art. 168(7).

With this question the British judges confronted the ECJ with an article of the EC Treaty that had not previously been taken into account by the ECJ in its relevant decisions on the freedom to provide services in the health care sector. This very article, Article 152 (5) of the Treaty Establishing the European Community (TEC),[45] was implemented by the Treaty of Amsterdam[46] in 1997 because of rising concerns of Member States over the loss of influence on health care matters; it declares that "Community action in the field of public health shall fully respect the responsibilities of the Member States for the organization and delivery of health services and medical care."

The ECJ, however, was unimpressed by the argument and followed its previous jurisprudence. First, the judges noted that the European legislation is not to be interpreted as imposing on the Member States an obligation to reimburse the cost of hospital treatment in other Member States without reference to any budgetary consideration but, on the contrary, is based on the need to balance the objective of the free movement of patients against overriding national objectives relating to management of the available hospital capacity, control of health expenditure, and financial balance of social security systems. Next, they noted that Article 152 (5) of the TEC does not exclude the possibility that EU Member States may be required under other Treaty provisions, such as Article 49 of the TEC, or Community measures adopted on the basis of other Treaty provisions, such as Article 22 of Regulation 1408/71, to make adjustments to their national systems of social security. In its typical apodictic manner, the ECJ then states: "It does not follow that this undermines their sovereign powers in the field." The ECJ concluded that the obligation of the competent institution to authorize a patient registered with a national health service to obtain, at that institution's expense, hospital treatment in another Member State where the waiting time exceeds an acceptable period having regard to an objective medical assessment of the condition and clinical requirements of the patient concerned does not contravene Article 152 (5) of the TEC.[47]

That said, the ECJ rulings expressly left unaffected the ability of Member States to define the scope of coverage of their health care system, but where the legislation of the competent Member State provides that a specific treatment is provided free of charge, the competent institution is required to establish that the waiting time for that treatment does not exceed the period that is acceptable on the basis of an objective medical assessment of the clinical needs of the person; that determination is to be made in the light of all of the factors characterizing the patient's medical condition at the time when the request for authorization is made or renewed. Under this ruling, a refusal to grant prior authorization for medical treatment in another EU Member State cannot be based merely on the existence of waiting lists intended to enable the

---

[45] Consolidated version of the Treaty Establishing the European Community, 2006 O.J. (C 321E) 37, 114 [hereinafter TEC].

[46] Treaty of Amsterdam Amending the Treaty on European Union, the Treaties Establishing the European Communities and Certain Related Acts, Oct. 2, 1997, 1997 O.J. (C 340) 1.

[47] Case C-372/04, Watts v. Bedford Primary Care Trust and Sec'y of State for Health, 2006 E.C.R. I-0 4325, 144–48.

supply of hospital care to be planned and managed on the basis of predetermined general clinical priorities without carrying out an objective medical assessment of the patient's medical condition, the history and probable course of the patient's illness, the degree of pain the patient is in, and/or the nature of the patient's disability at the time when the request for authorization was made or renewed.[48]

Thus, in addition to the EU regulation on cross-border health care based on Article 45 of the TFEU and, as some countries see it, in contradiction to the wording of Article 168 (7) of the TFEU, the ECJ has created a second form of individual right of EU citizens to reimbursement by their national health care system for medical treatment abroad.

III. The Codification of Case Law through the Services Directive

The first attempt to codify the jurisprudence of the ECJ on the freedom to provide services was presented by Commissioner Frits Bolkestein in 2004.[49] As a "horizontal Directive," the proposal covered a wide variety of economic service activities—with few exceptions, such as financial services—and applied to all service providers established in a Member State. The objective of the proposed Directive was to provide a legal framework that would eliminate the obstacles to the freedom of establishment for service providers and the free movement of services between the Member States, giving both the providers and recipients of services the legal certainty they need to exercise these two fundamental freedoms enshrined in the Treaty. The core piece of the Bolkestein draft was the establishment of the "country of origin principle," which means that service providers would be subject only to the national provisions of their Member State of origin.[50] The national provisions of the country where the service was provided relating to access to and the exercise of a service activity, in particular those requirements governing the behavior of the provider, the quality or content of the service, advertising, contracts, and the provider's liability, would not be valid for a service provider who moved to another Member State on a temporary basis. Unlike the Regulation mentioned in Section I of this chapter, this Directive was intended not only to coordinate different legal systems but to harmonize the national provisions relating to services.

These national provisions varied tremendously among Member States, ranging from very liberal to more interventionist approaches, making this a very ambitious attempt at regulation. There was much opposition to the liberalization of the posting of workers, especially from trade unions throughout Europe. They feared that the Directive would be a legal incentive for private companies to relocate to countries with

---

[48] *Id.* at 79, 119.

[49] Eur. Comm'n, *Proposal for a Directive of the European Parliament and of the Council on Services in the Internal Market*, COM (2004) 2 final/3 (Mar. 5, 2004) [hereinafter Bolkestein draft].

[50] *Id.* art. 16.

more permissive fiscal, social, and environmental requirements and then export their services from there to the other Member States, paving the way for social dumping. However, health care professionals were also concerned that Member States could lose control over health care in their territory. In addition to the general application of the country-of-origin principle to health care services, the draft included a special provision that codified the case law of the ECJ on the assumption of health care costs.[51] The Bolkestein Directive and the notorious "polish plumber" became the symbols of the free market bias and the lack of social content of the planned European Constitution and played an important role for the "no" votes on the European Constitutional Treaty in France and the Netherlands in 2005.[52]

After several heads of states suddenly discovered their opposition to the proposal,[53] the European Parliament adopted hundreds of amendments in its first reading of the proposal, which then lead to a watered-down proposal of successor commissioner Charlie McCreevy. The country-of-origin principle, the social provisions, and the provisions on health care were removed from the Directive.[54] But when it was adopted in 2006,[55] the Commission announced that it would develop an EU framework for safe, high quality, and efficient health services by reinforcing cooperation among Member States and providing clarity and certainty over the application of Community law to health services and health care.

IV. The New Directive on the Application of Patients' Rights in Cross-Border Health care

On February 28, 2011, the Council of the European Union approved the European Parliament's amendments on the draft Directive on the application of patients' rights in cross-border health care (Patient Rights' Directive).[56] This was the final step in an unusually long legislation process that reflected the typical problems of treatment abroad as well as the complex functioning of the European integration process. After the fiasco of the services Directive, the Commission initiated a lot of preparatory work in order to avoid a second failure. On initiative of the Commission, in June 2006, the Council of Ministers of the Member States adopted conclusions on common values and principles in EU Health Systems. The Council stated that it believes there is particular value in any appropriate initiative on health services ensuring clarity for European citizens about their rights and entitlements when they move from one EU Member

---

[51]   *Id.* art. 23.

[52]   Juan Delgado, *The European Services Directive, in* U.S.-EUROPE ANALYSIS SERIES 1 (2006).

[53]   Thus the draft became the "legislative hot potato of the early twenty-first century," Catherine Barnard, *Unravelling the Services Directive,* 45 COMMON MARKET L. REV. 323 (2008).

[54]   *Cf. id.* for the details and outcomes of the legislation procedure on the services.

[55]   Directive 2006/123/EC of the European Parliament and of the Council of December 12, 2006 on Services in the Internal Market, O.J. (L 376) 36 [hereinafter Services Directive].

[56]   *Supra* note 10.

State to another, and added that it "invites the European Commission to ensure that common values and principles contained in the Statement are respected when drafting specific proposals concerning health services."[57] The next step was a Communication of the Commission inviting stakeholders to take part in an official Consultation regarding Community action on health services.[58] In 2007 the European Parliament adopted two statements, one on cross-border health care[59] and one on the exclusion of health services from the services Directive.[60] In addition the Commission launched a study conducted by the European Observatory on Health Systems and Policies.[61] In 2008 the Commission presented its final proposal.[62]

Despite all this preparatory work, the legislation procedure was stopped several times by strong opposition of governments who expressed their concern that they could lose control over their health care systems.[63] This disagreement persisted for more than four years until, in December 2010, a final compromise on the "Directive on the application of patients' rights in cross-border healthcare" was reached in the so-called "Trialogue" tripartite negotiations among the Council,[64] Parliament,[65] and the Commission.[66] The final compromise therefore bears strong hallmarks of the Member States. The preamble with its sixty-four recitals suggests that some countries needed a "consolation prize"[67] for letting the Directive pass. Nevertheless, in the end, the Council of Ministers adopted the Directive by only a majority vote. Poland, Portugal, and Romania voted against it and put on record that they "regret that the Directive on the application of patients' rights in cross-border healthcare does not provide a sufficient guarantee of a high level of quality and safety to patients wishing to receive cross-border healthcare and does not

---

[57] Council of the European Union, Council Conclusions on Common Values and Principles in European Union Health Systems, 2006 O.J. (C 146) 1.

[58] Eur. Comm'n, *Consultation Regarding Community Action on Health Services (Communication)*, SEC (2006) 1195/4 (Sept. 26, 2006).

[59] Eur. Parliament, Resolution of March 15, 2007 on Community Action on the Provision of Cross-Border Healthcare, EUR. PARL. DOC P6_TA(2007)0073 (2007).

[60] Eur. Parliament, *Report on the Impact And Consequences of the Exclusion of Health Services from the Directive on Services in the Internal Market*, EUR. PARL. DOC. A6-0173/2007 final (2007).

[61] EUR. OBSERVATORY ON HEALTH SYS. & POLICIES, CROSS-BORDER HEALTHCARE: MAPPING AND ANALYSING HEALTH SYSTEMS DIVERSITY (Matthias Wismar et al. eds. 2007).

[62] European Commission, *Proposal for a Directive of the European Parliament and of the Council on the Application of Patients' Rights in Cross-Border Healthcare*, COM (2008) 0414 final.

[63] Press Release, Council of the European Union, Main Results of the 2947th Council Meeting, (June 8, 2009).

[64] Council of the European Union, Position (EU) No. 14/2010 of the Council at First Reading with a View to the Adoption of a Directive of the European Parliament and of the Council on the Application of Patients' Rights in Cross-Border Healthcare, O.J. (C 275E) 1.

[65] European Parliament, Committee on the Environment, Public Health and Food Safety, Draft Recommendation for Second Reading on the Council Position at First Reading with a View to the Adoption of a Directive of the European Parliament and of the Council on the Application of Patients' Rights in Cross-Border Healthcare, PE443.081

[66] European Commission, *Communication Concerning the Position of the Council at First Reading on the Adoption of a Directive of the European Parliament and of the Council on the Application of Patients' Rights on Cross-Border Healthcare*, COM (2010) 503 final.

[67] *Cf.* concerning Barnard, *Services Directive, supra* note 53, at 24.

entirely respect the responsibilities and competences of the Member States in relation to the organization and planning of national health systems."[68]

A. SECOND TRACK OF REIMBURSEMENT FOR PLANNED CROSS-BORDER HEALTH CARE

The core piece of the Patient Rights' Directive is the codification of the "second track" of statutory entitlement to benefits for planned cross-border health care in the European Union (discussed above), which supplements[69] Regulation 883/2004.[70] The first difference between this second track and the entitlements provided by Regulation 883/2004 is the fact that the "Member State of affiliation"[71] shall ensure that the costs incurred by an insured person who receives cross-border health care are reimbursed. The Member State of affiliation has to reimburse or to pay the costs of cross-border health care directly (not via the Member State of treatment). The second difference is that the costs are only reimbursed if the health care in question is among the benefits to which the insured person is entitled in the Member State of affiliation (not in the Member State of treatment). It is reimbursed up to the level of costs that would have been assumed by the Member State of affiliation had this health care been provided in its territory without exceeding the actual costs of health care received. The third difference is that the Member State of affiliation is not permitted to make the reimbursement subject to prior authorization except in the cases set out in Article 8 of the Patient Rights' Directive.

According to Article 8 (2) of the Directive, Member States may demand for a prior authorization for planned treatment in another Member State if the health care involves overnight hospital accommodation of the patient in question for at least one night or requires use of highly specialized and cost-intensive medical infrastructure or medical equipment. In these cases the demand for prior authorization is justified only if it is made subject to planning requirements relating to the object of ensuring sufficient and permanent access to a balanced range of high-quality treatment in the Home State or to the wish to control costs and avoid, as far as possible, any waste of financial, technical, and human resources.

Prior authorization requirements are also allowed if the health care involves treatments presenting a particular risk for the patient or the population or if the health care is provided by a health care provider that, on a case-by-case basis, could give rise to serious and specific concerns relating to the quality or safety of the care. If a specific kind of health care is, however, subject to Union legislation ensuring a minimum level of safety and quality throughout the Union, this argument does not justify prior authorization requirements.

---

[68] Council of the European Union, Statement of Poland, Portugal and Romania, Interinstitutional File 2008/0142 (COD) 6590/11 ADD 1 REV 2.

[69] Michael Tiedemann, *Koordinierung und Harmonisierung der Grenzüberschreitenden Patientenmobilität in Europa,* 11 NEUE ZEITSCHRIFT FUER SOZIALRECHT 887 (2011).

[70] *Cf. supra* Section II.

[71] The definition of the state of affiliation follows Regulation 883/2004, *supra* note 19, and means in practice the country where the person is insured (art. 3(c) of the Patients' Rights Directive, *supra* note 10).

If Member States make use of these derogations they have to notify the Commission of the categories of health care subject to prior authorization. These derogations are based on the jurisprudence of the ECJ[72] and reflect the compromise reached in the negotiations among the Commission, European Parliament, and Member States.

The difference between the new Directive and the original Bolkestein draft[73] with its "country of origin principle" becomes obvious with regard to the provisions imposed on the Member State of treatment.[74] Taking into account the principles of universality, access to good quality care, equity, and solidarity, cross-border health care shall be provided in accordance with legislation of the Member State of treatment, with standards and guidelines on quality and safety laid down by the Member State of treatment, and with Union legislation on safety standards.[75] The Member State of treatment has to ensure that there are transparent complaints procedures and mechanisms for patients to seek remedies in accordance with its legislation if they suffer harm arising from the health care they receive. The Member State of treatment shall also ensure that systems of professional liability insurance, a guarantee, or similar arrangement that is equivalent or essentially comparable as regards its purpose and that is appropriate to the nature and the extent of the risk, are in place for treatment provided on its territory.

In order to avoid any misunderstanding with regard to the non-application of the country-of-origin principle, Article 2(g) states explicitly that this Directive shall apply without prejudice to the regulations on the law applicable to contractual obligations (Rome I)[76] and noncontractual obligations (Rome II)[77] as well as to other EU rules on private international law, in particular rules related to court jurisdiction.[78]

B. ADVANTAGES FOR PATIENTS

The Directive contains several advantages for patients who seek health care services abroad or have received such health care. In order to ensure continuity of care, the Directive imposes new requirements on both states involved. In the Member State of treatment, patients who have received treatment are entitled to a written or electronic medical record of such treatment and access to at least a copy of this record. The Member State of affiliation shall ensure that where a patient has received cross-border health care and where medical follow-up proves necessary, the same medical follow-up

---

[72] *Cf. supra* Section III.

[73] *Cf. supra* Section IV.

[74] "Member State of treatment" means the Member State on whose territory health care is actually provided to the patient. In the case of telemedicine, health care is considered to be provided in the state where the health care provider is established. *See* Patients' Rights Directive, *supra* note 10, art. 3(d).

[75] *Id.*, art. 4.

[76] Regulation (EC) No. 593/2008 of the European Parliament and of the Council of June 17, 2008 on the Law Applicable to Contractual Obligations ("Rome I"), 2008 O.J. (L 177) 6.

[77] Regulation (EC) No. 864/2007 of the European Parliament and of the Council of July 11, 2007 on the law applicable to noncontractual obligations ("Rome II"), 2007 O.J. (L 199) 40.

[78] *Cf., e.g.*, Council Regulation (EC) No.44/2001 of December 22, 2000 on Jurisdiction and the Recognition and Enforcement of Judgments in Civil and Commercial Matters ("Brussels I Regulation"), 2001 O.J. (L 12) 1.

is available as would have been if that health care had been provided in its territory. It must also ensure that patients who seek to receive or do receive cross-border health care have remote access to or at least have a copy of their medical records. All data must be processed in conformity with, and subject to, national measures implementing EU provisions on the protection of personal data.[79] The Member State of affiliation shall take all necessary measures in order to ensure continuity of treatment in cases where a prescription is issued in the Member State of treatment for medicinal products or medical devices available in the Member State of affiliation and where dispensing is sought in the Member State of affiliation.[80]

Although the ECJ case law concentrated on discriminatory measures of the Member State of affiliation, the Directive also contains antidiscriminatory rules for the Member State of treatment. It states that the principle of nondiscrimination with regard to nationality shall be applied to patients from other Member States. Member States shall ensure that the health care providers on their territory apply the same scale of fees for health care for patients from other Member States as for domestic patients in a comparable medical situation, or that they charge a price calculated according to objective, nondiscriminatory criteria if there is no comparable price for domestic patients.

If prior authorization is required, the advantage of the "second track" compared to the "first track" of Regulation 883/2004 may be minimized or even become disadvantageous to the patient. Therefore, the Directive provides that the Member State of affiliation shall, with regard to requests for prior authorization for cross-border health care, ascertain whether the conditions laid down in Regulation (EC) No 883/2004 have been met. Where those conditions are met, the prior authorization shall be granted pursuant to that Regulation unless the patient requests otherwise.[81] In most cases it will be better for the patient to accept the application of the standard rules as in most countries he or she will receive the treatment as benefits in-kind, that is without having to pay cash in advance.

Many measures of the Directive address the information patients typically lack regarding foreign health care systems and the amount and procedures of reimbursement to which they are entitled. Each Member State shall designate one or more national contact points for cross-border health care and communicate those persons' names and contact details to the Commission.[82] The Member State shall ensure that the national contact points consult with patient organizations, health care providers, and health care insurers in order to facilitate the exchange of information and to cooperate closely with each other and with the Commission. National contact points shall provide

---

[79] This refers in particular to Directive 95/46/EC of the European Parliament and of the Council of October 24, 1995 on the Protection of Individuals with Regard to the Processing of Personal Data and on the Free Movement of Such Data, 1995 O.J. (L 281) 31, and to Directive 2002/58/EC of the European Parliament and of the Council of July 12, 2002 Concerning the Processing of Personal Data and the Protection of Privacy in the Electronic Communications Sector, 2002 O.J. (L201) 37.

[80] Patients' Rights Directive, *supra* note 10, art. 11(1).

[81] *Id.* art. 8(3).

[82] *Id.* art. 6.

patients on request with contact details of national contact points in other Member States. In order to enable patients to make use of their rights in relation to cross-border health care, national contact points in the Member State of treatment shall provide them with information concerning health care providers, including, on request, information on a specific provider's right to provide services or any restrictions on its practice, as well as information on patients' rights, complaint procedures, and mechanisms for seeking remedies, according to the legislation of that Member State, as well as the legal and administrative options available to settle disputes, including those applicable to harm arising from cross-border health care. The information shall be easily accessible and shall be made available by electronic means and in formats accessible to people with disabilities, as appropriate.

The Member States of treatment shall ensure that patients receive from the national contact point, upon request, relevant information on national quality standards and guidelines, including provisions on supervision and assessment of health care providers, information on which health care providers are subject to these standards and guidelines, and information on the accessibility of hospitals for persons with disabilities. The Member States have to guarantee that health care providers provide relevant information to help individual patients to make an informed choice, including information on treatment options and on the availability, quality, and safety of the health care they provide in the Member State of treatment. Health care providers also have to provide clear invoices and clear information on prices, as well as on the providers' authorization or registration status, their insurance cover or other means of personal or collective protection with regard to professional liability. However, to the extent that health care providers already provide domestic patients with relevant information on these subjects, the Directive does not oblige health care providers to furnish more extensive information to patients from other Member States.[83]

The Member State of affiliation shall ensure that there are mechanisms in place to provide, upon patient request, information on patient rights and entitlements in that Member State relating to receiving cross-border health care, particularly information regarding the terms and conditions for reimbursement of costs, procedures for accessing and determining those entitlements, and procedures for appeal and redress if patients believe that their rights have not been respected. In providing information about cross-border health care, the Member State must clearly distinguish rights that patients have by virtue of the new Directive regarding patients' rights and rights arising from Regulation (EC) No 883/2004.[84]

For patients seeking cross-border health care, the question they are most interested in is whether their costs for treatment abroad will be reimbursed, and if so to what level. For this reason the Directive requires the Member State of affiliation to have a transparent mechanism for calculation of costs of cross-border health care that are to be reimbursed to the insured person. This mechanism must be based on objective,

---

[83] *Id.* art. 4(2)(b).
[84] *Id.* art. 5(b).

nondiscriminatory criteria known in advance and applied at the relevant (local, regional, or national) administrative level.[85]

The restriction of reimbursement to the domestic level of benefits is a right, not a duty, of Member States. The Directive states that where the full cost of cross-border health care exceeds the level of costs that would have been assumed had the health care been provided in its territory, the Member State of affiliation may nevertheless decide to reimburse the full cost. It may also decide to reimburse other related costs, such as accommodation and travel costs, or extra disability-related costs that persons with disabilities might incur when receiving cross-border health care, in accordance with national legislation and on the condition that there be sufficient documentation setting out these costs.[86]

C. DISADVANTAGES FOR PATIENTS

Despite this overall positive impression from the point of view of patients, there are several provisions that show the strong influence of Member States and their legitimate intention to contain costs and to keep control over their health care systems.

With regard to the Member State of treatment, the Directive opens up the possibility of the Member State adopting measures regarding access to treatment aimed at fulfilling its fundamental responsibility to ensure sufficient and permanent access to health care within its territory. This possibility is limited to what is necessary and proportionate, may not constitute a means of arbitrary discrimination, and shall be made publicly available in advance.[87] This principle of proportionality is valid especially in case a Member State implements a system of prior authorization for reimbursement of costs of cross-border health care. Such a system of prior authorization, including the criteria and the application of those criteria, and individual decisions of refusal to grant prior authorization, may not constitute an unjustified obstacle to the free movement of patients.[88] The Member State of affiliation has to ensure that administrative procedures are based on objective, nondiscriminatory criteria that are necessary and proportionate to the objective to be achieved.[89]

Although these limited competencies of Member States may be in line with the case law of the ECJ, they could lose much of its exceptional character because of the mere fact of its codification. Each court judgment refers only to an individual case brought forward by the respective parties, but a written list of general derogations as part of the EU legislation creates new manoeuvring room for Member States concerning the decision on more or less restrictive rules on reimbursement of cross-border health care. Therefore, if the European internal market for health care services is to become real, it will depend on European citizens becoming aware of their new opportunities.[90]

---

[85] *Id.* art. 2(6).

[86] *Id.* art. 7(6).

[87] *Id.* art. 4(3).

[88] *Id.* art. 8(1).

[89] *Id.* art. 9(1).

[90] Walter Frenz & Christian Ehlenz, *Grenzüberschreitende Wahrnehmung von Gesundheitsdienstleistungen*, 29 MEDIZINRECHT 629 (2011).

Consequently, it is likely that future measures of Member States based on these provisions will be subject to further rulings of the ECJ.

This could also be the case with another derogation, relating to the Member State of affiliation. The latter may impose on an insured person seeking reimbursement of the costs of cross-border health care, including health care received through means of telemedicine, the same conditions, criteria of eligibility, or regulatory and administrative formalities (whether set at a local, regional, or national level) as it would impose if this health care was provided in its territory. This may include an assessment by a health professional or health care administrator providing services for the statutory social security system or national health system of the Member State of affiliation, such as the general practitioner or primary care practitioner with whom the patient is registered, if this is necessary for determining the individual patient's entitlement to health care. However, no conditions, criteria of eligibility, and regulatory and administrative formalities imposed according to this paragraph may be discriminatory or constitute an obstacle to the free movement of patients, services, or goods, unless such is objectively justified by planning requirements relating to the objective of ensuring sufficient and permanent access to a balanced range of high-quality treatment in the Member State concerned or to the wish to control costs and avoid, as far as possible, any waste of financial, technical, and human resources.[91] This exemption rule is based on the case law of the ECJ, but elaborating the alternatives of national steering measures, such as the gatekeeper role of general practitioners or the transfer of responsibilities to the regional or local level, could result in further restrictions for cross-border health care. Moreover, further ECJ rulings are foreseeable.

Reimbursement for medicinal products is excluded from the scope of the patients' rights Directive. Pharmaceuticals and medical devices are subject to different regulations,[92] but the Directive stipulates the recognition of prescriptions issued in another Member State.[93] The Member States shall ensure that prescriptions issued for such a product in another Member State for a named patient can be dispensed on the Member State's territory in compliance with its national legislation in force, and that any restrictions on recognition of individual prescriptions are prohibited unless such restrictions are "limited to what is necessary and proportionate to safeguard human health, and non-discriminatory" or "based on legitimate and justified doubts about the authenticity, content or comprehensibility of an individual prescription."[94]

According to the directive, the recognition of such prescriptions shall not affect national rules governing prescribing, dispensing, and reimbursement. In particular, the recognition of prescriptions shall not affect a pharmacist's right, by virtue of national rules, to refuse, for ethical reasons, to dispense a product that was prescribed

---

[91] Patients' Rights Directive, *supra* note 10, art. 7(7).
[92] *Cf.* Directive 2001/83/EC of the European Parliament and of the Council of November 6, 2001 on the Community Code Relating to Medicinal Products for Human Use, 2004 O.J. (L 311) 67.
[93] Patient's Rights Directive, *supra* note 10, art. 11.
[94] *Id.* art. 11(1).

in another Member State where the pharmacist would have the right to refuse to dispense had the prescription been issued in the Member State of affiliation.[95]

Finally, the biggest obstacle for individual patients to seek cross-border treatment remains the fact that they would have to rely on foreign complaints procedures and jurisdiction if they suffer harm arising from the health care they receive abroad and seek remedies for it.

Conclusion

More than fifty years after the foundation of the "Common European Market," it is still not commonplace for most European citizens to seek medicinal treatment in another Member State. Of course, there are some positive examples in specific border regions, but for the majority of patients in the European Union language barriers, lack of information and, in particular, complicated rules on reimbursement by national health care systems are still strong obstacles. The new EU Directive on the application of patients' rights in cross-border health care is only a first step to facilitate access to safe and high-quality cross-border health care in the European Union and to ensure patient mobility throughout Europe. There are additional measures inside and outside of the publicly funded and regulated health care systems necessary to give patients a better choice among different health care providers in different countries. It should, however, be recalled that the activities of the European Union go far beyond patient mobility and include many measures harmonizing the quality and safety standards of health care services,[96] medicinal products,[97] and exchange of health data[98] throughout all Member States of the Union.

---

[95] *Id.* art. 11(1).

[96] *Cf.* Miek Peeters, *Free Movement of Patients: Directive 2011/24 on the Application of Patients' Rights in Cross-Border Healthcare*, 19 Eur. J. Health L. 29 (2012).

[97] *Cf., e.g.*, Directive 2001/83/EC, *supra* note 92; Council Directive 93/42/EEC of June 14, 1993 Concerning Medical Devices, 1993 O.J. (L 169) 1.

[98] *Cf.* Paul Quinn & Paul De Hert, *The Patients' Rights Directive (2011/24/EU)—Providing (Some) Rights to EU Residents Seeking Healthcare in Other Member States*, 27 Computer L. & Sec. Rev. 497 (2011).

6

MEDICAL TOURISM AND GLOBAL JUSTICE

*I. Glenn Cohen**

Introduction

By promising lower-cost surgeries, medical tourism has represented a boon (although not an unqualified one[1]) for U.S. and other home-country patients. But what about the interests of those in the destination countries? From their perspective, medical tourism presents a host of cruel ironies. Vast medico-industrial complexes replete with the newest expensive technologies to provide comparatively wealthy medical tourists hip replacements and facelifts coexist with large swaths of the population dying from malaria, AIDS, and lack of basic sanitation and clean water. A recent *New York Times* article entitled "Royal Care for Some of India's Patients, Neglect for Others," for example, begins by describing the care given at Wockhardt Hospital in India to "Mr. Steeles, 60, a car dealer from Daphne, Alabama. [who] had flown halfway around the world last month to save his heart [through a mitral valve repair] at a price he could pay."[2] The article describes in great detail the dietician who selects Mr. Steele's meals, the dermatologist who comes as soon as he mentions an itch, and Mr. Steeles's "Royal Suite" with "cable TV, a computer, [and] a mini-refrigerator, where an attendant that afternoon stashed some ice cream, for when he felt hungry later."[3] This treatment contrasts

* Assistant Professor and Co-Director, Petrie-Flom Center for Health Law Policy, Biotechnology, and Bioethics, Harvard Law School. J.D., Harvard Law School. igcohen@law.harvard.edu. This chapter is adapted from I. Glenn Cohen, *Medical Tourism, Access to Health Care, and Global Justice*, 52 VA. J. INT'L L. 1 (2011). I thank the journal for all their excellent editing, as well as all those who gave me comments on the journal article, who are thanked therein.

[1] *See generally* I. Glenn Cohen, *Protecting Patients with Passports: Medical Tourism and the Patient-Protective Argument*, 95 IOWA L. REV. 1467, 1472 (2010) (reviewing the risks of malpractice and care quality created by medical tourism and proposing regulations to protect patients).

[2] Somini Sengupta, *Royal Care for Some of India's Patients, Neglect for Others*, N.Y. TIMES, June 1, 2008, at K3.

[3] *Id.*

with the care given to a group of "day laborers who laid bricks and mixed cement for Bangalore's construction boom," many of whom "fell ill after drinking illegally brewed whisky; 150 died that day."[4] "They had been wheeled in by wives and brothers to the overstretched government-run Bowring Hospital, on the other side of town," a hospital with "no intensive care unit, no ventilators, no dialysis machine," where "[d]inner was a stack of white bread, on which a healthy cockroach crawled."[5]

These kinds of stark disparities have prompted intuitive discomfort and critiques in the academic and policy literatures.[6] To highlight but one example, Professor Leigh Turner (who has also contributed a chapter to this book) suggests that "the greatest risk for inhabitants of destination countries is that increased volume of international patients will have adverse effects upon local patients, health care facilities and economies."[7] He explains that the kinds of investments destination-country governments must make to compete are in "specialized medical centres and advanced biotechnologies" unlikely to be accessed by "most citizens of a country [who] lack access to basic health care and social services."[8] Furthermore, higher wages for health care professionals resulting from medical tourism may crowd out access by the domestic poor.[9] Thus, "[i]nstead of contributing to broad social and economic development, the provision of care to patients from other countries might exacerbate existing inequalities and further polarize the richest and poorest members" of the destination country.[10] The same point has also been made in several regional discussions.[11]

Behind all of these claims—scholarly and popular—are some significant and interesting fundamental questions. How likely is medical tourism to produce negative consequences on health care access in Less Developed Countries (LDCs)? If those effects occur, does the United States (or other more developed countries or international bodies) have an obligation to discourage or regulate medical tourism to try to prevent such consequences?[12]

---

4 *Id.*

5 *Id.*

6 *E.g.*, David D. Benavides, *Trade Policies and Export of Health Services: A Development Perspective*, in TRADE IN HEALTH SERVICES: GLOBAL, REGIONAL, AND COUNTRY PERSPECTIVES 53, 55 (Nick Drager & Cesar Vieira eds., 2002), *available at* http://tinyurl.com/3crozzd; Rupa Chanda, *Trade in Health Services*, 80 BULL. WORLD HEALTH ORG. 158, 160 (2002); MILICA Z. BOOKMAN & KARLA K. BOOKMAN, MEDICAL TOURISM IN DEVELOPING COUNTRIES 176 (2007).

7 Leigh Turner, *"First World Health Care at Third World Prices": Globalization, Bioethics and Medical Tourism*, 2 BIOSCIENCES 303, 320 (2007).

8 *Id.*

9 *Id.*

10 *Id.* at 321.

11 *E.g.*, Laura Hopkins et al., *Medical Tourism Today: What Is the State of Existing Knowledge?*, 31 J. PUB. HEALTH POL'Y 185, 194 (2010); Rory Johnston et al., *What Is Known about the Effects of Medical Tourism in Destination and Departure Countries? A Scoping Review*, 9 INT'L J. FOR EQUITY HEALTH 1 (2010) (India).

12 In other work I have tackled the further regulatory question of what home-country governments or international bodies might do to prevent or mitigate these negative effects. *See* I. Glenn Cohen, *Medical Tourism, Access to Health Care, and Global Justice*, 52 VA. J. INT'L L. 1, 46–51 (2011); I. Glenn Cohen, *How to Regulatie Medical Tourism (and Why It Should Matter to Bioethicists)*, 12 DEV. WORLD BIOETHICS 9 (2012).

I examine those questions in this chapter. I hope the analysis developed here will serve as a template for discussion of similar problems in the globalization of health care, including migration of health care workers (brain drain).

Of course, medical tourism comes in multiple varieties. Let us distinguish three subtypes: The first is patients paying out of pocket. In the United States, this typically refers to uninsured or underinsured patients using medical tourism to achieve substantial cost savings for procedures such as hip replacements.[13] A second group consists of private-insurer–prompted medical tourism, where insurers provide incentives for patients to use medical tourism or merely cover services abroad.[14] A final form is government-prompted medical tourism, for example, in the European Union, where Member States face some obligations to reimburse their citizens for treatments received in other Member States.[15] I will argue that in the global justice analysis, these distinctions carry a lot of weight.

I. The Empirical Claim

While concerns about effects on health care access abroad are raised by academics and policy makers discussing medical tourism, they have been undertheorized. These concerns are best thought of as consisting of an empirical claim—that medical tourism diminishes health care access in the destination country, usually with a focus on its effects on the poorest residents—and a normative one—that such diminished access creates obligations on the United States and other tourist-patient home countries (or international bodies, or possibly corporations) to do something about medical tourism.

Although there have been a number of more anecdotal statements and analyses offered in favor of the empirical claim, there is very little in the way of statistical evidence supporting it. As such, this is an area where more developmental economic work is needed. Nevertheless, it is useful to identify six triggering conditions, which, when combined with substantial amounts of medical tourism, may lead to reduced access to health care for local populations and thus satisfy the empirical claim:

(1) *The health care services consumed by medical tourists come from those that would otherwise have been available to the destination country poor.* When medical tourists travel abroad for cardiac care, hip replacements, and other forms of surgery used by the destination country poor, the siphoning effect is straightforward. By contrast, the destination country poor are already unlikely to be able to access some boutique forms of treatment, such as cosmetic surgery and stem cell and fertility therapies. Thus, although medical tourism by U.S.

---

[13] Cohen, *supra* note 1, at 1479–81.
[14] *Id.* at 1486–88.
[15] Hilko Meyer discusses these rules in his chapter in this volume.

patients for these services would diminish access by, for example, Indian patients, it would not necessarily diminish access for *poor* Indian patients (which would remain steady at virtually none). Thus, one triggering condition focuses on whether medical tourism is for services currently accessed by destination-country poor.

That said, as discussed below, over time, the salience of the distinction is likely to break down, and even medical tourism for services currently inaccessible to destination-country poor may siphon resources away from the poor because increased demand for services such as cosmetic surgery may redirect the professional choices of graduating or practicing physicians who currently provide health care to India's poor into these niche markets. Whether that dynamic obtains would depend in part on the extent to which the destination country regulates specialty choice.

(2) *Health care providers are "captured" by the medical-tourist patient population, rather than serving some tourist clientele and some of the existing population.* Absent regulation, the introduction of a higher-paying market will likely cause health care providers to shift away from treating patients in the lower-paying market.[16] For example, Hopkins and her coauthors argue that this dynamic has taken place in Thailand, where "[a]lmost 6000 positions for medical practitioners in Thailand's public system remained unfilled in 2005, as an increasing number of physicians followed the higher wages and more attractive settings available in private care," and that due to medical tourism, "the addition of internal 'brain drain' from public to private health care may be especially damaging" for "countries such as Ghana, Pakistan, and South Africa, which lose approximately half of their medical graduates every year to external migration."[17] This has also been the dynamic when private options are introduced into public systems, even in the developed world; regulations that require providers to spend time in both systems are also more likely to produce positive externalities from the private to public health care systems. For example, a physician who receives extra training as part of her duties in the medical tourism sector may be able to carry that training over to her time spent treating poor patients, if regulation forces her facility to treat poor patients. That said, it is worth noting that in medical tourism havens such as India, even when such regulations are in place, many observers have been skeptical that they have been or will be enforced.[18]

(3) *The supply of health care professionals, facilities, and technologies in the destination country is inelastic.* Theoretically, if medical tourism causes increased

---

[16] *See* Johnston et al., *supra* note 11, at 11.

[17] Hopkins et al., *supra* note 11, at 194; *see also* Rupa Chinai & Rahul Goswani, *Medical Visas Mark Growth of Indian Medical Tourism*, 85 BULL. WORLD HEALTH ORG. 164, 165 (2007).

[18] *See, e.g.*, Ami Sen Gupta, *Medical Tourism in India: Winners and Losers*, 5 INDIAN J. MED. ETHICS 4–5 (2008): Johnston et al., *supra* note 11, at 5.

demand for health care providers and facilities in the destination country, the country could meet such demand by increasing the supply of these things. In reality, however, even developed nations have had difficulty increasing this supply when necessary.[19] As discussed, the need to match increased demand for the right specialties poses additional problems. In any event, investments in building capacity always entail an adjustment period. Thus, even countries that are unusually successful in increasing the size of their health care workforce to meet the demands of medical tourism will face interim shortages.

(4) *The positive effects of medical tourism in counteracting the "brain drain" of health care practitioners to foreign countries are outweighed by the negative effects of medical tourism on the availability of health care resources.* Medical migration, or "brain drain," represents a significant threat to health care access abroad. The issue is discussed in greater depth in other parts of this book, but to give one example, 61 percent of all graduates from the Ghana Medical School between 1986 and 1995 left Ghana for employment (of those, 54.9 percent worked in the United Kingdom and 35.4 percent worked in the United States), and a 2005 study found that 25 percent of doctors in the United States are graduates of foreign medical schools.[20] A recent study of nurses in five countries found that 41 percent reported dissatisfaction with their jobs, and one-third of those under age thirty planned on leaving to work elsewhere.[21] "Health care workers are 'pushed' from developing countries by the impoverished conditions: low remuneration, lack of equipment and drugs, and poor infrastructure and management," and "[t]hey are 'pulled' to developed countries by the allure of a brighter future: better wages, working conditions, training, and career opportunities, as well as safer and more stable social and political environments."[22] It is possible that for health care professionals tempted to leave their country of origin to practice in other markets, the availability of higher-paying jobs with better technology and more time with patients in the medical tourist sector of their country of origin will counteract this incentive.[23] Medical tourism may also enable the destination country to "recapture" some health care providers who left years earlier, or to change

---

[19] *See* Greg L. Stoddart & Morris L. Barer, *Will Increasing Medical School Enrollment Solve Canada's Physician Supply Problems?* 161 Can. Med. Assoc. J. 983 (1999).

[20] Fitzhugh Mullan, *The Metrics of the Physician Brain Drain*, 353 New Eng. J. Med. 1810, 1811 (2005); David Sanders et al., *Public Health in Africa*, in Global Public Health: A New Era 46 (Robert Beaglehole ed., 2003).

[21] Linda H. Aiken et al., *Nurses' Reports on Hospital Care in Five Countries*, 20 Health Aff. 43, 45–46 (2001).

[22] Lawrence O. Gostin, *The International Migration and Recruitment of Nurses: Human Rights and Global Justice*, 299 JAMA 1827, 1828 (2008).

[23] *See* Matthias Helble, *The Movements of Patients across Borders: Challenges and Opportunities for Public Health*, 89 Bull. World Health Org. 68, 70 (2011).

"brain drain" into "brain circulation."[24] But although some countries that experience medical brain drain are also developing strong medical tourism industries, many are *only* sources of medical brain drain and not destinations for medical tourism.[25] Thus, the creation of medical tourism hubs may actually exacerbate *intra*-regional medical migration.

(5) *Medical tourism prompts destination country governments to redirect resources away from basic health care services in a way that outweighs positive health care spillovers.* In order to compete for patients on quality and price against both the patient's home country and other medical tourism hubs, destination countries will need to invest in their nascent medical tourism industry through, for example, direct funding, tax subsidies, and land grants.[26] Unfortunately, such funding often comes from money devoted to other health programs, including basic health care and social services,[27] and those effects are likely to be felt most strongly by the destination-country poor. In other words, we need some sense of whether governments actually invest in health care services accessible by the poor (or at least do not take them away) in a counterfactual world where medical tourism is restricted. We also need to examine this dynamic as against a potential countervailing dynamic wherein medical tourism leads to a diffusion of Western medical technology or standards of practice or other health care spillovers that are beneficial to the entire patient population. In India, for example, some commentators have suggested that the product of these countervailing forces has ultimately been a net negative for the destination-country poor.[28]

(6) *Profits from the medical tourism industry are unlikely to "trickle down."* Successful medical tourism industries promise an infusion of wealth into the destination country, and the possibility that all boats will rise.[29] In practice, however, that possibility may not be realized. The reason for this might be something insidious such as rampant corruption, or it may be something more benign, such as a tax system that is not particularly redistributive, or a largely foreign-owned medical sector.[30] Thus, the fact that a destination country gains economically from medical tourism (for example, in GDP terms) does not necessarily mean that those gains are shared in a way that promotes health care access (or health) among the destination poor.

---

[24] For discussions of these possibilities in other contexts, see, for example, Ayelet Shachar, *The Race for Talent: Highly Skilled Migrants and Competitive Immigration Regimes*, 81 N.Y.U. L. REV. 148, 168 (2006).

[25] BOOKMAN & BOOKMAN, *supra* note 6, at 105–09.

[26] *Id.* at 65–82; Turner, *supra* note 7, at 314–15, 320.

[27] *See* Benavides, *supra* note 6, at 55; Johnston et al., *supra* note 11, at 5–6; Turner, *supra* note 7, at 320.

[28] *See, e.g.*, Hopkins et al., *supra* note 11, at 194.

[29] Nathan Cortez, *International Health Care Convergence: The Benefits and Burdens of Market-Driven Standardization*, 26 WIS. INT'L J. 646, 693–94 (2008) (citing Alain Enthoven, *On the Ideal Market Structure for Third-Party Purchasing of Health Care*, 39 SOC. SCI. & MED. 1413, 1420 (1994)).

[30] Helble, *supra* note 23, at 70.

Notice, as it will become relevant in the normative analysis, that many of these triggering conditions are themselves in the control of the destination-country government to some extent.

As I have said before, data on the effects of medical tourism on health care access in the destination country are scarce—in many cases, they rest on anecdote and speculation—and the analysis can only be done on a country-by-country basis, which is impossible, given the current paucity of data. In countries where the triggering conditions all obtain, one would expect medical tourism to cause some diminution in access to health care for the destination country's poorest due to medical tourism; as fewer factors obtain, this becomes less likely. This list of factors is certainly not exhaustive, and there may be additional factors in particular countries that push in the other direction. Although I cannot prove that this result obtains in any country, and some readers will no doubt be skeptical, the claim seems at least plausible enough to merit a normative analysis.

In the following analysis, I will merely assume we have a home-destination country pairing where the empirical claim obtains. For purposes of illustration, I will use U.S. medical tourists traveling to India as my example. From this point on, my analysis thus adopts a sort of disciplinary division of labor: I leave to development economists attempts to corroborate and further specify these triggering conditions and to show where they are satisfied. I instead focus on the normative questions about the obligations that flow from potential diminutions, and the legal and institutional design questions about how to satisfy those obligations.

II. The Normative Question

Suppose that U.S. medical tourism to India really does reduce health care access for India's poorest residents. Does the United States (or an international body) have an obligation to do something about it? In this section, I try to determine how much of an overlapping consensus there is among rival comprehensive moral theories.

I examine four types of theories that purport to find fault with medical tourism for this reason. The treatment here is by necessity brief, but I have explored these theories in more depth elsehwere.

A. SELF-INTEREST

The easiest argument to make for an obligation to restrict or regulate medical tourism would be based on the interests of the *home* country. In particular, one might press four claims: (1) medical tourism threatens home-country patients with poorer care or malpractice recovery, and results in negative externalities in meeting the needs of iatrogenically injured patients when they return home. Even assuming arguendo the factual elements of this claim are true, the cases where this particular self-interest argument might push us to curb medical tourism will map on only by coincidence, if at all, to cases posing concerns about the destination-country poor's health care access.

That is, there can be cases where this particular self-interest concern would urge action but there are no health care access concerns, and cases where there are health care access concerns but this particular self-interest argument is not operative. The same response applies regarding concerns about the importation of diseases (especially antibiotic-resistant strains or "superbugs") back to developed countries due to medical tourism, as has been reported in a few case studies.

There are three other arguments one might make in analogy to those deployed elsewhere in the health care globalization literature: (2) Medical tourism that results in decreased access to treatment for infectious diseases might increase the risk of transmission of those diseases to Americans; (3) Indians are valuable to the United States as producer-exporters of cheap goods and consumer-importers of our goods, so improving Indian citizens' basic health care will improve that country's development and ensure more productive trading partners and affluent markets in which to sell U.S.-made goods; and (4) Improving health care access abroad may reduce immigration pressures to the United States or increase national security by reducing global terrorism.

Unfortunately, these arguments are not very persuasive in this context. For the infection-transmission and consumer arguments, we should arguably be more concerned about the health of the higher socioeconomic-status strata of Indian society, who are more likely to travel to our shores and be better able to buy our goods. While diminishing health care access to India's poorest, medical tourism services may actually improve the health care of the wealthier strata, at least those who are able to buy into these better facilities or take advantage of the diffusion of knowledge and technology. This is not to say there are no infection concerns—Americans traveling to India for pleasure tourism may bring diseases back with them—but that they are less salient than in other contexts.

A more serious and general objection to deploying these self-interest arguments here is that even if it is in the American self-interest to help India's poor access health care for these reasons, it will frequently be even *more* in its self-interest to help its *own* poor citizens in this regard. Medical tourism promises to improve the health care of poor Americans even while it (by hypothesis) reduces health care access to poor Indians, and the former effect might be thought to dominate in terms of U.S. self-interest. This objection is particularly salient for medical tourism by those paying out-of-pocket or for government-prompted medical tourism. It is less forceful an objection with respect to insurer-prompted medical tourism, because if medical tourism were restricted, many of the users would continue to have access to health care; they would just pay more for it.[31] For similar reasons, this objection to the self-interest argument may be less forceful for certain subtypes of medical tourism such as cosmetic surgery.

B. COSMOPOLITAN THEORIES

Cosmopolitan theories share a commitment to ignoring geographic boundaries in the application of moral theory. As I have detailed elsewhere, they come in many

---

[31] Cohen, *supra* note 1, at 1546.

types—for example, Utilitarian, Prioritarian, and the Nussbaum/Sen Functioning/ Capabilities approach (which is in some senses Sufficientarian)—each of which would have somewhat different implications for medical tourism. To simplify: because the destination-country poor whose health care access is diminished by medical tourism are generally worse off than the home country patients who are seeking the care, each of these theories gives a prima facie reason to oppose medical tourism.

Although focusing on more Prioritarian Cosmopolitan approaches, Charles Beitz has eloquently captured the more general attraction of Cosmopolitan theories as twofold: (1) the desire to avoid moral arbitrariness in the distribution of primary goods—that is, "we should not view national boundaries as having fundamental moral significance"[32]—and (2) that a limitation of redistribution to the domestic sphere is only justifiable on an account of nations as self-sufficient cooperative schemes, a position he views as untenable in today's world of international interdependence, where those regulating trade (World Trade Organization (WTO)) and capital (International Monetary Fund (IMF) and World Bank)) "impose[] burdens on poor and economically weak countries that they cannot practically avoid."[33]

Although Cosmopolitan theories seem a promising ground for urging restrictions or regulation of medical tourism, there are several related problems with relying on them:

What Cosmopolitan theories offer us is *not* a theory of when we are responsible for harms *stemming from medical tourism*, but when we ought to improve the lives of the badly off *simpliciter*. In one sense, causation matters: only if restricting medical tourism causes an improvement in welfare for the worst off, the raising of health capabilities, etc., are we required to take the action. In another sense, however, causation in the historical and responsibility senses is irrelevant because it is the mere fact of the destination-country's citizens' needs that imposes upon us the obligation to help them in whatever way we can, and not anything about medical tourism specifically. Thus, in one direction, the duties may persist even when medical tourism is eliminated or its harms are remedied because the source of the obligation is not anything we have done, but instead the destitute state of those abroad. In the other direction, once the theories' goals are met (for example, they reach the threshold level on health capability, to use one variant), we do not bear an obligation (at least under distributive justice principles) to prevent medical tourism or remedy its ill effects, even if medical tourism continues to produce significant health care deficits for the destination-country poor that would not occur if it were curbed. Moreover, it is possible that other forms of aid or assistance might "cancel out" whatever negative effects medical tourism has in terms of the global Cosmopolitan calculus.

Further, these approaches face a "self-inflicted wounds problem," which suggests that on these views it is not relevant to the scope of the home country's obligation that some of the factors (discussed above) that cause medical tourism to negatively

---

CHARLES R. BEITZ, POLITICAL THEORY AND INTERNATIONAL RELATIONS 151 (1979).
33 Charles R. Beitz, *Justice and International Relations*, 4 PHIL. & PUB. AFF. 360, 374 (1975).

impact health care access in the destination country are within the *destination country's government's control* (i.e., that the destination country is partially responsible). The qualification is that to the extent that we could induce the destination country to alter these facts about its self-governance, such influence would be one tool to meet our obligations under these theories. But to the extent we are unable to prompt these alterations, under the Cosmopolitan approach, our responsibility to improve the welfare and capabilities of the poor in the destination country attaches even for policies for which its own sovereign is actually responsible.

To some, these implications may seem problematic; from others, the reply will be, "It is just not *that* kind of theory." More troubling, though, may be a pragmatic corollary: if we need to rely on these theories to persuade public policy makers to take action on medical tourism, they threaten to prove too much. These approaches threaten to become "oppressive in the totality of the claim they make on the moral agent";[34] addressing the harms caused by medical tourism is a small drop in the bucket in terms of what these theories would call upon us to do to right the balance between developed and developing countries. For starters, they would further demand that we radically increase taxes for all strata in our nation to fund large-scale water purification, housing, and other interventions in LDCs. As Thomas Pogge has stressed, unless a theory of Global Justice is politically feasible, it is "destined to remain a philosopher's pipe dream."[35] It seems hard to believe that a principle as broad and demanding as the one espoused by Cosmopolitans of this sort would be compelling to U.S. policy makers.

In any event, to find common ground with both those who would reject Cosmopolitanism as a *philosophical* matter and those who would reject it as a *pragmatic* matter, it would be desirable to show a normative obligation to correct health care access diminution from medical tourism on less demanding theories as well.

C. STATIST THEORIES

Unlike Cosmopolitans, Statists reach the conclusion that the obligations of distributive justice apply only within the nation-state and not to citizens of other nations; their reasoning is that "[w]hat lets citizens make redistributive claims on each other is not so much the fact that they share a cooperative structure," but that societal rules establishing a sovereign state's basic structure are "coercively imposed."[36] Nagel clarifies that this is because for Rawls (and contra the Cosmopolitans), the "moral presumption against arbitrary inequalities is not a principle of universal application"; rather "[w]hat is objectionable is that we should be fellow participants in a *collective* enterprise of *coercively imposed* legal and political institutions that generates such arbitrary

---

[34] CHARLES FRIED, RIGHT AND WRONG 13 (1978).

[35] Thomas W. Pogge, *Human Rights and Global Health: A Research Program*, 36 METAPHILOSOPHY 182, 185 (2005).

[36] Mathias Risse, *What We Owe to the Global Poor*, 9 J. ETHICS 81, 99–100 (2005); *see also* JOHN RAWLS, THE LAW OF PEOPLES 116 (1999); Michael Blake, *Distributive Justice, State Coercion, and Autonomy*, 30 PHIL. & PUB. AFF. 257, 285–89 (2001).

inequalities."[37] It is the "complex fact" that in societal rules establishing a sovereign state's basic structure "we are both putative joint authors of the coercively imposed system, and subject to its norms, i.e., expected to accept their authority even when the collective decision diverges from our personal preferences—that creates the special presumption against arbitrary inequalities in our treatment by the system."[38]

Increasing globalization does not change the picture, say Nagel and Rawls, because "mere economic interaction does not trigger the heightened standards of socioeconomic justice."[39] Nor does the existence of international institutions such as the United Nations or WTO trigger those obligations, according to Nagel, because their edicts "are not collectively enacted or coercively imposed in the name of all the individuals whose lives they affect."[40] That is, "[n]o matter how substantive the links of trade, diplomacy, or international agreement, the institutions present at the international level do not engage in the same kinds of coercive practices against individual agents"; it is "[c]oercion, not cooperation, [that] is the sine qua non of distributive justice."[41]

The medical tourism policies of home countries—permitting out-of-pocket purchases, insurer-prompted medical tourism, or government-prompted medical tourism whereby the state creates the incentives to use medical tourism—are not being imposed *in the name of destination-country citizens*, nor are those citizens or their governments being forced to open themselves up to medical tourism, and thus cannot ground Statist obligations.[42]

Nevertheless, I believe there may exist in Statist theories at least two open avenues for grounding some limited obligations of home countries and international bodies to regulate medical tourism or mitigate its negative effects on health care access in destination countries.

The first avenue stems from Rawls' recognition of a duty (separate from those relating to distributive justice) to assist "burdened societies"—those whose "historical, social, and economic circumstances make their achieving a well-ordered regime, whether liberal or decent, difficult if not impossible"—to "manage their own affairs reasonably and rationally" in order to become "well-ordered societies."[43] These societies "lack the political and cultural traditions, the human capital and know-how, and, often, the material and technological resources needed to be well-ordered" but, with assistance, can over time come to "manage their own affairs reasonably and rationally and eventually to become members of the Society of well-ordered Peoples."[44]

Grounding medical tourism–related obligations in this kind of duty, although possible, faces several challenges and will generate only a much more limited kind of obligation. Many of the destination countries in question may not be burdened societies;

---

[37] Thomas Nagel, *The Problem of Global Justice*, 33 PHIL. & PUB. AFF. 113, 127, 128 (2005) (emphasis added).

[38] *Id.* at 128–29; *see* Blake, *supra* note 36, at 265, 289.

[39] Nagel, *supra* note 37, at 138; *see also* RAWLS, *supra* note 36, at 115–19 (making a similar point).

[40] Nagel, *supra* note 37, at 138.

[41] Blake, *supra* note 36, at 265, 289.

[42] *Cf.* Nagel, *supra* note 37, at 129 (making a similar point as to immigration).

[43] RAWLS, *supra* note 36, at 90, 111.

[44] *Id.* at 106, 111.

India, Mexico, Thailand and Singapore, for example, may have poor populations facing deficits in health care access, but they seem to meet Rawls's more minimal criteria for being well-ordered. Second, there are restrictions on the kind of aid envisioned by this duty. Rawls seems focused on institution building, and Mathias Risse describes the duty's targets as building things such as "stable property rights, rule of law, bureaucratic capacity, appropriate regulatory structures to curtail at least the worst forms of fraud, anti-competitive behavior, and graft, quality and independence of courts, but also cohesiveness of society, existence of trust and social cooperation, and thus overall quality of civil society."[45] Foreign aid by home countries to help the destination countries improve their ability to produce more medical providers, or policy aid in designing health care system regulations designed to control how much time doctors spend in the public or private system—both factors likely to contribute to diminutions in access—seem to fit nicely into this category and are well-supported by this approach. Regulation aimed at trying to prevent or make it more expensive for home-country patients to travel for medical tourism fits less well. That kind of regulation may also run afoul of Rawls's caution that "well-ordered societies giving assistance must not act paternalistically."[46] Finally, it is possible that medical tourism may actually help build institutions in the destination country, aiding the burdened state *while* diminishing health care access for the destination-country poor. For example, the rise in GDP and the need for corporate accountability to support a medical tourism industry attractive to Westerners might carry with it benefits to the destination country in terms of establishing the rule of law or property rights. If so, medical tourism might itself represent aid to burdened states even while it diminishes health care access to the destination country's poor.

Thus, the approach justifies only a much smaller subset of possible interventions regarding medical tourism, but does not rule out a duty of home-state action entirely.

A second avenue for grounding a Statist duty is Nagel's separate conception of humanitarian duties of aid. Nagel suggests that "there is some minimal concern we owe to fellow human beings threatened with starvation or severe malnutrition and early death from easily preventable diseases, as all these people in dire poverty are," such that "some form of humane assistance from the well-off to those in extremis is clearly called for quite apart from any demand of justice, if we are not simply ethical egoists."[47] Although he is self-admittedly vague, he thinks "the normative force of the most basic human rights against violence, enslavement, and coercion, and of the most basic humanitarian duties of rescue from immediate danger, depends only on our capacity to put ourselves in other people's shoes," and speaks of obligations to relieve others, whatever their nation, "from extreme threats and obstacles to [the freedom to pursue their own ends] if we can do so without serious sacrifice of our own ends."[48]

Can this approach ground duties relating to medical tourism? Fisher and Syed suggest that a duty of Western countries to expand access to drugs in LDCs can be grounded

---

[45] Risse, *supra* note 36, at 85.
[46] RAWLS, *supra* note 36, at 111.
[47] Nagel, *supra* note 37, at 118.
[48] *Id*. at 131; *see also* Blake, *supra* note 36, at 271.

in these humanitarian duties because there "is little question that millions of people are suffering and dying from contagious diseases in developing countries and that the residents of developed countries could alleviate that suffering with relative ease."[49]

A parallel argument, however, seems somewhat harder to make in the context of medical tourism interventions. For one thing, the effects of medical tourism seem more marginal. Of course, lack of access to care is as sure a killer as is famine or lack of needed pharmaceuticals, and over a longer time horizon its effects may be more significant. Still, we should be cautious when specifying the level of deprivation needed to trigger these humanitarian duties because if we decide a particular kind of deprivation is enough to trigger our duty to intervene here, we will bear a comparable duty to all citizens of that foreign country in comparable conditions. That is, if the health care deficits experienced *due to medical tourism* are enough to ground humanitarian duties regarding medical tourism, should we not also open our immigration doors to those suffering comparable deficits in their home countries? Too expansive a conception would raise the very pragmatic and political concerns about the scope of the demands placed upon us that we aimed to avoid by seeking a non-Cosmopolitan approach.

Moreover, to ask whether we "could alleviate that suffering with relative ease" or "without serious sacrifice of our own ends" raises difficulties paralleling those faced by Cosmopolitan theories: At least for medical tourism by those paying out-of-pocket and, to a lesser extent, for some forms of government-prompted medical tourism, trying to satisfy humanitarian duties to the global poor by curbing medical tourism is more likely to come at the expense of our own poor than in the pharmaceutical case. Thus, in the exceptional case, we may face trade-offs not only between satisfying our humanitarian duties to our own poor versus those to the poor abroad, but also between our distributive justice duties to our poor and our humanitarian duties to the destination-country poor. Neglecting our duties to our own poor patients would seem to count as "serious sacrifice of our own ends," suggesting the obligations may more clearly attach to some forms of medical tourism, including insurer-prompted medical tourism, where paying more for health insurance is less clearly such a sacrifice. Similarly, the humanitarian-duty approach might more easily justify curbing medical tourism for services such as cosmetic surgeries that are more penumbral to health. This restriction may also limit us to interventions that do not restrict access to health care via medical tourism for our citizens but instead aid the destination country in building capacity; even that is tricky, though, for dollars spent on foreign aid could always be reallocated to improving Medicaid coverage for America's poor, to give but one example.[50]

---

49 William W. Fisher & Talha Syed, *Global Justice in Health Care: Developing Drugs for the Developing World*, 40 U.C. DAVIS L. REV. 581, 648 (2007).

50 Is it relevant that the United States has not "cleaned its own house" and adopted universal health care for its citizens, which in part causes the medical tourism need? Here is a place where it seems plausible to me that the philosophical and policy discourse split—it may be that the United States *ought* to deal with medical tourism by cleaning its own house first, but if we concede (as I think we should) that this is not within the political feasibility set, then we are back in a philosophically second-best world where we must ask what steps the United States should take regarding medical tourism directly.

Finally, notice that, like the Cosmopolitan theories, the duty toward humanitarian aid is actually somewhat divorced from medical tourism in the causal sense—we have a duty to give humanitarian aid whether or not we caused the need. Thus if one found this aspect of Cosmopolitan theories undesirable as a ground for duties as to medical tourism, the same problem applies here.

Although, as expected, the Statist theories reject grounding duties as to medical tourism in the distributive justice obligations to those abroad, there may be some room for obligations grounded in duties to aid burdened states or provide humanitarian aid.

D. INTERMEDIATE THEORIES

A final set of theories seeks to position itself between the Statist and Cosmopolitan camps. I examine one such intermediate theory, put forth by Joshua Cohen and Charles Sabel, and applied to health care by Norman Daniels; elsewhere I have discussed in-depth a different theory proposed by Thomas Pogge,[51] and there are still other versions. I think these are the most fertile grounds for a Global Justice–based theory of obligations to regulate medical tourism because they generate a *kind* of theory more appropriate for the task: one that focuses on the harms and institutions stemming from particular existing practices rather than one that focuses on the relative holdings of particular individuals at the current moment and that counsels a more general real-location of primary goods. That said, these theories are not without problems.

The Cohen, Sabel, and Daniels approach suggests the Statists are too demanding in requiring coercion as the touchstone of distributive justice principles and also too all-or-nothing in the deployment of those principles. Instead these authors propose lesser duties of "inclusion" internationally, which fall short of full-blown distributive justice but are greater than the minimal humanitarian duties endorsed by Statists: the state should treat those outside of the coercive structure of the nation-state as individuals whose good "counts for something" (not nothing) even if it falls short of the full consideration a state would give its own citizens.[52]

Cohen and Sabel suggest these duties of inclusion may be triggered inter alia by the "coercion-lite" (my term) actions of international bodies such as the WTO; that is, "[e]ven when rule-making and applying bodies lack their own independent power to impose sanctions through coercion," they still shape conduct "by providing incentives and permitting the imposition of sanctions" and "withdrawing from them may be costly to members (if only because of the sometimes considerable loss of benefits)," such that "[i]n an attenuated but significant way, our wills—the wills of all subject to the rule making–authority—have been implicated, sufficiently such that rules of this type can only be imposed with a special justification."[53]

---

[51] Cohen, *supra* note 12, at 42–46.

[52] *See* Joshua Cohen & Charles Sabel, *Extra Rempublicam Nulla Justitia?*, 34 PHIL. & PUB. AFF. 147, 154–55 (2006); NORMAN DANIELS, JUST HEALTH 351 (2008).

[53] Cohen & Sabel, *supra* note 52, at 165.

They offer the example of the WTO, suggesting that "[o]pting out is not a real option" because no country in the developed or developing world could really survive without participation in the WTO, and that "there is a direct rule-making relationship between the global bodies and the citizens of different states."[54] They argue that for the WTO, duties of inclusion would mean that the rulemakers are "obligated to give some weight to the reasonable concern of the rule takers (who are themselves assumed to have responsibility to show concern for the interests of their own citizens)."[55]

The authors also suggest consequential rulemaking by international bodies "with distinct responsibilities," such as the International Labor Organization (ILO), might require those bodies to adopt duties of inclusion, because the ILO has taken on the responsibility for formulating labor standards, the ILO claims that its rulemakings have significant consequences, and the ILO believes that, if it were to disappear, no comparable entity would emerge.[56]

Daniels adds that certain kinds of international independencies may also give rise to duties of inclusion, giving the example of medical migration ("brain drain"). He argues that the IMF's historical requirement that countries such as Cameroon make severe cutbacks in their publicly funded health care systems in order to reduce deficits that result in poorer working conditions for medical personnel (a "push" factor), combined with the attempt by the United Kingdom and other OECD countries to recruit medical personnel from developing countries (a "pull" factor), gives rise to a duty on the part of Western countries and the IMF to address the ill effects of this migration.[57] Among the methods to satisfy that obligation, he urges altering "the terms of employment in receiving countries of health workers from vulnerable countries," compensating for "the lost training costs of these workers," "prohibit[ing] recruitment from vulnerable countries," and "giv[ing] aid to contributing countries in order to reduce the push factor."[58]

Can this approach be readily applied to medical tourism? One might be tempted to draw three analogies, but each of them faces problems.

First, one might suggest that analogously to the ILO accreditors such as the Joint Commission International (JCI) bear some duties to build into their accreditation process consideration of the effects of medical tourism to a particular facility on health care access for destination-country poor. That is, JCI is like the ILO in that it has taken on responsibility for formulating standards, it claims its rules have significant consequences (determining who gets accredited, causing facilities to alter their procedures), and perhaps if it disappeared, no other institution would take its place.[59]

On reflection, though, the analogy is problematic. The JCI's role is to accredit foreign hospitals, specifically to examine their procedures and determine whether those

---

[54] *Id.* at 168.

[55] *Id.* at 172.

[56] *Id.* at 170–71.

[57] *See* DANIELS, *supra* note 52, at 337–39.

[58] *Id.*

[59] This last point of comparison seems more dubious.

procedures meet relevant standards of practice.[60] Although this might be loosely thought of as a kind of "rulemaking," the JCI does not purport to regulate the medical tourism market, let alone to weigh the advantages or disadvantages of a particular country or particular hospital opening itself up to medical tourism. The same points apply even more strongly to intermediaries who are largely for-profit entities.

Second, we might analogize to the medical migration example and say that, for patients paying out-of-pocket, the lack of affordable health insurance in the U.S. system and its failure to prevent insurer-prompted medical tourism drive medical tourism, much like the United Kingdom's recruitment of foreign nurses drives migration. In medical tourism, by patients paying out-of-pocket, we do not have the U.S. government or international bodies directly creating push and pull factors. True, the U.S. government has not taken steps to *prevent* travel to India for medical procedures. But if merely not acting and following a background norm of permitting travel to consume goods and services abroad is sufficient under Daniels's intermediate theory, the theory loses much of its attraction as a middle ground between the Cosmopolitan and Statist poles because so much of the day-to-day workings of international trade will trigger obligations under the theory.

That said, it seems that government-sponsored medical tourism initiatives might create home-country obligations to destination countries, at least insofar as tourism is incentivized and not merely covered in a way that is cost-neutral from the point of view of the patient. Medical tourism in universal health care countries prompted by long wait times might also better fit the analogy—the failure to produce sufficient medical practitioners in the patient's home country might prompt attempts either to recruit foreign providers (brain drain) *or* to incentivize medical tourism. However, it is unclear where the stopping point is from that analogy to the (problematic) conclusion the the fundamental organization of one's domestic health care system might trigger duties of inclusion *internationally* based on home-country patients' reactions to it.[61]

Third, one might focus on the obligations some destination countries have undertaken to open up their health care sectors to medical tourism under the General Agreement on Trade in Services[62] (GATS) and argue that it plays a "coercion-lite" role analogous to the obligations of WTO membership discussed by these authors.[63] I have discussed in-depth elsewhere whether the analogy holds as an empirical and normative matter, and found it faces several difficulties.[64]

---

[60] See Cohen, *supra* note 1, at 1485.

[61] Otherwise the underlying principle would be something like "for any domestic policy choice our country makes, be it health, education, transportation, etc., we are responsible for remediating any effects that follow, whether the conduit is changes in trade, consumption, or travel by our populace." If this is the principle that underlies the intermediate approach, it ceases to be a distinctive middle ground between the Cosmopolitan and Statist theories that can focus on particular institutional arrangements, coercion, and interdependency. Further, such a broad principle reintroduces the pragmatic policy-oriented worry I discussed above that the intermediate approach advantageously seemed poised to avoid.

[62] General Agreement on Trade in Services, Apr. 15, 1994, 33 I.L.M. 1167 (1994) [hereinafter GATS].

[63] See Patricia J. Arnold & Terrie C. Reeves, *International Trade and Health Policy: Implications of the GATS for US Healthcare Reform*, 63 J. BUS. ETHICS REFORM 313, 315 (2006); Cohen, *supra* note 1, at 1521 n.213.

[64] Cohen, *supra* note 12, at 37–40.

Even if the theory can ground a prima facie case that home countries face duties of inclusion relating to medical tourism's effect on the destination country poor, it still faces the self-inflicted wounds problems. Several of the triggering conditions for medical tourism's negative effects on health care access in the destination country—the supply of health care professionals, whether the system is regulated in such a way that requires professionals to spend time in both the public and private systems—are, as I stressed above, also at least partially within the control of the destination-country governments.

Does this blunt the claim that home-country governments or international bodies bear responsibility for deficits associated with medical tourism? Yes and no. As Daniels has argued, even countries with similar domestic policies experience significant differences in population health, such that "[e]ven if primary responsibility for population health rests with each state, this does not mean that the state has [the] sole responsibility."[65] In order to clarify home countries' obligations, we ought to try to factor out the elements of destination countries' population health deficits caused by medical tourism that are a result of domestic policy decisions[66] and then apply the Cohen, Sable, and Daniels duties of inclusion only to the remaining deficits that meet the theories' requirements.

This ability to apportion responsibility between the destination and home countries seems like a major theoretical advantage of this approach as against the prior ones discussed. Of course, although conceptually simple to state, actually doing such apportioning would be extremely difficult in practice, and the absolute best we can practicably hope for is a rough approximation. Thus, only in instances of medical tourism where a plausible case of "coercion-lite" or other pressure can be said to give rise to a duty of inclusion will such duties attach, and only then as to the proportion of the deficits caused by medical tourism to health care access by the destination-country poor that is outside the control of the destination country.

Even if one of these routes validly triggers a duty of inclusion on some home countries or international bodies for some sets of medical tourism, there is the further question of what that duty entails. The authors are self-admittedly somewhat vague about the contours of these kinds of duties, telling us that it is not a duty of "equal concern" or redistributive justice on the one hand, but that it requires more than mere humanitarian duties on the other, and that it requires treating individuals abroad as individuals whose good "counts for something" (not nothing) while making decisions that will impact their life.[67]

That leaves a fair amount of room to maneuver. One could imagine the duties mandating something such as "notice and comment rulemaking" in administrative law—which would merely require acknowledging that these interests were considered, but found to be outweighed—to something approaching a weighting formula in which the welfare of those abroad is counted as .8 while those in the nation state are counted as 1 (to use purely fictional discounting factors).

---

[65] DANIELS, *supra* note 52, at 345.

[66] *See id.* at 341–45.

[67] Cohen & Sabel, *supra* note 52, at 154–55; *see also* DANIELS, *supra* note 52, at 351 (making a similar point in the health context).

In discussing the brain drain example, Daniels seems to suggest duties of inclusion should have significant bite, arguing that they might prohibit recruitment from vulnerable countries, force recruiting countries to restrict the terms they offer foreign health workers, compensate for losses suffered when health care workers are lost, or give aid to help reduce push factors.[68] By analogy, in the context of medical tourism, such duties could perhaps require the United States to prevent its citizens from traveling abroad; channel its patients to medical tourism facilities or countries with programs to ameliorate the health care deficits that result; tax medical tourists, intermediaries, or insurers; and use that revenue as aid aimed at amelioration, or provide more general aid to build institutional health care capacity in the destination country, or more appropriately, regulate its health care sector.

Conclusion

A number of authors in both the popular and academic literature have expressed concern about the effects of medical tourism on access to health care for the poor of the destination country and have claimed that this is a normative problem calling for regulatory intervention. In this chapter, I have broken down this claim into its empirical and normative components and put pressure on both. On the empirical side, I have noted the current absence of evidence for diminutions in health care access by the destination-country poor due to medical tourism, and tried to specify triggering conditions that could be further studied by developmental economists under which this diminution would be most likely. Assuming arguendo that such negative effects occur, I then examined the normative question of destination-country governments and international bodies' obligations as to medical tourism having such effect. I canvassed Cosmopolitan, Statist, and Intermediate theories and suggested ways in which application of these theories to medical tourism highlights gaps and indeterminacies as well as reasons some of these theories may not be good fits for this kind of applied ethics inquiry, and built on existing discussions of pharmaceutical pricing and medical migration. I have tried to map divergences and convergences between these theories, and tentatively conclude that the claim for Global Justice obligations stemming from medical tourism is strongest (but not without problems) for insurer- and government-prompted medical tourism and for tourism for inessential services, such as cosmetic surgeries, while it is quite weak for medical tourism by those paying out-of-pocket for essential services. Elsewhere, I have outlined the types of regulatory policy levers available to developed countries and international bodies to seek to remedy deficits in destination-country health care access due to medical tourism.

Although my focus has been on medical tourism, as I suggested above, I think the discussion here has some important implications for analysis of other manifestations of the globalization of health care, and indeed, perhaps, for globalization more generally.

---

[68] DANIELS, *supra* note 52, at 353–54.

FOR SERVICES ILLEGAL OR UNAPPROVED IN

THE PATIENT'S HOME COUNTRY

7

THE PROPORTIONALITY PROBLEM IN CROSS-BORDER

REPRODUCTIVE CARE

Richard F. Storrow[*]

Introduction

The globalization of commerce and the international demand for a wider range of options in medical care have opened up markets for medical tourism in a multiplicity of countries. Governments and the private sector have responded eagerly to the opportunity to control a market share of this burgeoning area.[1] Current research indicates that patients travel abroad for treatment for many different reasons including the high cost of health care, wait times, access to services that might not be available locally, and, by some accounts, the ability to combine medical treatment with travel.[2] But much is still unknown about the effect of medical tourism on sending and destination countries, doctors and patients, and local and global economies. In response to this situation, researchers are delineating areas that warrant further inquiry.[3] One of these is the role that human rights, and the courts that enforce them, might play in addressing concerns arising from the increase in medical tourism. Cross-border reproductive care

[*] Professor of Law, City University of New York School of Law. I thank Mindy Mitchell for her excellent research assistance.
[1] Amanda Shaw & Anne-Line Crochet, *The Path of Asia*, MED. TOURISM, Feb.–Mar. 2011, at 8.
[2] Jason Behrmann & Elise Smith, *Top 7 Issues in Medical Tourism: Challenges, Knowledge Gaps, and Future Directions for Research and Policy Development*, 2 GLOBAL J. OF HEALTH SCI. 80, 81 (2010). This is not an exhaustive list. A recent survey of the literature specifies at least ten different motivations behind cross-border reproductive travel in particular. Zeynep B. Gürtin & Marcia C. Inhorn, *Travelling for Conception and the Global Assisted Reproduction Market*, 23 REPROD. BIOMED. ONLINE 535, 535 (2011).
[3] Behrmann & Smith, *supra* note 2, at at 81–85; Marcia C. Inhorn & Zeynep B. Gürtin, *Cross-Border Reproductive Care: A Future Research Agenda*, 23 REPROD. BIOMED. ONLINE 665, 668–69 (2011).

(CBRC) in particular, especially when it is triggered by restrictive reproductive laws, generates anxiety about whether states are adequately respecting private and family life, a right enshrined in the European Convention on Human Rights. Because the European Court of Human Rights looked favorably upon CBRC in its recent decision upholding Austrian restrictions on access to assisted reproduction, it is to be expected that CBRC will play a role in how governments in the future choose to shape their laws on assisted reproduction.

To be sure, CBRC bears many similarities to medical tourism for other purposes. Like many medical travelers, CBRC patients often seek more affordable infertility care than they can acquire at home. They, at times, travel to find medical care and avenues of delivery they perceive to be superior to what they can acquire in their country of residence.[4] Both medical tourism and CBRC trigger some common ethical concerns. For example, there is concern about the health of patients who suffer the physical and emotional strain of traveling for medical treatment or who may be subjected to inferior care or a substandard malpractice regime at the destination. There is, too, the potential for both medical tourism and CBRC to have a negative impact on the equitable delivery of health care in destination countries. Local doctors may seek to tap into a more lucrative market brought into the country by foreign patients and move from rural to urban areas or from public to private practice.[5] Finally, there is concern that medical tourism will release pressure that would otherwise fuel calls for structural change in the health care system at home.[6]

But despite the similarities between CBRC and other forms of medical travel, there are many salient differences. The first of these relates to terminology. Although there is very little controversy about the term "medical tourism" (it has in fact become the title of a magazine),[7] a vigorous debate has arisen around the proper term for CBRC. The concern about the term "tourism" is that it conjures visions of infertility patients on holiday,[8] and patients report feeling trivialized and scorned by this usage.[9] Physician Roberto Matorras, past president of the Spanish Fertility Society and director of

---

[4] LORRAINE CULLEY ET AL., TRANSNATIONAL REPRODUCTION: AN EXPLORATORY STUDY OF UK RESIDENTS WHO TRAVEL ABROAD FOR FERTILITY TREATMENT 10–12 (2011), *available at* http://www.transrep.co.uk/newsletters/TransrepReportJune2011.pdf.

[5] Leigh Turner, *"Medical Tourism" and the Global Marketplace in Health Services: U.S. Patients, International Hospitals, and the Search for Affordable Health Care*, 40 INT'L J. HEALTH SERVS. 443, 463 (2010); Françoise Merlet & Béatrice Sénémaud, *Prise en charge du don d'ovocytes: réglementation du don, la face cachée du tourisme procréatif* [Egg Donation: The Regulation of Donation and the Hidden Face of Procreative Tourism], 38 GYNÉCOLOGIE OBSTÉTRIQUE & FERTILITÉ 36 (2010); Elise Smith et al., *Reproductive Tourism in Argentina: Clinic Accreditation and Its Implications for Consumers, Health Professionals and Policy Makers*, 10 DEVELOPING WORLD BIOETHICS 59, 60, 65 (2010).

[6] Richard F. Storrow, *The Pluralism Problem in Cross-Border Reproductive Care*, 25 HUM. REPROD., 2939, 2941 (2010).

[7] *See* MEDICAL TOURISM MAGAZINE (Med. Tourism Ass'n), *available at* http://www.medicaltourismmag.com.

[8] Françoise Shenfield et al., *Cross Border Reproductive Care in Six European Countries*, 25 HUM. REPROD. 1361, 1362 (2010).

[9] Roberto Matorras, *Reproductive Exile versus Reproductive Tourism*, 20 HUM. REPROD. 3571 (2005).

Cruces Hospital's Reproductive Medicine Unit, has suggested "reproductive exile" as a term that more adequately captures the patient's perspective of, like a dissident or refugee, being forced by her country's political and social climate to seek medical assistance elsewhere.[10] This description of the patient's experience is documented in the ethnographic work of anthropologist Marcia Inhorn and others.[11] However, concluding that terms such as "tourism" and "exile" are too polarizing, ethicist Guido Pennings has suggested the more neutral "cross-border reproductive care,"[12] a term that is taking hold in the scientific literature.[13]

Second, the many procedures known collectively as "assisted reproduction" have been the subject of legal regulation, most prominently in Europe and Australia, since shortly after the first IVF child was born in 1978.[14] The Warnock Report, containing the findings of a British committee convened in 1982 to examine the social, ethical, and legal ramifications of assisted reproduction, remarked that surrogacy and research on human embryos in particular "arouse the greatest public anxiety."[15] The Report was prescient in remarking that "[d]ifferent countries are at different stages in the development both of services and of a policy response. They have different cultural, moral and legal traditions, influencing the way in which a problem is tackled and the ways in which it might be resolved."[16] Public anxiety, coupled with varying approaches to problem-solving, have given rise to a dizzying patchwork of differing laws in Europe, some enacted as early as 1984.[17]

One final difference between medical tourism and CBRC relates to motivations. Due to the restrictions on assisted reproduction that exist in many countries, CBRC patients often travel not to find attractive prices or a better standard of care but to find a jurisdiction where they can receive care that is legal. Many CBRC patients, then, attempting to escape exclusionary legal regimes at home, simply do not fit the common conception of the medical tourist as price-conscious or quality-conscious.[18] Furthermore, because CBRC travelers so often migrate to evade local laws, ethical concerns in connection with that evasion are implicated. These concerns are prominent within the European Union,

---

[10] *Id.*; interview with Roberto Matorras in Baracaldo, Spain (Nov. 11, 2010).

[11] Marcia C. Inhorn & Pasquale Patrizio, *Rethinking Reproductive "Tourism" as Reproductive "Exile,"* 92 FERTILITY & STERILITY 904, 905 (2009).

[12] Guido Pennings, *Reply to Reproductive Exile versus Reproductive Tourism,* 20 HUM. REPROD. 3571 (2005).

[13] *See, e.g., Symposium: Cross-Border Reproductive Care,* 23 REPROD. BIOMED. ONLINE 535, 535–676 (2011).

[14] Howard W. Jones et al., *Surveillance 2010,* INTERNATIONAL FEDERATION OF FERTILITY SOCIETIES (2011), http://www.iffs-reproduction.org/documents/IFFS_Surveillance_2010.pdf, at 10. The *Surveillance* reports that in approximately 40 percent of the surveyed countries, assisted reproduction is regulated by legislation. *Id.*

[15] U.K., DEP'T OF HEALTH & SOC. SEC., REPORT OF THE COMMITTEE OF INQUIRY INTO HUMAN FERTILISATION AND EMBRYOLOGY (1984).

[16] *Id.* at 6.

[17] Richard F. Storrow, *Religion, Feminism and Abortion: The Regulation of Assisted Reproduction in Two Catholic Countries,* 43 RUTGERS L.J. 725, 733 (2011).

[18] This is not to suggest that other classes of medical tourists never travel to evade the law. *See* I. Glenn Cohen, *Circumvention Tourism,* 97 CORNELL L. REV. 1309, 1312–13, 1319–27 (2012) (describing cases of "circumvention medical tourism").

where Member States are not permitted to impede the movement of goods and services across borders and thus cannot outlaw cross-border reproductive travel to other Member States. In countries without such limits, CBRC may itself be against the law,[19] raising important questions about the limits of legal extraterritoriality.[20]

One way of responding to CBRC, as does Kimberly Mutcherson in her contribution to this volume, is to focus on destination countries and the potential they have to foster pluralism in family formation.[21] This chapter's emphasis is on the laws of sending countries and whether the legal doctrine of proportionality, as employed in the jurisprudence of the European Court of Human Rights, might be used to dismantle restrictive laws that force patients to resort to CBRC. The analysis unfolds in three parts. Section I takes a closer look at how the law both triggers and responds to CBRC. Section II discusses how the legal doctrine of proportionality makes democracy responsive to human rights, and Section III introduces the role of the European Court of Human Rights in this project. Section IV examines the jurisprudence of the Court in connection with assisted reproduction. Finally, Section V predicts whether proportionality is a doctrine we can expect to be employed in human-rights jurisprudence to curb restrictions on assisted reproduction and the CBRC that is their result.

I. Cross-border Reproductive Care and the Law

Although not all CBRC is the result of legal restrictions, a significant amount of CBRC is either caused by or otherwise fraught with legal hazards for infertility patients. Legal regulation of assisted reproduction focuses primarily on what procedures are permitted and who may access them. Subsidiary laws may define the parentage that attaches to the use of particular procedures and the portion of their cost that will be absorbed by public health insurance. These laws are playing an increasingly important role in motivating those in need of reproductive assistance to travel to other more permissive countries to acquire treatment. These laws are also inspiring physicians to travel abroad to provide services outlawed at home and to refer patients to clinics in more permissive countries. Recent empirical work confirms that law is the primary impetus behind cross-border reproductive travel within Europe.[22]

The law and CBRC influence each other in three distinct ways. The most obvious of these is the way in which legal restrictions on assisted reproductive procedures or

---

[19] *See infra* notes 39–40 and accompanying text.

[20] Richard F. Storrow, *Assisted Reproduction on Treacherous Terrain: The Legal Hazards of Cross-Border Reproductive Care*, 23 REPROD. BIOMED. ONLINE 538, 541 (2011).

[21] Kimberly M. Mutcherson, *Open Fertility Borders: Defending Access to Cross Border Fertility Care in the United States*, Chapter 8 of this book.

[22] Shenfield, *supra* note 8, at 1362; Guido Pennings, *Cross-Border Reproductive Care in Belgium*, 24 HUM. REPROD. 3108, 3111 (2009). This recent data helps confirm earlier speculation that law was the primary driving force behind reproductive tourism from European countries. *See, e.g.,* Jean Cohen, *Procreative Tourism and Reproductive Freedom*, 13 REPROD. BIOMED. ONLINE 145, 145–46 (2006).

limitations on access to them trigger travel abroad for assisted reproductive services. Numerous examples of such restrictions exist throughout the world: Germany's ban on IVF with egg donation;[23] Italy's, Turkey's, and most Muslim countries' bans on any use of third-party gametes;[24] France's exclusion of nonheterosexual couples from infertility treatment;[25] Australia's ban on nonmedical sex selection;[26] the ban on surrogacy in many countries,[27] and the Netherlands' and the United Kingdom's bans on anonymous gamete donation.[28] Some countries also have laws prohibiting doctors from making referrals to clinics in countries where the procedures sought are legal[29] or even mentioning prohibited techniques to patients.[30]

Sometimes the law triggers reproductive tourism not because it is restrictive but because it is permissive. Although many destinations for reproductive tourism have no law on assisted reproduction, some states may attempt to enact laws that will encourage the development of a lucrative reproductive tourism industry. India, for example, having already developed a cross-border surrogacy industry that flourishes in a legal vacuum, now is considering legislation that would officially legalize commercial surrogacy by removing certain practical obstacles that have impeded some foreign patients from realizing through surrogacy in India their dream of becoming parents. The current bill contains language that would require potential parents to prove that surrogacy is permitted in their home country and that the child to be born will be permitted entry "as a biological child" of the parents, even if donor eggs and sperm were employed in the surrogacy arrangement.[31]

The second manner in which the law influences CBRC is when it prohibits crossing borders to obtain certain procedures illegal at home. This type of law has been recently enacted in Turkey and New South Wales and also exists in Malaysia, Queensland, and

---

[23] Sven Bergman, *Reproductive Agency and Projects: Germans Searching for Egg Donation in Spain and the Czech Republic*, 23 REPROD. BIOMED. ONLINE 600, 601 (2011).

[24] Giulia Zanini, *Abandoned by the State, Betrayed by the Church: Italian Experiences of Cross-Border Reproductive Care*, 23 REPROD. BIOMED. ONLINE 565, 567 (2011); Zeynep B. Gürtin, *Banning Reproductive Travel: Turkey's ART Legislation and Third-Party Assisted Reproduction*, 23 REPROD. BIOMED. ONLINE 555, 557 (2011); Marcia C. Inhorn, *Diasporic Dreaming: Return Reproductive Tourism to the Middle East*, 23 REPROD. BIOMED. ONLINE 582, 588 (2011).

[25] Petra De Sutter, *Considerations for Clinics and Practitioners Treating Foreign Patients with Assisted Reproductive Technology: Lessons from Experiences at Ghent University Hospital, Belgium*, 23 REPROD. BIOMED. ONLINE 652, 654 (2011).

[26] Andrea M. Whittaker, *Reproductive Opportunists in the New Global Sex Trade: PGD and Non-Medical Sex Selection*, 23 REPROD. BIOMED. ONLINE 609, 613 (2011).

[27] Amrita Pande, *Transnational Commercial Surrogacy in India: Gifts for Global Sisters?*, 23 REPROD. BIOMED. ONLINE 618, 619 (2011).

[28] De Sutter, *supra* note 25, at 654; Nicky Hudson & Lorraine Culley, *Assisted Reproductive Travel: UK Patient Trajectories*, 23 REPROD. BIOMED. ONLINE 573, 575 (2011).

[29] Wannes Van Hoof & Guido Pennings, *Extraterritoriality for Cross-border Reproductive Care: Should States Act against Citizens Travelling Abroad for Illegal Infertility Treatment?*, 23 REPROD. BIOMED. ONLINE 546, 552 (2011).

[30] B. Urman & K. Yakin, *New Turkish Legislation on Assisted Reproductive Techniques and Centres: A Step in the Right Direction?*, 21 REPROD. BIOMED. ONLINE 729, 730 (2010).

[31] The Assisted Reproductive Technologies (Regulation) Bill-2010 § 34(19), http://www.icmr.nic.in/guide/ART%20REGULATION%20Draft%20Bill1.pdf.

the Australian Capital Territory. Turkey has long banned all third-party assisted reproduction but now explicitly prohibits travelling abroad to procure donor gametes.[32]
Malaysia and the three Australian jurisdictions prohibit international commercial
surrogacy.[33]

CBRC's primary influence on the law is in the area of international commercial surrogacy. When parents who have travelled for surrogacy return home with their offspring to
a country that bans surrogacy, the children may be refused legal recognition. This form of
legal interference with the ultimate goal of reproductive tourism—to be legally recognized
as a family—is becoming increasingly common. For example, citizens of several European
and Asian countries, including the United Kingdom, France, Germany, Spain, Belgium,
and Japan have been refused travel documents for their children by their consular officials
abroad upon suspicion that they had engaged in international commercial surrogacy. If
they are able to return home, parents have sometimes encountered official refusal to recognize the parent-child relationships or to grant citizenship to the children.[34]

The most visible case of this kind is the recent case of the Mennesson family.
Surrogacy has been banned in France since 1991.[35] When couples travel abroad to engage
a surrogate and return home with a child, the birth certificates obtained abroad are
considered falsified and are not recognized by the French government. Only the biological connection between the male partner and the child is recognized.[36] In the case
of the Mennessons, consular officials in Los Angeles, suspicious that the couple had
employed a gestational surrogate in the United States in contravention of French law,
refused to issue a passport or a visa for their two infants.[37] After the children travelled
on U.S. passports back to France with their parents, French prosecutors charged the
couple with fraud and attempted to expunge their registration of parentage, thereby
depriving the children of French citizenship. With respect to the criminal charges, a
judge determined that France had no extraterritorial jurisdiction in the case, because
commercial surrogacy is legal in the United States. On the citizenship and parentage questions, although the court recognized the Mennessons' parentage, it refused
to grant the girls French citizenship that would normally flow by descent from their
French-citizen parents. Adoption is not a solution, because under French law, those
who have resorted to international surrogacy are not allowed to adopt because they
have attempted to circumvent legal adoption procedures.[38] The public minister alluded

---

[32] Urman & Yakin, *supra* note 30, at 730.

[33] Dennis Chong, *Police Probe Surrogacy Dad*, THE STANDARD, Dec. 2, 2010, *available at* http://www.the-
standard.com.hk/news_detail.asp?pp_cat=30&art_id=105592&sid=30489519&con_type=1;   Jenni
Millbank, *The New Surrogacy Parentage Laws in Australia: Cautious Regulation or "25 Brick Walls"?*, 35
MELBOURNE U. L. REV. 165, 185–86 (2011).

[34] Storrow, *supra* note 20, at 540.

[35] J. Bo, *La législation sera débattue au Parlement français en 2009*, LE MONDE, Aug. 5, 2008, at 3.

[36] *Id.*

[37] SYLVIE & DOMINIQUE MENNESSON, INTERDITS D'ENFANTS: LE TÉMOIGNAGE UNIQUE DE PARENTS
AYANT RECOURS À UNE MÈRE PORTEUSE 90, 86–92, 109 (2008).

[38] Myriam Hunter-Henin, *Surrogacy: Is There Room for a New Liberty between the French Prohibitive Position
and the English Ambivalence?*, *in* LAW AND BIOETHICS 329, 336–37 (Michael Freeman ed. 2008).

to being favorably disposed to the petition,[39] But finally, after five court decisions in the course of ten years, the Cour de Cassation ruled that the girls were not French citizens.[40] An editorial in *Le Monde* cried, "How do you justify depriving these children, now strangers in their parents' country, of all the rights connected with citizenship, based solely on the way they were conceived and when there is no dispute over their parentage? What are they guilty of, besides their birth, to merit such sanctions?"[41]

The Mennessons now plan to take their case to the European Court of Human Rights where they may rely on cases forbidding disparate treatment of nonmarital children.

II. Proportionality and Democracy

Any country committed to the ideal of democracy must establish the extent to which it will permit restrictions on an individual's freedom to act according to his or her system of values. Ideally, a democracy will strive to acknowledge and accommodate competing views of the common good through an authentically participatory process.[42] This rarefied vision of democracy can be difficult to implement, no more so than in plural societies grappling with highly volatile and polarizing issues. Such issues evoke deeply held and diametrically opposed moral reactions rendering dispassionate dialogue leading to mutual respect, tolerance, and consensus unlikely. As legal theorist Ralph Beddard sees it, "the difficulties of balancing the wishes of the individual and those of the community as a whole are not to be underestimated and may seem to encapsulate the major decision-making complexity of human rights law."[43]

Although it is extolled in international human rights documents, democracy is not always fertile ground for human rights.[44] Majoritarian regimes have a notorious tendency to violate human rights;[45] conversely, human rights may exist where there is no democracy.[46] There is, in short, no self-evident connection between democracy and human rights. Nonetheless, international bodies recognize that the advancement of human rights is best achieved within "effective," "workable," "well-functioning"

---

[39] Najat Vallaud Belkacem, *Gestation pour autrui: une question de responsabilité morale*, LE MONDE.FR, Apr. 7, 2011, *available at* http://www.lemonde.fr/idees/article/2011/04/07/gestation-pour-autrui-une-qu estion-de-responsabilite-morale_1504228_3232.html ("le ministère public avait lui-même fini par se déclarer favorable à cette reconnaissance au nom de l'intérêt de l'enfant et du droit à une vie familiale normale").

[40] Cour de cassation, 1e civ, arrêt n° 370 du 6 avril 2011 (10-19.053), *available at* http://www.courdecassa-tion.fr/jurisprudence_2/premiere_chambre_civil_568.

[41] Belkacem, *supra* note 39.

[42] Joshua Cohen, *Reflections on Habermas on Democracy*, 12 RATIO JURIS 385, 391 (1999).

[43] RALPH BEDDARD, HUMAN RIGHTS AND EUROPE 99 (3d ed.1993).

[44] Richard Burchill, *The Role of Democracy in the Protection of Human Rights: Lessons from the European and Inter-American Human Rights Systems*, *in* HUMAN RIGHTS AND DIVERSITY: AREA STUDIES REVISITED 137, 137 (David P. Forsythe & Patrice C. McMahon eds. 2003).

[45] *See* STEPHEN BREYER, MAKING OUR DEMOCRACY WORK: A JUDGE'S VIEW 5 (2010) (referring to the mistreatment of minorities by democratically elected governments).

[46] *Id.*

democracies.[47] These tags translate roughly as democracies with effective systems of constitutional judicial review that protect human rights.[48] It is thus recognized that courts have advantages over other branches of government in the protection of human rights. They are better positioned, relatively speaking, given that "they are *not* answerable to an electorate."[49] Without this outside pressure, their decisions are able to "reflect and safeguard the deeper and more enduring values of a liberal democracy" that are often overlooked by government.[50] An "effective" system of constitutional review, then, is one where there is compliance with judicial decisions assessing whether a governmental measure comports with constitutionally guaranteed rights.[51] By contrast, a government that does not respect certain fundamental rights is not a "genuine" democracy.[52]

In mediating the relationship between the citizen and the state, one tool courts use to evaluate the legitimacy of governmental action is the standard of proportionality. This standard requires that there be a reasonable relationship between the legitimate objective a governmental measure seeks to achieve and the means it employs to achieve that objective.[53] The standard thus operates as a judicial brake on legislative and executive power. Although some believe the content of the standard is insufficiently clear,[54] there is general agreement that proportionality in general requires governmental action to meet a standard of reasonableness. In assessing a statute's proportionality, courts are interested in knowing whether (1) the statute interferes with a protected interest; (2) the statute furthers a compelling interest; and (3) there are less restrictive means by which to accomplish the statute's aims.[55] Although the proportionality standard is not easy to apply, it figures prominently in the constitutional law of many

---

[47] Convention for the Protection of Human Rights and Fundamental Freedoms, pmbl., Nov. 4, 1950, E.T.S. 5; *see also* BREYER, *supra* note 45, at 5.

[48] Paul Mahoney, *Marvellous Richness of Diversity or Invidious Cultural Relativism?*, 19 HUM. RTS L.J. 1, 3 (1998).

[49] Lord Brown of Eaton-Under-Heywood, *The Unaccountability of Judges: Surely Their Strength and Not Their Weakness, in* EFFECTIVE JUDICIAL REVIEW: A CORNERSTONE OF GOOD GOVERNANCE 208, 210 (Christopher Forsyth et al. eds. 2010).

[50] *Id.*

[51] *See* Alec Stone Sweet, *Constitutionalism, Legal Pluralism, and International Regimes*, IND. J. GLOBAL LEGAL STUD. 621, 642 (2009) (citing by way of example, the European Court of Human Rights); Alec Stone Sweet & Jud Mathews, *Proportionality Balancing and Global Constitutionalism*, 47 COLUM. J. TRANSNAT'L L. 72, 91 (2008).

[52] VÍCTOR FERRERES COMELLA, CONSTITUTIONAL COURTS AND DEMOCRATIC VALUES: A EUROPEAN PERSPECTIVE 88 (2009). Burchill refers to such regimes as "illiberal." Burchill, *supra* note 44, at 137, 150.

[53] RICHARD CLAYTON & HUGH TOMLINSON, THE LAW OF HUMAN RIGHTS, 278 (2000); Arturas Panomariovas & Egidijus Losis, *Proportionality: From the Concept to the Procedure*, 2 JURISPRUDENCE 257, 263 (2010). If the government's objective is illegitimate, the measure would fail the test of constitutionality in the first instance without the necessity of evaluating its proportionality. Mahoney, *supra* note 48, at 4.

[54] Mark Elliott, *Proportionality and Deference: The Importance of a Structured Approach, in* EFFECTIVE JUDICIAL REVIEW, *supra* note 49, at 264, 265.

[55] BREYER, *supra* note 45, at 167.

countries,[56] and currently constitutes, in the view of some commentators, "the defining doctrinal core of a global, rights-based constitutionalism."[57]

III. The European Court of Human Rights and the Margin of Appreciation

The Council of Europe, created in the aftermath of World War II, was established to secure European unity and guarantee human rights.[58] Its Convention on the Protection of Human Rights and Fundamental Freedoms, which entered into force in 1953, created the European Court of Human Rights. All forty-seven members of the Council of Europe are bound by its terms. If human rights "express a moral commitment to objective principles of liberal democracy," then the European Convention on Human Rights reflects an agreement among the members of the Council of Europe "to be legally bound by certain fundamental principles of liberal democracy."[59] Such a commitment was particularly desirable at the end of World War II when faith in democratic governance was at a low point.[60] Thus, the Court was established against the "historical background of the Nazi experience"[61] and the belief that a certain amount of international monitoring of governmental practices could help promote the international peace and security that depends upon the domestic protection of individual rights.[62] It was hoped that the Convention would guard "against the revival of aggressive and repressive dictatorships by ensuring the enforcement of rights contained in the Universal Declaration of Human Rights."[63]

Today, the Court is considered Europe's de facto constitutional court enforcing its de facto bill of rights.[64] Although the effect of its jurisprudence is frequently contested,

---

[56] E. Thomas Sullivan & Richard S. Frase, Proportionality Principles in American Law: Controlling Excessive Government Actions 26–35 (2009) (citing Canada, Germany, France, Poland, Ukraine, and the European Union). Although the U.S. Supreme Court's levels of scrutiny framework bears a strong resemblance to proportionality, *id.* at 53–54, 58–62, 66, strict scrutiny is more outcome determinative, arguably functioning more like a "rulelike presumption" than does even the higher level of proportionality applied to interferences with fundamental rights in other systems, *id.* at ix, 11, 53, 54.

[57] Jud Mathews & Alec Stone Sweet, *All Things in Proportion? American Rights Review and the Problem of Balancing*, 60 Emory L.J. 797, 874 (2011).

[58] Nina-Louisa Arold, The Legal Culture of the European Court of Human Rights 19 (2007); Michael D. Goldhaber, A People's History of the European Court of Human Rights 3 (2007).

[59] George Letsas, A Theory of Interpretation of the European Convention on Human Rights 11 (2007).

[60] *Id.* at 18, 19.

[61] Comella, *supra* note 52, at 150.

[62] Letsas, *supra* note 59, at 18.

[63] Burchill, *supra* note 44, at 146.

[64] R.C. van Caegnegem, An Historical Introduction to Western Constitutional Law 134 (1995); Helen Keller & Alec Stone Sweet, *Introduction*, in A Europe of Rights: The Impact of the ECHR on National Legal Systems 3, 3 & n.1 (Helen Keller & Alec Stone Sweet eds. 2008). This is particularly so for states without their own bills of rights. Helen Keller & Alec Stone Sweet, *Assessing the Impact of the ECHR on National Legal Systems*, in A Europe of Rights, *id.* at 677, 689–99.

given that it "does not possess the authority to invalidate national legal norms judged to be incompatible with the Convention,"[65] it nonetheless commands broad allegiance thanks to the goodwill and good faith of most states.[66] The Convention's and the Court's growing political legitimacy have earned them a sterling international reputation as "the most effective human rights regime in the world."[67]

One of the primary functions of the Council of Europe is to protect and reinforce democratic pluralism.[68] At the same, time, it is concerned with articulating common solutions to the major societal problems encountered by member states.[69] Managing these two goals simultaneously requires choices to be made between diversity and uniformity. Although the Convention nowhere mentions proportionality,[70] the proportionality principle is nonetheless a "leitmotiv of jurisprudence of the Strasbourg organs."[71] In addition to proportionality, the Court's jurisprudence employs the doctrine of "margin of appreciation."[72] The Court developed the doctrine not only to help it manage the tension between uniformity and diversity in the protection of human rights[73] but also to help it negotiate the delicate political context in which it operates. By granting member states a zone of discretion that permits them to pursue solutions to human rights issues in different ways, the Court can promote diversity on questions of rights and also vindicate the rights of individuals when uniformity is demanded. Where a higher standard of proportionality must be attained, such as when a particularly important facet of an individual's existence or identity is at stake, the margin of appreciation accorded to a state will be restricted.[74] As the primary judicial tools employed by the Court, the margin of appreciation and the standard of proportionality enable it to achieve a "fair balance" of individual interests and broader public interests when a state places limitations on Convention guarantees.[75]

The margin of appreciation is most often described as wide or narrow. It applies most notably in areas of profound controversy—abortion, euthanasia, adoption of children by same-sex couples, and bans on in vitro fertilization in cases of unilateral withdrawal of consent. It is at its widest where "there is not some consensus between Member

---

[65] Keller & Sweet, *supra* note 64, at 13.

[66] *Id.* at 14.

[67] *Id.* at 19; *see also* AROLD, *supra* note 58, at 2; GOLDHABER, *supra* note 58, at 2.

[68] Burchill, *supra* note 44, at 146.

[69] *Id.*

[70] STEVEN GREER, THE EUROPEAN CONVENTION ON HUMAN RIGHTS: ACHIEVEMENTS, PROBLEMS AND PROSPECTS 217 (2006).

[71] LA CONVENTION EUROPÉENE DES DROITS DE L'HOMME: COMMENTAIRE ARTICLE PAR ARTICLE 338 (Louis-Edmond Pettiti, Emmanuel Decaux & Pierre-Henri Imbert eds. 1995).

[72] *Belgian Linguistic Case*, App. No. 1474/62, 1 Eur. H.R. Rep. 252, 278 (1968).

[73] Eva Brems, *The Margin of Appreciation Doctrine of the European Court of Human Rights, in* HUMAN RIGHTS AND DIVERSITY, *supra* note 44, at 81.

[74] Dickson v. United Kingdom, App. No. 44362/04, 46 Eur. H.R. Rep. 41, 959 (2008); *see also* GORDON ANTHONY, UK PUBLIC LAW AND EUROPEAN LAW: THE DYNAMICS OF LEGAL INTEGRATION 173–74 (2002).

[75] ANTHONY, *supra* note 74, at 171. The term "fair balance" appears for the first time in *Belgian Linguistic Case*, 1 Eur. H.R. Rep. at 255, 293.

States about the existence of this right or [where] the applicant's right consists solely in the treatment or the benefit upon which there is consensus."[76] Where there is a discernible consensus that a right exists, the Court grants a narrow margin to aberrant state action.[77] The Court has remarked, "[W]here there is little common ground amongst the Member States of the Council of Europe and, generally speaking, the law appears to be in a transitional stage, the respondent State must be afforded a wide margin of appreciation."[78] Conversely, the Court has struck down bans on homosexual sodomy based in part on the consensus that has emerged throughout Europe that such bans run counter to the human rights commitments of democratic societies.[79]

Many have criticized the inconsistency and vagueness with which the Court applies the margin of appreciation.[80] Some argue that the margin has been narrowed in ways the drafters of the Convention never intended.[81] This view holds that placing the threshold of deference too low risks undermining the credibility of the Court.[82] Others charge that the margin is so broad that it "completely override[s]" the proportionality principle, swallowing human rights.[83] As a practical matter, the doctrine reflects the political compromise necessary to gain signatories for the Convention. It acts as an accommodation of variations in the approaches different member states of the Council of Europe take in safeguarding Convention Rights[84] and may act as a brake against withdrawal from the Convention[85] and loss of the Court's political influence.[86] As such, as the Court negotiates this "political tightrope,"[87] the margin of appreciation helps define the limits within which it may adjudicate.

IV. The European Court of Human Rights and Assisted Reproduction

Restrictive reproductive laws that contribute to CBRC may not in all cases satisfy important democratic standards defining the limits of legislative competence in the first instance. On the one hand, as the margin of appreciation narrows and the

---

[76] LETSAS, *supra* note 59, at 12; *see also* COMELLA, *supra* note 52, at 152.

[77] HOWARD CHARLES YOUROW, THE MARGIN OF APPRECIATION DOCTRINE IN THE DYNAMICS OF EUROPEAN HUMAN RIGHTS JURISPRUDENCE 54 (1996).

[78] X, Y and Z v. United Kingdom, App. No. 21830/93, 24 Eur. H.R. Rep. 143, 169 (1997).

[79] Norris v. Ireland, App. No. 10581/83, 13 Eur. H.R. Rep. 186, 201 (1991); Dudgeon v. United Kingdom, App. No. 7525/76, 4 Eur. H.R. Rep. 149, 168 (1982).

[80] Burchill, *supra* note 44, at 147.

[81] *European Court of Human Rights Reform "Will Take Time,"* BBC NEWS, (Oct. 27, 2011), http://www.bbc.co.uk/news/uk-politics-15483272.

[82] Mahoney, *supra* note 48, at 4.

[83] Thomas Willoughby Stone, *Margin of Appreciation Gone Awry: The European Court of Human Rights' Implicit Use of the Precautionary Principle in Fretté v. France to Backtrack on Protection from Discrimination on the Basis of Sexual Orientation*, 3 CONN. PUB. INT. L.J. 271, 280 (2003); YOUROW, *supra* note 77, at 34.

[84] Burchill, *supra* note 44, at 147; *see also* COMELLA, *supra* note 52, at 150.

[85] LETSAS, *supra* note 59, at 14.

[86] Laurence R. Helfer, *Finding a Consensus on Equality: The Homosexual Age of Consent and the European Convention on Human Rights*, 65 N.Y.U. L. REV. 1044, 1052 (1990).

[87] YOUROW, *supra* note 77, at 49.

demands of the proportionality standard increase, the danger arises that restrictions on reproduction pose a proportionality problem, that is, too loose a fit between the law's objective and the means chosen to bring that objective about. On the other hand, there is some indication that the availability of CBRC itself will, however unjustifiably, embolden legislatures in their enactment of restrictions and persuade courts that the margin of appreciation need not be narrowed in such cases because CBRC affords an alternative means by which to realize one's reproductive goals.

The European Court of Human Rights has dealt on five occasions with questions involving the types of laws that contribute to CBRC. Four cases involved access to procedures and the fifth, *X, Y and Z*,[88] implicated the parentage ramifications of the use of assisted reproductive technology. The petitioners in all five cases claimed violations of Article 8, the Convention's guarantee of family and private life. Three of the cases, *Dickson*,[89] *Evans*,[90] and *S.H.*,[91] were heard by the Court twice, once by the Chamber and then by the Grand Chamber. In *Evans*, the Grand Chamber upheld the Chamber's decision against the petitioner; in *Dickson* and *S.H.*, it reversed the Chamber, ruling in favor of the petitioner in *Dickson* and in favor of the government in *S.H. S.H. v. Austria* and *Costa v. Italy* were the only two of the five cases not brought against the United Kingdom.

The first case, *X, Y and Z v. United Kingdom*, was brought by a female-to-male transsexual whose partner had given birth with the aid of artificial insemination using the sperm of an anonymous donor. X claimed the right to be legally recognized as the child's father, but the government took the position that only a biological man could be designated as the father of a child in a registration of birth.

The Court agreed with the Commission[92] that X, his partner, and their child were a de facto family entitled to protection under Article 8.[93] It did not agree with the Commission, however, that a trend in the direction of according legal recognition to a postoperative transsexual's reassigned sex meant that the government had gone beyond the bounds of its discretion in refusing to recognize X as the father of the child. Instead, it pointed out that recognizing a postoperative female-to-male transsexual as the social father of a child was not reflected in the trend toward legally recognizing a transsexual's gender reassignment.[94] Moreover, the Court emphasized that its previous declarations of the importance of recognizing familial ties arose in cases

---

[88] X, Y and Z v. United Kingdom, App. No. 21830/93, 24 Eur. H.R. Rep. 143 (1997).

[89] Dickson v. United Kingdom, App. No. 44362/04, 46 Eur. H.R. Rep. 41 (2008).

[90] Evans v. United Kingdom, App. No. 6339/05, 46 Eur. H.R. Rep. 34 (2008).

[91] S.H. v. Austria, App. No. 57813/00, Nov. 3, 2011, *at* http://hudoc.echr.coe.int/sites/eng/pages/search.aspx?i=001-107325.

[92] The European Commission on Human Rights was terminated in 1998 pursuant to a restructuring of the Court's function. Formerly, from 1953 until 1998, the Commission served a gatekeeping role by determining the admissibility of petitions to the Court and rendering preliminary decisions in those cases. GOLDHABER, *supra* note 58, at 4.

[93] X, Y and Z v. United Kingdom, 24 Eur. H.R. Rep. at 166.

[94] *Id.* at 169.

involving parents and children who had biological ties to each other.[95] The Court specifically mentioned the lack of "any generally shared approach" in how the law should treat the social parent–child relationships that result, as they did in this case, from the use of reproductive technology. Given the lack of common ground and the transitional nature of the law on this question, the Court resolved to grant the government a wide margin of appreciation.

The Court felt that, above all, the best interests of Z, the child in this case, had to be considered, and that it simply was not certain that legally recognizing the social relationship that existed between X and Z would be to the child's advantage. At the very least, it seemed, denial of recognition would not cause Z any undue hardship, particularly given that X could apply for and be granted parental responsibility.[96] In sum, the wide margin of appreciation in this case, combined with the sense that the child's best interests were not imperiled by the government's refusal of recognition, led the Court to decide in favor of the government.

In 2006, the Chamber decided a dispute over the right to use cryopreserved embryos. When medical tests revealed her need for an ovariectomy, the petitioner Evans and her partner decided to create embryos using her eggs and his sperm. The clinic they visited did not freeze unfertilized eggs. The two signed consents indicating their understanding that, under the law governing the transaction, each had the right to withdraw from treatment at any point before their embryos were placed in Evans's uterus. When thereafter Evans and her partner separated, he withdrew his consent to treatment and requested that the embryos be destroyed.[97] Evans's suit to establish her right to have children with the use of the embryos was unsuccessful, the trial court determining that the law fairly balanced the interests in reproductive autonomy and the welfare of the child that are implicated when a couple employs assisted reproduction to have children.[98] On appeal, the court agreed, citing its conviction that "no one should have the power to override the need for a genetic parent's consent."[99]

Having lost her appeal in the United Kingdom, Evans brought her claim to the European Court of Human Rights. The Chamber hearing the case framed the question presented as "whether there exists a positive obligation on the state to ensure that a woman who has embarked on treatment for the specific purpose of giving birth to a genetically related child should be permitted to proceed to implantation of the embryo notwithstanding the withdrawal of consent by her former partner, the male gamete provider."[100] In establishing the breadth of the margin of appreciation, the Court noted the lack of consensus regarding the regulation of in vitro fertilization in general and the point at which consent may be withdrawn in particular.[101] Several countries, it

---

95 *Id.*
96 *Id.* at 170–71.
97 Evans v. United Kingdom, App. No. 6339/05, 43 Eur. H.R. Rep. 21, 412 (2006).
98 *Id.* at 413.
99 *Id.* at 415.
100 *Id.* at 426.
101 *Id.* at 427.

observed, approach the problem in the same manner as the United Kingdom.[102] It then emphasized the care with which the government had approached the regulation of this area of medicine, including embodying in its legislation "the primacy of the continuing consent to IVF treatment by both parties to the treatment."[103] Given the highly sensitive nature of this field of medicine, the bright-line rule applied to this case by the government to promote legal certainty and public confidence was thought particularly appropriate.[104]

On reconsideration, the Grand Chamber upheld the decision of the Chamber. The point was made that although the withdrawal of her partner's consent prevented Evans from using the embryos, she was not thereby prevented from becoming a mother by adoption or by gestating a donor embryo.[105] That the government had prevented Evans from becoming a genetic parent, and only in the sense that the other genetic parent had withdrawn his consent, was a narrower issue. Although this deprivation fell within the scope of Article 8, so did the prospect of forcing him to become a genetic parent should Evans prevail. Moreover, the margin of appreciation on this question was broad, given the lack of consensus among member states and its sensitive nature.[106] Because at no point was Evans unaware that her partner could withdraw his consent or that the eggs she contributed to the treatment would be her last, no violation of Article 8 was evident.

The same year the Chamber handed down its decision in *Evans,* a panel of the Court decided a petition brought by a married couple denied permission to employ artificial insemination.[107] The husband was in prison for murder both at the time of the marriage and at the time of the application for a license to employ assisted reproduction. The government refused permission for several reasons, including that it was not possible to test whether the marriage would subsist after the husband's release, that any child to be born would not have the benefit of his father's presence for a significant portion of his childhood, and that the criminal law policies for incarcerating offenders would be undermined by permitting the couple to have a child through artificial insemination.[108] In short, the applicants had failed to prove that their case was "exceptional."[109]

The Chamber began its analysis by noting that imprisonment necessarily entails some curtailment of rights. The question, then, became what degree of curtailment of a prisoner's right to beget a child would be compatible with the Convention.[110] The Chamber noted the lack of consensus among the member states on the question of granting prisoners access to artificial insemination and determined that the

---

[102] *Id.* at 429.
[103] *Id.* at 427.
[104] *Id.* at 428.
[105] Evans v. United Kingdom, App. No. 6339/05, 46 Eur. H.R. Rep. 34, 761 (2008).
[106] *Id.* at 763.
[107] Dickson v. United Kingdom, App No. 44362/04, 44 Eur. H.R. Rep. 21 (2007).
[108] *Id.* at 422.
[109] *Id.* at 430.
[110] *Id.* at 428.

government's refusal deserved a wide margin of appreciation. It was observed that the government had attempted pursuant to an individualized assessment of the facts of the case to strike a balance among the rights of the prisoner, the welfare of the child, and the importance of public confidence in the penal system.[111] In light of the government's careful attempt to strike a fair balance and having in view the wide margin of appreciation enjoyed by the government, the Chamber determined that there had been no unreasonable curtailment of the petitioner's right to private and family life.

On reconsideration of this case by the Grand Chamber, the decision of the Chamber was overturned.[112] Initially, the Grand Chamber emphasized that prisoners do not relinquish their rights at the jailhouse door. Indeed, incarceration deprives them only of their liberty; other Convention rights are preserved until compelling reasons for their curtailment can be shown. The government had turned these understandings on their head by forcing a prisoner to demonstrate that exceptional circumstances supported his right to procreate. The government's pursuit of punitive aims in this manner, for all its appearance as an attempt to strike a fair balance, was tantamount to a blanket ban.[113] Underscoring the arbitrariness of the policy was its application to all prisoners no matter the gravity or nature of the crime.[114]

The most important feature of the Grand Chamber's decision was where it placed the margin of appreciation. Familiar considerations were brought to bear on this question:

> [W]here a particularly important facet of an individual's existence or identity is at stake (such as the choice to become a genetic parent), the margin of appreciation accorded to a state will in general be restricted. Where, however, there is no consensus within the Member States of the Council of Europe, either as to the relative importance of the interest at stake or as to how best to protect it, the margin will be wider.[115]

But in addition to these considerations is the basis for applying the margin at all. "The doctrine presupposes," in the words of Paul Mahoney, "as a condition for its application, the normal functioning of democratic processes at the national level."[116] Because the government's arbitrary policy, masquerading as careful balancing, in no way befitted "the preliminary conditions of normal democratic governance,"[117] its actions could not be deemed to fall within any acceptable margin, no matter how wide.[118] Thus, a violation of Article 8 was evident.

---

[111] *Id.* at 430.

[112] Dickson v. United Kingdom, App No. 44362/04, 46 Eur. H.R. Rep. 41 (2008).

[113] *Id.* at 951.

[114] *Id.*

[115] *Id.* at 959.

[116] Mahoney, *supra* note 48, at 4.

[117] *Id.*

[118] Dickson, 46 Eur. H.R. Rep. at 961.

The decision of the European Court of Human Rights relating to gamete donation in assisted reproduction is *S.H.*[119] The Court was asked to evaluate provisions of Austria's Artificial Procreation Act that banned egg donation altogether and banned sperm donation for in vitro fertilization but permitted it for artificial insemination in exceptional circumstances.[120] The restriction reflected the government's attempt to balance human dignity, procreative freedom, and the welfare of children by limiting assisted procreation to "homologous methods" save for artificial insemination, a well-known and not particularly sophisticated method.[121] It was believed that methods "too far removed from natural means of conception" would threaten the formation of "unusual personal relations" and might also lead to the exploitation of women.[122]

The applicants, all of whom required donor gametes to have children, claimed that the law treated them unjustifiably differently from couples who could use their own genetic material to have children. The Chamber hearing the case, in establishing the margin of appreciation, noted, as the Court in *Evans* had, the lack of consensus among member states regarding which techniques should be allowed and which should be outlawed.[123] The margin, therefore, was wide, as long as there was no breakdown in the democratic process that led to the enactment of the restriction.[124]

Regarding the ban on using a donor's egg to reproduce, the Chamber acknowledged that the government's reservations were serious but that a complete ban was unwarranted unless it was the only way to avert "serious repercussions."[125] Because the law permitted only medical professionals to provide treatment in this sphere, the Chamber felt the government could look to medical professionals, guided by their code of ethics, to safeguard against the feared harms.[126] Moreover, the Austrian legislature, having already banned the commercialization of ova and sperm, had the means at its disposal to enact further safeguards against abuse.[127] For these reasons, the Chamber found that Austria had not brought forth valid justifications for its ban on egg donation and thus that the discrimination between couples who require egg donation and those who do not was indefensible.

Regarding the law's approval of using donated sperm for artificial insemination but its disapproval of using donated sperm for in vitro fertilization, the Chamber noted first that most countries make no distinction between techniques based solely on the source of the sperm.[128] Moreover, in view of the fact that Austria did not ban either artificial insemination or in vitro fertilization outright, the Chamber required

---

[119] S.H. v. Austria, App. No. 57813/00, Nov. 3, 2011, *available at* http://hudoc.echr.coe.int/sites/eng/pages/search.aspx?i=001-107325.

[120] *Id.* at 30, 31.

[121] *Id.* at 19, 23, 66, 67.

[122] *Id.*

[123] S.H. v. Austria, App. No. 57813/00, 52 Eur. H.R. Rep. 6, 289 (2011).

[124] *Id.*

[125] *Id.* at 291.

[126] *Id.*

[127] *Id.*

[128] *Id.* at 283.

particularly persuasive justifications for the differential treatment.[129] Given that the justifications for banning ova donation were of little relevance in this context, the government described the justification for its differential treatment among types of sperm donation as necessitated not only by the fact that artificial insemination had been in use for quite some time at the point Austria enacted its restrictions but also by the practical difficulties of monitoring the use of a technique that does not require the intervention of medical professionals.[130] In the Chamber's estimation, this "efficiency" justification weighed little in the balance against the applicants' wish for a child, "a particularly important facet of an individual's existence or identity," and was consequently disproportionate.[131]

On reconsideration of this case by the Grand Chamber, the decision of the Chamber was overturned.[132] The Grand Chamber went beyond the Chamber's assessment of consensus to discern a "clear trend" among member states in the direction of allowing gamete donation for in vitro fertilization. The character of this consensus was not one, however, that would necessitate narrowing the margin of appreciation. Instead of being based on "settled and long-standing principles," this consensus was dynamic, subject to change in light of the sensitive moral and ethical responses to the "fast-moving medical and scientific developments" that generated it.[133] Despite the consensus, therefore, the margin of appreciation was to remain wide.

Regarding the ban on using a donor's egg to reproduce, the Grand Chamber reemphasized the fast pace of scientific developments in human reproduction. In light of these developments and their yet-unknown consequences, the Austrian legislature's caution in striking the balance between allowing access to new technologies and acknowledging the discomfort many experience toward them appeared sensible and measured.[134] In particular, the unknown consequences of "splitting motherhood" rendered the Chamber's view that the legislature could enact safeguards little better than theoretical.[135] The fact that the legislature could have struck a fairer balance did not mean it was bound to under the Convention.[136]

Regarding the law's approval of using donated sperm for artificial insemination but its disapproval of using donated sperm for in vitro fertilization, the Grand Chamber was similarly deferential. It did not, for instance, see the irrelevance of arguments the government raised against egg donation for sperm donation in the "highly technical medical process" of in vitro fertilization because sperm donation for artificial insemination had already become accepted in society at the time the restrictions

---

[129]   *Id.* at 293.
[130]   *Id.*; *see also* S.H. v. Austria, App. No. 57813/00, Nov. 3, 2011, at 68.
[131]   S.H., 52 Eur. H.R. Rep. at 294.
[132]   S.H. v. Austria, App. No. 57813/00, Nov. 3, 2011, *available at* http://hudoc.echr.coe.int/sites/eng/pages/search.aspx?i=001-107325.
[133]   *Id.* at 97.
[134]   *Id.* at 103, 104.
[135]   *Id.* at 105.
[136]   *Id.* at 106.

were enacted.[137] The choice the Austrian legislature made between permitting sperm donation for some techniques but not for others was a demonstration of its careful approach to reconciling social realities. Further evidence of this careful balancing was found in the lack of any proscription on CBRC in Austrian law and the existence of other provisions that would bestow legal parentage on those who successfully pursue gamete donation abroad.[138]

The most recent European Court of Human Rights decision in the area of restrictions on assisted reproduction, *Costa v. Italy*, concerned Italy's ban on preimplantation genetic diagnosis and its restriction of in vitro fertilization to infertile couples.[139] In this case, fertile and unaffected carriers of the gene for cystic fibrosis were refused access to very techniques that would allow them to select embryos unaffected by the disease for implantation. Their only option was to commence a pregnancy, submit to prenatal diagnosis, and terminate the pregnancy if the fetus turned out to be afflicted.[140] The Court judged it disproportionate to deny carriers of disease access to techniques of assisted procreation while allowing them access to abortion for the same reason.[141] Indeed, the Court determined that the harms the government sought to avoid were more gravely implicated by abortion than by assisted reproductive techniques.[142] A violation of Article 8 was thus evident. The decision will become final if no party requests review of the decision by the Grand Chamber.

V. Proportionality and Cross-border Reproductive Care

The five cases described above, taken individually, offer several insights into how the Court will respond in the future to matters arising from the use of assisted reproduction. *X, Y and Z* stands apart from the others because it is not an access case but instead one about the parentage ramifications of assisted reproduction. Nonetheless *X, Y and Z* is helpful in predicting what the Court's likely response to *Mennesson* will be. Both cases involve a government's refusal to recognize social parentage bonds that arise from the use of reproductive technology. But *Mennesson* contrasts sharply with *X, Y and Z* in that it involves an approach to assisted reproduction that has been widely condemned by the members of the Council of Europe. On the spectrum of controversial approaches to human reproduction, surrogacy is reviled in most parts of Europe but artificial insemination is not. Even if we believe that the decisive factor for the Court in *X, Y and Z* was the claim that the government must recognize a biological woman's fatherhood and that, in contrast, Sophie Mennesson's demand to be recognized as the

---

[137] *Id.* at 113.
[138] *Id.* at 114.
[139] Costa and Pavan v. Italy, App. No. 54270/10, Aug. 28, 2012, *available at* http://hudoc.echr.coe.int/sites/eng/pages/search.aspx?i=001–112992.
[140] *Id.* at 65.
[141] *Id.* at 64.
[142] *Id.* at 62, 66.

mother of her daughters will be more palatable to the Court, it bears noting that the question of transsexual parenthood is one that European legislatures have not tackled, leaving attitudes about the matter uncertain. The certainty with which European legislatures have expressed their opposition to maternity via surrogacy and the tenacity with which they have embraced the Roman law maxim of *mater semper certa est*[143] is so nearly universal that the margin of appreciation accorded them is likely to be substantial. In other words, if a *lack* of consensus warrants a wide margin of appreciation, then certainly a nearly full consensus that a right does not exist is likely to warrant an even wider one to a state that wishes to embrace that consensus.[144]

Of course, the *Mennesson* case may be approached from a different perspective. Some have remarked that the case implicates the consensus that has arisen in Europe on the need to dismantle laws that treat children born out of wedlock disadvantageously. Indeed, reflecting on the many couples who have faced the same response from government when they have engaged in international commercial surrogacy, lawyer Valérie Depadt-Sebag has designated the resulting children "a new category of pariahs"[145] that reintroduces a distinction between legitimate and illegitimate children long ago stricken from the law.[146] Consistent with this view, one of the courts hearing the *Mennesson* case remarked that Article 8 was probably implicated. Still, although the European Court of Human Rights' Article 8 jurisprudence on the rights of children born out of wedlock has transformed the laws of individual European countries on the question of their legal parentage, it is nonetheless a body of cases that vindicates the right to legal recognition of *biological* ties.[147] Perhaps the avenue most likely to be availing to the Mennessons, then, would be for them to pursue a claim against the government for refusing to allow Sophie to adopt her daughters. By virtue of the fact that the Mennessons are a married couple, the Court's recent decision against a woman who was refused permission to adopt her same-gender partner's child does not apply to them.[148]

---

[143] S.H. v. Austria, 52 Eur. H.R. Rep. at 291; *see also* S.H. v. Austria, App. No. 57813/00, Nov. 3, 2011, at 70 (describing the German government's commitment to "unambiguousness of motherhood."). "Mater semper certa est, etiamsi vulgo conceperit, pater est quem nuptiae demonstrant" or "maternity, even of illegitimate children, is always certain; paternity follows marriage" means that birth itself is conclusive of motherhood. JOHN GEORGE PHILLIMORE, PRIVATE LAW AMONG THE ROMANS FROM THE PANDECTS 64 (1863); Mary Ann B. Oakley, *Test Tube Babies: Proposals for Legal Regulation of New Methods of Human Conception and Prenatal Development*, 8 FAM. L.Q. 385, 391 (1974).

[144] *See supra* notes 76–79 and accompanying text.

[145] Charlotte Rotman, *"Filles fantômes" en mal de nom* [Nameless Girl Ghosts], LA LIBÉRATION, Feb. 18, 2010, at 10.

[146] Charlotte Rotman, *Gestation pour autrui: les enfants fantômes de la Republique* [Surrogacy: The Phantom Children of the Republic], LA LIBÉRATION, May 20, 2009, at 15 (quoting the Mennessons' attorney Nathalie Boudjerada).

[147] *See, e.g.,* Johnston v. Ireland, App. No. 9697/82, 9 Eur. H.R. Rep. 203 (1987); Kroon v. Netherlands, App. No. 18535/91, 19 Eur. H.R. Rep. 263 (1995). *See also* S.H. v. Austria, App. No. 57813/00, Nov. 3, 2011, at 105 (referring to "unusual family relations . . . which do not follow the typical parent-child relationship based on a direct biological link.").

[148] *See* Gas & Dubois v. France, App. No. 25951/07, Mar. 15, 2012, at 19, 62, 65, *available at* http://hudoc. echr.coe.int/sites/eng/pages/search.aspx?i=001-109571 (describing the adverse legal consequences that the adoption application would entail when brought by unmarried parties in a civil partnership).

The claim that barring access to assisted reproduction using donor gametes is a violation of the Convention may not stand on firmer ground. *S.H.* is most directly on point, and the fact that Austria's law was found not to violate the European Convention on Human Rights sends a strong signal that European countries are free to impose whatever restrictions on assisted reproduction they may desire. Even the Chamber's decision in *S.H.* stated plainly that member states may outlaw assisted reproduction altogether.[149] Given the Court's traditional vindication of the rights of genetic parents, it would be perfectly consistent for it to conclude in a future case that the margin of appreciation extends to countries who wish to legislate in the area of assisted reproduction to protect those who wish to create and raise children with the use of their own gametes, but to prevent those who require the gametes of third parties from doing so. It would appear that the availability of CBRC would at the very least be a factor in such an analysis. It played an important role in the Court's recent decision that Ireland was not compelled to liberalize its restrictions on abortion given the availability of abortion in other member states.[150]

Evans is of limited predictive use given that it involved a disagreement between biological progenitors over whether to proceed with treatment. *Dickson* is perhaps instructive with its forceful language narrowing the margin of appreciation where "a particularly important facet of an individual's existence or identity is at stake," but it, like *Evans* and *Costa*, refers specifically to "the choice to become a genetic parent."[151] The *Costa* decision, too, explicitly distinguishes *S.H.*, emphasizing that the applicants wished to procreate using their own gametes.[152] The Court might well hold, taking into consideration these statements about protecting genetic parenthood and the lesser protection accorded social parenthood exhibited by *X, Y and Z*, that the Convention's highest priority lies in protecting the rights of biological progenitors to reproduce and be recognized as parents. Even the reference the Court makes in *S.H.* to the familiarity of adoptive family relations[153] does not pertain directly to the question of whether couples should be able to reproduce with the gametes of others. The current state of the court's jurisprudence is more supportive of the proposition that the social parenthood that results from the use of donor gametes does not rise to the level of an "important facet" of identity and, thus, that access to a procedure that results in that form of parenthood need not be guaranteed.

Although the decisions of the member states' courts following their own constitutions are not necessarily predictive of the position the European Court of Human

---

[149] S.H. v. Austria, App. No. 57813/00, 52 Eur. H.R. Rep. 6, at 290 (2011). The statement has an odd ring, given developments in the inter-American system of human rights protection. The Inter-American Commission on Human Rights has ordered Costa Rica to lift its ban on in vitro fertilization. Murillo v. Costa Rica, Case No. 12.361, July 14, 2010, at 136, *available at* http://www.cidh.oas.org/demandas/12.361Eng.pdf. The case was recently heard by the Inter-American Court of Human Rights on September 5 and 6, 2012. Murillo v. Costa Rica, Case No. 12.361, *at* http://vimeo.com/48921880.

[150] A, B and C v. Ireland, App. No. 25579/05, 53 Eur. H.R. Rep. 13, 492–93 (2011).

[151] Dickson v. United Kingdom, App. No. 44362/04, 46 Eur. H.R. Rep. 41, 959 (2008).

[152] Costa and Pavan v. Italy, App. No. 54270/10, Aug. 28, 2012, at 69.

[153] S.H. v. Austria, App. No. 57813/00, Nov. 3, 2011, *at* 105.

Rights might take, because they typically do not involve deference to the consensus of sister states, the response of Italian courts to constitutional claims brought to challenge provisions of the Italian law provide interesting examples of how proportionality might apply to such claims. In striking down provisions in the Italian law mandating the production of at most three embryos in any one IVF cycle and the return of all embryos to the uterus, the Italian Constitutional Court expressed concern that the law rendered medical judgment irrelevant in the treatment of patients despite the individualized circumstances different patients invariably present. The Constitutional Court was unwilling to defer to the legislature where a less intrusive approach—the resort to medical judgment—was available. The Court also expressed concern that, in purporting to protect embryonic life, the law made no account of the medical fact that "it is impossible to procreate without a certain degree of early embryo loss."[154] This reasoning suggests that limitations on assisted reproduction must be harmonized not only with other permitted forms of assisted reproduction but with unassisted reproduction as well. The decision may not mandate the end of Italy's ban on the use of donor gametes, but it does suggest that the right to be free of legal interference in the decision to have a child does not end with one's infertility.

Other flaws in the Italian law suggest that the ban on donor gametes may not satisfy the standard of proportionality. The Italian legislature's stated objective in enacting the ban was to reaffirm the heterosexual couple as the only appropriate locus for family formation and to avert undesired ramifications, namely: (1) that the relationships of couples would be threatened by the presence of children not biologically related to both of them; (2) that children would be harmed by not knowing the identity of and not being raised by both biological parents; and (3) that Italian society would be harmed by increases in marital breakdown and psychologically damaged children. Ironically, it is CBRC itself that calls into question whether Italy's ban on donor gametes stands in adequate proportion to the aims of its law. Via cross-border reproductive travel, all of the feared dangers to patients, children, and society become subject to importation into Italy when patients return from abroad and give birth. Despite the supposed importance of biological ties, a gamete provider has no parental rights or obligations under the law. Despite the belief that third-party gamete donation renders family bonds fragile, the law contains no provision requiring the couple to adopt the child so as to solidify those bonds. The Italian law fails even to make a symbolic gesture in favor of the child's right to know his or her biological parents. The obvious lack of any connection between the Italian law and the harms it seeks to address is uncharacteristic of legislation that satisfies the standard of proportionality.

At the time the Grand Chamber's decision in *S.H.* was issued, Italy's Constitutional Court was considering the question pursuant to the appeal from a decision of a court in Milan that had declared the ban on gamete donation in violation of the right to form a

---

[154] Giuseppe Benagiano & Luca Gianaroli, *The Italian Constitutional Court Modifies Italian Legislation on Assisted Reproductive Technology*, 20 REPROD. BIOMED. ONLINE 398, 399 (2010).

family, including the right to have children.[155] The Constitutional Court remanded the case to the lower court to reconsider its decision in light of *S.H.*[156] This remand may be a signal that Italy's courts will not be vigorous sources of support, at least in the near term, for those who require the participation of gamete and embryo donors in order to have children but find themselves burdened by laws that prohibit these procedures. Other national courts may also look to *S.H.* as authority for upholding against constitutional challenges restrictions on assisted reproduction. Moreover, as the European Court of Human Rights looked favorably upon CBRC in *S.H.*, it is to be expected that the availability of CBRC will play a role in how governments choose in the future to shape their laws on assisted reproduction.

Conclusion

This chapter has explored the role the use of the doctrine of proportionality in the jurisprudence of the European Court of Human Right may play in curbing CBRC. Naturally, review by an institution that is not answerable to the electorate can place it into conflict with other governmental institutions. For this reason, judicial review has been referred to as a "democratic anomaly;" nonetheless, it is not "anomalously undemocratic."[157] Time and again we have seen that courts play an essential function in holding the more extreme manifestations of majoritarian control in check, thereby safeguarding unpopular minorities.[158] An effective judiciary is necessary to ensure that democracy will function well enough to respect minority rights.[159] This is the role that the members of the Council of Europe have agreed the European Court of Human Rights should fulfill.

Recent pronouncements of the European Court of Human Rights do not clearly indicate that restrictive reproductive laws may be unenforceable because of their lack of proportionality to the aims they seek to achieve. The jurisprudence displays a concern for protecting genetic parent-child relationships whether or not created in the context of marriage. The most common restrictions on assisted reproduction, however, tend to burden the creation and recognition of social parenthood relationships or single-parent families. Where restrictions have been found to be violations of the Convention, the primary problem for the Court has been their interference with a "typical parent-child relationship based on a direct biological link." Beyond protecting such traditional parent-child relationships, the Court has granted a wide margin of appreciation, most notably in *S.H.*, to member states that wish to place restrictions on reproduction-assisting techniques.

---

[155] Fabio Poletti, *Il Tribunale: La Legge 40 Viola il Diritto a Formare una Famiglia* [Court: Law 40 Violates Right to Form a Family], LA STAMPA, Feb. 4, 2011, at 18.

[156] Margarita De Bac, *Consulta, Rimane il Divieto della Fecondazione Eterologa*, CORRIERE DELLA SERA, May 23, 2012, at 29.

[157] BREYER, *supra* note 45, at 3, 5.

[158] Brown, *supra* note 49, at 211.

[159] BREYER, *supra* note 45, at 6; COMELLA, *supra* note 52, at 88.

Although it appears at this time that the Court is unlikely to strike down restrictions on the use of third-party gametes or the denial of citizenship to children born through international commercial surrogacy, it is fair to predict that, despite the Italian Constitutional Court's recent remand, proportionality review will assume, in the near term, a position of greater importance in the judicial review of restrictive reproductive laws in Europe. After all, the ECtHR is not the only rights-furthering organ in Europe. Countries throughout Europe have their own constitutional courts that possess the competence to declare that a law oversteps the constitutional limits placed on the exercise of legislative power. After *S.H.*, these courts will determine the future of restrictions on gamete donation in Europe. Were it willing to narrow the wide margin of appreciation currently accorded member states in the sensitive area of assisted reproduction, even the European Court of Human Rights, in response to an evolving consensus, could one day play a role in eliminating a major cause of much of the CBRC that originates in this part of the world.

8

OPEN FERTILITY BORDERS

Defending Access to Cross-Border Fertility Care in the United States

Kimberly M. Mutcherson[*]

Introduction

GENERALLY, WHEN ONE speaks of the length to which an individual will go to procreate, that conversation is not about geography. In our modern world, though, such a conversation may be about geographical distance as people seek access to fertility care away from their home countries. This phenomenon of cross-border fertility care (CBFC) is an offshoot of the more widely reported phenomenon of medical tourism and refers specifically to the act of traveling for fertility treatment.[1] Infertility is a global public health issue. Those with the resources and wherewithal can circumvent their fertility challenges through the use of assisted reproductive technology (ART), and some will do so even if it requires time and travel. Such travel is increasingly popular and possible in a world of growing infertility and accessible technology that allows the infertile to have biologically or genetically related children.

---

[*] Associate Professor of Law, Rutgers School of Law, Camden. Many thanks to Ashley Gagnon, Ross Mazer, and Brian Morrison at Rutgers and Erin Train and Jamie Gershkow at the Earle Mack School of Law at Drexel University for their research assistance.

[1] Many commentators use the term "reproductive tourism" to refer to such travel. However, as Dr. G. Pennings explains, "[t]ourism mainly refers to travelling for recreational reasons. Indirectly, this connotation devalues the desire motivating the journey; it implies that the fertility tourist goes abroad to look for something exotic and strange." G. Pennings, *Reproductive Tourism as Moral Pluralism in Motion*, 28 J. MED. ETHICS 337, 337 (2002). I think it inappropriate to perpetuate the use of a term that may belittle those to whom it is applied even if that is not the intent of the individual employing the phrase. Therefore, I embrace the term "cross-border fertility care" as used by other scholars. *See, e.g.,* Karl Nygren et al., *Cross Border Fertility Care—International Committee Monitoring Assisted Reproductive Technologies Global Survey: 2006 Data and Estimates*, 94 FERTILITY & STERILITY e4 (June 2010).

ART and the uses to which it has been put and will be put in the future spark substantial ethical anxieties about the use of that technology and the potential need for regulation. Coupled with the disquiet attendant to globalization, CBFC, especially when sought to make use of technology in a way forbidden by the laws of the home country, raises concern about high-tech procreation, exploitation of market players, commodification of children, and, even, the relationships among nations.

With its liberal attitude toward the fertility industry, the United States has substantial appeal as a destination country for those whose access to ART is limited or wholly barred in their home country. To the extent that inconsistencies in ART regulation raise anxieties, the idea of forum shopping for welcoming places to make babies draws criticism and concern. This chapter makes the case that the laissez-faire U.S. attitude toward CBFC is a good thing that, without creating significant detriments to others, benefits those seeking CBFC. Although the phenomenon of CBFC cannot resist being swallowed by general debates about ART, it is possible to imagine a subset of arguments that either as a matter of law or policy would lead down the road of forbidding or at least discouraging people from coming to the United States for CBFC. This chapter opposes any such effort and contemplates public policy concerns about CBFC and why those concerns do not warrant expression in law at this time. Ultimately, I conclude that a pluralist ethic of family formation and procreation urges wide access to fertility treatment across geographic borders.

I. Making Babies in The United States

The United States has a reputation as the Wild West of fertility treatment because of its comparative lack of strong regulation of the multimillion dollar fertility industry.[2] The vastness of this industry reflects the substantial number of people around the globe who experience difficulty in their attempts to become pregnant through coital reproduction. Medical infertility[3] is a global phenomenon with a worldwide estimate of 9 percent prevalence for current infertility and 16 percent prevalence for lifetime infertility in couples in fertile age groups.[4] Millions of people qualify as infertile under

---

[2] The American Society for Reproductive Medicine takes issue with this claim and argues that ART is "one of most highly regulated of all medical practices in the United States." American Society for Reproductive Medicine, *Oversight of Assisted Reproductive Technology*, *available at* http://www.asrm.org/uploadedFiles/Content/About_Us/Media_and_Public_Affairs/OversiteOfART%20%282%29.pdf (last visited Oct. 23, 2011).

[3] Medical infertility is a failure to achieve pregnancy after a year of unprotected heterosexual intercourse. Centers for Disease Control and Prevention, *Infertility FAQs*, *available at* http://www.cdc.gov/reproductivehealth/Infertility/index.htm (last visited Apr. 10, 2011). A person over the age of thirty-five will be labeled infertile if pregnancy is not achieved after six months of unprotected sexual intercourse. *Id.* Being able to get pregnant without being able to carry that pregnancy to term is also a form of infertility. *Id.*

[4] Nygren, *supra* note 1, at e5.

the medical definition of that term, and more qualify as socially infertile because although physically capable of becoming pregnant or creating a pregnancy through coital reproduction, they use ART due to social or other factors that are obstacles to procreating, including being single, being in a same-sex relationship, or carrying genes for disease or disability. Although the socially infertile may not comprise a large segment of those who use ART, they are an important part of a discussion of travelers seeking CBFC.

Across the categories of ART users, people pursue procreation and parenthood through technology with great vigor. For some individuals, the quest for a child will literally lead them around the world, and, for a variety of reasons, many of those world travelers will find themselves either physically or virtually pursuing that quest in the United States. And, although there are no especially good data about CBFC for a variety of reasons, "most of the experts who analyse the phenomenon agree that cross-border reproductive care will continue to increase in the coming years."[5]

There are multiple reasons individuals and couples seek CBFC, but saving money is unlikely to be one. Unlike in other medical tourism contexts, especially when travel is to developing nations, some number of those who travel to the United States for CBFC pay more for fertility care than at home because they are leaving nations with robust public health care financing. In those nations, the government pays for ART as a component of subsidized health care.[6] Ironically, the availability of payment for these services can lead to the situations that cause people to travel. This is because the exchange rates for public financing are often significant limits on who may use those government-financed fertility services. These access rules can be much more stringent than in the United States where ART treatment is self-financed or is covered by an individual's own health insurance if she is lucky.[7] The intricacies of local regulation may move a person to seek CBFC. So it is the case that although fertility treatment is available in many parts of the developed world, and even in some parts of the developing world, there are several reasons a person might travel to the United States in order to access ART.[8]

---

[5] Anna Pia Ferraretti et al., *Cross-Border Reproductive Care: A Phenomenon Expressing the Controversial Aspects of Reproductive Technologies*, 20 REPROD. BIOMED. 261, 265 (2010).

[6] Assuming that a patient meets the criteria, the National Health Service in the United Kingdom will cover the cost of fertility treatment for eligible patients. HFEA, *NHS Fertility Treatment*, HUMAN FERTILISATION & EMBRYOLOGY AUTHORITY, *available at* http://www.hfea.gov.uk/fertility-treatment-cost-nhs.html (last updated Aug. 29, 2009). Patients can also choose to access care privately if they are willing and able to pay the cost on their own. *Id.*

[7] *State Laws Related to Insurance Coverage for Infertility Treatment*, Nat'l Conf. St. Legislators, http://www.ncsl.org/default.aspx?tabid=14391 (last updated Apr. 2011).Sparse insurance coverage in the United States means "the costs of infertility treatment are usually borne by infertile couples, including an estimated 85% of the costs of IVF. As a result, in the United States, access to IVF services is limited primarily to older, white, middle-to upper-income individuals." Robert D. Nachtigall, *International Infertility Disparities*, 85 FERTILITY & STERILITY 871, 874 (Apr. 2006).

[8] It is the case that "[m]odern diagnostic and treatment services are available in most countries." Nygren et al., *supra* note 1 at e5.

Besides the physical lack of facilities or physicians to provide care (obvious reasons to leave one's home country), the reasons for travel frequently have to do with limits on ART accessibility rather than total unavailability of the technology.[9] One such limit is long waiting lists for access to gametes or surrogates in some countries. Specific types of restrictive regulation may impact the pool size.[10] For instance, in the United Kingdom, where ova cannot be sold anonymously and where those sellers can only be reimbursed for their services and not paid a fee, the wait to purchase ova can be as long as one to two years.[11] Many older women, whose chance of pregnancy with their own eggs is greatly diminished, leave the United Kingdom in order to purchase eggs to seek pregnancy.[12]

A further reason for fertility travel is to access a service unavailable in the home country because of legislative bans. Globally, the most banned procedures are "surrogacy, social sex selection, gamete donation, preimplantation genetic diagnosis (PGD) and screening (PGS)," and the countries that ban one of more of these procedures are a diverse group.[13] Austria, Germany, Italy, Tunisia, and Turkey do not allow the sale of sperm.[14] Italy, Tunisia, and Turkey prohibit the use of donor sperm outside of IVF, as do Hong Kong and Slovenia.[15] Sperm donors or sellers can be anonymous in France and Greece, but they must be identified or identifiable in the Netherlands, Norway, and Sweden.[16] Germany, Italy, Norway, Switzerland, Tunisia, Turkey, China, Croatia, Egypt, Japan, Morocco, and the Philippines forbid the use of donor or purchased ova by law or by guidelines, although their use is permitted in at least twenty-one other countries.[17] The United Kingdom and Canada make commercial surrogacy illegal.[18] Thirty-six countries, including India, Canada, China, Germany, Russia, Singapore, and the United Kingdom, have laws or policies that prevent sex selection.[19] Thus, across a

---

[9] According to the World Health Organization, "Most of those who suffer from infertility live in developing countries where infertility services in general, and ART in particular, are not available." WORLD HEALTH ORG., CURRENT PRACTICES AND CONTROVERSIES IN ASSISTED REPRODUCTION: REPORT OF A MEETING ON "MEDICAL, ETHICAL AND SOCIAL ASPECTS OF ASSISTED REPRODUCTION" xv (Effy Vayena et al. eds., 2001), *available at* http://whqlibdoc.who.int/hq/2002/9241590300.pdf; *see also* Nachtigall, *supra* note 7, at 873.

[10] Suzanne Leigh, *Reproductive Tourism*, USA TODAY, May 2, 2005, http://www.usatoday.com/news/health/2005-05-02-reproductive-tourism_x.htm (last visited Mar. 28, 2011).

[11] American Society for Reproductive Medicine, *IFFS Surveillance 2007*, 87 FERTILITY & STERILITY S 33 (SUPP. 2007).

[12] Sarah Boseley, *NHS Restrictions Prompt Fertility Tourism Boom*, GUARDIAN, JUNE 30, 2009,http://www.guardian.co.uk/society/2009/jun/29/women-over-40-fertility-tourism.

[13] Ferraretti et al., *supra* note 5, at 262.

[14] American Society for Reproductive Medicine, *supra* note 11, at S28.

[15] *Id.*

[16] *Id.*

[17] *Id.* at S31.

[18] Many countries ban commercial surrogacy. *See generally*, Mina Chang, *Womb for Rent*, HARV. INT'L REV. 11–12 (July 6, 2009).

[19] Memorandum by Marcy Darnovsky in preparation for April 13 New York Sex Selection Meeting, *Countries with Laws or Polices on Sex Selection*, Center for Genetics & Society (Apr. 2009), *available at* http://www.geneticsandsociety.org/downloads/200904_sex_selection_memo.pdf (last visited Apr. 8, 2011).

range of issues and nations a citizen might find his procreative desires thwarted by the laws that bind him on his home soil.

A final systemic driver of CBFC is laws that discriminate in access to ART on the basis of social status or demographic characteristics such as marital status and sexual orientation. As a result, same-sex couples; single gay people; couples who are cohabiting, but not married; or unmarried heterosexuals travel out of their home countries to find a friendlier forum in which to create a child. Examples of this situation are French law on ART that denies access for single people and further restricts the use of reproductive technology to people who are heterosexual.[20] Similarly, Italy's law limits use of ART to people who are legally married or in committed heterosexual relationships.[21]

For the reasons described in the preceding paragraphs, from waiting lists to discrimination to missing technology, people seek CBFC, and those who can afford the high price tag come to the United States to access equally high-quality fertility care. The remainder of this chapter concerns itself with analyzing whether movement of this type is good for those who travel, for the countries from which they leave and to which they will return, or for the countries that welcome their business.

II. Differentiating CBFC from Medical Tourism in General

Concerns about general medical tourism focus on issues such as whether medical care provided in destination countries is high quality;[22] what legal remedies an individual has for medical malpractice;[23] and whether the resource allocation to support medical travel detracts from the overall quality of medical care in a developing nation.[24] For several reasons, these concerns are either irrelevant or substantially less relevant in the context of people traveling to the United States for ART.

The United States is a world leader in providing ART, which means that the care provided in this country is among the best in the world in terms of quality. Although many aspects of the industry are not closely regulated, the actual provision of medical care is regulated by the system that regulates all medical care in this country, which requires licensed physicians in good standing.[25] There is also medical screening of those who sell

---

[20] Connie Cho, *Defining Parenthood: Assisted Reproduction in France*, 7 YALE J. MED. & LAW 19 (Apr. 7, 2011), *available at* http://www.yalemedlaw.com/2011/04/defining-parenthood-assisted-reproduction-in-fran ce/ (last visited May 25, 2011).

[21] V. Fineschi et al., *The New Italian Law on Assisted Reproduction Technology*, 31 J. MED. & ETHICS 536, 537 (2005).

[22] *Id.*

[23] *See, e.g.,* Nathan Cortez, *Recalibrating the Legal Risks of Cross-Border Health Care*, 10 YALE J. HEALTH POL'Y, LAW & ETHICS 1, 8–67 (2010).

[24] Priya Shetty, *Medical Tourism Booms in India, but at What Cost?* 376 LANCET 671, 672 (2010).

[25] As noted in a report from the American Society of Reproductive Medicine (ASRM):

> As with all medical practice in the United States, safety in reproductive medicine is assured by a combination of state and federal government regulation and professional self-regulation that includes facility accreditation and practitioner certification. On the state level, there is a strict physician licensure system. On the federal level, several agencies enforce standards and

gametes[26] and a system of professional self-regulation, which, although neither perfect nor binding, sets standards for how physicians should provide care.[27] Finally, the laboratories used to store gametes and provide a range of fertility services must be licensed and inspected.[28] Concern about substandard medical care is no reason to discourage people from traveling to the United States, and the availability of high-quality care is a justifiable reason to draw people to the United States for CBFC.

The availability of the tort system to redress wrongs where injury results from a provider's negligence also makes the concern about redress of injuries less relevant in the context of people traveling to the United States. Certainly, there is a broader critique of the U.S. medical malpractice system and its impact on the provision of health care, but that critique is unrelated to the use of ART in general or the use of ART by those seeking CBFC. Individualized barriers to accessing the legal system may exist for some, but the structure for seeking a legal response is intact and functioning. Finally, although there are many reasons to think that the U.S. health care system is flawed, a glut of people seeking to practice very specialized fertility treatment to the detriment of other necessary areas of medical care does not appear to be threatening the health care infrastructure in the country.

A final concern, raised explicitly in the context of ART given that using the technology often calls for third-party assistance, including that of gamete sellers and/or surrogate mothers, is that of exploitation of people in developing nations by citizens of developed nations. This is a serious possibility, but it is complicated in a conversation about travel from one developed nation to another or from a developing nation to a developed nation. Although economic insecurity and other substantial forms of disadvantage exist in the United States, the exploitation concerns that accompany these discussions when focused on the specific vulnerabilities of people in developing nations are of a different kind and degree than what exists when it comes to CBFC where the United States is the destination country. A woman in the United States who sells ova to help finance her college education or a military wife who signs on to be a surrogate is different in kind and character from a woman in a developing nation who participates in baby markets from a position of complete economic insecurity.

Further, where there are legitimate concerns about exploitation of third parties in the United States, those issues can and should be addressed through domestic laws and policies to protect those parties from exploitation no matter the travel status of the

---

practices designed to protect public health and safety. Several national groups accredit laboratories as well. In the realm of professional self-regulation, an on-going system of quality assurance includes specialty training and certification of physicians, accreditation of clinics and ethical and practice guidelines developed by professional organizations through consensus and evidence. AMERICAN SOCIETY FOR REPRODUCTIVE MEDICINE, OVERSIGHT OF ASSISTED REPRODUCTIVE TECHNOLOGY 4 (2010), *available at* http://www.asrm.org/uploadedFiles/Content/About_Us/Media_and_Public_Affairs/OversiteOfART%20%282%29.pdf.

[26] 21 CFR § 1271.80.

[27] The American Society for Reproductive Medicine and its affiliated agency, the Society for Assisted Reproductive Technologies (SART), are critical components of fertility industry self-regulation in the United States. *See* AMERICAN SOCIETY FOR REPRODUCTIVE MEDICINE, *supra* note 25, at 3.

[28] *What You Should Know—Reproductive Tissue Donation*, U.S. FOOD & DRUG ADMIN. (Nov. 5, 2010), http://www.fda.gov/BiologicsBloodVaccines/SafetyAvailability/TissueSafety/ucm232876.htm.

person from whom exploitation is feared. And the travel status of the person feared to be creating exploitation is irrelevant to any need for the United States to address that exploitation through policy.

III. The Good of Open Fertility Borders

Attempts to make policy about CBFC might coalesce around characteristics of fertility travelers and their reasons for leaving their home countries. Recognizing the potential for discrimination among the categories of those seeking CBFC, it is necessary to contemplate what fair principles might guide an effort to welcome some attempts at child creation and condemn others. The following scenarios offer a common text for considering this dilemma:

Scenario 1

A sixty-two–year-old British woman comes to the United States seeking insemination with the sperm of her deceased biological brother who bequeathed the frozen sperm to her with the request that she use it to become pregnant and bear a child.[29]

Scenario 2

A legally married lesbian couple from Canada comes to the United States to purchase and use sperm from an anonymous seller offered by a U.S.-based cryobank.

Scenario 3

A single man from France comes to the United States to purchase ova that will be fertilized with his sperm and transferred to a gestational carrier in California (not the woman who supplies the ova), to whom he will pay a fee of $15,000 for her reproductive labor.

Scenario 4

An opposite-sex unmarried Italian couple, both of whom are otherwise fertile, travels to the United States for IVF coupled with PGD, which will allow them to transfer only female embryos and avoid the risk of passing on a sex-linked disease.[30]

---

[29] It is possibly apocryphal, but one scholar references a story about a sixty-two–year-old French woman who came to the United States seeking a fertility specialist who would inseminate her with her brother's sperm. See Pennings, *supra* note 1, at 337. Given her age, it is unlikely that such a patient would be eligible for insemination as she would almost certainly be postmenopausal, and pregnancy would require the use of an egg from a much younger woman, which would then be fertilized with the brother's sperm and transferred to the womb of the patient/intended mother during an in vitro fertilization cycle. As explained later in the text, whether seeking artificial insemination or IVF, there will be significant barriers to this patient's quest for assistance in creating a pregnancy.

[30] "X-linked Diseases Are Single Gene Disorders That Reflect the Presence of Defective Genes on the X Chromosome." Richard Twyman, *X-Linked Diseases*, WELLCOME TRUST, *available at* http://genome. wellcome.ac.uk/doc_wtd020851.html (last visited Mar. 17, 2011).

Scenario 5

A couple from India travels to the United States to use PGD in conjunction with IVF to screen for male embryos for transfer in order to effectuate a preference for sons.

These scenarios, all plausible if not all equally likely, are illegal in the country of origin.[31] The woman in scenario 1 would be thwarted by the tight web of regulation governing ART in the United Kingdom where the Human Fertilisation and Embryology Act of 1990 established the legislative framework that governs ART and created the Human Fertilisation and Embryology Authority (HFEA).[32] The HFEA has ongoing responsibility for overseeing the use of ART.[33] Licensed clinics must "take account of the welfare of any child to be born as a result of the treatment to be provided (including the need of that child for supportive parenting)."[34] These requirements are a small slice of a lengthy guidance document.[35] In the highly regulated United Kingdom, high-tech incest, posthumous reproduction, even with consent, and postmenopausal pregnancy for a single woman will never pass muster.

In scenario 2, the couple could not make a child with an anonymous sperm seller because Canada made it illegal to sell sperm anonymously in 2004. Therefore they would be obliged to travel in order to access this service.[36] In scenario 3, the person seeking CFBC would need to leave France to engage in a commercial surrogacy arrangement because France made commercial surrogacy a criminal offense in 1994,[37] and because the country's control over ART includes refusing to provide this care to people who are single.[38] In scenario 4, Italy's strict laws on ART exclude unmarried individuals, though not unmarried couples, from using ART and forbid couples from refusing to transfer embryos even after PGD.[39] Finally, the couple in scenario 5 would leave India because that country has legislated against sex selection.[40]

By contrast, it is less clear that any of the possible scenarios are illegal in the United States where there is a brisk and legal market in the anonymous sale of gametes and surrogacy is explicitly legal in several states.[41] No state or federal laws specifically prevent people from using ART who are single or who are gay and, where inclusive

---

[31] The Human Fertilisation and Embryology Act, 1990, c. 37 (Eng.).

[32] *Id.*

[33] *Id.*

[34] *Id.* at § 13(5).

[35] HUMAN FERTILISATION & EMBRYOLOGY AUTHORITY, CODE OF PRACTICE: GUIDANCE NOTES § 8.11 (8th ed. 2009), *available at* http://www.hfea.gov.uk/5733.html.

[36] Assisted Human Reproduction Act, S.C. 2004, c.2, § 10 (Can.).

[37] CODE CIVIL [C. civ.] art. 16-7 (Fr.).

[38] Cho, *supra* note 20.

[39] LEGGE 19 febbraio 2004, n. 40 Norme in materia di procreazione medicalmente assistita, *available at* http://www.camera.it/parlam/leggi/04040l.htm; *see* Fineschi et al., *supra* note 21.

[40] The Prenatal Diagnostic Techniques (Regulation and Prevention of Misuse) Act, 1994, No. 57, Acts of Parliament, 1994 (India).

[41] Cal. Fam. Code § 7600 et seq. (West 2009).

antidiscrimination statutes exist, a person discriminated against in the use of ART based on a protected category, such as sexual orientation, may sue a health care provider for unlawful discrimination.[42] Finally, there are no state or federal laws banning the practice of PGD as such, nor are there statutes that would make a person civilly or criminally liable for choosing not to implant embryos of a specific sex.

As a starting point of analysis, I should note that formal legality of the desired act in each scenario does not guarantee that travel to the United States will be successful. Physicians may choose not to work with a prospective patient and parent so long as that refusal is not based on legally protected categories.[43] The lack of legal impediments means that fertility providers, frequently with guidance from professional agencies, must decide what do when faced with a would-be patient whose procreative desires are troubling.[44] Even in the absence of legal rules, it is doubtful that the woman in scenario 1 would leave the United States with her desires fulfilled.

For different reasons, the actors in scenario 5, the Indian couple coming to the United States to engage in sex selection, might raise red flags for fertility providers who are ethically troubled by acceding to such preferences even as other clinics tout their sex selection programs to an international audience.[45] The actors in the other scenarios, however, almost certainly would find satisfaction in the United States, which leads back to the initial concern that the search for neutral criteria to determine whether the United States should facilitate modes of babymaking that are rejected in a person's land of origin cannot be a successful one. Standing alone, unfairly or unintentionally biased criteria for excluding some from access to CBFC is a legitimate reason to avoid regulation in this arena, but there are several more positive reasons CBFC provided in the United States is a good that warrants encouragement and protection.

A. FACILITATING FREEDOM FROM OPPRESSION OR DISCRIMINATION

One might argue that the United States should not make itself a literal breeding ground for people whose home countries have determined that it is inappropriate for them to use ART either because of who they are or because of what they would like to do with the technology. However, there are equally strong arguments to be made on the other

---

[42] See, e.g., N. Coast Women's Care Med, Grp. v. San Diego Cnty. Super. Ct., 189 P.3d 959 (2008).

[43] Kimberly Mutcherson, *Disabling Dreams of Parenthood: The Fertility Industry, Anti-discrimination, and Parents with Disabilities*, 27 L. & INEQUALITY 311 (Summer 2009) (discussing discrimination on the basis of disability in the provision of fertility services).

[44] The ASRM provides several ethics opinions to guide practice among its members. *See, e.g.*, The Ethics Committee of the American Soc'y for Reproductive Med., *Child-Rearing Ability and the Provision of Fertility Services*, 92 FERTILITY & STERILITY 864 (Sept. 2009).

[45] *See* Ethics Committee of the American Soc'y for Reproductive Med., *Preconception Gender Selection for Nonmedical Reasons*, 75 FERTILITY & STERILITY 861 (May 2001). By contrast, the Fertility Institutes, with offices in Los Angeles, New York, and Mexico, prominently advertises the availability of sex selection through PGD to couples from all over the world. THE FERTILITY INSTITUTES, http://www.fertility-docs.com/fertility_gender.phtml (last visited Apr. 10, 2011).

side about the important character of procreation and the importance of equality and human freedom.

Even if travelers have a moral obligation to obey the law of their home countries no matter where they are, the question remains of which nation, home or destination, bears the responsibility of enforcing that obligation through law and policy. Therefore, even conceding such an obligation, the United States need not close its borders to these travelers because although there may be a "prima facie obligation of citizens to obey national law" there "is a wealth of precedents in reproductive healthcare, i.e. termination of pregnancy, sterilization and contraception" in which individuals, especially women, leave their home countries to access care.[46] Women from a long list of nations ranging from Spain to Ireland have fled their homes to access various aspects of reproductive health care, including abortion and birth control, denied to them on their home soil.[47]

A woman who left Ireland to have an abortion in New Jersey would not be denied access to that legal medical procedure. In fact, many would defend and praise U.S. willingness to allow a woman seeking abortion, birth control, or sterilization services banned or criminalized in her home country to access this care as a way of affirming an individual right to bodily integrity and a broad right to reproductive autonomy. In fact, as a historical matter, differing rules on access to reproductive health services were "the first cause of migration in the field of reproduction."[48]

In circumstances where the care sought outside of the home jurisdiction is of the type thought to be well within the parameters of acceptable health care in many parts of the world, condemning people to follow the precepts of their home nations while abroad would perpetuate an already dismal set of circumstances for affected individuals. Circumventing such rules is a praiseworthy act of defiance or civil disobedience to the extent that an individual refuses to be bound by a legal code that denies her the opportunity to express the full extent of her human freedom. That this may value one set of beliefs over another is a consequence of political pluralism among nations, which is also a good in that it allows sovereign nations to create and protect their own cultural norms while recognizing that those norms are questioned or rejected on other shores. It may be easier to see this link in the context of terminating an unwanted pregnancy or getting access to contraception that will aid in preventing pregnancy, but a central component of modern-day reproductive justice is a recognition that exercising control

---

[46] G. Pennings et al., *ESHRE Task Force on Ethics and Law 15: Cross-Border Reproductive Care*, 23 Hum. Reprod. 2182, 2182 (2008).

[47] As one commentator explained, "In Spain, we had a lot of experience with such reproductive exile; when oral contraceptives were banned, Spanish women acquired them in France; when termination of pregnancy was illegal, they went to England." Roberto Matorras, Letter to the Editor, *Reproductive Exile versus Reproductive Tourism*, 20 Hum. Reprod. 3571, 3571 (2005). According to a 2010 report issued by Human Rights Watch on abortion access in Ireland, that country's restrictive abortion laws mean that "all women living on Irish soil are forced to travel to access a medical procedure." Human Rights Watch, A State of Isolation—Access to Abortion for Women in Ireland 2 (2010), *available at* http://www.hrw.org/en/reports/2010/01/28/state-isolation (last visited May 13, 2011).

[48] Ferraretti et al., *supra* note 5, at 262.

over when to have a baby and the conditions of pregnancy and childbirth warrants the same level of care and concern as decisions not to procreate.[49]

Where a country denies access to tools of procreation and family expansion on the basis of invidious discrimination, such as on the basis of sexual orientation, the United States should proudly open its borders for those who would circumvent such rules. Allowing these acts is akin to providing a platform for people to express objections to the restrictive and discriminatory rules in their home countries. Certainly most people who travel to access ART will not think of themselves as making a political statement and will instead focus on building their families, but when they do build those families and go back home, their presence facilitates the process of breaking down the restrictions that drove them from home in the first place. To the extent that open fertility borders play a role in helping to dismantle unfair discriminatory structures in other countries, a decision not to restrict access to fertility care is an important policy choice.

Similarly, one could also argue in this context that the United States has an interest in acting so as to protect procreation and family building as a human right. However, the difficulty of this argument is similar to the difficulty that comes in the domestic context when one tries to make sense of whether ART is a constitutional right that emanates from the fundamental right to procreate. A person skeptical of ART as a form of human procreation might question whether access to ART is a human right that warrants sufficient respect so that it should be made available to fertility travelers. To many people, having a baby is not akin to traveling across borders for lifesaving care. Instead, one has to root the importance of ART in a belief that access to family formation and procreation are significant enough that those who seek those things through technology should be welcomed.

Here again, open fertility borders expand rather than restrict the definition of family, a process that is proceeding at a slower pace than some in the United States would like, and at a much more rapid pace than others would like to see, but a process that moves forward nonetheless. As states slowly grind their way to greater openness and inclusivity for diverse family structures as well as broader understandings of how children's best interests can be served, shutting borders to individuals similarly inclined to embrace this kind of expansion is a regressive move. The United States might want to be a safe haven for the married lesbian couple or the single gay man as a way of putting into practice a belief in both familial and procreative pluralism.

B. FACILITATING PRACTICES THAT CREATE MORAL AMBIGUITY

A more vexing set of concerns raised in the proffered scenarios is how to react to foreign rules and laws focused not on a desire to deprive individuals of access to genetic or biological parenthood, but on a governmental obligation to act in the interest of its citizens. This interest may be expressed by efforts to diminish practices such as sex

---

[49] Zakiya Luna, *From Rights to Justice: Women of Color Changing the Face of US Reproductive Rights Organizing*, 4 SOCIETIES WITHOUT BORDERS 343, 361 (2009).

selection that, on a global scale, disproportionately target girls.[50] More broadly, governments may believe that they have an obligation to protect the category of human procreation by refusing to allow market principles to overtake the process of creating and giving birth to new human beings. In these circumstances, striking the balance between protecting an individual interest in family and procreation against a societal interest is challenging.

A home country government might claim that it is precisely because the traveler will return with a child and integrate himself and his expanded family into the community that the United States owes it to other countries to be more restrained in its provision of fertility services. The crux of such an argument is that the societal consequences of choices made by people accessing CBFC are partially born by the country that hosts the traveler, but they weigh most heavily upon the countries to which those travelers return. As India attempts to reduce the number of missing girls, it must contend with those who travel abroad to avoid its strictures against sex selection. Italy's attempt to respect "natural" procreation and the human variation that it brings, including disease or disability, is thwarted by a country that turns a blind eye to its concerns. In these cases, open borders, unlike discrimination against single people or families created by gays and lesbians, facilitate and support an act the home country labels as discriminatory, rather than rejecting that act. If one gives merit to these claims, then CFBC may be so devastating to a country's character that not only should travelers feel bound by the laws of home, but the destination country should seek to effectuate the moral precepts that undergird those laws when foreign citizens are on their soil.

One response to this claim is that if there is such an obligation to respect the rules of one's home, it is the obligation and right of the home country to enforce these rules, rather than an obligation of the destination country. Countries that wish to assert power beyond their borders to restrict the actions of their citizens can make the option of CBFC less attractive. Some nations sanction physicians or others who promote CBFC.[51] Some countries have laws that make it complicated, if not impossible, for a would-be parent who accesses fertility services in a foreign country that are illegal in the home country to create a recognizable legal relationship with that child or to establish citizenship for the child.[52] Still other travelers will find that the adoption laws of their country will not let them create the legally recognized families that they seek even if they are able to bring a child into a relationship by accessing services in the United States. For instance, a same-sex couple not allowed to legally marry in a home country may be barred from being the adoptive parents of a child born through an arrangement

---

[50] *See, e.g.,* Sabu M. George, *Millions of Missing Girls: From Fetal Sexing to High Technology Sex Selection in India,* 26 PRENATAL DIAGNOSIS 604, 604–05 (2006); Ted Plafker, *Sex Selection in China Sees 117 Boys Born for Every 100 Girls,* 324 BRITISH M. J. 1233 (May 2002).

[51] Ferraretti et al., *supra* note 5, at 262.

[52] New Zealand warns its citizens who engage in international surrogacy arrangements that foreign birth certificates, adoption decrees, or passports might not be sufficient to meet New Zealand's immigration or citizenships requirements. INTERNATIONAL SURROGACY, http://www.docstoc.com/docs/134355871/International--Surrogacy--Information--Sheet (last visited Apr. 9, 2011).

facilitated in the United States that would not have been sanctioned in the home country. Arguably, where the laws of a home country will thwart the family-building goals of reproductive travelers, the travel should not be undertaken. But, for many people for whom having a child is paramount, and particularly having a child with whom they share a genetic connection, the risks inherent in engaging in CBFC will be worth it. These risks create an obligation on the part of any agency or attorney who brokers such deals to make sure that clients are well-informed of the potential pitfalls, legal and otherwise, of their choice to travel for access to ART, but this does not require official limitations on access to these procedures.

All of this discussion, though, begs the question of whether there is value in providing access to ART tools that will be used in ways that potentially denigrate whole communities of people, for instance through sex selection or discarding embryos that will create children with disabilities. As a starting point, one can reject the premise of the inquiry because the presumed remedy, denying access to specific reproductive tools, does not address the core issue, a cultural preference for one gender or against disability. Eliminating sexism or discrimination against people with disabilities requires fundamental transformation of societies and that change will almost certainly result in different practices related to the use of various technologies. However, it seems overly optimistic to believe that barring the use of technology is anything more than a symbolic move.

There are instances of worldwide cooperation to stamp out universally condemned practices, and it is appropriate for nations to seek and expect cooperation when it comes to citizens who cross borders to engage in these behaviors. For instance, as part of an international effort to protect minors from sex trafficking, the United States punishes its citizens who travel to foreign countries to engage in sexual conduct that is illegal in those countries and in the United States, such as sexual contact with minors.[53] In light of a worldwide consensus, enshrined in the laws of many nations, that sex crimes against minors deserve to be severely punished and deterred through the use of the substantial weight of the criminal law, it makes sense that the United States, along with other nations, finds ways to cooperate across national borders in stopping this behavior. CBFC, however, is not sex tourism. Although it involves the creation of children, it certainly does not involve the systematic sexual abuse and exploitation of children. Some may contend that commodification of reproduction is not good for a society, but it is difficult to argue that bringing wanted children into the world who will be cared for by loving parents is akin to abuse. The dissimilarities continue, but the end point is that the diversity of ART regulation speaks to the lack of international consensus on what is and is not acceptable reproductive behavior. Where such a consensus does not exist, the rationale for requesting extraterritorial cooperation to enforce culturally specifically laws dissipates.[54]

---

[53] 18 U.S.C. § 2423 (2006).
[54] *But see* I. Glenn Cohen, *Circumvention Tourism*, 97 CORNELL L. REV. 1309 (2012).

C. CBFC AS A SAFETY VALVE

Rather than undermining the lawmaking of other countries, it is possible to imagine that the role played by the United States in the global market for ART is critical and positive overall. Other countries may feel free to restrict choices within their borders because they know that access to such care exists elsewhere. Richard Storrow suggests that "fertility tourism acts as a moral safety valve permitting national parliaments to express local sentiments while simultaneously acknowledging the moral autonomy of those who do not agree with those sentiments."[55] Others describe the lack of harmonization of ART laws, which facilitates migration, as "reduc[ing] moral conflicts and contribut[ing] to the peaceful coexistence of different ethical and religious views."[56] If these scholars are correct, then a refusal to enforce the rules of a home country on U.S. soil is in keeping with the home country's attempt to create a particular type of society on its own soil while recognizing that its citizens might want things that the governments deems not in the interest of the society as a whole. Nations with freedom of movement are well aware that their citizens are not trapped within their borders. When those citizens use their passports to exercise a desire for a freedom not available to them at home, that is a fair and perhaps expected exercise of choice.

One might argue in this circumstance that the United States should be wary of embracing a role as a nation incapable of or unwilling to respond to ethically dubious procreative practices. On the other hand, the country could be playing a vital role within our flat world where it is good to support pluralistic choices about procreation and family. If it is right that countries feel less constrained to liberalize their laws because they know that their citizens can access care elsewhere, in keeping with the earlier discussion about accessing CBFC as an act of resistance, the United States can think of its open borders as a safe haven for those who would be denied fairness and equality in their countries of origin. This reinforces a vision of the United States as a pluralist nation with an ethos of equality in access to human goods, including freedom to procreate.

Of course, in many nations, only those with class privilege will be able to express their disagreement with their nation's laws by leaving. This does not mean that people who remain within the country will see no benefit from the availability of CBFC. Over time, the outward flow of citizens may force countries to reconsider the strictness of their own rules and perhaps even change those rules to respond to the needs of their citizens. The United Kingdom reconsidered its policy on preimplantation diagnosis after a widely publicized case of citizens leaving to access a variation of this service abroad.[57] If reconsiderations of this type occur, the United States should feel that its role in leading nations toward more inclusive policies is justified and productive.

---

[55] Richard Storrow, *Quests for Conception, Fertility Tourists, Globalization and Feminist Legal Theory*, 57 HASTINGS L.J. 295, 305 (2005–2006).

[56] Ferraretti et al., *supra* note 5, at 262.

[57] In 2004, Charlie Whitaker's parents sought permission from the HFEA to use preimplantation tissue typing (PTT) and IVF to create a child whose cord blood could be used to save Charlie, who was

Finally, a nation may seek to diminish access to CBFC not only because of the psychic consequences to the society, but because of potential costs to the local public health system. As Debra Spar explains, "[a] cross-border market for reproduction also means that societies that oppose assisted reproduction may nevertheless pay its costs. For who can prove that premature quintuplets born in Bremen were conceived in Istanbul?"[58] The unique nature of the care being provided means that the consequences of seeking CBFC impact "not just the health and well-being of one individual but also that of the child or children born of the process, as well as potential future generations."[59] This concern ostensibly has less to do with who is seeking to procreate and expand a family and more to do with the public health consequences of such choices for society, families, and children. The desire to protect patients and future children from objectively measured harms inherent in multiple gestations counsels changes in medical practice, but the genesis of those changes need not be legislation or other forms of hard law as there are other mechanisms for disseminating and encouraging change in medical practice even across borders. In the case of multiple gestations, there are concrete efforts to harmonize medical practice across borders. An example of this phenomenon is found in practices related to the number of embryos transferred during an IVF cycle. Even without the kind of extensive control exercised over fertility practices in other countries, reproductive physicians in the United States, through the professional associations that govern them, are following stricter standards for embryo transfer in IVF calculated to lead to reductions in the number of multiple gestations.[60] This puts U.S. practice closer in line with the practice in other parts of the world and shows that harmonization is possible when the need is clear and the resolution supported by medical science.

Further, where thought appropriate, a nation could refuse prenatal or neonatal care in high-risk pregnancies created with ART in other countries. It seems clear, though, that the end product of such a move, harm to pregnant women and to children, is so counterproductive as to strongly counsel against it. Countries might also satisfy

---

in desperate need of a bone marrow transplant. The HFEA refused permission for the procedure and the parents went to the United States where they successfully used technology to give birth to a child who was a perfect donor for Charlie, thus saving his life and bringing a healthy new baby into their family. In 2008, after Parliament determined that PTT was an acceptable use of technology, the HFEA reconsidered its stance on so-called savior siblings and decided that it would grant permission for this specific use of reproductive technology in certain cases. Human Fertilisation & Embryology Authority, *How Is PTT Regulated in the United Kingdom*, *available at* http://www.hfea.gov.uk/5932.html (last visited Oct. 21, 2011).

58 Debra Spar, *Reproductive Tourism and the Regulatory Map*, 352 NEW ENGLAND J. MED. 531, 533 (Feb. 10. 2005).

59 Lynn Mainland & Elinor Wilson, *Principles of Establishment of the First International Forum on Cross-Border Reproductive Care*, 94 FERTILITY & STERILITY e2 (June 2010).

60 *See* Practice Committee of the American Society for Reproductive Medicine and the Practice Comm. of the Society for Assisted Reproductive Technology, *Guidelines on Number of Embryos Transferred*, 92 FERTILITY & STERILITY 1518 (Nov. 2009).

this concern by educating citizens about the risks of multiple gestations and encouraging them to seek care from physicians abroad who respond to these risks in their practice.

Conclusion

For some, the United States has earned its reputation as a wild frontier where anything goes when it comes to ART. However, although the Wild West metaphor has dramatic appeal, it is not accurate and it denigrates those who work in the industry with care and conscience and those who travel to the United States to pursue a common desire to procreate and expand one's family.

In a world in which national borders have lost much of their rigidity, CBFC is one of many services that consumers seek in forums that are friendlier because of cost, availability of service, or less-stringent laws. In such a world, denying medical services simply on the basis of travel status may in fact thwart the will of other nations, which use the United States as a safety valve for their own citizens, and detract from attempts to position the United States as a nation that embraces variations in family structure. At some points, a respect for diverse familial structures may seem in conflict with other values related to public health or commodification and, where countries feel strongly about these issues, they have law and policy-making tools at their own disposal to use against their own citizens. Whether these uses are appropriate is a question for a different discussion. Here, it suffices to say that the U.S. position that sees wide access to procreative tools as furthering other important societal goals warrants respect and should be sustained.

9

TOURISM

A Matter of Life and Death in the United Kingdom

Hazel Biggs[*] *and Caroline Jones* [†]

Introduction

The availability of cross-border medical care presents numerous ethical and legal challenges. In the United Kingdom the most contentious of these have been assisted reproduction and assisted dying, where cross-border arrangements and interjurisdictional mechanisms influence the kinds of health care that are available and the legal responses to their outcomes. This chapter examines some of the ways in which the law has been inconsistent in relation to these issues, revealing a number of paradoxes associated with the operation of the law in this context that can result in failure to secure the protections the law was designed to afford. Of particular concern is the apparent focus of the current legal regime on the protection of those who are vulnerable to exploitation when using reproductive services abroad, and at the end of life. Although statutes, the common law, and prosecutorial policy are couched in terms of safeguarding the interests of vulnerable persons and groups, scant attention is paid to defining who genuinely is vulnerable. Consequently some will suffer injustice, or even harm, through the application of the law.

[*] Head of Law School and Professor of Health Care Law and Bioethics, School of law, University of Southampton.
[†] Senior Lecturer, School of law, University of Southampton.

I. Travel for Reproduction and Death

A. CROSS-BORDER REPRODUCTIVE CARE[1]

Research has shown that a complex mosaic of reasons prompt prospective parents to choose cross-border reproductive care. A recent study by the European Society of Human Reproduction and Embryology's (ESHRE) Taskforce on Cross-Border Reproductive Care[2] found that UK nationals were more likely to cite "better access to treatment than in country of origin" as a primary reason for seeking treatment overseas, whereas German, Norwegian, and Italian nationals frequently referred to "legal reasons." It is possible that "better access" may include the ability to purchase gametes and, if so, it would also constitute a legal reason.[3] However, the commercial purchase of gametes is not lawful in European jurisdictions under the EU Tissues and Cells Directive, which requires Member States to "endeavour to ensure voluntary and unpaid donations" of tissues, including gametes.[4] Hence, it appears that seeking parenthood via this route may have little or nothing to do with UK nationals directly seeking to circumvent the domestic regulatory regime established under the Human Fertilisation and Embryology Acts 1990 and 2008.

Nonetheless, interjurisdictional reproductive care raises concerns about the safety and efficacy of procedures undertaken, payment for surrogates, and citizenship for the resulting children, among others. Cross-border surrogacy exposes particular difficulties for the regularization of legal parenthood and citizenship, such that the Home Office United Kingdom Border Agency has produced specific guidance on these matters, and a spate of High Court decisions has resulted. Surrogacy raises particularly contentious issues, and there is a strong correlation between the social and ethical issues it raises and those prevalent in death tourism:

> The *unique* temper of surrogacy—one of the conundrums which it displays—is that it is socially and ethically divisive *because* it does not attract universal opprobrium, because it may be seen, indeed it is seen by some, as a natural and beneficial product of the reproduction revolution as much as an unnatural and abnormal artefact of it.[5]

---

[1] "Cross-border reproductive care" replaces "reproductive tourism" as the former is thought to better reflect the emphasis on the therapeutic purpose of the travel.

[2] F. Shenfield, J. de Mouzon, G. Pennings, A.P. Ferraretti, A. Nyboe Andersen, G. de Wert & V. Goossens, *Cross Border Reproductive Care in Six European Countries*, 25(6) HUM. REPROD. 1361, 1361 (2010).

[3] We are grateful to I. Glenn Cohen for this point.

[4] EU Tissues and Cells Directive, 2004/23/EC, Article 12(1). Compensation is nevertheless possible, albeit "strictly limited to making good the expenses and inconveniences related to the donation," Article 12(1). In terms of reimbursement Spain has interpreted "inconveniences" more generously than the United Kingdom (see Nuffield Council on Bioethics, Human Bodies: Donation for Medicine and Research 2.51 (2011)); although the Human Fertilisation and Embryology Authority has since revised its policy, bringing it in line with the Spanish model (*see* Human Fertilisation and Embryology Authority, HFEA Agrees New Policies to Improve Sperm and Egg Donation Services (Oct. 19, 2011), www.hfea.gov.uk/6700.html (last visited Jan. 15, 2012)).

[5] Derek Morgan, *Enigma Variations: Surrogacy, Rights and Procreative Tourism, in* SURROGATE MOTHERHOOD INTERNATIONAL PERSPECTIVES 75, 90 (Rachel Cook, Shelley Day Sclater & Felicity Kaganas eds., 2003).

Whether surrogacy should be examined in isolation from other contentious issues surrounding the inception or creation of life (let alone the fraught questions of end of life) is not for this court to say beyond the observation that these issues merit the widest public debate even if the ultimate conclusion be that they continue to be finally resolved on a case by case basis by judicial decision.[6]

With these statements in mind, this chapter will use surrogacy as a case study to exemplify issues connected with reproductive tourism alongside interjurisdictional assisted dying.

B. DEATH TOURISM

Euthanasia is prohibited under the common law of homicide in the United Kingdom; assisted suicide, where the death-inducing action is performed by the person who dies, is outlawed under the Suicide Act 1961. This statute decriminalized suicide but prohibited acts that assist suicide and has recently been amended by s59(2) of the Coroners and Justice Act 2009. The offense applies where a person intentionally performs an act that is capable of encouraging or assisting another person to commit suicide or attempt to commit suicide.[7] Alongside death tourism is a spate of suicides by young people thought to have been influenced by Internet Web sites promoting and glamorizing suicide provided the impetus to revise the law. Consequently, s59(2) includes the provision that a person may be guilty of the offense even if he or she does not know and cannot identify the suicidal person. The scope of such actions, and of the legislation, is clearly very wide.

Death tourism has been the subject of several legal challenges in the United Kingdom aimed at clarifying the circumstances under which a person who assists another to travel overseas for an assisted suicide will be prosecuted. There has never been a legal requirement that persons suspected of having committed a criminal offense must be prosecuted in the United Kingdom. Prosecution will generally occur "[w]herever it appears that the offence or the circumstances of its commission is or are of such a character that a prosecution in respect thereof is required in the public interest,"[8] but not normally otherwise. Section 2(4) of the Suicide Act 1961 provides explicitly that there can be no prosecution for the offense of assisted suicide other than by or with the consent of the Director of Public Prosecutions (DPP). Consequently, it has always been the case that unless the DPP believes that prosecution is necessary in the public interest, those who assist others to commit suicide may legitimately escape prosecution.

Several other more liberal European states[9] permit some forms of assisted dying, and uniquely, Switzerland, a non-EU Member State, extends the facility to non-domiciled

---

[6] *Re X and another (Foreign Surrogacy)*, [2008] EWHC (Fam) 3030, [29] (Hedley J.) (U.K.) (emphasis added).

[7] The definition was amended under the Coroners and Justice Act 2009, § 59, from the wording previously contained in the Suicide Act 1961, § 2(1), which encompassed "aiding and abetting, counselling or procuring the suicide of another."

[8] 483 Parl. Deb., H.C. (5th ser.) (1951) 681 (statement of Sir Hartley Shawcross, Attorney General).

[9] The Netherlands, Belgium, and Spain.

persons. It is believed that upward of two hundred British citizens have travelled to Switzerland for an assisted suicide, and more than 650 British citizens have joined Dignitas, the Swiss organization that provides assistance.[10] Most of those who have travelled to Switzerland for an assisted suicide have been accompanied by friends or relatives who helped with travel arrangements and sometimes physical support if the suicidal person had impaired mobility. Despite these actions clearly amounting to "acts capable of encouraging or assisting the suicide...of another,"[11] no one has yet been prosecuted. However, two specific legal challenges have been brought aimed at the clarification of individual rights with regard to the Suicide Act 1961, its application to those who are physically incapable of killing themselves, and in relation to the availability of assisted dying overseas.

Pretty v. UK involved a woman who suffered from Motor Neurone Disease (MND).[12] In a case reminiscent of *Rodriguez v. British Columbia*,[13] Diane Pretty sought an assurance from the DPP that her husband would not be prosecuted if he assisted her to commit suicide. She argued inter alia that the Suicide Act 1961 discriminated against people who experienced physical disability and claimed that this was contrary to her human rights under various provisions of the Human Rights Act 1998 and the European Convention on Human Rights (ECHR).

Subsequently, in *R (Purdy) v. DPP*, Debbie Purdy brought a case inviting the DPP to clarify the factors that would be influential in deciding whether to prosecute her husband if he helped her to travel to Switzerland for an assisted suicide.[14] More specifically, she sought clarification regarding when prosecution would be in the public interest. The case became the final judgment to be handed down by the United Kingdom House of Lords before it was transformed into the United Kingdom Supreme Court, and the Law Lords required the DPP to publish the prosecutorial guidelines that would apply in cases where British citizens are helped to travel abroad for assisted dying. These guidelines were published in February 2010. They apply to relevant actions performed after February 1, 2010,[15] and are designed to come into play only after a police investigation has already established that there is sufficient evidence to justify bringing a prosecution.[16] They include sixteen public interest factors that point in favor of a prosecution and six that operate to the contrary. The weight attached to each factor is nominally equal, with no one factor being regarded as determinative, making certainty as to when a prosecution might follow somewhat opaque. Thus, despite the call for

---

[10] Accurate figures are difficult to obtain because these acts give rise to potential criminal liability in the United Kingdom and there is no mechanism for reporting them.

[11] Suicide Act, 1961, as amended by s59 Coroners and Justice Act 2009.

[12] Pretty v. U.K., App. No. 2346/02 Eur. Ct. H.R. (2002). Also known as Amyotrophic Lateral Sclerosis (ALS) or Lou Gehrig's disease.

[13] Rodriguez v. British Columbia (Attorney General), [1993] 3 S.C.R. 519 (Can.).

[14] R (Purdy) v. DPP, [2009] UKHL 45 (appeal taken from Eng.).

[15] Any charge brought that relates to conduct prior to this date will require evidence that the accused aided, abetted, counselled or procured the suicide under the original Suicide Act 1961 and will proceed accordingly.

[16] This is known as the evidential stage.

clarity, the circumstances within which a death tourist's assistant might face prosecution in the domestic courts remain controversial.

Nevertheless, British nationals continue to travel abroad for assisted suicide, as they do for reproductive services denied them at home despite the physical and legal risks involved. With regard to death tourism the services being provided are not available in the United Kingdom, and those accessed by reproductive tourists may not meet the standards expected in the United Kingdom, often resulting in regulatory inconsistency that disadvantages those who use them. In order to expose some of these damaging inconsistencies, this chapter explores aspects of death and surrogacy tourism in relation to vulnerability and jurisdictional problems. Each of these headings reveals points of commonality and disjuncture, many of which are amplified in the UK publicly funded health care system.

II. Vulnerability

A. THE NATURE OF VULNERABILITY

The *Oxford Dictionary of English* defines the word "vulnerable" as meaning "exposed to the possibility of being attacked or harmed, either physically or emotionally."[17] Accordingly, the concept of vulnerability indicates a need to protect specific susceptible individuals or groups from exploitation. Who exactly might be vulnerable in this way is questionable however, because vulnerability is a socially constructed concept that differs depending upon the context. Some people are vulnerable because they are socially or intellectually disadvantaged, others because of the environment within which they find themselves or the relationships they encounter. One definition in relation to biomedical research involving human participants regards vulnerability as "a substantial incapacity to protect one's own interests owing to such impediments as lack of capacity to give informed consent, lack of alternative means of obtaining medical care or other expensive necessities, or being a junior or subordinate member of a hierarchical group."[18] Although specific to health care *research*, this portrayal includes factors that are relevant in relation to issues raised by both cross-border dying and reproductive care.

B. VULNERABILITY IN ASSISTED SUICIDE

The Suicide Act 1961 was primarily designed to decriminalize those who attempted suicide, in recognition of the fact that people who tried and failed to take their own lives usually required compassion and care rather than legal sanction. However, assisting the suicide of another remains a criminal act punishable by up to fourteen years imprisonment. This prohibition is clearly designed to safeguard those who might be vulnerable to coercion from being persuaded to kill themselves at the behest of somebody who could benefit from their death. This emphasis resonates with the rhetoric seen in

---

[17] OXFORD DICTIONARY OF ENGLISH (2d ed. rev. 2005).

[18] COUNCIL FOR INT'L ORGANISATIONS OF MED. SCIENCES (CIOMS), INTERNATIONAL ETHICAL GUIDELINES FOR BIOMEDICAL RESEARCH INVOLVING HUMAN PARTICIPANTS 10 (2002), *available at* www.cioms.ch/publications/layout_guide2002.pdf (last visited Oct. 10, 2011).

objections to recent proposals to legalize assisted suicide. The subsequently defeated End of Life Assistance (Scotland) Bill 2010 was met with claims that "tens of thousands of people would fall within its remit,"[19] implying that many people would be vulnerable to exploitation or abuse if the Bill was passed. Similarly, the British Geriatrics Society claimed, inter alia in relation to the Assisted Dying for the Terminally Ill Bill 2004 that "Older People are often unduly influenced by their families and carers. It is important to remember that not all these people will necessarily have the older person's well-being at heart."[20] Although it might be true that tens of thousands of people would qualify to use such provisions if they became law, both proposals included numerous safeguards to ensure that access to assisted dying would only be possible where clinicians were certain that the person's request was entirely voluntary. It is therefore far from clear how many such people are actually vulnerable.

Diane Pretty was in the late stages of her disease when she took her case before the United Kingdom and European Courts. She was wheelchair-bound, and experienced difficulties speaking, but appeared intellectually strong and determined; she was anything but vulnerable. To take her case to the ECtHR she applied for her first passport and travelled to the hearing, again denying her vulnerability. The court had scant regard for most of her claims, including that section 2 of the Suicide Act was discriminatory under Article 14 of ECHR because it prevented her from exercising rights that would be available to an able-bodied person. However, holding that it is through Article 8 of the Convention that "notions of quality of life take on significance,"[21] the Court acknowledged that Pretty was "prevented by law from exercising her choice to avoid what she considers will be an undignified and distressing end to her life."[22] Her Article 8(1) rights were therefore engaged, and her claim that the Suicide Act 1961 amounted to an interference with her right to respect for private life could not be denied. However, the Court had also to consider whether this interference with her rights was necessary, and being imposed by law "in pursuit of the legitimate aim of safeguarding life and thereby protecting the rights of others."[23] The court concluded that, under Article 8(2) it was, and that to do otherwise was potentially damaging to "the protection of health or morals, or the protection of the rights and freedoms of others who might be vulnerable" and whose protection is "paramount."[24] Hence, it was not the vulnerability of the claimant herself, but the potential vulnerability of other unknown persons, "especially those not in a condition to

---

[19] *End of Life Assistance (Scotland) Bill—Action for Scottish Supporters*, CHRISTIAN CONCERN (Nov. 29, 2010), http://www.christianconcern.com/our-concerns/end-of-life/the-end-of-life-assistance-scotland-bill—action-for-scottish-supporters (last visited Dec. 28, 2011).

[20] *Assisted Dying for the Terminally Ill Bill—BGS Response to the House of Lords*, BRITISH GERIATRICS SOCIETY (Aug. 31, 2004), www.bgs.org.uk/index.php?option=com_content&view=article&id=1216:assistedsuicide&catid=82:ethicslawcapacity&Itemid=552 (last visited Oct. 10, 2011).

[21] Pretty v. U.K., App. No. 2346/02 Eur. Ct. H.R. (2002), H18(d).

[22] *Id.* at H19(e).

[23] *Id.* at H20(f).

[24] *Id.* at 74–78.

take informed decisions against acts intended to end life or assist in ending life,"[25] which resulted in the court's failure to uphold her claim. The margin of appreciation, whereby states can assess specific risks and the likelihood of abuse within their own populations, thereby enabled the United Kingdom to rely on the restrictions in the Suicide Act 1961 designed to protect the weak and vulnerable.

Interrogation of the *Pretty* judgment reveals that it runs counter to the central premise behind much of UK health care law—respect for personal autonomy— because it is underpinned by assumptions that those who are dying are vulnerable to exploitation. For example, the Mental Capacity Act 2005 operates on the presumption that all adults have decision-making capacity unless the contrary is demonstrated. On this understanding the autonomous decisions of those who are mentally competent, expressed through the process of consent, should be respected regardless of the likely outcome, and even if death will result.[26] A competent adult has an absolute right to refuse consent to lifesaving medical treatment,[27] or to commit suicide, but the prohibition of assisted suicide even at the behest of the "victim" limits this right, because although "[I]t is not for society to tell people what to value about their own lives ... it may be justifiable for society to insist that we value their lives even if they do not."[28]

The characterization of a person who is assisted in suicide as vulnerable is inherent in the terminology used in the DPP's 2010 prosecutorial policy on assisted suicide.[29] In line with criminal law approaches, the assisted person is referred to throughout as the victim while the assistant is the suspect. This is at odds with the characteristics of the protagonists in most challenges to the legal prohibition on assisted suicide who voluntarily sought assistance because they were, or would be, physically incapable of committing suicide alone.[30] Diane Pretty and Debbie Purdy, for instance, brought their cases attempting to prevent their would-be assistants from being vulnerable to prosecution. Seemingly, this demonstrates the vulnerability of the assistant and the strength, or lack of evident vulnerability, of the suicidal person, thereby exposing an inherent contradiction in the legal approach.

Further inconsistencies are apparent in the fact that people are prepared to become tourists in order to access medicalized assisted suicide. One of the factors tending to favor prosecution refers to situations where the assistant "was acting in

---

[25] *Id.*, H22(h).

[26] Airedale NHS Trust v. Bland, [1993] A.C. 789 (H.L.) (appeal taken from Eng.).

[27] *Re* T, [1992] 3 W.L.R. 782 (U.K.).

[28] R (Purdy) v. DPP, [2009] UKHL 45, [68] (Baroness Hale) (appeal taken from Eng.).

[29] CROWN PROSECUTION SERVICE (CPS), INTERIM POLICY FOR PROSECUTORS IN RESPECT OF CASES OF ASSISTED SUICIDE (2009), *available at* http://www.cps.gov.uk/consultations/as_consultation.pdf (last visited Dec. 28, 2011).

[30] *E.g.*, Rodriguez v. British Columbia (Attorney General), [1993] 3 S.C.R. 519 (Can.); *Lindsell* case (unreported), TIMES (London), Oct. 29, 1997; *see also* BBC News, "Fighting for the Right to Die," Nov 28, 2000, *available at* http://news.bbc.co.uk/2/hi/health/background_briefings/euthanasia/332464.stm; Pretty v. U.K., App. No. 2346/02 Eur. Ct. H.R. (2002); *Re* Z (An Adult: Capacity), [2004] EWHC (Fam) 2817.

his or her capacity as a medical doctor, nurse [or] other healthcare professional."[31] In response the doctors' professional body, the British Medical Association (BMA), advises its members "not to offer or agree to provide medical reports if they are aware that they will be used to obtain assisted suicide, as this could be seen as facilitating that process. Similarly, doctors should not accompany a patient going abroad for assisted dying."[32]

Denying professional assistance to those who seek assisted suicide compels them, as Pretty and Purdy found, to rely upon friends and family to aid them, and may, in some instances increase the potential for abuse. Criminalizing assisted suicide, whether at home or abroad, means that external scrutiny of the motivations of those involved, both assisted and assistor, occurs only after the event, rendering the weak more vulnerable to exploitation rather than less. Accordingly, prohibiting professional assistance, along with the apparent preparedness of the DPP to tacitly condone death tourism, is a clear indictment of UK policy in this area.

C. VULNERABILITY IN SURROGACY

There has been considerable academic commentary on possible *exploitation* in surrogacy,[33] often premised on the *assumed vulnerability* of particular individuals or groups, especially women and children. In relation to interjurisdictional arrangements we have identified four key areas for consideration: (1) regulation as a form of protection; and the perceived need to protect (2) surrogates; (3) children; and (4) would-be parents.

1. Regulation as Protection: A Role for Professionals?

Early reviews of the law and ethics in this field in England and Wales typified surrogacy as a "risky undertaking,"[34] and an unethical venture for health care professionals to be involved in.[35] In 1984 the Warnock Committee recommended that legislation be introduced to criminalize the creation or operation of surrogacy agencies in the United Kingdom, irrespective of whether those bodies were commercial

---

[31] CROWN PROSECUTION SERVICE, POLICY FOR PROSECUTORS IN RESPECT OF CASES OF ENCOURAGING OR ASSISTING SUICIDE (Feb. 2010), 43(14), *available at* http://www.cps.gov.uk/publications/prosecution/assisted_suicide_policy.html (last visited Dec. 28, 2011).

[32] BRITISH MEDICAL ASSOCIATION, RESPONDING TO PATIENT REQUESTS RELATING TO ASSISTED SUICIDE: GUIDANCE FOR DOCTORS IN ENGLAND, WALES AND NORTHERN IRELAND (July 2010), *available at* www.bma.org.uk/images/assistedsuicideguidancejuly2010_tcm41-198675.pdf (last visited Oct. 25, 2011).

[33] *See generally* S. WILKINSON, BODIES FOR SALE: ETHICS AND EXPLOITATION IN THE HUMAN BODY TRADE 131–81 (2003); Rachel Cook, Shelley Day Sclater & Felicity Kaganas, *Introduction* to SURROGATE MOTHERHOOD INTERNATIONAL PERSPECTIVES 1–22 (Rachel Cook et al. eds., 2003).

[34] DAME MARY WARNOCK (CHAIR) ET AL., REPORT OF THE COMMITTEE OF INQUIRY INTO HUMAN FERTILISATION AND EMBRYOLOGY 8.6 (1984).

[35] MARGARET BRAZIER (CHAIR) ET AL., SURROGACY: REVIEW FOR HEALTH MINISTERS OF CURRENT ARRANGEMENTS FOR PAYMENTS AND REGULATION 3.3 (1998) (summarizing the BMA's views in 1984).

in nature; further, it made clear that the legislation should "render criminally liable the actions of professionals and others who knowingly assist in the establishment of a surrogate pregnancy."[36] Under its recommendations, private arrangements were not to be criminalized per se, but such contracts were to be deemed illegal and therefore unenforceable. Only two dissenting members of the Committee raised concerns that couples would be forced into informal arrangements, without professional assistance.[37]

The resulting legislation (Surrogacy Arrangements Act 1985, Human Fertilisation and Embryology Act 1990) followed a middle path[38] whereby commercial arrangements were prohibited, no advertising was permitted, and contracts were unenforceable against any party,[39] but where if certain conditions had been met, parental orders were available to commissioning couples in order to regularize their legal position in relation to the child.[40] Emily Jackson argues that this apparently conflicted legislative intent can be traced to the Warnock Committee: "Their judgement that surrogacy arrangements are flawed but inevitable led to the passage of two disparate goals: the rules are intended both to offer *some protection to the vulnerable parties* (believed principally to be the surrogate mother and the child), and to *discourage involvement* in surrogacy."[41]

Under the 1990 Act, most other forms of ARTs available at the time fell within the purview of the HFEA (the regulatory body), whereas surrogacy was not defined as a regulated activity per se. Accordingly, unless health professionals provide a licensed treatment (e.g., creation of an embryo outside the body, donation of eggs or sperm) in connection with a surrogate pregnancy, such arrangements fell outside its remit. By excluding "other" surrogacy arrangements where no licensed interventions were used, the provisions of the 1990 Act did little to bolster the purportedly protective role of medical professionals in relation to potentially vulnerable persons, including children.

By August 1990 the BMA had adopted a position whereby the involvement of professionals was deemed ethical in appropriate circumstances, and detailed guidance was issued for practitioners.[42] In 1996 the BMA went further still, expressing concern "about the lack of opportunity for *medical and psychological support* for individuals involved in surrogacy arrangements,"[43] and the lack of regulation of not-for-profit

---

[36] WARNOCK ET AL., *supra* note 34, 8.18.

[37] *Id.* at 88, 4.

[38] Lucy Theis, Natalie Gamble & Louisa Ghevaert, *Re X and Y (Foreign Surrogacy): A Trek through a Thorn Forest*, 39 FAM. L. 239, 239–43 (2009).

[39] *See* Surrogacy Arrangements Act, 1985, §§ 2, 3(1A), & 1A (as amended).

[40] Human Fertilisation and Embryology Act, 1990, § 30, since repealed and replaced by Human Fertilisation and Embryology Act, 2008, § 54.

[41] EMILY JACKSON, REGULATING REPRODUCTION. LAW, TECHNOLOGY AND AUTONOMY 262 (2001) (emphasis added).

[42] BRITISH MEDICAL ASSOCIATION, SURROGACY: ETHICAL CONSIDERATIONS 28–31 (1990).

[43] BRITISH MEDICAL ASSOCIATION, CHANGING CONCEPTIONS OF MOTHERHOOD: THE PRACTICE OF SURROGACY IN BRITAIN 3 (1996) (emphasis added).

surrogacy agencies operating (lawfully) in the United Kingdom.[44] Further, it advised that where health professionals suspected a person was being coerced, or the "anxieties of *vulnerable individuals*, (including existing children) are being ignored" that health professionals had an important role in trying to address such issues with the parties.[45] Yet the issue of cross-border surrogacy had not been raised in relevant reviews or guidance; the Warnock Report merely observed that private surrogacy agencies existed in other countries, without indicating that British nationals might make use of them.

In 1996 the BMA presciently highlighted the likelihood that "medical tourism" would increase.[46] Acknowledging the need to avoid the "disputes and exploitation" observed in other jurisdictions, and to "minimise the possibility of abuse in Britain" they highlighted some reported difficulties:

> During 1995 there were two press reports of the use of women from Eastern Europe as surrogate mothers for wealthy western couples. Plans were reported, of a scheme to take women from such countries as Poland, Romania and Hungary to Germany, Holland, Belgium, America and Canada....Counselling, support, legal advice and medical follow-up are not built into these kinds of schemes. It is the fear of this type of exploitation of economically or socially vulnerable women which has led to a complete ban on surrogacy in some countries such as France.[47]

The potential trafficking of women within Europe and beyond for surrogacy arrangements is clearly a grave concern. Despite the proactive approach alerting health care professionals to these issues as outlined in the BMA guidance, it is difficult to see how this kind of informal regulation of surrogacy can protect potentially vulnerable women from trafficking, especially when in many reported instances British nationals are travelling abroad for treatment, and the surrogate mother will remain abroad throughout. It is also questionable whether medical professionals are best positioned to deal with trafficking.

Further limitations were highlighted in a recent guidance letter on the HFEA's legal responsibilities with regard to *all* cross-border reproductive care, whereby: "The provision of information by centres about clinics in other countries, and the referral of patients to clinics overseas, are matters over which the *HFEA has little or no remit.*"[48] The onus lies with clinicians to inform patients of any potential consequences, a stance reiterated by the European Society of Human Reproduction and Embryology.[49] The Parliamentary decision to marginalize surrogacy from the otherwise comprehensive regulation of ARTs has therefore increased the potential for exploitation of the vulnerable.

---

[44] *Id.* at 11–12.

[45] *Id.* at 31 (emphasis added).

[46] *Id.* at xii.

[47] *Id.*

[48] HUMAN FERTILISATION AND EMBRYOLOGY AUTHORITY, CHIEF EXECUTIVE'S LETTERS, CE(10)03 (July 30, 2010) (emphasis added), www.hfea.gov.uk/6018.html (last visited Oct. 12, 2011).

[49] Francoise Shenfield et al., *ESHRE's Good Practice Guide for Cross-Border Reproductive Care for Centers and Practitioners*, 26(7) HUM. REPROD. 1625–27 (2011).

2. Protecting Surrogate Mothers?

The majority of the Warnock Committee opined "[t]hat people should treat others as a means to their own ends, however desirable the consequences, must always be liable to moral objection. Such treatment of one person by another becomes positively exploitative when financial interests are involved."[50] In contrast, the dissenting members of the Committee rightly questioned whether matters of exploitation and morality are always so clear-cut.[51] Similarly, Stephen Wilkinson has convincingly argued that there are considerable weaknesses in the traditional arguments around commodification and exploitation of women acting as surrogates, irrespective of whether the context of the arrangement is altruistic or commercial.[52]

In a recent case, Hedley J. suggested in obiter comments, the possible emergence of a niche market in unmarried surrogates might occur (as this would avoid a surrogate mother's husband being recognized as the resulting child's legal father), and cautioned that "*The unmarried surrogate mother may be more vulnerable, more prey to exploitation and be more likely to be motivated principally by material considerations. In my judgment that is a fair analysis of fact but whether it assists in statutory construction is more doubtful.*"[53] His observations about potentially "*more* vulnerable" single women are made without any evidence base in support, and are couched simply with the caveat that they "may" be so. The possibility that they might be *less* vulnerable is not explored.

Highlighting these unsupported assertions reveals a fine balance between protection and paternalism in the construction of who is vulnerable in any given scenario. Although there are clearly a number of issues of concern in many jurisdictions,[54] the evidence base for such concerns is less well established (if indeed there is any at all), especially when contrasted to, for example, the development of professional regulation and practice around single embryo transfer (SET), which has measurable potentially positive health impacts for pregnant women and the children to whom they give birth.[55] Evidence indicates that clinics in some jurisdictions may be transferring greater numbers of embryos per treatment cycle, thereby increasing the likelihood of multiple births and the attendant risks for the mother and child(ren)'s health.[56] Nevertheless,

---

[50] WARNOCK ET AL., *supra* note 34, 8.17.

[51] *Id.* at 87, 3.

[52] WILKINSON, *supra* note 33, at 134–81.

[53] *Re* X and another (Foreign Surrogacy), [2008] EWHC (Fam) 3030, [15] (U.K.).

[54] An oft-cited example in the United Kingdom media is India. *See, e.g.*, Nicola Smith, *Inside the Baby Farm*, SUNDAY TIMES MAG., May 9, 2011, at 22–29. In February 2011 the Indian Parliament began debating legislation to regulate the use of surrogacy.

[55] See HFEA's guidance, *Multiple Births and Single Embryo Transfer Review*, HUMAN FERTILISATION AND EMBRYOLOGY AUTHORITY (Apr. 7, 2009), www.hfea.gov.uk/530.html [hereinafter *Guidance*], which is currently under review by NICE. *NICE Outlines Review of Fertility Guidance*, NATIONAL INSTITUTE FOR HEALTH AND CLINICAL EXCELLENCE (Oct. 6, 2010), www.nice.org.uk/newsroom/pressreleases/ NICEOutlinesReviewOfFertilityGuideline.jsp. NICE's report is due in June 2012.

[56] *See, e.g.*, comments made by speakers at Progress Educational Trust's conference on "Passport to Parenthood: The Evidence and Ethics behind Cross Border Reproductive care," (Nov. 24, 2010), London, United Kingdom; summarized by Vivienne Raper, *Progress Educational Trust Conference: The Evidence for Cross-Border Reproductive Care*, 586 BIONEWS (2010), www.bionews.org.uk/page_83165.asp (last visited Jan. 15, 2012).

prospective parents may regard these risks as more acceptable than the prospect of failing to achieve a pregnancy.[57] ESHRE's recently published guidance has stipulated that SET "is the only acceptable option" in surrogacy;[58] hence, again, it is left to soft-law guidance—focused mainly on treatment provided in Europe—to establish protective norms in this context.

3. Protecting Children?

Two concerns regarding the vulnerability of resulting children were recorded by the Warnock Committee: the potential for harm to the child when the bonds with the "carrying mother" are broken, and the commodification argument: "for all practical purposes, the child will have been bought for money."[59] No evidence is provided in support of these assertions and, as Wilkinson demonstrates, the arguments based on commodification grounds are weak.[60]

Although the occurrence of "unforeseen events" was recognized, the Warnock Report did not directly address the possibility of neither party wishing to keep the child. There is no known recorded data on such incidents in the United Kingdom. We do not wish to be alarmist, but it is a concern. Although in the United Kingdom the care of such children would ultimately fall to the state, in interjurisdictional arrangements it is less clear as to which, if any, state is responsible. This is especially problematic in jurisdictions where surrogates (and, where relevant, their partners) are divested of any legal responsibilities for the child(ren) in question.[61] There seems to be a clear distinction between *vulnerability* and *exploitation* in these cases.

Parental orders cannot be made where money or benefits (other than "reasonably incurred" expenses) have been exchanged, unless payments are *retrospectively authorized* by the courts,[62] usually on the basis that an order is in the child's best interests.[63] The legislation lacks guidance as to the relevant factors the court should take into account,

---

[57] Shenfield et al., *supra* note 49, 2.4.

[58] *Id.* at 2.3.

[59] WARNOCK ET AL., *supra* note 34, 8.11.

[60] WILKINSON, *supra* note 33, at 143–49.

[61] *Re* X and Y (Foreign Surrogacy), [2010] EWHC (Fam) 3146, [8] (U.K.).

[62] For example, in *Re* Q (Parental Order), [1996] 1 F.L.R. 369, payment of £8280 was authorized; in *Re* X, [2002] EWHC (Fam) 157, £12,000 was authorized. More recently, in a complex cross-border case involving two simultaneous surrogacy agreements, the commissioning parents had paid approximately £27,405 to an Indian clinic, albeit each women received only circa £3,000 for their role, *Re* X and Y (Children—foreign surrogacy), [2011] EWHC 3147 (Fam), [24-28] (Sir Wall P.) (U.K.). In two other cross-border cases Hedley J. simply stated that the payments were beyond reasonable expenses without stipulating the amount, but the orders were nevertheless granted on the basis of welfare consideration of the child(ren) in question, discussed below; see *Re* L (A child) (Surrogacy: parental order), [2010] EWHC 3146 (Fam), [3, 12], *Re* IJ (A child) [2011] EWHC 921 (Fam), [2, 7].

[63] Under the HFEA 1990 and associated provisions, in deciding whether to make a parental order, the court was to give "first consideration . . . to the need to safeguard and promote the welfare of the child." Parental Orders (Human Fertilisation and Embryology) Regulations, Sch 1(1)(a) (1994). This version of the welfare principle was based on that in § 6 Adoption Act 1976 (as opposed to the "paramount" consideration of welfare in the Children Act 1989)—this Act has since been repealed and replaced by the Adoption and Children Act 2002).

nor has this issue ever been tested in the Court of Appeal.[64] In *Re X and another*,[65] involving a commercial agreement between a married couple from the United Kingdom and a married woman in the Ukraine, Hedley J. highlighted the difficulties faced by the courts in stark terms:

> What the court is required to do is to balance two competing and potentially irreconcilably conflicting concepts. Parliament is clearly entitled to legislate against commercial surrogacy and is clearly entitled to expect that the courts should implement that policy consideration in its decisions. Yet it is also recognised that as the full rigour of that policy consideration will bear on one wholly unequipped to comprehend it let alone deal with its consequences (i.e. the child concerned) that rigour must be mitigated by the application of a consideration of that child's welfare. That approach is both humane and intellectually coherent. The difficulty is that it *is almost impossible to imagine a set of circumstances in which by the time the case comes to court, the welfare of any child (particularly a foreign child) would not be gravely compromised (at the very least) by a refusal to make an order.*[66]

Hence, despite legislative policy against commercial surrogacy, in practice, when faced with the lifelong ramifications for the child(ren), the court will find it exceptionally difficult to do anything other than regularize the legal relationship with the commissioning parents,[67] provided the other statutory conditions have been met.

In the subsequent case of *Re L (A minor)* Hedley J. evaluated the statutory welfare provisions, arguing that the child's welfare is now the *paramount* consideration of the court:

> The effect of that must be to weight the balance between public policy considerations and welfare...*decisively in favour of welfare*. It must follow that it will *only be in the clearest case of the abuse of public policy* that the court will be able to withhold an order if otherwise welfare considerations supports (sic) its making. It underlines the court's earlier observation that, if it is desired to control commercial surrogacy arrangements, those controls need to operate before the court process is initiated i.e. at the border or even before.[68]

Ironically, it would seem that appeals to child welfare have not delimited commercial agreements, but rather, may now be used to justify the regularization of legal parenthood in the very kind of scenarios the Warnock Committee had sought to criminalize, especially where issues of citizenship may also arise.[69]

---

[64] *Re X and another (Foreign Surrogacy)*, [2008] EWHC (Fam) 3030, [19] (Hedley J.) (U.K.).

[65] *Id.*

[66] *Id.* at [22] (emphasis added).

[67] *See also Re S (Parental Order)*, [2009] EWHC (Fam) 2977, [7–8].

[68] *Re L (a minor)*, [2010] EWHC (Fam) 3146, [10] (emphasis added).

[69] *See, e.g., Re X and another (Foreign Surrogacy)*, [2008] EWHC (Fam) 3030, [9–10] (U.K.); *Re K (Minors) (Foreign Surrogacy)*, [2010] EWHC (Fam) 1180, [2011] 1 F.L.R. 533.

4. Protecting Would-Be Parents?

The Warnock Committee acknowledged strongly expressed views that surrogacy was "an attack on the value of the marital relationship" as it introduced a third party into procreation.[70] It considered whether the prohibition of surrogacy might address these concerns. The resulting legislation followed a middle path (outlined above) that may paradoxically encourage overseas arrangements for those who can afford them. In the absence of any international conventions governing intercountry surrogacy, difficulties ensue regarding the legal recognition of the commissioning couple as the resulting child's parents, not least as under English law the birth mother is automatically recognized as the child's legal mother, irrespective of the mode of conception or whose gametes were used.[71]

For commissioning couples to attain legal recognition as parents they must apply to the court for a "parental order" that the child should be treated in law as the child of the named applicants. The reference to "couples" throughout is not accidental, although it should be noted that until April 6, 2010, parental orders were restricted to married couples.[72] Under the revised provisions married couples, civil partners, and two people "living as partners in an enduring family relationship" may apply,[73] but single persons cannot.[74] Further hurdles arise as in order to successfully apply for a parental order the applicants must also satisfy the other statutory conditions[75] and take into account potential conflicts of law.

Many commissioning parents may not appear vulnerable due to their assumed secure financial and social status (in contrast to women acting as surrogates), but where surrogacy is being used as a last resort due to their infertility[76] there is clear potential for psychological or emotional vulnerabilities that may be exacerbated by the lack of enforceability of surrogacy contracts in the United Kingdom. Cross-border agreements do *not* create a specific vulnerability around the contract issue. However, recent cases illustrate two key "vulnerabilities" created by the statutory requirements for parental orders, in contrast to the *assumed* vulnerability of women and children (outlined above). We now turn to consider these jurisdictional problems.

III. Jurisdictional Problems

The existence of international markets in both "life" and "death" gives rise to some obvious (and some less immediately obvious) jurisdictional problems. Interestingly,

---

[70] Similar arguments were also made in relation to donor insemination.

[71] Human Fertilisation and Embryology Act, 2008, § 33. Under common law, see *The Ampthill Peerage Case*. [1977] A.C. 547 (appeal taken from Eng.).

[72] Human Fertilisation and Embryology Act, 1990, § 30(1).

[73] Provided they are not within prohibited degrees of relationship with one another. *See* Marriage Act, 1949 (as amended), Sch. 1.

[74] *See* Caroline Jones, *The (Im)possible Parents in Law*, *in* Taking Responsibility: Law and the Changing Family 201, 213 (Craig Lind, Jo Bridgeman & Heather Keating eds., 2011); A and another v. P and others, [2011] EWHC (Fam) 1738.

[75] Human Fertilisation and Embryology Act, 2008, § 54(1)–(8).

[76] As opposed to "convenience" arrangements undertaken for social reasons.

although "death" appears only to be an "export," cross-border surrogacy cases have both "import" and "export" aspects.

A. SURROGACY: IMPORTING AND EXPORTING LIFE

Key issues associated with interjurisdictional surrogacy arrangements include whether the child(ren) can enter the United Kingdom following birth so that an application for a parental order can be made, and questions regarding domicile when foreign nationals use UK-based surrogates. An example is *Re K*, a case concerning twins born following a commercial surrogacy arrangement between a married couple habitually resident in the United Kingdom and a married couple in India.[77] The surrogacy arrangement was made via a clinic on a commercial basis. The children were conceived using an egg from an anonymous donor fertilized with the sperm of the male applicant. Following birth in India, they were handed over to the applicants, and at the time of the application they were in the applicants' care at the grandparents' home in India. The applicants sought a parental order, but the case was adjourned with liberty to restore and proceed only if and when the children were in the jurisdiction.

Hedley J. noted that entry clearance[78] into the country was a "fundamental necessity," but it remained an *executive* decision rather than a judicial one. He referred to the Home Office United Kingdom Border Agency guidance on "*Inter-Country Surrogacy and the Immigration Rules*" issued in June 2009. This guidance permits applications for entry "outside" these rules in surrogacy cases at the discretion of the Secretary of State, where a parental order is sought within six months of the birth, there is a genetic connection to one of the applicants, and "*where evidence suggests that such an order is likely to be granted.*"[79] Although the genetic link and time conditions were clearly met here, Hedley J. expressed considerable unease in drawing any conclusions as to the likely success of the application. Because the children were not habitually resident in the United Kingdom the court had no jurisdiction over them;[80] their welfare needed to be considered by the court, and it also needed to approve payments under the commercial arrangement; the court should not usurp the role of the executive; and perhaps most crucially, "the giving of advisory opinions (as opposed to Declarations establishing rights or the lawfulness of an action) are alien to the traditional practice of the court."[81]

---

[77] *Re K* (Minors) (Foreign Surrogacy), [2010] EWHC (Fam) 1180, [2011] 1 F.L.R. 533.

[78] Defined as a visa or entry certificate permitting travel to the United Kingdom.

[79] *Re K*, [2010] EWHC (Fam) 1180, [5], (citing [41] of the *Guidance*, *supra* note 55) (emphasis added).

[80] As Rebecca Bailey-Harris, *Case Reports: Surrogacy*, [2010] FAM. L. 1281, correctly notes, Hedley J. did not cite any provisions regarding the jurisdiction matter. She suggests that the relevant provisions must be Article 8 of the Council Regulation (EC) No. 2201–2003, whereby jurisdiction is founded on a child's habitual residence.

[81] *Re K*, [2010] EWHC (Fam) 1180, [6].

This was the first English case to explicitly address the matter of jurisdiction in the surrogacy context,[82] and Hedley J. expressed some anxiety over the need for the court to act "correctly and not out of sympathy," not least because:

> The court is still at a comparatively early stage of its development in dealing with these foreign commercial surrogacy agreements. The need to obtain orders under section 30 is only gradually becoming fully appreciated. Many have been tempted to trust in the orders obtained in foreign jurisdictions believing that they will be valid (or recognised as such) here. The difficulty is (in stark contrast for example to adoption[83]) commercial surrogacy is unlawful in this jurisdiction and orders based entirely on its lawfulness may well not be capable of recognition.[84]

He therefore declined to state what the likely outcome of the application would be, although he went on to make obiter remarks, including an observation that most conditions were "fulfilled" in this case.

Although the commercial nature of the agreement would not necessarily prove fatal to the application, the case could not proceed until the children were present in the United Kingdom. Would-be parents might circumvent the statutory prohibition on commercial surrogacy, yet the soft-law guidance on border entry might prove a greater barrier to the regularization of their legal parental status. This is unique to cross-border agreements. At the very least we might observe that such parents are *legally vulnerable* in relation to exercising rights and responsibilities over those children—but unlike arrangements made in the United Kingdom, interjurisdictional cases also raise significant issues for the children regarding citizenship and nationality.[85]

The second observation pertains to the *immigration* of "tourists." In *Re G*, a married couple (Turkish nationals, domiciled in Turkey) sought a parental order following a surrogacy agreement with a British woman.[86] This order was refused due to the failure to comply with the statutory domicile requirement, but McFarlane J. made an alternative order ensuring the couple could lawfully leave the United Kingdom with the child and seek an adoption order in Turkey.[87] He condemned the lack of regulation in the most stringent terms.[88] Here, the "well-meaning amateurs," working for the not-for-profit organization Childlessness Overcome Through Surrogacy (COTS), are

---

[82] Bailey-Harris, *supra* note 80, at 1282.

[83] The Hague Convention on the Protection of Children and Co-Operation in Respect of Intercountry Adoption, May 29, 1993, S. Treaty Doc. No. 105–51 (1998), 1870 U.N.T.S. 167 (entered into force May 1, 1995).

[84] *Re K (Minors) (Foreign Surrogacy)*, [2010] EWHC (Fam) 1180, [8]. *See also Re L (A child) (Surrogacy: parental order)*, [2010] EWHC (Fam) 3146, [8].

[85] *See Re X and another (Foreign Surrogacy)*, [2008] EWHC (Fam) 3030, [8–10] (Hedley J.) (commenting about children being "marooned Stateless and parentless").

[86] *Re G (Surrogacy: Foreign Domicile)*, [2007] EWHC (Fam) 2814, [2008] 1 FLR 1047.

[87] Section 84, Adoption and Children Act 2002, confers parental responsibility on applicants prior to adoption abroad, and extinguishes the parental responsibility of any other person.

[88] *Re G (Surrogacy: Foreign Domicile)*, [2007] EWHC (Fam) 2814, [29] (emphasis added).

placed in stark contrast to the potentially protective role of health care professionals in advising couples, outlined above.

He also raised a salutary note regarding costs. The proceedings took nine months to conclude, and the total legal costs neared £35,000. No costs order was made against the couple, and the proceedings were paid for by the public purse. However, McFarlane J. issued a warning that in future cases on similar facts the courts would give "active consideration to the making of a costs order."[89] Consequently, commissioning couples might be placed under considerable financial pressure due to the courts' wish to discourage the involvement of domestic agencies in the future. This deterred COTS from advising and assisting foreign nationals,[90] which may exacerbate the potential difficulties outlined in this chapter.

B. EXPORTING DEATH

In contrast, death is purely an export; somewhat different jurisdictional issues arise in relation to death tourism, and specific issues have arisen in relation to Switzerland, the location to which UK death tourists travel. Revering the right to decide as the ultimate act of autonomy, Switzerland adopts a very liberal approach to assisted dying, which has been legally permissible since 1941 as long as the assistant has no vested interest in the death. However, in May 2011, in response to concerns about the influx of suicide tourists, voters in Zurich were invited to respond to proposals to limit to residents of the city the availability of assisted suicide. The illiberal attitudes of other jurisdictions has been condemned by some organizations there, with Bernhard Sutter, vice-president of *EXIT* arguing, "We cannot solve the dying problems of the rest of Europe... these other countries should solve their own problems... we would be happy if Germany or Great Britain would change their laws."[91] EXIT already assists only Swiss nationals, but Dignitas, which is based in Zurich, opens its doors to all who meet its qualifying criteria regardless of nationality. Yet 78 percent of Zurich residents voted against the proposed ban, enabling UK citizens to continue to access assisted suicide in Zurich.

The fact that no UK citizen has yet been prosecuted for assisting the suicide of a death tourist hints at the potential difficulties involved in bringing a successful prosecution in these cases. It is clear that defendants can be culpable for aiding and abetting acts to which they are not physically party, even where they do so from a remote location,[92] but there is no clear authority pertaining to complicity when the act is legitimate in the

---

[89] *Id.* at [52]. *See also* Darren Howe, *International Surrogacy—A Cautionary Tale,* [2008] FAM. L. 61.

[90] Its Web site now states that COTS can "no longer accept couples from outside the UK." *About COTS,* CHILDLESSNESS OVERCOME THROUGH SURROGACY, www.surrogacy.org.uk/About_COTS.htm (last visited May 6, 2011).

[91] *Switzerland: Zurich Votes on "Suicide Tourism" Laws,* BBC NEWS, May 15, 2011, http://www.bbc.co.uk/news/world-europe-13403074 (last visited Oct. 27, 2011).

[92] Director of Public Prosecutions for Northern Ireland v. Maxwell, [1978] 1 W.L.R. 1350.

jurisdiction in which it is performed. Philosophically these are murky waters, because criminalizing an act (assisting suicide) that is not itself a crime (suicide) is odd, making the perpetrator, as Huxtable says, "guilty for aiding the innocent."[93] To criminalize the same behavior (assisting suicide) when it is itself legitimate in the jurisdiction in which it is performed is even more peculiar. The contradictions are perhaps highlighted by the case of Mrs. Z,[94] where a woman under local authority care wished to travel to Switzerland for assisted suicide. Hedley J. held that being competent, she was entitled to make the journey, but her husband's position was less clear. Hedley J. explained that "by making arrangements and escorting Mrs. Z on the flight, Mr. Z will have contravened section 2(1),"[95] but in the event no prosecution was brought. The DPP guidelines stipulate at paragraph eight that the crime is committed so long as the acts that encourage or assist the suicide occur in England or Wales, even if the suicide happens somewhere else in the world; yet this remains a moot point, untested in court.

Conclusions: who bears the brunt?

The policy emphasis behind the current prohibition of legally authorized assisted dying and commercial surrogacy seems to be to protect the interests of potentially vulnerable individuals. However, in relation to cross-border arrangements that give rise to interjurisdictional uncertainty, the effect can be the exact opposite. Parents, children, and surrogates are rendered vulnerable because of their lack of access to demonstrably safe health care interventions and associated legal rights in relation to surrogacy. Those who seek assisted suicide must travel beyond their home territory to access professional assistance rather than rely upon their caregivers, but in so doing they expose their assistants to criminal investigation and potential prosecution despite the DPP's evident reluctance to press charges. Nevertheless, despite the risks, people are still prepared to become tourists in order to access medicalized assisted suicide and commercial surrogacy.

In such matters of life and death we question whether the interests of UK nationals would be better served by proper sympathetic regulation that safeguards the interests of all concerned. The failure to reform the domestic laws in the case of assisted suicide and the reliance on soft law and judicial discretion in relation to cross-border surrogacy arrangements gives rise to inequalities and uncertainties that persist over time, particularly for those involved in surrogacy arrangements and those who provide suicide assistance. The consequences might rightly be characterized as an indictment of the UK's inability to respond to contemporary issues in death and reproductive tourism.

---

[93] RICHARD HUXTABLE, EUTHANASIA, ETHICS AND THE LAW: FROM CONFLICT TO COMPROMISE 58 (2007).

[94] *Re Z* (Local authority: duty), [2005] 1 W.L.R. 959.

[95] *Id.* at 14.

10

THE ROLES AND RESPONSIBILITIES OF PHYSICIANS IN PATIENTS' DECISIONS ABOUT UNPROVEN STEM CELL THERAPIES[§]

Aaron D. Levine and Leslie E. Wolf[*]

Introduction

Stem cell science, using embryonic and tissue-specific stem cells, is advancing rapidly and promises future medical care improvements. Yet, except for hematopoietic stem cell transplantation, long used to treat certain blood system cancers, effective therapy is likely a long way off. Most current stem cell research focuses on basic scientific questions or preclinical data collection, and most clinical trials under way focus on safety. Nevertheless, numerous clinics worldwide offer stem cell "therapies" today.[1] Although it is unknown how many patients have received these stem cell–based interventions (SCBIs), anecdotal reports suggest a substantial number of people are willing to try them, despite questions about safety and efficacy. Because some patients travel from their home countries where access to these unproven SCBIs is restricted to other

[§] This chapter is adapted from the following article: *The Roles and Responsibilities of Physicians in Patients' Decisions about Unproven Stem Cell Therapies*, 40 J.L. MED. & ETHICS 122 (2012). We thank the journal for the permission to adapt the work.

[*] Aaron D. Levine, PhD, is an Assistant Professor in the School of Public Policy at Georgia Tech where his research explores the intersection between public policy, bioethics, and biomedical research; Leslie E. Wolf, J.D., M.P.H., is Professor of Law at Georgia State University's College of Law where she conducts research in a variety of areas in health and public health law and ethics, with a particular focus on research ethics.

[1] Darren Lau et al., *Stem Cell Clinics Online: The Direct-to-Consumer Portrayal of Stem Cell Medicine*, 3 CELL STEM CELL 591, 591–92 (2008); Alan C. Regenberg et al., *Medicine on the Fringe: Stem Cell-Based Interventions in Advance of Evidence*, 27 STEM CELLS 2312, 2312–13 (2009).

countries where these interventions are permitted, the practice is commonly known as "stem cell tourism."

Progress has been made in identifying and assessing the clinics that offer SCBIs. A 2006 article estimated that more than 4,800 patients had been treated in nine clinics offering SCBIs.[2] In 2007, there were an estimated twenty clinics offering unproven SCBIs.[3] By mid-2010, more than two hundred clinics existed worldwide.[4] Many SCBI clinics market their services directly to consumers, making claims that are generally "optimistic and unsubstantiated by peer-reviewed literature."[5]

Systematic analyses of clinic Web sites[6] and patient blogs[7] provide insight into the clinics' geographic distribution and the treatment modalities they claim to use. Asian countries, particularly China and India, have the most clinics. Central American and Caribbean countries, such as Mexico, Panama and the Dominican Republic, also host SCBI clinics. Clinics are less common in developed Western countries, where they typically face more stringent legal restrictions. Although the U.S. Food and Drug Administration has generally acted to close clinics operating in the United States relatively quickly,[8] several clinics maintain U.S. administrative offices for referring patients to foreign treatment locations.[9]

These clinics claim to use a wide variety of stem cell types, including autologous adult stem cells (stem cells isolated from patients, manipulated, and injected back into the same patients) and stem cells isolated from cord blood, aborted fetuses, and early human embryos. A few clinics offer treatment with animal cells.[10] Given the lack of regulatory oversight of these clinics in most countries where they operate, clinics may not actually treat patients with the stem cell type they claim or even use stem cells at all.[11]

Much less is known about the patients pursuing unproven SCBIs. Analysis of case studies posted on clinic Web sites and patient blogs identified common conditions for which patients engage in stem cell tourism such as spinal cord injury, amyotrophic lateral sclerosis, multiple sclerosis, cerebral palsy, and optic nerve hypoplasia.[12] The patient blogs suggested that this population was rapidly growing.[13] Nearly half of the blogs studied focused on pediatric patients.[14]

---

[2] Martin Enserink, *Selling the Stem Cell Dream*, 313 SCI. 160, 162 (2006).

[3] *See* Lau, *supra* note 1; *see* Regenberg, *supra* note 1, at 2313.

[4] Editorial, *Order from Chaos*, 466 NATURE 7, 7 (2010).

[5] Lau, *supra* note 1, at 591.

[6] *See* Regenberg, *supra* note 1.

[7] Kirsten A. Ryan et al., *Tracking the Rise of Stem Cell Tourism*, 5 REGENERATIVE MED. 27 (2010).

[8] *See, e.g.,* Alan Zarembo, *A Desperate Injection of Stem Cells and Hope*, L.A. TIMES, Feb. 20, 2005 at A1. *See also* Heidi Ledford, *Stem-Cell Scientists Grapple with Clinics*, 474 NATURE 550 (2011) (for a discussion of an important exception, stem cell clinics that claim their treatment methodologies are not subject to F.D.A. oversight).

[9] *See* Regenberg, *supra* note 1, at 2313.

[10] *See* Lau, *supra* note 1, at 591; *see* Regenberg, *supra* note 1, at 2314.

[11] Douglas Sipp, *Stem Cell Stratagems in Alternative Medicine*, 6 REGENERATIVE MED. 407, 408 (2011).

[12] *See* Regenberg, *supra* note 1, at 2313, 2315; *see* Ryan et al., *supra* note 7, at 30–31.

[13] *See* Ryan et al., *supra* note 7, at 29–30.

[14] *See id.* at 30.

Because of the politicization of stem cell research, scientists and policy makers are concerned that use of unproven SCBIs poses unacceptable risks to legitimate stem cell research, as well as to individual patients.[15] For example, negative outcomes, such as the glianeuronal-like tumors that developed in a thirteen-year-old boy after treatment with fetal neuronal stem cells[16] or the angiomyelo-proliferative lesions that developed in a forty-six-year-old woman following direct renal injection of autologous hematopoietic stem cells,[17] may hinder research and dampen investment in the field.[18] Negative results can inform ongoing research efforts if consistently tracked, but because knowledge about the cells used is limited, drawing appropriate conclusions will be difficult. Unproven SCBIs use may also reduce the pool of patients available for clinical trials.

This policy interest has led to efforts to discourage patients from engaging in stem cell tourism, and it provides the context for this chapter. Specifically, we consider the roles that physicians should and do play in patients' decisions about unproven SCBIs. We examine professional guidelines for physicians regarding medical and stem cell tourism and the legal obligations physicians have under U.S. law toward patients considering an unproven SCBI. We then use interviews with ten patients who engaged in stem cell tourism to describe how some patients interact with their physicians regarding unproven SCBIs and to assess preliminarily how well physicians are complying with these professional responsibilities.

I. Professional Guidelines for Health Care Providers

In this section, we examine professional guidelines that are relevant to stem cell tourism. Although these guidelines have a range of audiences, they offer insight into the behavior expected of physicians and, thus, the standard of care for physicians, in this context.

We focus on guidelines from the American Medical Association (AMA) and from the International Society for Stem Cell Research (ISSCR) because differences between them may inform future policy. The organizations' reaches are quite different: the AMA is a broad-based professional organization for physicians, regardless of specialty, whereas the ISSCR is a professional organization for the relatively small group of stem cell researchers. Second, the guidelines occupy opposite ends of the spectrum in their

---

[15] Insoo Hyun et al., *New ISSCR Guidelines Underscore Major Principles for Responsible Translational Stem Cell Research*, 3 CELL STEM CELL 607, 607–09 (2008); Bryn Nelson, *Stem Cell Researchers Face Down Stem Cell Tourism*, NATURE REPORTS STEM CELLS, June 5, 2008, http://www.nature.com/stemcells/2008/0806/080605/full/stemcells.2008.89.html (last visited July 7, 2011).

[16] Ninette Amariglio et al., *Donor-Derived Brain Tumor Following Neural Stem Cell Transplantation in an Ataxia Telangiectasia Patient*, 6 PUB. LIBR. SCI. MED. 221, 223 (2009).

[17] Duangpen Thirabanjasak et al., *Angiomyeloproliferative Lesions following Autologous Stem Cell Therapy*, 21 J. AM. SOC'Y NEPHROLOGY. 1218, 1218–19 (2010).

[18] Christopher T. Scott, *What Stem Cell Therapy Can Learn from Gene Therapy*, NATURE REPORTS STEM CELLS (Sept. 4, 2008), http://www.nature.com/stemcells/2008/0809/080904/full/stemcells.2008.123.html (last visited July 7, 2011).

scope. The AMA guidance applies broadly to medical tourism, which encompasses international travel to receive medical treatments that may be legal or illegal in a patient's home country. Unproven SCBIs typically fall in the latter category because appropriate regulatory bodies have not approved their use. In contrast, the ISSCR developed its guidance to facilitate translational stem cell research, which aims to bridge the gap between basic knowledge of stem cells and potential clinical applications, and to limit stem cell tourism.

A. GUIDELINES FROM THE AMERICAN MEDICAL ASSOCIATION

The AMA is the largest U.S. physician professional organization with roughly 217,000 members.[19] In July 2008, the AMA adopted nine guiding principles to ensure the safety of medical tourists (see Table 10.1).[20] The AMA indicated that these principles should be considered by patients, employers, insurers, and others coordinating medical travel.[21] Although the guidelines do not specifically address stem cell tourism, several principles are applicable to it. Principle (c), for instance, indicates that patients should be referred only to appropriately accredited institutions. Although most patients considering unproven SCBIs likely identify clinics themselves and are not "referred" in a traditional sense, it seems reasonable that physicians would consider accreditation when asked to help their patients evaluate potential SCBIs. Physicians' advice could be particularly useful in this situation as many patients may not be familiar with accreditation or be able to assess an institution's accreditation status.

AMA principle (g) might impose additional professional responsibilities on physicians. This principle calls for patients to have access to both physician licensing and outcome data for treatment outside the United States.

Although the destination institution is the most likely source of this data, patients may need assistance getting the data and interpreting them. As described more fully in the legal obligations section, physicians could reasonably be expected to provide assistance in response to patient requests. As previous examinations of stem cell tourism have generally found that the interventions offered were supported neither by the medical literature nor good outcome data, following this principle would likely lead physicians to advise against stem cell tourism in most cases.[22] In addition, physicians may be better positioned to help patients identify SCBI clinical trials or legitimate medical innovations outside the context of a clinical trial,[23] including those that may be offered outside their home country.

---

[19] AM. MED. ASS'N., 2011 ANNUAL REPORT OF THE AMERICAN MEDICAL ASSOCIATION 25 (2011), http://www.ama-assn.org/resources/doc/about-ama/2011-annual-report.pdf (last visited Oct. 24, 2012).

[20] AM. MED. ASS'N., NEW AMA GUIDELINES ON MEDICAL TOURISM (2008), http://www.ama-assn.org/ama1/pub/upload/mm/31/medicaltourism.pdf (last visited Oct. 24, 2012).

[21] Karen Caffarini, *AMA Meeting: Guidelines Target Safety of Medical Tourists*, AMEDNEWS (July 7, 2008), http://www.ama-assn.org/amednews/2008/07/07/prse0707.htm (last visited Oct. 24, 2012).

[22] *See* Lau, *supra* note 1, at 592–94; *see* Regenberg, *supra* note 1, at 2316.

[23] Olle Lindvall & Insoo Hyun, *Medical Innovation versus Stem Cell Tourism*, 324 SCI. 1664, 1664–65 (2009).

TABLE 10.1

AMA Guidelines on Medical Tourism

(a)	Medical care outside of the U.S. must be voluntary.
(b)	Financial incentives to travel outside the U.S. for medical care should not inappropriately limit the diagnostic and therapeutic alternatives that are offered to patients, or restrict treatment or referral options.
(c)	Patients should only be referred for medical care to institutions that have been accredited by recognized international accrediting bodies (e.g., the Joint Commission International or the International Society for Quality in Health Care).
(d)	Prior to travel, local follow-up care should be coordinated and financing should be arranged to ensure continuity of care when patients return from medical care outside the U.S.
(e)	Coverage for travel outside the U.S. for medical care must include the costs of necessary follow-up care upon return to the U.S.
(f)	Patients should be informed of their rights and legal recourse prior to agreeing to travel outside the U.S. for medical care.
(g)	Access to physician licensing and outcome data, as well as facility accreditation and outcomes data, should be arranged for patients seeking medical care outside the U.S.
(h)	The transfer of patient medical records to and from facilities outside the U.S. should be consistent with HIPAA guidelines.
(i)	Patients choosing to travel outside the U.S. for medical care should be provided with information about the potential risks of combining surgical procedures with long flights and vacation activities.

B. GUIDELINES FROM THE INTERNATIONAL SOCIETY FOR STEM CELL RESEARCH

The ISSCR, founded in 2002 to "encourage the general field of research involving stem cells,"[24] is a professional organization consisting primarily of stem cell scientists. In response to the growth of unproven SCBIs, the ISSCR created a task force in February 2008 to identify the "scientific, clinical, regulatory, ethical and societal issues that must be addressed to ensure that basic stem cell research is responsibly transitioned into appropriate clinical applications."[25] It subsequently published its "Guidelines for the Clinical Translation of Stem Cells."[26]

---

[24] See INT'L SOC'Y FOR STEM CELL RES., *Mission Statement*, ISSCR, http://www.isscr.org/Mission_Statement/2810.htm (last visited July 7, 2011).

[25] George Q. Daley, Insoo Hyun & Olle Lindvall, *Mapping the Road to the Clinical Translation of Stem Cells*, 2 CELL STEM CELL 139, 139 (2008).

[26] INT'L SOC'Y FOR STEM CELL RES., GUIDELINES FOR THE CLINICAL TRANSLATION OF STEM CELLS (2008), http://www.isscr.org/clinical_trans/pdfs/ISSCRGLClinicalTrans.pdf (last visited July 7, 2011).

The ISSCR guidelines focus on identifying the challenges associated with transla-tional stem cell research and developing guidelines to help clinician-scientists meet these challenges responsibly. They also include a section on addressing "the problem of unproven stem cell interventions being marketed directly to patients."[27] After carv-ing out a narrow exception for legitimate medical innovation outside the context of a clinical trial,[28] the guidelines state:

> In all other circumstances, the ISSCR condemns the administration of unproven
> uses of stem cells or their direct derivatives to a large series of patients outside of
> a clinical trial, particularly when patients are charged for such services. Scientists
> and clinicians should not participate in such activities as a matter of professional
> ethics. Health care institutions and research institutions should not participate
> in such activities.[29]

The ISSCR also created a patient handbook to "help patients and their doctors make informed choices when contemplating a stem cell-based intervention either locally or abroad."[30] This handbook contains answers to frequently asked questions designed to help patients and their doctors make decisions about potential SCBIs. For our analysis, two questions are most relevant: "What should I look for if I am considering a stem cell therapy?" and "What should I be cautious about if I am considering a stem cell ther-apy?" (see Table 10.2). In addition, the ISSCR has created a Web site to help patients and physicians considering SCBIs.[31]

TABLE 10.2

Key Questions from the ISSCR Patient Handbook on Stem Cell Therapies

What should I look for If I am considering a stem cell therapy?

- Preclinical studies have been conducted, published and replicated.
- Independent ethical oversight to ensure risks are minimized and outweighed by benefits.
- Regulatory approval from the appropriate national or regional regulatory agency.

What should I be cautious about if I am considering a stem cell therapy?

- Claims based on patient testimonials.
- Multiple diseases treated with the same cells.
- The source of the cells or how the treatment will be done is not clearly documented.
- Claims there is no risk.
- High cost of treatment or hidden costs.

---

[27] *Id.* at 4–5.
[28] *See* Lindvall & Hyun, *supra* note 23.
[29] *See* INT'L SOC'Y FOR STEM CELL RES, *supra* note 26, at 5.
[30] INT'L SOC'Y FOR STEM CELL RES., PATIENT HANDBOOK ON STEM CELL THERAPIES (2008), http://www.isscr.org/clinical_trans/pdfs/ISSCRPatientHandbook.pdf (last visited July 7, 2011).
[31] INT'L SOC'Y FOR STEM CELL RES., A CLOSER LOOK AT STEM CELL TREATMENTS, http://www.closer-lookatstemcells.org/ (last visited Jan. 4, 2012).

The ISSCR guidelines give physicians a set of specific responsibilities to follow when they are asked to help a patient evaluate a potential SCBI. The broadest interpretation of these responsibilities would direct physicians, when asked by an existing patient for assistance, to help identify if the proposed unproven SCBIs are being offered outside of a clinical trial or appropriate experimental setting and, if so, to discourage their patients from pursuing these treatment options. Similarly, physicians may be asked to assist in identifying and assessing relevant preclinical studies, determining if a SCBI has appropriate ethical oversight and regulatory approval, and assessing whether the particular treatment approach appears unreasonable, because, as the ISSCR patient handbook suggests, a single treatment is offered to treat a range of conditions. In addition, the ISSCR handbook suggests that physicians respond to patients' request for assistance in evaluating the information contained in the detailed treatment protocol such as the type of stem cells used and the method of administration.

C. IMPLICATIONS OF THE AMA AND ISSCR GUIDELINES

Notably, the AMA and ISSCR guidelines suggest that physicians are expected to have knowledge of stem cell-based medicine developments to help evaluate preclinical evidence and potential treatment modalities or be able to help patients access and interpret the medical literature. This knowledge requirement may not be a reasonable expectation for general practitioners who may not be in a position to keep up with advancing stem cell science in a range of fields for which they see patients only intermittently. Physicians' professional responsibilities in these cases are not clearly articulated in either the AMA or ISSCR guidelines, but a reasonable interpretation might be that physicians who are unable to fully evaluate a potential SCBI would be obligated to refrain from offering any recommendation and to instead refer the patient to a specialist (e.g., a neurologist, oncologist, or cardiologist) capable of fully evaluating the treatment option.

II. Legal Responsibilities for Health Care Providers

We next consider physicians' legal obligations to their patients concerning SCBIs. A physician's legal duty toward a patient arises when a physician–patient relationship is established, such as when a physician examines the patient to evaluate, diagnose, or treat the patient. The relationship—and, thus, the duty—may arise in other ways, such as being on call or through a consultation.[32] Once the relationship is formed, the duty is typically a continuing one.[33] Because most SCBI conversations in the home country will take place in existing physician–patient relationships where the legal duty is clear, we focus our discussion on what is required within those relationships concerning SCBIs.

---

[32] BARRY R. FURROW ET AL., HEALTH LAW § 6-1 (lst ed., 1995)
[33] See FURROW ET AL., *supra* note 32.

A. OBLIGATION TO INFORM

The legal requirement to obtain informed consent from patients for their treatment is based on the principle, famously articulated by Justice Cardozo, that "[e]very human being of adult years and sound mind has a right to determine what shall be done with his own body."[34] To exercise that right, patients must understand their condition and options. Thus, the informed consent doctrine requires physicians to disclose material information about the patient's diagnosis and prognosis, and the risks, benefits, and consequences of the proposed treatment, as well as any alternative treatments (including no treatment).[35] The majority of jurisdictions use a "reasonable physician" standard, whereas others apply the "reasonable patient" standard, which typically requires greater disclosure.[36] Under either standard, physicians must respond to patients' questions. Failure to obtain informed consent can give rise to legal liability. With this background, we can consider physician disclosure obligations regarding SCBIs.

1. Obligation to Disclose SCBI as a Treatment Alternative?

Because the informed consent doctrine requires physicians to inform patients about alternative treatment, the question arises whether physicians proposing a treatment must inform patients about the availability of unproven SCBIs, especially as patient interest in SCBIs grows for at least some conditions.

The California case of *Schiff v. Prados*[37] is instructive on this question. In *Schiff*, parents of a child who died from a malignant brain tumor brought suit against the child's University of California San Francisco (UCSF) neurosurgeon, Dr. Prados (among others). The Schiffs claimed that UCSF failed to get informed consent to treatment, which included surgery, aggressive radiation, and chemotherapy, because they were not told about an experimental treatment a Texas physician offered, after they specifically asked about alternative treatments.

The Schiffs found the experimental treatment through their own research after their daughter's tumor remained despite treatment. They spoke to Dr. Prados about the experimental treatment; he was "adamantly opposed" to it. Nevertheless, the Schiffs took their daughter to Texas for treatment and continued it at home in California, despite knowing that the treatment was not FDA-approved, that criminal and licensing actions were pending against the Texas doctor, and that transporting the experimental medicine across state lines was illegal.[38]

---

[34] For a general discussion of the legal requirement of informed consent, *see, e.g.,* Canterbury v. Spence, 464 F.2d 772 (D.C. Cir. 1972) and Schloendorff v. Soc'y of N.Y. Hosp., 105 N.E. 92 (N.Y. 1914).

[35] *See, e.g., Canterbury,* 464 F.2d 772.

[36] *See* FURROW ET AL., *supra* note 32, at § 6-9.

[37] 112 Cal. Rptr. 2d 171 (Ct. App. 2001).

[38] *Schiff,* 112 Cal. Rptr. 2d at 175. Several legal charges were resolved in the physician's favor, but only after the Schiff's daughter had been treated. *Id.* at 176–77. Mr. Schiff also acknowledged that he knew that the American Medical Association and American Cancer Society were critical of the Texas physician and his experimental treatment. *Id.* at 175–77.

The trial court determined that Dr. Prados had no legal duty to inform the Schiffs of a non–FDA-approved treatment that was illegal within California.[39] In affirming the trial court's decision, the California Court of Appeals noted that, although California follows the reasonable patient standard for informed consent, numerous opinions "have echoed the statement in *Cobbs v. Grant* ... that the duty of disclosure extends only to 'available choices.'"[40] Because the experimental treatment was not FDA-approved, it was not "available" in California. The Court further noted that, although "there is no general duty of disclosure with respect to *nonrecommended* procedures," whether an alternative treatment should be "recommended" will be determined by the reasonable physician standard.[41] The Court pointed to cases from other states that similarly rejected imposing a duty on physicians to inform patients about treatments not available within the state[42]

The consistent holdings of *Schiff* and similar cases suggest that physicians have no legal duty to tell patients about unproven SCBIs as alternative treatments if such treatments are not available within the physician's state. However, because the evaluation of recommended treatments is based on the reasonable physician standard, physician obligations regarding SCBI disclosure may change to the extent evidence develops about effectiveness of at least some SCBIs.

2. Obligations to Inform in Response to Patient Inquiries or Decisions?

SCBI discussions are most likely to arise when patients ask their physicians about them. A patient may ask her physician for information about a SCBI, for example, in response to a news story or if the patient is conducting internet research about treatment alternatives. Alternatively, a patient may ask his physician for advice after deciding to pursue a SCBI. In either case, the physician is providing medical advice that will be subject to malpractice standards. Thus, physicians must respond as would reasonable providers with their experience and expertise.

Physicians should provide when asked accurate information about what is currently known about SCBIs.[43] The ISSCR information may be particularly helpful in responding to this kind of inquiry. Referring the patient to other reputable Web sites, such as the National Institutes of Health, for information about stem cell research could

---

[39] *Id.* at 178.

[40] *Id.* at 179 (citing Cobbs v. Grant, 502 P.2d 1, 10, (Cal. 1972)).

[41] *Id.* (citing Vandi v. Permanente Med. Group Inc., 9 Cal. Rptr. 2d 463, 468 (Ct. App. 1992)).

[42] *Id.* at 183 (citing Spencer By and Through Spencer v. Seikel, 742 P.2d 1126 (Okla. 1987)).

[43] Lisa A. Vincler & Mary F. Nicol, *When Ignorance Isn't Bliss: What Healthcare Practitioners and Facilities Should Know about Complementary and Alternative Medicine*, 30 J. HEALTH & HOSP. L. 160, 160–78 (1997) (discussing physician obligations with respect to patient inquiries regarding complementary and alternative medicine (CAM)). They suggest that physicians in an ongoing relationship have an obligation to inquire about CAM usage and provide information about the risks and benefits of the particular CAM in use, and have a *minimum* obligation to obtain and share information regarding basic efficacy and safety of the CAM in use, which may be limited to the "reasonable efforts of a similarly trained practitioner."

also be helpful.[44] However, patients may need both assistance from their physicians interpreting SCBI information, including any clinical trials data, and recommendations from their physicians to guide decision making.[45] As the data presented below suggest, failure to make a clear recommendation may confuse patients. Physicians should be cautious about referring patients to providers or clinics providing SCBIs. A physician could be held liable for negligent referral if the physician knew or should have known that the physician to whom the referral was made was incompetent; the clinic was unaccredited or lacking in proper staff, equipment, or facilities; or the SCBI was ineffective and risky.[46] The AMA's guidance (c) speaks of referring only to accredited facilities, which can reduce the risk of a negligent referral. However, the ISSCR guidelines suggest physicians should also inquire about the physicians' qualifications and evidence of SCBI safety and efficacy before making any referral.

When a patient has previously decided on an unproven SCBI, the physician should inquire into the patient's decision and seek to persuade the patient to reconsider it. Physicians have ongoing duties to act in their patients' best interests.[47] In the case presented, the physician could discharge this duty by providing information about the risks, benefits, and uncertainties about the SCBI compared to other possible treatments, and the likely consequences of pursuing different actions, to dissuade the patient from pursuing the unproven SCBI. The AMA and ISSCR guidelines may be useful in determining what specific information to provide to these patient inquiries. In particular, the ISSCR's patient handbook describes the type of information that patients may need; it is a good source of basic information about SCBIs and the state of research. Importantly, the physician is not required to prevent a competent adult patient from pursuing an SCBI that appears fruitless (at best) or harmful (at worst) after attempts to dissuade the patient have failed. The "right to determine what shall be done with [one's] own body," is a broad one, extending to refusal of life-sustaining treatment.[48] Although patients may not have a right of access to experimental therapies[49] or to require that their physicians provide them,[50] they may choose unproven treatments where they are available. However, if the adult patient lacks decision-making capacity, there may be an obligation for the physician to intervene, as described for pediatric patients.

Physicians' legal and ethical obligations to their patients continue even when patients pursue SCBIs against physician advice. Patients returning home after receiving a SCBI

[44] *See, e.g.*, NAT'L INST. OF HEALTH, *Frequently Asked Questions*, STEM CELL INFORMATION (Aug. 2, 2010) http://stemcells.nih.gov/info/faqs.asp (last visited July 7, 2011).

[45] John Lantos, Ann Marie Matlock & David Wendler, *Clinician Integrity and Limits to Patient Autonomy*, 305 J. AM. MED. ASS'N 495, 497–98 (2011).

[46] Andrew W. Martin, *Legal Malpractice: Negligent Referral as a Cause of Action*, 29 CUMB. L. REV. 679, 682–84 (1999) (discussing the negligent referral cause of action and emphasizing the "duty of the referring physician to use reasonable care in making the recommendation").

[47] *See* Vincler, *supra* note 43; *see* Lantos et al., *supra* note 45.

[48] *See* Lantos et al., *supra* note 45.

[49] Abigail Alliance for Better Access to Developmental Drugs v. von Eschenbach, 495 F.3d 695 (D.C. Cir. 2007), *cert. denied*, 552 U.S. 1159 (2008).

[50] *See* Lantos et al., *supra* note 45.

abroad will likely turn to their physicians for post-intervention follow-up care, treatment of SCBI-related complications, and continuing medical care. Accordingly, physicians should explain that they will continue to provide care for their patients. In rare circumstances, a physician may feel that she cannot continue to provide care because the patient pursues unproven SCBI. In such cases, the physician must notify the patient of her intent to terminate the relationship to allow the patient to find another physician. Failure to do so could lead to a claim for abandonment, depending on the specific facts.[51]

B. OBLIGATIONS REGARDING PEDIATRIC PATIENTS

While a physician does not have a legal obligation to prevent competent adult patients from seeking SCBIs, he may have a duty to prevent parents from pursuing SCBIs for their minor children. The situation is different for children because they cannot protect themselves and must rely on others to make decisions on their behalf. Given their patients' vulnerability, pediatricians typically place stronger emphasis on the principle of beneficence—the obligation to affirmatively promote good, and the obligation to advocate on their patients' behalf, even against the patients' parents.[52]

Although parents typically have wide latitude in making decisions for their children under the assumption that the parents will act in their children's best interests, if a child is at risk of serious harm or death, that authority may be restricted.[53] If the parent persists in pursing an action that the physician believes is harmful to the child, she may seek a court order for the recommended treatment. The quintessential case where physicians seek to override parental decision making is when a Jehovah's Witnesses' child suffers a trauma requiring a blood transfusion—a highly effective treatment posing very little risk.[54] Although the parents' rights to raise their children within their religious beliefs is constitutionally protected, children may not embrace those beliefs as adults. Accordingly, courts have been willing to intervene in such cases to allow the child the opportunity to reach adulthood and exercise his or her choice. Courts intervene most often when the likelihood of success of the intervention is very high, the risks are low, and the intervention is of short duration. As the risks increase and the level of interference increases (e.g., intervention over months or years), courts are more hesitant to intervene, although courts have been willing to order some cancer treatments, despite negative side effects and typically long duration of treatment, when the likelihood of cure is very high.[55]

---

[51] See Vincler, *supra* note 43; Mark A. Hall, *A Theory of Economic Informed Consent*, 31 GA. L. REV. 511, 527–33 (1997)

[52] Leslie E. Wolf et al., *When Parents Reject Interventions to Reduce Postnatal Human Immunodeficiency Virus Transmission*, 155 ARCHIVES PEDIATRICS & ADOLESCENT MED. 927, 928 (2001); Amy Zarzeczny & Timothy Caulfield, *Stem Cell Tourism and Doctors Duties to Minors—A View from Canada*, 10 AM. J. BIOETHICS 3, 6 (2010).

[53] See Wolf, *supra* note 52; see Zarzeczny & Caulfield, *supra* note 52.

[54] See Wolf, *supra* note 52.

[55] See id.

Thus, the pediatric physician's obligation will depend on the proposed SCBI and the child's condition. The obligation to intervene will be strongest when there is evidence that the SCBI is likely to be harmful and where the SCBI will delay effective therapy. Even evidence of harm alone would provide strong justification for intervening to avert the harm. The obligation to intervene will be weakest when there is no evidence that SCBI is harmful, even if ineffective, and there is no available alternative therapy. In evaluating whether to intervene, the pediatric physician should also consider the impact of intervention on the relationship with the family.[56] The physician–family relationship may not survive court intervention and could potentially drive the parents away from conventional medicine, with consequences for the child's health. Thus, the physician should balance the SCBI risks against the risk of losing the opportunity to provide care and advocate for the child.

The pediatric physician must also consider whether she has a legal obligation to report a parent's decision to pursue SCBIs as child abuse or neglect.[57] All states mandate physician reporting of child abuse, in part, because children are vulnerable and unable to protect themselves.[58] Because physicians are mandated reporters in all states, it is important to consider reporting requirements in connection with SCBIs. Like the decision about court intervention, the physician should consider what is known about the SCBI's potential risks and benefits and what alternatives, if any, are available to the child. If there are no alternatives and no known risks from the intervention, there would not be an obligation to report. The child will not be harmed either by the SCBI or any delay in receiving conventional therapy. However, if the SCBI has known, serious harms with no known benefits, there may be an obligation to report, particularly if there are effective alternatives.[59] The more challenging SCBI situation is also the more common one, where harms are uncertain, but plausible. In such cases, a physician must ultimately rely on her own medical judgment. As with the decision whether to seek court intervention, a pediatric physician also should consider what reporting could do to the relationship with the patient's family. Where the physician learns about the SCBI only after the intervention, reporting will not avert any harm from the intervention, but could disrupt the physician–patient relationship and the chance to protect the child in the future.

III. Physicians' Roles in Patients' Decisions about Unproven Stem Cell Therapies

One of us (Levine) has conducted interviews to explore patient experiences with unproven SCBIs and the role that physicians play in patients' decisions; this was done with a small number of patients who had traveled internationally to receive unproven

---

[56] *See id.*

[57] *See* Zarzeczny & Caulfield, *supra* note 52.

[58] Nancy Kellogg, American Academy of Pediatrics Committee on Abuse and Neglect, *The Evaluation of Sexual Abuse in Children*, 116 PEDIATRICS 506, 511 (2005).

[59] *See* Zarzeczny & Caulfield, *supra* note 52 (reaching similar conclusions under Canadian law).

TABLE 10.3

Medical Conditions of Interview Subjects

Medical Condition	Number of Patients
Spinal Cord Injury	3
Autism	2
Multiple Sclerosis	2
Batten Disease	1
Optic Nerve Hypoplasia	1
Parkinson's Disease	1

SCBIs. Most interview participants were selected purposively from among patients or minor patients' parents who had blogged about their experiences.[60] Participants were given the opportunity to refer others, resulting in one interview. This sample was not intended to represent all patients receiving unproven SCBIs but rather to give an idea of the experiences that patients have when they pursue these treatments and the various roles that physicians play in these decisions.

During May and June 2010, ten interviews lasting forty-five to sixty minutes were conducted. Each interview was recorded and, portions of the recordings relevant to this analysis were transcribed. These ten patients sought unproven SCBIs for six different medical conditions (see Table 10.3) and visited clinics in China, India, Costa Rica, and Panama. The Institutional Review Boards at the authors' respective institutions approved this research.

Qualitative thematic analysis of the interview transcripts revealed several typical interaction patterns between patients and their physicians. At one extreme, an interviewed patient told of a case where a physician clearly recommended the unproven SCBI, while at the other extreme, patients described discussions where their physician strenuously argued against the unproven SCBI. Other patients reported that they had no discussions with physicians in their home country about their interest in an unproven SCBI.

Several interviewed patients indicated that they had chosen not to discuss their decisions to pursue an unproven SCBI with their home country physicians. These decisions were deliberate and based on assumptions about physicians' likely opposition to unproven SCBIs or their lack of knowledge about SCBIs. For example, one spinal cord injury patient explained:

> I started to get a little bit of publicity and they did this special [on tv] on me and in it they interviewed one of the big doctors at [a local] hospital and he just really just bashed me. So from there I just sorta had a bad taste in my mouth about trying to contact any doctors and get their opinions.

---

[60]   Ryan et al., *supra* note 7, at 28–29.

Another interviewee, whose wife has multiple sclerosis, explained their decision not to consult with his wife's neurologist as follows:

The neurologists just don't want to know. They're all driven by big pharma and they are [focused on] what drug to take and then they dish that out and most of the time [the drugs] don't work or they make it worse or whatever. There are two health systems, there is the kind of official system and then there is the parallel system where people do their own thing...The [doctors] wouldn't know what you were talking about. They would superficially but they're not interested. It's not part of their process.

When patients choose not to speak with their physicians prior to traveling to receive an unproven SCBI, their physicians have neither professional nor legal obligations. The prevalence of this interaction pattern suggests, however, that groups seeking to reduce demand for unproven SCBIs cannot rely solely on physicians as gatekeepers. Although dissuading a patient who makes this sort of decision without consulting a physician may be difficult, resources targeted directly at patients, such as the ISSCR's new Web site, may be a useful strategy. Some of these patients expressed skepticism of the Western medical establishment, however, and may doubt the intentions of an organization such as the ISSCR, suggesting that a resource provided by an independent third party that is not seen as part of the existing healthcare system might have a greater impact.

Interviews with patients who consulted physicians in their home countries before deciding to try unproven SCBI revealed three distinct interaction patterns. In two interviews, patients indicated that physicians unambiguously rejected these unproven treatments and attempted to persuade patients not to pursue them. In one, the father of a patient with a neurological disorder sought out leading experts at two different large academic medical centers and was told both times that the SCBI was a bad idea and might endanger his son. In the other, a patient's decision to try an unproven SCBI against her physician's advice had consequences for her future care. Responding to a question about pretreatment discussions with her doctor, the interviewee said, "We spoke with our neurologist and she was not in support of our decision and...she pretty much bailed on our case after that. Left us high and dry...She said, 'There's nothing good that comes out of China. You shouldn't do it.'" In both patients' cases, they were considering paying out-of-pocket for unproven treatments, and their physicians' responses were generally in line with the ISSCR guidelines to discourage the practice of stem cell tourism. However, the physician described in the second case appears to have abandoned her patient, which is ethically and legally problematic.

In other cases, physicians were consulted but provided more ambiguous advice. One patient recounted a discussion with a neurologist whom he described as "noncommittal." Another patient summarized his interactions with physicians as follows:

[Both family practitioners and specialists] knew I was going. Uncertainty...no recommendation. [They] pointed out that it hadn't gone through clinical trials or anything. It was just something to try. I discussed the procedure with my [disease] specialist and he thought that the bone marrow treatment had the best chance of working [for my condition].

This case is notable because although the patient's recollection of his physicians' advice overall was ambiguous, the conversation with the specialist could be interpreted as supporting one approach (bone marrow treatment), even if such support was not intended. Patients who have few, if any, conventional options may focus on *any* positive comments from their physician to justify a decision to pursue a SCBI; physicians should keep this possibility in mind in their discussions with patients.

Several explanations could plausibly account for these ambiguous responses. It may be that these physicians were not aware of the details of the proposed treatments and felt that sharing this uncertainty was the only accurate response they could provide. If this is the case, these doctors may be fulfilling their professional obligations to the best of their abilities. It would be important, however, for physicians who find themselves in this position to either conduct the research necessary to provide advice to their patients or refer their patients to other doctors who can help guide these sorts of decisions. Alternatively, it may be that these physicians found value in the hope these unproven SCBIs provided to their patients[61] and chose to give ambiguous answers to avoid eliminating this hope. In this scenario, the physicians would be going against the guidance provided by the ISSCR and, potentially, the AMA as well.

In addition to these negative and unclear responses, several physicians gave advice that was interpreted by patients as supporting their pursuit of unproven SCBIs. In one case, the only one of the ten, a U.S.-based specialist directly recommended an unproven SCBI:

He said to us, "I usually don't suggest this, but you are at the end of the road with everything you've done" ... He had been talking to [a doctor at a foreign stem cell clinic] and was really convinced that stem cells could help ... He was absolutely convinced that it was worth our time and effort to seek out the stem cells.

This sort of recommendation, which, according to the interviewee, was based primarily on case reports from a doctor affiliated with the clinic offering the unproven SCBI, certainly violates the ISSCR guidelines. Whether such a referral would violate AMA guidelines is difficult to assess without knowing the details of the physician's interaction with the international clinic, its accreditation status, and the types of outcome data, if any, available from the clinic.

In other cases, physicians were supportive of their patients receiving an unproven SCBI, although they did not originate the suggestion. One interviewee reported providing information from the clinic's Web site to his doctor, who concluded, "Well it doesn't look like it's going to hurt you, and it might do some good." Another patient

61 Charles E. Murdoch & Christopher T. Scott, *Stem Cell Tourism and the Power of Hope*, 10 AM. J. BIOETHICS 16, 20 (2010).

reported a similar encounter. "We mentioned it to our pediatrician and he said, you know, from a research standpoint it sounds logical, and he didn't see why there would be anything wrong with it. He just urged us to use caution when deciding which center to go to."

Although in these cases, the patients' physicians did not claim to have any specialized knowledge of the unproven SCBIs, their opinions as medical professionals played an important role in convincing patients to pursue them. It is difficult to know on what information these physicians based their recommendations. It may be that these positive reactions reflected rather superficial assessments of these SCBIs based on patient descriptions. In such cases, the better approach would be to defer offering an opinion until the physician could conduct some research in the medical literature or refer patients to a specialist with greater knowledge of stem cell–based medicine. Alternatively, it may represent a situation where a physician's best judgment, based on available information, is that the SCBI is worth trying, which may violate the ISSCR guidelines, depending on the physician's specific reasoning. If the recommendation resulted from a belief that the hope provided by the SCBI was sufficient to justify trying it, perhaps due to the lack of other medical options for the patient, this would violate the ISSCR guidelines. On the other hand, if the physician concluded that the SCBI under consideration was a legitimate medical innovation, such a recommendation may be acceptable.

Analysis of this small series of interviews identified four distinct patterns of interaction between patients and their home-country physicians. In addition to the "no interaction" approach, the interviews identified patients who chose to pursue an unproven SCBI over the strenuous objection of academic specialists. In other cases, patients received at least a positive endorsement, if not an outright recommendation of the SCBIs. This range of interactions suggests that targeting physicians remains a promising area for organizations such as the ISSCR seeking to discourage the practice of stem cell tourism. At the same time, the identification of a group of patients who did not discuss their plans with their home physician suggests that efforts to control stem cell tourism will require a broader approach than simply issuing professional guidelines and hoping physicians will discourage patients from pursuing these unproven options.

Conclusion

In recent years, patient pursuit of unproven SCBIs has inspired substantial policy interest because of the risks they pose to individual patients and the stem cell research field. We have focused on one element of patients' decisions to pursue unproven SCBIs and examined the legal obligations and professional responsibilities of physicians when their patients are considering these treatments. Although these obligations and responsibilities vary with the details of each specific patient, even among the small set of interviews with returning patients, we identified physician behavior that differed from these legal obligations and professional expectations.

We are unable to determine if the gap between physician behavior and legal and professional obligations is because physicians are unaware of their obligations with respect to unproven SCBIs, unfamiliar with the medical literature on stem cell research and the growing practice of unproven SCBIs, or support unproven SCBIs in some cases. Regardless, the data reported here call for further investigation of physicians' roles in the practice of stem cell tourism and action to help physicians understand and fulfill their roles appropriately.

Additional research or investigation of physicians' roles in stem cell tourism and additional efforts to help them fulfill their legal, professional, and ethical obligations is important because the concerns raised by unproven SCBIs apply broadly to other areas of medicine. Indeed, patient interest in unproven medical interventions, ranging from ancient herbal remedies to cutting-edge technologies, is a recurring issue in numerous serious medical conditions. Particularly in our modern, interconnected world, where patients routinely access medical information online and can easily communicate with practitioners and patients around the world, physicians must be prepared to address questions and advise their patients about a range of alternative and unproven interventions.

Our analysis here points to ways to help prepare physicians to provide appropriate advice about alternative and unproven interventions. Professional organizations, such as the AMA and the ISSCR, have sought to educate their members through guidance development. The ISSCR guidance is more specific than the AMA's in terms of topic (stem cell tourism versus medical tourism generally) and the guidance given (e.g., providing specific questions for evaluating SCBIs). To our knowledge, the AMA has provided only limited guidance on unproven medical interventions[62] and no guidance that specifically addresses international travel for unproven medical interventions—the challenge posed by the rise of stem cell tourism. We believe that the ISSCR approach likely will be more helpful to physicians unfamiliar with the field. However, the ISSCR is a relatively small organization of individuals interested in stem cell research, and who may not be clinicians. The AMA, which brings together physicians from a variety of specialties within the United States, has a much larger audience and is also more likely to reach physicians. Perhaps the best approach would be to join subject matter experts (in this case, the ISSCR) with the group who will need to provide advice (i.e., the AMA) to provide specific guidance that reaches the appropriate audience.

---

[62] See, e.g., AMERICAN MEDICAL ASSOCIATION, H-480.964 ALTERNATIVE MEDICINE (2006), http://www.ama-assn.org/resources/doc/omss/omss-handbook.pdf (outlining the AMA policy on alternative medicine, highlighting the lack of safety or efficacy information on most alternative therapies and calling for such studies and for physicians to routinely inquire into their patients' use of such alternative therapies and to educate both themselves and their patients about the state of scientific knowledge on these options). See also AMERICAN MEDICAL ASSOCIATION, D-480.981 INCREASING AWARENESS OF THE BENEFITS AND RISKS ASSOCIATED WITH COMPLEMENTARY AND ALTERNATIVE MEDICINE (2010), http://www.ama-assn.org/ad-com/polfind/Directives.pdf. (calling on the AMA to "promote awareness among medical students and physicians of the wide use of complementary or alternative medicine, including its benefits, risks, and evidence of efficacy or lack thereof.").

In developing such guidance, attention should be paid to the ultimate goal of helping physicians provide patients considering alternative and unproven therapies appropriate advice to inform their decision making. We believe that the following considerations should be included: the location of the treatment (e.g., is it an unproven intervention administered in the patient's home country or does it involve travel for the purpose of receiving the treatment?), the nature of the intervention, the rationale for seeking the intervention, the seriousness of the medical condition, and the age and decision-making capacity of the patient. Focusing on the needs of physicians and their patients likely will result in a richer set of guidance that will better help physicians address the range of questions raised by patient interest in and pursuit of unproven medical interventions in today's world.

Medical Worker Migration

11

GLOBAL POLICIES AND LOCAL PRACTICE IN THE ETHICAL

RECRUITMENT OF INTERNATIONALLY TRAINED HEALTH

HUMAN RESOURCES

*Vivien Runnels, Corinne Packer, and Ronald Labonté**

Introduction

The multidirectional migration of health human resources (HHR) is not a recent phenomenon, but flows from developing countries to developed countries continue to dominate, exacerbating deficits of HHR in many developing countries.[1] These deficits prevent developing countries from implementing disease prevention and health promotion efforts; sustaining primary health care systems; carrying out health-focused

* Affiliated with the Globalization and Health Equity Research Unit, Institute of Population Health, University of Ottawa and the Population Health Intervention Research Network of Ontario. Financial assistance for the study reported in this chapter was provided through a grant from the Social Sciences and Humanities Research Council of Canada (Grant # 410-2006-1781 ID No: 20986). Vivien Runnels was supported by a Social Sciences and Humanities Research Council of Canada doctoral award and a University of Ottawa Excellence scholarship during the conduct of the research. Ronald Labonté is supported by the Canada Research Chairs Program of the Government of Canada. Thanks are extended to the study participants who generously shared their time, practices, knowledge, and opinions, and to administrative support staff and students (Michelle Payne, Phyllis Hartwick, Nathan Klassen, Jodie Karpf, Chloe Davidson, Tanya Black, Kitley Corey, Kathleen McGovern, and Taslenna Shairulla).

[1] TOWARDS A GLOBAL HEALTH WORKFORCE STRATEGY (Paulo Ferrinho & Mario Dal Poz eds., 2003); ANDRÉS SOLIMANO, THE INTERNATIONAL MOBILITY OF TALENT: TYPES, CAUSES AND DEVELOPMENT (2008); Corinne Packer et al., *Globalization and the Cross-Border Flow of Health Workers, in* GLOBALIZATION AND HEALTH: PATHWAYS, EVIDENCE AND POLICY 213 (Ronald Labonté et al. eds., 2010); Linda Ogilvie et al., *The Exodus of Health Professionals From Sub-Saharan Africa: Balancing Human Rights and Societal Needs in the Twenty-First Century*, 14 NURSING INQUIRY 114 (2007). For a summary of push-and-pull factors associated with HHR Migration, *see* Packer et al., at 222.

campaigns; limiting responses to context-specific events such as civil wars, humanitarian disasters, and global health crises such as HIV/AIDS and SARS; and meeting global goals such as the Millennium Development Goals.[2] Developed countries, in comparison, are better able to respond to any shortages they experience by increasing capacity for domestic training and by recruiting internationally trained health professionals to their health care workforces, some of whom are from developing countries. Direct recruitment in which there is deliberate targeting of overseas HHR is generally acknowledged as unethical and health-inequitable but seems particularly unfair when developed countries do this while knowing the harmful consequences of outmigration from under-resourced developing countries. An emerging literature that suggests international professional mobility can be a good thing does not appear to apply to the migration of HHR who leave progressively weakened health systems behind them.[3]

For a number of years, the World Health Organization, governments, workforce alliances, individual researchers, and other actors have worked to solve the problem of global HHR shortages.[4] The outcomes of these efforts are policies that include control or management of HHR migration, transfers of financial resources from developed to developing countries, use of novel ways of delivering services by staff with less training, and planning to prevent shortages, all of these having the potential to reduce the harmful impacts on health systems caused by migrating HHR. A coherent and coordinated policy approach to the complexity of practices and policies could help to address unethical recruitment of internationally trained health professionals. However, the policy context is complex and implicates multiple levels of governance, sectors of government, systems, and actors, raising the chances for gaps, inconsistencies, and discontinuities in policy and policy implementation.

In order to understand better the overall policy context for the ethical recruitment of internationally trained health professionals, we conceive a framework populated with examples of current policies regarding the ethical recruitment of migrating HHR. We include examples of policies that are particularly relevant for the Canadian context. Because recruiters and the tools that they use to recruit HHR play an important role in enabling the employment of HHR, and because recruiters are users or potential users of recruitment policy, we report from our study of the local practice, knowledge, and roles of recruiters in Canada.[5] We discuss implications of these findings for the implementation of a coherent and ethical recruitment policy framework.

---

[2] Joint Learning Initiatives. Human Resources for Health: Overcoming the Crisis (Global Equity Initiative, Harvard University. 2004). WORLD HEALTH ORG. THE WORLD HEALTH REPORT 2006: WORKING TOGETHER FOR HEALTH (World Health Organization, 2006). Lindsay J. Mangham & Kara Hanson, *Scaling Up in International Health: What Are the Key Issues?* 25 HEALTH POLI'Y & PLAN. 85–96 (2010). Anthony D. Harries, Erik J. Schouten & Edwin Libamba, *Scaling Up Antiretroviral Treatment in Resource-Poor Settings*, 367 LANCET 1870–72 (2006).

[3] SOLIMANO, *supra* note 1; Packer et al., *supra* note 1.

[4] Stephen Bach, *International Mobility of Health Professionals: Brain Drain or Brain Exchange*, in THE INTERNATIONAL MOBILITY OF TALENT: TYPES, CAUSES, AND DEVELOPMENT IMPACT 202 (Andrés Solimano ed., 2008).

[5] Vivien Runnels et al., *Reflections on the Ethics of Recruiting Foreign-Trained Human Resources for Health*, 9 HUM. RESOURCES HEALTH 2 (2010).

I. Recruitment of HHR: A Multilevel Policy Framework

Different levels of policy are implicated in the recruitment of internationally trained HHR (Figure 11.1). These are the global or macro-level, the national, single country or meso-level, and the organizational and authority or micro-level. The level of governing bodies that determine HHR recruitment policy has ramifications on the form and authority of the policy, its reach, and the involvement of different actors. Recruitment policies can be issued by global decision-making bodies such as the World Health Organization and the World Medical Association that have global reach, but these policies function as normative codes and lack enforcement authority. At the national level, policies may take on different forms such as "a law, a rule, a statute, an edict, a regulation or an order," with each of these carrying state enforcement power and sanctions but only reaching domestic policy users.[6] At the local level in Canada as for other countries, governing boards of local health organizations and hospitals, which have degrees of autonomy to establish their own recruitment policies, have reach and authority only within their own organization.

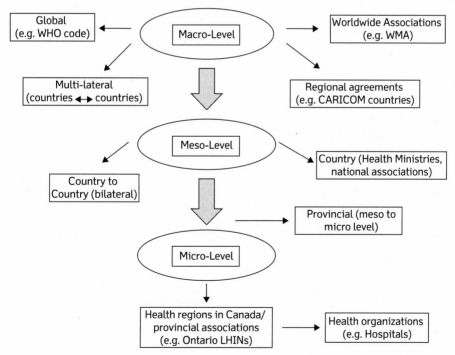

FIGURE 11.1 Levels and Decision-Making bodies for Ethical Health Human Resources Recruitment Policies

---

[6] Frank Fischer, Reframing Public Policy: Discursive Politics and Deliberative Practices (2003).

A. MACRO-LEVEL

1. Global Level Policies—Codes and Associational Instruments

In 2010 the World Health Assembly passed the WHO Global Code of Practice on the International Recruitment of Health Personnel (hereafter "the Code").[7] The Code's objectives include: "(to) establish and promote voluntary principles and practices for the ethical international recruitment of health personnel."[8] Intended in part to address recruitment practices generally viewed as unfair for source countries, the Code was designed to be used alongside other WHO guidelines that address closely related problems such as health human resources management and retention of health workers in rural and remote areas.

Participation in the Code is voluntary and intended for WHO member states. It is not a legal instrument to which countries are bound; therefore, unlike international health regulations, it carries significantly less weight at the country level. If it is not observed, there is little consequence other than the possibility of social or diplomatic sanctioning. Article 4.1 of the Code recognizes that there is a range of actors at different levels of society who are encouraged to work together to implement the Code. The Code might be said to provide a moral standard to support other policy levels.[9]

2. Associational Position Statements and Resolutions

Other macro-level policies establishing ethical principles for international HHR recruitment include the World Medical Association's (WMA) 2003 Statement on Ethical Guidelines for the International Recruitment of Physicians.[10] The WMA Council's 2005 Resolution on the Healthcare Skills Drain reaffirmed the original statement and summarized other important components of an ethical policy to address the

---

[7] WORLD HEALTH ORGANIZATION. THE WHO GLOBAL CODE OF PRACTICE ON THE INTERNATIONAL RECRUITMENT OF HEALTH PERSONNEL 2010, *available at* http://www.who.int/hrh/migration/code/code_en.pdf. The WHO is "the directing and coordinating authority for health" within the United Nations system. *About WHO*, WORLD HEALTH ORGANIZATION, www.who.int/about/en/ (last visited Feb. 28, 2012); *Governance*, WORLD HEALTH ORGANIZATION, http://www.who.int/governance/en/index.html (last visited Feb. 28, 2012).

[8] WORLD HEALTH ORGANIZATION, *supra* note 7, Article 1(1)3. Codes of practice can also be used to support other policy approaches by providing a standard, and by providing the "moral force and the normative content around the development of bilateral agreements." IBADAT S. DHILLON ET AL., THE HEALTH WORKER MIGRATION INITIATIVE, INNOVATIONS IN COOPERATION: A GUIDEBOOK ON BILATERAL AGREEMENTS TO ADDRESS HEALTH WORKER MIGRATION 11 (Aspen Institute 2010).

[9] RONALD LABONTÉ, GLOBALIZATION & HEALTH EQUITY INSTITUTE OF POPULATION HEALTH, GLOBAL HEALTH POLICY: EXPLORING THE RATIONALE FOR HEALTH IN FOREIGN POLICY (University of Ottawa, 2010), http://www.globalhealthequity.ca/electronic%20library/Global%20health%20Policy%20Exploring%20the%20Rationale%20for%20Foreign%20Policy%20version%201.5.pdf (last visited Feb. 28, 2012).

[10] *WMA Statement on Ethical Guidelines for the International Recruitment of Physicians*, WMA (Sept. 2003), http://www.wma.net/en/30publications/10policies/e14/ (last visited Feb. 28, 2012).

migration of HHR from developing to developed countries.[11] This resolution is supported widely and in Canada, by the Canadian Medical Association.[12] Another associational statement, "A Code of Practice for the International Recruitment of Health Care Professionals," or "The Melbourne Manifesto," was issued by the World Organisation of National Colleges, Academies and Academic Associations of General Practitioners/Family Physicians (WONCA) at the World Rural Health Conference in 2002.[13] All delegates but one were reported to have adopted the document.[14]

3. Multilateral Codes

Some policies have also been agreed to between groups of countries such as the Commonwealth nations.[15] The voluntary Commonwealth Code of Practice for the International Recruitment of Health Workers and its accompanying documents provide guidelines "for the international recruitment of health workers in a manner that takes into account the potential impact of such recruitment on services in the source country" as well as for the protection of rights and émigré HHR professional standing in destination countries.[16] The Commonwealth Code has reportedly been the basis for several bilateral agreements between Commonwealth countries; however, not all Commonwealth countries have subscribed to the Code.[17] Canada, for one, was not one of its early signatories.[18]

The Managed Migration Program of the Caribbean is a regional strategy that features a number of agreements between several countries that includes a focus on nurse

---

[11] *WMA Council Resolution on the Healthcare Skills Drain*, WMA (May 2005), http://www.wma.net/en/30publications/10policies/30council/cr_2/ (last visited Feb. 28, 2012).

[12] *See, e.g.,* CMA's February 23, 2008 letter to James Rajotte, MP Chair, Standing Committee on Industry, Science and Technology: Review of the Service Sector in Canada, *available at* http://www.cma.ca/multimedia/CMA/Content_Images/Inside_cma/Submissions/2008/rajotte-en-08.pdf (last visited Feb. 28, 2012).

[13] *Available at* http://www.srpc.ca/PDF/MelbourneManifesto.pdf (last visited Feb. 28, 2012).

[14] CATHERINE PAGETT & ASHNIE PADARATH, EQUINET DISCUSSION PAPER NO. 50, A REVIEW OF CODES AND PROTOCOLS FOR THE MIGRATION OF HEALTH WORKERS (EQUINET 2007), *available at* http://www.equinetafrica.org/bibl/docs/Diss50HRHpaggett07.pdf (last visited Feb. 28, 2012).

[15] COMMONWEALTH SECRETARIAT, http://www.thecommonwealth.org/subhomepage/191086/ (last visited Feb. 28, 2012).

[16] COMMONWEALTH HEALTH MINISTERS, COMMONWEALTH CODE OF PRACTICE FOR THE INTERNATIONAL RECRUITMENT OF HEALTH WORKERS 7, at 4 (2003); COMMONWEALTH HEALTH MINISTERS, COMPANION DOCUMENT TO THE COMMONWEALTH CODE OF PRACTICE FOR THE INTERNATIONAL RECRUITMENT OF HEALTH WORKERS (2003); Ann Keeling & Peggy Vidot, *The Politics of Health Worker Migration in the Commonwealth: The Implementation of the Commonwealth Code*, COMMONWEALTH SECRETARIAT, *available at* http://www.thecommonwealth.org/shared_asp_files/GFSR.asp?NodeID=172878 (last visited Feb. 28, 2012); Ann Keeling & Jacqueline Wilson, Directors, Governance and Institutions Development Division, Keynote Speech at the Commonwealth Health Professionals Meeting (Nov. 19, 2007), *available at* http://www.thecommonwealth.org/speech/34293/35178/172875/healthkeynote.htm (last visited Feb. 28, 2012).

[17] PAGETT & PARADATH, *supra* note 14.

[18] *Id.*

migration.[19] This program led to the creation of partnerships "in order to maximize the benefits and minimize the costs to the countries and to the professionals," not only within the Caribbean countries but also with countries and associations outside the region. One such extra-regional agreement includes a Caribbean–Canadian accord in which Caribbean nurses receive training in the Caribbean by Canadians and work for short periods of time in Canadian hospitals, thereby increasing nursing capacity in the Caribbean countries.[20] However, in 2006, Dawson suggested that this project had stalled, while Salmon and colleagues noted that it was too early to demonstrate any success, with both authors suggesting that there has been little progress in implementing the Program.[21]

B. MESO-LEVEL

1. Single-Country Policies

The United Kingdom's Code of Practice for the International Recruitment of Healthcare Professionals is a single-country policy that aims to stop the active recruitment of HHR from developing countries "unless there exists a government-to-government agreement to support recruitment activities."[22] One section of the Code of Practice is also designed to ensure that the standards used by the NHS in international recruitment are used by third-party recruitment agencies working for the NHS.[23] Norway also has a code of ethical recruitment that states that Norway will recruit only from European Union countries.[24] However, as the Norwegians have noted, this policy has potential for encouraging unethical recruitment because the European countries from which Norway recruits are likely to fill their own shortages from low-income countries. Norway's seemingly "ethical" recruitment policy could therefore indirectly contribute to unethical recruitment in other countries.[25] In Canada, the College of Physicians and

---

[19] Marla E. Salmon et al., *Managed Migration: The Caribbean Approach to Addressing Nursing Services Capacity*, 42 HEALTH SERVICES RES. 1354 (2007).

[20] *See* LAURA RITCHIE DAWSON, CENTER FOR TRADE POLICY & LAW, A MANAGED TEMPORARY MOVEMENT PROGRAM FOR NURSES FROM THE CARIBBEAN TO CANADA: THE SHORT (BUT INTERESTING) LIFE OF A POLICY ADVOCACY PROPOSAL (FOCAL 2006). *See also* WORLD BANK, REPORT NO. 48988-LAC, THE NURSE LABOR & EDUCATION MARKETS IN THE ENGLISH-SPEAKING CARICOM: ISSUES AND OPTIONS FOR REFORM (2009), *available at* http://siteresources.worldbank.org/INTJAMAICA/Resources/The_Nurse_Labor_Education_Market_Eng.pdf (last visited Feb. 28, 2012).

[21] DAWSON, *supra* note 20. Salmon et al., *supra* note 19.

[22] DEP'T OF HEALTH, THE CODE OF PRACTICE FOR NHS EMPLOYERS INVOLVED IN THE INTERNATIONAL RECRUITMENT OF HEALTHCARE PROFESSIONALS 4 (2004).

[23] *Id.*

[24] *See more generally,* NORWEGIAN MINISTRY OF FOREIGN AFFAIRS, A PROPOSAL FOR MEASURES UNDER NORWEGIAN FOREIGN AND INTERNATIONAL DEVELOPMENT POLICY TO COMBAT THE GLOBAL HEALTH WORKFORCE CRISIS, *available at* http://www.regjeringen.no/upload/UD/Vedlegg/helse/EN%20Arbeidsgrupperapport_helsepersonellkrisen.pdf (last visited Feb. 28, 2012).

[25] THE POLICY COHERENCE COMMISS'N, COHERENT FOR DEVELOPMENT? HOW COHERENT NORWEGIAN POLICIES CAN ASSIST DEVELOPMENT IN POOR COUNTRIES 147–48 (Official Norwegian Reports, Report No. 2008: 14, 2008).

Surgeons of Ontario (CPSO), and the Canadian Nurses Association have acknowledged some recruitment as unethical, and have issued position statements on the ethical recruitment of internationally trained health professionals.[26] The CPSO statement of principle on ethical recruitment states that "active recruitment efforts must employ strategies that are cognizant of physician resource needs in source jurisdictions and adequately protect those jurisdictions and the recruited physicians."[27]

2. Bilateral Policies

Bilateral HHR agreements explicitly recognize the inequitable results that recruitment from developing to developed countries creates, and may include provisions for cost underwriting, training additional staff, and recruiting staff for fixed periods.[28] These policies are typically designed at higher levels of government to be disseminated and implemented at local levels. Examples of bilateral agreements include the 2003 Memorandum of Understanding between South Africa and the United Kingdom. The United Kingdom has also forged memoranda of understanding with India and the Philippines.[29] Potential migrants to the United Kingdom are warned that applications from countries that appear on the Code's list of prescribed countries will not be considered, except in the case of bilateral agreements or with prior approval from their respective governments."[30]

The Health Worker Migration Initiative (HWMI) at the Aspen Institute lists some bilateral agreements that are intended to "better manage health worker migration," with some focusing specifically on the recruitment of HHR,[31] as well as a report designed for policy makers to guide the development of bilateral agreements addressing health worker migration.[32]

C. MESO-TO-MICRO–LEVEL POLICIES: CANADIAN PROVINCIAL AND TERRITORIAL HEALTH MINISTRY POLICIES

Canadian provinces and territories are mid-level domestic governments whose ministries of health oversee the majority of health care delivery. Ostensibly, these provincial

---

[26] CANADIAN NURSES ASSOC'N, POSITION STATEMENT: REGULATION AND INTEGRATION OF INTERNATIONAL NURSE APPLICANTS INTO THE CANADIAN HEALTH SYSTEM (2005); *Ethical Recruitment of International Medical Graduates*, THE COLLEGE OF PHYSICIANS & SURGEONS OF ONTARIO (June 2007), *available at* http://www.cpso.on.ca/policies/positions/default.aspx?id=1732 (last visited Feb. 28, 2012).

[27] THE COLLEGE OF PHYSICIANS & SURGEONS OF ONTARIO, *supra* note 26.

[28] JAMES BUCHAN & DELANYO DOVLO, DFID HEALTH SYSTEMS RESOURCE CENTER, INTERNATIONAL RECRUITMENT OF HEALTH WORKERS TO THE UK: A REPORT FOR DFID 42 (2004).

[29] PAGETT & PARADATH, *supra* note 14.

[30] BUCHAN & DOVLO, *supra* note 28, at 10.

[31] Aspen Global Health & Development, *Databank of Bilateral Agreements*, THE ASPEN INSTITUTE, *available at* http://www.aspeninstitute.org/policy-work/global-health-development/ news/hwmi-databank -bilateral-agreements (last visited Feb. 28, 2012).

[32] DHILLON ET AL., *supra* note 8.

and territorial health ministries could adopt and enforce HHR recruitment policies but none of the ten provinces and three territories has done so.

Health regions in Canada are governing structures put in place by provincial government policy, which have their own policies and guidelines: provinces, for instance, may have multiple health regions within their boundaries. These health regions and hospitals are the smallest level of organization that can develop policies. For example, a statement developed by the Saskatoon Health Region Nurse Recruitment trip to the Philippines featured terms of reference to govern their practice in recruiting foreign-trained health professionals.[33] However, with the exception of the Saskatoon Health Region's statement, we have not been able to find other evidence of health-organization– or hospital-level policies that relate to the ethical recruitment of foreign-trained HHR.

Outside the health care system itself, some municipalities (local councils) and local ad hoc committees in Canada have engaged in recruitment efforts. For instance, in 2006, the Kingston City Council in the province of Ontario approved the final report of an Ad Hoc Committee to Recruit, Retain and Recognize Family Physicians, to pursue recruitment efforts, although whether recruitment targets domestic and/or internationally trained physicians is not specified.[34]

This framework forms the overall environment of HHR recruitment policies. The authority that accompanies macro- and meso-level policy, particularly meso-level policy where a country's policies have legislative power and implementable sanctions, has potential to reach governance at the micro-level. However, implementation of policy is weak when authority is lacking or when knowledge of policy is not transferred to other levels. Because policy makers' priorities and interests are different between disparate levels, there is also the potential for policy incoherence.

II. The Canadian Context with Regard to Recruitment of Internationally trained HHR

Canada is a country that has historically received immigrants from all skills sectors, with internationally trained health professionals forming a significant percentage of Canada's health labor force. In 2009, the percentage of physicians in Canada who had received their training abroad was 23.6 percent.[35] In the same year, of a total of 348,499

[33] *Nurse Recruitment Trip to the Philippines*, SASKATOON HEALTH REGION, http://www.saskatoonhealthregion.ca/news_you_need/media_centre/media/2008/recruitment_trip_ethics.htm (last visited Feb. 28, 2012).

[34] *Opportunities for Family Physicians in Kingston*, CITY OF KINGSTON ONTARIO, http://www.cityofkingston.ca/business/kedco/doctors.asp (last visited Feb. 28, 2012).

[35] CANADIAN INSTITUTE FOR HEALTH INFORMATION, SUPPLY, DISTRIBUTION, AND MIGRATION OF CANADIAN PHYSICIANS, 2010 (2010).

regulated nurses (7.0 percent) were internationally trained, with these percentages remaining relatively stable for a decade.[36] Projections and planning for HHR requirements in Canada incorporate the assumption that internationally trained HHR are included as a resource.

HHR planning for Canada is a responsibility of the Federal, Provincial and Territorial (F/P/T) Advisory Committee on Health Delivery and Human Resources (ACHDHR). The recruitment of internationally trained health professionals is viewed as beneficial. As well as filling vacancies, internationally trained HHR also bring culturally competent care to Canada's diverse population. Remittances and other ways of contributing to home countries are seen as an important ethical counterbalance to recruitment of internationally trained HHR.[37] Although ACHDHR supports the ethical principles in the Commonwealth Code of Practice for the International Recruitment of Health Workers, the formal standing of its support is not clear. The current context for the recruitment of internationally trained HHR in Canada is therefore one in which Canada's HHR shortages are recognized, and recruitment of internationally trained HHR is not discouraged.

Programs outside the health sector support the recruitment of internationally trained HHR. In collaboration with the federal government's citizenship and immigration ministry, provincial governments operate programs such as Provincial Nominee Programs that encourage and enable immigration of certain professions and fast-track their employment.[38] These programs, which are provincial- or employer-driven initiatives to address labor shortages, can be used to recruit HHR directly. Recruitment of internationally trained HHR may also occur in other ways. For example, representatives of the provincial government of Manitoba have traveled to other countries on recruitment missions to meet potential applicants. People interviewed may be formally invited to apply to the MPNP (Manitoba Provincial Nominee Program).[39] In addition to these general recruitment drives, several ministries of health have conducted international recruitment campaigns, or implemented programs intended to facilitate recruitment of internationally trained medical graduates (IMGs).[40]

---

[36] CANADIAN INSTITUTE. FOR HEALTH INFORMATION REGULATED NURSES: TRENDS, 2005 TO 2009 (2010), https://secure.cihi.ca/free_products/nursing_report_2005-2009_en.pdf (last visited Feb. 28, 2012).

[37] Federal/Provincial/Territorial Advisory Committee on Health Delivery and Human Resources, *How Many Are Enough? Redefining Self-Sufficiency for the Health Workforce—A Discussion Paper*, HEALTH CANADA, *available at* http://www.hc-sc.gc.ca/hcs-sss/pubs/hhrhs/2009-self-sufficiency-autosuffisance/index-eng.php#a16 (last visited Feb. 28, 2012).

[38] *See, e.g.*, Opportunities Ontario: About the Program, *available at* http://www.ontarioimmigration.ca/en/pnp/OI_PNPABOUT.html (last visited Feb. 28, 2012).

[39] Strategic Initiatives, Immigrate to Manitoba, Canada, MANITOBA, *available at* http://www.immigrate-manitoba.com/how-to-immigrate/strategic-initiatives/ (last visited Feb. 28, 2012).

[40] JEAN-CHRISTOPHE DUMONT ET AL., ORG. FOR ECONOMIC CO-OPERATION & DEVELOPMENT, WORKING PAPER NO. 40, INTERNATIONAL MOBILITY OF HEALTH PROFESSIONALS AND HEALTH WORKFORCE MANAGEMENT IN CANADA: MYTHS AND REALITIES (2008).

III. Recruiting Internationally Trained HHR: Local practice

Our research study sought to understand how recruitment of internationally trained HHR was taking place (if at all) at the local level in five Canadian provinces historically known to be recipients of HHR from developing countries.[41] The study also sought to acquire responses to a variety of potential policy options intended to mitigate health-inequitable outcomes resulting from the recruitment of internationally trained HHR. We interviewed thirty-two recruiters, retrieving information about recruitment methods, and their ratings and comments on the different policies.

The recruiters worked in primary and acute publicly funded health care organizations in urban areas as well as underserved, rural, and sparsely populated Northern areas in Canada. The majority of the respondents were from Ontario, Canada's largest province by population. Recruiters answered the questions primarily with reference to the recruitment of physicians and nurses, but other health professions were sometimes mentioned. Recruiters were responsible for the recruitment of both domestically trained HHR and internationally trained HHR. They enabled HHR recruitment and placement and often assisted with the settlement of internationally trained HHR. Many recruiters possessed considerable knowledge and expertise in helping potential recruits navigate the complexity of federal and provincial government levels and the different ministries involved with health, employment, and immigration, as well as regulatory and educational bodies.

According to most of the recruiters, in their experience, direct or active recruitment in which there is deliberate targeting of overseas HHR was never or only very rarely used. To their knowledge, most internationally trained potential recruits had already immigrated to Canada prior to seeking employment with their organizations. Some respondents were aware of existing and recent recruitment campaigns conducted overseas. These campaigns are mostly conducted by provincial government bodies, such as the HealthForceOntario Marketing and Recruitment Agency, or by health regions in conjunction with provincial governments, such as the Government of Saskatchewan and Saskatchewan Health Region.

IV. Recruitment Methods

Recruitment methods generally included Internet and print advertising, recruiter attendance at conferences and job fairs, radio and television campaigns, and receptions. Word of mouth and personal contact were reported by most respondents as the best means of recruiting staff. In addition to the use of Internet "classified" advertising on government and hospital Web sites and electronic job boards, social media and social networking were used extensively by some recruiters to contact potential

---

[41] Runnels et al., *supra* note 5.

recruits. Respondents recognized that the Internet played an increasingly important and effective role in reaching different age groups and health professions, rapidly replacing other methods of advertising.

Some health organizations contracted recruitment services with outside firms. Third-party recruiters, colloquially referred to as "headhunters," may have performed recruitment tasks that organizations and their human resources staff lack time, resources, or expertise to pursue, and as one respondent suggested, the recruiters can perform tasks that the organization may not see as "ethical," such as the direct recruitment of internationally trained HHR. Respondents suggested that third-party recruitment was expensive and used mostly for specialist and/or higher-level clinical administrative positions.

In general, widespread use of the Internet means that information is readily available throughout the world, and unrestricted access to the Internet in most countries has ended any idea of limiting advertising to only domestic audiences. As one respondent noted, "whether you're in South Africa or in India or in...Saskatchewan or in Ottawa...The information is the same, the message is the same, the opportunity is the same."

V. Local Policy Environment for Recruiting HHR

The majority of recruiters reported no guidance for recruitment from organizational policy, and none of the recruiters reported being involved with policy making. Only a very small number of recruiters reported any knowledge of specific policy with regard to HHR recruitment, and those who did referred to reimbursement-of-expenses policies during the recruitment process. Some recruiters felt that organizational policy was needed, and one respondent reported there were plans to develop such a policy.

VI. Policy Options

Prior to the interviews, respondents had an opportunity to review a selection of policy options drawn from the literature designed to mitigate the effects of HHR migration. The policies are listed in the key to Figure 11.2. Recruiters were asked to indicate support for a policy on a five-point scale from *No Support* (1) through to *High Support* (5). In the absence of organizational policy, scores were based on personal knowledge and opinions. Some recruiters reported having informal conversations with colleagues about the policy options prior to the interview and before scoring. For some respondents, the study's questions and the list of mitigating policies raised the notion of "ethical" recruitment of internationally trained HHR for the first time.

Of eleven policy options presented, the highest-rated policy option was, *c) better health human resource planning in receiving countries such as Canada to minimize recruitment outside Canada*. Ninety percent of respondents selected "high support" for this option because most felt that lack of planning and implementation was the root cause

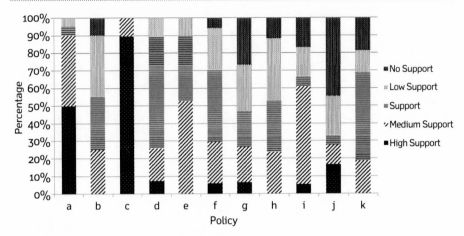

FIGURE 11.2 Recruiters' Scores on Policy Options

a) Ethical codes on recruitment from developing countries where there is an existing shortage of health professionals.

b) Government reparations to source countries for training and health system loss that has resulted from the migration of health professionals.

c) Better health human resource planning in receiving countries such as Canada to minimize recruitment outside Canada.

d) Increased development assistance to strengthen health systems in source countries that minimize some of the health system factors that encourage people to leave — or "push" factors.

e) Requiring mandatory in-country work after graduation of trained health workers in source countries, i.e. for a specified time in a specified location (sometimes called bonding).

f) Requiring financial repayment by trained health workers to public training institutes in the case when no in-country work takes place after graduation.

g) Focus on training auxiliary or lower-skilled workers in source countries, which might decrease their attractiveness to health systems in receiving countries.

h) Management of migration through bilateral or multilateral agreements that encourage temporary stays only and return health workers to their source country.

l) Two-way staff flows which allow health workers from the receiving country to provide a period of service to the source country.

j) Voluntary financial contributions from those who have emigrated to be directed to the health systems of the source country.

k) Assigning a share of income tax payments made by migrants to a development fund, or some other form of bilateral tax agreement.

of HHR shortages in Canada. As one respondent said, "We definitely need to have better HHR planning and I don't believe there's virtually any right now." Another reported, "We wouldn't need to do international nurse recruitment if we had enough resources in our own country." One respondent reported that "going after foreign training is done to offset poorer planning. If we hadn't cut the number of health care seats in the early '90s we'd probably be in a different situation right now," referring to reductions made at that time to the numbers of training seats for physicians, and the discouraging of recruitment of migrating internationally trained physicians in order to restrain health care costs and decrease a surfeit of doctors.[42]

[42] Morris Barer & Greg Stoddart, Health Policy Research Unit, Toward Integrated Medical Resource Policies for Canada: Background Document. (1991).

The second-highest–rated policy option was *a) Ethical codes on recruitment from developing countries where there is an existing shortage of health professionals*. As one respondent put it, "I think that we have a responsibility outside of our national issues...to ensure that developing countries and their infrastructure including their people working in health care is respected and that it is not irreparably damaged by us recruiting the professionals from their country," summarizing a feeling of responsibility that many recruiters had for developing countries. Another respondent pointed out the necessity of involving multiple actors in ethical recruitment policy: "for our organization (a policy) wouldn't suffice because we have the licensing bodies that would also have to adhere to those ethical codes and adopt them."

Combining the three positive rating categories of Support, Medium Support, and High Support, another preferred option was *d) Increased development assistance to strengthen health systems in source countries to minimize "push" factors*. Not all respondents were in agreement with this option. As one respondent said, "I think I'd probably put that pretty low on the possibility list. We have enough trouble funding our own health care system in Canada much less paying for someone else's." One respondent suggested a disconnect between the health organization and other levels of policy in terms of the relevance of a policy: "I don't think it (increased development assistance) would matter either way to our organization, I don't think our organization would say that's really their core business." Another option, *e) Requiring mandatory in-country work after graduation of trained health workers in source countries, sometimes called bonding*, was acceptable in principle but difficult to implement.[43] Some respondents thought it was only acceptable when training is publicly funded. One said, "For those countries that need these professionals then probably yes (for mandatory in-country work), probably like for in Canada. If we're going to train them here we would like them to work here." This particular response also reflected those of other respondents who thought that a test for policies being proposed for developing countries should be their acceptability in the Canadian context.

The least-popular policy option was one designed to obtain voluntary financial contributions from those who have emigrated, with contributions being redirected to the health systems of the source country. One respondent referred to physicians being held to a different standard than other migrants such as engineers and teachers, whereas another noted, "How do you know the funds are going to get back to what they're intended for?" However, one respondent supported this option as long as it was "completely voluntary and ideally (counted as) a tax deductible contribution within Canada." A second–least-popular policy option focused on training auxiliary or lower-skilled workers in source countries, which might decrease workers' attractiveness to health systems in receiving countries. This was an interesting option that was included because the idea for the policy has been voiced in meetings, although not referred to directly in the literature. This policy was seen as "abhorrent" by one respondent. Another thought, " [Y]our patients drive what level of care and what level of skilled health care worker

---

[43] *See, e.g.,* Till Bärnighausen & David E. Bloom, *Financial Incentives for Return of Service in Underserved Areas: A Systematic Review,* 9 BMC HEALTH SERVS. RES. (2009).

you need. It sounds like you'd train lesser skilled people just to keep them in their home country and that doesn't really sound very ethical to me." Recruiters were concerned about the level of care that patients require, but the question did not encourage discussion about the often successful use of cadres of community health workers at the primary-care level in many developing countries.[44]

If there was agreement among the respondents on the need for an ethical statement on the recruitment of HHR, the contents were open for discussion. The perspective of some authorities was that direct recruitment of internationally trained HHR from source countries was not unacceptable; neither was recruitment at arms' length by them through third parties as long as it was done "ethically." One interpretation of "ethical" recruitment was to minimize possible harmful impacts on overseas organizations and families by limiting the numbers of experienced staff to be recruited. Views about what is "ethical" are different enough that interpretation of "ethical" recruitment for one organization cannot be assumed to be in agreement with policies made elsewhere.

Although recruiters reported they were not party to policy discussions on recruitment, they indicated a discussion is needed. As one recruiter noted, "Canada would be well suited to create a list of countries where it would be acceptable to actively recruit . . . versus ones where we put a moratorium on active recruitment, certainly (it would include) that list of developing countries. But there's probably also some developed countries that have significant shortages to the point where their own health care system [is] in jeopardy. I don't know what the criteria might look like but it may well be worth a discussion."

VII. Discussion

HHR recruiters in Canada generally work without institutional policy and sometimes work without knowledge of ethical recruitment policies, such as the WHO Code. Recruiters' lack of knowledge of higher-level codes and policies suggests that there is little knowledge transfer or exchange to the micro-level, as proposed by the dotted arrows in Figure 11.3, with little transfer and exchange taking place from the meso-level. Capacity for policy development, diffusion, and implementation may be present at some levels rather than others.

However, even with knowledge of such policies and intentions or sanctions to comply, local level recruiters are situated between a rock and a hard place. Although advertising through electronic media may not deliberately target health professionals in other countries, widespread use of the Internet means that information is readily available throughout the world. Distinguishing between active or passive recruitment to determine if recruitment is "ethical" or not was more useful at a time before global connectivity became possible.

---

[44] EARTH INSTITUTE, ONE MILLION COMMUNITY HEALTH WORKERS: TECHNICAL TASK FORCE REPORT (2011), http://millenniumvillages.org/files/2011/06/1mCHW_TechnicalTaskForceReport.pdf (last visited Feb. 28, 2012).

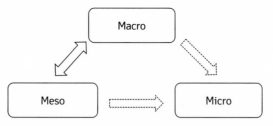

FIGURE 11.3 Levels & Transfers of HHR Recruitment Policy

The notion of ethical recruitment, although acceptable in principle to respondents, clashes with the operation of HHR labor markets in Canada. Highly competitive environments for recruits, including internationally trained HHR, exist across provinces and between regional health authorities and individual organizations in the same health care system. Although competition is to be expected in the normal operations of labor markets, even in a public system, not all organizations compete on a level playing field. Study respondents suggested that preferences for metropolitan and urban areas, higher remuneration levels, and the availability of other incentives in some areas are making recruitment to less well-resourced northern and rural areas and some smaller urban areas considerably more challenging. At the same time, provincial ministries of health have enhanced their roles and activities in marketing and recruitment. Although these efforts are intended to bring recruits and benefits to all, from local recruiters' perspectives, who were at a significant disadvantage because of their smaller size and resources, this felt like additional competition for recruits. Adopting an ethical recruitment policy at the provincial, regional, and local level therefore competes with the importance of filling vacancies.

At the local level the development and implementation of corporate, socially responsible policy has potential to raise organizational and public awareness of the issues. A corporate, socially responsible policy indicates awareness of an organization's connection to a global problem, and can outline the organization's values and responses through monitoring and accounting of its recruitment practices, assessment of the organization's specific mitigation of any health inequities that arise from recruitment and associated migration flows, while extending its policies to external or third-party agents to observe only those practices that are acceptable to the organization.[45] This places certain responsibilities at the level in which policies are developed and enacted.

VIII. A Role for Research

Our earlier research and the literature garnered several policy options. Some preliminary work we conducted as part of this study to identify, analyze, and evaluate the costs and benefits of the workforce integration of internationally trained health

---

[45] Runnels et al., *supra* note 5.

professionals in Canada suggests that any estimation of true costs (that include social or taxpayer costs) is a task worth undertaking in order to demonstrate if there is any evidence of "perverse" subsidies for sending or source countries, and for receiving countries to determine if investments in recruitment, settlement, and integration programs for internationally trained health professionals are more socially desirable investments than domestic investments in education and training of health human resources. We are not aware of any studies to date that have attempted a full economic evaluation, although studies that contribute components have been found. In Canada, the Western Alliance for Assessment of International Physicians (WAAIP), through the MAX project, estimated the costs to prepare internationally trained physicians (which WAAIP refers to as international medical graduates—IMGs) for practice readiness (in which "a physician is qualified to provide unsupervised patient care within a defined domain and a defined setting") as approximately CAN$82,193 per IMG.[46] Investing time and resources in developing in-country methodology and carrying out economic evaluations of active and nondirect recruitment of internationally trained health human resources is suggested. The considerable expense of some methods such as recruitment junkets, and the implementation of complex programs that assess and facilitate integration of internationally trained health professionals, may unearth some cost surprises or sufficient evidence to encourage developed countries to direct their attention toward training sufficient HHR domestically.

Another approach to assessing recruitment policies associated with the migration of health professionals should be the measurement and assessment of health impacts on the population as a whole as well as on disadvantaged groups. Such assessments are variously known as health impact or health equity impact assessments, and could be used in conjunction with other measures to demonstrate policy impacts at different levels in both sending and receiving countries.[47]

Conclusion

In the absence of specific organizational policies, the exigencies of local labor market requirements at the local and regional levels and the transfer of information through the Internet are likely to open up recruitment initiatives to internationally trained job seekers in source countries.[48] Evidence of unethical recruitment suggests a need for ongoing critical review and attention to the complexity of influences that can

---

[46] RODNEY A. CRUTCHER ET AL., MAX PROJECT REPORT: MAXIMIZING THE GAINS FROM WAAIP (2007).

[47] See GÖRAN DAHLGREN & MARGARET WHITEHEAD, INST. FOR FUTURES STUDIES, POLICIES AND STRATEGIES TO PROMOTE SOCIAL EQUITY IN HEALTH (1991). MINISTRY OF HEALTH AND LONG TERM CARE, HEALTH EQUITY IMPACT ASSESSMENT, available at http://www.health.gov.on.ca/en/pro/programs/heia/ (last visited Feb. 28, 2012). Health impact assessment: questions and guidance for impact assessment, available at http://www.dh.gov.uk/en/Publicationsandstatistics/Legislation/Healthassessment/Browsable/DH_075622 (last visited Feb. 28, 2012).

[48] Packer et al., supra note 1.

undermine ethical recruitment policy. This requires political support and diplomacy, policy coherence at different levels of government, intersectoral vigilance and support, and incentives of varying forms to participate in policy implementation and enforcement. Pursuit of policy coherence offers some promise for closing loopholes.[49] Although evidence of the effectiveness of interventions for controlling migration of health professionals from source countries has yet to be determined, recruitment strategies themselves can be controlled by recipient countries with the aid of normative agreements.[50] At the global level, however, there are no international or global regulations in force or likely to be developed in the foreseeable future to set the conditions.

We look forward to learning the results of the public hearing on the WHO Code, and particularly the first review of the relevance and effectiveness of the Code to be presented to the World Health Assembly in 2015. In the meantime, developing and sharing country plans for ethical recruitment of internationally trained HHR, and learning about intended methodologies for assessing the real costs of the recruitment of foreign-trained health professionals, will all add useful knowledge. We are not optimistic that the Code's intentions and activities by themselves will make much in the way of real progress in addressing active and "unethical" recruitment efforts, but are optimistic that combining efforts at multiple levels, such as through bilateral agreements with developing countries, can help to affirm ethical principles and health equity. At the local level this means adopting and developing ethical approaches to recruitment through corporate, socially responsible policy that addresses the recruitment of internationally trained HHR in Canada.

---

[49] *Id.*

[50] *See, e.g.*, Blanca Peñaloza et al., *Interventions to Reduce Emigration of Health Care Professionals from Low-and Middle-Income Countries,*, COCHRANE DATABASE OF SYSTEMATIC REVIEWS: PROTOCOLS (2009).

12

CONDITIONING MEDICAL SCHOLARSHIPS ON LONG,

FUTURE SERVICE

A Defense

Nir Eyal and Till Bärnighausen[*]

I. Background: Physician Scarcity, Conditional Scholarships, and Long-Commitment Scholarships (LCS)[1]

In many developing countries, progress toward the delivery of essential health interventions ranging from antiretroviral treatment to childhood vaccinations is thwarted by a critical scarcity of health workers,[2] especially physicians.[3] Deficits are especially severe in many areas of sub-Saharan Africa and some Asian countries where some of

---

[*] Nir Eyal is Associate Professor in Global Health and Social Medicine (Medical Ethics) at the Harvard Medical School and an affiliate of the Harvard University Program in Ethics and Health. Till Bärnighausen is Associate Professor of Global Health, Department of Global Health and Population at the Harvard School of Public Health and Senior Epidemiologist, Africa Centre for Health and Population Studies, at the University of KwaZulu-Natal.

[1] For helpful comments, we would like to thank Lincoln Chen, who commented on our paper during the conference, and conference organizer I. Glenn Cohen, as well as members of the audience and Speranta Dumitru, Ezekiel Emanuel, Samia Hurst, Nancy Pellerin, Brendan Saloner, Lucas Stanczyk, Madeline Taskier, David Weakliam, Dan Wikler, Andrew Williams, Jurgen de Wispelaere, and audiences at the Harvard Medical School, the Harvard Program in Ethics and Health, and Trinity College Dublin.

[2] World Health Organization, The World Health Report 2006—Working Together for Health (2006); Committee for the Evaluation of the President's Emergency Plan for AIDS Relief (PEPFAR) Implementation Institute of Medicine, PEPFAR Implementation: Progress and Promise (2007); Till Bärnighausen, David E. Bloom & Salal Humair, *Universal Antiretroviral Treatment: The Challenge of Human Resources*, 88 Bull. World Health Org. 951, 952 (2010).

[3] Sudhir Anand & Till Bärnighausen, *Human Resources and Health Outcomes: Cross-Country Econometric Study*, 364 Lancet 1603, 1609 (2004); Sudhir Anand & Till Bärnighausen, *Health Workers and Vaccination Coverage in Developing Countries: An Econometric Analysis*, 369 Lancet 1277, 1285 (2007).

the world's poorest and sickest populations live. Many developed countries also face shortages of physicians in so-called medically underserved areas, albeit at less critical absolute levels. For instance, about fifty-million North Americans live in medically underserved areas.[4]

One existing mechanism to increase the supply of physicians to medically underserved areas is the so-called conditional scholarships, that is, scholarships for medical education in return for a commitment to serve for a number of years after graduation in an underserved area. Such scholarships exist both in developing and in developed countries.[5]

Although conditional scholarships currently operate in several countries, they continue to generate ethical controversy. In relation to commitment to medical service, one writer recently warned that, in developing countries, such schemes risk:

> trespassing on the basic rights of... citizens. After all, the very idea that a group of people should have to work off their debts before being set free will sound suspiciously like a form of debt bondage, serfdom or even outright slavery to some. Moreover, such a system would involve fairly drastic limits on the international movement of people.[6]

Likewise, the U.S. National Health Service Corps (NHSC), a conditional scholarship scheme, has been considered "coercive" and "top-down,"[7] and Australia's equivalent scholarship was branded "unjust," "deceptive and coercive," and "entirely inappropriate."[8] Indeed, although conditional scholarships may provide a partial fix to the shortages of health workers that can be intractable otherwise, the question of when they are justified remains complex. Such scholarships often result in confining a person who grew up in a city to working and living in a desolate rural location, not just for a short period, but for years, merely because he or she signed up for the scholarship as a youth. In rural locations, this physician may find herself separated from her friends and relatives. Her children may lack access to the sort of education that she enjoyed, and cultural opportunities and even access to running water, electricity, and communication facilities could be severely limited.

These worries have been expressed with regard to the common practice of conditional scholarships requiring one year of service in an underserved area for each year

---

[4] *The Affordable Care Act Is Already a Success* (2012), CENTER FOR AMERICAN PROGRESS, http://www.americanprogress.org/issues/2012/01/aca_success.html (last visited Feb. 15, 2012).

[5] Donald E. Pathman, Thomas R. Konrad & Thomas C. Ricketts, *The National Health Service Corps Experience for Rural Physicians in the Late 1980s*, 272 JAMA 1341, 1348 (1994); Delanyo Dovlo & Frank Nyonator, *Migration by Graduates of the University of Ghana Medical School: A Preliminary Rapid Appraisal*, 3 HUM. RES. DEV. J. 1, 16 (1999); Andrew J. Ross, *Success of a Scholarship Scheme for Rural Students*, 97 S. AFR. MED. J. 1087, 1090 (2007); Till Bärnighausen & David E. Bloom, *Financial Incentives for Return of Service in Underserved Areas: A Systematic Review*, 9 BMC HEALTH SERV. RES. 1, 17 (2009).

[6] Carywn R. Hooper, *Adding Insult to Injury: The Healthcare Brain Drain*, 34 J. MED. ETHICS 684, 687 (2008).

[7] Thomas C. Ricketts, *Workforce Issues in Rural Areas: A Focus on Policy Equity*, 95 AM. J. PUBLIC HEALTH 42, 48 (2005).

[8] Joseph V. Turner, Jeremy Brammer & Carl M. Vogler, *Will Bonded Medical School Places Do More Harm Than Good?*, 12 AUST. J. RURAL HEALTH 227 (2004).

of scholarship.[9] We shall argue that conditional scholarships are not only ethically permissible for the currently common commitment times, usually one year commitment per year of scholarship (i.e., between four and six years of total commitment, depending on the length of time in medical school in the country of training), but also for significantly longer commitment times, such as three years commitment per year of scholarship (or twelve to eighteen years for the entire length of time in medical school). We shall call scholarships that are conditional on such long periods of later service "long-commitment scholarships" (LCS). The precise upper bound on the morally acceptable length of service commitment will depend on a multitude of factors (such as the projected needs and the acceptability of physicians' work and life conditions in the commitment areas and alternative employments available to young medical school graduates).[10] Here, we shall merely argue that commitment times that are substantially longer than current practice are permissible. We propose that at least so long as the length of required commitment still allows signatories not only a rich set of possible life plans (which we believe practice in medically underserved areas usually allows) but also sufficient potential to revise personal and professional life plans, then the length of commitment remains clearly below an upper acceptable bound. We believe that commitment times as long as twelve to eighteen years can be acceptable.

Again, this is not to endorse scholarships that would commit applicants to career-long service in rural medicine (such commitment length could undercut a person's important capacity to revise his or her life plan).[11] We do, however, defend a twelve-to-eighteen year commitment to service that is significantly longer than present practice, so long as an affordable (if steep) buyout option is in place,[12] work conditions are otherwise reasonable, and other conditions that we expound below apply. LCS or near-LCS for medical students already exist in a few places,[13] but are overall much less common than short-term scholarship schemes. We shall build on our previous work on

---

[9] Till Bärnighausen & David E. Bloom, *The Global Health Workforce, in* THE OXFORD HANDBOOK OF HEALTH ECONOMICS (Peter Smith & Sherry Glied eds., 2011).

[10] Nir Eyal & Till Bärnighausen, *Precommitting to Serve the Underserved,* AM J. BIOETHICS (forthcoming 2012).

[11] JOHN RAWLS, POLITICAL LIBERALISM, *e.g.* at 19 (1993).

[12] A buyout option allows medical students and graduates to replace their commitment with a payment. The payment usually covers the entire amount of money (with interest) that a student has received plus an additional financial penalty for breaking the commitment. Till Bärnighausen & David E. Bloom, *Designing Financial-Incentive Programmes for Return of Medical Service in Underserved Areas: Seven Management Functions* 7 HUM. RES. HEALTH 1, 14 (2009).

[13] In the Jichi Medical University in Japan, commitment length is rather long—nine years, reflecting equally long medical education. Importantly, since 1972 the program has successfully recruited thousands of physicians for underserved service, and larger proportions of participating physicians stay in underserved areas after completing their service commitment than participants in many other conditional scholarship programs. Masatoshi Matsumoto, Kazuo Inoue & Eliji Kajii, *A Contract-Based Training System for Rural Physicians: Follow-Up of Jichi Medical University Graduates (1978–2006),* 24 J. RURAL HEALTH 360, 368 (2008). Some study scholarships in Singapore are fairly long-term and facilitate training in less urgently needed fields than medicine: *see Awards and Scholarships,* THE AGENCY FOR SCIENCE TECHNOLOGY AND RESEARCH, http://www.a-star.edu.sg/AwardsScholarships/Overview/tabid/170/Default.aspx (last visited Feb. 10, 2012). We thank Nino S. Levy and William Chin for the Singapore example. We argue that more liberal regimes are also compatible with LCS.

the same topic,[14] and discuss in detail the ethics of committing students in advance to work for many years in underserved areas.

II. The Effectiveness of Conditional Scholarships and LCS

Conditional scholarships can potentially increase the supply of physicians in underserved areas, thanks to their impact on scholarship recipients, on other physicians, and on potential medical students. Many studies have examined the impact of conditional scholarships on the supply of physicians in underserved areas.[15] They show that conditional scholarship programs have placed substantial numbers of physicians and other health workers in such areas,[16] and that they could substantially contribute to the attainment of the population health goals.[17] For instance, America's NHSC has placed more than thirty thousand health professionals in underserved areas since its inception in 1972.[18] Some studies compare the probability of working in an underserved area between scholarship recipients and non-recipients. These studies find that recipients are far more likely than students who did not receive conditional scholarships to provide service to an underserved population, not only during the formal commitment period, but at many later points in time, as late as twenty-nine years past graduation.[19] However, in none of these studies were students randomly assigned to the scholarships, and we therefore cannot rule out that the observed effect is biased

---

[14] Eyal & Bärnighausen, *supra* note 10.

[15] Donald E. Pathman, Thomas R. Konrad & Thomas C. Ricketts, *The Comparative Retention of National Health Service Corps and Other Rural Physicians: Results of a 9-Year Follow-Up Study*, 268 JAMA 1552, 1558 (1992); Howard K. Rabinowitz et al., *The Impact of Multiple Predictors on Generalist Physicians' Care of Underserved Populations*, 90 AM. J. PUBLIC HEALTH 1225, 1228 (2000).; Judith D. Singer et al., *Physician Retention in Community and Migrant Health Centers: Who Stays and for How Long?*, 36 MED. CARE. 1198, 1213 (1998); Robert G. Brooks et al., *The Roles of Nature and Nurture in the Recruitment and Retention of Primary Care Physicians in Rural Areas: A Review of the Literature*, 77 ACAD. MED. 790, 798 (2002); George M. Holmes, *Increasing Physician Supply in Medically Underserved Areas*, 12 LAB. ECON. 697, 725 (2005); Donald E. Pathman et al., *National Health Service Corps Staffing and the Growth of the Local Rural Non-NHSC Primary Care Physician Workforce*, 22 J. RURAL HEALTH 285, 293 (2006).

[16] Bärnighausen & Bloom, *supra* note 5.

[17] Till Bärnighausen & David E. Bloom, *"Conditional Scholarships" for HIV/AIDS Health Workers: Educating and Retaining the Workforce to Provide Antiretroviral Treatment in Sub-Saharan Africa*, 68 SOC. SCI. MED. 544, 551 (2009).

[18] *The National Advisory Council on the National Health Service Corps' Priorities for Reauthorization and Legislative Updates*, NAT'L HEALTH SERVICE CORPS, http://nhsc.hrsa.gov/downloads/priorites.pdf (last visited Feb. 10, 2012).

[19] Rabinowitz et al., *supra* note 15; Gang Xu et al., *Factors Influencing Physicians' Choices to Practice in Inner-City or Rural Areas*, 72 ACAD. MED. 1026 (1997); Gang Xu et al., *The Relationship between the Race/ Ethnicity of Generalist Physicians and Their Care for Undeserved Populations*, 87 AM. J. PUBLIC HEALTH 817, 822 (1997); Robert G. Brooks, Russell Mardon & Art Clawson, *The Rural Physician Workforce in Florida: A Survey of US- and Foreign-Born Primary Care Physicians*, 19 J. RURAL HEALTH 484, 491 (2003); Donald E. Pathman et al., *Medical Training Debt and Service Commitments: The Rural Consequences,*16 J. RURAL HEALTH 264, 272 (2000). It cannot be completely ruled out that the observed results are due to selection effects, rather than scholarship effects, on recruitment and retention. Medical students who chose

due to selective participation in the scholarships of those most inclined to work in underserved areas.[20] George M. Holmes thus examines the effect of scholarships using selection models to control for selective participation on observed and unobserved factors in the United States He confirms that the conditional scholarship programs are effective in increasing the number of doctors in underserved areas.[21]

In addition, the existing evidence suggests that conditional scholarships also increase the supply of nonparticipating physicians. U.S. communities that received physicians through the NHSC experienced larger increases in nonparticipating physicians than eligible communities that did not receive an NHSC participant,[22] which is plausible because the addition of a scholarship recipient to an area where few physicians practice could make the area more attractive for other physicians. For instance, the addition of an NHSC physician could decrease workload and professional isolation of other physicians working in the same area. Finally, it is plausible that in countries where some of the places available in medical education remain unfilled because interested, qualified students cannot afford it,[23] conditional scholarships can increase the total number of physicians by eliminating the financial barriers to a medical education.[24]

III. The Moral Legitimacy of Conditional Scholarships and LCS

Assume that we are right in arguing that conditional scholarships, and especially LCS, work or could be made to work. On this assumption, we now argue, there is a strong initial case for using conditional scholarships, and especially for using LCS.

A. A FAIR DISTRIBUTION OF BURDENS

First, higher physician density in currently underserved areas would significantly promote people's basic health interests, which may well be a matter of basic rights

---

to participate in conditional scholarship programs may have been more likely than nonparticipants to work in underserved areas, even if they had counterfactually not participated. However, studies that control for selection effects in the analysis consistently confirm that scholarship recipients are more likely than non-recipients to work in underserved areas in the long run. Pathman et al., *supra* note 5; Pathman et al., *Comparative Retention*, *supra* note 15; Rabinowitz et al., *supra* note 15.

[20] Bärnighausen & Bloom, *supra* note 5.

[21] George M. Holmes, *Does the National Health Service Corps Improve Physician Supply in Underserved Locations?*, 30 EAST ECON. J. 563, 581 (2004).

[22] Pathman et al., *National Health Service Corps Staffing*, *supra* note 5.

[23] Bärnighausen & Bloom, *supra* note 5.

[24] Conditional scholarships are only one type of financial incentive to increase the supply of physicians to underserved areas. Other financial incentives include educational loans with service requirement, service-option educational loans, loan repayment programs, and direct financial incentives (Bärnighausen & Bloom, *supra* note 5). These other financial incentives differ from conditional scholarships in various ways: the time of commitment relative to the start of medical education is different, the time when the participant receives the incentive is different, and restrictions on the spending use of the incentive are different. The present chapter focuses on conditional scholarships because there is substantially more evidence suggesting that conditional scholarships are effective than there is for any of the other types of financial incentive.

and fundamental equity. Moreover, the populations living in areas with low physician densities are commonly disadvantaged in many other respects, such as having less access to safe water and sanitation, opportunities for good education, and employment prospects, and are usually relatively sick and poor. Hence, conditional scholarships considerably help many among humanity's, and the relevant nations', worst-off members—in many cases, the badly off in absolute terms. Because a single physician touches the lives of many patients, often dozens a day, many patients benefit from a single conditional scholarship agreement. In philosophical parlance, the scholarships may therefore serve the utilitarian[25] and communitarian[26] goal of increased collective benefit. These reasons—promoting the basic health interests of disadvantaged populations—also increase distributive justice or equity: they probably promote egalitarian,[27] prioritarian,[28] and sufficientarian[29] goals, and perhaps the goal of rights-fulfillment.[30] As such, they may allow societies to promote and express virtues such as social solidarity and compassion.[31]

B. CONTRACT

Undoubtedly, even if conditional scholarships promote noble ends and distribute burdens and benefits fairly, they may still be deemed wrong, all things considered, because they violate other individual rights along the way. For example, conditional scholarships may coercively introduce serious harm, risk, or coercive intrusion to one person as a means of helping others, desperate and numerous though the latter may be. To use an extreme analogy, enslaving innocent members of the urban middle class to build a rural hospital could also boost social utility and the basic health interests of worse-off rural residents. But most of us would consider it wrong because coercively introducing serious harm or risk to an innocent person and demanding specific performance, even as a means of saving others, violates that person's rights. This chapter therefore adduces further moral justifications.

In particular, conditional scholarships always commit trained physicians to work in rural areas based on contracts that they previously signed. It is in return for this

---

[25] PETER SINGER, THE LIFE YOU CAN SAVE: ACTING NOW TO END WORLD POVERTY (2009).

[26] AMITAI ETZIONI ET AL., THE COMMUNITARIAN READER: BEYOND THE ESSENTIALS (2004).

[27] Larry S. Temkin, *Inequality and Health, in* WHAT'S WRONG WITH HEALTH INEQUALITY? (Nir Eyal et al. eds., forthcoming); Kasper L. Rasmussen & Nir Eyal, *Equality and Egalitarianism, in* ENCYCLOPEDIA OF APPLIED ETHICS (Ruth Chadwick ed., 2011). We interpret egalitarianism as the view that it is in itself bad, perhaps for being unjust, if some are worse off than others (through no fault or choice of their own).

[28] Derek Parfit, *Equality and Priority*, 10 RATIO 202, 221 (1997). Prioritarianism is the view that benefits have greater moral value the worse off the recipients.

[29] Harry Frankfurt, *Equality as a Moral Ideal*, 98 ETHICS 21, 43 (1987). Sufficientarianism is the view that it is in itself bad or unjust if not everyone has enough (where "enough" means different things for different thinkers), and that other concerns about maldistribution are weaker or nil.

[30] AMARTYA K. SEN, THE IDEA OF JUSTICE (2009).

[31] Roger Crisp, *Equality, Priority, and Compassion*, 113 ETHICS 745, 763 (2003).

signature that funding was secured. In that way, conditional scholarships differ from dictates. Strictly speaking, they are not initially coercive. All signatories will have enjoyed at least the formal option of not studying medicine with conditional funding. For many, the contract will have been advantageous—or too few would sign it. Once the choice is made to take up the offer and sign a contract to study medicine with a commitment to work in underserved areas later, such service may seem to be legitimately expected.

C. SUFFICIENTLY INFORMED, VOLUNTARY, COMPETENT, AND AUTHORIZED CONSENT

Still, absent further arguments, this response might be insufficient. Choices and contracts do not always suffice for legitimate expectation. Not all signed contracts are ethically permissible to offer, not all are ethically valid, and not all are ethically enforceable. Some involve, for example, uninformed, involuntary, incompetent, or unauthorized consent. Others involve an agreement that is too straining on the individual to keep later on. Still others involve agreement to do things that a person is not permitted to agree to do.

Let us start with the worry about uninformed, involuntary, incompetent, or unauthorized consent. Some may worry that conditional scholarships, and especially LCS, are ethically wrong, null and void, or nonenforceable, because of the poor quality of consent on which they rely. For example, the worry that "exploiting students' arguably premature ideals at so early a stage in their lives is both deceptive and coercive" seems to express such concerns.[32] More specifically, worries have or could arise concerning:

- Signatories' tender age;
- Signatories' relative ignorance about the realities of work in underserved areas;
- Signatories' tendency to irrationally "discount" the harsh realities that, as practitioners, they would endure many years later;
- An "optimism bias" that may drive young school applicants to imagine away these harsh realities;
- The allegedly "undue inducement" involved in offering immediate scholarship money in return for reduced future freedom, especially for the poor;
- Poor applicants' lack of decent alternatives to accepting the contracts on offer;
- Changes in the personal identity of signatories during their many formative years in medical training, which might undermine their authority to commit their future selves.

Worries about poor-quality consent seem to be bolstered by the observation that students' willingness to serve the needy commonly undergo substantial transformations in medical school. Across societies, medical school applicants desire very different futures than medical school graduates. In particular, while surveyed anonymously

---

[32] Turner et al., *supra* note 8.

upon applying or beginning medical school, both Africans and Americans cite motivations based on altruism, service to mankind, self-realization, and vocation;[33] but, as we already said, few medical graduates seek work where the need for health care is greatest, and most seek higher salaries and technologically intensive practice.[34] This might be thought to indicate that early consent to prolonged rural service would rarely have been fully informed and fully voluntary.

Elsewhere we have expounded on the worries about the quality of consent, as well as many responses to each worry.[35] Here we would like to focus on three responses, which address several worries. First, governments already allow individuals of the same age as young medical school applicants to enter many types of contracts with long-term personal implications. For example, there are no legal barriers on most young adults' ability to take out loans and mortgages. In the proposal described below, all signatories would be legal adults.

Second, although medical students tend to become *less* inclined to assist the underserved over the course of their studies, this does not establish that their decisions are better or more "authentic" upon graduation. The strongest case for the position that graduating students are better positioned to make a more authentic or rational decision is that medical education will have given them new information and experience relevant to the decision to work in underserved areas. However, people who go on to complete a commitment period upon graduation will have gained far more detailed information and firsthand experience about working in underserved areas. If more information and experience make decisions more rational, then the latter will be even better positioned to decide whether to work in underserved areas. Interviews expounding attitudes toward compulsory service in underserved communities in South Africa *once that service is over* suggest that fresh school graduates' predictions about what they will get out of their compulsory rural service are overly pessimistic.[36] Additionally, as already mentioned, scholarship signatories are more likely than other physicians to work in an underserved area past their commitment periods, suggesting that they found caring for underserved populations to be a satisfying professional choice.[37] Whom should we "trust" then—the fresh school graduate, whose judgment may conflict with that of the (even earlier) rurally motivated signatory, or the far more experienced graduate of rural service, whose judgment often converges with that of the rurally motivated earlier self? If regret for having accepted a conditional scholarship

[33] Olumuyiwa O. Odusanya, Wole Alakija & Fatiu A. Akesode, *Socio Demographic Profile and Career Aspirations of Medical Students in a New Medical School*, 7 Niger Postgrad. Med. J. 112, 115 (2000); Ian D. Coulter, Michael Wilkes & Claudia Der-Martirosian, *Altruism Revisited: A Comparison of Medical, Law, and Business Student's Altruistic Attitudes*, 41 Med. Educ. 341, 345 (2007); Fernando Sousa Jr. et al., *The Training and Expectations of Medical Students in Mozambique*, 5 Hum. Res. Health 1, 7 (2007).

[34] Joint Learning Initiative, Human Resources for Health: Overcoming the Crisis (2004).

[35] Eyal & Bärnighausen, *supra* note 10.

[36] Steve Reid, *Compulsory Community Service for Doctors in South Africa—An Evaluation of the First Year*, 91 S. Afr. Med. J. 329, 336 (2001).

[37] Bärnighausen & Bloom, *supra* note 5; Pathman et al., *Comparative Retention, supra* note 15.

lasts only a few years and fades away sometime after rural service begins, it may matter less than the later, but potentially lifelong, satisfaction derived from providing health care to the neediest populations. The reason for this change of approach years past graduation may be that fresh medical school graduates will often have been socialized in a medical system that values highly specialized services in urban hospitals more than primary care in rural areas, commonly leading to a (temporary) bias for the former.[38]

A final response to the concerns that signatories of conditional scholarship contracts are insufficiently cognizant and insufficiently concerned with future events due to ignorance, irrational future discounting, undue inducement, and so forth, is practical. We propose that conditional, including LCS, loans be signed midway through the first year of medical school, after students have completed a rural externship that is required for eligibility for a conditional scholarship. Such externships could enlighten potential signatories on the realities of rural service, displaying a balanced picture of prudential and altruistic arguments for and against long service in such settings. The scholarship installments could also be deferred, so that potential signatories compare the distant future only to a less distant one, and not to the immediate future, circumventing potentially extreme bias for immediate gratification. For instance, enrollment in conditional scholarships could take place around the middle of the first year of medical school, while students enjoy an initial, unconditional scholarship payment for their first year in school. Because installments of the conditional scholarship would begin only after the first year, and not immediately, the decision would lack immediate consequences, mitigating some cognitive biases.

D. NOT AN OVERLY STRAINING COMMITMENT

Andrew Williams raised the Rawlsian concern that conditional scholarships place too much strain on citizens' commitments.[39] The "strains of commitment" concern has special bite in relation to LCS, which involves long commitments. The Rawlsian concern arises when compliance with a social arrangement is tremendously hard for some. In this case, Rawlsians point out, severe practical problems may arise. Overly straining legal commitments criminalize what is a natural human choice and jeopardize liberal stability, inter alia by forcing the authorities to use increasingly harsh enforcement measures to deal with what is likely to be widespread noncompliance. In fact, authorities must prepare in advance, potentially by training police and judges who possess the ruthlessness to enact harsh measures against noncompliance. Such preparation may

---

[38] At the very least, it is highly unclear whether the school applicant or the school graduate is the more autonomous one. Therefore, and because the force of autonomy requirements comes in degrees (Nir Eyal, *Informed Consent, in* STANFORD ENCYCLOPEDIA OF PHILOSOPHY (Edward N. Zalta ed., 2011)), it remains plausible that in our case, social welfare generally prevails. Surely the needs of many desperate third parties can serve as a tiebreaker.

[39] RAWLS, *supra* note 11, at 17.

have negative repercussions, for example, in terms of ruthless treatment of other matters by the police. Therefore, Rawls says, enforceable contracts should never be very straining. In our context, one might conclude, a conditional scholarship, especially a long-commitment scholarship, may be too straining.

Our main reply to this challenge is that a technological solution exists. No ruthless agents and harsh measures are necessary for enforcing commitments to perform underserved service. The system can be designed to enforce contracts without them. Suppose that administration computers were programmed to grant medical degrees only once all required service is completed.[40] A general implication would be that high strains of commitment could remain unproblematic. Mechanical precommitment could achieve compliance without harsh measures, special police forces, and the like.

Admittedly, such arrangements may still seem too straining where they force breach of deep personal commitments, but our own context is different. As we argued elsewhere,[41] service commitments may be uncomfortable for physicians, but they are hardly a violation of personal integrity, especially not in the presence of an affordable buyout option (which is discussed further below).

E. NONDOMINATION

Conditional scholarships, including LCS, are subject to two broad types of worries about domination. The first type is literal domination. As mentioned, some opponents have likened conditional scholarships to "a form of debt bondage, serfdom or even outright slavery."[42] The concern here may be about bonded labor, serfdom, slavery, or indentured servitude in the most literal sense. After all, even proponents call Ghana's conditional scholarships a "system for bonding,"[43] and Australia's, "Bonded Medical Places."[44] Because literal bonded labor and enslavement can constitute extreme wrongs, examining whether such tags make sense is urgently important.

It is true that, both in actual bondage and in conditional scholarships, a person sells away several years of labor and his or her freedom to pursue certain personal aspirations during later years in return for financial benefits now. Worries about specific performance initially arise, both about LCS and about any other conditional scholarship. In most legal systems, "even a contract of short duration that calls for the performance of routine and unobjectionable tasks is a contract of self-enslavement and therefore legally unenforceable if it bars the employee from substituting money damages for his promised performance."[45] Conditional scholarships that do not offer buyout options,

[40] Till Bärnighausen & David E. Bloom, *Changing Research Perspectives on the Global Health Workforce* (National Bureau of Economic Research, Working Paper No. 15168, 2009).

[41] Eyal & Bärnighausen, *supra* note 10.

[42] Hooper, *supra* note 6, at 686.

[43] Dovlo & Nyonator, *supra* note 5.

[44] *Bonded Medical Places (BMP) Scheme*, AUSTRALIAN DEPARTMENT OF HEALTH AND AGEING, http://www.health.gov.au/bmpscheme (last visited Feb. 10, 2012).

[45] Anthony T. Kronmant, *Paternalism and the Law of Contracts*, 92 YALE L. J. 763, 798 (1983).

opponents may argue, are, quite literally, null and void slavery contracts. That would obviously cast doubt on the legitimacy and application of many conditional scholarship contracts.

There are a number of responses to this worry. First, actual enslavement and bonded labor exhibit many evils that service in return for scholarships clearly does not. A slave cannot take anyone to court, not least his master, but scholarship recipients remain full legal persons. Slavery contracts often curtail legal constraints on how the master and others treat the slave, but conditional scholarship contracts involve nothing of the sort. Slavery alone imposes enforceable legal duties to obey one's master even outside the workplace and in relation to the body, and conditional scholarships do not. Slavery contracts demand specific performance, whereas the conditional scholarship arrangements that we support involve buyout options. Even when no affordable buyouts are available, bankruptcy laws may provide protection.[46] Conditional scholarships thus differ from enslavement and bondage on multiple accounts.[47]

Some may argue that scholarships in return for students' future work for the underserved are impermissible because students should not be allowed to sell their freedom of choice, even when a buyout protection exists; our ability to choose freely is too valuable to be traded for a price, and to work is precisely to make a less-than-fully free choice. Our reply is simple: If this argument were valid, then paying physicians a salary or bonus in return for earlier work for the underserved would have to be similarly impermissible. Such a salary or bonus would constitute financial transfer in lieu of services rendered earlier and thus, allegedly, sale of earlier "freedom." Because salaries and special bonuses are perfectly legitimate ways to increase physician density in underserved areas, this argument against conditional scholarships must fail.

Alternatively, conditional scholarships might be said to involve "domination" in the Republican sense of *arbitrary power*—a situation in which someone has the capacity to profoundly impact, with impunity, the lives of others, and not as their proxy or

---

[46] The present U.S. situation might be thought to leave NHSC participants no affordable choice except to render service. Extremely steep buyout prices for NHSC loans are coupled with a statute making government-provided student loans generally nondischargeable for any chapter of bankruptcy. Opponents may allege that effectively—albeit informally—NHSC loans currently demand specific performance—just like many loan bondage contracts elsewhere, which give bonded laborers the formal legal "option" to buy their freedom in return for exorbitant debt payments or fines. However, as Nancy Pellerin clarified in correspondence, a U.S. debtor may discharge student loans under 11 U.S.C. § 523(a)(8)(2000), provided he or she can demonstrate that repaying the loans would cause "undue financial hardship." We thank Pellerin, as well as Dan Brock, Glenn Cohen, Drew Schroeder, and Lucas Stanczyk, for related discussions.

[47] Interestingly, despite the resolute present legal rebuke, political philosophers have recently advanced a powerful case for the occasional legitimacy of specific-performance demands—for performances of certain types or in extreme circumstances. Cecile Fabre, *Distributive Justice and Freedom: Cohen on Money and Labour*, 22 UTIL. 393, 412 (2010); Lucas Stanczyk, Justice in Production (doctoral dissertation, Harvard University, 2011). The present chapter does not take a position on this matter, which affects only the assessment of conditional scholarships where neither affordable buyouts nor bankruptcy protections apply.

advocate.[48] Precisely because conditional scholarships increase pressure to stay in service, initially the worry arises that they can create situations where someone else, such as a clinic manager, will have physicians "under his or her thumb." In general, employees have the protection of "exit" available to them (with some exposure to potential civil action for damages). Not so under conditional scholarships, the worry goes. Being indebted would prevent scheme participants from leaving bad jobs. Managers would have near-arbitrary power over them, giving rise to domination and, with it, vulnerability to abuse, the need to cajole and to please, and the humiliation and indignities that transpire.[49]

Our response is that, in the proposed schemes, physicians would not need to serve in any particular clinic or hospital in an underserved area, but would merely need to work in one of many such health care facilities, and would be able to change the facility several times during the period of commitment. This feature of the scholarships largely rules out the worst kinds of domination by local senior colleagues. In addition, scheme participants could always use their buyout option, normally prorated for every year of service, as a last resort. Buyout options should remain affordable, only steep enough to prevent abuse. The exact amount can depend on the signatory's economic status.[50] Strong independent bureaus to address graduates' complaints could be formed. In many jurisdictions, discharging debts in bankruptcy may be an option of last resort. Alternatively, graduates who prefer not to use "exit" can use "voice"[51]: they can speak out publicly on problems in rural service. The power of the latter protection should not be dismissed, precisely because young signatories' continued willingness to sign up for the scheme depends on its reputation, greatly delimiting the impunity with which scheme management can maltreat any participating physician.

IV. Trying out LCS

Above, we argued for LCS with the following features:

- Enrollment in LCS takes place around the middle of the first year of medical school. During that year students enjoy an unconditional scholarship that covers both fees and a living allowance.
- Enrollment in LCS takes place only once students have completed a rural externship and have received multiple sessions on rural medicine, LCS, and what enrollment may mean for their lives and careers. There is some

---

[48] PHILIP PETTIT, REPUBLICANISM: A THEORY OF FREEDOM AND GOVERNMENT (1997); Frank Lovett, *Republicanism, in* STANFORD ENCYCLOPEDIA OF PHILOSOPHY (Edward N. Zalta ed., 2010).

[49] Carole Pateman, *Self-Ownership and Property in the Person: Democratization and a Tale of Two Concepts*, 10 J. POL. PHIL. 20, 53 (2002); PETTIT, *supra* note 48.

[50] Eyal & Bärnighausen, *supra* note 10.

[51] ALBERT O. HIRSCHMAN, EXIT, VOICE, AND LOYALTY: RESPONSES TO DECLINE IN FIRMS, ORGANIZATIONS, AND STATES (1970).

screening for students who lack the competence to enroll, and all are legal adults at the time of signing.

- For students who sign up for LCS, the scholarships fund both medical school fees and a generous living allowance from the second year of study onward.
- By signing up for LCS, students commit to twelve-to-eighteen years of work in underserved areas upon completion of their studies, with the exact length depending on country-specific, area-specific, and (sometimes) personal circumstances.
- Once studies are completed, students are matched with posts in underserved areas.
- There is a strong advance guarantee of good work conditions during the commitment period, including acceptable salaries and living conditions, and the ability to switch jobs within underserved areas depending on available vacancies.
- A steep-yet-affordable buyout option exists. The size of the buyout may be responsive to the financial standing of the student's family. It is prorated for met commitments.
- M.D. degrees can be assigned at the end of the commitment period (or once the full buyout payment is made).

We have argued that, insofar as LCS that have these features are effective in increasing the supply of physicians to medically underserved areas, LCS withstand a host of ethical worries. The scholarships distribute burdens fairly and are based on contractual commitments. The contract is sufficiently informed, voluntary, competent, and authorized. The commitment does not seem overly straining or excessively vulnerable to domination. Thus, where LCS further the basic health interests of some of the world's poorest and least healthy populations, LCS should usually be implemented.

We believe that the evidence of the effectiveness of conditional scholarships is strong enough to justify their increased use. We also believe that the evidence of the potentially greater effectiveness of LCS is encouraging enough to justify experimenting with LCS that have the features listed above. We therefore propose that in countries with pockets of critical or severe physician shortages, governments and donors initiate pilot LCS. These LCS schemes should be studied prospectively so that their feasibility and effectiveness can be evaluated to the benefit of local and global authorities.

13

A GLOBAL LEGAL ARCHITECTURE TO ADDRESS THE

CHALLENGES OF INTERNATIONAL HEALTH WORKER

MIGRATION

A Case Study of the Role of Nonbinding Instruments in

Global Health Governance

*Allyn L. Taylor and Ibadat S. Dhillon**

Introduction

The loss of highly skilled personnel, colloquially referred to as "brain drain," has been a central concern of developing countries for the last half century. Despite a call by developing countries, only limited international structure has emerged to equitably manage the gains and losses from the largely asymmetric movement of skilled workers.

---

* Allyn L. Taylor is a Visiting Professor of Law at Georgetown University Law Center, where she is a faculty Member of the O'Neill Institute for National and Global Health Law, and was the senior legal adviser to the World Health Organization (WHO) for the negotiation and adoption of the WHO Global Code; Ibadat S. Dhillon served as the associate director of Health Workforce at Realizing Rights, a program of the Aspen Institute, during the period leading to adoption of the WHO Global Code. This chapter has been adapted from the article: Allyn L. Taylor & Ibadat S. Dhillon, *The WHO Global Code of Practice on the International Recruitment of Health Personnel: The Evolution of Global Health Diplomacy*, GLOBAL HEALTH GOVERNANCE, Fall 2011, available at http://blogs.shu.edu/ghg/files/2011/11/Taylor-and-Dhillon_The-WHO-Global-Code-of-Practice-on-the-International-Recruitment-of-Health-Personnel_Fall-2011.pdf. The opinions expressed herein are those of the authors alone and do not necessarily reflect the views of the WHO or Realizing Rights.

Over this last decade, in the context of a global health workforce crisis, the international migration of health personnel and associated negative impacts on health systems in source countries has been identified as a particular concern by many developing and some developed nations.[1] The escalating demand for health workers in middle-and high-income nations is increasingly being met through reliance on foreign health workers, very often from low-income countries. The Organisation for Economic Co-operation and Development (OECD) identifiedthat 18 percent of physicians and 11 percent of nurses working in OECD nations were foreign-born and that the international migration of health workers to OECD nations was increasing.[2]

The migration of health workers to middle-and high-income countries is exacerbating existing inequities in the health workforce.[3] For example, over half of the physicians from Angola, Antigua and Barbuda, Grenada, Guyana, Haiti, Liberia, Mozambique, Saint Vincent and the Grenadines, Sierra Leone, Tanzania, and Trinidad and Tobago—countries already facing critical health workforce shortages—practice as expatriates in OECD countries.

At their core, the challenges associated with health worker migration point to a lack of coherence between the global health-related development agenda and the domestic health workforce policies of many donor nations. Ameliorating the negative effects of health worker migration demands an international structure to further dialogue and guide cooperation among states on issues related to the international recruitment and migration of health workers.[4] Without serious engagement on these issues, improvements to health in low-income countries, as well as significant donor investments and credibility, are placed in jeopardy.

The May 2010 adoption by the World Health Assembly (WHA or Health Assembly) of the World Health Organization (WHO) Global Code of Practice on the International Recruitment of Health Personnel (the "Code" or "WHO Global Code") puts in place a global architecture, including the identification of ethical norms as well as institutional and legal arrangements, to guide international cooperation on the issue of health worker migration and to serve as a platform for continuing dialogue.[5] Although this is only the second code of its kind promulgated by the WHO, the process toward development of the Code evidences a growing maturity of global health diplomacy. Multilateral agreement among all 193 WHO Member Stateshas been achieved on an issue of

---

[1] Outflow of Trained Professional and Technical Personnel at All Levels from the Developing to the Developed Countries, Its Causes, Its Consequences and Practical Remedies for the Problems Resulting from It, G.A. Res. 2417 (XXIII), U.N. Doc. A/7406 (Dec. 17, 1968).

[2] Jean-Christophe Dumont & Pascal Zurn, Organization For Economic Co-Operation and Development, *Immigrant Health Workers in OECD Countries in the Broader Context of Highly Skilled Migration*, in INTERNATIONAL MIGRATION OUTLOOK 161, 162–63 (2007), *available at* http://www.oecd.org/dataoecd/22/32/41515701.pdf.

[3] WHO, THE WORLD HEALTH REPORT 2006: WORKING TOGETHER FOR HEALTH xvii–xviii (2006), *available at* http://www.who.int/whr/2006/en/.

[4] Mary Robinson & Peggy Clark, *Forging Solutions to Health Worker Migration*, 371 LANCET 691 (2008).

[5] WHO, WHO Global Code of Practice on the International Recruitment of Health Personnel, WHA Res. 63.16, WHO Doc. A63/8 (May 21, 2010), *available at* http://www.who.int/hrh/migration/code/code_en.pdf.

long-standing concern to developing countries, one that until recently was viewed as irreconcilable with the interests of high-income nations. The choice of a nonbinding approach to address an issue that is dynamic, complex, and highly sensitive also reflects more nuanced understanding by Member Statesof the nature and utility of binding and nonbinding international legal instruments to further global health.

I. The Development of the Who Global Code of Practice

A. INITIATION OF THE WHO GLOBAL CODE PROCESS

In order to advance a global framework for dialogue and cooperation among states on international health worker recruitment issues, in May 2004 the Health Assembly, the legislative body of WHO, adopted Resolution 57.19 mandating that the Director-General, in consultation with Member States and all relevant partners, develop a nonbinding code of practice on the international recruitment of health workers.[6] The resolution marked the first time that the WHA had invoked the constitutional authority of WHO to develop a nonbinding code since the 1981 International Code of Marketing of Breast Milk Substitutes.

The WHO Global Code process was preceded by a number of initiatives to address international health worker recruitment concerns on a country-by-country, multilateral, or transnational basis. Over the last decade countries have adopted a number of nonbinding instruments aimed at tackling the challenges associated with international health worker recruitment, including the Commonwealth Code of Practice on the International Recruitment of Health Workers,[7] the Pacific Code of Practice for the International Recruitment of Health Workers in the Pacific Region,[8] and the United Kingdom National Health Service Code of Practice for the International Recruitment of Healthcare Professionals.[9] Bilateral agreements between source and destination countries that formalize ongoing dialogue and address rights and responsibilities in ethical international recruitment also multiplied over the ten years prior to the adoption of the Code.[10]

---

[6] WHO, International Migration of Health Personnel: A Challenge for Health Systems in Developing Countries, WHA Res. 57.19 (May 22, 2004), *available at* http://apps.who.int/gb/ebwha/pdf_files/WHA57/A57_R19-en.pdf.

[7] COMMONWEALTH HEALTH MINISTERS, COMMONWEALTH CODE OF PRACTICE FOR THE INTERNATIONAL RECRUITMENT OF HEALTH WORKERS (2003), *available at* http://www.thecommonwealth.org/shared_asp_files/uploadedfiles/%7B7BDD970B-53AE-441D-81DB-1B64C37E992A%7D_CommonwealthCodeofPractice.pdf.

[8] WHO W. PAC. REGION OFFICE [WHO WPRO], PACIFIC CODE OF PRACTICE FOR RECRUITMENT OF HEALTH WORKERS AND COMPENDIUM (2007), *available at* www.hrhresourcecenter.org/node/3448

[9] U.K. DEP'T OF HEALTH, CODE OF PRACTICE FOR THE INTERNATIONAL RECRUITMENT OF HEALTHCARE PROFESSIONALS (2004), *available at* http://www.dh.gov.uk/prod_consum_dh/groups/dh_digitalassets/@dh/@en/documents/digitalasset/dh_4097734.pdf.

[10] IBADAT S. DHILLON, MARGARET E. CLARK & ROBERT H. KAPP, THE ASPEN INSTITUTE, INNOVATIONS IN COOPERATION: A GUIDEBOOK ON BILATERAL AGREEMENTS TO ADDRESS HEALTH WORKER MIGRATION 11–12 (2010), *available at* http://www.aspeninstitute.org/sites/default/files/content/docs/pubs/Bilateral%20Report_final%20code.pdf.

Existing voluntary codes of practice and other similar nonbinding instruments have been widely criticized as weak and ineffective in addressing the core challenges of health worker migration and its impact on health systems. Critics have argued, for example, that such nonbinding instruments have been largely ineffective in limiting health worker migration from poor countries or protecting the human rights of health workers because the instruments lacked meaningful mechanisms to collect data and to monitor national compliance.[11] In addition, unlike the WHO Code, none of the earlier instruments set forth a global approach necessary to address a global problem or mobilized the funding required for implementation.

Despite early support for the development of a WHO Global Code, the initiative lacked political support, resources, and policy direction. However, in early 2008, the Code effort reemerged as the issues surrounding health systems and health worker recruitment rose in stature in the global health policy agenda of states. Development and drafting of the Code were led by the WHO's Human Resources for Health Division (WHO/HRH), and a framework for the proposed Code was first presented by WHO/HRH in March 2008 in Kampala at the Global Forum on Human Resources for Health.

The efforts of the Health Worker Migration Global Policy Advisory Council (the Council), a partnership between Realizing Rights, the Global Health Workforce Alliance (GHWA), and WHO, with Realizing Rights serving as Council secretariat, were also critical to the renewed focus on Code development. The idea of the partnership, linking rigorous research and evidence with high-level political leadership and engagement, emerged in 2006 on the occasion of the United Nations (UN) General Assembly Special Session on Migration and Development. The Council, cochaired by the Honorable Mary Robinson, former President of Ireland and UN High Commissioner for Human Rights, and Dr. Francis Omaswa, former Executive Director of GHWA, played a significant role in supporting the development of the Code. The Council was comprised of forty high-level sitting and former policy makers from sending and receiving nations, as well as high-level representatives from international organizations. Through its members and meetings, the Council provided political and technical support to the work of the WHO Human Resources for Health Division in the development of the Code.

Despite growing support for the international cooperation many observers continued to dismiss the potential contribution that a nonbinding code of practice could make to issues surrounding international health worker recruitment. It was argued that the proposed Code was not "legal" or could have no impact in state practice because it would be technically nonbinding as a matter of international law. To gather and respond to such concerns, as well as galvanize stakeholder interest, at its May 2008 meeting in Geneva, the Council commissioned a paper to facilitate discussion on the potential strengths of nonbinding instruments in international legal practice

---

[11] Annie Willetts & Tim Martineau, *Ethical International Recruitment of Health Professionals: Will Codes of Practice Protect Developing Country Health Systems?* 13–15 (2004), *available at* http://www.medact.org/content/health/documents/brain_drain/Martineau%20codesofpracticereport.pdf.

and how the proposed code could best be structured and negotiated to advance global action on international health worker migration issues.[12]

B. PREPARATION OF FIRST DRAFT TEXT AND EARLY STAGES IN THE NEGOTIATION PROCESS

Technical legal work and the preparation of the first draft of the Code commenced in earnest in July 2008 at WHO headquarters in Geneva, and the draft of the Code prepared under the auspices of the WHO/HRH, headed by Dr. Manuel Dayrit, was ready for consideration by Member States by the end of the summer in 2008.

The first draft of the Code endeavored to establish a global architecture for national and international dialogue and action on international health worker recruitment and migration. The brief first draft, consisting of eleven articles, did not aim to address and resolve all of the substantive issues raised by international health worker recruitment and migration. Rather, the goal of the first draft was to set forth a brief, straightforward framework and platform for substantive negotiations. It was expected that WHO Member States would negotiate more detailed commitments in the final text of the Code or in later instruments.

Notably, the first draft of the Code did aim to respond to criticisms of other nonbinding instruments in this realm by recommending voluntary measures to promote national compliance. Consistent with contemporary international practice in other realms of international law, the first and all of the following drafts of the Code recommended a robust and transparent framework for global governance, including voluntary mechanisms for effective and periodic information sharing, reporting, and supervision of implementation.[13]

In September 2008, the WHO Secretariat launched a Web-based global public hearing on the first draft of the proposed Code. In addition, the draft text was presented by the WHO/HRH and considered at WHO Regional Committees in September and October 2008 in the European Region, South-East Asian Region, and Western Pacific Region. The Council also met for two days in September 2008, with members including the then-chair of the WHO Executive Board ("the Executive Board" or "the Board") reviewing the text line by line and providing specific input through the online process. Based on the input provided by the regional committee meeting, the global public hearing, and the comments provided by the Council, the WHO Secretariat prepared a second draft of the proposed Code in November 2008.

The second draft of the Code was considered by the Executive Board in January 2009 at one regular session and in one closed informal session. Although there was wide

---

[12] Allyn L. Taylor, The Proposed WHO Code of Practice on Health Worker Migration: Issues of Form, Substance and Negotiation (May 18, 2008) (unpublished manuscript presented at Health Worker Migration Global Policy Advisory Council) (on file with author).

[13] Allyn L. Taylor, *The Draft WHO Code of Practice on the International Recruitment of Health Personnel*, INSIGHTS (American Society of International Law, Washington, D.C.), Nov. 11, 2008, *available at* http://www.asil.org/insights081111.cfm.

agreement on many parts of the text, there was also divergence on some key aspects of the draft that reflected the underlying complexity of the issues and differences among states regarding health worker recruitment and migration. For example, a number of industrialized countries, including the United States, and Hungary on behalf of the European Union, expressed concern that the Code was overly prescriptive for a nonbinding instrument. Japan, the United States, and other delegations intervened that provisions on monitoring and implementation were inappropriate for a nonbinding instrument. In contrast, however, a number of countries, including Mauritania on behalf of the WHO Regional Office for Africa (WHO AFRO region), as well as Malawi and South Africa, emphasized that the Code needed to be "enforced."

As a further example, Sri Lanka, Member States of the WHO AFRO region, and others expressed the view that the Code must also include mechanisms to compensate developing countries for the migration of health workers to high-income states. Other participants, in particular some destination states, indicated that bilateral support was a preferred alternative and that a compensatory mechanism should not be included in the Code.

Notably, many Member States, including Mauritania on behalf of the WHO AFRO region, Hungary on behalf of the European Union, Brazil, Djibouti, Bahamas, and China expressed the view that the second draft paid insufficient attention to the impact of migration on the health systems of developing countries. Some delegations also argued that the draft overemphasized the rights of health workers at the expense of the health systems of source states and could be interpreted as encouraging migration.

In recognition of the important differences among countries on issues surrounding health worker recruitment, there was widespread agreement that the draft Code required further consultation among Member States and subsequent revision before it could be forwarded to the Health Assembly for negotiation and adoption. At the same time, some state delegates privately expressed the view that delaying negotiation and adoption of the Code for one year could create a more fertile negotiating environment by allowing time for a new United States presidential administration to take office and establish policy that might be more supportive of the Code effort. Consequently, it was agreed that the Secretariat should initiate a consultative process on the draft Code, including consideration of the draft Code at the WHO regional committee meetings in the fall of 2009 before the issue of the Code would be revisited by the Executive Board in January 2010.

Following the January 2009 Executive Board session, issues related to the Code were considered in national, regional, and international meetings in preparation for fall 2009 regional committee sessions. Some Member States held national consultations, and some regional offices convened regional and sub-regional meetings. In July 2009, the Group of Eight (G8) countries encouraged WHO to develop a Code of practice on the international recruitment of health personnel by 2010, and the ministerial declaration of the 2009 High-Level Segment of the United Nations Economic and Social Council called for the finalization of a WHO Code.[14]

---

[14] Group of Eight (G8), Responsible Leadership for a Sustainable Future, 121 (July 8, 2009), *available at* http://www.g8italia2009.it/static/G8_Allegato/G8_Declaration_08_07_09_final%2co.pdf.

The Secretariat revised the text and prepared a third draft of the Code in order to take into account the views and comments expressed by members of the Board in January 2009 and the outcome of the subsequent sessions of the Regional Committees.[15] In particular, the Code was deftly revised to considerably strengthen the emphasis of the text on the interests and concerns of source states in the health worker migration process, but, at the same time, it reflected the views of destination states by, among other things, softening the perceived "prescriptive" language of the draft text.

In January 2010 the draft Code was once again before the Executive Board. Although some states expressed disagreement with some aspects of the draft text, or proposed mechanisms for improvement, it was unanimously agreed that the draft Code was a good basis for negotiation and should be forwarded to the May 2010 Health Assembly for negotiation and possible adoption.

Alongside the formal WHO process, Council members and others supported a political process to both inform and engage Member States around support for a substantive WHO Code. Norway's leadership, both in its capacity as a Member State and as an active member of the Council, was invaluable in this process. The Council, through its meetings and partnerships, additionally worked to highlight the content and import of a substantive WHO Code to both source and destination Member States. Particular emphasis was placed on engaging constructively with President Obama's incoming administration. The Honorable Mary Robinson and others reached out on numerous occasions to the highest levels of U.S. government, including to President Obama through his advisors, to encourage support for the WHO Code. Through his speech in Ghana, President Obama, as part of his first presidential visit to Sub-Saharan Africa, specifically articulated the link among donor incentives, health worker migration, and gaps created in primary care in Africa. This important speech was critical to easing strong U.S. administration opposition to development and adoption of the WHO Code.

Although it was African countries that championed the call for development of the Code, their engagement with the initial drafts of the proposed WHO Code was relatively limited. A week before formal Code negotiations at the WHA in May 2010, Norway and the WHO Regional Office for Europe (WHO EURO region) supported the Council to host a two-day Inter-Regional Dialogue around the text and contentious issues of the Code. Norway particularly supported the Council in ensuring strong representation of African nations at the meeting. The meeting included fifty-five participants from thirty-two countries, fifteen from Africa. Some of the national governments represented at the meeting included South Africa, Norway, the United States, Botswana, Ghana, Uganda, Kenya, Brazil, Zimbabwe, the United Kingdom, France, Hungary, and Spain (which held the EU presidency)—many of whom were to play a leading role in Code negotiations. The two-day meeting was perhaps most important in familiarizing some participants with the text and underlying points of contention associated with

---

[15] WHO Secretariat, International Recruitment of Health Personnel: Draft Global Code of Practice, WHO Doc. A63/8 (Apr. 15, 2010), *available at* http://apps.who.int/gb/ebwha/pdf_files/WHA63/A63_8-en.pdf.

the draft Code before formal negotiations took place, as not all of the Member States had participated in the Executive Board deliberations over the past two years. The participants were united in recognizing that the areas of contention could not be allowed to jeopardize adoption of the Code.

C. NEGOTIATION OF THE WHO GLOBAL CODE AT THE MAY 2010 WORLD HEALTH ASSEMBLY

On May 17, 2010, the Sixty-Third WHA established a "drafting committee" open to all Member States to negotiate the text of the Code that had been forwarded by the Executive Board. Under the chairmanship of an experienced negotiating chair, Dr. Viroj Tangcharoensathien of Thailand, and with the support of the WHO Secretariat, led by Dr. Manuel Dayrit, the final text of the WHO Global Code was negotiated in this closed drafting group that met over three days during the May 2010 Health Assembly, including a final negotiating session that lasted until 4:30 a.m. on Thursday, May 20, 2010.

Over thirty countries, including many of the key players in the global health recruitment debate, such as South Africa, Norway, the United States, Botswana, Switzerland, Uganda, Kenya, Brazil, Thailand, Zimbabwe, New Zealand, Australia, and Canada—and the European Union, represented by Spain as well as some of its Member States such as the United Kingdom, France, Belgium, and Germany—participated in the global negotiations.

Although there remained important differences among countries, under the keen stewardship of Dr. Viroj the negotiating group forged a consensus document that contains voluntary recommendations on many of the issues surrounding international recruitment of health personnel. The draft was negotiated by first identifying the key issues in dispute and then proceeding through the text provision by provision until consensus was achieved.

Global health workforce recruitment and migration is a complex and multidimensional global health challenge, and a number of the critical issues that had challenged the development of the text throughout the negotiation process were central to the debates of the drafting group. However, as the draft text had been revised by the Secretariat several times prior to the Health Assembly, the differences among countries had been considerably narrowed. Consequently, the final text of the Code can be fairly described as only subtly different from the last draft prepared by the Secretariat, reflecting fine differences in tone and precision, but only limited substantive changes.

A recurring issue in the discussions leading up to the Health Assembly and the drafting group itself was the perceived "prescriptive" nature of the voluntary Code. As described above, during the Executive Board debates a number of high-income countries argued that the tone of the draft Code was too prescriptive or mandatory for a nonbinding instrument. Most of the high-income countries present in the drafting sessions joined in support for modification of the draft Code during the Health Assembly, including Canada, New Zealand, Spain on behalf of the European Union, the

United States, Monaco, and others. Without any objection from low-income states, the draft Code was revised to eliminate terms such as "standards" and "comply." At the same time, Member State commitments under the Code were modified throughout the text from the word "should" to terms such as "should consider" or "should encourage." It can well be argued that because the Code is nonbinding and only makes recommendations to governments that these subtle changes have no impact on the substance of the Code and are likely to make no meaningful difference in state practice. However, the case can also be made that such changes, by undermining the precision of the commitments in the text, could potentially impact or even soften the sense of duty among Member States to comply with the underlying norms in the Code.

Another key issue that arose during the consultations surrounding the draft Code was whether the instrument should narrowly focus on establishing voluntary principles and practices related to international recruitment or whether the scope of the instrument should be broadened to address the impact of health worker migration on health systems generally. Revisions to the text during the drafting committee did not fully clarify this issue. Early in the drafting group, high-income states tailored the text of the Code, particularly the objectives in Section 1, to focus exclusively on recruitment and to leave out the larger issues of migration. However, a careful reading of the final text of the Code reveals that broad issues of health workforce migration, the "brain drain" from developing countries, comprise a substantial part of the substance of the text. For example, Article 5 focuses on general issues surrounding health system sustainability, and Articles 6 and 7 are centered upon collection and exchange of information on health personnel migration.

An important area of concurrence among high- and low-income states during the drafting group revolved around human rights issues under Article 4 of the Code. As described above, issues surrounding how to honor the right of developing countries to strengthen their health systems and the rights of health workers to migrate to countries that wish to admit and employ them was a long-standing concern in the drafting of the Code. During the Health Assembly deliberations, the right to health of source countries became the dominant concern in this balance as interests among high-income and low-income participating states aligned. Consistent with international human rights law and preexisting codes, such as the Commonwealth and the Pacific Codes of Practice, the draft WHO Code had emphasized in several articles the human rights of health workers in Article 4 to fairness and equality of treatment. High-income countries modified the language in this Article by, among other things, subjecting rights to "applicable law." The effort of high-income countries to limit the broad recognition of rights aligned with the interests of developing countries who had long argued that the draft Code had overemphasized the rights of workers at the expense of the health systems of developing countries.

Throughout most of the negotiation process at the Health Assembly, high-income states, particularly the participating states from the European Union, Canada, the United States, and New Zealand, dominated the interventions and advanced recommendations for change in the draft text. Developing countries, particularly the delegates from African States, frequently remained silent during discussions of the substantive provisions of the draft Code, with Norway and Brazil often voicing the position of source countries. However, an important change occurred after midnight on May 20, 2010, as the delegates moved from negotiations of the substantive aspects of the Code to discussions of the detailed procedural mechanisms involving data collection, information exchange, monitoring, and implementation, and the ranks of negotiators thinned from a high of over thirty participating states to a core group of delegates from just over twenty Member States. As described above, a number of high-income states had strongly opposed the Secretariat's detailed inclusion of these critical procedural and institutional mechanisms in the voluntary instrument. An information document prepared by the Secretariat, consisting of Member State proposals to the draft text, evidenced that countries such as Canada and the United States, as well as the European Union, preferred that such provisions be strictly circumscribed or deleted.[16] However, starting with the deliberations on data collection, the delegations from African states, including South Africa, Zimbabwe, Kenya, and Botswana, established a united front in favor of maintaining the strong legal and institutional provisions in the draft text against all efforts to modify and limit such provisions. In the end, the detailed legal, institutional, and data-sharing provisions established in the final text remained substantively unchanged from the draft prepared by the Secretariat.

In addition, although developing countries had long pushed during the early stages of the Code process for strengthening the financial mechanisms to promote "compensation" from destination states to source states, there was no effort to negotiate more detailed commitments on financial provisions in the final negotiations. Indeed, there was a keen recognition among developing country delegates at the Health Assembly that high-income states would simply not agree to deeper provisions on financial support to developing countries. As the delegate of Brazil essentially noted, the Code effort should not be held back by lack of agreement on compensation, and that maybe, in the future, there could be meaningful discourse on compensation.

The three-day negotiation of the WHO Global Code of Practice occurred during what was a well-attended and highly charged WHA. The agenda of the Health Assembly included negotiation of contentious issues in other substantive and procedural areas. It also saw the launch of President Obama's new Global Health Initiative. While negotiations on the WHO Global Code were occurring at Committee A, there were negotiations around WHO governance structures, in particular the process to appoint the Director-General, occurring in Committee B. Delegates to the negotiations were highly sensitive to shifts in alliances due to negotiation positions taken on other topics.

The drafting committee's final text of the Code was brought forward on May 21, 2010, to Committee A for further discussion before the text was to be accepted by

---

[16]   WHO, Provisional Agenda Item 11.5: International Recruitment of Health Personnel: Draft Global Code of Practice, WHO Doc. A63/INF.DOC./2 (Apr. 15, 2010), *available at* http://apps.who.int/gb/ebwha/pdf_files/WHA63/A63_ID2-en.pdf.

Committee A as final. Many of the negotiators from both source and destination countries privately expressed the view that they remained apprehensive that the process toward adoption achieved by the drafting group could still be derailed by ongoing discussion and negotiation at Committee A. However, the WHO Global Code of Practice elicited no discussion at Committee A. Once accepted for adoption, there was spontaneous applause by all present in the room. According to observers, the applause in the room reflected both the magnitude and urgency of the challenge of health worker migration, as well as the ability to achieve multilateral agreement on such a complex and sensitive subject.

II. The Who Global Code of Practice

The WHO Global Code was officially adopted at the closing session of the Sixty-Third WHA on the evening of Friday, May 21, 2010. Director-General Margaret Chan identified the adoption of the WHO Global Code as one of the major achievements of the Health Assembly, referring to adoption of the Code as a "real gift to public health everywhere."

The final text of the WHO Global Code includes a preamble and ten articles, including: Objectives; Nature and Scope; Guiding Principles; Responsibilities, Rights, and Recruitment Practices; Health Workforce Development and Health Systems Sustainability; Data Gathering and Research; Information Exchange; Implementation of the Code; Monitoring and Institutional Arrangements; and Partnerships, Technical Collaboration, and Financial Support.

The Code is a voluntary instrument that identifies global ethical norms, "principles and practices" around the international recruitment and migration of health workers. The instrument's norms link to an array of critical challenges associated with the migration of health workers—encouraging health personnel development in countries with critical shortages, the development of a sustainable health workforce in all countries, greater cooperation on issues of recruitment and migration, equitable treatment of migrant health personnel, and coordination and collection of relevant data. The Code is explicitly a dynamic text to be updated based on the changing nature and impact of health worker migration.

Most important, the WHO Code incorporates strong procedural mechanisms for data collection, information sharing, reporting, monitoring, and systematic review by the Health Assembly. The WHO, through the Director-General, in particular, is called to report to the Health Assembly every three years on implementation of the Code, after initial data reporting in 2012. Notably, nonstate actors have a critical role to play in the implementation regime as they are also called upon to report to the Secretariat their observations on Code implementation. Based upon Member State and other reports, the Director-General is also called upon to submit a report every three years to the WHA on the status of the Code along with recommendations for its strengthening. These reporting mechanisms are designed to keep the topic of health worker migration and the Code on the active agenda of Member states, WHO, and civil society. Importantly, whereas Member States are encouraged to report to the WHO, WHO's reporting on the Code is mandatory.

The WHO Global Code is neither a perfect text nor a solution to the challenges associated with health worker migration. The substantive norms advanced by the Code remain relatively general and are advanced in a soft manner to Member States. It should be recognized, however, that the Code was never intended to be the final answer or encompass the whole solution to the challenges associated with health worker migration. Rather, the goal of the drafters was to establish a global platform that could provide a framework for continuing dialogue and cooperation among states. The Code, in particular the key legal and institutional arrangements, does provide a robust instrument for ongoing global cooperation that may lead to a deepening of commitment over time.

Although the long-term impact of the WHO Global Code is yet undetermined some positive developments have already resulted from the process of its negotiation and adoption. First and foremost, the long-ignored issue of health worker migration is now centrally on the global political agenda. This has been made most evident by inclusion of the WHO Global Code, as well as some of its relevant norms, in the Outcome Document of the September 2010 UN Millennium Development Goals Summit.

The legal and institutional arrangements present in the WHO Global Code will further ensure that the issue remains on the agenda of the WHA for the foreseeable future, with reporting by the Director-General mandated every three years. As of October 2011, as called for by the Code, more than sixty-nine countries have designated a national authority responsible for Code implementation. In addition, in order to assist states in meeting their first reporting obligations in May 2012, the WHO Secretariat took a key step by releasing draft guidelines on monitoring the Code's implementation, including a model national reporting instrument. Notably, the guidelines break new ground at WHO and significantly democratize the global health governance process by setting forth a second formal reporting instrument for all other stakeholders concerned with the international recruitment of health personnel. In accordance with the Code's principle of transparency, the draft guidelines provide that regular national reports from WHO Member States and reports from other stakeholders will be made publicly available through the WHO Web site. Collectively, these features are likely to make certain that the effectiveness of the Code will be kept under public scrutiny and continuous review, thereby increasing accountability.

One of the historic obstacles to comprehensively addressing the challenges associated with the international recruitment and migration of health personnel has been the need for and difficulty in engaging with the various sectors within national governments. These include the Ministries of Foreign Affairs/International Development, Health, Labor, Education, and Immigration. Prior to the WHO Global Code negotiations, only a few countries—notably Norway and the Philippines—had engaged in a whole-of-government approach in reflecting on the issue of health worker migration. In the process of developing a negotiation position, a number of additional Member States engaged across these multiple sectors within their governments. This process of engagement is itself important, with the networks created potentially an important step toward greater internal coherence and meaningful implementation of the norms articulated by the WHO Global Code.

III. Lessons Learned for Future Negotiations

In any political context, the organization of negotiations is a question of political mapping that must respond to political realities and resource constraints. Issues, interests, and strategies need to be organized to reduce complexity and promote coalition building and consensus. With that said, there were specific aspects of the legislative process that contributed to the success of the Code endeavor.

The lessons to be learned from the Code negotiations go beyond the mere spectrum of the nuts and bolts of international negotiation processes, and provide some deeper insight into the evolution in global health diplomacy over the past decade. The senior author of this case study initiated, with the late Professor Ruth Roemer, the idea of the Framework Convention on Tobacco Control (FCTC), the first treaty negotiated under the auspices of WHO, and was the senior legal adviser to WHO during the negotiations of the FCTC and during the negotiations of the WHO Global Code.[17] A comparison of the negotiating processes of the Code and the FCTC clearly is not a scientific endeavor that can fully reveal transformations in global health diplomacy over the past decade. Among other things, there are important differences between the two processes, including the fact that the analysis involves a comparison of the negotiations of binding and nonbinding instruments, with the FCTC negotiations also being much larger in scale. Despite these differences, the experience of the Code negotiations does appear to evidence some growing maturity and, perhaps, an evolution, in global health diplomacy at WHO among the different actors in the process—the Secretariat, civil society and, most important, Member States.

A. THE POTENTIAL CONTRIBUTION OF NON-BUILDING INSTRUMENTS TO GLOBAL HEALTH GOVERNANCE

Recent developments in global health diplomacy have led to increasing calls for international standard setting. However, consistent with other international realms, the pattern that is beginning to emerge is a marked preference for binding global health law instruments. This preference for expanding treaty law appears among state actors, civil society, and academia and is reflected in the proliferation over the last decade of proposals for new global health treaties.

The experience of the WHO Global Code evidences the important and largely overlooked contribution that nonbinding instruments can make to global health diplomacy

---

[17] Ruth Roemer, Allyn Taylor & Jean Lariviere, *Origins of the WHO Framework Convention on Tobacco Control*, 95 Am. J. Pub. Health 936 (2005).

and may serve as a model for future global health law negotiations.[18] Undoubtedly, there is no alternative to treaties when states want to make credible commitments. However, treaties are not the only source of norms in the international system. It is increasingly recognized that the challenges of global governance demand faster and more flexible approaches to international cooperation than can be provided by traditional and heavily legalized strategies. Consequently, in other realms of international concern ranging from the environment to arms control, the world community is increasingly turning to the creation of nonbinding international norms.

Like binding international instruments, nonbinding instruments have important strengths and limitations as international legal tools. Chief among the limitations of nonbinding instruments is that such voluntary agreements are not subject to international law and, in particular, its fundamental principle of *pacta sunt servanda*. There are no rules of international law that regulate or supplement nonbinding instruments such as the Vienna Convention on the Law of Treaties. Many nonbinding instruments are purposefully designed as way stations or even detours from hard-binding legal commitments. Consequently, many if not most, nonbinding instruments are purely rhetorical and have no impact on state practice.

However, nonbinding instruments have some important advantages as mechanisms for international cooperation and can, at times, make important contributions to shaping state behavior. A key advantage of nonbinding instruments is their flexibility. Flexibility is an essential component of international negotiations. Nonbinding agreements can facilitate compromise, and agreement may be easier to achieve than with binding instruments, especially when states jealously guard their sovereignty, because nonbinding standards do not involve formal legal commitments. Notably, the FCTC was negotiated in six separate rounds of two-week negotiation sessions open to all WHO Member States over five years whereas the WHO Global Code was negotiated in just a fraction of that time. In addition, by removing concerns about legal noncompliance, nonbinding instruments may, at times, promote deeper commitments with stricter compliance mechanisms than comparable binding instruments. Notably, the WHO Global Code incorporates procedural mechanisms to advance implementation that are more potent than those incorporated in the FCTC. Although both the FCTC and the Global Code set forth a shallow substantive framework, the Code sets forth a deep legal and institutional framework.

B. THE WHO PROCESS: DEVELOPMENT OF A SIMPLE DRAFT
TEXT EARLY IN THE NEGOTIATIONS

An important factor contributing to the success of the Code negotiation process is that the Secretariat introduced a simple negotiating text early in the process and maintained control of the drafting of the text until formal negotiations at the WHA in 2010.

---

[18] Intergovernmental Negotiating Body on the WHO Framework Convention on Tobacco Control, Chair's Text of a Framework Convention on Tobacco Control, WHO Doc. A/FCTC/INB2/2 (Jan. 9, 2001), *available at* http://apps.who.int/gb/fctc/PDF/inb2/e2inb2.pdf.

At first instance, a key strategy was to establish concise and carefully drafted commitments for states to bargain over and flush out. In addition, Secretariat control over the drafting process helped prevent the document from spiraling out of control.

The first draft of the Code and process of developing subsequent drafts can be contrasted sharply with the negotiating experience during the FCTC negotiations, in which the first draft text prepared by the Secretariat for the negotiating chair contained an entire catalog of potential substantive obligations.[19] In addition, during the process of negotiating the FCTC in six formal rounds of negotiations open to all Member States, each and every recommendation by Member States, sometimes amounting to nothing other than mere wording and stylistic differences, was incorporated into the draft, leading to remarkably complex texts and unnecessarily prolonged negotiating sessions. In the case of the Code, the Secretariat contributed to advancing negotiations by maintaining control of the drafting process and incorporating the key themes proposed by Member States but not verbatim text during the early stages of the negotiation process.

C. THE WHO PROCESS: STAGING AND SEQUENCING

Negotiations tend to be marked by a series of stages that narrow the agenda and differences among countries. There is not one formula for successful negotiations, and different structures can be used. In some respects, the Code negotiations reflect a good example of sequencing in that Secretariat draft text went through several political scrubs by a small group of states' representatives at the WHO regional committees and the WHO Executive Board before it was opened up for broader negotiation for all WHO Member States at the WHA. Consequently, the text was largely acceptable before it was opened up to broad negotiations. However, a critical last stage of the negotiation process involved the mMember states taking control and ownership of the document in the final negotiations at the WHA.

Cementing broad stakeholder participation is critical in a negotiation process, and a cautionary tale is provided by some international negotiations that fail to incorporate effective participation by relevant stakeholders, particularly states. For example, in the case of the United Nations Guidelines on Internal Displacement, the draft text of the Guidelines were developed by an expert group and never negotiated by governments. When brought for adoption to the United Nations General Assembly, certain countries complained that because states were not involved in the drafting, the Guidelines lacked legitimacy. Such objections were overcome only by the arguments that the Guidelines merely reflected existing international law and did not set forth new standards.

With that said, it should be recognized that the Code negotiation process was also hampered by the absence of a truly global negotiation prior to the WHA in May 2010.

---

[19]   Allyn L. Taylor, *Global Health Law*, *in* TEXTBOOK ON GLOBAL HEALTH DIPLOMACY (Ilona Kickbusch ed., forthcoming 2012).

Although the Code was considered at various international fora and regional committees prior to the Health Assembly negotiations, there was no formal global consultation necessary to advance consensus, and to move the text and the consensus forward.

D. POLITICAL LEADERSHIP

Political leadership is a critical factor in international negotiations to broker deals and bring innovative thinking. Leadership can come from many sources, including the executive head of an international organization, as was the case of Dr. Mostafa Tolba for many years at the United Nations Environment Programme. It can also be brought by states. Notably, it is often mid-sized countries such as Australia, Canada, Switzerland, New Zealand, and Norway that have provided leadership in areas ranging from the environment to health.

In the context of the Code negotiations, Norway led the way among the states. Recognizing the challenges associated with health worker migration, Norway had previously engaged across its ministries to make coherent its domestic need for foreign health workers with its international development efforts. In February 2009, Norway released its internal policy coherence strategy. However, Norway also recognized that singular action alone could not meaningfully address the global nature of the challenge. As such, Norway was a strong advocate for development of a Code. Moreover, Norway was cognizant throughout the process of its own unique economic position and the need to engage other, particularly source country, champions.

In addition to country leadership, a strong chair is an essential ingredient of effective negotiations, and the Code negotiations were expertly steered throughout the WHA process by Dr. Viroj Tangcharoensathien.

E. THE ROLE OF CIVIL SOCIETY

The unique partnership between WHO/HRH, GHWA, and Realizing Rights was integral to development of the Code. Realizing Rights's formation of the Council, an independent body and authority, in particular, allowed for a channel that could run parallel to the formal WHO process in shaping and advancing negotiations. The Council, through its Secretariat, members, and meetings, was able to compliment WHO Secretariat's efforts by reaching out to specific Member tates and hosting an inter-regional discussion in order to clarify and further consensus around contentious issues. The Code effort reflects a new type of civil society participation in global health negotiations at WHO. Through the Health Worker Migration Initiative partnership, Realizing Rights, an organization with experience in global governance, was involved with the Code development from the very inception of the process. Realizing Rights's method of work focused on supporting its partners' and Member States' capacity to move forward mutually acceptable solutions. Moreover, Realizing Rights staff—led by Mary Robinson—had knowledge and experience in international law and global negotiations and were able to bring this depth to Council meetings and its contacts with

Member tates. Robinson's ability to convene and engage stakeholders and key decision makers was undoubtedly an important additional asset.

Notably, neither the Council nor or its Secretariat were ever directly involved in drafting the text of the Code, but rather worked with Member States to provide detailed commentary on draft text and raised awareness and support for a substantive Code. Moreover, enabled by the technical legal work of the WHO Secretariat on the Code, the Council was able to point to a tangible vision and action that political leadership, from both source and destination nations, could further.

The role of civil society in the negotiation of the Code stands in contrast with that of the negotiation of the FCTC from 1998 to 2003. Civil society played a much more limited role in participating and guiding the FCTC negotiations primarily because of its lack of expertise and experience in international lawmaking and the limited opportunities to work with mMember tates and WHO in the closed negotiation sessions that dominated the negotiation process. It should be recognized, of course, that FCTC was the first binding treaty negotiated at the WHO. Civil society organizations participating in the treaty negotiations were largely domestic tobacco control organizations, with no experience in international law and negotiations. However, in recent years, through the Framework Convention Alliance, civil society has acquired depth and experience in the international lawmaking process and has played an increasingly important role in guiding the implementation of the FCTC.

F. MEMBER STATES AND THE EVOLUTION OF DIPLOMATIC CAPACITY

Similar to the apparent growth in legal capacity among members of civil society, the Code negotiations evidence a deepening or maturing of diplomatic capacity to engage in global health negotiations among low-income country delegations. Indeed, there was a striking difference between delegations engaged in the FCTC negotiations and the Code negotiations. During the FCTC negotiations, the vast majority of low-income Member States' delegations were new to the international law negotiation process and were comprised of representatives from the health ministries accompanied by junior mission lawyers or no lawyers at all. During the FCTC negotiation process, such inexperienced delegates were simply and frequently out-lawyered by the experienced negotiators, including highly skilled international lawyers from high-income states.

The difference in negotiating capacity, including legal expertise, largely, though not exclusively, explains the textual outcome of the FCTC that consists of soft substantive obligations and shallow institutional and procedural mechanisms. A lack of realistic assessment about the scope of the treaty and the depth of commitments haunted the negotiations of the FCTC. Health ministers from low-income countries clearly thought it possible to have deep and wide substantive commitments on tobacco control without losing any participants. During the final days of the negotiations, high-income states were able to negotiate substantially softer substantive commitments in the seventeen articles of the text that set forth tobacco control commitments. But, at the same time that low-income delegations were focused on the substantive obligations, they neglected attention to the key procedural and institutional mechanisms necessary in a framework convention to strengthen and deepen the regime over time. Although a robust procedural framework had been set forth by the Secretariat in the drafts of the FCTC, many of the key legal and institutional mechanisms of global governance were deleted in a side meeting open to all Member States in the final negotiations round in March 2003 in which no developing countries participated. Although the FCTC has, in practice, been remarkably successful in a number of respects,[20] an important consequence of a lack of negotiation experience among delegates from low-income countries is a framework convention with uniquely shallow procedural and institutional mechanisms.

In contrast, in the Code negotiations, the character of the state delegations differed markedly and was reflected in the negotiations and the final text. Delegations from developing countries, particularly Sub-Saharan Africa, consisted of senior diplomats and highly experienced international lawyers. Such delegations came to the table with a keen understanding of what agreement was possible and targeted critical areas of negotiations. Unlike the FCTC negotiations, these delegations, recognizing the realities of underlying politics of the negotiations, spent precious little time trying to hammer out deep substantive commitments to limit recruitment or create compensatory mechanisms. Rather, the skilled delegates and veteran negotiators focused attention on the critical legal and institutional mechanisms of information exchange and monitoring and reporting that are necessary to maintain the legal regime and, perhaps, deepen it over time.

The differences in character of the negotiating teams at the FCTC and Code negotiations may reflect a deepening of interest in global health among Member States and an evolution of global health negotiations. As global health has risen on the political agenda, more and more states may be identifying global health negotiations as a priority and bringing more experienced diplomats and lawyers to the table. If this is the case, it is a welcome development to balance the negotiation dynamics and put high-income and low-income countries on a more even footing in terms of negotiating expertise although not, of course, negotiating power. However, the limited participatory scope of the Code negotiations may mean that it is too soon to draw a definitive conclusion regarding whether the Code negotiations reflect a genuine evolution in global health diplomacy.

Conclusion

The WHO Global Code of Practice, only the second of its kind promulgated by WHO, was adopted almost three decades after adoption of its predecessor, the International

---

[20] Allyn L. Taylor, Douglas W. Bettcher & Richard Peck, *International Law and the International Legislative Process: The WHO Framework Convention on Tobacco Control, in* GLOBAL PUBLIC GOODS FOR HEALTH: HEALTH ECONOMIC AND PUBLIC HEALTH PERSPECTIVES 212 (Richard Smith et al. eds., 2003).

Code of the Marketing of Breast Milk Substitutes. The historic nature of the WHO Global Code adoption makes evident the gauntlet of a process associated with promulgating global health "law" at the WHO. Without the range of factors identified in this case study, including recognition of the value of nonbinding instruments, development of a simple negotiating text, appropriate staging and sequencing, strong civil society engagement, political leadership, and support for the negotiation capacity of developing countries, work toward development of the Code could very easily have resulted in a failed effort.

However, the WHO Member States have come together to make available a powerful and unique instrument to begin addressing the challenges associated with health worker migration. Long ignored, the issue of health worker migration is and, thanks to the Code's reporting requirements, will remain on the global health agenda for the foreseeable future. As one African government representative at the Health Assembly stated, the issue of health worker migration long "under the table, is now squarely on the table."

Despite the goodwill and multilateral spirit exhibited as part of the WHO Global Code adoption process, there is real danger that the norms articulated in the WHO Global Code may not be reflected in national and international laws, policies, and programs. This is due in significant part to the scarcity of resources made available to the WHO Secretariat in support of implementation as a consequence of the general reform process under way at WHO. Though heralded as a "real gift to public health everywhere," the success of the WHO Global Code will ultimately be judged by whether its norms are implemented and lead to tangible improvement in the lives of individuals and communities of those most affected. Work to this end is under way and must immediately be supported and intensified. Nothing less than progress toward the health-related Millennium Development Goals and donor credibility is at stake.

III

The Globalization of Research and Development

14

CLINICAL TRIALS REGISTRATION AND RESULTS REPORTING

AND THE RIGHT TO HEALTH

*Trudo Lemmens and Candice Telfer**

Introduction

Access to medicine remains one of the core challenges of global health. Innovative approaches to promote access to medicines, such as Canada's proposed improved access to medicines regime, continue to encounter resistance by industry.[1] At the same time, an increasing number of domestic court decisions also acknowledge that access

* LicJur, LLM, DCL, Dr. William M. Scholl Chair in Health Law and Policy, Faculty of Law, University of Toronto (TL); JD, Ministry of the Attorney General of Ontario (CT). The authors thank the organizers and participants of the Petrie-Flom Center's Conference on "Globalization of Medicine" and of the Central European University's Conference on "An Enforceable Right to Health" (June 2011) for useful feedback. Kevin Outterson and Saad Abughanm gave us particularly detailed comments. Special thanks also to colleagues of the Pan American Advisory Committee on Health Research, particularly Luis Gabriel Cuervo and Ludovic Reveiz, and to Karmela Krleža-Jerić, for discussions in the context of related policy work and publications. Finally, Alvin Wong and Shannon Gibson did excellent work on the references. Research for this chapter was supported by a Social Sciences and Humanities Research Council grant on "Promoting the Integrity of Biomedical Research: The Janus Face of Regulation" and by the Cancer Stem Cell Consortium with funding from the Government of Canada through Genome Canada and the Ontario Genomics Institute. This chapter is a short revised version of Trudo Lemmens & Candice Telfer, *Access to Information and the Right to Health: The Human Rights Case for Clinical Trials Transparency*, 38 AM. J.L. & MED. (2012).
[1] *See* Richard Elliot, *Delivery Past Due: Global Precedent Set under Canada's Access to Medicines Regime*, 13(1) HIV/AIDS POL'Y & LAW REV. 1 (2008), *available at* http://www.aidslaw.ca/publications/interfaces/downloadFile.php?ref=1345 (discussing the recent pressure exercised to halt legislative reform of much-needed revisions to Canada's *Access to Medicines* legislation); Paige E. Goodwin, *Right Idea, Wrong Result—Canada's Access to Medicines Regime*, 34 AM. J.L. & MED. 567, 569 (2008).

to lifesaving therapies can be seen as a component of the right to health.[2] In contrast, access to reliable information about the safety and effectiveness of medical therapies has received little attention in human rights discourse. This is to some extent understandable: pharmaceutical products must first be available and affordable in order for the lack of reliable information about those products to become a matter of public health concern.

Yet, promoting access to medicine without paying attention to the need for reliable safety and effectiveness information may ultimately undermine gains made in the improvement of public health through better access, particularly in developing and semi-industrialized countries. If no considerable efforts are made to promote proper knowledge creation and distribution, we will likely have to shift our focus from promoting access to medicines to reducing the public health burden of adverse drug effects resulting in part from overconsumption and improper prescription. This is already a major public health challenge in the industrialized world.

One of the means to promote better information about health product safety and effectiveness is the implementation of clinical trials and results-reporting registries. In the last decade, various initiatives have been undertaken to promote transparency and access to safety and effectiveness data through the establishment of such registries. Yet, these initiatives rely in many, if not most, countries, and at the international level, largely on the goodwill and collaboration of research sponsors and on those involved in conducting clinical trials.[3] Most countries have neither a strong regulatory framework nor the legal impetus to provide access to information about therapeutic products. International trade agreements are still invoked as an impediment to promoting the transparency of clinical trials data, and the momentum in favor of full transparency may be disappearing.

In this chapter, we argue that access to information about clinical trials and the safety and effectiveness of drugs and medical devices ought to be recognized as a fundamental component of the right to health, and that this link should be used to promote the establishment of solid knowledge creation systems based on transparent data. Although on a practical level, significant definitional and enforcement challenges exist with regard to the concept of the right to health, we suggest that it can function in this context not only as a rhetorical and interpretative tool (particularly in the interpretation of international trade obligations), but also as a concrete right that can be invoked to impose duties upon states to provide access to specific sets of information.

The claim that access to health information should be seen as a component of the right to health is compatible with the argument developed by some commentators

---

[2] E.g., The Minister of Health v. Treatment Action Campaign (TAC) 2002 (5) SA 721 (CC) (S. Afr.); Glenda Lopez v. Instituto Venezolano de Seguras Sociales 487-060401 (Venezuela); Cruz del Valle Bermudez y otros v. MSAS, and Asociacion Benhalensis y otros v. Ministerio de Salud y Accion Social, case 323:1339, June 1, 2000 (Bermuda) (discussing access to HIV/AIDS medicines).

[3] See, e.g., Karmela Krleža-Jerić et al., Prospective Registration and Results Disclosure of Clinical Trials in the Americas: A Roadmap towards Transparency, 30(1) PANAM. J. PUB. H. 87 (2011) (discussing trial registration and results-reporting initiatives, particularly in the Americas).

that clinical trials information ought to be considered a public good.[4] For example, according to Jerome Reichman, a public goods approach implies that states ought to be directly involved in the creation of these data.[5] The claim that the production of clinical trials data ought to be organized by the state as part of an accountable and independent drug regulatory process has also been made by health policy analysts.[6] Consideration ofi access to information as part of the right to health is reconcilable with this approach, but in our view also offers distinct advantages, particularly in the absence of fundamental reform of the clinical trials industry. Although we support the public goods approach, it is unlikely that we will see in the near future a shift to a publicly organized clinical trials system. We therefore believe it is essential to look at more immediate solutions that take into consideration the need for better scrutiny and critical assessment of industry-produced data. A *human rights approach* to clinical trials registration and results reporting fulfills this need. It shifts the approach from one of transparency as an exception, to transparency as an essential component of allowing individuals to assess and evaluate (with expert support) health information relevant for them personally, and of creating reliable knowledge-production systems.

I. Clinical Trials Registration and Results Reporting in Context

Various groups and medical organizations have been arguing since the 1960s for the introduction of some system of trial registration.[7] However, real progress has only been made since the exposure of some major controversies around the turn of this century. One controversy involved the research and marketing practices of pharmaceutical giant SmithKlineBeecham related to Paxil, which was approved for the treatment of depression in adults. The company had conducted several safety and effectiveness trials on the use of Paxil for depression in children and adolescents; it had been seeking to obtain data for a label change to enable more aggressive marketing of the drug

---

[4] *See, e.g.*, Tracy R. Lewis, Jerome H. Reichman & Anthony D. So, *The Case for Public Funding and Oversight of Clinical Trials*, 4 ECONOMISTS' VOICE 1 (2007), *available at* http://www.bepress.com/ev/vol4/iss1/art3/; Jerome H. Reichman, *Rethinking the Role of Clinical Trial Data in International Intellectual Property Law: The Case for a Public Goods Approach*, 13(1) MARQUETTE INT. PROP. L. REV. 1 (2009). The "public good" approach seems also embraced by reports of the Knowledge Ecology International. *See* Judit Rius Sanjuan, James Love & Robert Weissman, *Protection of Pharmaceutical Test Data: A Policy Proposal*, KEI RESEARCH PAPER 1 (2006), *available at* http://keionline.org/content/view/86/1.

[5] Reichman, *supra* note 4.

[6] *See, e.g.*, SHELDON KRIMSKY, SCIENCE IN THE PRIVATE INTEREST: HAS THE LURE OF PROFIT CORRUPTED BIOMEDICAL RESEARCH? 229 (2003); Wayne A. Ray & C. Michael Stein, *Reform of Drug Regulation— Beyond an Independent Drug-Safety Board*, 354 N. ENG. J. MED. 194 (2006); MARCIA ANGELL, THE TRUTH ABOUT THE DRUG COMPANIES: HOW THEY DECEIVE US AND WHAT TO DO ABOUT IT (2004). In an earlier publication, one of us supported these recommendations. *See* Trudo Lemmens, *Leopards in the Temple: Restoring Scientific Integrity to the Commercialized Research Scene*, 32(4) J.L. MED. & ETHICS 641, 652–53 (2004).

[7] *See* Kay Dickersin & Drummond Rennie, *Registering Clinical Trials*, 290 JAMA 516 (2003) (providing an excellent historical overview of trial registration).

for use in that population. When the data indicated safety and effectiveness concerns, the company failed to publish them. Allegedly, it managed to selectively publish partially positive data of only one study, claiming that Paxil was safe and effective for the treatment of major depressive disorders in children and adolescents.[8] In 2004, the attorney general of New York prosecuted the company for these practices.[9] Around the same time, another notorious controversy involving the pain medication Vioxx created awareness about the importance of timely access to reliable research data. It is estimated that the drug caused hundreds of thousands of acute myocardial infarctions and cardiac deaths. Analyses of internal company documents also revealed a lack of reporting of data, in addition to other problematic publication practices such as the use of company-paid ghost authors.[10]

The Paxil and Vioxx controversies erupted at the "right time" to create a real momentum for transparency initiatives, as developments in computer technology and the Internet facilitated publicly accessible databases and exchange of information at a global level. The very public nature of these controversies, the fact that they involved hiding serious risk to children in one case and hundreds of thousands of premature deaths in another, certainly made it difficult to reject the claim that public health was at stake.

In reaction, various actors, including some pharmaceutical companies themselves, as well as the International Council of Medical Journal Editors, embraced the idea of a publicly available registration system for clinical research. The most powerful boost to trial registration came from the World Health Organization (WHO), which established the International Clinical Trial Registry Platform (ICTRP) in 2005. The ICTRP was set up to coordinate the creation of international standards for registration of clinical trials. It developed a search portal and a unique identifier numbering system and identified a set of key items to be entered into the registries. By 2007, the ICTRP search portal and registration system was up and running, using a minimal data set as the basis of its system.

Legislative initiatives were also undertaken by a handful of states. The United States was the first country to introduce stringent registration and results reporting requirements by legislation. The 2007 FDA Amendment Act (FDAA) imposes a duty to register all phase II, III, and IV trials of pharmaceutical products submitted for approval and all medical device trials other than feasibility studies with ClinicalTrials.gov, and to report the results after finalization of the trial.[11] The European Commission also mandated

---

[8] See Jon N. Jureidini, Leemon B. McHenry & Peter R. Mansfield, Clinical Trials and Drug Promotion: Selective Reporting of Study, 20 INT'L J. RISK & SAFETY MED. 73 (2008).

[9] New York v. GlaxoSmithKline, No. 04-CV-5304 MGC (S.D.N.Y. Aug. 26, 2004); see also Drummond Rennie, Trial Registration: A Great Idea Switches from Ignored to Irresistible, 292 JAMA 1359 (2004).

[10] Richard Horton, Vioxx, the Implosion of Merck and Aftershocks at the FDA, 364 LANCET 1595 (2004); Eric J. Topol, Failing the Public Health—Rofecoxib, Merck, and the FDA, 351 NEW ENG. J. MED. 1707 (2004); Joseph S. Ross et al., Guest Authorship and Ghostwriting in Publications Related to Rofecoxib: A Case Study of Industry Documents from Rofecoxib Litigation, 299 JAMA 1800 (2008).

[11] Food and Drug Administration Amendments Act of 2007, Pub. L. No. 110-85, § 801, 121 Stat. 823 (2007).

that all phase II, III, and IV trials with at least one site in the European Community be registered with the EuroPharm database.[12] Trial registration has also been made mandatory in Brazil, Argentina, India, and Japan through regulatory requirements of the ministries of health.[13] In Canada, the research ethics policy of the major Canadian funding agencies, the Tri-Council Policy Statement, introduced trial registration and results reporting as essential requirements to pass ethics reviews.[14]

Despite this progress, major challenges remain. To obtain meaningful transparency, international collaboration and comprehensive national implementation and enforcement of standards are essential. Although most of the world's clinical trials focus on product development for industrialized countries and regions, in particular the United States, Europe, and Japan, the clinical trials business itself is increasingly global.[15] Booming clinical trials markets are found in the developing countries of Asia, Africa, Latin America, and among the former Communist countries in Eastern Europe. India, Brazil, Russia, and China have been identified as new powerhouses of the clinical trials industry, an industry whose worth has been estimated at $50 billion.[16] Yet global compliance with the WHO-supported call for universal registration remains a challenge.

The WHO ICTRP system is not a registry: it is a platform that provides a unique identifier (a Universal Trial Number) to clinical trials that are registered in primary registries, enabling linkages between data sets and the identification of all clinical trials undertaken on a specific disease at any given time. Although the ICTRP is key in providing an internationally coherent system, it has itself no clear enforcement mechanism; enforcement has to take place at the national level. Unfortunately, only a few

---

[12]   European Commission, *Regulation (EC) No. 726/2004 of the European Parliament and of the Council of March 31, 2004 Laying Down Community Procedures for the Authorisation and Supervision of Medicinal Products for Human and Veterinary Use and Establishing a European Medicines Agency*, 2004 O.J. (L 136) 1; European Commission, *Communication from the Commission regarding the Guideline on the Data Fields Contained in the Clinical Trials Database Provided for in Article 11 of Directive 2001/20/EC to be Included in the Database on Medicinal Products Provided for in Article 57 of Regulation (EC) No 726/2004 (2008/C 168/02)*, 2008 O.J. (C 168) 3, *available at* http://ec.europa.eu/health/files/eudralex/vol-10/2008_07/c_16820080703en00030004_en.pdf.

[13]   *See* Ministerio de Salud, *Resolucion 102/2009, Ministerio de Salud, Créase el Registro de Ensayos Clínicos en Seres Humanos. Del 02/02/2009; Boletín Oficial 10/02/2009*, LEGISALUD ARGENTINA, *available at* http://test.e-legis-ar.msal.gov.ar/leisref/public/showAct.php?id=12916; Registration of Clinical Trial in ICMR Clinical Trial Registry, 2009, F.No. 12-01/09-DC-(Pt-32)(India), *available at* http://cdsco.nic.in/CTRegistration.doc; Japanese Ministry of Health, Labour and Welfare, *Statement on Japan Primary Registries Network*, MINISTRY OF HEALTH, LABOUR AND WELFARE (2008), *available at* http://www.mhlw.go.jp/topics/2008/10/tp1017-1.html; Roderik F. Viergever & Davina Ghersi, *The Quality of Registration of Clinical Trials*, 6PLoS ONE 1, 7 n.13 (2011). South Africa has indicated its intention to do the same. *See Registration and Regulation*, SOUTH AFRICAN NATIONAL CLINICAL TRIAL REGISTER, http://www.sanctr.gov.za/Registrationandregulation/tabid/194/Default.aspx.

[14]   CAN. INST. OF HEALTH RESEARCH, NATURAL SCI. AND ENG'G COUNCIL OF CAN., SOC. SCI. AND HUMANITIES RESEARCH COUNCIL OF CAN., TRI COUNCIL POLICY STATEMENT: ETHICAL CONDUCT FOR RESEARCH INVOLVING HUMANS, art. 11(3)-11(12) (Dec. 2010).

[15]   *See* Seth W. Glickman et al., *Ethical and Scientific Implications of the Globalization of Clinical Research*, 360 NEW ENG. J. MED. 816 (2009).

[16]   *Global Clinical Trial Business Report & Analysis 2008-2018*, VISIONGAIN (2009), http://www.visiongain.com/Report/315/Global-Clinical-Trial-Business-Report-Analysis-2008–2018.

countries have actually introduced trial registration obligations through legislation or regulation with significant sanctions attached for noncompliance.

Even more worrisome is that progress toward greater transparency may have stalled. The global introduction of trial registration and the creation of universal trial numbers were never intended to mark the end of the initiative, but rather were seen as a crucial and achievable first step.[17] However, the WHO has made no further progress following its registration portal in the implementation of a results-reporting requirement. And further, the ICTRP office has recently been decimated by budget cuts, suggesting that this is no longer seen as a key priority for the WHO.

II. Industry Concerns Related to Trial Registration and Results Reporting: Trips and the Protection of Clinical Trials Data

Overall, industry opposition seems the main stumbling block to detailed prospective trial registration and even more so to the implementation of results reporting. Industry has cited various concerns in its opposition to trial registration and to results reporting: the costs of the implementation of these systems, the risk of misinterpretation of research data by patients, the impact on patents, the loss of competitive advantage, and the investments made in creating clinical trials data. We have discussed elsewhere in more detail why the first four reasons are not convincing.[18] We discuss here only the most important barrier to the implementation of trial registries: the existence of confidentiality obligations under international trade agreements.

Commentators and regulatory agencies have warned that implementing mandatory registry or results reporting would force regulators to violate data protection obligations under the Trade-Related Aspects of Intellectual Property Rights (TRIPS) Agreement, as well as the bilateral trade agreements that the United States has entered into with a number of countries with data exclusivity provisions offering more protection for innovators than TRIPS itself (TRIPS-plus agreements). The issue of the tension between access to information and TRIPS or TRIPS-plus agreements merits further discussion.

Article 39 of TRIPS obliges states to protect confidential commercial information "from being disclosed to, acquired by, or used by others, without their consent in a

---

[17] See Group Signatories, OTTAWA STATEMENT ON TRIAL REGISTRATION (2005), http://ottawagroup.ohri. ca/signatories.html; Karmela Krleža-Jerić, et al., *Principles for International Registration of Protocol Information and Results from Human Trials of Health Related Interventions: Ottawa Statement (Part 1)*, 330 B.M.J. 956 (2005); Charlotte Haug, Peter C. Gøtzsche & Torben V. Schoeder, *Registries and Registration of Clinical Trials*, 353 NEW ENG. J. MED. 2811, 2812 (2005).

[18] See Trudo Lemmens & Candice Telfer, *Access to Information and the Right to Health: The Human Rights Case for Clinical Trials Transparency* 38 AM. J.L. & MED. 63 (2012) ; Trudo Lemmens & Ron Bouchard, *Mandatory Clinical Trial Registration: Rebuilding Trust in Medical Research*, GLOBAL FORUM FOR HEALTH RESEARCH, GLOBAL FORUM UPDATE ON RESEARCH FOR HEALTH VOL. 4: EQUITABLE ACCESS: RESEARCH CHALLENGES FOR HEALTH IN DEVELOPING COUNTRIES 40 (2007). See also Matthew Herder, *Unlocking Health Canada's Cache of Trade Secrets: Mandatory Disclosure of Clinical Trials Results*, 184 CAN. MED. ASS. J. 194 (2012).

manner contrary to honest commercial practices."[19] It also obliges states to protect against unfair commercial use undisclosed tests or data submitted to regulators in the context of marketing approval for pharmaceutical or agricultural products. The obligations under article 39 do not create an absolute right of exclusive use of the data.[20] Rather, they aim at preventing unfair commercial use by others of data that has been created with significant effort and remains "undisclosed."

Article 39(2) specifies three criteria for information to fall within the category of protected information. First, the information has to be secret, and not generally known or readily available to specialists dealing with this type of data. Second, the secrecy must add commercial value to the data, for example in preventing generic manufacturers from relying on originators' data. Third, reasonable steps must have been taken by the person in control of the information to maintain the confidentiality of the data. Companies must refrain from undertaking any actions that could result in the disclosure of data, for example through publication in an academic journal.

Article 39(3) specifies that undisclosed tests or other data created with "considerable effort" and submitted to state regulators for marketing approval (i.e., of pharmaceutical products) must be protected against "unfair commercial use" and disclosure "except where necessary to protect the public, or unless steps are taken to ensure that the data are protected against unfair commercial use."[21] The term "unfair commercial use" refers to norms with considerable regional and cultural variables, thus providing states with considerable interpretive leeway. The term "considerable effort" is undefined, but the significant organizational efforts and investment involved in preclinical research and clinical trials are generally accepted as fulfilling this requirement.

TRIPS arguably leaves sufficient room to allow states to implement some level of registration and results reporting or to use in such systems data that is in some form shared within the scientific community. First, the obligation to protect data exists only with respect to data that is "undisclosed."[22] Under article 39(2), data are protected only if they are secret and if reasonable steps have been taken by the holder of the data to keep them secret. In the context of trial registration, when companies have widely shared their data within the scientific community, the regulator is no longer under an obligation to keep the same data confidential in the approval process. In other words, drug regulators cannot be obliged to keep secret what is already publicly available elsewhere. Second, according to article 39(3), the obligation to keep data secret comes with two broad exceptions. States can disclose either "where necessary to protect the public" or where "steps are taken to ensure that the data are protected against unfair

---

[19] Agreement on Trade-Related Aspects of Intellectual Property Rights art. 39, Apr. 15, 1994, Marrakesh Agreement Establishing the World Trade Organization, Annex 1C, 1869 U.N.T.S. 299 [hereinafter TRIPS Agreement].

[20] *See* Carlos M. Correa, Protection of Data Submitted for the Registration of Pharmaceuticals: Implementing the Standards of the TRIPS Agreement 14 (2002).

[21] TRIPS Agreement, *supra* note 19, at art. 39(2).

[22] Or more practically, data disclosed only "selectively and under precise conditions." Daniel Gervais, The TRIPS Agreement: Drafting History and Analysis 424 (3d ed. 1998).

commercial use." This means that TRIPS will be respected if states disclose data but provide adequate protection against unfair commercial use, even if that disclosure is not "necessary" to protect the public. Both provisions leave room for the development of trial registries and results-reporting systems.

Europe, the United States, and several commentators have argued that article 39 inevitably refers to the need to ensure some period of data or market exclusivity. The United States has pursued this interpretation in its TRIPS-plus agreements, introducing requirements that explicitly impose a duty on states to provide a period of exclusivity for the data submitted by innovators.[23] The WHO Commission on Intellectual Property Rights, Innovation and Public Health, however, rejects this position.[24] Commentators have pointed out that there are various ways in which the investment in the creation of the data by the original holder of the data can be fairly dealt with, and that TRIPS article 39(3) does not require data exclusivity. An ordinary reading of the terms in article 39(3) suggests that it obliges the states only to protect the data submitted to regulators against dishonest commercial practices; it in no way prevents governments from using this data in the exercise of their regulatory role.[25]

Yet the data exclusivity approach does provide an advantage for countries wanting to establish trial registration and results-reporting systems. When data exclusivity protects clinical trials data from being used by competitors in the approval process, the duty to protect against unfair commercial use seems fulfilled, allowing a regulator to disclose those data to the wider public even if disclosure is *not* demonstrably necessary for public protection. Although exclusivity approaches are problematic, in particular because they create barriers for generic companies that disproportionately affect access to medicines in developing countries, the existence of exclusivity protection can at least be invoked by those states that have entered into TRIPS-plus agreements, allowing the states to defend the introduction of trial registration and results reporting.

The TRIPS agreement does not provide guidance on what protection of the "public" or "public interest" really means, and does not refer explicitly to health in this context.

Commentators have pointed out that the discussion about exceptions to a state's duty of confidentiality with regard to clinical trials' data focused primarily on the ability of a state to protect against unfair commercial use. The public interest exception has not received the same attention as the "protection against unfair commercial use" exception.[26] Yet, the lack of definition of "public interest" offers the advantage of providing states with a reasonable degree of discretion in determining for themselves what constitutes a public interest that justifies an exception to the otherwise binding

---

[23] Kevin Outterson, *Pharmaceutical Arbitrage: Balancing Access and Innovation in International Prescription Drug Markets*, 5 YALE J. HEALTH POL'Y L. & ETHICS 193, 215–16 (2005).

[24] *See Report of the Commission on Intellectual Property Rights, Innovation and Public Health*, at 124 (2006), *available at* http://www.who.int/entity/intellectualproperty/documents/thereport/ENPublicHealthReport.pdf (last visited Sept. 20, 2011). *See also* United Nations Conference on Trade and Development, New York and Geneva, 1996, *The TRIPS Agreement and Developing Countries*, 48 U.N. Doc. UNCTAD/ITE/1.

[25] CORREA, *supra* note 20, at 41–46; Gervais, *supra* note 22, at 429.

[26] *See* CORREA, *supra* note 20, at 22; SUSAN K. SELL, PRIVATE POWER, PUBLIC LAW: THE GLOBALIZATION OF INTELLECTUAL PROPERTY RIGHTS 139 (2003).

rule. Under traditional public interest tests in international law, such as the so-called "necessity test" under WTO/GATT provisions and jurisprudence, those invoking the public interest are allowed some discretion in the implementation of "public interest"–focused rules. A public interest–focused necessity test is therefore deferential to states, although states have an obligation to provide evidence of the existence of the necessity and of how the public disclosure will assist in addressing the problem.[27]

Those in favor of a more stringent obligation on the state to justify "necessity" would argue that to respect TRIPS, states must have a disclosure regime in place that determines specific categories of data for which disclosure is really "necessary" for public protection. Disclosure could only be deemed "necessary" to protect the public if there is a clear indication that the lack of disclosure of specific data sets will result in concrete harm to specific patients. A related approach is to look at the proportionality of the disclosure and the goal of the data protection itself. The goal of the disclosure—the protection of the public—is weighed against the harm caused by the disclosure for the interests the data secrecy provision aims to protect: commercial interests associated with competitive advantage. However, this approach is less desirable, because the concept of weighing of interests suggests that if the likely impact on the competitive interests of the company is very significant, the regulatory agency might accept a higher level of risk of harm to the public. When it comes to people's lives and physical integrity, regulatory agencies should err on the side of prudence, regardless of potential commercial harm. This seems particularly important in the context of health care. Although society may arguably benefit from the economic interests in health care product development, surely the regulatory agencies mandated to protect the public must remain focused on the ultimate reason for promoting the integration of health products in the market: to improve health care. We would argue that it is cynical and highly problematic to start calculating how many individual lives can be balanced against, say, the $200 million reputational damage associated with the public exposure of confidential data related to a blockbuster drug.

TRIPS itself provides in article 8 that states may "adopt measures necessary to protect public health and nutrition, and to promote the public interest in sectors of vital importance to their socio-economic and technological development." Furthermore, article 1(1) allows states the necessary flexibilities to determine what appropriate measures would help to realize these provisions. This, in our view, leaves the door open to defend the need for a much more flexible, "disclosure friendly" interpretation of necessity, which does not make the use of the public interest exception dependent on how the disclosure of very specific data sets will be directly relevant for protecting health interests of individuals. That is to say, a regime of detailed prospective trial registration and results reporting (and the disclosure of pharmaceutical test data that comes with it) would be in and of itself defensible under a public interest exception. The implementation of a stringent (yet incomplete) disclosure obligation system in the United States is a helpful indication in this respect. If the U.S. regulator, with decades of investments in highly

---

[27] Carlos M. Correa, *Unfair Competition under the TRIPS Agreement: Protection of Data Submitted for the Registration of Pharmaceuticals*, 3 CHI. J. INT'L L. 69, 76 (2002) (with references to MICHAEL TREBILCOCK & ROBERT HOUSE, THE REGULATION OF INTERNATIONAL TRADE 140 (2d ed. 1999)).

sophisticated drug regulatory review, has not been able to counter some of the problematic aspects of industry control over clinical trials through other regulatory means, including the imposition of stiff penalties for regulatory transgressions, it seems fair to conclude that countries with many fewer resources will have even greater difficulties. The move in the United States under the FDAA toward mandatory trial registration and results reporting should certainly help make the case for the "necessity" of such measures at a global scale. In countries where fewer governmental experts are involved in inspecting pharmaceutical products, civil society groups and independent researchers may play an even greater role in scrutinizing and analyzing industry-produced data to detect problems and alert the community about safety and efficacy issues. In addition, global collaboration may be needed to enable various regulatory agencies, civil society, and independent researchers to scrutinize data sets residing in different jurisdictions and to work together to identify potential problems.

It is also worth mentioning here that that one can assume that the United States, with the adoption of the FDAA, considers that limited mandatory trial registration and results reporting are compatible with its trade secrecy obligations under TRIPS-plus agreements.[28]

III. The Right to Information and Human Rights

We have discussed, by invoking the data protection exception under TRIPS, how it may be possible to impose clinical trials registration and results-reporting obligations through regulation if governments also provide protection against unfair commercial use of the data. We want to show in this section, however, that the public interest exception provided under TRIPS offers a much wider basis for governments to impose trial registration and results reporting.

Our argument is that trial registration and results reporting can be placed under the rubric of obligations imposed by the fundamental human right to health. We argue that access to meaningful information is a critical determinant of the right to the highest attainable standard of health, and requires a reliable system of knowledge production.[29] Given

---

[28] For a related argument in the context of compulsory licensing, see Saad Abughanm, The Protection of Pharmaceutical Patents and Data under TRIPS and US–Jordan FTA: Exploring the Limits of Obligations and Flexibilities: A Study of the Impact on the Pharmaceutical Sector in Jordan 217–22 (SJD Thesis, University of Toronto, 2011).

[29] Dhir and Salinas have also made the claim that the right to health requires access to information of clinical trials. See Aaron A. Dhir, Corporate Selective Reporting of Clinical Drug Trial Results as a Violation of the Right to Health, in CRITICAL PERSPECTIVES ON HUMAN RIGHTS AND DISABILITY LAW 341 (Lee Ann Basser, Melinda Jones & Marcia H. Rioux, eds., 2010), in particular at 356–64; Rodrigo Salinas, Open Access to Research Protocols and Results: Intellectual Property and the Right to Health, in GLOBAL FORUM FOR HEALTH RESEARCH, GLOBAL FORUM UPDATE ON RESEARCH FOR HEALTH VOL. 4: EQUITABLE ACCESS: RESEARCH CHALLENGES FOR HEALTH IN DEVELOPING COUNTRIES 47, 47–48 (2007). There is an interesting connection also to arguments about the human right to enjoy the benefits of scientific progress. See Audrey R. Chapman, The Human Rights Implications of Intellectual Property Protection, 5 J. INT'L ECON. L. 861, 867–72 (2002).

this integral relationship, detailed trial registration and results reporting can be justified by invoking the public interest exception under TRIPS and TRIPS-plus agreements.

Firmly grounding transparency measures such as trial registration and results reporting in the context of human rights has significant advantages. As already argued, we believe that a comprehensive knowledge production system is needed to ensure the protection of patients and consumers and that health care systems are not negatively affected by biased research. This requires, in our view, a shift in the thinking about clinical trials data, away from access to data as an exception and toward seeing access to data as a crucial component of credible, accountable, and public safety–oriented research. The argument for access to all data also reflects a view of medical research on drug safety and effectiveness as inherently complex, and as necessitating an ongoing scientific dialogue and exchange among regulatory agencies, industry, patient advocacy groups, and independent public health–oriented research organizations such as the Cochrane Collaboration.[30] The Cochrane Collaboration, for example, with its international network of researchers, has the capacity and the credibility to scrutinize the available medical evidence and to provide a critical independent and public voice in the context of drug safety and effectiveness. In particular, at a time when drug regulators are criticized for their relatively limited role in ensuring the accuracy of the public presentation of scientific data, publicly accountable promotion of evidence-informed medicine through active contributions of civil society organizations such as Cochrane seems key. Yet, to function appropriately, the scientific community needs access to the data.

Medical experts who have argued for clinical trial transparency and full access to clinical trials' data have provided convincing examples of instances where access to early clinical trials, even phase I exploratory trials, could have provided useful information about potential safety issues with pharmaceutical products on the market. Klim McPherson and Elina Hemminki argue, for example, that better access to and publication of small clinical trials and observational studies related to hormone replacement therapy (HRT) would have allowed researchers to reveal the increased risks associated with combined HRT much earlier than the large National Institutes of Health–sponsored randomized controlled study by the Women's Health Initiative.[31] Kaye Dickersin and Drummond Rennie, for their part, invoke the delays in reporting of important data related to antiarrhythmic drugs to support their call for trial registration and results reporting. In this case, one study conducted in 1980, which could have helped prevent the flawed prescription of this medication, was not published

---

[30] The Cochrane Collaboration is an independent international network of more than 28,000 researchers and academics. The goal of the organization is to help health care providers, governments, patients, and others to make well-informed health care decisions based on the best available medical evidence. The organization publishes the highly credible Cochrane Reviews. *See* THE COCHRANE COLLABORATION, http://www.cochrane.org/.

[31] *See* Klim McPherson & Elina Hemminki, *Synthesising Licensing Data to Assess Drug Safety*, 358 B.M.J. 518 (2004).

until 1993. According to Dickersin and Rennie, the drug is estimated to have caused 20,000 to 75,000 deaths per year in the United States throughout the 1980s.[32]

Situating transparency within the larger context of the right to health and connecting it to the duty of states to contribute to reliable knowledge creation can be a powerful tool to argue for an expansion of the obligation to register clinical trials and results reporting, so that these obligations involve all forms of research involving health care products, including phase I clinical trials.

A. THE RIGHT TO INFORMATION AS A CRITICAL DETERMINANT OF THE RIGHT TO HEALTH

How does a right to information about clinical trials data fit under the concept of the right to health? The right to health has received considerable recognition in both domestic and international law. Many countries around the world now explicitly or implicitly recognize the right to health in their constitutional documents and case law,[33] and the right to health has been deemed a freestanding right by both the UN and the WHO.[34] The UN gave particular force to the international right to health by creating, in 2002, the office of Special Rapporteur on the Right to Health, and recognition of the right to health has since become increasingly prevalent, with discussions integrated into the agendas of significant international fora.[35]

The international right to health is an inclusive right, incorporating a myriad of freedoms and entitlements, with significant individual and public components. Although it is in essence an individual right, requiring the ability to make one's own choices about one's own health care, it also mandates government support in the realization of broad public goals, such as availability, accessibility, and quality.[36] Such goals, we would argue, necessarily require the creation of independent and effective knowledge systems.

There has also been much discussion in human rights discourse around the right to information. Unlike the right to health, there is not as yet consistent and universal recognition of a freestanding right of access to information. It has been integrally tied to

---

[32] Dickersin & Rennie, *supra* note 7, at 517.

[33] The South African constitution explicitly recognizes the right to health; *see* Soobramoney v. Minister of Health (Kwazulu-Natal) 1997 (1) SA 765 (CC) (S. Afr.); The Minister of Health v. Treatment Action Campaign (TAC) 2002 (5) SA 721 (CC) (S. Afr.). In India, the constitutionally protected right to life has been interpreted as including a right to health dimension; *see* Paschim Banga Khet Mazdoor Samity & Ors v. State of West Bengal and Anor, A.I.R. 1996 S.C. 2426 (India).

[34] *See* International Covenant on Economic, Social, and Cultural Rights, G.A. Res. 2200A (XXI), U.N. GAOR, 21st Sess., Supp. No. 16, U.N. Doc. A/6316 (1966) at 49 [hereinafter ICESCR]; Rep. of Paul Hunt, Special Rapporteur of the Commission on Human Rights, U.N. Doc. E/CN.4/2004/49/Add.1 (Mar. 8, 2004) [hereinafter Report of the Special Rapporteur]; *Constitution of the World Health Organization, Preamble,* WORLD HEALTH ORGANIZATION, http://apps.who.int/gb/bd/PDF/bd47/EN/constitution-en.pdf.

[35] Paul Hunt, *Towards Development: Human Rights and the WTO Agenda,* Panel Presentation at WTO Ministerial Conference (Sept. 12, 2003), *available at* http://www.3dthree.org/pdf_3D/Righttohealthan deconomicpolicy-English09-03.pdf.

[36] Report of the Special Rapporteur, *supra* note 34, at 18, 33–38.

two well-recognized rights: the right to freedom of expression and the right to health. Because of the somewhat undefined status of access to information in human rights law, the lines are not always clear between the different fundamental rights to which it is tied. This has been particularly highlighted in the context of reproductive rights, for example in litigation over whether denying information about abortion services violates international human rights conventions.[37] Although such decisions grapple with the right to access to information specifically in the context of freedom of expression, they undoubtedly provide a persuasive precedent for advocates of abortion rights as necessary to women's reproductive health.

The UN has also acknowledged that the right to health extends to the "underlying determinants of health," including "access to health-related education and information," and that states have positive obligations to ensure "information accessibility" in protecting the "right to seek, receive and impart information and ideas concerning health issues."[38] Paul Hunt, former UN Special Rapporteur on the Right to Health, asserts that "reliable information about medicines must be accessible to patients and health professionals so they can make well-informed decisions and use medicines safely."[39]

Domestic courts are also grappling with the status of access to information in relation to recognized rights. In the context of freedom of expression, the Supreme Court of Canada has addressed the issue by characterizing access to information as a "derivative right," defined as a "necessary precondition of meaningful expression."[40] It later provided further clarification (in the context of freedom of association and labor relations) by holding that denying derivative rights renders the original right itself effectively useless and therefore impairs the exercise of that right.[41] The basic idea seems to be that access to information is critical to allowing full expression and realization of the right in question. We characterize this as being a "determinant"[42] of the right,

---

[37] *See, e.g.*, Open Door and Dublin Well Women v. Ireland, 15 Eur. Ct. H.R. (ser. A) (1992). The European Court of Human Rights found that the absolute prohibition on information about an activity that was not in fact illegal (i.e., it was not illegal to travel abroad for an abortion) was overbroad and disproportionate, violating the freedom-of-expression provision under the European Convention on Human Rights; see 67–77. For a discussion of access to information and abortion, see Joanna Erdman, *Access to Information on Safe Abortion: A Harm Reduction and Human Rights Approach*, 34 HARV. J.L. & GENDER 413 (2011).

[38] U.N. Educ., Sci. and Cultural Org., Comm. on the Right to the Highest Attainable Standard of Health, 12(b), 14, U.N. Doc. E/C.12/2000/4 (2000). Although not binding instruments, general comments are generally viewed as having "considerable legal weight." MATTHEW C.R. CRAVEN, THE INTERNATIONAL COVENANT ON ECONOMIC, SOCIAL, AND CULTURAL RIGHTS: A PERSPECTIVE ON ITS DEVELOPMENT 91 (1995).

[39] RAJAT KHOSLA & PAUL HUNT, HUMAN RIGHTS GUIDELINES FOR PHARMACEUTICAL COMPANIES IN RELATION TO ACCESS TO MEDICINES: THE SEXUAL AND REPRODUCTIVE HEALTH CONTEXT 8 (2009), *available at* http://www.escr-net.org/docs/i/1312215].

[40] Ontario (Public Safety and Security) v. Criminal Lawyers' Association, 2010 SCC 23, [2010] 1 S.C.R. 815 at 30 (Can.).

[41] Ontario (Attorney General) v. Fraser, 2011 SCC 20 at 54 (Can.).

[42] The characterization as "determinant" is borrowed from Paul Hunt, former UN Special Rapporteur on the Right to Health, who broadly defines the scope of the right to health to include both freedom from discrimination in the delivery of health care as well as access to the underlying determinants of health such as potable water, sanitation, and access to essential medicines (and we would argue information about those medicines); Report of the Special Rapporteur, *supra* note 34, at 18–19.

and we argue specifically that in the context of clinical trials registration and results reporting, access to information is a critical determinant of the right to health.

The UN refers to essential drugs as an underlying determinant of the right to health and counts the availability of essential drugs as a key obligation of states in protecting and ensuring the right to health. The right to health is not simply the right to be healthy, but rather a complex notion of freedoms and entitlements. The determinants of the right to health, such as access to essential drugs and, we would argue, access to information about those drugs, provide content to those entitlements by allowing participation in health-related decisions at all levels (community, national, and international).[43] As such, access to information plays a significant role in self-determination and empowerment in health care and physical integrity, principles that must surely underlie the notion of the right to health if it is to have any meaningful force and content.

On the level of individualized rights, where the right to health is seen as a personal right to participation in one's own health and health care choices, access to information is implied in the very notion of "participation," which in language adopted by the UN must be "active and informed."[44] Accessible medicines must be of good quality, the assurance of which requires effective regulation as well as a rigorous system of scientific debate and scrutiny. However the obligations imposed by the international right to health are not (or at least not directly) on the scientific community but rather on state parties to the foundational human rights covenants. This vocabulary, then, imposes on governments the duty to promote and protect scientific rigor, even in the face of persuasive industry opposition.

Although the right to information about the safety and effectiveness of medical therapy may seem at first glance to be primarily about the right to make self-regarding health care decisions, our argument moves beyond this goal. We stress that this information is created in a complex economic, social, health care, and research context. Many clinical trials data do not have immediate implications for individuals. Yet connecting these data with other data sets, and appropriately assessing them in a complex interactive system of scientific inquiry, often reveals important information for both individuals and populations. In this process of knowledge creation and interpretation, civil society groups, medical researchers, patient advocacy groups, industry scientists, government regulators, and others all participate in an interactive exchange, often at a global level, in which those involved often have conflicting interests.[45] Access to information is in this context an important component of ensuring public accountability and enabling scrutiny of governmental decisions by civil society groups.[46]

---

[43] ICESCR, *supra* note 34, at 8, 11.

[44] U.N. Secretary-General, *The Right of Everyone to the Enjoyment of the Highest Attainable Standard of Physical and Mental Health*, 49, 61, U.N. Doc. A/61/338 (Sept. 13, 2006).

[45] *See* Lemmens, *supra* note 6, at 652–53.

[46] *See* Társaság a Szabadságjogokért v. Hungary (No 37374.05), Eur. Ct. H.R. 618 (2009), in which the European Court of Human Rights ruled, after weighing the interest in accessing the information against the privacy interest in the information held by the government, that a state party could not

Although most national governments have signed on to TRIPS and TRIPS-plus agreements, accepting obligations of patent and intellectual property protection, there is an equal, if not greater, global commitment to the protection of the right to health. By 2006, the WHO estimated that "[e]very country in the world is now a party to at least one international treaty that recognizes health-related human rights."[47] We argue that the fundamental human right to health cannot be subservient to the TRIPS obligations, especially in light of this elevated status in international law. Human rights must trump patent and commercial interest concerns.

B. COUNTERING INDUSTRY ARGUMENTS: HUMAN RIGHTS AND ACCESS TO INFORMATION AS INTERPRETIVE TOOLS

The pharmaceutical industry has argued that stringent registry and reporting requirements violate the standards of intellectual property and data protection assured by TRIPS and TRIPS-plus agreements. The TRIPS system, it is argued, necessarily interferes with governments' abilities to fulfill their obligations under international human rights treaties. However, this sort of argument is inconsistent with statements made at the highest levels of international governance. The UN has stated that intellectual property rights, such as those protected under the TRIPS agreement, must be seen to serve internationally recognized human rights. Rather than use TRIPS as a way to interpret and limit obligations under human rights regimes, in fact the reverse is appropriate and possible.[48] International human rights law must be seen as an interpretive tool in establishing the parameters of trade and intellectual property regimes. In other words, states pursuing policies under TRIPS and TRIPS-plus agreements have an obligation to assess the impact of such policies on human rights, including the right to health.

The risk of loss of competitive advantage and the speculative nature of the impact on innovative drug development strategies must be weighed against the importance of public access to clinical trial data. TRIPS explicitly allows states to disclose commercially sensitive information of pharmaceutical companies because of public health interests. This should be seen as international recognition of the fact that, in the balancing act, public health interests outweigh trade-related interests.

---

refuse to release information to a civil society organization. The ruling situated the right to information as an essential component of freedom of expression. See, however, the earlier decision in *Guerra and Others v. Italy* (No 14967.89) 26 Eur. H.R.R. 357 (1998) in which the same court situated the right to obtain relevant health risk information from the government under the right to protection of private and family life and not freedom of expression.

[47] WORLD HEALTH ORGANIZATION, ENGAGING FOR HEALTH: ELEVENTH GENERAL PROGRAMME OF WORK, 2006–2015 (2006), *available at* http://whqlibdoc.who.int/publications/2006/GPW_eng.pdf.

[48] Comm. on Econ., Soc. and Cultural Rights, *Human Rights and Intellectual Property*, 4–6, U.N.Doc. E/C.12/2001/15 (2001); *see* Chapman, *supra* note 28; Laurence R. Helfer, *Human Rights and Intellectual Property: Conflict or Coexistence?*, 5 MINN. INTELL. PROP. REV. 47 (2003) (with references to Robert Howse and Makau Mutua, and to Richard Elliott).

This has also been recognized in the World Trade Organization Ministerial Conference's 2001 Doha Declaration on TRIPS and Public Health,[49] which recognizes the general right of states to interpret and implement TRIPS in a way that supports their "right to protect public health." The Doha Declaration thus emphasizes the importance of interpreting and implementing TRIPS through the human rights lens of the right to health and the supremacy of public health and human rights over trade interests.[50] A flexible interpretation of the "public health" exception in TRIPS, which recognizes the importance of access to trial data as an important component of promoting public health, is consistent with the Doha Declaration.

C. CHALLENGES UNDER THE HUMAN RIGHTS APPROACH

Employing a human rights approach in the context of advocating for trial registration and results reporting is not without its challenges and drawbacks. For one thing, there is an inherent contradiction to economic, social, and cultural rights, including the right to health, under international law. Although international bodies make strong statements about the equal status of economic, social, and cultural rights with civil and political rights, the former category is often not justiciable.[51] As a result, socioeconomic rights have not yet been given real juridical content. In this context, governments have had no real impetus to ensure health-related obligations.

Furthermore, socioeconomic rights are subject to "progressive realization" rather than the more immediate and assertive obligations inherent to civil and political rights. The concept of progressive realization was adopted to recognize "that full realization of all economic, social and cultural rights will generally not be able to be achieved in a short period of time."[52] It entails a gradual implementation of protection and promotion measures as resources, knowledge, and expertise become available. Progressively realizable rights are in general not directly enforceable, as enforcement depends on whether, in the socioeconomic context of a country, it is reasonable to expect the state to introduce specific measures to enable these rights. Furthermore, because these rights are "progressively" realizable, infringements are in reality very difficult to quantify, and given the issue of justiciability there is virtually no international case law to draw upon for precedents on infringement measurement.

---

[49] World Trade Organization, Ministerial Declaration of Nov. 20, 2001, WT/MIN(01)/DEC/2 (2001); *see in particular id.* at 4–5.

[50] *See* Christopher Butler, *Human Rights and the World Trade Organization: The Right to Essential Medicines and the TRIPS Agreement*, 4 J. INT'L L. & POL'Y 1 (2007).

[51] *See* Office of the High Comm'r for Human Rights, *Fact Sheet No. 6 (Rev. 1), The Committee on Economic, Social and Cultural Rights*, UNHCR (1991), http://www.ohchr.org/Documents/Publications/FactSheet16rev.1en.pdf; Inter-American Comm'n on Human Rights, *Annual Report of the Inter-American Commission on Human Rights, 1983–1984*, § V(II)(2), U.N. Doc. OEA/Ser.L/V/II.63/doc.10 (1984); TARA MELISH, PROTECTING ECONOMIC, SOCIAL AND CULTURAL RIGHTS IN THE INTER-AMERICAN HUMAN RIGHTS SYSTEM: A MANUAL ON PRESENTING CLAIMS 54 (2002).

[52] U.N. Educ., Sci. and Cultural Org., *General Comment 3: The Nature of States Parties' Obligations*, 9, U.N. Doc. E/1991/23 (1990).

Nevertheless, there are minimum core obligations in international covenants that are of immediate effect and cannot be deferred due to lack of resources. Nor can they be interfered with, as discussed above, because of intellectual property policy such as TRIPS-plus obligations. "Essential primary health care" is cited as one such minimum core obligation. We would argue that the most minimal primary health care provided by the state must fundamentally be health care based on reliable data. Essential primary health care necessarily requires reliable, credible systems of knowledge production that are enabled and protected through state regulatory regimes based, in our view, on accessible data.

Conclusion

The limits of a human rights approach notwithstanding, we believe that approaching clinical trial registration and results reporting from this perspective provides significant advantages. It gives advocacy groups, the research community, national governments, and international organizations both a strong moral and legal foundation to reduce the limits imposed on access to clinical trials data by international trade obligations and related national rules. It should enable advocacy groups and health policy makers to argue for the national implementation of mandatory trial registration and results reporting, and should stimulate international organizations such as the WHO and the Pan American Health Organization to continue with the development of a coherent international system of research transparency. It should also inspire civil society to assist with the development of further tools to promote the transparency and the reliability of medical research. Civil society plays a crucial role in this context. Considering the serious problems associated with the design, conduct, and especially reporting of industry-controlled clinical research, as well as the limits of regulatory control, immediate steps must be taken to safeguard the reliability of this crucial component of evidence-informed health care decision making. Clinical trials registration and results reporting are crucial pillars of health information governance. A meaningful realization of the right to health is only possible if health care decisions can build on well-governed and publicly accountable health information systems.

15

THE NEW GLOBAL FRAMEWORK FOR PANDEMIC INFLUENZA VIRUS- AND VACCINE-SHARING

*Robert Gatter**

Introduction

In May 2011, the World Health Assembly (WHA) approved the "Pandemic Influenza Preparedness Framework for the Sharing of Influenza Viruses and Access to Vaccines and Other Benefits."[1] The Framework identifies international norms with respect to sharing novel influenza viruses with pandemic potential as well as sharing pandemic vaccines developed from those viruses. It is the result of negotiations organized by the World Health Organization (WHO) over a four-year period starting in 2007 among representatives of developing and wealthy nations as well as representatives of pharmaceutical companies that manufacture influenza vaccines or antiviral medications.[2]

Under the Framework, WHO member states are to provide novel animal and human influenza virus samples to laboratories operating as part of the WHO's Global Influenza Surveillance and Response System (GISRS) and to further agree that the WHO may provide those samples to others, including pharmaceutical manufacturers.[3] In return,

---

* Professor of Law and Co-Director of the Center for Health Law Studies, Saint Louis University School of Law.

[1] *See* Rep. of the Open-Ended Working Group of Member States on Pandemic Influenza Preparedness: Sharing of Influenza Viruses and Access to Vaccines and Other Benefits, WHO, 64th Sess., May 5, 2011, WHO Doc. A64/8 (2011).

[2] *See* David P. Fidler & Lawrence O. Gostin, *The WHO Pandemic Influenza Preparedness Framework: A Milestone in Global Governance for Health*, 306 JAMA 200 (2011); Catherine Saez, *WHO Group Strikes Landmark Deal on Global Framework for Flu Pandemics*, INTELL. PROP. WATCH, Apr. 18, 2011, http://www.ip-watch.org/weblog/2011/04/18/who-group-strikes-landmark-deal-on-global-framework-for-flu-pandemics/.

[3] *See* World Health Organization, *supra* note 1, at para. 5.1.1.

pharmaceutical companies receiving virus samples through GISRS must commit contractually to some minimal benefit-sharing, and they also are asked to go beyond that contractual commitment to provide the WHO and developing nations with greater access to, among other things, pandemic influenza vaccines, antiviral medications, and intellectual property necessary to develop those vaccines and medications.[4] Additionally, pharmaceutical companies agree to fund 50 percent of the operating costs of GISRS. The WHO may use these funds for any number of purposes, including purchasing pandemic vaccine that the WHO can then distribute as needed to developing nations during a pandemic and assisting in the development of surveillance capacity in developing nations.[5]

This chapter provides an overview of the Framework. It explains the dispute that arose in 2007 between developing and wealthy nations related to influenza virus- and vaccine-sharing, and it describes the negotiations that resolved that dispute and led to the Framework. It also reviews the elements of the Framework, focusing especially on the form contract it endorsed as the legal mechanism through which to enforce the sharing of vaccines and other benefits. Finally, this chapter analyzes the pros and cons of the Framework, concluding that it stabilizes the GISRS and therefore is a major contribution to pandemic influenza preparedness.

I. The Dispute and Negotiations

The Framework adopted by the WHA in 2011 is the result of a mediated negotiation to resolve a dispute between developing and wealthy nations that came to a head in 2007 when Indonesia took the dramatic step of refusing to submit samples of human influenza collected within its borders to the network of laboratories within GISRS.[6] This network is the world's primary system for identifying influenza viruses with pandemic potential and recommending to pharmaceutical manufacturers the content of a vaccine to combat that virus.[7] Without the cooperation of member states in sharing influenza samples, GISRS cannot fulfill its vital role in the prevention of pandemic influenza. To make matters worse, Indonesia is an international hot spot for novel influenza, having experienced 179 human infections with avian influenza that resulted in 147 deaths from 2003 through mid-October 2011.[8] Thus, Indonesia's refusal to share its influenza samples was a serious threat to global health.

---

[4] *See id.* at para. 6.

[5] *See id.* at para. 6.14.

[6] *See* David P. Fidler, *Negotiating Equitable Access to Influenza Vaccines*, 7(5) PLoS MED. e1000247 (2010), http://www.plosmedicine.org/article/info:doi/10.1371/journal.pmed.1000247; Simone Vezzani, *Preliminary Remarks on Envisaged WHO Pandemic Influenza Preparedness Framework*, 13 J. WORLD INTELL. PROP. 675 (2010); *see also* Endang R. Sedyaningsih et al., *Towards Mutual Trust, Transparency and Equity in Virus Sharing Mechanism: The Avian Influenza Case of Indonesia*, 37 ANNALS ACAD. MED. SING. 482 (2008).

[7] *See* World Health Organization, WHO Global Influenza Surveillance and Response System, http://www.who.int/influenza/gisrs_laboratory/en/ (last visited Mar. 6, 2012).

[8] *See* World Health Organization, Cumulative Number of Confirmed Human Cases for Avian Influenza A(H5N1) Reported to WHO, 2003–2012, http://www.who.int/influenza/human_animal_interface/EN_GIP_20120810CumulativeNumberH5N1cases.pdf,NumberH5N1cases.pdf (last visited Mar. 6, 2012).

Indonesia withheld its virus samples to protest the inequities it experienced in the distribution of vaccine developed through GISRS.[9] In 2005, Indonesia had shared avian influenza samples with a GISRS laboratory; later, the country discovered that its samples had been used by that laboratory—and a private pharmaceutical manufacturer to which the WHO laboratory had transferred the samples—to create a vaccine. (Transferring influenza virus samples from public health laboratories to private drug manufacturers had been and continues to be standard practice.[10] Private manufacturers develop nearly all of the world's supply of influenza vaccine, and the virus samples are an essential raw material in that process.[11]) The vaccine developed from Indonesia's 2005 virus samples was patented by the manufacturer and sold primarily to wealthy countries at a price that made it inaccessible to most Indonesians.[12] This despite Indonesia's cooperation in submitting its virus samples to GISRS and despite its being among the countries hardest hit by the 2005 avian flu.[13]

Although no other developing nation has refused to share its influenza samples with GISRS, several made public statements in support of Indonesia's action,[14] likely because Indonesia's experience was not an isolated one. There are several instances, for example, in which private entities have profited by securing patent rights over influenza gene sequences based on samples provided at no cost to GISRS by developing countries.[15] Not only are these nations cut out of any share of patent profits, but, more important, they must also pay market prices to access vaccines developed from those gene sequences, even during a public health emergency, and they must compete with wealthy nations in doing so.

Tensions eased somewhat in 2007 when the WHO agreed to lead intergovernmental meetings to negotiate the sharing of benefits associated with participation in GISRS, including, in particular, the benefit of timely access to pandemic vaccines developed through that system.[16] In response to the announced negotiations, Indonesia began sharing at least some influenza samples with GISRS later in 2007,[17] and it has shared all of its samples through a different network than GISRS.[18] Most notably, the Director

---

[9]   *See* Rachel Irwin, Indonesia, H5N1, and Global Health Diplomacy, 3 GLOBAL HEALTH GOVERNANCE (No. 2) (Spring 2010), http://www.ghgj.org; Fidler, *supra* note 6; Vezzani, *supra* note 6.

[10] See Testimony on Influenza Vaccine Supply Before the H. Comm. on Energy and Com., 109th Cong. (2005) (statement of Jesse L. Goodman, Dir. of the Ctr. for Biologics, Evaluation and Res.), http://www.fda.gov/NewsEvents/Testimony/ucm161669.htm; Dennis O'Mara, Keiji Fukuda & James A. Singleton, Influenza Vaccine: Ensuring Timely and Adequate Supplies, MEDSCAPE NEWS (Feb. 2, 2004), http://www.medscape.com/viewarticle/465438_2.

[11] *See Testimony on Influenza Vaccine Supply*, *supra* note 10; O'Mara et al., *supra* note 10; *see also* CDC, Questions and Answers: Seasonal Flu Vaccine, http://www.cdc.gov/flu/about/qa/fluvaccine.htm#dhhs-role (last visited Mar. 6, 2012).

[12] *See* Irwin, *supra* note 9; Vezzani, *supra* note 6.

[13] See Irwin, *supra* note 9; Vezzani, *supra* note 6.

[14] *See* Fidler, *supra* note 6.

[15] *See* Vezzani, *supra* note 6.

[16] *See* Fidler, *supra* note 6; Irwin, *supra* note 9.

[17] *See* Fidler, *supra* note 6.

[18] *See* Irwin, *supra* note 9.

of the WHO's Initiative for Vaccine Research confirmed during the recent H1N1 pandemic that Indonesia shared its H1N1 samples with the WHO.[19] Yet, the country continues at times to withhold samples.[20]

The WHO-led intergovernmental negotiations were especially contentious over the critical question of whether to require pandemic influenza vaccine–sharing as a condition of GISRS participation. Developing nations argued that those donating influenza samples to GISRS are entitled in return to share equitably in the benefits—and in particular any vaccine—derived from GISRS' work, and they claim that member states are further entitled to withhold their samples from GISRS if fair access to vaccine is not guaranteed.[21] Meanwhile, wealthy nations countered that there are many benefits linked to GISRS participation, of which access to novel influenza vaccine is only one, and that equity requires only that member states share generally in the benefits derived from GISRS. At that point, wealthy nations endorsed voluntary, but not mandatory, vaccine-sharing.[22] They also claimed that member states were required to share virus samples with WHO.[23]

International law did not—and still does not—resolve the dispute. On the one hand, the 2005 International Health Regulations (IHR) can be interpreted to support the position espoused by wealthy nations. IHR requires member states to report to the WHO all "events which may constitute a public health emergency of international concern within its territory" and to provide the WHO with "public health information" about such events.[24] Additionally, IHR instructs state officials to identify such an event using a decision aid adopted as part of IHR, an aid that specifically identifies the detection of a human influenza case caused by a new viral subtype as a reportable event.[25] Thus, one viable interpretation of IHR is that all member states are obligated to share samples of novel human influenza with the WHO via GISRS because those samples constitute public health information about a potential international public health emergency.[26] Moreover, the obligation of member states to report events and share public health information is not conditioned, under IHR, on a guarantee of access to GISRS benefits.

On the other hand, there are several reasons member states might retain the right to withhold influenza samples despite the current IHR. For one thing, IHR specifically recognizes the sovereign right of each member state to adopt its own domestic health policy.[27] Additionally, WHO statements have distinguished between "biological

---

[19] *See* Martin Enserink, *The Challenge of Getting Swine Flu Vaccine to Poor Nations*, SCIENCE (Nov. 3, 2009), http://news.sciencemag.org/scienceinsider/2009/11/the-challenge-o.html.

[20] *See* Irwin, *supra* note 9.

[21] *See* Fidler, *supra* note 6.

[22] *See id.*

[23] *See* Vezzani, *supra* note 6.

[24] World Health Organization, Int'l Health Regs. art. 6, 2005.

[25] *See id.* at annex 2.

[26] *See* David P. Fidler, *Influenza Samples, International Law, and Global Health Diplomacy*, 14(1) EMERGING INFECTIOUS DISEASES (Jan. 2008), http://www.cdc.gov/EID/content/14/1/88.htm.

[27] *See* World Health Organization, *supra* note 24, at art. 3, para. 4.

samples" and "public health information" in the past, suggesting that a nation's duty to share public health information does not include a duty to share influenza samples.[28] Finally, and most important, the current IHR must be read in conjunction with the international Convention on Biological Diversity (CBD); the CBD recognizes a virus discovered in a nation's territory as the "genetic resource" of that nation, which cannot be shared or used without that nation's consent.[29] In late 2010, CBD was amended to address, among other things, genetic resource–sharing and benefit-sharing in the special context of a potential public health emergency. The amended CBD instructs each nation to account for the value of its genetic resources to others during an international health emergency when that nation is regulating international access to its genetic resources.[30] Yet, it also authorizes nations to consider whether there will be "expeditious, fair and equitable sharing of benefits arising out of the use of such genetic resources, including access to affordable treatments by those in need, especially in developing countries."[31] This authorization appears to permit a developing nation to withhold samples of a novel influenza virus identified in its territory if, after considering the importance of those samples to the WHO and the global effort to prepare for a potential pandemic, the nation determines that it or other developing nations lack sufficient access to pandemic vaccine to justify international sharing of a virus sample.

Given the uncertainty of international law, the WHO-led intergovernmental negotiations over influenza virus and vaccine–sharing were vitally important. They represented a way to reach a stable solution to the ongoing dispute.

Throughout the four years of negotiations, the parties agreed that all nations and pharmaceutical companies should share virus samples with the WHO through GISRS as well as the benefits derived from the work of GISRS, especially in the case of an influenza pandemic; the dispute was over whether and, if so, when such sharing is mandatory.[32] Over time, the negotiations resulted in a "commitment" of member states to share virus samples and GISRS benefits "on an equal footing."[33] Additionally, negotiations increasingly focused on two broad categories of benefit-sharing: what I refer to here as "medical benefits" and "vaccine production benefits."

Negotiations over sharing medical benefits concerned access by developing nations to the means of diagnosing and treating novel influenza during a pandemic. In return for permitting GISRS to transfer shared virus samples to pharmaceutical companies,

---

[28] *See* Fidler, *supra* note 26.

[29] *See* United Nations Convention on Biological Diversity art. 15, par. 5, 1992, *available at* http://www.cbd.int/convention/text/.

[30] *See* United Nations Nagoya Protocol on Access to Genetic Resources and the Fair and Equitable Sharing of Benefits Arising from Their Utilization to the Convention on Biological Diversity, art. 6 (2011), *available at* http://www.cbd.int/abs/doc/protocol/nagoya-protocol-en.pdf.

[31] *Id.* at art. 8(b).

[32] *See* Kaitlin Mara, *Last-Minute Progress Made on Pandemic Flu: More Still to Come*, INTELL. PROP. WATCH (Dec. 15, 2008), http://www.ip-watch.org/weblog/2008/12/15/last-minute-progress-made-on-pandemic-flu-though-more-still-to-come/.

[33] *See id.* This language was retained in the Framework as approved by the WHA in May 2011. *See* World Health Organization, *supra* note 1, at art. 1, para. "PP3."

developing nations sought guaranteed access to "benefits" such as pandemic vaccines developed from those samples as well as access to antiviral medications and diagnostic kits.[34] These negotiations were driven by the need during an influenza pandemic to aid nations that do not have the means to either produce their own vaccine or purchase vaccine internationally.

Meanwhile, negotiations over vaccine production benefits concerned intellectual property rights for pharmaceutical companies and new vaccine production capabilities for developing nations. As a condition of a pharmaceutical company's acquiring intellectual property rights in a virus isolate, gene sequence, or medication developed from a virus transferred to that company by GISRS, developing nations sought royalty-free access to such intellectual property as well as vaccine production know-how.[35] In this way, developing nations sought the means to free themselves at some future point from dependence on pharmaceutical companies in wealthy nations for medical benefits during a pandemic.

Wealthy nations and pharmaceutical companies did not dispute that shared "benefits" includes both medical benefits and vaccine production benefits. They did, however, disagree that benefit-sharing be mandatory or linked to intellectual property rights.[36] And these disagreements defined a stalemate that persisted among the parties for several years.[37]

The 2009 H1N1 pandemic proved to be a pivotal event in breaking through this stalemate by plainly confirming the inequity of global pandemic vaccine distribution. First, wealthy nations controlled virtually all of the world's supply of H1N1 vaccine even before it was manufactured. They had entered into massive preproduction purchasing agreements with vaccine developers, leaving little if any opportunity for other nations to purchase vaccine directly from a manufacturer.[38] Second, the H1N1 pandemic demonstrated that the stated intentions of many wealthy nations to donate some of their influenza vaccine supplies are unreliable. The United States, for example, was reluctant to donate or even sell *any* of its expected supply of vaccine despite having made a commitment to the international community to share 10 percent of its supply with poorer nations.[39] As it happened, the United States completely disregarded that

34 *See* Report of the Open-Ended Working Group of Member States on Pandemic Influenza Preparedness: Sharing of Influenza Viruses and Access to Vaccines and Other Benefits, WHO, 63rd Sess., May 14, 2010, WHO Doc. A63/48, annex 2 (2010) (containing three different proposed terms for virus-transfer agreements, each of which address benefits in the form of vaccines, antiviral medications, and diagnostic kits as well as benefits in the form of intellectual property rights and know-how for the independent production of pandemic vaccines).

35 *See id.*

36 *See id.*

37 *See* Fidler, *supra* note 6.

38 John M. Barry, *The Next Pandemic*, 27 WORLD POL'Y J. 10 (2010); Chan Chee Khoon, Conference Paper, Equitable Access to Pandemic Flu Vaccines, WHO CONFERENCE ON STRENGTHENING HEALTH AND NON-HEALTH RESPONSE SYSTEMS IN ASIA (Mar. 18–19, 2010), http://www.twnside.org.sg/title2/health.info/2010/health20100303.htm.

39 Chris Neefus, *Sebelius Says U.S. Will Donate Part of H1N1 Vaccine Supply to Foreign Nations before Meeting This Nation's Demand*, CNSNews (Oct. 21, 2009), http://www.cnsnews.com/node/55907.

commitment out of concern that it would not have a sufficient supply to serve all of its at-risk citizens first, a concern that only heightened when production of the vaccine was delayed.[40]

Indeed, the game-changing effect of the H1N1 pandemic is reflected in the 2010 report of the WHO's intergovernmental working group. This was the earliest report on the negotiations following the pandemic, and it reflected an important concession by wealthy nations. Remarkably, countries in the WHO's European Region proposed that pharmaceutical companies receiving virus samples through a GISRS laboratory be required to participate in benefit-sharing, at least to a minimal degree.[41] This proposal is the first instance in which a group of wealthy nations departed from their position that benefit-sharing should be purely voluntary.

It seems likely that the H1N1 pandemic also played a key role in the WHO's selection of Juan José Gomez Camacho, Mexican Ambassador to the United Nations (UN), to cochair the working group that led the intergovernmental negotiations on virus- and benefit-sharing in June 2010.[42] The first human infections with H1N1 in 2009 occurred in Mexico, and the Mexican government was quick to report the novel influenza outbreak and provide virus samples to GISRS.[43] Yet, despite its cooperation and its ability to pay for medications, Mexico was unable to acquire the pandemic vaccine until January 2010, close to ten months after identifying the first infection.[44] The glaring inequity of Mexico's experience undoubtedly provided its ambassador to the UN with the moral authority to extract concessions from pharmaceutical companies as well as representatives of developing and wealthy nations in order to craft the Framework that was adopted by the WHA in May 2011.

II. Core Features of the Framework

The central principle of the Framework is that member states commit to sharing both influenza virus samples and the benefits of participation in GISRS "on an equal footing."[45] It implements this principle through a combination of aspirations, incentives, and requirements.

---

[40] *See* Fidler, *supra* note 6.

[41] *See* World Health Organization, *supra* note 24, annex 2, white paper 4.

[42] *See* Bente Molenaar, *Continued Negotiations to Finalize the Pandemic Influenza Preparedness Framework*, 1 HEALTH DIPL. MONITOR 14 (June 2010).

[43] *See* World Health Organization, Influenza-Like Illness in the United States and Mexico, Global Alert and Response Update (Apr. 29, 2009), http://www.who.int/csr/don/2009_04_24/en/index.html; Kaitlin Mara, *WHO Flu Misconduct Debate Polarising as Independent Review Advances*, INTELL. PROP. WATCH (July 7, 2010), http://www.ip-watch.org/2010/07/07/who-flu-misconduct-debate-polarisin g-as-independent-review-advances/, (reporting that Mexico shared its virus samples internationally).

[44] *See* Public Health Agency of Canada, Canada to Bridge Mexico's H1N1 Flu Vaccine Requirements, News Release (Jan. 6, 2010), http://www.phac-aspc.gc.ca/media/nr-rp/2010/2010_0106-eng.php; *see also* Mara, *supra* note 32.

[45] World Health Organization, *supra* note 24.

As for aspirations, member states are encouraged, but not required, under the Framework to share with GISRS laboratories samples of influenza viruses identified within their borders and to do so in a timely manner.[46] To account for the requirement in the recently amended CBD that the genetic resources of a member state be used only with the consent of that state, the Framework declares that, by providing a virus sample to a GISRS laboratory, a member state necessarily consents to the onward transfer of the virus within the WHO network of laboratories and to entities outside of the WHO, including pharmaceutical companies.[47] This authorizes GISRS laboratories to provide donated virus samples to pharmaceutical manufacturers that, in turn, use those samples to produce vaccines.

Additionally, there is an incentive for countries to submit their influenza viruses to GISRS. The Framework requires that the WHO and its laboratories complete a Standard Material Transfer Agreement (SMTA) as a condition of transferring a donated virus or its components to a pharmaceutical company for use in developing a vaccine or other medication.[48] The SMTA, in turn, imposes a contractual obligation on the recipient of the virus to participate in benefit-sharing, at least to a minimal degree. Specifically, the form contract requires a recipient that manufactures influenza vaccines or antiviral medications to commit to at least two of the following six options:

Donate 5–20 percent of pandemic vaccine production to the WHO;

Reserve 5–20 percent of pandemic vaccine production for sale to the WHO at affordable prices;

Donate a specified number of treatment courses of anti-viral medications to the WHO;

Reserve a specified number of treatment courses of anti-viral medications for sale to the WHO at affordable prices;

License manufacturers in developing countries at affordable rates intellectual property rights the recipient owns for the production of influenza vaccines, adjuvants, anti-viral medications, and/or diagnostics;

Grant royalty-free licenses to manufacturers in developing countries or grant to the WHO royalty-free, non-exclusive licenses for intellectual property, which can be sub-licensed by the WHO to manufacturers in developing countries, for the production of influenza vaccines, adjuvants, anti-viral medications, and diagnostics needed in a pandemic.[49]

Companies that receive virus samples from the WHO or its laboratories and that do not manufacture either influenza vaccines or antiviral medications are obligated under

---

[46] *See* World Health Organization, *supra* note 1, at para. 5.1.1.

[47] *See id.* at para. 5.1.2.

[48] *See id.* at para. 5.4.2. A different SMTA must also be used for transfers of viral material among laboratories within GISRS, and that SMTA prohibits the recipient from acquiring any intellectual property rights in the transferred material. *See id.* at para. 5.4.1 and annex 1.

[49] *See id.* at annex 2, para. 4.1.1.

the SMTA to commit either to one of the licensing benefits described above or to one of the following:

Donate to the WHO a specified number of diagnostic kits needed for
pandemics;

Reserve for sale to the WHO at affordable prices a specific quantity of diagnostic kits needed for pandemics;

Coordinate with the WHO to support the strengthening of influenza laboratory
and surveillance capacity in developing countries;

Coordinate with the WHO to support the transfer of technology, know-how,
and/or processes for pandemic influenza preparedness and response in developing countries.[50]

In this way, the SMTA is a vehicle through which the Framework imposes benefit-sharing on pharmaceutical companies while still respecting intellectual property rights and incentivizing developing countries to provide their virus samples to GISRS. In short, by providing virus samples to GISRS, a developing nation triggers the use of SMTA under the Framework and thereby guarantees some minimal benefit-sharing, a guarantee that is contractually enforceable.

The Framework not only requires direct benefit-sharing by pharmaceutical companies that receive virus samples through the WHO, it also obligates those companies to fund each year half of the cost of operating GISRS.[51] The WHO estimates the total annual cost of operating GISRS to be $56.5 million.[52] This annual contribution by the pharmaceutical industry will be used to improve pandemic preparedness by "conducting disease burden studies, strengthening laboratory and surveillance capacity, [and improving] access and effective deployment of pandemic vaccines and anti[-]viral medicines."[53] In particular, the Framework authorizes the WHO in consultation with an Advisory Group to use this funding to, among other things, purchase as many as 150 million doses of pandemic vaccine that the WHO will distribute to affected and developing nations dur-ing a pandemic.[54] Thus, the financial obligation on pharmaceutical companies working with GISRS indirectly imposes an additional benefit-sharing requirement.

The Framework also provides for the creation of an eighteen-member Advisory Group with representatives from each of the WHO's regions, balanced between devel-oped and developing nations, and including experts in public health and influenza.[55] The group will advise the WHO in the determination of the amount that each phar-maceutical company must contribute annually toward the operation of GISRS and of spending priorities for those funds. Additionally, the group will assist the WHO in

---

50 *See id.*
51 *See id.* at para. 6.14.3.
52 *See id.*
53 *Id.* at para. 6.14.4.
54 *See id.* at para. 6.9.5.
55 *See id.* at Art. 7.

monitoring the implementation of the Framework generally, which includes making a biennial report to the WHO's Director-General.[56] This Advisory Group appears to be different from the experts who will assess the public health needs and resources of various countries so that the WHO can determine how to best distribute the benefits during a pandemic.[57]

Moreover, the Framework requires that the WHO implement a mechanism for electronically tracing influenza virus samples shared with GISRS.[58] This will allow stakeholders to track samples as they are transferred inside and outside of the WHO.

Finally, the Framework provides for its own review and revision. The WHO must organize a review of the Framework in 2016 so as to propose any needed revisions to the WHA in 2017.[59]

III. Pros and Cons of the Framework

The Framework is a major contribution toward global preparedness for an influenza pandemic. Its benefit-sharing system resolves at least some of the inequities that result from relying on private manufacturers to develop and distribute scarce vaccine and antiviral medication during a pandemic. In so doing, it helps assure that developing nations will continue to share novel influenza virus samples they discover within their borders. Thus, the Framework will help stabilize GISRS.

This contribution is particularly important in the short-run given the WHO's push pursuant to the Global Action Plan to expand influenza vaccine production capacity.[60] Although the world community is well behind on its goal of having the capability by 2016 to produce nearly seven billion doses within six months of an outbreak,[61] it is making substantial progress. By 2015, eleven new vaccine manufacturing plants will be operational in eleven low- or middle-income nations.[62] Annual global vaccine production capacity at that time will increase to 1.7 billion doses.[63] By increasing the global supply of influenza vaccine during a pandemic, and by locating new portions of that supply in developing nations, the Global Action Plan will slowly ease the dependence of developing nations on wealthy nations to share an extraordinarily scarce supply of vaccine. As vaccine technology is improved and production capacity continues to expand beyond that which is scheduled for 2015, that dependence is likely to be eased

---

[56] *See id.*

[57] *See id.* at para. 6.1.2(iii).

[58] *See id.* at para. 5.3.

[59] *See id.* at para. 7.4.2.

[60] *See* World Health Organization, *Global Pandemic Influenza Action Plan to Increase Vaccine Supply*, WHO Doc. 06.13 (2006).

[61] *See id.*

[62] *See* Catherine Saez, *WHO Enters Phase of Global Plan to Increase Flu Vaccine Production*, Intell. Prop. Watch (July 14, 2011), http://www.ip-watch.org/2011/07/14/who-enters-next-phase-of-global-plan-to-increase-flu-vaccine-production/.

[63] *See id.*

even further. Thus, in the short-run, the Framework is uniquely important as a bridge, addressing some of today's inequities that arise from extreme vaccine scarcity while allowing the world community to reduce the likelihood of those inequities in the long-run by increasing vaccine supply.

Yet the Framework is not a magic bullet, not even in the short-run. Although significant, the level of benefit-sharing it requires of pharmaceutical companies remains modest. The SMTA provides a variety of benefit-sharing options for manufacturers receiving virus samples through GISRS, and so there is no guarantee that companies will choose to share pandemic vaccine or antiviral medications. Likewise, although it is a marked improvement that the WHO will have external funding to create a stockpile of 150 million doses of pandemic vaccine, such a small supply would make only a minute difference in developing countries during a particularly virulent pandemic. In short, the Framework addresses only the worst of the inequities that drove Indonesia to withhold its virus samples in 2007, the ones on glaring display during the 2009 H1N1 pandemic. Because of the Framework, developing nations will have some access to vaccines and other medications during the next pandemic, but not the degree of access enjoyed by wealthy nations.

Some may also be concerned that the Framework does not require virus-sharing by member states and instead only pronounces that member states "should" provide GISRS laboratories with influenza viruses they discover within their borders.[64] Although the WHO has the authority to adopt binding international law,[65] it likely made a prudent decision not to exercise that authority, but instead to balance aspirations, incentives, and requirements in the Framework as it did. This approach reflects the political context in which the WHO was operating in 2007 and continues to operate today. Governments of developing nations must find a way to protect their citizens during a pandemic. In the absence of access to vaccine or antiviral medication, at least one such nation—Indonesia—withheld its influenza samples as leverage to gain access to needed medicine, and it received public statements of support from other developing nations. Moreover, it appears that the WHO's promise to lead intergovernmental negotiations over benefit-sharing was instrumental in causing Indonesia to begin sharing its virus samples again. Had the WHO merely adopted a regulation declaring that member states must submit virus samples to GISRS, it is quite possible, if not probable, that Indonesia and perhaps other nations would have refused to share virus samples as a form of protest and self-preservation. Additionally, a diplomatic approach was prudent because the WHO has only limited legal authority over the pharmaceutical companies on which the global community depends to develop influenza vaccine during a pandemic. Accordingly, the only real choice was to pursue a negotiated resolution.

Furthermore, the Framework is not purely aspirational. As described above, it creates an incentive for developing nations to share their influenza viruses with GISRS

---

[64] *See, e.g.*, Fidler & Gostin, *supra* note 2.

[65] See World Health Organization, Constitution of the World Health Organization art. 21, 2005, http://www.who.int/governance/eb/who_constitution_en.pdf.

so as to trigger the obligation of the WHO to use the SMTA as the exclusive vehicle for transferring donated virus samples to private vaccine manufacturers. The SMTA, in turn, imposes legally enforceable benefit-sharing obligations on those manufacturers. Additionally, recall that the Framework obligates pharmaceutical companies to make an annual financial contribution that WHO may use to acquire pandemic vaccine or to provide other benefits to developing nations.

Nonetheless, there is reason to criticize the Framework for failing to impose any requirements on wealthy nations.[66] Unlike pharmaceutical manufacturers under the Framework, wealthy member states are simply encouraged to "contribute" to the pandemic influenza benefit-sharing system by, for example, donating vaccines or antiviral medication, providing information from pandemic surveillance, or helping nations develop their own surveillance and vaccine production capacity.[67] The 2009 H1N1 pandemic clearly established that wealthy countries will delay fulfilling, if not break altogether, promises to donate pandemic vaccine to developing nations. Consequently, it seems particularly egregious that the WHO did not obtain an agreement from its wealthiest member states that those nations would make enforceable benefit-sharing commitments. Although representatives of those nations might have argued that it would be politically irresponsible of them to commit to giving away scarce, lifesaving vaccine during a pandemic, the WHO could have pursued other benefit-sharing commitments. For example, it could have sought regular financial donations from wealthy member states to a WHO fund that would be used to purchase pandemic vaccines on behalf of developing nations.

Another point of critical concern is that the Framework is vulnerable to inappropriate influence by the pharmaceutical industry, as revealed in the Framework's governance provisions. The implementation of the Framework is overseen by the WHA and Director-General based, at least in part, on the reports, assessments, and recommendations of an expert Advisory Group.[68] The Advisory Group's charge is to assess and make reports and recommendations to the Director-General and the WHA with respect to every aspect of the Framework, including the extent and timeliness of virus-sharing, the use of financial and nonfinancial contributions, and the fairness and equity of benefit-sharing.[69] Although WHO regulations applicable to expert panels would likely preclude a member of the pharmaceutical industry from serving in the Advisory Group,[70] the Framework nonetheless permits the Advisory Group to consult with industry members when carrying out its work.[71] Thus, the Advisory Group is a potential conduit through which pharmaceutical industry interests could unduly influence policy with respect to virus- and benefit-sharing.

---

[66] *See* Fidler & Gostin, *supra* note 2.

[67] *See* World Health Organization, *supra* note 1, at para. 6.1.1.

[68] *See id.* at art. 7 and annex 3.

[69] *See id.* at annex 3, sec. 2.

[70] *See* World Health Organization, Regulations for Expert Advisory Panels and Committees, at para. 4.6 (requiring panelists to disclose potential conflicts of interest), http://apps.who.int/gb/bd/PDF/bd47/ EN/regu-for-expert-en.pdf.

[71] *See* World Health Organization, *supra* note 1, at annex 3, para. 1.2.

Whether or not this potential is ever realized, the WHO has created the appearance of impropriety. First, beginning in 2012, the pharmaceutical industry will be contributing upward of $28 million annually to WHO for the operation of GISRS. This, along with the fact that the industry depends on GISRS to provide it with virus samples as raw material for the development of vaccines and antiviral medications, creates a powerful incentive for industry to exercise what influence it has over GISRS operations. Second, the WHO is vulnerable to such industry influence because it is experiencing a budget crisis of its own. The WHO finances its operation primarily through the donations of its member states. In 2011, contributions by member states dropped, and, as a result, the UN agency fell $300 million short of meeting its budgeted spending.[72] Moreover, the WHA approved a WHO budget for 2012 that is 20 percent (nearly $1 billion) less than WHO officials had proposed, forcing the agency to cut, among other things, three hundred administrative jobs.[73] Consequently, the WHO is becoming more dependent on the funds provided by industry.[74] Third, the public image of the WHO was dealt a severe blow over similar conflict-of-interest allegations in 2010. Evidence exists suggesting that scientists on a WHO influenza advisory panel had financial relationships with pharmaceutical companies that stood to benefit if the H1N1 outbreak was declared a "pandemic."[75] Moreover, those scientists were working under the influence of those financial ties at the time they advised the WHO and other governments with respect to the H1N1 pandemic.[76] Thus, although there is never a good time for a major public health organization to create the appearance of a conflict of interest, this seems like a particularly bad time for the WHO to have done so in the Framework. Under the circumstances, the WHO should screen the members of the Advisory Group very carefully to rule out members with ties to the pharmaceutical industry, it should publicize the names and qualifications of each member of the Advisory Group, and the Advisory Group should scrupulously avoid private consultations with industry.

Finally, the Framework can be criticized for continuing to rely on private contract law—even in this more regulated form—as the means for achieving the public good of pursuing equitable access to novel influenza virus strains and the pandemic medications created from them. For one, there is no guarantee that these individual contracts will, in the aggregate, result in affordable access by developing nations to vaccine in the event of a pandemic. Instead, we may find that manufacturers typically avoid the contractual option of providing free or low-cost access to those vaccines.

---

[72] *See* Stephanie Nebehay & Barbara Lewis, *WHO Slashes Budget, Jobs in New Era of Austerity*, REUTERS NEWS (May 19, 2011), http://www.reuters.com/article/2011/05/19/us-who-idUSTRE74I5I320110519; *see also* Catherine Saez & William New, *WHO Future in Question; Debate over Industry Representation*, INTELL. PROP. WATCH (Jan. 17, 2011), http://www.ip-watch.org/2011/01/17/who-future-in-question-debate-over-industry-representation/.

[73] *See* Nebehay & Lewis, *supra* note 72.

[74] *See id.*

[75] See Deborah Cohen & Philip Carter, *WHO and the Pandemic Flu "Conspiracies"*, 340 BRIT. MED. J. 2912 (2010), http://www.bmj.com/content/340/bmj.c2912.full.

[76] *See id.*

Additionally, private ordering in this context burdens developing nations to enforce that contract if it is breached by a manufacturer during a pandemic, which is unlikely to result in a meaningful remedy given the speed with which a pandemic influenza might spread around the world and the time it would take to pursue contract enforcement. Moreover, the Framework's reliance on contract suggests that the WHO lacks the political legitimacy to impose public rules and thus it is settling for a less-intrusive form of regulation. Whether this perception occurs will likely turn on the force with which the WHO aids developing nations with enforcing benefit-sharing contracts, or the willingness of the WHO to impose public regulations should these benefit-sharing contracts prove to be inadequate.

Conclusion

Despite its shortcomings, the Framework is a major achievement in pandemic influenza preparedness. The negotiations leading to the Framework and the Framework itself appear to have appeased developing nations and secured their commitment to virus-sharing, at least in the short-run. In the long-run, however, the reliability of GISRS to identify novel influenza virus strains with pandemic potential and to trigger the development of a vaccine will depend on substantially increasing vaccine production capacity in developing nations. And, in the interim between the short-run and the long-run, the success of GISRS will depend on the WHO's commitment to use the new Framework to benefit developing nations in the ongoing effort to prepare the world for an influenza pandemic.

This state of experiment-as-health care...consti-
tutes an unsettled legal frontier...Auditing and
oversight must be coupled with innovative legal
strategies that would make pharmaceutical companies responsible...

[Petryna, *When Experiments Travel*][1]

16

OFFSHORING EXPERIMENTS, OUTSOURCING PUBLIC HEALTH

Corporate Accountability and State Responsibility for Violating the

International Prohibition on Nonconsensual Human Experimentation

*Bethany Spielman**

I. Pfizer's Trovan Experiment

In March 1996, an epidemic of bacterial meningitis broke out in the state of Kano, Nigeria. The timing could not have been more disastrous: Kano was already dealing with dual epidemics of measles and cholera. Médecins Sans Frontières (MSF), also known as Doctors Without Borders, arrived in Kano shortly after the initial meningitis outbreak to provide medical aid. MSF began to treat the victims at Kano's state-owned Infectious Disease Hospital with the intravenous form of ceftriaxone, the World Health Organization–endorsed generic antibiotic for bacterial meningitis in low-income countries. Within several weeks, Pfizer drew up a plan to test an oral form of an antibiotic called Trovan on infected children at the Kano clinic. At the time, Pfizer was seeking to gain FDA approval for Trovan's use on children. Pfizer researchers selected 200 sick children, aged one to thirteen, from lines of those awaiting treatment and redirected them to the experiment. Other patients were directed to the MSF area. Pfizer divided the subjects into two groups, treating half with Trovan and half with a lower-than-recommended dose of the standard treatment. Five children who received Trovan and six children to whom Pfizer administered the low dose of ceftriaxone died. Others suffered blindness, deafness, and paralysis.

---

[1] ADRIANA PETRYNA, WHEN EXPERIMENTS TRAVEL: CLINICAL TRIALS AND THE GLOBAL SEARCH FOR HUMAN SUBJECTS 134, 189 (2009).

* PhD, JD, Professor, Southern Illinois University Schools of Medicine and Law.

In 2001, families of the children filed two class action lawsuits against Pfizer in the United States under the Alien Tort Statute (ATS)[2] for violating a norm of customary international law prohibiting nonconsensual medical experimentation. The ATS, a provision in the 1789 Judiciary Act, states: "The district court shall have original jurisdiction of any civil action by an alien for a tort only, committed in violation of the law of nations or a treaty of the United States."[3] The ATS permits non-U.S. citizens to bring tort actions in U.S. courts for alleged violations of the law of nations. Plaintiffs claimed that they did not know that the children were participating in an experimental drug trial. Pfizer characterized the problem as a procedural error and stated that "verbal consent was obtained." Plaintiffs also claimed that researchers failed to follow protocol as they omitted blood testing prior to administering Trovan (which could determine whether the strain of meningitis might be responsive to Trovan); failed to determine that the children in the test had meningitis, and left without following up. The two U.S. suits were consolidated.

After eight years of litigating whether U.S. courts had jurisdiction to hear the case, the U.S. Court of Appeals for the Second Circuit affirmed in *Abdullahi v. Pfizer* that the allegation of nonconsensual medical experimentation on human subjects stated a claim under the ATS for a violation of the law of nations.[4] The Second Circuit distinguished between information at the "core" of the norm, such as the fact that an experiment is occurring, which must be disclosed to subjects, and information at the "fringes" of the norm, such as the design of a placebo-controlled trial. The court also found that plaintiffs had adequately pled that Pfizer acted under color of law. Pfizer sought certiorari, asking the U.S. Supreme Court to consider two questions, one of which was framed as follows: "Whether ATS jurisdiction can extend to a private actor based on alleged state action by a foreign government where there is no allegation that the government knew of or participated in the specific acts by the private actor claimed to have violated international law."[5] The Court rejected Pfizer's request, allowing the plaintiff's claims to go to trial. The parties settled in February 2011.

Abdullahi v. Pfizer helped to underscore the problem of corporate accountability in offshored clinical trials. Ten years of legal proceedings resulted in a development that may facilitate greater legal accountability: recognition by the Second Circuit of an international law norm prohibiting nonconsensual human experimentation, enforceable under the ATS. In part because *Abdullahi* was settled at a "very early stage of proceedings,"[6] however, several important legal issues remain unresolved. These issues are critical to victims' opportunities for compensation under the ATS.

This chapter argues that a much-needed step toward enforcement of the prohibition against nonconsensual human experimentation is attending to the relationships

---

[2] Alien Tort Statute, 28 U.S.C. § 1350 (2006).

[3] *Id.*

[4] Abdullahi v. Pfizer, Inc., 562 F.3d 163 (2d Cir. 2009) (holding that allegation of nonconsensual medical experimentation on human subjects stated a claim under the ATS for a violation of the law of nations).

[5] Brief of Petitioner-Appellant at (i), Pfizer, Inc. v. Abdullahi, 130 S. Ct. 3541 (2010) (No. 09-34).

[6] Brief for the United States as Amicus Curiae at 19, *Pfizer*, 130 S. Ct. 3541.

between U.S.-based multinational corporations and the foreign states that host these companies' clinical trials. Although international clinical trials in which the fact of experimentation is not disclosed to subjects will continue, as long as courts require state responsibility in ATS cases, the odds are against actually holding multinational pharmaceutical corporations, their CEOs, or contract research organizations liable unless judges attend to two phenomena when inquiring into state responsibility: "double outsourcing" and delegations of public functions.[7]

II. The Alien Tort Statute Could Fill an Accountability Gap

Nonconsensual offshore experiments by U.S. pharmaceutical corporations have occurred since the Trovan experiment; they will persist because they are lucrative.[8] Clinical research is now a worldwide, hugely profitable, multibillion dollar "data-making enterprise."[9] The global business of clinical trials was estimated to be worth $50 billion in 2008, with an expected growth rate of 10 percent through 2018.[10] On $800–880 million invested in research in 2001, the U.S. pharmaceutical industry made a return of

---

7 Numerous ATS decisions involving nonstate defendants have required state action. *See* BETH STEPHENS ET AL., INTERNATIONAL HUMAN RIGHTS LITIGATION IN U.S. COURTS (2d ed. 2008).

8 *See* Kelly Hearn, *The Rise of Unregulated Drug Trials in South America*, THE NATION, Sept. 21, 2011, *available at* http://www.thenation.com/article/163547/rise-unregulated-drug-trials-south-america (reporting nonconsensual outsourced clinical trials in Central South America, which account for 26 percent of all subjects enrolled in foreign trials). According to Dr. V.N. Bhattathiri of the Regional Cancer Center in Thieruvananthapuram, India, the majority of the twenty-five patients at the Regional Cancer Center on whom the 1999–2000 first-in-human trials of G4N and M4N anticancer drug were conducted did not realize that the injections they received were part of an experiment, rather than part of their treatment. Madhur Singh, *Should Clinical Trials Be Outsourced?*, TIME, Aug. 7, 2008, *available at* http://www.time.com/time/health/article/0,8599,1830334,00.html; R. Krishnakumar, *Trial and Errors*, FRONTLINE, Dec. 3–16, 2005, *available at* http://www.flonnet.com/fl2225/stories/20051216005102200.htm. Only 18 percent of published trials carried out in China in 2004 reported that participants gave informed consent to research. Dalu Zhang et al., *An Assessment of the Quality of Randomised Controlled Trials Conducted in China*, TRIALS, Apr. 24, 2008, *available at* http://www.trialsjournal.com/content/9/1/22. A *St. Petersburg Times*' prizewinning series reported on human experiments in India, some of which were nonconsensual. *Times Series on Drug Testing in India Wins Award*, ST. PETERSBURG TIMES, July 15, 2009, *available at* http://www.tampabay.com/news/article1018501.ece; *see also The Latest Industry Being Outsourced to India: Clinical Drug Trials*, ST. PETERSBURG TIMES, Dec. 14, 2008, *available at* http://www.tampabay.com/news/business/article934677.ece; *see also Deaths Raise Questions in Indian Hospital*, ST. PETERSBURG TIMES, Dec. 14, 2008, *available at* http://www.tampabay.com/news/business/article934633.ece; *see also* Kris Hundley, *Testing Grounds: Drugs Are Expensive. Life Is Cheap.*, ST. PETERSBURG TIMES, Dec. 14, 2008, *available at* www.tampabay.com/specials/2008/reports/india; *see also* Sharon Lafraniere et al., *The Dilemma: Submit or Suffer*, WASH. POST, Dec. 19, 2000, at A01 (reporting numerous nonconsensual international experiments).

9 PETRYNA, *supra* note 1, at 189. One third of phase 3 trials of the twenty largest U.S. pharmaceutical companies are being conducted solely outside the United States. For those same firms and studies, a majority of study sites (13,521 of 24,206) are outside the United States. Seth W. Glickman et al., 360 NEW ENG. J. MED. 816 (2009).

10 *Global Clinical Trial Business Report and Analysis 2008–2018*, VISION GAIN (Oct. 7, 2008), http://www.visiongain.com/Report/315/Global-Clinical-Trial-Business-Report-Analysis-2008–2018.

$1–10 billion.[11] (Wall Street analysts had predicted that, had the FDA approved Trovan in its oral form, Trovan would be a $1 billion blockbuster drug.)[12] The corporate financial advantage of offshore as compared to U.S.-based trials, regardless of consent, is considerable. In 2008, a *Harvard Business Review* article reported that "by switching 50% of its trials from high-cost places such as the United States and Western Europe to low-cost places such as India and South America, a midsize pharmaceutical company with 60,000 patients in clinical trials could save $600 million annually."[13]

Pharmaceutical corporations and their agents can easily include "boilerplate" informed consent language in an experiment's written protocol so that the possibility of failing to disclose the experimental nature of the intervention appears precluded—in fact, Pfizer did this during the Trovan experiment. But actually preventing nonconsensual experimentation, especially in a different language and culture, is time-consuming and difficult.[14] It is especially difficult when cultures lack concepts such as "research," "hypothesis," and "randomization."[15]

The Second Circuit explicitly excluded from the international norm's coverage a failure to ensure understanding of placebo-controlled trial design, which it described as at the "fringes."[16] Identifying and excluding what was at the "fringe" was necessary to establish that there was, by contrast, a core sufficiently specific to meet the Supreme Court's requirement in *Sosa v. Alvarez Machain* that international norms cognizable under the ATS be "defined with specificity." But the Second Circuit's "core" v. "fringe" distinction does not correspond to a distinction between information that is relatively easy and quick to communicate, and information that is difficult and time-consuming to communicate. Communicating ideas and information at the core rather than the margins of the norm may at times be more difficult, time-consuming, and unprofitable—and as a result, it may also not be undertaken by pharmaceutical companies.

---

[11] Robert M. Califf, *Global Landscape of Medical Research* (Feb. 2011), http://www.bioethics.gov/background/ (presentation to The Presidential Commission for the Study of Bioethical Issues. Slide titled "Economic Proposition to Industry from Globalization."). *See also id.*, Mar. 1, 2011 transcript, http://www.bioethics.gov/background/.

[12] J. Stephen, *Where Profit and Lives Hang in Balance*, WASH. POST, Dec. 17, 2000, at A1.

[13] Jean-Pierre Garnier, *Rebuilding the R&D in Big Pharma*, HARV. BUS. REV. 68 (May 2008). The number of trials abroad has increased 250 percent in the last twenty-five years.

[14] Mwanamvua Boga et al., *Strengthening the Informed Consent Process in International Health Research through Community Engagement: The KEMI-Wellcome Trust Research Program Experience*, PLoS MEDICINE, Sept. 2011, at 1.

[15] E.O. Ekunwe & R. Kessel, *Informed Consent in the Developing World*, 14 HASTINGS CTR. REP. 22 (June 1984); K. Moodley, *HIV Vaccine Trial Participation in South Africa—An Ethical Assessment*, 27 J. MED. & PHIL. 197 (2002); K.M. MacQueen et al., *Ethical Challenges in International HIV Prevention Research*, 11 ACCOUNTABILITY IN RES. 49 (2004); C.S. Molyneux et al., *Understanding Informed Consent in a Low-Income Setting: Three Case Studies from the Kenyan Coast*, 59 SOC. SCI. & MED. 2547 (2004); L. Dawson & N.E. Kass, *Views of U.S. Researchers about Informed Consent in International Collaborative Research*, 61 SOC. SCI. & MED. 1211 (2005). *See Ethical and Policy Issues in International Research: Clinical Trials in Developing Countries*, Vol. 1 (2001) (Report and Recommendations of the National Bioethics Advisory Commission); L. Dawson & N.E. Kass, *Views of U.S. Researchers about Informed Consent in International Collaborative Research*, 62 SOC. SCI. & MED. 1211 (2005).

[16] Abdullahi v. Pfizer, Inc., 562 F.3d 163, 185, 185 n.15 (2d Cir. 2009).

The risk of nonconsensual offshored human experiments increases when pharmaceutical corporations' disincentives to undertake difficult communication with potential subjects are aligned with the incentives of foreign resource-poor governments and physicians to receive money, equipment, and supplies from pharmaceutical corporations in exchange for quickly making citizens available for research.[17] In the face of these disincentive and incentive structures, regulatory oversight of multinational corporations can be of only limited effectiveness.[18] After surveying international regulations and guidelines in 2010, Lee concluded that there is a regulatory enforcement vacuum.[19] Petryna argues that the norm in offshored environments "[is] that it takes injury, scandal, or sustained patient advocacy to hold trial sponsors accountable."[20] As a result of these harsh realities, litigation under the ATS may continue to be the only route through which pharmaceutical corporations will be held accountable for nonconsensual experimentation. Significant obstacles remain, however, for victims of nonconsensual experimentation who would use the ATS to actually hold transnational pharmaceutical corporations liable.

III. The State Responsibility Challenge Under the Ats

A. 42 U.S.C. § 1983

1. Nexus Theory: Challenges in Demonstrating State Responsibility for Violating the Norm

Given the peculiarity of the norm prohibiting nonconsensual medical experimentation, pleading and proving state responsibility presents a significant obstacle to enforcement through the ATS itself. Because the original purpose of the ATS included responding to torts committed by nonstate rather than state entities—and the foundational document of this particular norm is the Nuremberg Code, which says nothing about states—one may question whether courts should require state action for this norm. Nonetheless, the Second Circuit did so, relying on its own *Kadic* decision both to categorize the prohibition on nonconsensual human experimentation as a norm that would not apply directly to private actors without any connection to state action,

---

[17] Shirley S. Wang, *Most Clinical Trials Done Abroad*, WALL ST. J., Feb. 18, 2009, *available at* www.wsj.com/article/SB123499424805316443.html; Adriana Petryna, *Clinical Trials Offshored: On Private Sector Science and Public Health*, 2 BIOSOCIETIES 21, 27 (2007). *The Globalization of Clinical Trials: A Growing Challenge in Protecting Human Subjects*, Dept. of Health and Human Services, Office of Inspector General, Sept. 2001; *The Promise and Pitfalls of Clinical Trials Overseas*, 322 SCI. 214 (2008), *available at* http://www.sciencemag.org/content/322/5899/214.full.pdf?sid=ca9e11b5-600c-4a05-8e8e-db30b4240206.

[18] Molly McGregor, *Uninformed Consent: The United Nations' Failure to Appropriately Police Clinical Trials in Developing Nations*, 31 SUFFOLK TRANSNAT'L L. REV. 103 (2007).

[19] Stacey B. Lee, *Informed Consent: Enforcing Pharmaceutical Companies' Obligations Abroad*, 12(1) HEALTH & HUM. RTS.: AN INT'L J. 12 (2010), *available at* http://www.hhrjournal.org/index.php/hhr/article/view/200/297; Molly McGregor, *Uninformed Consent: The United Nations' Failure to Appropriately Police Clinical Trials in Developing Nations*, 31 SUFFOLK TRANSNAT'L L. REV. 103 (2007).

[20] PETRYNA, *supra* note 1, at 136.

and to "transform" a private party into the state by means of 42 U.S.C. § 1983.[21] If state action continues to be required for this norm, as it has been for several other norms under the ATS, the analysis should focus on outsourcing of public functions under the delegation-of-public-function theory.

Constitutional law scholars typically identify four specific state action "tests" in § 1983 jurisprudence: delegation of a public function, joint participation, close nexus, and pervasive entwinement. Scholars sometimes reduce the tests to two central "theories" that I will use in this chapter: nexus theory, which looks for significant contacts or links between the state and the violation; and delegation of a public function theory, which inquires whether the state has delegated one of its own functions to a private entity.

a. Tight Link to Challenged Conduct: Difficult to Plead/Prove

In *Abdullahi*, the state responsibility question was whether the Nigerian state was responsible for Pfizer's alleged violation. Several § 1983 tests other than those for delegation of a public function were relied upon. The Second Circuit cited *Kadic* for "acting in concert with" and "acting together with state officials or with significant state aid," *Brentwood Acad. v. Tennessee Secondary Assn.* and *Jackson v. Metropolitan Edison Co.* for the "nexus" test, and *Gorman Bakos v. Cornell Extension* for the "joint action" test and for the standard of "willful participation in joint activity."[22]

The Second Circuit reached the conclusion that the state action requirement had been met. Yet the question of state action presented significant difficulties in *Abdullahi* and is likely to present difficulties in future cases involving nonconsensual experimentation.[23] Dissenting in *Abdullahi*, Judge Wesley objected to general pleading of a loose nexus between the alleged facts and state actors, writing, "At most [the plaintiffs] alleged... that the Nigerian government acquiesced to or approved the Trovan program in general without knowing its disturbing details."[24] In its unsuccessful petition for certiorari, Pfizer framed the question as follows: "Whether ATS jurisdiction can extend to a private actor based on alleged state action by a foreign government where there is no allegation that the government knew of or participated in the specific acts by the private actor claimed to have violated international law."[25] A question

---

[21] The ATS lay largely dormant until 1980. After more than a decade of use in suits directed primarily against state perpetrators, the Second Circuit's 1995 holding in *Kadic v. Karadzic*—that the ATS can also apply to private actors—triggered a wave of litigation against multinational corporations that had allegedly aided and abetted human rights abuses in countries where they did business.

[22] Abdullahi v. Pfizer, Inc., 562 F.3d 163, 188 (2d Cir. 2009).

[23] Brief of Petitioner-Appellant at 14–18, Pfizer, Inc. v. Abdullahi, 130 S.Ct. 3541 (2010) (No. 09–34); Brief for the United States as Amicus Curiae at 10–14, Pfizer, Inc. v. Abdullahi, 130 S. Ct. 3541 (2010) (No. 09–34). In order for the Second Circuit to find state action adequately pled, it drew upon facts absent from the original complaint. *Abdullahi*, 562 F.3d at 210 (Wesley, J., dissenting); *Recent Cases: Federal Statutes—Alien Tort Statute—Second Circuit Looks beyond Complaint to Find State Action Requirement Satisfied;* Abdullahi v. Pfizer, Inc., *562 F.3d 163 (2d Cir. 2009),* 123 HARV. L. REV. 768 (2010).

[24] *Abdullahi*, 562 F.3d at 212 (Wesley, J., dissenting).

[25] Brief of Petitioner-Appellant at (i), Pfizer, Inc. v. Abdullahi, 130 S. Ct. 3541 (2010) (No. 09–34).

more tightly focused on this case could have been posed: "In a chaotic, triple-epidemic hospital environment where subjects were recruited in one location and treated in a separate ward, and after Pfizer had communicated to the state (by protocol) that consent would be sought, did any state actors know that informed consent was not being sought?"

To answer the latter question, one would need a developed ATS jurisprudence regarding state knowledge of corporate violations. But ATS jurisprudence regarding state knowledge of corporate violations has not developed as quickly as has ATS jurisprudence on corporate knowledge of state violations. The latter, part of "aiding and abetting" jurisprudence, has explored mens rea issues, but is not directly transferable to state responsibility questions. Only one circuit (the Eleventh, in *Aldana v. Del Monte Fresh Produce NA Inc.*) has even considered reaching the question of state knowledge of a corporate violation—specifically Guatemalan police knowledge of torture allegedly committed by Del Monte[26]—and that court declined to reach the question. Had it done so, however, it would be clear that, in comparison to pleading and proving state knowledge of torture, pleading and proving state knowledge of nonconsensual experimentation is quite difficult. This is because of the latter norm's peculiarities.[27]

What are the peculiarities of the norm? The norm, drawn from numerous source documents, including the Nuremberg Code, the World Medical Association's Helsinki Declaration, guidelines authored by the Council for International Organizations of Medical Sciences, and Article 7 of the International Covenant on Civil and Political Rights, has three peculiar features.[28] The first peculiarity is that the norm prohibits only a very limited subset of problematic human experiments; it does not prohibit any experiments that are illegal, exploitative, or unethical unless they are nonconsensual. A second peculiarity is that the prohibition is conditioned only on omission, that is, a lack of disclosure of certain facts about, and a lack of consent to, the experiment. It is in this respect distinguishable from (hypothetical) norms against nonconsensual experimentation involving the use of force, or nonconsensual experimentation taking place in a concentration camp, which would be norms with additional conditions involving affirmative acts. (The latter was the basis of one of Judge Wesley's objections

---

[26] Aldana v. Del Monte Fresh Produce N.A. Inc., 578 F.3d 1283 (11th Cir. 2009).

[27] That Guatemalan state actors who were positioned at some distance from the alleged torture knew that torture was taking place is a fact more susceptible to proof than that Nigerian state actors located in a separate ward knew disclosure did not take place in the hospital's waiting line.

[28] The Nuremberg Code, Trials of War Criminals before the Nuremberg Military Tribunals, Vol. 2 (1946), *available at* http://www.hhs.gov/ohrp/archive/nurcode.html; World Med. Ass'n., Declaration of Helsinki (1964), *available at* http://www.wma.net/en/30publications/10policies/b3/index.html; Council for Int'l Orgs. of Med. Scis., International Ethical Guidelines for Research Involving Human Subjects at General Ethical Principles (1993), *available at* http://www.cioms.ch/?frameguidelinesnov202.htm; International Covenant on Civil and Political Rights art. 7, Dec. 16, 1996, 999 U.N.T.S. 171, *available at* http://www2.ohchr.org/english/law/ccpr.htm. Other sources include the 1997 Council of Europe Convention on Human Rights and Biomedicine; the 2001 European Parliament Clinical Trials Directive; the 2005 UNESCO Universal Declaration on Bioethics and Human Rights; and several countries' domestic codes. *Abdullahi*, 562 F.3d at 175.

to recognizing the norm).[29] Insofar as no force is required for violation of this norm, it is also distinguishable from international law norms such as prohibitions against torture, slave trading, and genocide. And a third peculiarity is that the inaction on which the prohibition is conditioned is subtle—communicative inaction—that is, a failure to communicate information and a lack of an affirmative communication about the choice that the subject (or in the case of the Trovan experiment, the guardian) has made.

Because of these features, state knowledge that the norm was being violated would have been nearly impossible for the *Abdullahi* plaintiffs to prove. Kano's own Investigation Committee on the Clinical Trial found it difficult to determine which state actors knew that Pfizer was conducting a trial; it follows that it would have been exponentially more difficult for plaintiffs, seeking to establish a tight nexus between the state and Pfizer's violation, to demonstrate that state actors knew consent was not being sought.

b. Loose Link to Challenged Conduct: Disincentive for Corporations and Host Governments to Collaborate to Ensure Consent

In *Abdullahi*, plaintiffs did not need to establish that state actors knew consent was not being sought, because a loose nexus was used. For the Second Circuit, state "participation" at any stage of the international project counted as "state participation." It would be poor policy, however, for courts to consistently use such a loose approach to the link between the state and the complained-of violation. The reason it would be poor policy is not the business community's claim that pharmaceutical corporations will refuse to invest internationally if the prospect of lawsuits is high. (Pharmaceutical corporations will continue to carry out international clinical trials because even after factoring in litigation costs for occasional ATS suits, they are hugely profitable.) A loose nexus approach would be poor policy because it creates an incentive for pharmaceutical corporations to minimize collaborations that may be necessary to develop linguistically and culturally appropriate disclosures. With a loose nexus, even contacts with the host government that are largely irrelevant to a possible consent violation would increase the probability of corporate liability (because any such contacts might increase the probability of sufficiently pleading state action necessary for suits under the ATS). But creating incentives for pharmaceutical corporations to minimize contacts with host governments runs counter to current understandings of the ethics of international clinical trials, which emphasize host state and host community involvement.[30]

---

[29] Judge Wesley's dissent refers to concentration camp conditions such as those that resulted in the Nuremberg Code, which the majority used as a source for the international law norm prohibiting nonconsensual experimentation. *Abdullahi*, 562 F.3d at 206 (Wesley, J., dissenting). The lack of force in the Trovan experiment may have been the reason the plaintiff's claims included other disturbing, but legally irrelevant issues such as low dosing the control group rather than providing standard care, and deviating from protocol.

[30] *See* Presidential Comm'n for the Study of Bioethical Issues, *Research across Borders: Proceedings of the International Research Panel of the Presidential Commission for the Study of Bioethical Issues* (2011), *available at* http://www.bioethics.gov/cms/sites/default/files/IRP-Proceedings%20and%20 Recommendations_0.pdf.

Under a looser nexus approach, exemplified by the Second Circuit proceedings, the more collaboratively a pharmaceutical company worked with a host government, the more vulnerable the corporation would be to an ATS suit holding it accountable for nonconsensual experimentation. Under a sounder policy, a corporation that undertakes experimentation with input from state actors in the host county (as well as with others familiar with the culture) should be less, rather than more, vulnerable to ATS suits. State action jurisprudence built on a loose nexus approach therefore gets the matter backward.

Subjects of international clinical trials can be harmed either through the high burden on the plaintiff associated with a tight nexus, or through a loose nexus resulting in strategic corporate avoidance of contacts with those necessary to develop an ethical experiment. The practical effect of either version of the nexus approach may be to immunize pharmaceutical corporations rather than to enhance their accountability. Therefore, judicial attention should not be directed to links between pharmaceutical corporations and host governments that may be irrelevant to consent, but instead should focus on features of corporate–host state partnerships that can influence whether the experimentation is consensual.

2. Delegation of a Public Function

a. Background

One such feature is whether the host state has delegated—or outsourced—a public function to a pharmaceutical corporation. Focusing on such delegations of public functions would help U.S. law develop in a way that not only avoids creating inappropriate incentives for pharmaceutical corporations but also connects facts about current corporate–state relationships with the underlying purpose of state responsibility law. The fundamental notion underlying a public function inquiry is that when the government delegates one of its functions to a private entity, the private entity must execute the delegated function within the limits of the U.S. Constitution, domestically, or, with regard to the ATS, within the bounds of international law. Legal accountability is thus not limited to the government proper but extends even to those private entities exercising governmental powers.

A delegation of a public function test has seldom been argued successfully in recent years except when the function is not only traditionally, but also exclusively public. An inquiry into public function, however, need not be so narrow, nor must it be considered either a discrete or a dispositive test; it can be treated as one factor to be analyzed.[31] The Second Circuit was not asked to consider a possible delegation of public function even as a factor to be analyzed. Except for a comment by dissenting judge Wesley, one would think no such test or theory existed,[32] despite the fact that the concept of

---

[31] Rendell-Baker v. Kohn, 457 U.S. 830, 842 (1982); Mark v. Borough of Hatboro, 51 F.3d 1137, 1143, n.7 (3d Cir. 1995).
[32] *Abdullahi*, 562 F.3d at 211 (Wesley, J., dissenting).

delegating a public function is clearly on display in *Brentwood Academy* and *Gorman Bakos*, which the Second Circuit cited.

b. Delegation of a Public Function (Outsourcing) Applied to the Trovan Experiment

The Nigerian state delegated some of its public functions to Pfizer; therefore Pfizer, in all fairness, could have been described as a Nigerian government actor in the Trovan experiment. If judicial attention had been directed toward "outsourcing" of a public health function, two governmental acts could have come to the fore.

First, during the Nigerian epidemic the state accepted responsibility for the public health emergency by seeking help from the Nigerian federal government, appointing a task force with members from MSF and the International Red Cross "to control an epidemic of CSM in Nigeria,"[33] and carrying out public education campaigns. But the government also delegated some of its public health responsibilities to Pfizer. This example could be analogized to delegating decisions about suppressing a raging fire to a private company (which in U.S. law might then be subject to a section 1983 action[34]). In fact, Pfizer itself drew the analogy between a fire and an epidemic in its opening statement to the Investigation Committee in Kano, stating "the CSM/cholera outbreak started in November 1995 and was spreading like wild fire, ravaging most states in the north."[35]

Second, what could have come to the fore is that the Nigerian government delegated to Pfizer the decision whether to treat patients within a state hospital. This is an exclusive public function. The Infectious Disease Hospital was organized under the Hospital Management Board of the Kano State Ministry of Health.[36] The Kano State Ministry of Health's Director of Personnel Services gave written permission to Pfizer staff to "treat patients" in the hospital.[37] (In the United States, public hospitals are themselves vulnerable to section 1983 suits. Medical facilities owned and managed by a state have long been recognized as proper defendants in claims of federal rights deprivations.)[38]

By handing over a hospital ward for an experiment when the hospital was overcrowded, the Nigerian state delegated to Pfizer the authority to prevent access of members of the Kano public to treatment in a public hospital setting. Pfizer's experiment prevented or delayed access to standard treatment for individuals not suffering from meningitis and not between the ages of one and thirteen.

An incentive for pharmaceutical corporations to work collaboratively with host states to avoid nonconsensual experiments would be created if corporations knew that judges would undertake a public function inquiry and consider features such as these.

---

[33] I. Mohammed, Academics Epidemics and Politics: An Eventful Career in Public Health 73 (2007).

[34] *See* Goldstein v. Chestnut Ridge Volunteer Fire Co., 218 F.3d 337 (9th Cir. 2000).

[35] Fed. Ministry of Health, *Report of the Investigation Committee on the Clinical Trial of Trovan by Pfizer, Kano, 1996,* at 18 (2001) (Nigeria), *available at* http://www.circare.org/info/trovan_clinicaltrialreport.pdf.

[36] *Id.* at 35.

[37] *Id.* at xxii.

[38] *Annotation, Action of Private Hospital as State Action under 42 U.S.C.A. § 1983 or Fourteenth Amendment,* 42 A.L.R. Fed. 463 (2009). *See* Chudacoff v. Univ. Med. Ctr., 2011 U.S. App. LEXIS 11586 (9th Cir. 2011).

Judicial consideration of a public function delegation is more appropriate for global clinical trials than a consideration based on a nexus theory. A section 1983 delegation of public function analysis may carry particular weight in the narrow circumstances of a public health crisis.

B. STATE RESPONSIBILITY UNDER ARTICLE 5 OF THE INTERNATIONAL LAW COMMISSION'S ARTICLES ON STATE RESPONSIBILITY

1. Article 5

a. Background

Although the Second Circuit chose to use section 1983 for the analysis of state responsibility, one may ask whether a different approach to state responsibility might be better suited to evaluating a broader set of experimental circumstances. Some commentators have argued that domestic law is the wrong body of law to apply. Priselac has argued that using section 1983 color-of-law jurisprudence may be in tension with *Sosa*,[39] and Bradley has argued that there are important differences between the purposes of section 1983 and the purpose of the ATS that preclude section 1983's use.[40] In *Kadic*, the Second Circuit itself turned to section 1983 for state responsibility doctrine but used international law for the definition of a "state." International law, as well as section 1983, may be used to draw attention to a delegation of a public function. The International Law Commission's (ILC) Articles on the Responsibility of States for Internationally Wrongful Acts, adopted by the ILC in 2001, summarize rules for deciding when a state can be held responsible for acts (or omissions) of nonstate actors.[41] Because the articles codify rather than create international law, scholars, as well as the Second Circuit (in another case), give the Articles authoritative weight.[42]

Chapter II, Article 5, of the ILC's Articles deals with the conduct of entities, such as Pfizer, that the state has empowered to exercise governmental authority.[43] The central question under Article 5 is whether the private entity is exercising governmental functions. It reads: "The conduct of a person or entity which is not an organ of the State

---

[39] Jessica Priselac, *The Requirement of State Action in Alien Tort Statute Claims: Does SOSA Matter?*, 21 EMORY INT'L L. REV. 789 (2007) (arguing that using § 1983 is at odds with Sosa n.20).

[40] Curtis A. Bradley, *State Action and Corporate Human Rights Liability*, 85 NOTRE DAME L. REV. 1823, 1828 (2010). Koebele, however, argues for the use of § 1983.

[41] The ILC was established by the United Nations General Assembly in 1948.

[42] David Caron, *The ILC Articles on State Responsibility: The Paradoxical Relationship between Form and Authority*, 96 AM. J. OF INT'L L. 857, 867 (2002), surveying the views of prominent academics on the articles. The Second Circuit cited Article 4 as an axiomatic principle of international law in "Compagnie." Compagnie Noga D'Importation et D'Exportation v. The Russian Fed'n., 361 F.3d 676, 689 (2d Cir. 2004). The court wrote, "An axiomatic principle of international law is that the conduct of any state organ shall be considered an act of that state under international law, whether the organ exercises legislative, executive, judicial or any other functions, whatever position it holds in the organization of the state, and whatever its character as an organ of the central government or of a territorial unit of the state."

[43] JAMES CRAWFORD, THE INTERNATIONAL LAW COMMISSION'S ARTICLES ON STATE RESPONSIBILITY: INTRODUCTION, TEXT AND COMMENTARIES 100–02 (2002).

under Article 4 but which is empowered by the law of that State to exercise elements of governmental authority shall be considered an act of the State under international law, provided the person or entity is acting in that capacity in the particular instance."[44] Even when wrongful acts are outside the scope of the authority granted to the private entity, or if the corporation was not acting in an official capacity, Article 7 provides that "[t]he conduct of an organ of a State or of a person or entity empowered to exercise elements of the governmental authority shall be considered an act of the State under international law if the organ, person or entity acts in that capacity, even if it exceeds its authority or contravenes instructions."[45]

b. Article 5 Applied to the Trovan Experiment

According to Crawford's commentary, Article 5 applies in "special cases" to private corporations. To establish that a private corporation's acts are attributable to the state, the state must have empowered it to "exercise functions of a public character normally exercised by state organs," and the conduct must relate to the exercise of the governmental authority concerned. The drafters did not attempt to define the "scope of government authority," and, unlike many U.S. jurists, did not limit government authority to that which is "exclusively" governmental. Rather, the drafters encouraged looking beyond the substance of the powers granted to consider the way in which the authority was granted, the purposes for which the government granted that authority, and the extent to which the corporation is accountable to the government. The ILC drafters cite specific examples, including state-owned airlines empowered to carry out immigration and quarantine functions.[46] The purposes for which the authority was granted and the way in which authority was granted could be those outlined above; the extent to which Pfizer was accountable to the Nigerian government, however, seems to be minimal.

Considering a delegation of a public function though either federal or international law, therefore, brings the legal inquiry about state responsibility closer than does nexus theory to the fundamental question "Should human experimentation have been done at all in this situation, and, if so, under what conditions?" For this reason, it might be considered a constructive policy move. When interviewed about the Trovan experiment, the former president of MSF France, an organization that had been on the scene at the Kano hospital, focused on this question, stating "It was not a time for a drug trial at all."[47] Recent work in ethics tries to flesh out the conditions and constraints under which human experimentation during epidemics is morally acceptable.[48] A search for

---

[44] *Id.* at 100.

[45] *Id.* at 106–09.

[46] *Id.* at 101.

[47] Sarah Boseley & David Smith, *As Doctors Fought to Save Lives Pfizer Flew in Drug Trial Team*, GUARDIAN, Dec. 9, 2010, *available at* http://www.guardian.co.uk/business/2010/dec/09/doctors-fought-save-lives-pfizer-drug.

[48] Some of the conditions described by Ezeome are that uncertainty must exist that can only be resolved by doing research during epidemics, and Emanuel's principles. Emmanuel R. Ezeome & Christian Simon, *Ethical Problems in Conducting Research in Acute Epidemics: The Pfizer Meningitis Study in Nigeria as an Illustration*, 10 DEVELOPING WORLD BIOETHICS 1 (2008).

delegation of a public function, such as the one taken up here, draws attention to the possibility that the pharmaceutical corporation may have been empowered to conduct an experiment under conditions that were woefully unconstrained—perhaps so unconstrained as to make the Nigerian government responsible for the corporation's violation.

c. Attributing State Responsibility in Contexts Other Than Public Health Crises

Pharmaceutical corporations have gravitated to crises—situations that may give a veneer of "humanitarian" legitimacy to actions that would otherwise be unacceptable.[49] Public health crises have attracted corporate experiments in situations other than the Nigerian meningitis epidemic—for example, Sandoz's test of rhGM-CSF following the Chernobyl nuclear disaster.[50] Both Article 5 and the section 1983 public function test could be used to hold pharmaceutical corporations accountable for nonconsensual experiments in those situations. Still, the outsourcing of public health functions in other situations, and the state–corporate dynamics that create and facilitate such outsourcing, should also be explored. Space permits only a brief exploration of corporate–host state relationships in contexts other than public health crises. A necessarily abbreviated consideration of Petryna's and others' descriptions of those dynamics and their relation to ILC Articles 8 and 9 follows.

2. Article 8

Article 8 defines exceptions to the general rule that under international law acts of private entities are not attributable to the state: when a private entity, acting on the instructions of the state, carries out an act that violates international law; and when a private entity acts under the state's direction or control.[51]

After studying international clinical trials in both wealthy and poor settings, particularly in Latin American and Eastern Europe, anthropologist Adriana Petryna concluded that pharmaceutical corporations feed upon public health systems[52] and are adaptable, mobile, and parasitic.[53] Corporations, she writes, "piggy back trials on existing health care structures."[54] These observations are consistent with advice from an

---

[49] ADRIANA PETRYNA ET AL., GLOBAL PHARMACEUTICALS: ETHICS, MARKETS, PRACTICES 43 (2006).

[50] ADRIANA PETRYNA, LIFE EXPOSED: BIOLOGICAL CITIZENS AFTER CHERNOBYL 44–48 (2002); Adriana Petryna, *Globalizing Human Subjects Research, in* GLOBAL PHARMACEUTICALS: ETHICS, MARKETS, PRACTICES 33, 51 (Adriana Petryna et al. eds., 2006). Anne C. Roark, *Chernobyl "Hero": Dr. Gale— Medical Maverick*, L.A. TIMES, May 5, 1988, *available at* http://articles.latimes.com/1988-05-05/news/mn-3615_1_bone-marrow-transplant.

[51] Article 8 states: "Conduct directed or controlled by a State. The conduct of a person or group of persons shall be considered an act of a State under international law if the person or group of persons is in fact acting on the instructions of, or under the direction or control of, that State in carrying out the conduct." CRAWFORD, *supra* note 43, at 62.

[52] PETRYNA, *supra* note 1, at 96, 197.

[53] Petryna, *supra* note 17, at 23.

[54] PETRYNA, *supra* note 1, at 5.

international law firm to its pharmaceutical clients to "maximize the public healthcare settings in developing countries: India, Brazil, Russia, Ukraine."[55]

The difficulty with attempting to apply Article 8 (as well as with some section 1983 jurisprudence requiring control of the private party by the state[56]) is that clinical trials are increasingly taking place in stressed, poor-state health settings whose states occupy weak bargaining positions relative to U.S.-based pharmaceutical corporations. Such foreign host states do not "instruct" U.S. pharmaceutical giants to experiment without consent, and U.S. pharmaceutical corporations are not likely to submit to their "direction or control."[57]

3. Article 9

Article 9 addresses situations where the state does not instruct, direct, or control the pharmaceutical corporation because the state itself is absent or has defaulted.[58] Article 9 commentary indicates that it is meant to cover circumstances in which the state apparatus has partially or totally collapsed or the state has lost control over a certain locality.[59] The conduct must have been carried out in the "absence" or "default" of the official authorities under circumstances that "call for the exercise of those elements of authority."[60] Situations covered by Article 9 are so extreme that it is likely that only humanitarian organizations, not pharmaceutical corporations, would venture into them. Many situations in which nonconsensual pharmaceutical experiments could occur would, therefore, fall through the cracks between Article 8 and Article 9.

4. The Gap between Article 8 and Article 9

In the clinical trials that Petryna studied, official authorities were neither absent nor had they defaulted. They may have been impotent, or shirked their responsibilities to protect the public because of their conflicts of interest. They may have turned a blind eye to consent problems, but they were still exercising their functions. As Petryna noted, "host countries have proven themselves quite adaptive to business demands."[61]

Corporate–host state relations may be collusive as well as collaborative. Idris Mohammed, head of the Nigerian Task Force to deal with the Nigerian epidemic, wrote "In the third world, authoritarian regimes and corrupt local government official and

---

[55] John Manthei et al., *Global Clinical Trials: Potential Pitfalls of Offshore Trials*, BAY-BIO (Apr. 17, 2008), *available at* http://www.baybio.org/pdf/AC08_T4S3_Global_Clinical_Trials.pdf.

[56] Pennsylvania v. Bd. of Dir. of City Trusts of Phila., 353 U.S. 230, 231 (1957) (holding that board of directors of racially segregated school for orphans was state agency).

[57] *See* Bradley, *supra* note 40, at 1830.

[58] Article 9 states: "The conduct of a person or group of persons shall be considered an act of a state under international law if the person or group of persons is in fact exercising elements of the governmental authority in the absence or default of the official authorities and in circumstances such as to call for the exercise of those elements of authority." CRAWFORD, *supra* note 43, at 62.

[59] *Id.* at 115.

[60] *Id.* at 114.

[61] PETRYNA, *supra* note 1, at 19.

health authorities are eager to be paid off by first-world organizations and to have good relations with them. They 'encourage' entire villages or provinces to enroll in research programs while local doctors enrich themselves by providing human subjects."[62] A set of interlocking corporate and host state interests is at play, sometimes to the detriment of potential research subjects.[63]

To the extent that public institutions "mediate" the participation of research subjects in low-income nations,[64] subjects' opportunities to know that they are involved in experimentation may be sacrificed. Petryna has described the relationships between pharmaceutical corporations and host states as "convoluted,"[65] resulting in local public health systems that "have become cogs in the outsourced research enterprise."[66] This dynamic between pharmaceutical corporations and host state governments might be viewed as a double outsourcing. First, the U.S. pharmaceutical corporation outsources its clinical trial to a relatively poor ("inexpensive") country; in turn, the relatively poor country outsources its health delivery to the U.S. pharmaceutical corporation, which substitutes the experimental drug for standard treatment.[67]

Conclusion

Pharmaceutical corporations will continue outsourcing some experiments from the United States to relatively poor nations, and the leaders of those nations or states will outsource some of their public health responsibilities to pharmaceutical corporations. These exchanges characterize the convoluted contexts in which corporate nonconsensual clinical trials occur.

Further steps toward accountability of pharmaceutical corporations for nonconsensual international human experimentation require that, if state action is found to be

---

[62] MOHAMMED, *supra* note 33, at 192.

[63] PETRYNA, *supra* note 50, at 50.

[64] PETRYNA, *supra* note 1, at 13.

[65] *Id.* at 9.

[66] *Id.* at 197.

[67] The gap between Article 8 and 9 is not completely out of reach of "color of law" jurisprudence, where symbiosis, collusion, and covert encouragement can matter. State encouragement may be "overt or covert." Blum v. Yaretsky, 457 U.S. 991, 1004 (1982). Petryna's use of the term *surrogate* to characterize state–pharmaceutical relationships is reminiscent of the term in *Brentwood Academy v. Tennessee Secondary School Athletic Assoc.*: "It is, of course true that the time is long past when the close relationship between the surrogate association and its public members and public officials acting as such was attested freely . . . the state Board once freely acknowledged the Association's official character but now does it by winks and nods." 531 U.S. 288, 300 (2001). "The significance of winks and nods in state-action doctrine seems to be one of the points of the dissenters' departure from the rest of the Court . . . [I] f formalism were the sine qua non of state action, the doctrine would vanish owing to the ease and inevitability of its evasion, and for just that reason formalism has never been controlling. For example, a criterion of state action like symbiosis . . . looks not to form but to an underlying reality." *Id.* at 301 n.4.

necessary for this norm, judicial attention should be focused on delegations of public functions. With this focus, the law may eventually be better able to come to terms with nonconsensual experiments that take place during public health emergencies. When nonconsensual experiments occur in contexts that are not public health emergencies, however, a state responsibility requirement may prove an insurmountable obstacle, and U.S. corporations will remain unaccountable.

17

BEYOND PATENTS

Global Challenges to Affordable Medicine

*Cynthia M. Ho**

Introduction

A major challenge to global health care is the current state of access to affordable medicine. Many citizens in developing countries currently lack affordable access to lifesaving and life-sustaining medicines.[1] Citizens of these countries often have higher out-of-pocket expenses on drugs than citizens in wealthier countries, in addition to having fewer resources to begin with.[2] Accordingly, laws that shield drugs from competition may result in patients choosing between basic needs such as housing versus medication.[3]

---

* Clifford E. Vickrey Professor of Law, Loyola University of Chicago.

[1] *See, e.g.*, MDG Gap Task Force, U.N., The Global Partnership for Development: Time to Deliver 51–55 (2011), *available at* http://www.un.org/en/development/desa/policy/mdg_gap/mdg_gap2011/mdg8report2011_engw.pdf (discussing current lack of access to affordable medicines).

[2] In many developing countries, the cost of medicine can compete with other essentials, such as food and shelter because the highest component of household health-related expenditure is on medicines that are obtained through out-of-pocket payments. Dele Abegund, World Health Organization [WHO], Background Paper: Essential Medicines for Non-Communicable Diseases (NCDs) 5 (2011), *available at* http://www.who.int/medicines/areas/policy/access_noncommunicable/EssentialMedicinesforNCDs.pdf. The higher out-of-pocket costs may be due to a number of factors. First, many citizens in poor countries lack insurance. Also, many developing countries do not provide price controls on the cost of drugs. This is very important because drug companies may often sell drugs in developing countries for close to the same price sold in wealthier countries. In addition to all of these factors, costs can also be exacerbated by other issues, such as tariffs on imported drugs. Also, although this chapter focuses on cost of drugs, other issues that exacerbate access include problems with supply and delivery of drugs.

[3] *See, e.g., id*; Ajita Singh, *Hepatitis C: Govt Apathy Means Debt or Death for Millions*, Statesman, Oct. 23, 2011, http://www.thestatesman.net/index.php?option=com_content&view=article&show=archive&id=387370&catid=36&year=2011&month=10&day=23&Itemid=66.

Although patents represent the prototypical type of legal protection for drugs, they are actually just the most well-known method of protecting drugs from competition (and the resulting lower drug prices that come with increased competition).[4] There are other types of protection of drugs under regulatory laws of some countries known as "data exclusivity"[5] and "patent linkage" that are generally less well-known yet also impact access to affordable medicine. Understanding these regulatory protections is important for developing countries because they are increasingly pressured to recognize them[6]—despite the objections of some—when signing free trade agreements (FTAs) that are often contingent upon adopting such protections.[7]

Although regulatory protections will be discussed in more detail, this introduction provides a brief overview of each type and its implications. Data exclusivity prevents a generic company from relying on the clinical data submitted by an originator company that would help the generic company establish the safety and efficacy of the proposed generic drug by inference during the period of exclusivity. This reliance permits generic companies to seek approval by simply showing that its drug is bioequivalent to the previously approved drug. Although there are many rationales cited, a common one is that data exclusivity is necessary to prevent "free riding" on an originator's investment. The second type of protection, patent linkage, bars a national regulatory agency from approving a generic drug if it is "linked" to one or more existing and unexpired patents, such that the generic drug would theoretically infringe the linked patents if it were made and sold. Patent linkage is argued to be a logical method to ensure that regulatory approvals do not unduly promote patent infringement; opponents, however, assert that it is inappropriate for regulatory officials to police areas beyond the scope of their expertise.

---

[4] After all, the owner of a patented drug can legally exclude others from making the patented drug, which usually means that the owner can charge a premium for the drug during the patent term (unless there is some type of price control beyond patent laws).

[5] Although this chapter uses the phrase *data exclusivity*, the same protection is often referred to as *test data exclusivity* or *data protection*. The term *data protection* is particularly confusing and thus not used here because it is more applicable to a lesser type of protection than data exclusivity that is required under the Agreement on Trade-Related Aspects of Intellectual Property Rights (TRIPS). *Market exclusivity* is a totally different type of protection provided under some laws that does not involve reliance on another's data; rather, if market exclusivity exists, a country will not approve a second drug applicant during that term, even if the second applicant does not need to rely on another's data. However, some have confusingly used the term *market exclusivity* interchangeably with *data exclusivity*. To help minimize confusion, only *data exclusivity* is used here.

[6] The United States was the first country to recognize regulatory protections of drugs and has also been at the forefront of efforts to expand adoption of such protections.

[7] Those who oppose such requirements for developing countries include not only some scholars and public interest groups, but also some politicians. *See, e.g.,* Letter from Rep. Henry Waxman et al. to the Honorable Ron Kirk, U.S. Trade Representative (Oct. 19, 2011), http://democrats.energycommerce.house.gov/sites/default/files/documents/Letter_Kirk_10.19.11.pdf; Doctors Without Borders/ Médecins Sans Frontières, *How the Trans-Pacific Partnership Agreement Threatens Access to Medicine* (2011), http://www.doctorswithoutborders.org/press/2011/MSF-TPP-Issue-Brief.pdf; Brook K. Baker, *Ending Drug Registration Apartheid: Taming Data Exclusivity and Patent/Registration Linkage*, 34 Am. J.L. & Med. 303, 303–13 (2008).

These regulatory protections provide independent legal bases for protecting drugs beyond patents. Such protection is very important because it can preclude traditional exceptions to patent rights intended to promote faster access to low-cost drugs. For example, many countries permit an exception to patent rights called a compulsory license. Essentially, a compulsory license is a government-granted license to an entity to make and sell a patented drug without permission of the patent owner; the patent owner is given a "reasonable royalty" as compensation, but this is generally far below the patent owner's preferred retail price. However, even if a government grants a compulsory license to make a patented drug, such a license may be a moot point if the licensee cannot obtain regulatory approval to bring the drug to market. This is a real issue because every drug—including those made under compulsory licenses—must be approved as safe and effective by a regulatory authority before being sold.

Lower-cost generic drugs can be marketed more quickly in countries that do not recognize data exclusivity or patent linkage. In India, for example, where no such protections exist,[8] the government can approve a generic version immediately after the originator has obtained approval. This is true in part because without data exclusivity, there is nothing to prevent the generic company from immediately relying on the data of the originator in seeking to show that the proposed generic is equivalent to the original. In addition, without patent linkage, a generic drug will be approved without regard to whether it might infringe an existing patent once it is made and sold. Of course, a generic company that markets a patented drug will likely be sued for patent infringement. Nonetheless, a generic company may be willing to take this risk because patents are often found invalid or not infringed.[9]

This chapter examines the existence and implications of data exclusivity and patent linkage. After an explanation of the basic parameters of each of these regulatory protections along with the respective policy rationale, the global context is discussed. Finally, the chapter concludes with a summary of solutions that may serve to minimize the harm likely to occur in developing countries that are forced to adopt such regulatory regimes.

---

[8] India is, however, under pressure to adopt data exclusivity in a pending FTA with the European Union. *See, e.g.*, Amiti Sen, *India, EU Settle Generics Dispute, Pave Way for FTA Talks in April*, ECON. TIMES, Mar. 15, 2011, http://articles.economictimes.indiatimes.com/2011-03-15/news/28691669_1_data-exclusivity -trade-and-investment-agreement-patent-protection; Doctors Without Borders, Briefing Documents: Background on the EU–India FTA, *available at* http://www.doctorswithoutborders.org/publications/ article.cfm?id=5757&cat=briefing-documents. In addition, some companies have tried, albeit unsuccessfully, to persuade Indian regulatory authorities to adopt patent linkage through litigation. Bayer sued Indian generic company Cipla as well as the Indian regulatory agency; however, the Delhi High Court as well as the Delhi High Court Division Bench declined to grant Bayer's request to create patent linkage via judicial fiat, and also imposed costs on Bayer for bringing frivolous litigation. Bayer v. Cipla, (2008) WP(C) No. 7833/2008 (Del. H. C., Nov. 20, 2008), *rev'd by* Del. H.C. Court (Aug. 18, 2009, Judge S. Ravindra Bhat), *aff'd by* Del. H.C. Division Bench (Feb. 9, 2010, Judge S. Muralidhar).

[9] *See, e.g.*, FED. TRADE COMM. GENERIC DRUG ENTRY PRIOR TO PATENT EXPIRATION: AN FTC STUDY 13 (2002) (finding that generic applicants successfully challenged pharmaceutical patents as invalid or not infringed in 73 percent of the cases).

I. Data Exclusivity

A. BACKGROUND ON DRUG APPROVAL

To understand the impact of data exclusivity, a brief sketch of the process of drug approval is necessary. Most countries do not permit the sale or marketing of new drugs unless and until they have been approved by the government as safe and effective. In places such as the United States and European Union, where strong infrastructures exist to assess safety and efficacy, the government undertakes to evaluate the extensive clinical data submitted by companies seeking to obtain approval of their drugs. However, in many developing countries without such infrastructures, drugs may be approved on the basis of approval in other countries, such as the United States.

In addition to requiring preapproval of new drugs that have never been sold, most countries also require some type of approval process for new versions of previously approved drugs (what would be considered a "generic" drug to most consumers). Most countries provide a streamlined approval process where the proposed generic manufacturer only has to show that its product is "bioequivalent" to the prior drug for the same dosage. This streamlined process means the generic manufacturer does not need to duplicate the more extensive clinical studies submitted by the first manufacturer of a drug. Instead, the generic manufacturer need only show that its proposed product would be chemically equivalent, such that a government can assume that the generic product would be as safe and effective as the originally approved drug.

B. DATA EXCLUSIVITY'S IMPACT ON THE APPROVAL OF GENERICS

If clinical data is subject to data exclusivity, no one else can rely on that data for the term of exclusivity. This means that, even though there may be a streamlined approval process for generics that requires less data to establish that the proposed generic is safe, that process cannot start until the data exclusivity period expires.[10] Because data exclusivity exists separate and apart from the patent system, the bar on reliance exists even if the original drug is unpatented or the patent has expired.

During the term of data exclusivity, a generic company could theoretically conduct its own clinical tests to show that its proposed drug is safe and effective. Indeed, originator companies often point this out as a reason data exclusivity provides only modest protection compared to patents. However, such data generally takes many years and great expense to develop because it involves multiple phases of animal and human testing. It is typically not cost-effective for a generic company to undertake such expense, especially as the resulting drug would have neither patent rights nor data exclusivity to protect it from competition. Before 1984, when the United States

---

[10] This is a broad overview. In some countries, applicants of proposed generics may submit applications during the period of exclusivity, but regulatory approval will not be granted until after the terms of the exclusivity expires.

provided an essentially unlimited term of data exclusivity, there were often no generic versions of even expired drug patents.[11] Moreover, demanding that generic manufacturers essentially reinvent the wheel is both unnecessary and unethical because it requires duplicate tests of drugs *already known* to be safe and effective. In essence, then, data exclusivity may provide a type of de facto market exclusivity separate from patent rights because generic companies will rarely have an adequate economic incentive to conduct the duplicative testing necessary for market approval.

Although data exclusivity is generally less well-known than patent protection, it may in some cases provide more effective market protection than patent rights. Technically, patent rights are considered most exclusive in precluding others from making, using, or selling a drug; data exclusivity, by contrast, does not prevent others from making or trying to sell the protected drug. Data exclusivity, however, is easier to obtain. Whereas a patent is granted only for an invention that is new and inventive, data exclusivity is automatically granted with marketing approval of a drug based on the lower threshold of being safe and effective. A further benefit of the automatic grant of data exclusivity is that it is not subject to challenge, unlike patent protection.

C. THE TERM OF DATA EXCLUSIVITY

As with all intellectual property rights, the term of data exclusivity is very important. The shortest term of data exclusivity is usually five years from approval, but terms of ten or twelve years are not unusual. At first glance, this may seem to be of no importance because patent terms are calculated as ending twenty years from the filing of a patent application. However, because patent applications are filed long before drug approval is even sought, the terms are in fact much closer. In particular, the *effective* patent term—the period of the patent term during which a drug has been approved for sale by the regulatory authorities—is usually about eleven years. Thus, in some cases at least, the data exclusivity term may be roughly equivalent to the patent term and possibly longer than the patent term. Moreover, an important issue is that data exclusivity will provide exclusivity in the marketplace even for drugs that are unpatentable.

---

[11] Between 1972 and 1984 (before data exclusivity, when the United States provided essentially infinite exclusivity), there were 150 drugs whose patents had expired, but for which there were no generics. *See* Gerard J. Mossinghoff, *Overview of the Hatch-Waxman Act and Its Impact on the Drug Development Process*, 54 FOOD & DRUG L.J. 187, 187 (1999). In addition, only two of the top thirteen drugs had generic competitors within a year of patent expiration before 1984, whereas, more recently, eleven of the top thirteen drugs had generic competition within a mere two months of patent expiration. David Reiffin & Michael R. Ward, *Generic Drug Industry Dynamics* 6 (F.T.C., Working Paper, 2002), citing CONG. BUDGET OFFICE, HOW INCREASED COMPETITION FROM GENERIC DRUGS HAS AFFECTED PRICES AND RETURNS IN THE PHARMACEUTICAL INDUSTRY (1998) and R. Caves, M. Whinston & M. Hurwicz, *Patent Expiration, Entry, and Competition in the U.S. Pharmaceutical Industry*, in BROOKINGS PAPERS ON ECONOMIC ACTIVITY: MICROECONOMICS 1 (1991), *available at* http://www.ftc.gov/be/workpapers/industrydynamicsreiffenwp.pdf.

D. EXPLORING THE RATIONALE FOR DATA EXCLUSIVITY

In examining the rationale for data exclusivity, it is useful to consider its genesis. The United States was the first country to provide data exclusivity. Interestingly, data exclusivity was not enacted based on a need to protect the data of innovators. Rather, at the time, the United States considered such data to be a trade secret that could be protected indefinitely. The current form of data exclusivity (i.e., the kind with a limited term) was actually part of a grand legislative compromise that also created a stream-lined process for approving generics. This streamlined process permitted a generic company to rely on the clinical data of the originator company after data exclusivity expired in conjunction with limited data that its proposed generic was bioequivalent to the originator's drug. To originator pharmaceutical companies, data exclusivity provides less protection than drug companies previously enjoyed under trade secret law. From this perspective, the only alternative to data exclusivity is absolute and indefinite exclusivity.

A frequently cited rationale for data exclusivity is that it is a just reward to compensate the expense and effort of conducting clinical trials.[12] Alternatively, data exclusivity is sometimes cited as necessary to prevent free riding by another company that did not engage in such efforts.[13] The research-based pharmaceutical industry has repeatedly noted that whereas clinical data for a new drug may well exceed $100 million—including ones that never make it to market—the costs necessary for limited testing by generic companies is only about $1 million.[14] Although some critics contest the exact cost of developing a new drug, it is unquestionably more expensive than the limited testing required to approve a generic drug. The more important question, however, is whether data exclusivity is needed at all. Notably, drug companies cite the same development costs to justify both patent and data exclusivity. To the extent that data exclusivity and patent protection offer independent protection, some critics have asserted that there is no need for both.[15]

Alternatively, even if some protection beyond patents were considered necessary to prevent free riding, that does not necessarily require data exclusivity as a solution. Some

---

[12] A less compelling rationale that is nonetheless often cited as a reason that countries should embrace data exclusivity is that without it, companies would have no incentive to generate such data. Although companies recognize that patents can protect new compounds, they suggest that data exclusivity is critical for those compounds that are unpatentable—without considering whether what patent policy has deemed unpatentable should otherwise be protected. *See* Int'l Fed'n of Pharmaceutical Manufacturers Ass'n (IFPMA), Encouragement of New Clinical Drug Development—The Role of Data Exclusivity 2 (2000), *available at* http://www.who.int/intellectualproperty/topics/ip/en/DataExclusivity_2000.pdf.

[13] *See, e.g., id.* (suggesting that originators would be at an unfair commercial disadvantage if generic competitors did not face similar costs).

[14] *Id.* at 6–7.

[15] *E.g.,* Yaniv Heled, *Patents vs. Statutory Exclusivities in Biological Pharmaceuticals—Do We Really Need Both?* 56–63 (Georgia State Univ. College of Law, Legal Studies Research Paper No. 2011-17, June 28, 2011), *available at* http://papers.ssrn.com/sol3/papers.cfm?abstract_id=1874130 (arguing that biological products should not receive both patent and regulatory protection).

patient advocates have recommended cost sharing instead of data exclusivity as a solu-tion that would prevent undue free riding while simultaneously promoting rapid entry of generic drugs.[16] Under this approach, a generic company could be approved without any delay after an originator drug, but the generic company would need to compensate the originator company in order for the generic company to rely on the originator com-pany's clinical data in showing bioequivalence. There is some limited precedent for this: in the analogous area of agricultural products, the United States provides a mechanism for subsequent companies to rely on the originator's data if they *share* in costs, albeit after a period of exclusivity.[17] Although this proposal may seem reasonable, it is unlikely to gain traction because pharmaceutical companies do not even bother to criticize this concept, which suggests that they do not consider it a serious option.

II. Regulatory Protection Through Patent Linkage

Another regulatory protection for drugs is patent linkage. In countries that recognize patent linkage, the national regulatory authorities may deny approval of generic drugs that are "linked" to an existing unexpired patent—usually based on information sub-mitted by self-interested patent owners regarding what patents are linked to certain drugs.[18] Thus, a proposed generic drug that would allegedly infringe a patent if sold in the market will be denied regulatory approval. Importantly, denial is not based on the usual regulatory standards of drug safety and efficacy, but solely on a presumed *poten-tial* patent problem where there is generally no independent assessment of whether the listed patent(s) are relevant, let alone valid. This lack of assessment is not surpris-ing, as regulatory authorities have no competency in the area of patents.

Patent linkage holds important implications. As with data exclusivity, patent link-age operates independently of patent defenses and exceptions. The implication of this is that even if a country grants a manufacturer the right to use a patented drug under a compulsory license, such a license may be ineffective if due to patent linkage the manufacturer cannot get regulatory approval to market the drug. This problem can be avoided if there is an exception to patent linkage for compulsory licenses, but that is often not the case.

---

[16] *E.g.*, JUDIT RIUS SANJUAN ET AL., CONSUMER PROJECT ON TECH., POLICY BRIEF NO. 1, A COST SHARING MODEL TO PROTECT INVESTMENTS IN PHARMACEUTICAL TEST DATA 3–8 (2006); *see also* TAHIR AMIN ET AL, INITIATIVES FOR MEDICINES, ACCESS & KNOWLEDGE (I-MAK), THE IMPACT OF ARTICLE 39.3 IN INDIA: A PRACTICAL PERSPECTIVE 13–167 (July 2006); Robert Weissman, *Public Health-Friendly Options for Protecting Pharmaceutical Registration Data*, 1 INT'L. J. INTELL. PROP. MGMT. 113, 117–20 (2006).

[17] U.S. Federal Insecticide, Fungicide, and Rodenticide Act, 7 U.S.C. § 136a(c)(1)(F) (providing complete exclusivity for the first ten years and then cost sharing in years eleven through fifteen).

[18] For example, in the United States, this information is in what is referred to as the "Orange Book." Although the U.S. FDA compiles the list, the data solely reflects information given by applicants with-out any independent review. In addition, the FDA has been found not to have any legal duty to analyze whether the listed patents are actually relevant. *See* Alphapharm v. Thompson, 330 F. Supp. 2d 1, 9 (D.C. Cir. 2004).

A. EXPLORING THE RATIONALE FOR PATENT LINKAGE

The policy rationale for patent linkage focuses primarily on efficiency. Originator companies assert that patent linkage is important because the government should not promote infringement of patents by granting marketing approval for a drug that will infringe a patent granted by another government entity.[19] Companies acknowledge that they could alternatively sue for infringement, but suggest either that they cannot always obtain injunctions, or that patent linkage is simply a preferable mechanism for resolving legal disputes without the expense of litigation.[20]

What is unstated is that patent linkage does not actually resolve legal disputes. To the contrary, because regulatory agencies tend not to evaluate whether patents on a list are valid, patent linkage results in a dramatic change to the status quo where a patent owner must otherwise prove likelihood of success against an accused infringer—both that the patent is valid and infringed—before a preliminary injunction is granted. Against this backdrop, patent linkage turns traditional enforcement of patent rights upside down in that the patent owner is granted a de facto injunction against the purported infringer without any evaluation of facts, let alone a showing of likely validity and infringement.[21] No proof of patent validity or actual infringement is required for a generic company to be barred from approval on the basis of theoretical patent infringement.

Perhaps even more troubling is the fact that in countries where there is some ability to challenge linked patents, many are ultimately found invalid or not infringed during litigation. This result is unsurprising because self-interested patent owners are responsible for listing "relevant" patents. Even if the listed patents are valid, however, they may bear a weak relation to the "linked" drug as regulatory agencies do not evaluate whether patents are relevant, and indeed do not have the technical competency to do so.

Some critics argue that patent linkage promotes the "evergreening" of patents.[22] Although patents do expire, it may seem that the original patent is "evergreen" because subsequent patents can improperly bar generic versions of the original drug after the

---

[19] *E.g.*, PHARMACEUTICAL RESEARCH AND MANUFACTURERS OF AMERICA (PhRMA), SPECIAL 301 SUBMISSION 2011 14 (2011), *available at* http://www.phrma.org/sites/default/files/304/phrma2011special301submission.pdf ("Such a mechanism provides a 'procedural gate' or safeguard, because it ensures that drug regulatory entities do not inadvertently contribute to infringement of patent rights granted by another government entity by granting marketing rights to a competitor of the innovative company.").

[20] *E.g.*, PHARMACEUTICAL RESEARCH AND MANUFACTURERS OF AMERICA (PhRMA), SPECIAL 301 SUBMISSION 2010 14 (2010), *available at* http://keionline.org/sites/default/files/USTR-2010-0003-0245.1.pdf ("Legal mechanisms that allow for early resolution of patent disputes before the generic product in question gains marketing approval avoid the need for complex litigation over damages for marketing an infringing product.") [hereinafter PhRMA 2010].

[21] A generic applicant can sometimes challenge the validity and/or infringement issue, but during the pendency of that challenge be nonetheless barred from regulatory approval.

[22] *E.g.*, COMMISSION ON THE FUTURE OF HEALTH CARE IN CANADA, BUILDING ON VALUES: THE FUTURE OF HEALTH CARE IN CANADA 208 (2002), *available at* http://www.cbc.ca/healthcare/final_report.pdf; Andrew A. Caffrey & Jonathan M. Rotter, *Consumer Protection, Patents and Procedure: Generic Drug Market Entry and the Need to Reform the Hatch-Waxman Act*, 9 VA. J.L. & TECH. 1, 13 (2004).

original patent expires. For example, a drug company could patent a new variation of an already approved drug. A proposed generic of the originally approved drug would not actually infringe the new variation. However, the generic company may not have an opportunity to prove in court the product does not infringe if its product is barred from approval due to patent linkage of an irrelevant patent.

If a country permits legal challenges to patent linkages, there may be an opportunity to mediate the harm of patent linkage that results from improper linking combined with lack of regulatory oversight. For example, in the United States, a generic company can challenge whether a linked patent is either invalid or not infringed.[23] However, even if a country does permit challenges, there may be other barriers to prompt access to generic drugs. Generic companies may not have the financial resources to mount such challenges.[24] An additional complication is that even when generic companies challenge a patent, they sometimes agree to accept a large financial payment from the originator company in exchange for promising not to enter the market until the patents expire.[25]

B. THE IMPACT OF PATENT LINKAGE ON TRADITIONAL PATENT EXCEPTIONS

As with data exclusivity, patent linkage can present an independent bar to marketing a generic drug even when there are no underlying patent problems. For example, patent linkage may thwart the utility of a well-recognized exception to patent rights often referred to as the "Bolar" exception. Under this exception, generic companies are permitted to make limited amounts of a patented drug so that they may seek regulatory approval during the patent term, with the goal of selling the generic drug as soon as the patent expires. There is global support for this policy because, without the Bolar exception, the patent owner would continue to have market exclusivity for several years after the patent expired while generic companies engaged in necessary testing and awaited the results of regulatory approval. Patent linkage may undermine the Bolar exception because, although generic companies can apply for regulatory approval, the patent linkage process may prevent approval during the term of the original patent. Moreover, as noted above, if there are additional patents "linked" to a product that a generic company wants to be marketed, there will be additional delay beyond the term

---

[23] The generic company technically only raises the defense of invalidity or lack of infringement as a defense to a special type of patent infringement. During the period of litigation, approval of the generic drug is stayed. Generic companies can also challenge linked patents in Canada, but in Canada, generic companies after receiving regulatory approval are vulnerable to subsequent patent infringement litigation.

[24] Maurice Ross, *Leveling the Playing Field—The Role of Venture Capital in Hatch-Waxman Patent Litigation*, 79 PAT TRADEMARK AND COPYRIGHT J. (BNA) 730 (2010).

[25] This practice of what is called "pay for delay" is strongly criticized by a number of academics and is under scrutiny by the Federal Trade Commission. *E.g.*, FTC, PAY FOR DELAY: HOW DRUG COMPANY PAY OFFS COST CONSUMERS BILLIONS (2010), *available at* http://www.ftc.gov/os/2010/01/100112payfordelayrpt.pdf; Scott Hemphill, *Paying for Delay: Pharmaceutical Patent Settlement as a Regulatory Design Problem*, 81 N.Y.U. L. REV. 1533 (2006).

of the original patent. Indeed, the European Union has thus far resisted adopting patent linkage on the ground that it would undermine the Bolar exception.

III. The International Context for the Regulatory Protection of Drugs

To understand regulatory protection in the international arena, one must understand two issues. First, existing or future international agreements, as well as less formal political pressure, may force countries to adopt at least data exclusivity and potentially also patent linkage. Second, there may be inadequate policy justification for requiring countries, especially developing countries, to adopt regulatory protection.

A. INTERNATIONAL OBLIGATIONS

The starting place for any discussion of international norms concerning intellectual property protection relating to drugs is the World Trade Organization (WTO) and, in particular, the requirement that all WTO members comply with the Agreement on Trade Related Aspects of Intellectual Property Rights (TRIPS). Under TRIPS, all WTO members must not only provide patent rights, but also protection of some clinical data submitted to national governments in conjunction with obtaining regulatory approval to sell a new drug.[26] A major issue since TRIPS was concluded is whether TRIPS requires data exclusivity.[27] Although there are good arguments that TRIPS does not in fact require data exclusivity, this point of debate is moot for many countries that are obligated to provide such protection after signing agreements that require more than TRIPS does—the so-called TRIPS-plus agreements. Similarly, although there is no serious dispute about the fact that TRIPS does not require patent linkage, this is likewise a moot point for countries that have agreed to TRIPS-plus agreements that explicitly require patent linkage.

B. POLICY CONCERNS FOR DEVELOPING COUNTRIES

Although the underlying policies for data exclusivity and patent linkage were discussed (and questioned) above, their justification for developing countries deserves special scrutiny. After all, such countries have only limited economic means, and the case

---

[26] TRIPS: Agreement on Trade-Related Aspects of Intellectual Property Rights, Marrakesh Agreement Establishing the World Trade Organization, Apr. 15, 1994, Annex 1C, 1869 U.N.T.S. 299, art. 39.

[27] *See, e.g.*, PHRMA 2010, *supra* note 20, at 7 (suggesting that TRIPS requires data exclusivity); CYNTHIA M. HO, ACCESS TO MEDICINE IN THE GLOBAL ECONOMY 80 (2011) (noting that many scholars do not consider TRIPS to require data exclusivity). Others suggest that TRIPS does not require absolute exclusivity, but does require compensation. *E.g.* Aaron Xavier Fellmeth, *Secrecy, Monopoly and Access to Pharmaceuticals in International Trade Law: Protection of Marketing Approval Data under the TRIPS Agreement*, 45 HARV. INT'L L. J. 443, 464 (2004); Shamnad Basheer, *Protection of Regulatory Data under Article 39.3 of TRIPS: The Indian Context*, 28–29 (2009), *available at* http://papers.ssrn.com/sol3/papers.cfm?abstract_id=934269.

for such protection is not ironclad even in countries with greater economic means. Indeed, some countries, such as those in the European Union, reject patent linkage as unduly encroaching on fundamentally recognized exceptions to patent rights, making it questionable why poorer countries should be required to adopt such linkage.[28]

Academics and policy makers have questioned the claim by pharmaceutical companies that stronger protection of drugs—whether through stronger patent or regulatory laws—will necessarily promote greater innovation and foreign direct investment in developing countries.[29] The claim that economic benefits flow from stronger protection of drugs was first made in the context of TRIPS; however, countries that have adopted stronger patent laws and even regulatory protections have not seen greater innovation or foreign direct investment.[30] In fact, countries such as China have received strong foreign direct investment while providing only weak protection of intellectual property.[31] In addition, many skeptics of the claim for stronger protection note that intellectual property rights alone do not promote innovation; rather, a nation must be at a certain level of economic sufficiency before such rights can do so. Most developing countries lack adequate economic capacity to stimulate local innovation. Moreover, even in countries with adequate resources, such as the United States, despite strong legal protection and increasing financial investments the amount of innovation has actually been decreasing.[32]

The argument that patent or regulatory protections are essential to promote innovation is particularly weak with respect to the needs of developing countries. First, the

---

[28] EUROPEAN COMMISSION, PHARMACEUTICAL SECTOR INQUIRY FINAL REPORT 130 (2009) [hereinafter FINAL REPORT], *available at* http://ec.europa.eu/competition/sectors/pharmaceuticals/inquiry/staff_working_paper_part1.pdf.

[29] *E.g.*, COMMISSION ON INTELLECTUAL PROPERTY RIGHTS, INTEGRATING INTELLECTUAL PROPERTY RIGHTS AND DEVELOPMENT POLICY 79–89 (3d ed. 2003) (suggesting increased patent rights may not be optimal for developing countries).

[30] After introducing patent protection and data exclusivity pursuant to an FTA, Jordan reported no such benefits. *See, e.g.*, Hamed El-Said & Mohammed El-Said, *TRIPS-Plus Implications for Access to Medicines in Developing Countries: Lessons from Jordan–United States Free Trade Agreement*, 10 J. WORLD INTELL. PROP. 438, 452–57 (2007); Oxfam Int'l, *All Costs, No Benefits: How TRIPS-Plus Intellectual Property Rules in the US–Jordan FTA Affect Access to Medicines* 7 (Oxfam Briefing Paper, 2007), *available at* http://www.oxfam.org.uk/resources/issues/health/downloads/bp102_trips.pdf.

[31] Frederick M. Abbott, *The International Intellectual Property Rider Enters the 21st Century*, 29 VAND. J. TRANSNAT'L L. 471, 474 (1996) (noting that countries with the weakest levels of intellectual property rights (IPR) protection—the People's Republic of China, Taiwan, Brazil, Argentina, Thailand, etc.— over the past decade have routinely been recipients of the largest net foreign direct investment (FDI) inflows). Others have also noted that the argument between stronger rights and increased FDI is weak. *E.g.*, F.M. Scherer & S. Weisburst, *Economic Effects of Strengthening Pharmaceutical Patent Protection in Italy*, 26 INT'L REV. INDUS. PROP & COPY. L. 1009 (1995); E. Mansfield, *Intellectual Property Protection, Direct Investment, and Technology Transfer* (Int'l Finance Corporation, Discussion Paper, No. 27, 1995).

[32] *See, e.g.*, CONG. BUDGET OFFICE, PUB. NO, 2589, RESEARCH AND DEVELOPMENT IN THE PHARMACEUTICAL INDUSTRY 11–12 (2006) (noting that despite increased spending on research, there is no corollary increase in innovation); MOLLY REDFIELD WART, KNOWLEDGE ECOLOGY INT'L, NOTES ON THE 2004 TO 2009 UNITED STATES FOOD AND DRUG ADMINISTRATION APPROVAL OF NEW MOLECULAR ENTITIES (2010), *available at* http://keionline.org/misc-docs/research_notes/kei_rn_2010_3.pdf (noting that many recently approved drugs do not provide major advances in treatment).

United States and other developed countries constitute the vast majority of sales and profits for pharmaceutical companies, such that any revenue generated in developing countries as a result of data exclusivity and patent linkage is likely to be relatively minimal. Moreover, the marginal additional revenue that may be theoretically generated by these protections should be balanced against the fact that developing countries have only minimal resources. In fact, some scholars have argued that expanding data exclusivity and patent linkage to developing countries would simply provide a windfall to companies that are already more than adequately compensated by protections in wealthier countries.[33] Even if increased protection would promote some innovation, it would likely promote the most profitable treatments, which may not necessarily be the ones most helpful or economically accessible to developing countries. Indeed, in India, where there is some innovative capacity in pharmaceuticals, the focus is on drugs to treat first-world needs, rather than those of local consumers.[34]

In addition to these broad policy concerns, the impact of strong regulatory protection should also be considered in conjunction with patent protection. In particular, in some countries, data exclusivity has been a greater barrier to entry than patent protection. Even when patent protection is available, some companies are electing to rely solely on data exclusivity rather than patent protection. As explained earlier, data exclusivity is automatic and cannot be challenged,[35] which can have a significant impact on the availability of affordable drugs. For example, after Guatemala enacted data exclusivity to comply with a free trade agreement with the United States, medicine prices rose substantially despite the fact that only a limited number of drugs were patented.[36] Similarly, after Jordan implemented TRIPS-plus measures, medicine prices rose by 20 percent.[37] There is no real data yet on the impact of patent linkage on drug prices in developing countries because drugs are only just beginning to be patented in such countries, but patent linkage would likely only compound the existing problems seen with data exclusivity.

The potential harms of data exclusivity and patent linkage for developing countries have not gone unnoticed. As early as 2001, developing countries attempted to clarify that TRIPS did not require data exclusivity. As noted above, although there continues to be an academic debate, this issue is moot for countries that have expressly agreed to data exclusivity in TRIPS-plus agreements. The U.S. Congress seemed to also recognize

---

[33] *E.g.*, Jerome H. Reichman & Catherine Hasenzahl, UNCTAD-ICTSD Project on IPRs and Sustainable Development, Non-Voluntary Licensing of Patented Inventions 6 (2003), *available at* http://www.iprsonline.org/resources/docs/Reichman%20-%20Non-voluntary%20Licensing%20-%20Blue%205.pdf.

[34] *E.g.*, David Operdeck, *Patents, Essential Medicines and the Innovation Game*, 58 Vand. L. Rev. 501, 520 (2005).

[35] An additional issue is that patent filings can be expensive and also cumbersome if a developing country is not a member of the Patent Cooperation Treaty that enables streamlined applications in many countries.

[36] Ellen R. Shaffer & Joseph Brenner, *A Trade Agreement's Impact on Access to Generic Drugs*, 31 Health Affairs 957, 964 (2009), *available at* http://content.healthaffairs.org/content/28/5/w957.full.

[37] *See, e.g.*, El-Said & El-Said, *supra* note 30, at 452–57 (2007); Oxfam Int'l, *supra* note 30.

the harms of regulatory protection in 2007 when it concluded that patent linkage would be made voluntary, rather than mandatory for the then-pending trade agreements with Peru and Panama.[38]

Beyond the already recognized harms of foreign-imposed regulatory protection, developing countries may face further problems. The United States is in negotiations with a number of countries for a new agreement referred to as the Trans-Pacific Partnership (TPP). Although the negotiations are in secret, leaked text suggests that current provisions would backtrack on the 2007 congressional agreement.[39] For example, whereas patent linkage was optional for Peru under the 2007 agreement, the TPP may make it mandatory for Peru, and also create an absolute bar to regulatory approval until the patent issue is litigated. The TPP may also extend data exclusivity beyond five years and even preclude reliance on information that is publicly available.[40] Even more worrisome is that the TPP will likely have broader repercussions; the TPP provisions will be a template for future agreements with other developing countries because the United States has generally sought increased protections in subsequent agreements across-the-board.

IV. Mediating the Harms of Regulatory Protection

Although many public health advocates suggest that developing countries should avoid further adoption of data exclusivity and patent linkage, that is not realistic for most developing countries interested in enhanced market opportunities in the United States. Some countries may feel compelled to agree to some type of regulatory protection in the context of a free trade agreement, separate and apart from whether they believe that such protection is sound from a policy perspective. In such circumstances, the details of the protection are critical. This next section focuses on those crucial details as a means to provide practical solutions.

---

[38] Peru & Panama FTA Changes 8 (May 10, 2007), *available at* http://waysandmeans.house.gov/Media/pdf/110/05%2014%2007/05%2014%2007.pdf. This is the most affirmative action to recognize the public health interests of developing countries; it goes substantially beyond resolutions by the U.S. Congress and the EU parliament that simply recognize the principle of public health as an interest. *See, e.g.*, Resolution of July 12, 2007 on the TRIPS Agreement and Access to Medicines, Eur. Parl. Doc. B6-0288 (2007); S. Res. 241, 110th Cong. (2007); H. Res. 525, 110th Cong. (2007).

[39] The TPP is being negotiated with Australia, Brunei, Chile, Malaysia, New Zealand, Peru, Singapore, the United States, and Vietnam. *See* Office of the U.S. Trade Representative, Trans-Pacific Partnership Agreement, http://www.ustr.gov/tpp (last visited on Oct. 29, 2011).

[40] Not only does the text explicitly suggest that countries may provide more than five years ("at least five years"), but PhRMA is actively suggesting twelve years for biologics. The Trans-Pacific Partnership: Intellectual Property Rights Chapter, art. 9(2)(a)–(b) (Feb. 10, 2011 leaked draft), *available at* http://www.citizenstrade.org/ctc/wp-content/uploads/2011/10/TransPacificIP1.pdf   [hereinafter Draft TPP]; PhRMA, PhRMA Views: Intellectual Property (IP) Chapter for the Trans-Pacific Partnership (TPP) Agreement 1 (Apr. 2011), *available at* http://freepdfhosting.com/b862d1fe3a.pdf (suggesting at least five years for traditional drugs and at least twelve years for biologics—with the ability for "adjustments" as needed in the future).

A. DATA EXCLUSIVITY LIMITATIONS

The most ambitious alternative to data exclusivity is to instead adopt data *sharing*. In other words, generic entrants would not have completely free reliance on the data developed by another, but they would pay a fair amount to have immediate access. As noted above, this model already exists for agricultural products in the United States. Unfortunately, although popular with some public health advocates, its likelihood of adoption is very slim because pharmaceutical companies generally do not even bother to consider it a serious option, and suggest that the only alternative is *unending* exclusivity.

If data exclusivity itself is adopted, the key issue is limiting its scope. For example, there should be no exclusivity provided where the underlying data is now in the public domain. Similarly, it should only exist where there was considerable effort or expense involved in developing the clinical data because there would otherwise be no real rationale for providing the protection—even assuming that it was justified separate from patent protection. In addition, the term of the data exclusivity is very important. The term is a current issue because the United States is proposing that, at least for some drugs, data exclusivity would last as long as ten or twelve years.

No matter the length of time, the harm of data exclusivity could be mediated substantially if the term began from the first global approval. A recent white paper released by the Obama administration suggests that the United States plans to propose data exclusivity for developing countries, but such exclusivity will be conditioned upon companies promptly seeking approval in those countries.[41] Although this is not optimal to promote the fastest access to generics and has thus been roundly criticized, if data exclusivity is required, this would at least eliminate some harm by limiting the term in developing countries to ensure that generic drugs are available at the same time in these countries as in wealthier ones.[42] However, the devil is in the details and, although the official details are as yet undisclosed, leaked text suggests that countries will merely have the *option* of requiring pharmaceutical companies to promptly file to get the benefit of a longer patent term.[43]

---

[41] OFFICE OF THE U.S. TRADE REPRESENTATIVE, TRANS-PACIFIC PARTNERSHIP TRADE GOALS TO ENHANCE ACCESS TO MEDICINE 1 (2011). On the other hand, the leaked test suggests that this is only an *option* and not a mandatory requirement. Draft TPP, *supra* note 40, at art. 8(6)(e) (stating that to receive patent extensions for curtailment of term from marketing approval, a country "may" require marketing approval to begin "within [X] years" of first marketing approval, with the critical period of X yet to be defined.).

[42] Even though some harm is mitigated, some are critical of any requirement of data exclusivity or patent linkage for developing countries. *E.g.*, William New, *USTR White Paper on Trade in Medicines Raises Questions*, INTELL. PROP. WATCH (Sept. 14, 2011), http://www.ip-watch.org/weblog/2011/09/14/ustr-white-paper-on-trade-in-medicines-raises-questions/; Doctors Without Borders, *supra* note 7, at 5–6.

[43] Draft TPP, *supra* note 40, at art. 6(e) (suggesting that parties *may* require an applicant that has submitted an application for marketing approval to commence the process "within [X] years of the date of first marketing approval of the same" product as a condition for an extension of the patent term). This optional requirement has been criticized. *E.g.*, Brook Baker, *US-Trade-Enhancing Access to Medicines (Access Window) in Its Proposed TPP IP Text Is a Sham*, INFOJUSTICE.ORG (Oct. 25, 2011), http://infojustice.org/resource-library/trans-pacific-partnership/us-trade-enhancing-access-to-medicines-access-window-in-its-proposed-tpp-ip-text-is-a-sham.

B. PATENT LINKAGE LIMITATIONS

The best "type" of patent linkage would be one that most companies would not consider to be true linkage at all, in that it would not completely bar approval of a generic; rather, it would provide notice to the patent owner, who could then initiate an infringement suit after the generic enters the market.[44] The benefit of this system is that, although the patent owner is on notice that the generic company is planning to launch a new product, the generic company is not completely thwarted from the ability to not only market its product, but also to challenge validity and infringement.

This system is not a completely theoretical option. In Australia, for example, after patent linkage was reluctantly adopted as a result of a free trade agreement with the United States, the regulatory authorities give notice to patent owners about generic applicants, but do not bar approval of generics.[45] Peru and Panama were also permitted to use this diluted form of patent linkage after the U.S. Congress in 2007 announced that pending agreements with such countries would be so modified (as noted above).[46]

Harm from patent linkage may be ameliorated further if generic companies have not only the opportunity to challenge validity, but also incentives to do so. Indeed, the first country to provide patent linkage, the United States, permits legal challenges to either infringement or validity, although the procedures are quite complex and permitted only during the last year of data exclusivity; nonetheless, challenges are common because the first successful challenger is awarded a six-month period of exclusivity as the only generic, which may result in an increase in market share among consumers.[47] Although most agreements requiring patent linkage have not included such provisions, the leaked provisions of the current TPP suggest providing an "effective reward" for such successful challenges when a country delays marketing approval to a proposed generic that is linked to a previously approved drug that is patented.[48]

Another option is to limit the scope of patents that can be "linked." For example, although in the United States, a generic version of a previously approved drug will be

---

[44] This assumes a situation where something is required beyond no linkage at all.

[45] Therapeutic Goods Act 1989 (Cth) s 26D (Austl.).

[46] The United States now seems to be requiring patent linkage that bars regulatory approval of generics in pending free trade agreements. Draft TPP, *supra* note 40, at art. 9(5) (providing not only notice, but an automatic delay of marketing approval for generic drugs to permit the patent owner time to adjudicate patent issues).

[47] This incentive may be diluted because originator companies often market authorized generics during this term, which significantly reduces the benefit of the exclusivity from other generic competition. *E.g.*, FEDERAL TRADE COMMISSION, AUTHORIZED GENERIC DRUGS: SHORT-TERM EFFECTS AND LONG-TERM IMPACT (2011). In addition, as noted earlier, another problem is that an originator company may pay the generic not to market its drug during the exclusivity period. The Federal Trade Commission, legislators, and scholars suggested solutions to address these issues. *E.g.*, S. 27, 112th Cong. (2011) (limiting pay for delay settlements); S. 373, 112th Cong. (2011) (banning authorized generic drugs); H.R. 741, 112th Cong. (2011) (banning authorized generic drugs); C. Scott Hemphill & Mark A. Lemley, *Earning Exclusivity: Generic Drug Incentives and the Hatch-Waxman Act*, 77 ANTITRUST L. J. 947 (2011) (suggesting non-legislative solution that utilizes the FDA).

[48] Draft TPP, *supra* note 40, at art. 9(5)(d).

denied approval if it is linked to a patent on a new use of the drug that was previously approved, that does not need to occur. Patent linkage could be limited such that it only bars approval of drugs based on patents on the identical composition that was first approved. This option would also bar denial of patents based on subsequent patents that merely change the dosage strength. Another possibility would be to bar denial when the composition is modified slightly. All of these options are difficult to police in practice because regulatory authorities do not have the expertise to evaluate whether patents are properly listed. On the other hand, even if the list of linked patents cannot be effectively policed by regulatory authorities, it could possibly be effectively policed if there are penalties for invalid claims of patent validity or infringement—if generic companies have the option to litigate this issue.[49]

Conclusion

The ultimate conclusion to this chapter remains to be seen. Although the impact of data exclusivity and patent linkage can be described and predicted, whether developing countries will adopt such measures is yet to be determined. In addition, although regulatory protections do have an impact on access to medicine, these are not the only factors besides patents that impact access to affordable medicine. Drug costs can also be affected, for example, by rules in FTAs that limit the ability of countries to set price caps.[50] By focusing on the narrow but influential field of regulatory protections, this chapter has sought to promote a better understanding of a select number of laws that greatly impact access to affordable medicine.

---

[49] Australia requires the pioneer company to certify that litigation against generic companies is in good faith, has a reasonable prospect of success, and will be conducted without unreasonable delay. Therapeutic Goods Act 1989 (Cth) s 26C(3)–(4) (Austl.). If the certification is later discovered to be false or materially misleading, the company may be subject to a fine of up to $10 million. *Id.* at s 26C(5). The generic applicant may also be subject to a penalty. For a more in-depth discussion of Australia's law, see Thomas Faunce & Joel Lexchin, *"Linkage" Pharmaceutical Evergreening in Canada and Australia*, 4 N.Z. Health Pol'y, 1,1 (2007).

[50] *See, e.g.*, US–Austl. FTA, Annex 2-C; US–Korea FTA, art. 5.2; The Trans-Pacific Partnership: Transparency Chapter—Annex on Transparency and Procedural Fairness for Healthcare Technologies (June 22, 2011 leaked draft), *available at* http://www.citizenstrade.org/ctc/wp-content/uploads/2011/10/TransPacificTransparency.pdf; *see also* Ho, *supra* note 27, at 246–49 (explaining FTA strategy of minimizing price controls, as well as encouraging use of patented drugs); Sean Flynn, Statement: Leaked US Proposal for a TPP Pharmaceutical Chapter (Oct. 22, 2011), *available at* http://infojustice.org/archives/5814#more-5814 (discussing impact of TPP provisions on price controls).

18

COMBATING ANTIBIOTIC RESISTANCE THROUGH

THE HEALTH IMPACT FUND

Kevin Outterson, *Thomas Pogge,†and Aidan Hollis* **

Introduction

On April 7, 2011, the World Health Organization (WHO) embarked on a yearlong campaign to combat antibiotic resistance. The project is driven by several related concerns: resistance is rising, drug companies are producing fewer innovative antibiotics, and yet antibiotics continue to be used inappropriately.[1] Resistance distorts markets for innovative antibiotics in unusual and counterintuitive ways, giving major stakeholders economic incentives to waste these precious resources.[2] An insurance reimbursement system that rewards companies primarily for unit sales of antibiotics undermines public health goals such as the rational use of antibiotics. Conversely, rational use,

* Associate Professor & Co-Director of the Health Law Program, Boston University School of Law, mko@bu.edu. Mark Nickas, Boston University School of Law, provided research assistance.

† Leitner Professor of Philosophy and International Affairs, Yale University, thomas.pogge@yale.edu.

** Professor of Economics, University of Calgary, ahollis@ucalgary.ca.

[1] WORLD HEALTH ORGANIZATION, WORLD HEALTH DAY—APRIL 7, 2011, http://www.who.int/world-health-day/2011/en/index.html; A.D. So, N. Gupta, S.K. Brahmachari, I. Chopra, C. Nathan, K. Outterson, J.P. Paccaud, D.J. Payne, R.W. Peeling, M. Spigelman & J. Weigelt, *Towards New Business Models for R&D for Novel Antibiotics*, 14 DRUG RESISTANCE UPDATES 88 (2011); Infectious Diseases Soc'y of America, *Combating Antimicrobial Resistance, Policy Recommendations to Save Lives*, 52 CLINICAL INFECTIOUS DISEASES S397 (Supp. 5 2011).

[2] So et al., *supra* note 1; Kevin Outterson, *The Legal Ecology of Resistance: The Role of Antibiotic Resistance in Pharmaceutical Innovation*, 31 CARDOZO L. REV. 613, 628 (2010); Aaron S. Kesselheim & Kevin Outterson, *Fighting Antibiotic Resistance: Marrying New Financial Incentives to Meeting Public Health Goals*, 29 HEALTH AFFAIRS 1689 (2010); RAMANAN LAXMINARAYAN & ANUP MALANI, EXTENDING THE CURE: POLICY RESPONSES TO THE GROWING THREAT OF ANTIBIOTIC RESISTANCE (2007), *available at* http://www.extendingthecure.org/report; Rachel Nugent, Emma Back & Alexandra Beith, THE RACE AGAINST

infection control, and antibacterial vaccine programs significantly reduce antibiotic sales, undermining company research and development (R&D) incentives.[3] As a result, a prominent drug industry leader recently stated that antibiotic "incentives that separate the financial return from the use of a product are the only way to change this behavior."[4] Such mechanisms are called "de-linkage" in that they separate the markets for medicines from R&D cost recovery. In de-linkage, product sales revenues are not the sole source of R&D cost recovery and profits, but are supplemented or replaced by other mechanisms such as prizes.

One prominent de-linkage mechanism is the Health Impact Fund (HIF), which would reward companies for the health impact of their drugs.[5] The HIF is a global mechanism, which is especially valuable in the field of antibiotics. Effective antibiotics are a global common pool, a potentially exhaustible resource that should be managed effectively on a global basis.[6]

This chapter is organized as follows. In Section I, we describe the original HIF proposal in greater detail, including some of the criticisms that have been lodged concerning generic competition. The legal and biological complexities of resistance are explored in Sectiont II. The legal ecology of resistance strongly suggests that new antibiotic incentives must be conditioned on meeting long-term public health goals. Otherwise, the rush to produce new antibiotics will only hasten the arrival of resistance. The confluence of antibiotic resistance and the HIF is the subject of Section III, evaluating whether antibiotics might be an appropriate test of the HIF and whether the HIF might be an effective global coordination mechanism for antibiotics. We conclude that antibiotics as a class may be an appropriate first application of the HIF, but that the problems of cross-resistance will probably require all antibiotics to participate. Significant questions and limitations are noted.

The stakes are huge for getting these policies right: the Infectious Diseases Society of America (IDSA) warns that the alternative may be a global ecological collapse in antibiotic effectiveness.[7]

DRUG RESISTANCE (2010), *available at* http://www.cgdev.org/content/publications/detail/1424207/; Elias Mossialos, Chantal M. Morel, Suzanne Edwards, Julia Berenson, Marin Gemmill-Toyama & David Brogan, POLICIES AND INCENTIVES FOR PROMOTING INNOVATION IN ANTIBIOTIC RESEARCH (2010), *available at* http://www.euro.who.int/__data/assets/pdf_file/0011/120143/E94241.pdf.

3   Outterson, *supra* note 2.

4   So et al., *supra* note 1, at 92.

5   Aidan Hollis & Thomas Pogge, THE HEALTH IMPACT FUND: MAKING NEW MEDICINES ACCESSIBLE FOR ALL (2008), *available at* http://healthimpactfund.org/e-library. *See* www.healthimpactfund.org for many publications and media discussions about the HIF as well as information about HIF supporters and their work.

6   LAXMINARAYAN & MALANI, *supra* note 2; Nugent et al., *supra* note 2; Mossialos et al., *supra* note 2.

7   Infectious Diseases Soc'y of America, *supra* note 1; Infectious Diseases Soc'y of America, BAD BUGS, NO DRUGS: AS ANTIBIOTIC DISCOVERY STAGNATES...A PUBLIC HEALTH CRISIS BREWS (2004), *available at* http://www.idsociety.org/uploadedFiles/IDSA/Policy_and_Advocacy/Current_Topics_ and_Issues/Advancing_Product_Research_and_Development/Bad_Bugs_No_Drugs/Statements/ As%20Antibiotic%20Discovery%20Stagnates%20A%20Public%20Health%20Crisis%20Brews. pdf#search=%22BAD BUGS NO DRUGS%22 [hereinafter BAD BUGS, NO DRUGS].

I. The Health Impact Fund

A. PAYING FOR GLOBAL HEALTH IMPACT

Financed primarily by governments, the Health Impact Fund is a proposed pay-for-performance mechanism that would offer innovators the option—completely voluntary[8]—to register any new medicine.[9] By registering a product, the innovator would undertake to make it available, during its first ten years on the market, wherever it is needed at no more than the lowest feasible cost of production and distribution. The innovator would further commit to allow, at no charge, generic production and distribution of the product after these ten years have ended (if the innovator still has unexpired patents on the product). In exchange, the registrant would receive, during that ten-year period, annual reward payments based on the product's health impact. The reward payments would be part of a large annual payout, with each registered product receiving a cash payment from the HIF proportional to its share of the assessed health impact of all HIF-registered products in the relevant year.[10] If the HIF were found to work well, its annual reward pool could be scaled up to attract an increasing share of new medicines.[11]

The HIF would foster the development of new high-impact medicines—including against diseases concentrated among the poor, who are now neglected because innovators cannot recover their R&D costs from sales to the poor.[12] The option of an alternative reward based on health impact would transform heretofore neglected diseases into some of the most lucrative pharmaceutical R&D opportunities. For example, many have suggested that antibiotic research is not financially rewarding for large pharmaceutical companies.[13] The HIF would help to reverse that problem by offering an alternative revenue stream of up to several billion dollars per drug over the ten-year registration period.

The HIF would also promote appropriate financial access to new medicines by contractually limiting the price of any registered product to the lowest feasible cost of production and distribution. In addition, because the HIF pays only for actual health impact, the companies themselves are economically motivated to maximize access. The HIF rewards drug company registrants when their products are appropriately available to the neediest patients, perhaps at prices below marginal cost, and when they are competently prescribed and optimally used. Registrants would be rewarded not for

---

[8]   As noted below, the problem of cross-resistance might require antibiotics to join the HIF in an all-or-nothing system.

[9]   Under certain conditions, the HIF might also permit a company to register a traditional medicine or a new use of an existing medicine.

[10] In some cases, the HIF may want to create contractual minimum and maximum payout amounts to reduce uncertainty for registrants.

[11] Hollis & Pogge, *supra* note 5.

[12] The HIF is limited to new medicines, and perhaps new uses for existing molecules. It does not directly change incentives for existing generic drugs, but if HIF-registered drugs are fully deployed, they may effectively compete with generic drugs at lower prices.

[13] So et al., *supra* note 1.

selling their products, but for making them effective toward improving global health. For antibiotics, health impact will be maximized not necessarily through aggressive sales, but also through careful long-term stewardship and appropriate use. HIF incentives would need calibration to the unique characteristics of antibiotics.

If some pharmaceutical R&D were financed through tax-funded HIF rewards, most of the cost would be borne by affluent populations and people—just like today. But there are important differences. First, innovators would make no profit from the sale of their medicine as such—they would profit only insofar as this medicine is actually used to improve patient health. Second, in order to profit from serving affluent patients, innovators would not need to exclude poor patients. On the contrary, they would profit equally from serving poor patients, too, even if the drugs were offered at very low prices. Health gains achieved for any patients—rich or poor—would contribute equally toward the innovator's bottom line.

The HIF will provide optimal incentives only if potential registrants are assured that the rewards will actually be there in the decade following market approval. Core funding of the HIF is therefore best guaranteed by a broad partnership of countries. If governments representing one-third of global income agreed to contribute just .03 percent of their gross national incomes (3 of every 10,000 currency units), the HIF could get started with $6 billion annually. This fixed pool of funds will be divided annually among registrants in proportion to the health impact of the registered drug. Thus, the HIF can be seen as an ongoing competition among innovators that ranges over all countries and all diseases, with firms earning more money if their product has a larger impact on health.

Health impact can be measured in terms of the number of quality-adjusted life years (QALYs)[14] saved worldwide. The QALY metric is already extensively used by private and state insurers in determining prices for new drugs, so employing it in calculating HIF rewards is not a big leap. Taking as a benchmark the pharmaceutical arsenal available before a registered medicine was introduced, the HIF would estimate to what extent this medicine has added to the length and quality of human lives. This estimate would be based on surveillance data and clinical trials (including pragmatic trials in real-life settings), combined with data on sales volumes and the demographic and clinical characteristics of patients using the product. Additional tools that could be used include tracking randomly selected medicines (identifiable by serial numbers) to their end users, and statistical analysis of sales data as correlated with data about the global burden of disease. These estimates would necessarily be imperfect. But so long as any errors are random and small, or at least not exploitable by registrants,[15] HIF incentives would remain correct in their direction and relative sizes.

The reward rate, in terms of dollars per QALY, would be calculated annually for each registered drug in the HIF. This rate would vary, depending on the total number of

---

[14] For additional details on using QALYs to measure health impact, see Hollis & Pogge, *supra* note 5.

[15] Because registrants are competing for shares of a fixed pool, public monitoring will be supplemented by the private monitoring efforts of other firms in the HIF.

QALYs in the HIF for a given year. With the HIF so designed, innovators would choose to register products that can reduce the global burden of disease most cost-effectively. Products with the largest health impact would make the most money—creating exactly the right incentives for innovation. And because the HIF would be an optional system, the reward rate is self-adjusting. If rewards were too high, new registrants would enter and reduce the annual reward rate (money per QALY). If profits were too low, the reward rate would naturally increase as firms would choose, for more of their new products, to forgo HIF registration in favor of exploiting the ordinary patent-based marketing system. Competition would ensure that registered products are rewarded at a rate that is profitable for innovators and maximizes the effect of the HIF.

To be certain that the HIF is cost-effective relative to other public health expenditures, a maximum reward rate can be stipulated; if one year's funds are not fully used, the remainder can be rolled over into future years. To reassure potential innovators, some protection against unreasonably low rewards can be added.[16]

B. ADVANTAGES OF THE HEALTH IMPACT FUND

Let us sketch how the original HIF proposal would, without revision of global intellectual property agreements,[17] provide systemic relief for seven failings of the present system. These seven problems are prominent weaknesses with the current global market for pharmaceuticals, as we have detailed elsewhere.[18]

High Prices would not exist for HIF-registered medicines. In local markets where buyers were particularly price sensitive, innovators would have strong incentives to reduce prices, possibly even below the cost of production, in order to increase health impact rewards through increased volume.

Diseases concentrated among the poor, insofar as they contribute substantially to the global disease burden, would no longer be neglected. In fact, the more destructive among them would come to afford some of the most lucrative research opportunities for biotechnology and pharmaceutical companies. The HIF counts health benefits to the poorest of patients equally with health benefits to the richest.

Bias toward maintenance drugs would be absent from HIF-encouraged research. Drugs for long-term chronic conditions may be sold to the same patients for many years, providing a longer and more stable market. By contrast, an antibiotic is generally given only for a short course, and a vaccine is generally delivered in a single dose. Drug company executives complain that the market is therefore biased in favor of maintenance drugs.[19] The HIF assesses each registered medicine's health impact in terms of

---

[16] Hollis & Pogge, *supra* note 5.

[17] The Trade-Related Aspects of Intellectual Property Rights (TRIPS) Agreement sets global minimum standards for intellectual property law through the World Trade Organization. *See* http://www.wto.org/english/tratop_E/trips_E/t_agmo_E.htm.

[18] Hollis & Pogge, *supra* note 5.

[19] *See, e.g.,* Steven J. Projan, *Why Is Big Pharma Getting Out of Antibacterial Drug Discovery?*, 6 CURRENT OPINION IN MICROBIOLOGY 427 (2003).

how its use reduces mortality and morbidity worldwide—without regard to whether it achieves this reduction through cure, chronic treatment, or prevention. This would guide firms to deliberate about potential research projects in a way that is also optimal for global public health, namely in terms of the expected global health impact of the new medicine relative to the cost of developing it. The profitability of research projects would be aligned with their value in terms of global public health.

Wastefulness would be dramatically lower for HIF-registered products. There would be no deadweight losses from large markups.[20] There would be less costly patent litigation as generic competitors would lack incentives to invalidate weak patents and innovators would have less incentive to suppress generic products (as these would enhance the innovator's health impact reward). Innovators might therefore often not even bother to obtain, police, and defend patents in many national jurisdictions. To register a medicine with the HIF, innovators need show only once that they have an effective and innovative product, avoiding the need to repetitively demonstrate inventive step or non-obviousness to patent offices around the world.[21]

Excessive marketing would also be much reduced for HIF-registered medicines. Because each innovator is rewarded for the health impact of its addition to the medical arsenal, incentives to develop "me-too" drugs to compete with an existing HIF-registered medicine would be weak. And innovators would have incentives to urge a HIF-registered drug upon doctors and patients only insofar as such marketing results in measurable therapeutic benefits for which the innovator would then be rewarded. In antibiotics, this feature will be especially welcome, as it removes financial pressures to promote resistance through excessive sales.

Counterfeiting of HIF-registered products would be less attractive. With the genuine item widely available near or even below the marginal cost of production, there is less to be gained from producing and selling counterfeits.[22]

The Last-Mile Problem[23] would be mitigated because each HIF-registered innovator would have strong incentives to ensure that patients are fully instructed and properly provisioned so that they make optimal use (dosage, compliance, etc.) of its medicines, which will then, through wide and effective deployment, have their optimal public health impact. Rather than ignore poor countries as unprofitable markets, pharmaceutical companies would, moreover, have incentives to work with one another and with national health

---

20. Sean Flynn, Aidan Hollis & Michael Palmedo, *An Economic Justification for Open Access to Essential Medicine Patents in Developing Countries*, 37 J.L. MED. & ETHICS 184 (2009).

21. Talha Syed, SHOULD A PRIZE SYSTEM FOR PHARMACEUTICALS REQUIRE PATENT PROTECTION FOR ELIGIBILITY? (Incentives for Global Health, Discussion Paper No. 2, 2009).

22. Kevin Outterson & Ryan Smith, *Counterfeit Drugs: The Good, The Bad, and the Ugly*, 16 ALBANY L.J. SCI. & TECH. 525 (2006).

23. In the early days of the Internet, the "last mile" problem was framed in the United States as the difficulty in delivering bandwidth from a neighborhood fiber optic node to homes via copper telephone wires. The term has now taken on a much broader meaning to include many logistical barriers to delivering technological innovation to the end of the distribution chain. In our context, overcoming the last mile problem is ensuring that low-income populations across the world have excellent access to pharmaceutical innovation, and that this access greatly improves human health.

ministries, international agencies, and nongovernmental organizations (NGOs) toward improving the health systems of these countries in order to enhance the impact of the pharmaceutical companies' HIF-registered medicines there.

C. CRITIQUES OF THE HEALTH IMPACT FUND

James Love of Knowledge Ecology International has criticized the HIF in a number of forums.[24] Love has proposed several global de-linkage mechanisms to pay for R&D outside of the market reimbursement system.[25] His primary substantive criticism is that the HIF leaves patents in the hands of the patent owners, thereby delaying market-based generic competition from multiple producers. Others share this concern in the broader context of prize proposals that rely on contractual access provisions.[26] In response to these criticisms, the HIF proposal was adjusted to permit: (a) subcontracting (licensing) to generic firms, (b) tender systems, and (c) administratively determined prices.[27] The final form of the HIF is flexible, which permits a variety of contract options to be explored so that the HIF is most attractive for different classes of medicines. With respect to antibiotics, because of the interest in conservation, there is a stronger rationale to prefer to limit the rights to produce and sell the drug, as we explore below.

Other practical concerns include measuring health impact in order to determine the prize payments and obtaining sufficient financial support to fund the HIF. Measurement will be a complex task, with many real-world epidemiological problems to solve, including tracking and disentangling the various causal factors implicated in health impact. Substantial work is underway to articulate appropriate metrics, but will not be detailed here, as it was the subject of a two-day conference at Harvard Law School in November 2009 and ongoing work thereafter. In addition to measuring the health impact from antibiotics in a specific year, further work is needed to consider the future health impact of inappropriate antibiotic use today.

---

[24] See JAMES LOVE, THE HEALTH IMPACT FUND PROPOSAL (2008), *available at* http://keionline.org/hif. For a response from the HIF project, see Thomas Pogge & Jake Hirsch-Allen, *A Response from the Authors of the Health Impact Fund*, INTELLECTUAL PROP. WATCH (Oct. 3, 2011), *available at* http://www.ip-watch.org/weblog/2011/10/03/a-response-from-the-authors-of-the-health-impact-fund/.

[25] James Love, *Prizes, Not Prices, to Stimulate Antibiotic R&D*, SCI. & DEV. NETWORK (Mar. 26, 2008), *available at* http://www.scidev.net/en/opinions/prizes-not-prices-to-stimulate-antibiotic-r-d-.html; James Love & Tim Hubbard, *The Big Idea: Prizes to Stimulate R&D for New Medicines*, 82 CHI.-KENT L. REV. 1519 (2007); James Love & Tim Hubbard, *Prizes for Innovation of New Medicines and Vaccines*, 18 ANNALS HEALTH L. 155, 159–60 (2009).

[26] Paul Wilson & Amrita Palriwala, PRIZES FOR GLOBAL HEALTH TECHNOLOGIES: AN ASSESSMENT WITH A CASE STUDY IN TB DIAGNOSTICS (2010), *available at* http://healthresearchpolicy.org/sites/healthresearchpolicy.org/files/assessments/files/R4D%20Prizes%20Assessment%20Draft%20Report_2.pdf; Donald W. Light, *Making Practical Markets for Vaccines*, 2 PLoS MED. 934 (2005); Donald W. Light, *Is G8 Putting Profits before the World's Poorest Children?*, 370 LANCET 297 (2007); Donald W. Light, *GAVI's Advance Market Commitment*, 375 LANCET 638 (2010).

[27] Aidan Hollis, THE HEALTH IMPACT FUND AND PRICE DETERMINATION (Incentives for Global Health Discussion Paper No. 1, 2009), *available at* healthimpactfund.org/files/papers/DP1_Hollis.pdf .

The funding question will be dependent upon the political will to initiate a realistic test of the HIF. This chapter outlines a therapeutic category of drugs for a potential large-scale test, namely systemic antibacterials.

II. The Legal Ecology Of Antibiotic Resistance and the Need for Global Coordination

Before turning to the potential case of a special-purpose HIF limited to antibiotics (aHIF), we must briefly explore some of the unique legal and biological aspects of antibiotics. These unique characteristics make antibiotics an appealing candidate for a test of the HIF, but also suggest some aHIF modifications to account for the problem of resistance.

Antibiotics may be the greatest single medical success of the twentieth century. If antibiotics were to lose their effectiveness, some of the advances in health over the previous seventy-five years would be threatened. The edifice of modern medicine rests upon the foundation of effective antibiotic therapies. But this achievement rests on an insecure foundation. As antibiotics are used, they create evolutionary pressure that threatens their undoing through resistance.[28] Resistance is an evolutionary dynamic.

Antibiotic effectiveness can also be understood as an ecological issue, a valuable common pool resource akin to productive fisheries. Common pools are prone to depletion and collapse through uncoordinated withdrawals: a stark example is the destruction of the vast herds of North American buffalo in the Great Plains in the nineteenth century.[29] In the case of antibiotics, withdrawals occur as antibiotic resistance grows through use and misuse, including antibiotic pollution when resistance externalities are spread across populations and drugs. The common pool is renewed through conservation and the addition of new antibiotic therapies. We face a tragedy of the antibiotic commons as uncoordinated use, misuse, and pollution of precious antibiotics may prematurely destroy these important drugs.[30] Incentives for new antibiotics must therefore be conditioned on addressing both ecological and evolutionary (Eco/Evo) factors,[31] to ensure that long-term public health goals are achieved.[32]

---

[28] BAD BUGS, NO DRUGS, *supra* note 7; Infectious Diseases Soc'y of America, *supra* note 1; Mossialos et al., *supra* note 2; Nugent et al., *supra* note 2; LAXMINARAYAN & MALANI, *supra* note 2.

[29] M. Scott Taylor, *Buffalo Hunt: International Trade and the Virtual Extinction of the North American Bison*, 101 AMER. ECON. REV. 3162 (2011).

[30] Timo Goeschl & Timothy Swanson, *The Interaction of Dynamic Problems and Dynamic Policies: Some Economics of Biotechnology*, *in* BATTLING RESISTANCE TO ANTIBIOTICS AND PESTICIDES: AN ECONOMIC APPROACH (Ramanan Laxminarayan ed., 2003); Kevin Outterson, *The Vanishing Public Domain: Antibiotic Resistance, Pharmaceutical Innovation and Intellectual Property Law*, 67 U. PITT. L. REV. 67, 122 (2005)].

[31] Fernando Baquero, Teresa M. Coque & Fernando de la Cruz, *Ecology and Evolution as Targets: The Need for Novel Eco-Evo Drugs and Strategies to Fight Antibiotic Resistance*, 55 ANTIMICROBIAL AGENTS & CHEMOTHERAPY 3649 (2011) ("Classical measures trying to contain or slow locally the progress of antibiotic resistance in patients on the basis of better antibiotic prescribing policies have clearly become insufficient at the global level. Urgent measures are needed to directly confront the processes influencing antibiotic resistance pollution in the microbiosphere. Recent interdisciplinary research indicates that new eco–evo drugs and strategies, which take ecology and evolution into account, have a promising role in resistance prevention, decontamination, and the eventual restoration of antibiotic susceptibility.").

[32] Kesselheim & Outterson, *supra* note 2.

Resistance creates at least six important policy issues for antibiotic incentives, as described in the chart below and the text that follows:

Policy Issue	Implications
1. Conservation dampens R&D incentives for new antibiotics	Optimal solutions must balance conservation and new production; faster introduction of new molecules may harm global public health
2. Companies have financial incentives to maximize unit sales of antibiotics, wasting antibiotics through resistance	De-linkage enables companies to profit from meeting public health goals
3. Resistance stimulates innovation by clearing the field of competitive antibiotics	New antibiotic molecules should be well-timed, arriving when needed due to resistance rather than as quickly as possible
4. Patents are clumsy policy levers for antibiotic policy because pollution externalities differ in each drug–bug combination	Alternative de-linkage mechanisms should be explored, such as reimbursement, prizes, and aHIF
5. Resistance is a global problem	Solutions must be scalable across the globe and cannot depend on the existence of highly functional governments and infrastructure in poor countries
6. Antibiotic innovation is broken	Managing antibiotic pollution externalities is difficult and complex

The first is the effect of conservation upon incentives for R&D of new antibiotics.[33] Both conservation and R&D are laudable, but in many ways conservation and R&D work at cross-purposes, and difficult choices must be made between them. For example, insofar as antibiotic conservation is successful in curbing inappropriate use and maintaining the effectiveness of existing products, it will suppress demand for new antibiotics. Viewed from the dynamic perspective of R&D into new drugs, conservation programs undercut market incentives by dampening future demand.[34] But from the static perspective of public health, conservation is an unqualified success when infections are prevented or antibiotic resistance averted. In an optimally coordinated market, current antibiotics would be conserved for as long as possible and new ones introduced on a "just in time" basis, perhaps with some antibiotics held in a Strategic Antibiotic Reserve for emergencies.[35] This sort of coordination is terribly difficult at present, but might be a key advantage of the aHIF.

---

[33] Outterson, *supra* note 2, at 628.
[34] *Id.*
[35] Kesselheim & Outterson, *supra* note 2.

The second problem is the financial incentives that the market gives to drug companies, hospitals, physicians, pharmacists, and informal health care workers around the globe.[36] All of these parties are rewarded by moving product, especially through increased unit sales of antibiotics. A sale yields the same profit whether the use is actually appropriate or not. In ordinary drugs, this situation is wasteful if money is spent unnecessarily, or dangerous if patients are needlessly exposed to pharmaceutical risks. With antibiotics, the damage of inappropriate use is multiplied because misuse promotes resistance, destroying the power of the drug for future patients as well.

Companies also sell antibiotics for animal use. Most U.S. antibiotic sales (by volume) are for use in healthy animals, which raises the potential of resistant organisms developing in animal hosts. Restricting such sales might promote human health, but would lower profits for drug companies and raise costs for some farmers. The aHIF would give companies an incentive to limit nontherapeutic agricultural uses, saving antibiotics for human use.

Patent systems recover R&D costs through pricing above marginal cost. Firms will have incentives to exploit their patent through overproducing (relative to the social optimum) during the exclusivity period. Nor is it clear that society would be well-served by pricing at marginal cost: unlike many drugs with deadweight losses due to lost sales, overuse of antibiotics could be welfare-reducing due to resistance. The aHIF could rationalize these incentives by paying for health impact, not just product sales.

The third quandary is the relationship between resistance and innovation. The conventional wisdom assumes that resistance is a problem in antibiotic innovation, but resistance may also stimulate innovation.[37] In other drug classes, new entrants must compete against generic drugs with proven records of safety and efficacy. Lipitor (atorvastatin) is an excellent statin, and when it transitions to fully generic status, atorvastatin will set a high bar against which new statin drugs must be measured. Importantly, the use of atorvastatin by one person does not undermine its value for any other person: the billionth dose is just as effective as the first. None of this is true for antibiotics. Penicillin was an outstanding antibiotic, perhaps better than almost anything we have seen in many decades. But resistance makes highly effective antibiotics obsolete over time, which clears the competitive field before a new drug enters the market. This trend of declining effectiveness favors entry of new antibiotic molecules. Paradoxically, speeding market entry of antibiotics may actually accelerate resistance, by flooding the market with competing drugs that trigger another round of resistance.[38] The aHIF would reward well-timed antibiotic introductions, which arrive to address the greatest human health needs.

The fourth issue concerns the policy levers employed in the battle against antibiotic resistance. Prior scholarship has been perhaps too quick to turn to patent law as the

---

[36] So et al., *supra* note 1; Kesselheim & Outterson, *supra* note 2; Aaron S. Kesselheim & Kevin Outterson, *Improving Antibiotic Markets for Long Term Sustainability*, 11 Yale J. Health Pol'y L. & Ethics 101, 155 (2011) [hereinafter *Improving Antibiotic Markets*].

[37] Projan, *supra* note 19; So et al., *supra* note 1; Outterson, *supra* note 2, at 637.

[38] Outterson, *supra* note 2.

preferred policy lever. For example, the Infectious Diseases Society of America (IDSA) has catalogued the thin pipeline of new antibiotic therapies, but called for significant changes in patent law to remedy the problem, including patent extensions and wildcard patent extensions for antibiotics.[39] In our view, patent law mechanisms are ill-suited to address the resistance problem, in part because patent law is not flexible enough to be carefully calibrated to the biological complexity of resistance.[40] The traditional advantage of patent law is its reliance on market pricing; many pharmaceutical prices, however, are not really set by the market, but are instead governed by public reimbursement systems. In effect, elements of the pharmaceutical market are already de-linked, but not in a system that prioritizes global health impact.[41] To the extent that market-based pricing is an important element of the patent system, its absence in pharmaceuticals is quite troubling. If the primary market signals are muddled or broken, additional modifications to patent law should not be rolled out before the reimbursement system is fixed.[42] The aHIF sidesteps these problems by creating a new de-linkage mechanism to focus reimbursement on the most socially desirable pharmaceutical innovations.

Resistance spreads globally across political and geographic boundaries, giving rise to our fifth policy concern: antibiotic resistance is an ecological pollution problem that requires global coordination mechanisms that are not currently being provided by the market. Global coordination through the WHO is poorly funded and focused on conservation. Global coordination through the patent system is unhelpfully devoted to selling new drugs. As described above, conservation and new drug R&D incentives work at cross-purposes. By paying for human health impact anywhere on the planet, the aHIF would be uniquely well-placed to globally coordinate these issues.

Finally, the antibiotic innovation system is not functioning well. Compare antibiotic innovation with information technology: what if successive generations of laptops were larger and slower with diminished capabilities? Or suffered incremental safety problems with each new model? No one would consider that situation acceptable for laptop innovation, and yet that is the landscape for antibiotics. Today's antibiotics are in many ways inferior to the drugs available in 1950; although some accounts treat the 1980s as the "glory days" of new antibiotic introductions,[43] many of these drugs were subsequently withdrawn from the market, often with safety problems.[44] Antibiotics suffer from an innovation deficit.

But a significant increase in antibiotic drug approvals may not solve the problem.[45] Companies are rewarded based on antibiotic unit sales, so they often focus on the wrong

[39] BAD BUGS, NO DRUGS, *supra* note 7; Infectious Diseases Soc'y of America, *supra* note 1.

[40] Outterson, *supra* note 33; *Improving Antibiotic Markets*, *supra* note 36.

[41] Kesselheim & Outterson, *supra* note 2.

[42] *Id.*

[43] BAD BUGS, NO DRUGS, *supra* note 7; Infectious Diseases Soc'y of America, *supra* note 1.

[44] Enrique Seoane-Vazquez, Jing Hao & Rosa Rodriguez-Monguio, *Exploring the Relationship between Drug Patent Life and Drug Approvals*, AM. PUBLIC HEALTH ASS'N (2011), *available at* http://apha.confex. com/apha/139am/webprogram/Paper246364.html.

[45] Kevin Outterson, John H. Powers, Ian M. Gould & Aaron S. Kesselheim, *Questions about the 10 x '20 Initiative*, 51 CLINICAL INFECTIOUS DISEASES 751 (2010).

types of innovation. In many antibiotic drugs, resistance can be transmitted within the antibiotic drug class to other drugs in the class, permitting market rivals to pollute their competitors' drugs. These resistance patterns can vary between different bacterial species. In this ecological context, bringing additional "me-too" drugs to market within an existing class can speed the destruction of all drugs in the class. Cross-class resistance complicates the problem even more, as the pollution affects more distant drugs.[46] A patent race that results in too many new antibiotics reaching the market at the same time is not success, but failure. Multiple simultaneous entries of antibiotics with pollution externalities should be considered uncoordinated withdrawals by competitors from a potentially exhaustible common pool.[47] Such races may drive resistance instead of improving human health.

Antibiotic pollution externalities could potentially be managed by Coasian contractual mechanisms among companies producing antibiotics. The number of patent-owning firms involved is relatively small, but cooperation in this fashion would run afoul of the antitrust statutes in the United States and competition laws around the world. As a result, limited antitrust waivers would be required for any coordinating mechanism among the companies.[48] But antibiotic pollution also affects society at large, greatly increasing the number of persons involved. Once the patent expires, the number of polluting firms can increase significantly. Finally, antibiotic pollution externalities vary significantly depending on how the antibiotic is used, making the contractual solution even more difficult to manage.

A related problem involves truly innovative antibiotics, especially drugs with entirely new mechanisms of action. These antibiotics are the first entrant into a new "functional resistance group."[49] To the extent that competitors' actions do not damage the new drug, then the patent owner need not fear obsolescence through resistance pollution. But the patent clock ticks on for the patent on each new antibiotic molecule, because the company owns a time-limited property right. The company has every incentive to bring this molecule to market quickly, even absent either urgent clinical need or pollution risk. This market introduction begins the countdown to resistance for a new functional resistance group of antibiotics. In short, the patent holder has strong financial incentives to waste the antibiotic, even if clinically appropriate alternatives exist.[50] For these first-in-class antibiotics, society would be better served by keeping these drugs off the market until clinically necessary. One potential solution is the Strategic Antibiotic Reserve (Reserve), which would pay patent owners handsomely to entirely forgo marketing the drug class until the day that resistance to other drugs necessitated a withdrawal from the Reserve.[51] The analogy is to the strategic petroleum reserve, saving an exhaustible resource for a day of utmost need. The Reserve is distinguished

[46] Outterson, *supra* note 30; *Improving Antibiotic Markets, supra* note 36.
[47] LAXMINARAYAN & MALANI, *supra* note 2.
[48] *Improving Antibiotic Markets, supra* note 36, at 112.
[49] LAXMINARAYAN & MALANI, *supra* note 2.
[50] Outterson, *supra* note 30, at 103–04.
[51] Kesselheim & Outterson, *supra* note 2; *Improving Antibiotic Markets, supra* note 36, at 160–61.

from the aHIF in that it pays for not using a drug, based on estimated future health impact. The Reserve and the aHIF are complementary but distinct proposals.

III. The Antibiotic Health Impact Fund

In the following pages, we explore first the details of how the aHIF would impact R&D incentives for antibiotics before turning to the issue of conservation. In both cases, the aHIF may be able to solve vexing problems in this sector, serving as a global coordinating mechanism to simultaneously promote appropriate use as well as boosting incentives for bringing important new antibiotics to market at the right time. The aHIF could encompass all systemic antibacterials for human use, or it could be more narrowly focused on antibiotics for hospital use, where the resistance problems are greatest and the potential for conservation gains more readily attainable.

A. THE ANTIBIOTIC HEALTH IMPACT FUND AS A GLOBAL COORDINATION
MECHANISM FOR NEW ANTIBIOTIC DEVELOPMENT

The aHIF is very appealing as a global coordination mechanism for antibiotic R&D. For the first time, companies would be rewarded for producing antibiotics that were better than existing therapies, with the target being actual improvement in human health as opposed to mere growth in unit sales. The aHIF would not function as a bureaucratic expert panel picking "winning" research programs. Companies would continue to evaluate and prioritize their own research programs, but the aHIF reward would be proportional to the health impact rather than the ability to generate sales in high-income countries through aggressive marketing. The aHIF would offer little or no reward to a company for switching patients from an older but still effective antibiotic to its own brand-new, aHIF-registered product because the incremental health impact would be slight. Under aHIF, the new market entrant does not appropriate the entire profit the other company derived from its existing sales, but gets rewarded only if and insofar as the switch is beneficial to patients' health. New antibiotics will receive aHIF rewards only to the extent that they address unmet needs in human health, which will dramatically reorient antibiotic R&D goals in a socially desirable way.

The HIF has been initially scaled in the range of $6 billion per year over ten years. The aHIF would test the HIF concept by limiting all of that funding to systemic antibiotics for human use. Although $6 billion is a relatively small percentage of global pharmaceutical sales, the aHIF would have a much more salient impact within the antibiotic class of drugs. In 2008, U.S. sales of systemic antibacterial drugs were $11.2 billion;[52]

---

[52] IMS HEALTH, http://www.imshealth.com. Sales at ex-manufacturer prices (manufacturer invoice). Includes rebates and certain discounts. Sales at consumer prices would include wholesaler cost and pharmacy fees.

global sales were approximately $42 billion in 2009.[53] If additional focus was desired, the aHIF could be limited at first to antibiotics for hospital use, where we already noted that the most serious resistance and infection issues are located. The aHIF would dramatically boost innovation incentives in this drug class, and serve an important coordinating function by steering the work toward antibiotics with the greatest potential global health impact. Investing $6 billion per year in this fashion would likely be very efficient, because the social value of the unmet need for antibiotics is at least an order of magnitude higher.[54]

B. THE ANTIBIOTIC HEALTH IMPACT FUND AS A COORDINATION MECHANISM FOR GLOBAL ANTIBIOTIC CONSERVATION

The current global pharmaceutical market balances access and innovation primarily upon the fulcrum of generic entry. The global rollout of low-cost antiretroviral medicines was made possible by the entry of generics.[55] Access to many medicines improves after generic entry, due to the significant price reductions driven by generic competition. On a static level, deadweight loss is reduced through marginal cost production and generic distribution as soon as possible. A persistent criticism of the HIF raises the question of inadequate incentives for generic production.[56] Whatever traction this criticism may or may not have in general, the calculus is different for antibiotics. For antibiotics, paradoxically, maximizing production and access may be globally counterproductive.[57] Policy makers should avoid indiscriminately flooding the market with vast quantities of low-priced generic antibiotics. Inappropriate use must be restricted through antibiotic conservation if long-term human health is to be maximized. As a result, concerns about generic access are uniquely less salient for the aHIF.

If we focus solely on producing new antibiotics to the exclusion of long-term conservation, then all we have done is to accelerate the final ecological collapse of every functional resistance group of antibiotics. Consider the following two charts. The first is the oft-repeated chart on the decline in FDA approvals for antibiotics over the previous decades:[58]

---

[53] Bashar Hamad, *The Antibiotics Market*, 9 NATURE REVS. DRUG DISCOVERY 675, 675–76 (2010).

[54] Kesselheim & Outterson, *supra* note 2.

[55] JAMES LOVE, COST BENEFIT ANALYSIS FOR UNITAID PATENT POOL (2008), http://www.keionline.org/misc-docs/1/cost_benefit_UNITAID_patent_pool.pdf.

[56] *See* Love, *supra* note 24.

[57] Much empirical work is needed to fully understand this dynamic. If significant human health needs are currently unmet due to inadequate access to existing antibiotics, widespread generic access could improve human health. On the other hand, if antibiotics are already widely misused for inappropriate conditions, increased generic access could accelerate resistance without offsetting benefits to human health. One ancillary benefit to the aHIF would be the collection and dissemination of surveillance data on these issues.

[58] Modified from BAD BUGS, NO DRUGS, *supra* note 7.

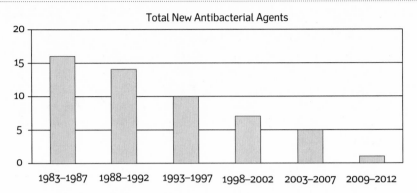

Total New Antibacterial Agents

This decline might actually be a hopeful sign since antibiotics must be managed for long-term ecological and evolutionary balance, but the IDSA uses this chart to ask Congress for additional financial and patent incentives to spur production of new anti-biotics.[59] Conservation efforts are included in this proposed legislation, but the new financial incentives are not conditioned on meeting conservation goals. The failure to view antibiotic resistance as an ecological problem can lead to grave errors. Consider the second chart, historical data on a previous ecological collapse: the near-extermination of the North American buffalo herds in the 1870s. M.S. Taylor has estimated buffalo hide exports from the United States from 1870 to 1886.[60]

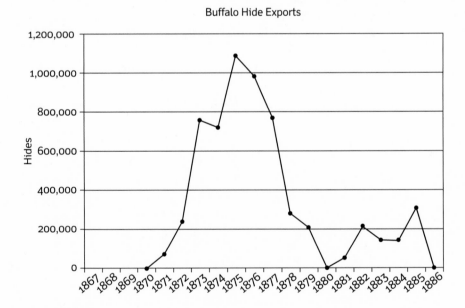

Buffalo Hide Exports

---

[59] *Antibiotic Resistance: Promoting Critically Needed Antibiotic Research and Development and Appropriate Use ("Stewardship") of These Precious Drugs: Before the Subcomm. on Health of the H. Comm. on Energy and Commerce*, 111th Cong. (2010) (statement of Brad Spellberg, Infectious Diseases Society of America).

[60] *See also* Taylor, *supra* note 29.

Confronted with this buffalo hide export data, the rational response in 1877 should be to stop hunting buffalo. It would have been a grave error if Congress had increased financial incentives for hunting. The buffalo population was a common pool resource that suffered ecological collapse through unsustainable withdrawals following a post–Civil War innovation in tanning techniques. Prices stayed high—and the profitability of exploiting the herd was maintained—because of the large export market for hides in Europe.[61] This led to the wholesale slaughter of the buffalo population in about a decade.

Any analogy between antibiotics and buffalo markets should be approached with caution. However, the common pool problems are similar. Both common pools are potentially expandable through breeding (for buffalo) and new drug introductions (for antibiotics), and can be depleted through uncoordinated withdrawals (buffalo hunting or antibiotic pollution). If private benefits from the use of polluting antibiotics are perceived to be high, but private cost are kept very low, we can anticipate many withdrawals (antibiotic use), leading to the onset of resistance unless the common pool resource is managed for long-term sustainability. Put another way, we must understand global antibiotic policy as a primarily ecological and evolutionary management question.[62] The battle against microbes cannot be "won." Indeed, microbes are a significant percentage of our body weight and cellular census, with complex effects on health. The long-term goal is a sustainable balance between microbes and humanity.

In the HIF, long-term sustainability could be addressed by making additional rewards available to the extent that long-term antibiotic conservation goals are achieved. Conservation is the second major feature of our proposal, after de-linkage. Conservation rewards are the mechanism for global antibiotic coordination through the HIF.

The HIF will require the assistance of public health experts to develop appropriate antibiotic conservation goals. Outterson and Kesselheim have described one possible model, which would focus on surveillance data of actual resistance levels as the key metric. Governments would set the conservation targets, but leave implementation to the companies themselves, perhaps in partnership with governments and appropriate NGOs.[63] The defining feature of this model is the reluctance to use government to specify detailed regulations, assuming that the companies and NGOs have important information about the contours of the antibiotic markets and the heterogeneous policy tools available to reduce inappropriate use. Although other models are certainly possible, reliance on the companies, in partnership with governments and NGOs, while holding the companies accountable for actual resistance targets, yields several interesting implications. The following chart summarizes these issues, which are then discussed in more detail in the text:

---

[61] *Id.* Other economists focus on the late arrival of property rights as a factor in the near extermination of the herd. Dean Lueck, *The Extermination and Conservation of the American Bison*, 31 J. LEGAL STUD. 609, 638–39 (2002).

[62] Baquero et al., *supra* note 31.

[63] Kesselheim & Outterson, *supra* note 2; *Improving Antibiotic Markets*, *supra* note 36, at 146–47.

The aHIF as a Coordination Mechanism for Global Antibiotic Conservation.

Conservation incentives to companies	Examples of company implementation	Challenges for the aHIF approach
1. Manage their antibiotics to maximize health impact without exceeding specific resistance targets	Cease sales of animal antibiotics for nontherapeutic uses; companies can focus their considerable marketing and government relations functions on appropriate use	Relies primarily on the companies to lead the process after governments have set the aHIF conservation targets
2. Coordinate activities across companies to minimize pollution	Contractual agreements to minimize pollution; joint support for conservation programs, infection control, and vaccines	Requires waivers to antitrust law; potential spillovers of anticompetitive behavior; all-or-nothing aHIF might be necessary
3. Manage antibiotics for longer time horizons	aHIF contracts might need to be significantly longer than the patent term, tied more to clinical realities rather than patent life	Delays generic entry; longer aHIF registration periods might be necessary
4. Solving "last mile" problems	Subsidize rapid point-of-care diagnostics that limit unit sales to appropriate use; support (rather than oppose) hospital formulary restrictions that support appropriate use	Companies control this process and must be held accountable
5. Maximize global health impact	aHIF payment and conservation targets would be based on global health impact; aHIF becomes an effective global coordination mechanism independent of the quality of local governmental support or competence	Targets must be set appropriately, without company gaming; surveillance likewise must be independent and reliable

First, companies would have a significant financial incentive to manage their antibiotics for long-term public health, rather than short-term sales. Companies would benefit most from getting the right drug to the right person at the right price, and would deploy their remarkable marketing talents to discourage inappropriate use. Companies might also make strategic market decisions. For example, Bayer owned the patents on both ciprofloxacin and a related antibiotic used in agriculture. The battle to restrict nontherapeutic uses of antibiotics in animal feeds would be transformed if the company's profits from exploitation of these two products were contingent on meeting conservation goals. In the current regulatory battle over animal antibiotics, the government and companies question each other's data; in the aHIF, companies would use their own private data to make decisions to forgo animal sales.

Second, as described above, the biology of resistance might require multiple companies to coordinate their actions in order to hit resistance targets, maximize health impact, and minimize antibiotic pollution. Limited antitrust waivers (or state action protection via the aHIF) may be required. Antibiotic pollution might require aHIF registration to be an all-or-nothing offer to all antibiotic drugs in a functional resistance group. Unlike other therapeutic categories, antibiotics in the aHIF face special challenges if some drugs are in the program but others—polluters with low health impact—remain outside. It should be noted that any company with an aHIF-registered antibiotic would have a clear incentive to manage its entire portfolio in order to achieve the aHIF resistance targets, even if this required changes to marketing plans for unregistered drugs. In this way, companies with one or more registered products would enjoy financial rewards for carefully managing even their antibiotics that are outside the aHIF.

It must be conceded that some companies might remain entirely outside the aHIF and yet choose to market their drugs in a fashion that polluted other antibiotics, including registered products. Such extreme cases might call for other remedies, including denying (or revoking) market access for such polluting, low-value drugs on public health grounds, or mandating registration with the aHIF. This is an empirical question that should not be answered a priori; we simply do not know yet whether cross-company antibiotic pollution from non-aHIF companies will undermine aHIF conservation goals to a significant degree.

Third, because resistance emerges gradually over time, the proper time frame for the aHIF might be much longer than ten years. If an antibiotic remained in the aHIF for twenty years or more with significant continuing health impact, then the company should continue to receive the reward, so long as it met the resistance targets. New antibiotics might be delayed, especially ones not quite as good as existing drugs, but that need not bother us. Indeed, social welfare over the coming decades would be enhanced by just such a delay, saving these drugs for a time when resistance to other drugs has improved the relative effectiveness of this new drug. In addition to stretching the aHIF reward period beyond the usual ten years for antibiotics, delaying the start of the aHIF period for some antibiotics that are not urgently required might be considered. Here the aim would be to encourage the innovator to delay efforts to achieve extensive use of its product to the future period in which such wide use can make the greatest contribution to global health. Limited use for extreme cases might be appropriate during these Strategic Antimicrobial Reserve periods.

Fourth, companies will be incentivized to solve many significant "last mile" problems in antibiotics. One such problem involves the availability of rapid point-of-care diagnostics to distinguish between viral and bacterial infections. In the absence of such a test, many clinicians resort to empiric therapy with broad-spectrum antibiotics. Treating a virus with antibiotics does not affect the virus, but may negatively affect the health of the patient while also facilitating resistance. From the financial perspective of a drug company that is selling antibiotics under the current system of incentives, these diagnostics can only decrease its sales and are therefore financially undesirable. In contrast, under the aHIF, the company would have a significant financial incentive to promote appropriate use of diagnostics. Likewise, antibacterial vaccines dampen the demand for antibiotics by reducing the incidence of bacterial illness. Companies with antibacterial vaccines in the aHIF would be financially rewarded for preventing the spread of disease through vaccination. Similar infrastructure issues include infection control measures and resistance surveillance; these tasks do not have an insurance billing code in most countries and are frequently left to public health agencies with limited budgets. Companies with antibiotics in the aHIF would have a financial incentive to support these efforts in whatever way the companies thought maximized health impact. In a similar fashion, the companies would deploy their impressive marketing, public relations, and lobbying operations in support of antibiotic conservation, rather than opposing these efforts through aggressive marketing and other tools.

Finally, most current efforts to conserve antibiotics are not global in scope. Global coordination is a significant collective action problem, akin to unregulated depletion of fisheries or pollution that falls on distant countries. Many of the benefits of antibiotic use are internalized, but many of the costs are externalized. The WHO's program in 2011–2012, although laudable in aspirations, was not well funded and lacked both enforcement and norm-setting mechanisms. The aHIF could serve a significant global coordination role here, leveraging funding from the aHIF sponsors into a true global strategy implemented with the enthusiastic support of private actors. The aHIF would give the global drug companies a direct stake in reducing the global health impact of communicable bacterial diseases while managing the common pool resource of antibiotics for the long-term health of the global population. The companies are well positioned to influence the utilization of their products in every region of the planet. Because the companies themselves largely undertake the task, this mechanism can succeed without regard to the quality of local governance institutions. The aHIF is therefore scalable throughout the world, despite weak health governance in many countries.

C. PATENT-RELATED ISSUES FOR THE ANTIBIOTIC HEALTH IMPACT FUND

As described above, the precise patent policy of the HIF is not an essential design feature, but a functional and practical choice at this stage. We can think of several reasons various patent policies might work with the HIF generally, but in many cases the analysis is significantly different for the aHIF.

First, by transferring the patent, the company would lose the right to control certain follow-on innovations, which are commercially important in many drug classes. For the aHIF, this issue may be less salient, as a successful aHIF will delay the clinical and financial need for follow-on antibiotics. In antibiotics, we do not necessarily want to promote additional drugs in class on an accelerated timetable. Society may be better off with spreading antibiotic approvals across a larger number of years, so long as this is coupled with strong conservation incentives. In any event, the aHIF might need to be an all-or-nothing program, especially if cross-drug and cross-class pollution could not otherwise be controlled.

Second, retaining the patent gives the company additional control over operational issues such as how the drug is used in drug combinations, with companion diagnostics, and potential early exit rights under the aHIF contract. All of these issues are enmeshed with the antibiotic pollution externalities described above: in many cases, combination drugs offer much lower resistance profiles; companion diagnostics target the right drug against the right bug without inappropriate use; but early exit may need to be discouraged or contractually limited in order to protect from pollution drugs remaining in the aHIF.

One advantage of an immediate transfer (or open license) of the patent for a HIF-registered product is that it shifts competition from the molecule to finding more efficient manufacturing methods that might significantly reduce the marginal cost of production. Although the company contractually promises production at marginal cost, the HIF does not necessarily create competitive conditions wherein companies strive to drive those costs down. In economic terms, the HIF will address the great majority of the deadweight loss associated with patent-based pricing, but may forgo some opportunities for additional social welfare gains through reduced marginal costs. Insofar as manufacturing is outsourced, the incentive to reduce the marginal cost of production for HIF-registered products is powerful, as competing manufacturers will want to be able to submit the lowest bid. Insofar as manufacturing is not outsourced, the firm will still want to lower its manufacturing cost, for even if the firm's best option is to sell at cost, regardless of what this cost is, the firm will achieve more health impact if the product is sold at a lower price. The firm is better off producing and selling at $4 than at $5.

In the context of antibiotics, these issues are muted somewhat, because maximizing production volume and minimizing unit costs are not the primary objectives. Indeed, universal misuse of free antibiotics would be a public health problem. A key issue here is that although the aHIF could stretch out or delay the reward period for antibiotics, such that the incentives for conservation were adequate, patents would inevitably expire, opening a path for uncontrolled generic production. Therefore, to the extent that cross-molecule and cross-class pollution cannot otherwise be controlled, a key component of antibiotics in the aHIF would be an international agreement not to permit other firms to sell aHIF-rewarded antibiotics, regardless of the patent status. Put another way, pollution externalities might require all antibiotics to be in the aHIF.

Some have suggested longer patents for antibiotics.[64] Without the aHIF, simply extending exclusivity rights is a nonstarter, because it opens up opportunities for exploitation of consumers by innovators without any clear conservation gains.[65] Within the

---

[64] Eric Kades, *Preserving a Precious Resource: Rationalizing the Use of Antibiotics*, 99 Nw. U. L. Rev. 611 (2005); Infectious Diseases Soc'y of America, *supra* note 1.

[65] Outterson, *supra* note 30.

aHIF mechanism, extending exclusivity rights is consistent with maintaining roughly the same level of profits while improving clinical and conservation outcomes.

James Love has criticized the HIF for not relying on generic production to ensure the lowest possible marginal cost of production.[66] As discussed above, we find these concerns to be addressed by the companies' incentives to realize the greatest health impact at the lowest possible contractual price. But in the context of antibiotics, this criticism gains even less traction. Global public health is clearly advanced by wide dissemination of quality generic statins to treat cardiovascular disease; the same cannot be said for antibiotics with resistance problems. We suggest that unconstrained generic production of antibiotics might make the global conservation effort more difficult, tipping the long-term ecological and evolutionary balance in the wrong direction. Further empirical research is clearly needed on this question.

Finally, the patent holder may hesitate to transfer the patent in advance of the ten-year HIF reward payments. The HIF will gain credibility as a trusted reimbursement partner over time, so perhaps this issue will diminish in importance in future years. Antibiotics do not appear to present novel questions for this specific issue.

Conclusion

The antibiotic sector is an attractive but complex candidate for testing the Health Impact Fund. Poor market incentives have led both industry and academic researchers to suggest de-linkage mechanisms as a means to simultaneously address problems with conservation and R&D. The looming crisis of antibiotic resistance is an important global problem. Resistant diseases are significant health risks throughout the world. This problem threatens both high- and low-income populations, and it may prove impossible to solve without an effective global coordination mechanism. The aHIF demonstration, although modestly sized compared to global pharmaceutical markets, is probably large enough to alter incentives in the antibiotic sector. Some of the criticisms raised about the HIF apply with less force in the antibiotic sector, making it an attractive candidate for a full-scale test.

The aHIF is not without significant challenges. Financing must be robust and sustainable. Adequate and realistic resistance targets will have to be set globally, without political meddling. Achieving these targets will be partially delegated to the companies, but they will also be accountable to the aHIF for failing to hit the mark. Drug companies will therefore be encouraged to cooperate for global public health in unprecedented ways, with equally impressive impacts on global health.

The aHIF can serve a key role as a global coordination mechanism for antibiotics, ensuring that this important drug class does not fade away, but continues to serve humanity.

---

[66] See Love, *supra* note 24.

IV

Telemedicine

19

ELECTRONIC MEDICAL TOURISM AND THE MEDICAL WORLD

WIDE WEB

*Gil Siegal**

Introduction

There are numerous contributing factors to the growing dominance of health care in our lives, including our collective transition from "patients" to consumers, the progress of medicine and science, and the large-scale economic implications of health care, such as the daunting and growing portion of health-related expenditures of the GDP/GNP. The very nature of health care and health delivery systems is changing, and these changes are not limited to one country or continent but rather represent global trends. Indeed, such commonality lends itself to multilateral global solutions.

This chapter aims at advancing policy changes needed to create the infrastructure for a *global* web of modern health care services, a construction that would allow numerous communities within and among nations access to the tremendous promise of modern medicine. Too little attention to date has been devoted to *information technology's* potential to propel the globalization of health care as a top-down governmental policy goal.[1] Therefore, my aim is to make the case for the United States and

* MD; LLB; SJD; Professor of Law, University of Virginia School of Law; Chair, Center for Health Law and Bioethics, Kiryat Ono College, Israel; Senior Researcher, The Gertner Institute for Health Policy and Epidemiology, Israel; gs6x@virginia.edu; gil.siegal@ono.ac.il.

I wish to thank Richard Bonnie, Karen Rheuban, and Mark Rothstein for helpful comments on this chapter, and the Petrie-Flom Center, Harvard Law School, for inviting me to present the original paper at the annual conference "Globalization of Health Care: Legal and Ethical Challenges," May 2011, and for reviewing and preparing this chapter for publication.

1 *See generally* Jon D. Blum, *The Role of Law in Global E-Health: A Tool for Development and Equity in a Digitally Divided World*, 46 ST. Louis U. L.J. 85 (2002); Thomas R. McLean, *The Global Market for Health Care: Economics and Regulation*, 26 Wis. INT'L L.J. 591, 591–645 (2008); Leah B. Mendelsohn, *A Piece of the*

other international parties to invest further in information technology (IT) in order to promote the globalization of health care both for domestic and international arenas. Information technology refers to the spectrum of applications that arise from the advent and continuous progress of the computing and communication sciences and applications: the Internet (e-health) and social networks; electronic health/medical records; medical databases; and telemedicine (defined here as the use of medical information exchanged from one site to another via electronic communications to improve patents' health status),[2] which I use as my key case study.

In creating such a global medical web, various areas of law are implicated—both public and private international law, as well as domestic public and private law and regulation. While delineating only the most central legal issues that must be addressed, I argue for a convergence of domestic and international regulatory efforts to allow for a better and more efficient dissemination and utilization of modern IT-driven health care. I make use of the flourishing medical tourism phenomenon and introduce the concept of "*Electronic* Medical Tourism" (EMT) as a helpful avenue for overcoming contemporary conceptual legal barriers, and a way to propel telemedicine's dissemination. In a nutshell, I argue that what is permitted or not prohibited in the physical world (e.g., traveling to another country for medical care), should be allowed prima facie in the electronic/digital world, notwithstanding legality, safety, and quality requirements, thereby alleviating most current legal impediments.

Sections I and II outline some leading features of modern health care—the evolving technologies that bring changes about, and prevailing regulatory response. The introduction of IT to health care allowed for e-health and telemedicine to move from vision to reality, and the driving forces and current barriers are briefly summarized. Section II concludes with some American, European, and international responses to e-health and telemedicine, which reveal the possibility of enhancing the globalization of affordable, high-quality health care via a stronger commitment to IT exploitation. Section III then takes a closer look at current legal regulation, with a special emphasis on licensure and liability. Section IV offers some directions on facilitating IT contribution to the globalization of health care. This section calls for a more robust dedication of international resources and greater efforts toward concerted action in order to promote IT health care systems that stand to benefit both the contributing and recipient countries plus their respective citizenry. Toward this end, the basic elements of a medical World Wide Web (M-WWW) platform are introduced.

I. The Changing Face of Modern Health care

The changing face of modern health care involves all stakeholders—patients, medical institutions, health insurance providers, and national agencies.

Puzzle: Telemedicine as an Instrument to Facilitate the Improvement of Healthcare in Developing Countries, 18 Emory Int'l L. Rev. 151 (2004).

[2] These issues are further discussed in the chapter by Sao, Gupta, and Gantz in this volume.

People today expect to live longer and healthier lives than in the past. Individuals as health care consumers, especially in developed countries, now have better access to information pertaining to their health, various alternative providers or treatments, and information on cutting-edge medical technology that might improve their health or ameliorate current ailments. Thanks to the Internet, easy access to information offers many more options. In the United States, as well as in other countries, individuals dissatisfied with their current options of care, or individuals without access to local health services (usually due to lack of insurance or unavailability) are able to explore solutions to their health problems elsewhere. In this sense, globalization of health care is about the process of long-distance exchange of medical services in an informed society.[3] And although citizens of developed countries are the prime drivers of this transformation in self-management of care, citizens in developing countries are also gradually reaping the benefits. Although this process can continue to be propelled in a bottom-up fashion by "e-patients" (who are equipped, enabled, empowered, and engaged),[4] a top-down institutional/governmental thrust would have far-reaching impacts with respect to resource allocation, dissemination, and surmounting of regulatory barriers.

Medical institutions are striving to increase their capabilities, improve quality, and assure financial stability. Technology that can offer efficient yet improved care is the prime target of institutions, while they attempt to increase their capacities to offer treatment to an optimal number of patients in order to generate needed revenues. Toward this end, many institutions seek to offer care to international or out-of-state audiences by making use of IT and telemedicine. Finally, outsourcing medical services (most notably in teleradiology) to other countries allows significant cost-savings and round-the-clock services.[5]

Health insurance providers attempt to meet their legal obligations to assure adequate health care, contain rising costs, and guarantee financial sustainability. IT/telemedicine has much to offer for strategic restructuring of services provision. Enhanced IT capabilities also allow for improved organizational performances (relying, for example, on sophisticated data-mining and utilization reports), and identifying pockets of under-/overutilization and disparities in health outcomes.

National stakeholders (policy makers and regulators in the health/treasury/finance departments), especially in countries with a national health system, need to accommodate competing interests while guaranteeing respect for budgetary constraints; further, they need to be convinced that investments in health care will pay off. The prospect of harnessing IT/telemedicine to improve the public's health is promising, offering possibilities such as providing better service to chronic patients via telemonitoring, helping patients manage their drug-taking regimen with cellular reminders, or addressing public health emergencies.

---

[3] *See, e.g.*, Case C-372/04, Watts v. Bedford Primary Care Trust, 2006 E.C.R. I-04325.

[4] TOM FERGUSON, E-PATIENTS: HOW THEY CAN HELP US HEAL HEALTH CARE (2007), *available at* http://e-patients.net/e-Patients_White_Paper.pdf.

[5] *See* Rebecca S. Lewis, Jonathan H. Sunshine & Mythreyi Bhargavan, *Radiology Practices' Use of External Off-Hours Teleradiology Services in 2007 and Changes since 2003*, 193 AM. J. ROENTENOLOGY, 1333, 1333–39 (2009).

A growing commitment on the part of developed nations and supranational bodies to the health of less-fortunate countries has generated a steady influx of resources to build and maintain needed infrastructure, education, training, and supply of medication. Although some of these efforts have had tremendous impacts, overcoming local cultural, political, and social conditions has lowered the overall success. Intellectual technolgy and telemedicine offer an important addition to the armory of international health aid efforts by offering new, efficient ways to provide care.

Thus, it seems clear that IT has been and is in the midst of revolutionizing the ways health care is provided. Yet are we doing enough to expand the range of benefits available, both domestically and on a global scale?

A. THE EVOLVING LANDSCAPE OF TELEHEALTH

At this stage of the chapter, an overview of the technological avenues available to enhance health care is due. The following list represents a bird's-eye view of some of the salient ways in which IT is reshaping the health care scene:

- Electronic medical/patient records that allow round-the-clock access to/ sharing of a patient's medical history, medication plan, or imaging studies
- Remote patient care (teledermatology, telepsychiatry, or telesurgery)
- Safety and quality support systems, including medication, diagnostics, and treatment decision support systems
- Health e-commerce and e-prescription
- Mobile health (m-Health)[6]

The above list is a vivid testament to the immediate availability of health IT, and hence the urgent need to exploit its benefits on a large scale. Yet, as with every new technology, benefits need to be ascertained.

B. DEMONSTRATED BENEFITS

Generally, clinical outcomes of telemedicine seem to have a positive trend,[7] yet hype around telemedicine should be avoided and medical benefits need to be clearly proven.[8] Cost-cutting has been demonstrated in several areas of home-care or in teleradiology,[9] but economic benefits also require further proof.[10] Some beneficial aspects of

---

[6] *Mobile e-Health Solutions for Developing Countries*, INTERNATIONAL TELECOMMUNICATIONS UNION (2010), http://www.itu.int/ITU-D/cyb/app/e-health/mhealth.html (last visited Dec. 30, 2011).

[7] *E.g.*, Melinda Beeuwkes Buntin et al., *The Benefits of Health Information Technology*, 30 HEALTH AFF. 464, 464–71 (2011).

[8] Joanne Spetz & Dennis Keane, *Information Technology Implementation in a Rural Hospital*, 54 J. HEALTH MGMT. 337, 337–47 (2009).

[9] Maria E. Dávalos et al., *Economic Evaluation of Telemedicine*, 15 TELEMED. J. & E-HEALTH 933, 933–48 (2009).

[10] Trine S. Bergmo, *Economic Evaluation in Telemedicine—Still Room for Improvement*, 16 J. TELEMED. TELECARE 229, 229–31 (2010).

telemedicine seem hard to refute, such as offering access to health care in rural areas where such care is absent or garnering ancillary savings by avoiding travel time lost.[11] The beneficial possibilities of IT are much more powerful once we consider the provision of care to developing countries, and especially to rural areas in those countries. In India, for example, .9 percent of the GDP is spent on health care for 70 percent of its rural poor, whereas 4.2 percent is allocated to the urban sector.[12] In such circumstances, IT is the sole realistic vehicle to provide health care or public health education to the masses.

II. National and International Responses

There is a growing sense that regulators have finally realized the need to take advantage of IT and telemedicine to improve society's health. Many institutions and agencies have funded IT/telemedicine demonstration projects: on the U.S. front, the list includes the Departments of Health and Human Services, Agriculture, Defense, and Education; the Centers for Medicare and Medicare Services; the Agency for Health Care Research and Quality; and NASA.[13] Nevertheless, the pace of IT incorporation is inadequate, relying instead on a bottom-up, market-driven process led mostly by enthusiastic providers and the telecommunication industry and not by a proactive regulatory effort.[14] Thus, not only do IT companies need to come up with science and technology solutions, but they also must overcome law and regulation that, for the most part, has been hostile or at least unsympathetic—reaping the benefits of IT clearly requires a different state of mind on the part of regulators and legislators. Recently, pertinent parts of the American Recovery and Reinvestment Act and the Obama administration's health care reform legislation have set forth the clear intention of broadly utilizing IT in health care.[15] However, these efforts must be accompanied by a much broader legal scheme that would enable easier dissemination of medical IT, taking into account issues such as licensure or liability.

In 2008, the European Union Commission published a Communication on "Telemedicine for the Benefit of Patients, Healthcare Systems and Society." This communication put forward a plan of action for three strategic goals: "(1) Building confidence in and acceptance of telemedicine services, (2) Bringing legal clarity, (3) Solving

---

[11] Peter M. Yellowlees et al., *Telemedicine Can Make Healthcare Greener*, 16 TELEMED. J. & E-HEALTH 229, 229–32 (2010).

[12] McLean, *supra* note 1, at 612.

[13] VIRGINIA ROWTHORN & DIANE HOFFMANN, LEGAL IMPEDIMENTS TO THE DIFFUSION OF TELEMEDICINE—WHITE PAPER (2010), *available at* http://digitalcommons.law.umaryland.edu/cgi/viewcontent.cgi?article=2194&context=fac_pubs.

[14] Maurice Mars & Richard E. Scott, *Global E-Health Policy: A Work in Progress*, 29 HEALTH AFF. 239, 239–45 (2010).

[15] *See Medicare and Medicaid Electronic Health Records (EHR) Incentive Programs*, U.S. DEP'T HEALTH & HUM. SERVS., https://www.cms.gov/ehrincentiveprograms (last visited Dec. 30, 2011); Medicare and Medicaid Programs & EHR Incentive Program, 42 CFR §§ 412, 413, 422 et seq (2010).

technical issues and facilitating market development."[16] The Commission provides funds for conducting trials and creating guidelines for "consistent assessment of the impact of telemedicine services, including effectiveness and cost-effectiveness." In order to provide legal clarity in the area of telemedicine, the Commission has called on Member States to adopt national regulations addressing licensing, reimbursement, and privacy issues.[17] This recommendation was accepted in connection with a European Parliament Resolution in 2007 that encouraged "Member States to actively support the introduction of eHealth and telemedicine, particularly by developing interoperable systems allowing the exchange of patient information between health care providers in different Member States."

In line with the EU's official actions to promote telemedicine, a Communication from the European Parliament on the Europe 2020 Flagship Initiative calls for:

Accelerating the creation of the necessary framework conditions and demand, which will need to include...regulatory requirements such as measures to protect medical and personal data, reimbursement through NIH schemes and coordinated procurements by the public sector, ensuring interoperability and setting standards and reference specifications for new equipment and services for telemedicine and independent living....[18]

Additionally, the Commission has announced two Key Actions: to work with Member States "to equip Europeans with secure online access to their medical health data by 2015 and to achieve by 2020 widespread deployment of telemedicine services"[19] and to reach the definition of "a minimum common set of patient data for interoperability of patient records to be accessed or exchanged electronically across Member States by 2012." The Commission also laid out its goal to "foster EU-wide standards, interoperability testing and certification of eHealth systems by 2015 through stakeholder dialogue."

The examples of the U.S. and European responses to telemedicine relate to attempts to regulate IT and telemedicine only with regard to these entities' own citizens. Far less attention is given in these places to the powers of IT/telemedicine to change the health of people on a global scale. Clearly, both the United States and EU Member States are heavily invested in the promotion of health in developing countries too, and IT may greatly influence the benefits of allocated resources as well as provide a higher return-on-investment.

On the international front, in 1998 the Valetta Declaration of the International Telecommunication Union (the United Nations' specialized agency for information and communication technologies) stated firm support for telemedicine projects in

[16] *Telemedicine for the Benefit of Patients, Healthcare Systems and Society*, at 6, COM (2008) 689 final (Apr. 11, 2008).

[17] *Commission's Recommendation on Cross-Border Interoperability of Electronic Health Record Systems*, at 4, No. 2008/594/EC (July 2, 2008).

[18] *Europe 2020 Flagship Initiative: Innovation Union*, at 33, COM (2010) 546 final (June 10, 2010).

[19] *Id*. at 20.

developing countries.[20] In 1998, the G-8 countries agreed on active cooperation to promote global telemedicine.[21] The World Health Assembly adopted a 2005 resolution that established an eHealth strategy for the World Health Organization (WHO).[22] To implement its formal program on eHealth, the WHO itself created the Global Observatory for eHealth, providing evidence-based guidance to countries and institutions about the broad range of eHealth activities that are being implemented throughout the world. An atlas of eHealth profiles of 119 countries was assembled in 2009, allowing a state-by-state comparison with respect to existing frameworks: policy, legal, and ethical; eHealth expenditures and funding sources; capacity building; and eHealth application. The results of these decade-long activities are yet to materialize in a more concrete and robust way. Thus although the prospects are exciting, they are subject to significant legal barriers.

III. Current Legal Barriers

In developed countries, fulfillment of the promise of high-quality medicine that enables enhanced access and availability and decreases costs is contingent not only on computing and communication sciences but on successfully crossing the legal battleground.[23] This part summarizes the germane developments with respect to licensure and liability in the United States and the European Union. Solutions presented here reflect my sincere belief that leaving things "as they are" is unacceptable, as the interests of patients, providers, and the health system at large are not adequately served. Although the intra-continental approach dominates current legal discussion, this section focuses on the resolutions needed to enable dissemination of greater access to health care in developed *as well as* developing countries resolving licensure and liability issues.

A. LICENSURE

In most jurisdictions, practicing medicine without a valid license is a criminal offense.[24] In the United States, licensure has traditionally been the states' prerogative, resulting in the need to obtain a license for every state where one wishes to practice. Founded on the need to protect the public from the practice of medicine by unqualified providers, state-by-state licensure also restricts unwanted competition. This restrictive policy for

---

[20] Second World Telecommunications Development Conference, Nov. 24–27, 1998, *Valletta Declaration*, (Nov. 27, 1998), *available at* http://www.itu.int/newsarchive/press/WTDC98/Declaration.html.

[21] André Lacroi et al., *International Concerted Action on Collaboration in Telemedicine: Recommendations of the G-8 Global Health Care Applications Subproject-4*, 8 TELEMED. J. & E-HEALTH 149 (2002).

[22] WORLD HEALTH ORGANIZATION, GLOBAL eHEALTH SURVEY (2005); WORLD HEALTH ORGANIZATION, eHEALTH TOOLS AND SERVICES: NEEDS OF MEMBER STATES (2005).

[23] This section of the chapter relies on Gil Siegal, *Legal Aspects of Telemedicine*, 44 OTOL CLINICS N. AM. 1375–84 (2011).

[24] *E.g.*, CAL. BUS. & PROF. CODE 2052; Hageseth v. Superior Court of San Mateo Cnty., 59 Cal. Rptr. 3rd 385 (Cal. Ct. App. 2007).

practicing medicine across state lines has been subject to growing criticism.[25] First, it is hard to defend a locally based licensure process to protect the "public safety," as citizens of all states should enjoy the practice of medicine by qualified professionals. Second, medical malpractice jurisprudence throughout the Unites States has repeatedly endorsed a higher "national standard" for determining if a provider rendered "reasonable care."[26] In effect, then, a national standard of practice has been deployed already. It seems a very small leap to accept that the safety and qualifications requirements can and should be harmonized across states, thereby allowing easier access to health care by facilitating free movement of professionals. The establishment of the National Practitioner Data Bank containing robust medical malpractice information on providers and its incorporation in daily practices of hiring and granting privileges was a significant step in this direction.[27] Thus, although I add my voice to the critics of the overall current licensure structure, my ambition here is to illuminate the regulation's negative impact with respect to telemedicine's licensure requirements in particular. Indeed, IT and telemedicine alike support strong dissent from today's parochial protectionist segregation, and lead to the call for a more uniform licensure process based on accepted requirements that are already in place.[28]

As the practice of telemedicine requires a license, and assuming the patient and the physician are not located in the same state or country, under which jurisdiction is the telemedical event taking place? There are at least three options: in the location of the patient, in the location of the provider, or in the abstract cyberspace. Legislators and policy makers usually opt for the first option, assuming that a physician is considered to be practicing medicine in the state where the *patient* is located (termed the "originating site"). The physician must therefore comply with the originating site's state licensure requirements. Requiring practitioners to acquire state-by-state licensure is very cumbersome in the United States, and even more so globally. To facilitate transborder practice, approximately ten states[29] have adopted some version of a limited/special purpose licensure. This scheme allows practitioners to obtain a limited license for the delivery of specific health services under particular circumstances, which can then be regarded as suitable for the telemedicine care. Practitioners are required to maintain a full and unrestricted license in at least one state, while practicing telemedicine in others. Noticeably, a telemedicine license authorizes an out-of-state physician to practice *only* telemedicine.

---

[25] Sarah E. Born, *Telemedicine in Massachusetts: A Better Way to Regulate*, 42 NEW ENG. L. REV. 195 (2007–2008). *See also* FEDERATION OF STATE MEDICAL BOARDS, REPORT OF THE SPECIAL COMMITTEE ON LICENSE PORTABILITY (2002), *available at* http://www.fsmb.org/pdf/2002_grpol_License_Portability.pdf.

[26] Logan v. Greenwich Hosp. Ass'n, 465 A.2d 294, 301 (Conn. 1983); Young v. Univ. of Mississippi Med. Ctr., 914 So. 2d 1272, 1276 (Miss. Ct. App. 2005).

[27] *The Data Bank: National Practitioner Healthcare Integrity & Protection*, U.S. DEP'T HEALTH & HUM. SERVS., http://www.npdb-hipdb.hrsa.gov/ (last visited Dec. 30, 2011).

[28] These issues are further discussed in the chapter by Sao, Gupta, and Gantz in this volume.

[29] Siegal, *supra* note 23; see also CENTER FOR TELEHEALTH AND E-HEALTH LAW, *available at* http://www.ctel.org/library/research/ (last visited Dec. 30, 2011).

Another option for the United States could be a national system that would issue a telemedicine license based on national standards.[30] This national system could be constructed in a way that did not necessarily preempt state sovereignty and thus would avoid unnecessary opposition. Uniform legislation in health care has been successful in the past after all; consider, for example, the Uniform Anatomical Gift Act of 1968, which harmonizes the law on organ donation and was adopted by all states.[31] Some steps in this direction on other fronts of health care can serve our purpose, such as the establishment of the National Practitioner Data Bank,[32] or the expanding reach of the FDA over health issues.

Another, less ambitious and less productive option for resolving the licensure barrier is by *endorsement*, where state boards can award (upon a physician's request) licenses to professionals in other states with equal standards. However, because states may require additional qualifications or documentation before endorsing a license issued by another state, endorsement can be time-consuming and expensive for a multi-state telemedicine practitioner.

Reciprocity requires the authorities of each state to reach agreements to recognize licenses issued by the other states (bilateral or multilateral) without further review of individual credentials. Such a requirement may be waived by mutual recognition when one state's licensing authority legally accepts the licensure of another without further action. An example of this situation was the nurse licensure compact, which allows nurses to practice in other states and became legally accepted in twenty-four states.[33]

The corrective measures that I have presented thus far relate to regulating the practice of telemedicine within the United States, where national standardization has been shaping already. How should these solutions apply to a global world? Severing the Gordian knot should be considered on both a U.S. and a global scale—the most sensible and productive solution to telemedicine licensure would be "electronic medical tourism" (EMT), which views telemedicine as being rendered at the location of the physician, as is the case for medical tourism.[34] After twenty years of telemedicine and the dramatic increase in medical tourism, this revised way of thinking should not be hard to accept. Just as a patient may travel to another state or country to be treated,[35] so too should patients be allowed to "travel" electronically, thereby saving money, time, and the environment.

---

[30] *See generally* United States v. Lopez, 514 U.S. 549 (1995); Pharm. Mfrs. Ass'n v. FDA, 484 F. Supp. 1179, *aff'd* 634 F.2d 106 (3d Cir. 1980). These issues are further discussed in the chapter by Sao, Gupta, and Gantz in this volume.

[31] Health Care Quality Improvement Act of 1986, Pub. L. 99–660, § 401–32, 100 Stat. 3784–94 (as amended by § 402 of Pub. L. 100–177), 101 Stat. 1007–1008 (42 U.S.C. §§ 11101–11152).

[32] U.S. DEP'T HEALTH & HUM. SERVS., *supra* note 27.

[33] Siegal, *supra* note 23.

[34] Arnold Milstein & Mark Smith, *America's New Refugees—Seeking Affordable Surgery Offshore*, 355 NEW ENG. J. MED. 1637, 1637–40 (2006). *See also* Levi Burkett, *Medical Tourism: Concerns, Benefits, and the American Legal Perspective*, 28 J. LEG. MED. 223, 223–45 (2007).

[35] *See generally* I. Glenn Cohen, *Protecting Patients with Passports: Medical Tourism and the Patient-Protective Argument*, 95 IOWA L. REV. 1467 (2010).

Other legal issues deserve at least several short notes. For example, provider's authentication (i.e., ascertaining the identity of the telemedicine provider) remains a challenge. However, telemedicine should not be restricted on these grounds, as authentication requirements are shared by all IT-based modern enterprises (including banking, credit, and e-learning), and have been reasonably resolved. Practically, responsibility for authentication should belong to the institution that provides the medical service, and appropriate regulations should be instituted and monitored (passwords, event log/access archives, log-in logs, etc.). In contrast, authentication of non-affiliated Internet providers in cyberspace becomes much more problematic. In these circumstances, responsibility should be shifted to consumers, whom we should expect to utilize only credible sources. At the same time, consumers should be informed on the hazards of receiving medical care or consultation from nonaffiliated practitioners, along with a list of flawed sources/sites.

A final related question refers to choice of venue and of law. Assume, by way of example, that we are settling a dispute arising from a multi-state or multinationality telemedicine interaction. In this example, which court should have jurisdiction, and what legal norms should be used?[36] Because telemedicine will undeniably create legal disputes—such as malpractice claims or breach of privacy/confidentiality—dispute resolution must be determined proactively. However, this facet is shared by all IT-based modern enterprises, and most uncertainties can be resolved by adopting the EMT concept. Alternatively, or possibly in addition to the EMT concept, binding arbitration[37] as commonly seen in multinational commercial interactions can provide clearer ex ante solutions.[38]

B. LIABILITIES—MEDICAL MALPRACTICE AND INFORMED CONSENT

This section briefly surveys health law jurisprudence viewed through the prism of using IT to create a patient–provider relationship. Such liabilities stem from traditional tort doctrines such as negligence, thereby providing us ample case law to draw from.[39] At the outset, it should be noted that in health systems around the world, most notably in the Unites States, medical malpractice litigation has resulted in an insurance coverage crisis and costly defensive medicine,[40] but has had an insufficient impact on patients' safety.[41] Expanding or transforming medical services to the digital market is bound to

---

[36] See, e.g., Jeffrey L. Rensberger, *Choice of Law, Medical Malpractice and Telemedicine*, 55 U. MIAMI L. REV. 31 (2000); Paul Schiff Berman, *The Globalization of Jurisdiction*, 151 U. PA. L. REV. 311 (2002).

[37] E.g., Madden v. Kaiser Found. Hosps., 552 P.2d 1178, 1180–85 (Cal. 1976).

[38] These issues are further discussed in the chapter by Sao, Gupta, and Gantz in this volume.

[39] See Jon D. Blum, *Internet Medicine and the Evolving Legal Status of the Physician–Patient Relationship*, 24 J. LEG. MED. 413, 413–55 (2003).

[40] David M. Studdert et al., *Defensive Medicine among High-Risk Specialist Physicians in a Volatile Malpractice Environment*, 293 J. AM. MED. ASS'N 2609, 2617 (2005).

[41] Michelle M. Mello & Troyen A. Brennan, *Deterrence of Medical Errors: Theory and Evidence for Malpractice Reform*, 80 TEX. L. REV. 1595, 1604–05 (2002).

evoke a "med-mal knee-jerk reaction" (mostly on the part of providers and insurers) and hence a need to address liability issues in advance. Some adjustments or even concessions can be acceptable in order to reduce decision makers' angst and reluctance to fully engage in telemedicine for fear of increased exposure. The following analysis presupposes that the current silo mentality still prevails—no harmonization or global agreements have been achieved, thus creating only local standards and remedies for liability.

It is important to be aware of the fact that telemedicine interactions are conducted in different models, which can impact liability.[42] Some models involve direct provider-to-patient interaction such as in direct-to-consumer enterprises, or in telemonitoring or telepsychiatry. Others stipulate the presence of another provider at the originating site (the consulting "P2P," or provider-to-provider, model), practiced in telesurgery. Yet another model is devoid of patient presence altogether (e.g., teleradiology). These different models have important legal implications insofar as creating binding patient–provider relationships. Thus, one should reject any notion that "telemedicine is telemedicine is telemedicine" and rather identify within each telemedicine interaction the relevant components that can impact liabilities.

1. Medical Malpractice

To invoke malpractice, a plaintiff must establish that the provider has breached the duty of care owed to the patient (based on a legally binding patient–physician relationship) by performing below the standard of care expected from a reasonable professional under the same circumstances, a breach that directly brought about the patient's legally compensable injuries.[43] Delineation of the standard of care in telemedicine is still in its infancy. To date, no court ruling has grappled with telemedicine's standard of care; thus, we must assume that traditional malpractice precedents will fill the void and serve telemedicine cases. This in turn dictates complying with reasonable care with respect to the medical care: taking a medical history taking, employing appropriate diagnostics, reaching a diagnosis based on adequate differential diagnosis, choosing and providing the accurate treatment in a reasonable manner, engaging in appropriate follow-up, and intervening in a timely way if the need arises. It also refers to institutional practices such as recruiting and privileges policies, assuring that only competent practitioners are providing care, or that the institution's infrastructure is adequate.[44] As I have indicated in a previous section (see section III(A)), the fact that many courts have declared a de facto national standard of care seems to help the establishment of a general standard of care for the telemedicine industry. These standards in turn can provide greater predictability of what is expected from providers with respect to equipment, training, and performance.

---

[42] Siegal, *supra* note 23.

[43] Edward B. Hirshfeld, *Practice Parameters and the Malpractice Liability of Physicians*, 263 J. AM. MED. ASS'N 1556, 1556–62 (1990).

[44] *See* McClellan v. Health Maint. Org. of Pa., 604 A.2d 1053 (Pa. Super. Ct. 1992).

The challenge of creating internationally accepted standards is daunting at first. Yet there are reasons for optimism. First, North American–generated guidelines already serve many other nations' medical/professional associations, and common ground can be reached if the stakes (such as becoming part of a global telemedicine market) are high enough. The growing credibility and the much-sought-after Joint Commission International standardized approval is a vivid testament. Second, as discussed below, the leverage power of the U.S. massive investments in foreign aid should suffice in bringing all parties to the table. Finally, all standards should be prepared and launched as an international collective effort, thus hopefully diminishing national resistance that stems from international politics.

Until an international initiative is successfully instated, the question of whose standard of care should be used to determine negligence must be addressed. A genuine legal debate with respect to telemedicine's standard of care will arise only if a provider attempts to refute a plaintiff's allegation by reverting to a lower standard practiced in the provider's locality. In this case, accepting the rule of locality with respect to the provider's licensure should also establish the chosen standard of care.

Within the United States, the locality standard has lost favor in comparison with a national one. The same legal evolution should occur in international forums. If an international telemedicine license option should prevail, and once prior agreement on standard of care can be developed, most providers are likely to abide by the accepted international standards. Providers' acquiescence should be part of both the review procedure and the informed consent process prior to their providing telemedical care.

Finally, what constitutes a compensable injury currently varies from one jurisdiction to another. For example, caps on noneconomic damages or dignitary damages are dealt with differently in the United States than in other countries. In Section IV, I briefly describe how this debate is tackled by pretreatment agreements on the governing legal regime and its rules for compensable injuries.

2. Informed Consent

In an explicit attempt to abandon physician paternalism and to empower patients to make their own health care decisions, the informed consent doctrine has become a foundational precept in medical ethics and health law.[45] The underlying ethical principle is that because individuals are rational moral agents, they should be in command of decisions that relate to *their* lives and bodies.[46] The corollary obligation of the physician is to respect and facilitate patient autonomy. In telemedicine, consent should be given to the medical interaction itself (be it diagnosis, treatment, monitoring, etc.), which requires a deliberation regarding the procedures, benefits, risks, and available

---

[45] *E.g.*, JESSICA W. BERG, PAUL S. APPELBAUM, CHARLES W. LIDZ & LISA S PARKER, INFORMED CONSENT: LEGAL THEORY AND CLINICAL PRACTICE (2001); Gil Siegal, Richard J. Bonnie & Paul S. Appelbaum, *Personalized Disclosure by Information-on-Demand: Attending to Patients' Needs in the Informed Consent Process*, 40 J.L. MED. ETHICS 359 (2012).

[46] *See* Canterbury v. Spence, 464 F.2d 772, 781 (D.C. Cir. 1972).

alternatives, with the additional information that results from providing the service via telecommunication. In obtaining informed consent for a telemedicine procedure, one must clarify whether a particular telemedicine interaction is materially different than its non-telemedicine counterpart. For example, consent to a telesurgery removal of a gallbladder involves all the risks of the medical procedure with the addition of "telerisks" such as the spontaneous failure of communication lines, or a need to abort a telesurgery, perhaps or most probably to then be continued by a different practitioner. Conversely, if the telemedicine procedure does not carry special or significant additional risks (such as is safe to speculate in respect to telepsychiatry), the informed consent process should be basically identical to the processes currently employed.

As with the discussion regarding licensing and medical malpractice above, in obtaining informed consent, an underlying legal question of what standard to use must be considered. Some countries and U.S. states have adopted the "reasonable patient" standard in determining the nature and amount of information that should be provided, whereas others adhere to the "reasonable physician" standard.[47] If a telemedicine interaction involves countries or states with different standards of information disclosure, such a conflict might be resolved in a similar fashion as was suggested above for the licensure or standard of care qualm—assuming the electronic tourism metaphor succeeded, it seems reasonable to implement the provider's domestic standard. However, prior notice on this matter should be the norm.

Furthermore, I strongly recommend that professional bodies such as the AMA or specific professional associations and patients' advocacy groups evaluate all proposed telemedicine interactions and clearly define the information required for valid informed consent.

Finally, all involved parties (especially in multinational interactions) should verify the accuracy and adequacy of the informed consent process, and maintain access to the signed informed consent forms for future reference. New Web-based, multilingual platforms (iMedConsent and EMMI Solutions, for example)[48] enable providers to obtain standardized, automatic, computerized informed consent; manage legal risks; and improve patients' education. Documentation of informed consent remains essential, and many information technologies are available to record and archive ICs should the need for them arise.

IV. Mobilizing IT-Driven Health care—Suggestions for Future Directions

Harnessing IT to promote globalization of health care requires a substantial legal and regulatory effort. In this section, I delineate several areas where I anticipate that

---

[47] Jaime Staples King & Benjamin W. Moulton, *Rethinking Informed Consent: The Case for Shared Medical Decision-Making*, 32 AM. J.L. & MED. 429, 493–501 (2006).

[48] *See* Deborah Franklin, *Uninformed Consent: Tech Solutions for Faulty Permissions in Health Care*, SCIENTIFIC AM., Mar. 15, 2011, *available at* http://www.scientificamerican.com/article.cfm?id=uninformed-consent-mar-11.

successful engagement may assist in a more robust exploitation of IT/telemedicine to promote globalization. The basic premises I rely on have been set forth in previous sections, and their aggregated form creates a modest proposal for future progress: First, individuals may travel to other states/countries where medical care is readily available to them. However, a great number of patients who could have benefited from medical tourism will not, or cannot, travel for their health care needs. Second, medical facilities, current practices, and workforce qualifications can be reliably subject to external, independent, effective, and standardized review. Providers and institutions in turn will willingly submit to such review if it is conceived as a prerequisite to partake in the global market of EMT. Third, the need to protect patients is a constant concern. Arguing for patients' protection has two major facets—protecting their health during and following telecare (the quality and safety argument), and protecting their legal rights when injury does occur and redress is sought (the legal rights argument). The quality and safety argument has been pivotal in fueling a negative attitude toward traditional medical tourism generally and toward telemedicine in particular. However, the quality and safety argument is neither proven nor well-founded.[49] Finally, redress for avoidable injuries and mishaps is required to prevent a situation wherein injured patients face substantial loss or devastating outcomes, or a situation wherein such losses are externalized to the home country's social security system.

A. M-WWW—APPROVED/ELIGIBLE PROVIDERS

A collective process of international/supranational official recognition based on established accreditation processes (JCI-like accreditation) should enable the creation of a medical World Wide Web (M-WWW)—where national bodies, institutions, and providers all subscribe to standardized infrastructure and equipment, accepted standards of practice, and normalized data management and privacy safeguards. The formation of this trusted web should be a concerted effort, bringing in the private sector as well as governments. The private–public aspect of the partnership is crucial—the private sector is essential to infuse the enthusiasm and efficiency of entrepreneurship; the public partner is critical in harnessing the state's police power to allow cross-border health care, to enable the resolution of current legal obstacles, and to assure that patients and public interests are adequately promoted. In addition, supranational health organizations such as the WHO have an important leadership role.[50]

Successful establishment of the M-WWW depends primarily on addressing the following: instituting appropriate privileges/credentials to verify professional competence; introducing safeguards to prevent unauthorized access, use, and fraud; and

---

[49] See Cohen, *supra* note 35, at 1471–73.

[50] Gil Siegal, *Enabling Globalization of Health Care in the Information Technology Era*, 35 VA. J.L & TECH. 1 (2012); Scott Borris & Evan D. Anderson, *A Framework Convention on Global Health: Social Justice Lite or a Light on Social Justice?*, 38(3) J.L. MED. & ETHICS 580 (2010), *available at* http://papers.ssrn.com/sol3/papers.cfm?abstract_id=1685858.

implementing sanctions (including revocation of institutional certification, agreed penalties, mechanisms of complaints to institution's home national authorities) in case of a breach. The responsibility for compliance and quality of care should rest on provider institutions. These institutions must assure that only licensed and qualified professionals are practicing telemedicine and that the institution has guaranteed their authentication; additionally, institutions must meet their own standards of care, and protect patients' confidentiality and privacy according to predetermined criteria.

Furthermore, participating parties should establish "contact points" in participating countries and states that will provide interested patients with information concerning the recognition of professional qualifications, the standards of practice, and, where appropriate, the pertinent rules of health law and medical ethics.[51] In this regard, for example, some countries and some U.S. states have adopted the "reasonable patient" standard in determining the nature and amount of information that should be provided to patients by their doctors, whereas others adhere to the "reasonable physician" standard.[52] If a telemedicine interaction involves countries or states with different standards of information disclosure, prior notice on this matter should be available to patients. Noticeably, EMT allows states and countries to maintain their sovereign legal regimes, as patients explicitly accept the local law (*lex domicilii*) of the provider.

Responsibility for consuming health care from nonaccredited providers should be shifted to consumers. Indeed, health care consumers should be well-informed on the hazards of receiving medical care or consultation from nonaffiliated practitioners. Dealing with patients who have been injured using non–M-WWW members deserves serious deliberation, especially if they are left without means to recuperate or are forced to absorb the costs of their injuries. Accordingly, creative means to address such eventualities, as well as means to dissuade patients from using non-approved providers, should be discussed.

B. FINANCING

I shall not attempt to identify the likely provider of the funds ultimately needed to promote a more extensive dissemination and utilization of IT and telemedicine—including infrastructure, standardization, workforce training, and ancillary costs. That said, the thriving medical tourism industry, with its estimated price tag of $200 billion by 2020,[53] is a vivid testimony to the ability to generate sufficient economic incentives for parties involved in cross-border medicine; it stands to reason, then, that IT and telemedicine hold a similar chance of success, even in the abstract.

Unlike medical tourism, utilizing IT capabilities should become a prime target for national players, including governments, when addressing their citizens' needs and

---

[51] Miek Peeters, *Free Movement of Medical Doctors: The New Directive 2005/36/EC on the Recognition of Professional Qualifications*, 12 EUR. J. HEALTH L. 385 (2005).

[52] King & Moulton, *supra* note 47, at 493–501.

[53] *See* Mclean, *supra* note 1, at 599.

when reviewing their foreign health aid investments. In this respect, another important source of funding should be added to the discussion: money dedicated by nations to foreign aid.[54] Adding new expenses in today's economy is politically hard; diverting existing ones can be acceptable, especially if geared toward multiple beneficiaries. Dedicated allocation from existing foreign aid to global health should be earmarked to promote IT and telemedicine programs. By allocating resources to the development of high-tech medicine, developing countries may do a better job of retaining their qualified workforce, as the current departure of health professionals tends to create severe and disadvantageous results for poorer countries.[55] Additionally, a dedicated portion of funds should be earmarked for reinvestment in providers and manufacturers operating within donating countries to create substantial incentives (including tax incentives) to participate in these projects and, as a consequence, boost the capabilities in developed countries as well. Indeed, the expected spillage to the domestic arena in developed countries would have a beneficial effect, benefiting all stakeholders.

C. REDRESS

Patients interested in receiving cross-border telemedicine will be prompted to learn about the legal remedies available to them in case of an injury. The first remedy involves the continuous reliance on the tort system either in the provider's host country or in the patient's originating one. As a result, many now-familiar problems emerge (choice of law, appropriate forum, setting of the applicable standard, determination of compensable injuries, etc.). However, as scholars have noted, the availability of adequate compensation in certain leading telemedicine sites is doubtful with respect to the likelihood of litigation's success, the amount awarded, and the prospects of enforcement of judgments.[56] Thus, two alternative approaches should be considered: a no-fault administrative compensation scheme, or a mandated insurance program.

The first alternative might operate similarly to schemes implemented in Nordic countries such as Sweden, Norway, and Denmark, or in New Zealand, where compensation for injuries attributed to avoidable events is granted by government-operated bodies.[57] I find this option unsuitable for the current global telemedicine market for the following reasons. First, it would be extremely difficult to establish multiple schemes for every country, adjusting to each country's nuanced political and legal institutions. The pace of progress can never be synchronized globally, leading to a

---

[54] *Public Policy Update*, GLOBAL HEALTH COUNCIL, http://www.globalhealth.org/test.html#IMG_case_statement.

[55] *See generally* Fitzhugh Mullen, *The Metrics of the Physician Brain Drain*, 353 NEW ENG. J. MED. 1810 (2005); C.R. Hooper, *Adding Insult to Injury: The Health Care Brain Drain*, 34 J. MED. ETHICS 684–87 (2008); Jeremy Snyder, *Is Health Worker Migration a Case of Poaching?*, 9 AM. J. BIOETHICS 3–7 (2008).

[56] *See* Cohen, *supra* note 35.

[57] David M. Studdert & Troyen A. Brennan, *No-Fault Compensation for Medical Injuries: The Prospect for Error Prevention*, 286 JAMA 217 (2001). *See also* R.G. Jorstad, *The Norwegian System of Compensation to Patients*, 21 MED. L. 681, 683 (2002).

piecemeal implementation and an extended period of legal uncertainty. Second, the nascent phase of telemedicine requires much expertise, and it is highly unlikely that an independent and disperse system that is based in every country can evade an extended period of a learning curve, which again results in an extended period of legal uncertainty. Finally, I would advise against embarking on an attempt to establish a central, supranational authority in light of the obvious managerial difficulties it represents.

The second alternative is mandatory insurance with differential pricing—both in insurance acquisition (the premium) and in respect to compensation. Patients contemplating using EMT will want to purchase "telemedicine accident insurance." Indeed, Assurance Company Limited (Aos) is already offering "Patient Medical Malpractice Insurance" that insures against "the risk of suffering Medical Malpractice abroad."[58] Similar to personal injury coverage (which does not require proof of negligence), patients in this alternative will be entitled to compensation should predetermined adverse effects of care transpire. Insurance payments will be subject to the originating site's local insurance laws. "Glocal" (global and local) works very nicely for telemedicine, as the premium as well as the compensation for damages will reflect local (patient's) values in a transparent, upfront fashion, while allowing individuals to enjoy the benefits of global medicine (as the risk of non-compensable injuries is contained). Locally based insurance has an important role in such a system, as it is best situated to assess local (country-specific) costs of harm. Given local standards, insurance premiums are expected to be lower in poor countries, as is compensation. Troublingly, the ability of poor patients to purchase such insurance initially is obviously questionable, and more thought should be given to ways to provide them compensation.

The major drawback of an insurance model most be acknowledged: providers will be enjoying liability-free practice, thus creating the need to replace tort's prime role in deterring negligent conduct.[59] Several tools can be used to create positive as well as negative incentives. Leveraging the commercial value of reputation, insurance companies could publish the number of patients who were injured in a particular telemedicine interaction by a particular provider, and premiums within states could adjust accordingly. Ultimately, insurance companies could refuse to cover telemedicine interactions by a particular provider if that provider's record falls below industry standards. Compensating patients should be closely linked to reporting requirements to providers' national authorities and/or to a central M-WWW database so as to allow disciplinary and market-based measures both locally and internationally.

In its mature form, the M-WWW would consist of qualified providers in certified institutions who abide by a supranational standard of care, making use of cutting-edge technology and serving an international audience of patients who consume high-quality telecare and are financially protected in case of mishaps.

---

[58] Cohen, *supra* note 35, at 1536.

[59] MAXWELL J. MEHLMAN & DALE A. NANCE, MEDICAL INJUSTICE: THE CASE AGAINST HEALTH COURTS (2007).

Conclusion

In order to promote the globalization of health care, this chapter reviewed the existing impediments to a more robust exploitation of IT. After addressing current barriers, the need to develop a cross-border approach to health care seems evident. Toward this end, I have proposed a dedicated effort to establish a formal M-WWW. The following elements need to be in place in order to make that happen: funding for demonstration projects and subsequent translation to large-scale sustainable programs; a strong commitment to quality evidenced by appropriate training of the workforce and established guidelines, protocols, and accepted accreditation processes with adequate sanctions; transparent and trusted information on treatment offered; and assurance of patients' rights and remedies for those injured. Importantly, current legal obstacles such as licensure requirements, liabilities, and privacy must be overcome in a manner that enables sensible solutions with appropriate adaptation of traditional health care law and ethics. The materialization of M-WWW depends on a bifurcated maneuver— the bottom-up drive of the industry and providers as well as medical tourists/patients seeking optimal health care must be met by the top-down efforts of governments and supranational organizations to facilitate legal and regulatory requirements and direct the appropriate resources. Only such a dually engaged partnership will enable us to reap the benefits of IT in modern health care for the betterment of our global citizenry.

20

LEGAL AND REGULATORY BARRIERS TO TELEMEDICINE IN THE

UNITED STATES

Public and Private Approaches toward Health Care Reform*

Deth Sao,[†] Amar Gupta,[**] and David A. Gantz[‡]

Introduction

The United States spends one-and-a-half times more per person on health care than any country in the world,[1] yet lags behind other industrialized nations in health care system performance.[2] Telemedicine has the potential to play a central role in resolving

---

* Some of the contents of this chapter have been previously published in journals. See Deth Sao, Amar Gupta & David A. Gantz, Disputes Related to Healthcare across National Boundaries: The Potential for Arbitration, 42 GEO. WASH. INT'L L. REV. 3 (2011); Amar Gupta & Deth Sao, The Constitutionality of Current Legal Barriers to Telemedicine in the United States: Analysis and Future Directions of Its Relationship to National and International Health Care Reform, 21 HEALTH MATRIX 385 (2011);

[†] J.D. 2010, James E. Rogers College of Law, University of Arizona; B.A. 2001, Wellesley College.

** Dean and Professor, Seidenberg School, PACE University. Formerly Thomas R. Brown Endowed Professor, Eller College of Management, University of Arizona; concurrent appointments in the College of Science, College of Public Health, College of Social and Behavioral Sciences, James E. Rogers College of Law, and the College of Pharmacy (HOPE Center); Ph.D. 1980, Indian Institute of Technology Delhi; M.S. 1980, Massachusetts Institute of Technology Sloan School of Management; Bachelor of Technology 1974, Indian Institute of Technology Kanpur.

[‡] Samuel M. Fegtly Professor of Law and Director, International Trade and Business Law Program, James E. Rogers College of Law, University of Arizona; J.S.M. 1970, Stanford Law School; J.D. 1967, Stanford Law School; A.B. 1964, Harvard College.

[1] U.S. President Barack Obama, Remarks by the president to the Joint Session of Congress on Health Care (Sept. 9, 2009) (transcript available at http://www.whitehouse.gov/the_press_office/remarks-by-the-pr esident-to-a-joint-session-of-congress-on-health-care/).

[2] Mary Mahon & Bethanne Fox, *U.S. Ranks Last among Seven Countries on Health System Performance Based on Measures of Quality, Efficiency, Access, Equity, and Healthy Lives*, THE COMMONWEALTH FUND

this ongoing disparity. Defined as "the use of medical information exchanged from one site to another via electronic communications to improve patients' health status,"[3] telemedicine offers the capabilities to deliver health care across distances at reduced costs while maintaining or even increasing the quality of treatment and services.[4] However, U.S. state legal and regulatory regimes currently inhibit the full realization of telemedicine's benefits by subjecting interstate telemedicine providers to differing standards and requirements and by creating legal uncertainty in the event of cross-border disputes.[5] These barriers call for a uniform means of redress and regulation.[6]

A combination of public and private approaches should be adopted to accommodate the interstate and international practice of telemedicine. Section I discusses the importance of telemedicine in U.S. health care reform. Section II analyzes legal and regulatory barriers to telemedicine in the United States. Section III offers proposals for a national telemedicine regime, including private and public approaches to uniformity in regulation and dispute resolution mechanisms. Section IV concludes with an assessment of the feasibility of applying such proposals on a global scale. The U.S. experience shares similarities with other nations, and represents a microcosm of the international community's need and struggle to develop a uniform telemedicine regime, as well as to deploy nontraditional options to resolve the dilemmas of rising costs and discontent in the delivery of quality health care services.

I. The Role of Telemedicine in U.S. Health Care Reform

There are two critical and central failings of the U.S. health care system that telemedicine may help to resolve. First, health care spending in the United States is the highest among all economically advanced countries,[7] making health care services (increasingly) unaffordable for a wide range of consumers.[8] In the attempt to finance such exorbitant costs, public and private health insurers have more than doubled insurance premiums in the past decade—an increase that far outpaces the growth of U.S. wages and cost of

---

(June 23, 2010), http://www.commonwealthfund.org/Content/News/News-Releases/2010/Jun/US-R anks-Last-Among-Seven-Countries.aspx. Six other countries in the 2010 Commonwealth Fund study include: Australia, Canada, Netherlands, New Zealand, and the United Kingdom. *Id.*

[3] *About Telemedicine*, AMERICAN TELEMEDICINE ASSOCIATION, http://www.americantelemed.org/i4a/ pages/index.cfm?pageID=3331 (last visited May 3, 2011).

[4] *See* Susan E. Volkert, *Telemedicine: Rx for the Future of Health Care*, 6 MICH. TELECOMM. & TECH. L. REV. 147, 155 (2000).

[5] *Id.* at 156.

[6] *Id.* at 158–59.

[7] CHRIS L. PETERSON & RACHEL BURTON, CONG. RESEARCH SERV., RL 34175, U.S. HEALTH CARE SPENDING: COMPARISON WITH OTHER OECD COUNTRIES 1 (2007).

[8] *U.S. Health Care Costs*, THE HENRY J. KAISER FAMILY FOUNDATION, http://www.kaiseredu.org/topics_i m.asp?imID=1&parentID=61&id=358#1t (last visited Jan, 15, 2010) (citing CENTER FOR MEDICARE & MEDICAID SERVICES, DEPARTMENT OF HEALTH & HUMAN SERVICES, UPDATED NHE HISTORICAL PROJECTIONS (1965–2019).

living.[9] Second, many individuals lack geographic access to health care. These populations include, for example, those requiring home health care, those confined to correctional facilities,[10] and those residing in rural communities.[11]

Telemedicine has the capacity to reduce health care expenditures, improve quality of care, and deliver services to underserved populations by offering treatment at a distance. This form of "distance medicine" includes: online communications between physician and patient; consultations via electronic communications between patients' primary care physicians and tertiary care specialists; and real-time examination, treatment, and diagnosis through interactive television and emergency centers where physicians remotely evaluate a patient's symptoms.[12] Such applications not only enable immediate delivery of health services when circumstances delay or prevent traditional face-to-face treatment, but also greatly mitigate or avoid related costs such as travel expenses and duplicative administrative and specialist services.[13] Furthermore, these applications represent a few of the many ways in which telemedicine has and is expected to improve the quality of health care. By improving or creating new approaches to treatment such as workload redistribution,[14] home-based telemedical services for enhanced communications between clinicians and patients,[15] and remote access to and sharing of patient data for stronger care coordination and reduced medical errors,[16] telemedicine is able to achieve comparable if not superior delivery of health services.

II. Barriers to Telemedicine in the United States

Present and potential uses of telemedicine are constrained by overlapping and often inconsistent and inadequate regulatory and legal frameworks and technical standards imposed by governments and professional medical organizations.[17] In the United States, states have both the authority to regulate health professionals who practice in

---

[9] *Id.;* HEALTHCARE.GOV, HEALTH INSURANCE PREMIUMS, PAST HIGH COSTS WILL BECOME THE PRESENT AND FUTURE WITHOUT HEALTH REFORM 1 (2011), http://www.healthcare.gov/law/resources/reports/premiums01282011a.pdf.

[10] Volkert, *supra* note 4, at 156.

[11] Joy Elizabeth Matak, *Telemedicine: Medical Treatment via Telecommunications Will Save Lives, but Can Congress Answer the Call?*, 22 VT. L. REV. 231, 236 (1997).

[12] Volkert, *supra* note 4, at 153. Additionally, promising developments include advances in information technology to resolve security and data privacy concerns and offshore outsourcing of diagnostic services. Amar Gupta, *Prescription for Change*, WALL ST. J., Oct. 20, 2008, at R6.

[13] FEDERAL TRADE COMMISSION AND THE DEPARTMENT OF JUSTICE, IMPROVING HEALTH CARE: A DOSE OF COMPETITION 31 (2004).

[14] Gupta, *supra* note 12, at R6.

[15] WILLIAM R. HERSH ET AL., TELEMEDICINE FOR THE MEDICARE POPULATION: UPDATE 6 (2006), [http://archive.ahrq.gov/downloads/pub/evidence/pdf/telemedup/telemedup.pdf.

[16] Farzad Mostashari, *Aging in Place: The National Broadband Plan and Bringing Health Care Technology Home*, U.S. DEPARTMENT OF HEALTH & HUMAN SERVICES (Apr. 19, 2011), http://www.hhs.gov/asl/testify/2010/04/t20100422e.html.

[17] *See* Volkert, *supra* note 4, at 156–57.

their territories and jurisdiction over medical malpractice claims.[18] The federal government plays a relatively limited role in these areas, and often permits states to impose stricter standards in areas of overlapping regulation.[19] For instance, the 1996 Health Insurance Portability and Accountability Act (HIPAA) mandates privacy and security requirements for personal health information at the federal level,[20] but its effectiveness is limited by its deference to state laws that do not conflict and are more stringent.[21] An examination of these regulatory and legal barriers will demonstrate how overlapping, inconsistent, and inadequate obligations imposed by governments and professional organizations impede the practice and growth of telemedicine.

A. REGULATORY BARRIERS TO INTERSTATE TELEMEDICINE

The following regulatory barriers raise transaction costs and keep patients and health care providers from reaping the benefits of interstate telemedicine: licensure and insurance requirements, information privacy compliance, and reimbursement processes. The practice of telemedicine across state lines subjects health care providers to the licensing requirements of more than one state because all states require physicians to be licensed in the state in which they practice medicine.[22] The lack of consensus among states on licensing requirements, and telemedicine licensure requirements in particular, force health care providers to incur higher business costs in order to meet compliance with differing state statutes.[23] Compliance with states' medical malpractice insurance coverage requirements is also costly and complicated, as states have the authority to establish and regulate insurance for health care providers.[24] Although there is overlap between state insurance codes, each state has its own unique definitions, coverage schemes, and procedures.[25] Additionally, concurrent federal and state regulations force telemedicine providers to comply with multiple standards for protecting the privacy of health care information—compliance is a process that is expensive, difficult, and time-consuming.[26] Finally, interstate telemedicine is impeded by health care reimbursement

---

[18] *The Role of the State Medical Board*, FEDERATION OF STATE MEDICAL BOARDS, http://www.fsmb.org/grpol_talkingpoints1.html (last visited Jan. 8, 2010) [hereinafter Fed'n of State Med. Bds.].

[19] *See, e.g.*, 42 U.S.C. § 1320d(7)(a) (2006).

[20] 42 U.S.C. § 1320(d) to (d)(8) (2000).

[21] 42 U.S.C. § 1320d(2).

[22] Thomas R. McLean, *The Future of Telemedicine & Its Faustian Reliance on Regulatory Trade Barriers for Protection*, 16 HEALTH MATRIX 443, 462 (2006); *see also* Matak, *supra* note 11, at 242. *See, e.g.*, ALASKA STAT. § 08.64.170; COLO. REV. STAT. § 12–36–106 (2010); DEL. CODE ANN. tit. 24, § 1702 (2008); FLA. STAT. ANN. § 458.327 (West 2010); HAW. REV. STAT. § 453–2; IDAHO CODE ANN. § 54–1804; KAN. STAT. ANN. § 65–2803 (West 2010); LA. REV. STAT. ANN. § 37:1271 (2010); MISS. CODE ANN. § 73–25–1; NEV. REV. STAT. § 630.160; OKLA. STAT. tit. 59, §§ 491, 492(C)(2)(b); S.C. CODE ANN. § 40–47–30 (2009). Gil Siegal discusses these issues in his chapter in this volume, *Electronic Medical Tourism and the Medical World Wide Web*.

[23] *See* McLean, *supra* note 22, at 462.

[24] *See* Paul v. Virginia, 75 U.S. (8 Wall) 168, 183–84 (1869).

[25] *See, e.g.*, KY. REV. STAT. ANN. § 304.40–250 to – 320 (West 2009).

[26] *See* Joy Pritts, *Preemption Analysis under HIPAA—Proceed with Caution*, American Health Information Management Association (Apr. 2003), http://library.ahima.org/xpedio/groups/public/documents/

processes, as public and private insurers alike may not pay for telemedicine services or may pay only for some services under limited circumstances.[27]

B. LEGAL BARRIERS TO INTERSTATE TELEMEDICINE

The need to develop a standardized approach toward a uniform regulatory regime further highlights the following legal dilemmas related to medical malpractice disputes involving telemedicine providers and patients in different U.S. states or countries: determining the potentially liable parties; asserting personal jurisdiction and forum selection; discerning choice of law considerations and appropriate theories of liability for injuries and damages; and, in cases involving non-U.S. based defendants, enforcing foreign judgments.[28] A brief overview of these legal issues demonstrates the increasing necessity of implementing uniform procedures and standards for cross-border telemedicine disputes.

1. Determining Potentially Liable Parties

In any telemedicine dispute, the potentially liable parties may include a remote health care provider, any affiliated local health care provider working in consultation or contracting with that remote provider,[29] and the supplier of the telemedical device.[30] The fact that telemedicine usually involves several parties in different locations and at varying capacities in the course of medical treatment complicates the nature and scope of a defendant's liability in medical malpractice claims.[31] In the United States, one of the essential elements a plaintiff must prove is that the defendant owed a duty to the patient arising out of the traditionally conceived physician–patient relationship.[32] In the modern world of telemedical care, technologically enabled departures from face-to-face physician–patient relationships make it difficult to determine when such a duty arises.[33]

---

ahima/bok3_005197.hcsp?dDocName=bok3_005197#sidebar. For analysis on this issue, see Siegal, *supra* note 22.

[27] HEALTH RES. AND SERVICES ADMIN., DEPARTMENT OF HEALTH AND HUM. SERVICES, 2001 TELEMEDICINE REPORT TO CONGRESS (2001), *available at* ftp://ftp.hrsa.gov/telehealth/report2001.pdf.

[28] Barring few exceptions, U.S. states will likely enforce sister state judgments in accordance with the full faith and credit clause of the federal Constitution, which dictates: "Full Faith and Credit shall be given in each State to the public Acts, Records, and judicial Proceedings of every other State." U.S. CONST. art. IV, §1. Most exceptions arise where there is nonmonetary relief or monetary relief is collateral to the judgment. Jean A. Mortland, *Interstate Federalism: Effect of Full Faith and Credit to Judgments*, 16 U. DAYTON L. REV. 47, 53 (1990).

[29] Heather L. Daly, *Telemedicine: The Invisible Legal Barriers to the Health Care of the Future*, 9 ANNALS HEALTH L. 73, 99–100 (2000).

[30] *Id.* at 100.

[31] *Id.*

[32] *Id.*

[33] *Id.*

2. Asserting Personal Jurisdiction and Forum

For disputes involving telemedicine providers offering services in the United States, federal and state case law and legislation provides little guidance for determining personal jurisdiction—a rule of U.S. civil procedure that determines whether the court has jurisdiction over the parties involved in the action.[34] Although it is likely that personal jurisdiction will be established in accordance with the Supreme Court's proscribed analysis of a defendant's "minimum contacts" with the forum state,[35] the test's flexible, multifactor approach is open to different interpretations and offers no reliable outcome to either party in a claim.[36] Even if a plaintiff succeeds in asserting personal jurisdiction in the preferred forum state, the defendant may utilize the complex common law doctrine of *forum non conveniens* to dismiss the claim.[37] *Forum non conveniens* empowers courts to dismiss cases under particular circumstances—including the existence of undue burdens on the defendant[38]—and its application varies from state to state.[39] As with personal jurisdiction, there is currently little guidance for courts and litigants alike when telemedicine disputes lead to forum debates.

3. Discerning Choice of Law and Adequacy of Existing Laws

Cross-border telemedicine disputes are further complicated by choice-of-law considerations. When a legal dispute involves the interests of two or more states, a court must decide which state's laws apply.[40] There is no uniform approach to choice-of-law determinations, as U.S. state courts follow the particular rules adopted by their respective jurisdictions.[41] Even after choice-of-law considerations are settled, the selected law may be unable to offer adequate theories of liability and damages arising out of the

---

[34] *See generally* Nathan Cortez, *Patients without Borders: The Emerging Global Market for Patients and the Evolution of Modern Health Care*, 83 IND. L.J. 71, 77 (2008); Deth Sao, David A. Gantz & Amar Gupta, *Disputes Related to Healthcare across National Boundaries: The Potential for Arbitration*, 42 GEO. WASH. INT'L L. REV. 3 (2011).

[35] *See, e.g.*, Archie A. Alexander, *American Diagnostic Radiology Moves Offshore: Is This Field Riding "The Internet Wave" into a Regulatory Abyss?*, 20 J.L. & HEALTH 199, 232–36 (2006–07); Mark S. Kopson, *Medical Tourism: Implications for Providers & Plans*, 3 J. HEALTH & LIFE SCI. L. 147, 182–83 (2010); Thomas R. McLean, *The Offshoring of American Medicine: Scope, Economic Issues and Legal Liabilities*, 14 ANNALS HEALTH L. 205, 247 (2005); Asahi Metal Indus. Co. v. Superior Court, 480 U.S. 102 (1987).

[36] *See, e.g.*, Burger King Corp. v. Rudzewicz, 471 U.S. 462, 471–79 (1985); Hanson v. Denckla, 357 U.S. 235, 251–53 (1958); World-Wide Volkswagen Corp. v. Woodson, 444 U.S. 286, 291–98 (1980); *Asahi Metal*, 480 U.S. at 108–13.

[37] *See* Martine Stückelberg, Lis Pendens *and* Forum Non Conveniens *at The Hague Conference*, 26 BROOK. J. INT'L L. 949, 954–55 (2001).

[38] Nathan Cortez, *Recalibrating the Legal Risks of Cross-Border Health Care*, 10 YALE J. HEALTH POL'Y, L. & ETHICS 1, 11 (2010).

[39] David W. Robertson, *Access to State Courts in Transnational Personal Injury Cases: Forum Non Conveniens and Antisuit Injunctions*, 68 TEX. L.REV. 937, 949–50 (1990).

[40] WILLIAM M. RICHMAN & WILLIAM L. REYNOLDS, UNDERSTANDING CONFLICT OF LAWS 2 (2002), http://www.lexisnexis.com/lawschool/study/understanding/pdf/ConflictsCh1.pdf.

[41] *See generally* William Tetley, *New Development in Private International Law: Tolofson v. Jensen and Gagnon v. Lucas*, 44 AM. J. COMP. L. 647 (1996).

practice of telemedicine. One area of legal ambiguity concerns the appropriate standard of care to determine a defendant's fault in a medical malpractice suit. The standard of care is generally defined as what a reasonable and prudent physican would do in similar circumstances.[42] Currently, it is not clear whether technological innovations and practices associated with telemedical services should change the existing standard, or if courts should create a new standard altogether.[43] Another legal point of confusion is whether today's understanding of the duty of confidentiality and informed consent extends to telemedical services.[44]

4. Enforceability of Judgments against Non–U.S. Based Defendants

Unlike U.S.-based telemedicine providers, a claim involving their foreign counterparts presents the added challenge of enforcing any judgment rendered. Absent regional or international agreements, no general consensus exists among countries to enforce another's court-issued decrees.[45] Similar to the legal challenges of adjudication in state courts, the unreliablity of enforceable judgments further affirms the uncertainties associated in pursuing a cross-border malpractice claim and the tremendous investment in cost and time of such a process.

III. Public and Private Approaches Toward a National Telemedicine Regime

In light of the present barriers to telemedicine, it is crucial that we consider national and international approaches to establishing standards, regulations, and forums for redress involving out-of-state parties and transactions. Although state authority over health care regulation is historically rooted in the Tenth Amendment of the U.S. Constitution,[46] the Constitution also arguably provides grounds for federal authority

---

[42] Tanya Albert, *Studies Define Standard of Care, even When They Conflict*, AMEDNEWS.COM (Apr. 14, 2003), [http://www.ama-assn.org/amednews/2003/04/14/prca0414.htm.

[43] McLean, *supra* note 35, at 252–53.

[44] Dr. Puteri Nemie J. Kassim, *Medicine beyond Borders: The Legal and Ethical Challenges*, 28 MED. & L. 439, 448 (2009); *see* Sanjiv N. Singh & Robert M. Wachter, *Perspectives on Medical Outsourcing and Telemedicine—Rough Edges in a Flat World?*, 358 NEW ENG. J. MED. 1622, 1624 (2008), *available at* [http://www.uapd.com/wp-content/uploads/Perspectives-on-Medical-Outsourcing-and-Telemedicine-%E2%80%941.pdf; for analysis on this issue, see Siegal, *supra* note 22.

[45] Singh & Wachter, *supra* note 44, at 1624.

[46] *See, e.g.*, Dent v. West Virginia, 129 U.S. 114, 122 (1889) (under the police power, a state can impose regulation for the general welfare even if it prevents a person from practicing his or her profession); Hawker v. New York, 170 U.S. 189, 191–93 (1898) (determining that state had broad discretion in describing qualifications necessary to practice medicine in state); Watson v. Maryland, 218 U.S. 173, 179–80 (1910) (holding that a state statute barring practice of medicine without state registration does not violate Fourteenth Amendment); Jacobson v. Massachusetts, 197 U.S. 11, 38–39 (1905) (upholding state law allowing boards of health to require mandatory small pox vaccinations); McNaughton v. Johnson, 242 U.S. 344, 349 (1917) (upholding state regulation defeating ophthalmologist on a Fourteenth Amendment claim); Semler v. Oregon State Bd. of Dental Examiners, 294 U.S. 608, 612 (1935) (holding that a state has discretion to regulate the practice of dentistry). For analysis on the constitutionality of U.S. state laws regulating the practice of interstate telemedicine, see Amar Gupta & Deth Sao,

over the practice of cross-border telemedicine through the Interstate Commerce[47] and Spending Power Clauses.[48] Just as the Commerce Clause may be invoked to limit state and local regulation, it may also be invoked to authorize federal action.[49] Second, the Spending Power grants Congress the broad power to spend for the general welfare so long as this does not violate other Constitutional provisions.[50] Such a solid legal basis for federal reform opens the door to the considerations of workable and successful national alternatives to current state regulatory and legal frameworks.

A. PROPOSALS FOR REGULATORY REFORM

Public measures, such as transferring state authority to regulate the practice of inter-state telemedicine to the federal government, are optimal for several reasons.

1. Federal Regulation Lowers Transaction Costs and
Advances Public Policy Goals

The imposition of national standards and regulations in interstate telemedicine would reduce or remove the transaction costs that currently dissuade telemedicine providers from operating across state borders. For example, a national system may eliminate the administrative difficulties and costs of obtaining licenses in each state's jurisdiction and allow for "a greater degree of flexibility in the health professional's practice with the confidence that his compliance with basic quality standards was assured."[51] Additionally, federal licensure standards promise greater access to health care by enabling health professionals to treat underserved populations, such as rural residents, without requiring these professionals to live in the areas that they serve.[52] Uniformity in other areas, such as medical malpractice coverage, further advance public policy goals of greater access, quality care, and reduced costs. Presently, differing state insurance requirements influence where health professionals choose to practice, as evidence suggests that health care providers avoid jurisdictions with higher malpractice damage

---

The Constitutionality of Current Legal Barriers to Telemedicine in the United States: Analysis and Future Directions of Its Relationship to National and International Health Care Reform, 21 HEALTH MATRIX 385 (2011).

[47] *See* Gibbons v. Odgen, 22 U.S. (9 Wheat.) 1, 195–96 (1824) ("But, in regulating commerce with foreign nations, the power of Congress does not stop at the jurisdictional lines of the several States...The power of Congress, then, whatever it may be, must be exercised within the territorial jurisdiction of the several States"). For analysis on the constitutional basis for federal authority over health care regulation, see Gupta & Sao, *supra* note 46.

[48] *See* United States v. Butler, 297 U.S. 1, 66 (1936).

[49] *Gibbons*, 22 U.S. at 19–196 (J. Marshall) ("But, in regulating commerce with foreign nations, the power of Congress does not stop at the jurisdictional lines of the several states...The power of Congress, then, whatever it may be, must be exercised within the territorial jurisdiction of the several states").

[50] United States v. Butler, 297 U.S. 1, 66 (1936).

[51] *See* Alison M. Sulentic, *Crossing Borders: The Licensure of Interstate: Telemedicine Practitioners*, 25 J. LEGIS. 1, 36 (1999).

[52] *Id.*

awards and unfavorable laws, such as the absence of caps in damages and malpractice premium rates.[53]

2. Foundations for Federal Regulation Are Currently in Place for Interstate Telemedicine

Several aspects of the health care industry are already subject to national standards and procedures. For example, educational and specialization requirements have come to follow a national standard, and existing federal licensing models are in place in limited circumstances.[54] Another related example is accreditation requirements, as Medicare and Medicaid already impose operational standards on health care entities in exchange for funding.[55] The precedents of health-related standards on a national level underscores the feasibility of implementing uniform standards and requirements for interstate telemedicine on a national scale.

3. Operational National and Regional Health Care Delivery Models Are Already in Place

The United States should look to notable examples, such as Malaysia and the European Union, for guidance in the move toward the the establishment of uniform regulations and standards for telemedicine. With its Telemedicine Act of 1997, Malaysia became a forerunner in enacting laws that regulate telemedicine providers licensed within the nation and abroad.[56] On a regional level, the European Union has broken down geographic barriers with regards to ensuring access to quality medical treatment. The EU's "Doctor's Directive 93/16" permits a physician to practice in all Member States provided that he or she obtains a diploma from one Member State that meets the Directive's minimum training requirements.[57] Although the European Union does not directly address telemedicine, the implementation of such a measure supports the proposition that the development of a cross-jurisdictional approach to the delivery of health care is a more feasible and desirable alternative than geography-based initiatives.

---

[53] Lars Noah, *Ambivalent Commitments to Federalism in Controlling the Practice of Medicine*, 53 U. KAN. L. REV. 149, 186 (2004); *see* U.S. CONGRESS, GEN. ACCOUNTING OFFICE, MEDICAL MALPRACTICE INSURANCE: MULTIPLE FACTORS HAVE CONTRIBUTED TO INCREASED PREMIUM RATES, NO. GAO-03-702 (2003).

[54] *See* Volkert, *supra* note 4, at 177–78.

[55] *See* 42 U.S.C. § 1395x(e) (2006) (defining "hospital" within the context of Medicare regulations); 42 U.S.C. § 1395x(m) (2006) (defining "home health services" within the context of Medicare regulations); 42 C.F.R. §§ 484.1-.55 (2001) (regulating various types of providers).

[56] Hsing-Hao Wu, *Evolving Medical Service in the Information Age: A Legal Analysis of Applying Telemedicine Programs in Taiwan*, 27 MED. & L. 775, 784 (2008) (Malaysia's telemedicine law "specifically addresses legal issues concerning telemedicine, such as licensure, informed consent and telemedicine standard development."); *see* Telemedicine Act, Act 564 cl. 4(1) (1997) (Malay).

[57] Council Directive 93/16/EEC, of the Council of the European Communities of April 5, 1993 to Facilitate the Free Movement of Doctors and the Mutual Recognition of Their Diplomas, Certificates and Other Evidence of Formal Qualifications 93/16/EEC, 1993 O.J. (L 165) 1, 1–24.

B. PROPOSALS FOR FORUMS OF REDRESS FOR INTERSTATE TELEMEDICINE DISPUTES

In anticipation of the legal uncertainties sure to arise from cross-border telemedicine disputes, two promising forums for redress merit further consideration.

1. Adjudication in Federal Courts

Congressional imposition of federal jurisdiction and federal laws governing telemedicine disputes may help to resolve jurisdiction and choice-of-law concerns as to which state law applies when parties are from different states and to determine whether substantive federal laws should be enacted. In light of the legal principles that presently guide the U.S. judicial system, such a proposition may be considered unworkable at this time and in the short-term future.[58] Although the Supreme Court has affirmed that states govern medical malpractice law,[59] the Court's jurisprudence has upheld concurrent or preemptive federal involvement in interstate activities implicating traditionally local concerns.[60] Promisingly, members of Congress have long signaled their intent to federalize aspects of medical malpractice litigation; indeed, proposals for federal involvement have been continuously discussed since the late 1960s.[61] Although these proposals have failed to be enacted into law,[62] past instances of congressional consensus for intervention in areas of traditional local concern offer encouragement that federal legislators will eventually move more assertively into federal health care regulation. This has already happened in small part, for example, with the enactment of the federal Mammography Quality Standards Act in 1992, which requires Federal Drug Administration certification for all mammography facilities.[63]

---

[58] The *Erie* Doctrine mandates that citizens from different states may bring a claim in federal court, but such a claim is governed by state law unless it is based upon a federal question to be decided by federal law. Erie R.R. Co. v. Tompkins, 304 U.S. 64, 78 (1938). One may bring a telemedicine dispute in a state court, but such claims may be removed by the defendant to federal court, under the federal court's diversity jurisdiction. *See* 28 U.S.C. § 1332(a) (2006). Regardless of forum, state law would apply in federal court diversity actions as Congress has yet to enact any telemedicine statutes seeking to modify state jurisdiction or liability rules. *See* 28 U.S.C. § 1652 (2006) ("The laws of the several states, except where the Constitution or treaties of the United States or Acts of Congress otherwise require or provide, shall be regarded as rules of decision in civil actions in the courts of the United States, in cases where they apply.")

[59] *Erie*, 304 U.S. at 78.

[60] Instances include upholding the following federal measures: the Labor Standards Act of 1938, which bans the shipment of interstate commerce of goods made by employees paid less than minimum wage (United States v. Darby, 312 U.S. 100, 125–26 (1941)); imposition of penalties on the interstate transportation of lottery tickets (Champion v. Ames (*The Lottery Case*), 188 U.S. 321, 362–64 (1903)); banning interstate transportation of women for immoral purposes (Hoke v. United States, 227 U.S. 308, 323 (1913)); and banning the mailing of obscene matter (Roth v. United States, 354 U.S. 476, 492–93 (1957)).

[61] *See* Abigail R. Moncrieff, *Federalization Snowballs: The Need for National Action in Medical Malpractice Reform*, 109 COLUM. L. REV. 844, 857 (2009).

[62] *Id.*

[63] 42 U.S.C.A. § 263(b) (West 2010); Mammography Quality Standards Act of 1992, Pub. L. No. 102–539.

In the short-term, it may be realistic to envision limited federal procedural involvement that would require interstate telemedicine disputes be removed to federal court. Although litigants still face several of the legal challenges discussed earlier—such as choice-of-law determinations—having federal courts hear telemedicine cases would help to reduce legal liability uncertainty and costs by restricting parties' opportunities to forum shop in order to gain advantage in litigation. In the long-term, should complete federal authority over interstate telemedicine disputes be realized, the costs of uncertainty and conflicts as to where jurisdiction lies and the treatment of similar issues in different states will be reduced.

2. Arbitration of Interstate Telemedicine Disputes

As the following analysis will demonstrate, arbitration is a private means of redress that is more flexible and predictable than litigation in the courts. As a form of alternative dispute resolution (ADR) that has been successfully utilized on national and international levels,[64] arbitration is more efficient as well as more adaptive to changes in the field of telemedicine than litigation and has binding force that is enforceable in court.[65] Arbitration is a streamlined adjudication process overseen by an arbitrator, a judge-like neutral third party who ensures compliance with procedural rules and renders enforceable judgments.[66] Arbitration is a viable approach for the following reasons, which are analyzed below: jurisdictional and choice-of-law concerns are bypassed as parties to the dispute contractually agree to a set of procedural and substantive rules to govern the process and to choose an arbitrator;[67] the existence of a comprehensive arbitration framework in place in the United States and abroad provides a solid foundation for widespread acceptance of arbitration of cross-border telemedicine disputes; and precedent of practicible approaches toward implementation of an arbitration model for cross-border telemedicine disputes is established. Arbitration is a viable approach for several additional reasons that we lay out below.

a. Arbitration Resolves Legal Ambiguities and Uncertainties of Interstate Telemedicine Claims

In addition to settling jurisdiction and choice-of-law concerns, arbitration resolves the dilemma of whether substantive law provides for appropriate theories of liability for injuries and damages arising from cross-border delivery of telemedical services. This is achieved by parties' selection of qualified decision makers for evaluating complex,

---

[64] Martha Neil, *International Arbitration Has Become a Lucrative Field after a Decade of Disfavor*, A.B.A. J. 28 (Sept. 2002); Katherine Benesch, *The Increasing Use of Arbitration and Mediation in Adjudicating Healthcare Cases*, N.J. LAW. 28, 28 (2007).

[65] *See* Keith Maurer, *Implementing Effective Health Care ADR Mediation, Arbitration, and "I'm Sorry" Programs*, 47 VOICE OF THE DEFENSE BAR 37, 6 (2009).

[66] *Id.* at 5.

[67] William S. Fiske, *Should Small and Medium-Size American Businesses "Going Global" Use International Commercial Arbitration?*, 18 TRANSNAT'L LAW. 455, 458–59 (2005).

specialized cases such as medical malpractice claims.[68] Parties in medical malpractice cases typically select arbitrators from a list of qualified candidates.[69] Arbitrators are more appropriate decision makers than juries because parties to the dispute most often select arbitrators who have expertise in the subject matter of the claim.[70] In the ever-changing field of telemedicine, it is crucial to have decision makers who are able to apply existing substantive legal principles to new conflicts that arise from continuous transformations to telemedical services.[71]

The participation of parties in the selection of decision makers in an arbitration system also contributes to a sense of confidence and fairness in the process.[72] The process of choosing an arbitrator customarily requires each party to select its own arbitrator, and then the selected arbitrators together decide upon a third arbitrator who serves as the only judge.[73] Although this approach is not the sole, or necessarily the best method, the interests of all parties are represented at all stages, thereby diminishing suspicions of bias in the selection process.

Additionally, arbitration eliminates most of the uncertainty surrounding enforceability of judgments against foreign defendants.[74] Arbitration agreements and decisions are binding on the parties, all jurisdictions are empowered by legislation enabling courts to enforce arbitration awards,[75] and all countries that are signatories to various regional and international treaties recognize other members' arbitration awards.[76] Alternatively, if a country is a non-signatory to the relevant treaties, arbitration agreements and awards may still be enforced in some instances under customary law through Friendship Commerce and Navigation Treaties[77] (FCN treaties) or general principles of comity.[78] Both applications of customary law encourage enforcement of arbitration agreements and awards, as FCN treaties were designed to foster private international investment[79] and the principle of comity may appeal to a national

---

[68] Kenneth A. DeVille, *The Jury Is Out:Pre-Dispute Binding Arbitration Agreements for Medical Malpractice Claims*, 28 J. LEGAL MED. 333, 369 (2007).

[69] *Id.* at 338.

[70] *Id.* at 341; Ljiljana Biukovic, *International Commercial Arbitration in Cyberspace: Recent Developments*, 22 NW. J. INT'L L. & BUS. 319, 344 (2002).

[71] *See* McLean, *supra* note 35, at 252.

[72] Thomas J. Stipanowich, *Contract and Conflict Management*, 2001 WIS. L. REV. 831, 871 (2001).

[73] S. Spencer Elg, *Health Care Arbitration Agreements in Tennessee*, 45 TENN. B.J. 15, 16 (2009).

[74] JOSEPH LOOKOFSKY, UNDERSTANDING THE CISG 10 (3d ed. 2008).

[75] Elg, *supra* note 73, at 16.

[76] Karim Benyekhlef & Fabien Gélinas, *Online Dispute Resolution*, 10 LEX ELECTRONICA 1, 51 (2005), *available at* http://www.lex-electronica.org/articles/v10-2/Benyekhlef_Gelinas.pdf.

[77] *See* Treaty of Friendship, Commerce and Navigation, U.S.-S. Kor., Nov. 28, 1956, 8 U.S.T. 2217, T.I.A.S. No. 2947; Treaty of Friendship, Commerce and Navigation, U.S.-W. Ger., Oct. 29, 1954, 7 U.S.T. 1839, T.I.A.S. No. 3593; Treaty of Friendship, Commerce and Navigation, U.S.-Japan, Apr. 2, 1953, 4 U.S.T. 2063, T.I.A.S. No. 2863; Treaty of Friendship, Commerce and Navigation, U.S.- Greece, Aug. 3, 1951, 8 U.S.T. 1829, T.I.A.S. No. 3057 [hereinafter FCN treaties].

[78] 8 AM. JUR. *Trials* § 236 (1965).

[79] Gerald D. Silver, *Friendship, Commerce and Navigation Treaties and United States Discrimination Law: The Right of Branches of Foreign Companies to Hire Executives "Of Their Choice,"* 57 FORDHAM L.REV. 765, 765 (1989).

court's sense of international duty and regard for the rights of persons under another nation's laws.[80]

b. A Comprehensive Arbitration Framework Is in Place in the United States

The existence of a comprehensive arbitration framework in the United States also makes this forum a feasible mechanism for redress. Arbitration commands legislative federal and state support and is the favored choice among private actors in the health services industry. Federal and state judicial systems encourage the resolution of health care cases by ADR, as courts direct cases to these forums with parties' consent.[81] Additionally, when parties enter into a written contract with an arbitration clause and one party seeks litigation, most federal courts return the case to arbitration.[82] When the arbitration clause is upheld and an arbitration organization is identified in the contract, that organization's rules and procedures will govern the claim.[83] A variety of arbitration organizations with a national reach have authority to preside over these cases.[84] Furthermore, some state legislatures have enacted laws requiring medical malpractice claims to be arbitrated or requiring that arbitration panels include physicians.[85] The Maryland Health Care Malpractice Act, for example, requires court-ordered mediation or mandatory arbitration.[86]

Just as important, arbitration has been applied in business-to-consumer disputes among participants in the health care industry.[87] A notable example is Kaiser Permanente (Kaiser), a nonprofit health management organization, which has mandated arbitration among its members since 1971.[88] In 2009, 91 percent of these cases were medical malpractice disputes.[89] In the same year, a report on Kaiser's arbitration system revealed that a majority of participants preferred the process over resolution by the courts[90] and that arbitration resolved the dispute in an average of twelve

---

[80] 8 Am. Jur. *Trials*, *supra* note 78, at § 236.

[81] Benesch, *supra* note 64, at 29. These referred cases must be governed by rules of the jurisdiction in which they were filed. *Id.*

[82] *Id.*

[83] DeVille, *supra* note 68, at 338.

[84] *Id.*

[85] Christopher J. Marchand, *Arbitration and Long-Term Health Care*, 38 Md. B.J. 32, 34 (2005).

[86] *Id.* at 34.

[87] *See, e.g.,* Law Offices of Sharon Lybeck Hartmann, First Annual Report of the Office of the Independent Administrator of the Kaiser Foundation Health Plan, Inc. Mandatory Arbitration System for Disputes with Health Plan Members FN 1, 14 (2000), *available at* http://www.oia-kaiserarb.com/oia/Forms%20&%20Reports/annrptyr1.pdf.

[88] In 1997, Kaiser handed administrative control of its arbitration process to an independent body in response to a California Supreme Court decision that cited Kaiser's self-administration approach as the source of undue delay in resolving claims. *Id.* at 23.

[89] Law Offices of Sharon Lybeck Hartmann, Eleventh Annual Report of the Office of the Independent Administrator of the Kaiser Foundation Health Plan, Inc. Mandatory Arbitration System for Disputes with Health Plan Members 4 (2009), *available at* http://www.oia-kaiserarb.com/oia/2009%20report.htm.

[90] *Id.* at 3.

months[91] in comparison to the four- to five-year average for payouts from litigation.[92] Additionally, arbitration is standard practice in business-to-consumer disputes related to long-term care[93] and business-to-business disputes in the health care industry.[94] The experience that so many industry participants have with ADR supports the feasibility of transferring business-to-consumer medical malpractice claims to these forums.

c. Proposal of a Workable Arbitration Model for Interstate Telemedicine Disputes

An arbitration model could be tailored with some complementary steps to minimize legal ambiguity and allocate risk between businesses and consumers to the fullest extent practicable. A no-fault compensation scheme, with its proven capacity to eliminate many contestable issues of liability and adequate relief, is one potential complementary mechanism.[95] The combination of no-fault and arbitration models has been successfully implemented on national levels.[96] Building upon such existing models, we advocate a two-step claim evaluation process that first utilizes a no-fault compensation scheme and secondarily mandates arbitration when a dispute arises concerning any aspect of a decision regarding award compensation.

I. CONSIDERATIONS FOR THE ESTABLISHMENT OF A NO-FAULT SCHEME

Successful implementation of a no-fault scheme requires consideration of the following issues. Businesses should conduct due diligence in avoiding any public policy defenses of unconscionability and failure to provide informed consent. The most common challenge raised against the legitimacy of arbitration agreements involving businesses and consumers is unconscionability, which requires that a party knowingly enter into a contract and understand its terms in order to be bound to that contract.[97] First, patients must give informed consent in order to be bound to no-fault and arbitration dispute resolution mechanisms.[98] This means that agreements should be drafted in such a way that makes it clear that arbitration is voluntarily entered into

---

[91] *Id.*

[92] Cortez, *supra* note 38, at 27.

[93] Benesch, *supra* note 64, at 31.

[94] *Id.* at 28.

[95] For analysis on no-fault compensation, see Siegal, *supra* note 22; *see generally*, Thomas Douglas, *Medical Injury Compensation: Beyond "No Fault,"* 17 MED. L. REV. 30 (2009); Jeremy Coylewright, *No Fault, No Worries…Combining a No-Fault Medical Malpractice Act with a National Single-Payer Health Insurance Plan,* 4 IND. HEALTH L. REV. 31 (2007); Henry Huang & Farzad Soleimani, *What Happened to No-Fault? The Role of Error Reporting in Healthcare Reform,* 10 HOUS. J. HEALTH L. & POL'Y 1 (2009); Duncan MacCourt & Joseph Bernstein, *Medical Error Reduction and Tort Reform through Private, Contractually-Based Quality Medicine Societies,* 35 AM. J.L. & MED. 505 (2009); Peter H. Schuck, *Tort Reform, Kiwi-Style,* 27 YALE L. & POL'Y REV. 187 (2008); David M. Studdert et al, *Can The United States Afford a "No-Fault" System of Compensation for Medical Injury?,* 60 LAW & CONTEMP. PROBS. 1 (Spring 1997).

[96] *See* Huang & Soleimani, *supra* note 95, at 11–15.

[97] Meredith R. Miller, *Contracting Out of Process, Contracting Out of Corporate Accountability: An Argument against Enforcement of Pre-Dispute Limits on Process,* 75 TENN. L. REV. 365, 376 (2008).

[98] *See* Huang & Soleimani, *supra* note 95, at 26.

through the informed consent of the consumer, and is not a condition to receiving treatment.[99] Second, a designated body is required to implement and oversee the processing and evaluation of cross-border malpractice claims. Although some countries, such as New Zealand and Sweden, appoint a government agency,[100] the political climate and plethora of private vendors in the health care industry make it more practicable and politically feasible for insurers to take on these duties in the United States. This arrangement offers a fair and efficient allocation of legal liability and redress, as insurers are increasingly exposing consumers to potential disputes by providing coverage for health services performed by foreign health care providers[101] and cross-border health coverage.[102] Third, the determinations of compensation eligibility and appropriate recovery amounts must be considered in order to minimize any contestable issues of coverage.[103] Finally, businesses must also address an allowance for arbitration or litigation of certain actions that otherwise would be inadequately compensated by a no-fault scheme.[104] In order to not only minimize legal liability exposure and costs to businesses and consumers, but also to advance mechanisms that deter substandard care, a cross-border no-fault model should include public policy–based exclusions in order for it to have lasting success.[105]

II. APPEALING ADVERSE DECISIONS AND ADJUDICATING EXCEPTIONS: THE ARBITRATION PROCESS

In instances where the no-fault approach fails to satisfactorily resolve a claim or the issues in question qualify under a no-fault exception, these contested issues should be handled through binding arbitration. An arbitration process tailored specifically for these types of claims should account for the following considerations. First, the involvement of parties from different states or countries requires that choice-of-law considerations be resolved. To minimize any appearance of bias, a third state or country approach is recommended whereby selection of substantive law is based upon a state's or country's well-developed jurisprudence and prominent status in medical malpractice law, not on a party's domicile. For instance, in cases involving a foreign telemedicine provider, Australia would be an appropriate candidate, as several countries defer to Australian case law for guidance in interpreting legal principles.[106]

Second, a key consideration is the choice of forum for the arbitration process. This issue is significant because it implicates cost considerations, which are dispositive in

---

[99] Marchand, *supra* note 85, at 36.

[100] Schuck, *supra* note 95, at 190. Huang & Soleimani, *supra* note 95, at 15.

[101] Thomas R. McLean, *Shaping A New Direction for Law and Medicine: An International Debate on Culture, Disaster, Biotechnology and Public Health*, 10 DePaul J. Health Care L. 131, 163 (2007).

[102] Cortez, *supra* note 34, at 100.

[103] David M. Studdert & Troyen A. Brennan, *Toward a Workable Model of "No-Fault" Compensation for Medical Injury in the United States*, 27 Am. J.L. & Med. 225, 231 (2001).

[104] *See* Huang & Soleimani, *supra* note 95, at 26.

[105] *Id.*

[106] Kumaralingam Amirthalingam, *Judging Doctors and Diagnosing the Law: Bolam Rules in Singapore and Malaysia*, Singapore J. Legal Stud. 125, 135 (2003).

parties' ability to seek legal redress and successfully resolve disputes. The fact that courts in some jurisdictions may invalidate arbitration agreements in consumer disputes when the process incurs unreasonable fees underscores the importance of cost considerations.[107] It is worth considering online arbitration as a viable alternative, as this forum can "increase access to justice and ensure greater legal certainty on the Internet by reducing the cost and time required to settle disputes."[108] One of the biggest arguments against arbitrating cross-border medical malpractice disputes online is that such disputes are simply too complex.[109] Concern over complexity may lose its force, however, in the face of technological advances in communications and the increasing use of online mechanisms by arbitral institutions. Examples of innovation include software applications enabling users to perform all procedural steps in arbitration;[110] permanent online technical support;[111] networks in place of neutral and expert third parties;[112] and the availability of Web cameras to facilitate human interaction when required.[113] These online procedural mechanisms and the availability of forums to administer and oversee such mechanisms demonstrates the feasibility of using online arbitration for cross-border health services claims, regardless of the level of their complexity.

Additionally, the process of selecting an arbitrator warrants consideration. Medical malpractice arbitration panels traditionally have three arbitrators comprised of the following: an attorney, a physician or hospital administrator, and a layperson.[114] Although it is understandable that such a mixed panel is preferable to account for any bias and to ensure a well-informed and thorough evaluation of the claim, parties should also be open to other arrangements. To minimize the appearance of bias, adoption of a third state or country approach similar to that discussed above for choice-of-law selection may be a viable option. Alternatively, in the context of online arbitration, a software program may choose an arbitrator randomly from a list of qualified candidates or based on open criteria.[115]

Finally, consideration of additional mechanisms may facilitate deterrence of substandard care. A major critique of the arbitration process is that its decisions are

---

[107] *See* Green Tree Fin. Corp. v. Larketta, 531 U.S. 79, 92 (2000) (party seeking to invalidate contract must show likelihood of incurring prohibitive costs, and "mere risk" of incurring prohibitive costs not sufficient ground for invalidating arbitration clause); Brower v. Gateway 2000, Inc., 676 N.Y.S.2d 569 (1st Dept. 1998).

[108] Benyekhlef & Gélinas, *supra* note 76, at 9.

[109] *Cf.* Nicolas de Witt, *Online International Arbitration: Nine Issues Crucial to Its Success*, 12 AM. REV. INT'L ARB. 441, 455 (2001) (online arbitration's "objectives are to cut down the registration fee by virtue of its standardized and computerized process, and to reduce the arbitrator's fee, considering the lack of complexity of most of the cases that should be presented").

[110] Benyekhlef & Gélinas, *supra* note 76, at 5.

[111] *Id.*

[112] *Id.*

[113] Jason Krause, *Settling It on the Web: New Technology, Lower Costs Enable growth of Online Dispute Resolution*, A.B.A. J. (Oct. 1, 2007, 12:12 PM), http://www.abajournal.com/magazine/article/settling_it_on_the_web/.

[114] Nancy M. Simone, *Medical Malpractice Litigation: A Comparative Analysis of the United States and Great Britain*, 12 SUFFOLK TRANSNAT'L L. REV. 577, 597 (1989).

[115] de Witt, *supra* note 109, at 480.

confidential, thereby removing any stigma associated with fault and reducing incentives to prevent mistakes.[116] Publication of arbitration decisions could easily eliminate the protection such confidentiality affords. For instance, the Swedish government recently began annually publishing all arbitration decisions related to medical malpractice in order to encourage public awareness and scrutiny.[117] To make these decisions even more accessible to the public, publication should also be online.[118] Increased consumer awareness of those health care providers with a record of adverse decisions will impact consumer choice and willingness to pay a certain amount based on a health care provider's reputation; consequently, it should go far in helping to prevent substandard care.

IV. The Potential for a Global Telemedicine Regime

Proposals for a national telemedicine framework in the United States can provide workable models for an international telemedicine regime. Currently, no international telemedicine framework is in place. Although existing multilateral trade agreements pertaining to cross-border services may evolve to include provisions liberalizing trade in health services,[119] these agreements are ill-equipped to deal with unique health-related barriers. For instance, the enforcement of the General Agreement on Trade and Services (GATS) under the World Trade Organization's (WTO) dispute settlement mechanism is unavailable to private parties involved in medical malpractice disputes. The WTO restricts standing to member governments for a GATS-based violation, and private parties are afforded no legal protection unless they can garner enough political support for a government to bring a claim on their behalf.[120] Even when a private party *does* persuade a government to represent him or her or a group of individuals or enterprises on a claim, the claim may only be made against another government, and the only relief available is a prospective remedy of correction of the GATS violation.[121] With respect to regulatory challenges, the WTO offers no recognized authoritative platform by which uniform standards or regulations may be promulgated to member states related to the delivery of health care. Additionally, dissenting WTO

---

[116] Mijha Butcher, *Using Mediation to Remedy Civil Rights Violations When the Defendant Is Not an Intentional Perpetrator: The Problems of Unconscious Disparate Treatment and Unjustified Disparate Impacts*, 24 HAMLINE J. PUB. L. & POL'Y 225, 266–67 (2003).

[117] Patricia M. Danzon, *The Swedish Patient Compensation System*, 15 J. LEGAL MED. 199, 216 (1994).

[118] As an example, India provides the option of adjudicating a medical malpractice claim involving businesses and consumers in a government agency hearing, known as the Consumer Forum. Decisions of this forum are published online for public viewing. *See* CONSUMER LAW INDIA: CONSUMER LAW ISSUES & FORUM, http://consumerlaw.in/category/consumer-cases/ (last visited Nov. 11, 2010).

[119] *E.g.*, McLean, *supra* note 22, at 501.

[120] *See* Josè E. Alvarez, *The New Dispute Settlers: (Half) Truths and Consequences*, 38 TEX. INT'L L.J. 405, 415 (2003).

[121] *See* Understanding on Rules and Procedures Governing the Settlement of Disputes, Apr. 15, 1994, Marrakesh Agreement Establishing the World Trade Organization, Annex 2, 1869 U.N.T.S. 401, *available at* http://www.wto.org/english/docs_E/legal_E/28-dsu.pdf.

members may invoke the GATS exception clause allowing noncompliance for public health protection under Article XX(b).[122] The difficulties involved in bringing telemedicine within the scope of the GATS suggests the need for prompt consideration of other feasible alternatives.

A. PROPOSALS FOR INTERNATIONAL REGULATORY REFORM

The establishment or allocation of an entity or mechanism with established expertise in the health field may help the promulgation of supranational regulatory frameworks and standards.[123] The World Health Organization (WHO) is a possibility, as it has the global expertise, reputation, and resources to act as an authoritative body with similar responsibilities as the U.S. federal government has in the health care field.[124] Notably, the WHO is comprised of 193 member nations,[125] representing one of the largest memberships of an international body or treaty.[126] Because the WHO embraces and incorporates more countries than many other organizations, there may be greater acceptance by the international community for WHO-initiated measures in the health care arena. The WHO might establish and ensure compliance with regulations and standards pertaining to the international practice of telemedicine.[127] For example, the WHO has recent experience in this capacity in promulgating the International Health Regulations (IHR), an international legal instrument that is binding on all WHO member states. Thus, in the interests of advancing the policy goals of greater quality and access to health care, nations may be increasingly willing to defer authority in various aspects of transnational health care services to global institutions such as the WHO.

B. PROPOSALS FOR INTERNATIONAL FORUMS FOR REDRESS

Because arbitration requires the participation of private parties in any setting, the arbitration model proposed earlier for the United States may also be implemented at the international level. Just as in the United States, a comprehensive international arbitration framework is in place with similar foundations—national and subnational

---

[122] *See* Nicolas F. Diebold, *The Morals and Order Exceptions in WTO Law: Balancing the Toothless Tiger and the Undermining Mole*, 11 J. INT'L ECON. L. 43, 43–44 (2008).

[123] *See generally* Amar Gupta & Deth Sao, *Harmonization of International Legal Structure for Fostering Professional Services: Lessons from Early U.S. Federal-State Relations*, 18 CARDOZO J. INT'L & COMP. L. 239 (2010).

[124] *See* John D. Blum, *The Role of Law in Global E-Health: A Tool for Development and Equity in a Digitally Divided World*, 46 ST. LOUIS U. L.J. 85, 89–91 (2002).

[125] *Governance of WHO*, WORLD HEALTH ORGANIZATION, http://www.who.int/about/governance/en/index.html (last visited Oct. 2, 2010).

[126] In comparison, there are 140 signatory countries to the GATS. *The General Agreement on Trade in Services (GATS): Objectives, Coverage and Disciplines*, THE WORLD TRADE ORGANIZATION, http://www.wto.org/english/tratop_E/serv_E/gatsqa_E.htm#2 (last visited Jan. 13, 2011).

[127] P. Greg Gulick, Note, *The Development of a Global Hospital Is Closer Than We Think: An Examination of the International Implications of Telemedicine and the Developments, Uses and Problems Facing International Telemedicine Programs*, 11 IND. INT'L & COMP. L. REV. 183, 212 (2000).

legislation enabling courts to enforce arbitration awards,[128] and the ratification of international and regional commercial arbitration agreements by many countries, recognizing and enforcing foreign arbitration agreements and awards of member states and International Commercial Arbitration Organizations.[129] For instance, the 1958 United Nations Convention on Recognition and Enforcement of Foreign Arbitral Awards (New York Convention) is one of the most prominent and effective international commercial agreements, with more than 135 member countries.[130] Similar to the comprehensive arbitration framework already in place in the United States, these preexisting agreements and networks establish a foundation upon which an arbitration framework for international telemedicine disputes may be built.

Conclusion

Telemedicine offers the potential to improve existing health care systems on national and international levels. At the same time that telemedicine provides a feasible and ready solution to health care crises in nations such as the United States, it motivates reconsideration and realignment of the degree of sovereignty that local, county, state, and national governments have traditionally held or have assumed over the years. The interstate nature of telemedicine involves opportunities and challenges, as the ability to deliver health care across distances not only achieves public policy goals of greater quality and access to health care, but also creates legal and regulatory conflicts within and among nations. The experience of the United States shows that such challenges, if resolved appropriately, could be regarded as a positive rather than a negative consequence of the development of telemedicine.

As we look at the dilemma of health care, with its mounting costs and current poor quality of delivery, we must hasten our advocacy for more revolutionary changes. The dilemma confronting us now is similar to the Year 2000 Problem (otherwise known as Y2K or the Millenium bug), which forced the financial industry and other companies to embrace nontraditional solutions in order to prevent computer failures when clocks rolled over into 2000.[131] These nontradtional solutions included outsourcing work abroad or sponsoring foreign programmers to come to the United States.[132] Until 1999, such practices were frowned upon for reasons ranging from violation of corporate policies to breach of customer data privacy.[133] The firm deadline of December 31, 1999, forced the companies to become more flexible in adopting nontraditional and

---

[128] Elg, *supra* note 73, at 16.

[129] de Witt, *supra* note 109, at 458–59.

[130] David Buoncristiani, *Enforcement of International Arbitration Awards in the United States*, 27 CONSTRUCTION LAW. 14, 14 (2007).

[131] Amar Gupta et al., *Outsourcing in the Healthcare Industry: Information Technology, Intellectual Property, and Allied Aspects*, 21 INFO. RESOURCES MGMT. J. 1, 7–8 (2008).

[132] *Id.*

[133] *Id.*

more cost-effective solutions in order to address new challenges within the limited time frame available.[134]

Similarly, in the area of check processing in the U.S. banking industry, technologies were available for electronic transmission and processing in the 1990s, but the industry was unwilling to embrace them on a broad scale.[135] The incidents of September 11, 2001, halted air and ground transportation, making it very difficult to quickly send paper checks from one part of the country to another.[136] Resulting disruptions to the national economy spurred rapid adoption of electronic transmission and processing of checks, which led to greater efficiencies and cost reductions in the check collection process.[137] As we face a similar dilemma in health care marked by escalating costs and growing discontent, but with no "very hard deadline" to force cohesive action,[138] our policy makers will be compelled to look at nontraditional options that involve rethinking the relationships between state and national governments on various facets of health care. Although there is widespread agreement that changes are needed in the health care industry, various constituencies in that industry want their respective parts to remain unchanged. This, in turn, makes it very difficult to introduce new business processes that could benefit both the patients and the organizations that pay for such costs. Just as the advent of interstate trade led to widespread economic growth across U.S. states,[139] the elimination of state barriers to health care offers the potential for significant innovation, improvement in quality of health care, and reduction of costs. It remains to be seen if such a change will happen without a major crisis on the level of Y2K or September 11.

---

[134]   *Id.*

[135]   Jefferey Barry, *The Check Clearing for the 21st Century Act ("Check 21")*, 24 ANN. REV. BANKING & FIN. L. 130, 132 (2005).

[136]   *Id.* at 131–32.

[137]   *Id.* at 131; Darrell Payne, *A Report Card on Check 21*, 13 ANDREWS' BANK & LENDER LIAB. LITIG. REP. 2, 2 (2007).

[138]   *See* Gupta et al., *supra* note 131, at 7.

[139]   *See generally* Gupta & Sao, *supra* note 123.

V

Health Care Globalization, Equity, and Justice

21

GLOBAL HEALTH GOVERNANCE AS SHARED HEALTH

GOVERNANCE*

Jennifer Prah Ruger[†]

Introduction

This chapter presents shared health governance (SHG) as an alternative theory of global health governance (GHG), one based on a moral conception of global health justice called "provincial globalism." It contrasts SHG with the existing model and identifies opportunities for GHG reform. Although discussed extensively elsewhere and only briefly here, provincial globalism asserts a general duty to reduce shortfall inequalities in, and address threats to, central health capabilities (premature mortality and escapable morbidity), and stipulates shared global and domestic responsibilities.[1] Responsibility allocations rest on the specific duties and effectiveness of different actors. This framework respects self-determination by groups and individuals and seeks voluntary commitments. SHG embodies the moral

---

* Adapted from Jennifer P. Ruger, *Global Health Governance as Shared Health Governance*, 66 J. Epidemiology & Community Health. 653-61 (2012).

† Yale University School of Public Health, 60 College Street, P.O. Box 208034, New Haven, CT 06520 USA. E-mail: jennifer.ruger@yale.edu, Phone: 203-785-3710, Fax: 203-785-6297. I would like to thank the participants in the Values and Moral Experiences in Global Health conference in 2007 at Harvard University and in the Medical Anthropology at the Intersections conference in 2009 at Yale University for comments on earlier versions of this chapter. Parts of this chapter have been presented at the PAHO/WHO Equity and Health conference in 2010 and the Globalization of Health Care conference at Harvard Law School in 2011. I would also like to thank Christina Lazar, Nora Ng, and Betsy Rogers for research and editing assistance and Sarah Pallas for comments. This research was supported, in part, by the Open Society Institute of the Soros Foundation and the Whitney and Betty MacMillan Center for International and Area Studies. Dr. Ruger is supported in part by an Investigator Award from the Patrick and Catherine Weldon Donaghue Medical Research Foundation (grant DF06–112) and a Guggenheim Fellowship.

1 Jennifer P. Ruger, *Global Health Justice*, 2 Pub. Health Ethics 261 (2009).

principles of this global health justice theory. It rests on internalizing the public moral norms it promotes as shared authoritative standards. The moral conception of global health justice set out in provincial globalism builds on and expands globally the "health capability paradigm" developed for the domestic realm in *Health and Social Justice*.[2] This theory is grounded in a particular view of the good life, "human flourishing," valuing health intrinsically and giving special moral importance to "health capability," a person's ability to be healthy.

Global health has experienced a record entry of private and public actors with unprecedented funding levels. This hyper-pluralism and fragmentation have received popular and academic attention, characterizing them as anarchic and requiring coordination and control. Figures 21.1A, 1B[3] illustrate the congested, chaotic, and complex nature of the activities of various global health actors.

Public and private actors each pursue their own goals and preferences and not necessarily those of their "beneficiaries." Overlapping interests among donors can cause confusion and paralysis that dissipate or delay aid.[4] Conflicts in donor priorities and requirements create competition and duplication of activities that overwhelm recipient countries' institutional capacities. By creating parallel facilities, systems, and procedures, donors distort the design, implementation, and sustainability of health programs.[5] So far, attempts to coordinate proliferating global health actors have fallen short.

No dominant overarching theory has emerged to elucidate current GHG or to provide principles upon which a new approach might develop. Rather, older international relations frameworks (realism and institutionalism), which continue to recycle various perspectives (sovereign states' self-interest and international human rights law), have shaped international health relations over time.[6] The global public goods perspective emphasizes the need for international collective action to provide services (e.g., disease control and surveillance, rules and standards) for the mutual benefit of rich and poor countries alike.[7] Attention to mutual benefit, however, may neglect health issues more

---

[2] JENNIFER P. RUGER, HEALTH AND SOCIAL JUSTICE (2009).

[3] U.K. HOUSE OF LORDS, *Chapter 3: International Health: The Institutional Labyrinth*, INTERGOVERNMENTAL ORGANISATIONS COMMITTEE—FIRST REPORT (2008), *available at* http://www.publications.parliament. uk/pa/ld200708/ldselect/ldintergov/143/14306.htm (last visited June 2, 2011); NICK DRAGER, GLOBAL HEALTH GOVERNANCE (June 2009), http://graduateinstitute.ch/webdav/site/iheid/shared/summer/ GHD%202009%20Summer%20Course/Drager_Global%20Health%20Governance_June%2015_2009. pdf (last visited June 2, 2011).

[4] A. BROOKS ET AL., CHILDREN'S VACCINE INITIATIVE & U.S. AGENCY FOR INT'L DEV., POLICY STUDY OF FACTORS INFLUENCING THE ADOPTION OF NEW AND UNDERUTILIZED VACCINES IN DEVELOPING COUNTRIES (1999).

[5] Gill Walt & Kent Buse, *Global Cooperation in International Public Health*, in INTERNATIONAL PUBLIC HEALTH: DISEASES, PROGRAMS, SYSTEMS, AND POLICIES 649–80 (Michael Merson et al. eds., Jones & Bartlett Learning, 2d ed. 2006); Susannah H. Mayhew et al., *Donor Agencies' Involvement in Reproductive Health: Saying One Thing and Doing Another?*, 35 INT'L J. HEALTH SERVS 579 (2005).

[6] Jennifer P. Ruger, *Toward a Theory of a Right to Health: Capability and Incompletely Theorized Agreements*, 18 YALE J.L. & HUMAN. 273 (2006); Jennifer P. Ruger, *Normative Foundations of Global Health Law* 2 GEO. L.J. 423 (2008); Nora Ng & Jennifer P. Ruger, *Global Health Governance at a Crossroads*, 3 GLOBAL HEALTH GOVERNANCE 1 (2011).

[7] Richard Smith, *Global Public Goods and Health*, 81 BULL. WORLD HEALTH ORG. 475 (2003); Inge Kaul & Michael Faust, *Global Public Goods and Health: Taking the Agenda Forward*, 79 BULL. WORLD HEALTH ORGAN. 869 (2001).

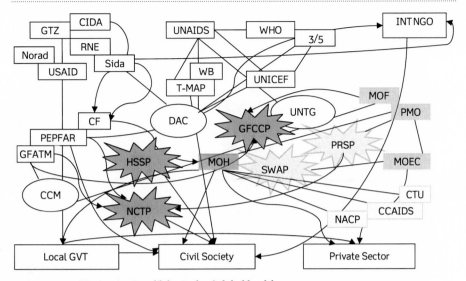

FIGURE 21.1A[1] The institutional labyrinth of global health

Adapted from Mbewe, WHO. 3/5, 3 by 5 initiative; CCAIDS, Christian Communicators Against HIV/AIDS; CCM, country coordination mechanism; CF, Clinton Foundation; CIDA, Canadian International Development Agency; CTU, clinical trials unit; DAC, development assistance committee; GFATM, Global Fund to Fight AIDS, Tuberculosis, and Malaria; GFCCP, Global Fund Country Coordination Plan; GTZ, Germany Agency for Technical Cooperation; HSSP, health sector support program; INTNGO, international non-governmental organization; LOCAL GVT, local government; MOEC, ministry of economy and commerce; MOF, ministry of finance; MOH, ministry of health; NACP, national HIV/AIDS control project; NCTP, national care and treatment plan; Norad, Norwegian Agency for Development Cooperation; PEPFAR, United States President's Emergency Plan for AIDS Relief; PMO, Prime Minister's Office; PRSP, poverty reduction strategy papers; RNE, Royal Netherlands Embassy; Sida, Swedish International Development Cooperation Agency; SWAP, sector-wide approach; T-MAP, Tanzania Multisectoral AIDS Project; UNAIDS, Joint United Nations Programme on HIV/AIDS; UNICEF, United Nations Children's Fund; UNTG, United Nations Theme Group; USAID, United States Agency for International Development; WB, World Bank; WHO, World Health Organization.

[1] UNITED KINGDOM HOUSE OF LORDS, CHAPTER 3: INTERNATIONAL HEALTH: THE INSTITUTIONAL LABYRINTH (Select Committee on Intergovernmental Organisations First Report, 2008) <http://www.publications.parliament.uk/pa/ld200708/ldselect/ldintergov/143/14306.htm> accessed June 2, 2011.

particular to the poor.[8] The utopian or human rights approach, also present in global health, has put forth the "right to health" in domestic case law,[9] but it has also been employed to mobilize support for addressing disease and morbidity worldwide. Yet, the human rights strategy has only been moderately effective, and some would argue ineffective—for example, in efforts to control and mitigate the HIV/AIDS epidemic.[10]

---

[8] Lincoln Chen, Tim Evans & Richard Cash, *Health as a Global Public Good*, in GLOBAL PUBLIC GOODS: INTERNATIONAL COOPERATION IN THE 21ST CENTURY 284 (Inge Kaul, Isabelle Grunberg & Marc Stern eds., 1999).

[9] Treatment Action Campaign v. Minister of Health, 2002 (4) SA 721 (CC); George J. Annas, *The Right to Health and the Nevirapine Case in South Africa*, 248 NEW ENG. J. MED. 750 (2003).

[10] David P. Fidler, *Fighting the Axis of Illness: HIV/AIDS, Human Rights, and U.S. Foreign Policy*, 17 HARV. HUM. RTS. J. 99 (2004).

FIGURE 21.1B[2] The global health landscape is increasingly crowded

Adapted from Drager.
[2]Nick Drager, *Global Health Governance* Presentation for the Global Health Diplomacy Summer Course at The Graduate Institute in Geneva, Switzerland, June 2009 http://graduateinstitute.ch/webdav/site/iheid/shared/summer/GHD%202009%20Summer%20Course/Drager_Global%20Health%20Governance_June%2015_2009.pdf accessed June 2, 2011.

A vague, underspecified conception of a "right to health" and unclear, inadequate allocation of obligations to meet rights claims undermine this approach.[11] On its own, it is an insufficient framework for GHG. The current regime of global health is neither orderless nor uncooperative. With the exception of key "proven successes" in global health, which operate primarily at a programmatic level, the regime comprises transnational actors with their own specific interests operating under a rational actor model of international cooperation. But the global health enterprise lacks collective principles representing the needs and interests of all whose health is compromised or threatened. National, group, or self-interest alone fails to justify an obligation to help meet the health needs of others. We need an ethical commitment to provide all with health capability.

GHG has failed to develop and effectuate a moral norm of equity in health. A theory of global health justice is needed to bind actors together in cooperation for health. Provincial globalism provides one such theoretical framework. In the rational actor and rational choice framework, agents (actors) act on their own or on behalf of principals (national governments, foundations, private institutions) that may or may not share common goals of health equity, which necessitate common commitments and "shared health governance." Such actors may work together in pursuit of enlightened

---

[11] Allen Buchanan & Matthew Decamp, *Responsibility for Global Health*, 27 THEORETICAL MED. & BIOETHICS 95 (2006); Onora O'Neill, *The Dark Side of Human Rights*, 81 INT'L AFF. 427 (2005).

self-interest, as in the global public goods perspective. This cooperation based on self-interest alone, in contrast to SHG, does not recognize that the provision of public goods is also a collective exercise in which people and organizations play roles and have responsibilities toward a social goal that is undergirded by moral conceptions about equity and capability. SHG separates health and disease control from powerful countries' narrow interests, the self-interest of wealthy nongovernmental organizations (NGOs) and foundations, and international legal instruments. It does not refute or abolish entirely self- or national interest; rather, it seeks to align them with shared goals through ethical commitments. It grounds GHG in principles of justice.

I. Rational Actor Model of GHG

Under the current rational actor model, individual actors in the global health environment are rational decision makers. They include individuals (e.g., a health minister), NGOs, multilateral public institutions such as the World Bank and the World Health Organization (WHO), public–private partnerships such as the Global Alliance for Vaccines and Immunization, and nation-states (and their constituent parts). In the rational actor model, each actor has its own set of goals and objectives, and these actors take actions based on analysis of the costs and benefits of various available options. Moreover, within many multilateral institutions, the most powerful actors can dominate and effectively direct policy and resource allocations toward their goals and objectives. International organizations, too, pursue their own interests, which may or may not coincide with those of states. Even NGOs, which have a distinctly populist flavor, operate out of their own interests.

The current global health landscape includes record numbers of actors and financial resources, both public and private. [Figure 21.1B] In addition to the WHO, World Bank, and the European Union, some of the largest players are relatively new; they include the Gates Foundation; the United States President's Emergency Plan for AIDS Relief; The Global Fund to Fight AIDS, Tuberculosis, and Malaria (Global Fund); and corporations (e.g., pharmaceutical companies). The Global Fund, for example, now provides roughly 20 percent of international public HIV/AIDS program funding, 65 percent of malaria funding, and 65 percent of TB funding for twenty-two high-burden countries.[12] The Global Fund is the quintessential contemporary initiative, focused on selective aid for narrow disease control programs in particular countries and on monitoring and evaluating intermediate indicators rather than developing broader health systems – even though health systems, while not as high profile as disease-specific initiatives, are essential building blocks for sustainable health.

One study identified several key characteristics in donor funding. These include narrowly defined success criteria (e.g., performance results based on organizational measures – number of loans disbursed, dollars provided – rather than health

---

[12] THE GLOBAL FUND, MAKING A DIFFERENCE: GLOBAL FUND RESULTS REPORT 2011 EXECUTIVE SUMMARY (2011), www.theglobalfund.org/documents/publications/progress_reports/Publication_2011Results_ExecutiveSummary_en/ (last visited Aug. 5, 2011).

outcomes), overlapping mandates, competition and duplication of health activities, shifting power structures, and poor coordination.[13] As a result, most technical assistance and funding conform to donor rather than recipient countries' policies and values. And because donor-driven development is evaluated by organizational criteria, it eludes critical scrutiny of its ultimate impact on health and disease control. In 2006, the World Bank estimated that half of health aid in Sub-Saharan Africa fails to reach intended clinics and hospitals.[14] Another study of children's immunization programs found that confusing priorities and policies at the global and country level delayed new vaccine delivery, and recommended that overlap among the WHO, the World Bank, the Gates Foundation's Children's Vaccine Program, and other organizations be addressed.[15]

Developing countries are required to manage each donor's project according to the donor's demands. This can conflict with the recipient country's needs and abilities. Donors undermined essential drug distribution in Tanzania[16] and integration of reproductive health services in Kenya[17] by creating their own parallel systems and by adding vertical programs. Most donor funding is disease- and program-specific and fails to address weak in-country institutional capacity.

The burdens and mayhem are evident in numerous recipient countries. A 2003 Organization for Economic Cooperation and Development study in eleven recipient countries revealed that five of the recipient countries' heaviest burdens were: difficulties with donor procedures, donor-driven priorities and systems, uncoordinated donor practices, excessive demands on time, and delays in disbursements.[18] Another study in Mozambique, Tanzania, Uganda, and Zambia – all Global Fund recipients – found that all four countries had difficulties incorporating additional resources and meeting donor requirements. It concluded that the need to learn the management of a new financial mechanism and to juggle proliferating activities among multiple donors overwhelmed these countries.[19]

Self-interest maximization leads to suboptimal results in global health policy. A review of the literature points to eight counterproductive elements: (1) electoral considerations, political and social power; (2) donor ideology and preference; (3) turf; (4) inter-NGO competition for funding and excessive demand for accountability; (5) profits; (6) geopolitical and strategic interests; (7) recipient manipulation of aid; and (8) mutual dependence on ineffective aid. Table 21.1 offers limited examples. Efforts to

---

[13] Walt & Buse, *supra* note 5.

[14] Laurie Garrett, *The Challenge of Global Health*, 86 FOREIGN AFF. 14 (2007).

[15] BROOKS ET AL., *supra* note 4.

[16] Walt & Buse, *supra* note 5.

[17] Mayhew et al., *supra* note 5.

[18] Organization for Economic Co-Operation & Devevelopment, *Harmonizing Donor Practices for Effective Aid Delivery*, 2003 DAC GUIDELINES & REFERENCE SERIES 1, http://www.oecd.org/dataoecd/0/48/20896122.pdf (last visited Feb. 7, 2011).

[19] Ruairi Brugha et al., *The Global Fund: Managing Great Expectations*, 364 LANCET 95 (2004).

TABLE 21.1

Examples of self-interest maximization and suboptimal results in global health

Interest Being Maximized	Examples
Political and social power	• Focus on health on foreign policy agenda dominated by infectious diseases and bioterror – on how the West is affected by health risks from the developing world, rather than on promotion of global public health.[1]
	• Governments in low-income countries often direct disproportionate resources to politically important urban and elite populations; for example, in Ghana in 1994, the richest fifth of population received 33% of public spending in health, while the poorest fifth received 12%.[2]
	• Birth control arbitrarily dispensed by community-based distributors wishing to develop prestige and respect.[3]
Donor ideology and preference	• IMF's neoliberal economic approach called for fiscal austerity and imposed public spending ceilings, which rendered Ugandan government nearly unable to accept $52 million from The Global Fund.[4]
	• Some faith-based organizations stress abstinence and faithfulness but marginalize or exclude condoms from HIV/AIDS prevention campaigns; HIV and those infected are often stigmatized.[5]
	• Uncoordinated focus on specific diseases lead to lopsided health funding and neglect of overall health system development.[6]
Turf protection	• Attempts to streamline UN system thwarted by disagreements on how to redefine duplicating and overlapping functions.[7]
	• Botswana physicians hindered scale-up of antiretroviral therapy by resisting use of phlebotomists to ease medical staff shortage.[8]
	• Honduran town receiving UN World Food Program aid wished to participate in a project run by NGO CARE; WFP threatened to leave if town accepted CARE assistance.[9]
Inter-NGO competition	• To remain competitive for funding, NGOs sometimes withhold information about ineffective programs, undertake projects in areas for which they have little expertise and tolerate recipient misbehavior; NGOs offered Kyrgyzstani politicians bribes to maintain good relations.[10]
	• To satisfy donor demands for accountability and ensure continued funding, aid recipients deal with duplicate paperwork and onerous monitoring requirements at the expense of substantive work;[11] Tanzania in 2001–2002 had 1000 donor meetings and 2400 donor reports each quarter.[12]
Profits	• 10/90 gap: lack of drug R&D for tropical diseases.[13]
	• Price of Pentamidine, a previously cheap treatment for sleeping sickness, rose 500% after it was discovered to be effective for AIDS-related *pneumocystic carinii* pneumonia; the drug disappeared from the markets of poor African and Southeast Asian countries.[14]
	• Tobacco industry lobbies government and UN agencies (e.g., FAO) to resist WHO's tobacco control programs;[15] tobacco companies in many developing countries also use marketing strategies banned in many developed countries.[16]
	• Corruption and theft in public sector medical supply chain.[17]
Geopolitical interests	• Rich countries direct aid to strategic allies, former colonies or regions they wish to influence, rather than giving aid based on need;[18] the poorest countries receive just 40 cents of every dollar sent overseas.[19]
	• A 2007 UN resolution addressing Myanmar's failure to respond to its HIV epidemic was vetoed by China, which considered Myanmar a long-term strategic ally and did not desire the introduction of U.S. influence into the region.[20]

(Continued)

Interest Being Maximized	Examples
Recipient manipulation of aid	• Ethiopian government denied food aid to rebel-controlled territories during the 1983–1985 famine.[21] • Filipino government was dealing with insurgency during the WHO Malaria Eradication Program, and stopped malaria spraying on at least one important island in order to allow the spread of malaria among the insurgent population.[22]
Mutual dependence on ineffective aid	• Madagascar continued to receive aid despite poor performance in meeting goals, due to mutual dependence of donors and recipient. Donors depended on continuing need for aid as a reason to pursue interests such as maintaining/expanding spheres of influence and containing terrorism. NGOs benefited from persisting justification for their existence, Madagascan elites received material benefits, whereas the government derived legitimacy from attracting aid and dealing with donors.[23] • NGOs in Honduras opted for uncoordinated chaos rather than be told that their project might not be needed; Honduran government opted for allowing chaos to persist rather than have funding cut off, and did not enforce coordinated plan.[24]

[1] Colin McInnes & Kelley Lee, *Health, Security and Foreign Policy*, 32 Rev, Int'l Studies 5–23 (2006).

[2] C. Blouin, *Economic Dimensions and Impact Assessment of GATS to Promote and Protect Health*, in International Trade in Health Services and the GATS 169–202 (Chantal Blouin et al., eds., 2006).

[3] Amy Kaler & Susan Watkins, *Disobedient Distributors: Street-Level Bureaucrats and Would-Be Patrons in Community-Based Family Planning Programs in Rural Kenya*, 32 Stud. Fam. Plann. 254–69 (2001).

[4] Global Health Watch, Global Health Watch 2005–2006: An Alternative World Health Report (2005).

[5] Sara Woldehanna et al., Faith in Action: Examining the Role of Faith-Based Organizations in Addressing HIV/AIDS (2005).

[6] Gill Walt et al., *Mapping the Global Health Architecture*, in Making Sense of Global Health Governance: A Policy Perspective 47–71 (Kent Buse et al. eds., 2009).

[7] *Id.*; Julio Frenk et al., *The Future of World Health: The New World Order and International Health*, 314 Brit. Med. J. 1404–07 (1997).

[8] Ann Swidler, *Syncretism and Subversion in AIDS Governance: How Locals Cope with Global Demands*, 82 Int. Aff. 269–84 (2006).

[9] Jeffrey Jackson, The Globalizers: Development Workers in Action (2005).

[10] Alexander Cooley & James Ron, *The NGO Scramble: Organizational Insecurity and the Political Economy of Transnational Action*, 27 Int'l Security 5–39 (2002).

[11] Anthony Bebbington, *Donor–NGO Relations and Representations of Livelihood in Nongovernmental Aid Chains*, 33 World Dev. 937–50 (2005).

[12] Ilona Kickbusch, *Action on Global Health: Addressing Global Health Governance Challenges*, 119 Public Health 969–73 (2005).

[13] Bernard Pecoul et al., *Access to Essential Drugs in Poor Countries: A Lost Battle?* 281 JAMA 361–67 (1999).

[14] Caroline Thomas, *Trade Policy and the Politics of Access to Drugs*, 23 Third World Q. 251–64 (2002).

[15] Kent Buse & Chris Naylor, *Commercial Health Governance*, in Making Sense of Global Health Governance: A Policy Perspective 187–208 (Kent Buse et al., eds., 2009).

[16] R. Beaglehole & D. Yach, *Globalisation and the Prevention and Control of Non-Communicable Disease: The Neglected Chronic Diseases of Adults*, 362 Lancet 903(2003).

[17] Maureen Lewis, Governance and Corruption in Public Health Care Systems (Working paper number 78, Center for Global Development 2006).

[18] Anup Shah, *Foreign Aid for Development Assistance*, Apr. 8, 2012, http://www.globalissues.org/article/35/foreign-aid-development-assistance, accessed Nov. 7, 2012.

[19] Thalif Deen, *Three Decades of Missed Aid Targets*, Apr. 18, 2005, http://www.ipsnews.net/2005/04/development-three-decades-of-missed-aid-targets/, accessed Nov. 7, 2012.

[20] Yanzhong Huang, *Pursuing Health as Foreign Policy: The Case of China*, 17 Ind. J. Global Legal Studies 105–46 (2010).

[21] Ondine Barrow, *International Responses to Famine in Ethiopia 1983–85*, in The Charitable Impulse: NGOs and Development in East and North-East Africa 63–80 (Ondine Barrow & Michael Jennings eds., 2001).

[22] Javed Siddiqi, World Health and World Politics (1995).

[23] Nadia R. Horning, *Strong Support for Weak Performance: Donor Competition in Madagascar*, 107 African Affairs 405–31 (2008).

[24] Jeffery T. Jackson, The Globalizers: Development Work in Action (2005).

improve cooperation and coordination have occurred primarily at a practical level,[20] leaving theoretical issues unaddressed. A theoretically grounded normative approach is lacking.

II. Common Goals and Common Commitments: The Social Agreement Model

Although the rational actor model predominates, specific examples of successful collective action exemplify global health cooperation. Successful coordination among agencies occurs, for example, in the Onchocerciasis Control Programme, the Task Force on Child Survival, and the Global Polio Eradication Initiative. Table 21.2 provides three examples. Additional illustrations of success include campaigns to eradicate polio and the guinea worm, and to eliminate lymphatic filariasis. These efforts involve the participation of numerous international and national actors as well as corporate and nonprofit entities, such as the WHO, UNICEF, U.S. Centers for Disease Control and Prevention, the Carter Center, the Gates Foundation, Du Pont, and Merck.[21] Global measles mortality has also greatly declined since 2000 due to a drive to eliminate the infection by national governments, the WHO, UNICEF, and the International Federation of Red Cross and Red Crescent Societies.[22] These examples exhibit four general characteristics: partnerships defined by a shared goal; clear objectives and agreed-upon roles and responsibilities; delineation of complementary expertise and accountability in pursuing goals; and donors' willingness to cede the lead to others.[23]

Common goals are essential to successful collective action. To achieve consensus, GHG should move beyond the rational actor model to a normative model of social agreement theory, in which actors embrace shared values to produce stability and social unity. John Rawls's notion of "overlapping consensus" clarifies this dynamic, emphasizing the necessity of identifying shared values – even values shared for various reasons – and social agreement for making decisions collectively.

Rawls distinguishes between political bargaining models – associated with a rational actor model – and conceptual models rooted in political philosophy. He suggests that

---

[20] Ng & Ruger, *supra* note 6. Examples of efforts to improve cooperation include: Paris and Accra principles (harmonization and alignment); Comprehensive Development Framework (country ownership); Poverty Reduction Strategy Papers; International Health Partnership; Health 8; Health Clusters; committee "c"; proposals such as global action networks; a Framework Convention on Global Health; issue-specific global health laws, etc.

[21] RUTH LEVINE & WHAT WORKS WORKING GROUP WITH MOLLY KINDER, MILLIONS SAVED: PROVEN SUCCESSES IN GLOBAL HEALTH (2004); Rebecca Voelker, *Global Partners Take Two Steps Closer to Eradication of Guinea Worm Disease*, 305 JAMA 1642 (2011); David Molyneux, *Lymphatic Filariasis (Elephantiasis) Elimination: A Public Health Success and Development Opportunity*, 2 FILARIA J. 13 (2003), *available at* http://www.filariajournal.com/content/2/1/13.

[22] William J. Moss & Diane E. Griffin, *Global Measles Elimination*, 4 NAT'L REVS. MICROBIOOGY 900 (2006); World Health Organization, *Global Elimination of Measles: Report by the Secretariat*, 125 EXECUTIVE BOARD SESSION 1 (2009), *available at* http://apps.who.int/gb/ebwha/pdf_files/EB125/B125_4-en.pdf.

[23] MARK L. ROSENBERG ET AL., REAL COLLABORATION: WHAT IT TAKES FOR GLOBAL HEALTH TO SUCCEED (2010).

TABLE 21.2

Three examples of global health successes and shared health governance principles

- *Onchocerciasis Control Programmes*

    The OCP and the Merck ivermectin donation program administered by the Task Force for Child Survival and Development are widely considered to be exemplary.[1] The 1974 OCP covered West Africa, and was a collaboration among the World Bank, WHO, UNDP, and FAO; the 1995 African Programme for Onchocerciasis Control (APOC) expanded the effort to central, southern and eastern Africa, and extended participation to 21 bilateral and multilateral donors, more than 30 NGOs (including the Carter Center, Helen Keller International, Lions Clubs, and the River Blindness Foundation), and more than 100,000 rural communities.[2] Both programs used ivermectin donated by Merck. The programs halted parasite transmission in 11 West African countries and made 25 million arable hectares safe for resettlement.[3] Factors driving the success of these programs include: *a shared goal to control onchocerciasis; willingness of actors to be coordinated regionally for OCPs and into an ivermectin distribution network by the Task Force; clear delineation of roles facilitated mutual accountability; community involvement and grassroots empowerment increased health agency.*[4]

- *HIV/AIDS in Brazil*

    In Brazil, an egalitarian ethos underlies the health care system, with health care considered a duty of the state. Civil society is involved in health policy planning, and the government funds health advocacy groups. The Brazilian effort to combat HIV/AIDS is held up as a model to be emulated; between 1996 and 2002, Brazil halved mortality from AIDS.[5] Part of this Brazilian undertaking has been funded by the World Bank, which made loans despite the divergence of Brazilian health policies from World Bank positions, showing a "respect for different values and social choice."[6] Factors driving the success of these healthcare systems include: *a shared commitment to HIV/AIDS prevention and control; clear recognition of the state's obligation to provide healthcare in Brazil; health agency-enhancing civil society involvement, country ownership of health policies.*

- *WHO global influenza surveillance*

    First established in 1948, WHO's global influenza surveillance programme involves 110 collaborating laboratories in 82 countries. It is an example of a "highly successful global partnership." National case detection systems and labs are strengthened according to internationally accepted norms; virus isolates from national labs are further analyzed in one of four WHO influenza collaborating centers, and this data is then used in the annual influenza vaccine design process. The 1997 H5N1 outbreak in Hong Kong was effectively handled, with rapid identification of the virus strain by a collaborating lab in the Netherlands, and mobilization and coordination of investigating team from US WHO collaborating centers. Scientific studies, public information and diagnostic test kits were quickly developed and distributed, resulting in a "timely, ordered, and effective response."[8] Factors driving the success of this program include: *shared goal of outbreak surveillance and control; mutual obligation to detect and report outbreaks; coordination and cooperation to provide a global public health good.*

[1] Ruth Levine & What Works Working Group, *Controlling Onchocerciasis in Sub-Saharan Africa*, in Millions Saved: Proven Successes in Global Health 57–64 (Ruth Levine & What Works Working Group eds., 2004).

[2] *Id.*

[3] *Id.*

[4] M. N. Katabarwa et al., *Community-Directed Interventions Strategy Enhances Efficient and Effective Integration of Health Care Delivery and Development Activities in Rural Disadvantaged Communities in Uganda*, 10 Tropical Med. Int'l Health 312–21 (2005).

[5] Susan Okie, *Fighting HIV: Lessons from Brazil*, 354 N. Engl. J. Med. 1977–81 (2006).

[6] Ruben A. De Mattos et al., *World Bank Strategies and the Response to AIDS in Brazil*, 27 Divulgação em Saúde para Debate 215–27 (2003), http://www.columbia.edu/itc/hs/pubhealth/p8725/mattos.pdf (accessed Feb. 10, 2011).

[7] David L. Heymann & Guenael R. Rodier, *Global Surveillance of Communicable Diseases*, 4 Emerg. Infect. Dis. 362–65 (1998).

[8] *Id.*

political bargaining models are akin to a modus vivendi – a consensus on "accepting certain authorities, or on complying with certain institutional arrangements, founded on a convergence of self- or group interests."[24] If power relations shift or players' positions change, and powerful actors are no longer in a position to keep the bargain, the convergence would no longer hold. For example, an international agreement among the G-8 nations based on trading favors would be unstable because the bargain would be "contingent on circumstances remaining such as not to upset the fortunate convergence of interests."[25] Additionally, an international consensus such as the Millennium Development Goals does not necessarily signify a true consensus or guarantee achieving those goals. Successful polio and smallpox eradication, for instance, requires each country to continue to immunize its children, even if that country has been disease-free for some time, to reduce the chance of cross-border transmission. Each country must commit to this underlying goal, and if not all countries continue to immunize, eradication is compromised.

Additional distinctions separate social agreements based on overlapping consensus and those resulting from political bargaining. First, as Rawls notes, the object of an overlapping consensus "is itself a *moral* conception," valued in itself.[26] Second, the overlapping consensus is "affirmed on moral grounds" and includes "conceptions of society and of citizens as persons, as well as principles of justice, and an account of the political virtues through which those principles are embodied in human character and expressed in public life."[27] It represents a consensus on the public good among both elites and citizens, rising above group- or self-interest. Third, the overlapping consensus is more stable because it is a reasonable consensus, not simply a balance of power. A modus vivendi, by contrast, reflects a temporary agreement among different and opposing actors. Thus, the overlapping consensus framework has lasting power through subsequent shifts in influence.[28] Fourth, a social agreement framework endeavors to educe "certain fundamental ideas viewed as latent in the public political culture of a democratic society."[29] It attempts to tap into individuals' shared core values, even if individuals and their representatives have difficulty articulating those values completely. Fifth, this framework contrasts legitimate political authority with political power, differentiating authentic authority from the self-interest so often inherent in power.[30] It rejects coercion,[31] recognizing that stability comes from a reasonable consensus on a political conception that is politically legitimate, based on appeals to the "public reason" of "free and equal citizens."[32] From this social agreement perspective, legitimate political authority has pragmatic advantages in forging consensus and

---

[24] JOHN RAWLS, POLITICAL LIBERALISM 147 (1993).
[25] *Id.*
[26] *Id.* (emphasis added.)
[27] *Id.*
[28] *Id.* at 148.
[29] *Id.* at 175.
[30] *Id.* at 143–44.
[31] *Id.* at 143.
[32] *Id.* at 144.

cooperative coalitions. Compared to political bargaining based on expedience, a social agreement involves actors' commitment and consensus on values, which render that agreement more sustainable over time and in the face of difficulties.

At the national level, a social agreement model emphasizes public deliberation, responsible leadership, and mass communication; it relies on popular sovereignty and political leadership to reach agreement on the common good. In many countries, common ground on ethical principles governing health and health care remains elusive. Achieving health equity requires finding it.

III. Global Health Governance as Shared Health Governance

A. VALUES, IDEAS, AND NORMS IN GHG

Values, ideas, and norms have a critical role to play in GHG: a role inadequately studied and lacking a theoretical framework. Global health problems require joint action for their resolution and require analysis within a normative framework. This framework evaluates actors' ethical commitments to making sacrifices and effectuating policies and programs transcending self-interest and narrow notions of individual rationality, which also play an important role in behavior. Whereas values are embedded in ideas, providing norms' content, norms are internalized, having a "taken for granted" quality. Public moral norms, their degree of internalization, and the level of social consensus around them demand study in the GHG context.

In international relations theory,[33] "ideas" influence international public policy in several ways, the first of which is to provide a "road map" "that increase[s] actors' clarity about goals or ends-means relationships."[34] Principled ideas or beliefs, when expressed as values, can have a significant impact on global political action. In 1989, for example, Eastern Europeans, who placed a high value on liberty, put their lives on the line for freedom when they defied and overthrew the communist regimes.[35] Global health requires a set of principled ideas to shift the focus from material and power interests to moral concerns.

Second, ideas play a role in coordinating behavior to solve collective problems, particularly where there is no unique equilibrium. "[I]deas affect strategic interactions, helping or hindering joint efforts to attain 'more efficient' outcomes."[36] They serve as "focal points" defining cooperative solutions "or act as coalitional glue" helping particular groups cohere.[37] "[I]deas focus expectations and strategies" especially where incomplete agreement occurs.[38] As Garrett and Weingast note, "given that most agreements

---

[33] IDEAS AND FOREIGN POLICY: BELIEFS, INSTITUTIONS, AND POLITICAL CHANGE (Judith Goldstein & Robert O. Keohane eds., 1993).

[34] Judith Goldstein & Robert O. Keohane, *Ideas and Foreign Policy: An Analytical Framework*, *in* IDEAS AND FOREIGN POLICY, *supra* note 33, at 3.

[35] *Id.*

[36] *Id.* at 12.

[37] *Id.* at 12.

[38] *Id.* at 18.

are likely to be incomplete . . . shared beliefs about the spirit of agreements are essential" to maintain cooperation.[39]

Third, "[o]nce institutionalized . . . ideas continue to guide action,"[40] as they become embedded as rules and institutionalized norms, leading to "reinforcing organizational and normative structures."[41] Jackson, for example, explains European foreign policy shifts toward decolonization by normative ideational changes favoring self-determination among former colonies.[42] "Epistemic communities" are also important here as these networks of experts possess knowledge of both social scientific and normative information[43] that facilitates idea institutionalization and enforcement.

B. PROVINCIAL GLOBALISM: A FUNCTIONAL APPROACH TO RESPONSIBILITY ALLOCATION

Provincial globalism allocates responsibility for effectuating global health justice based on functional requirements and voluntary commitments. These obligations, set out in "Global Health Justice,"[44] will not be reiterated here. However, Figure 21.2 offers a preliminary pragmatic sketch of certain elements.[45] Table 21.3 illustrates how respective roles and responsibilities of global health institutions may shift over time. A provisional road map for GHG is necessary to avoid "dumping" duties on various state and global actors without sufficient moral justification.[46] Duty dumping can prompt parties to skirt responsibility.

Another key road map feature is the willing assumption of duties among individuals and institutions. This voluntary participation enhances their autonomy and boosts effective implementation. Individuals and institutions that have embraced ethical commitments and internalized public moral norms are more likely to discharge specific duties than those that have not.[47] The public moral norm incorporates self- and national interest, as well as others' interests, in the context of a global society.

---

[39] Geoffrey Garrett & Barry R. Weingast, *Ideas, Interests, and Institutions: Constructing the European Community's Internal Market, in* IDEAS AND FOREIGN POLICY, *supra* note 33, at 176.

[40] Goldstein & Keohane, *supra* note 34, at 5.

[41] *Id.* at 13.

[42] Robert H. Jackson, *The Weight of Ideas in Decolonization: Normative Change in International Relations, in* IDEAS AND FOREIGN POLICY, *supra* note 33, at 111.

[43] Peter M. Haas, *Introduction: Epistemic Communities and International Policy Coordination*, 46 INT'L ORG. 1 (1992).

[44] Ruger, *supra* note 1.

[45] This preliminary sketch requires further refinement to bring respective roles and responsibilities into greater focus, given the considerable overlap and redundancies in functions among actors that complicate clear delineation of duties.

[46] Buchanan & DeCamp, *supra* note 11.

[47] Raymond De Young, *Recycling as Appropriate Behavior: A Review of Survey Data from Selected Recycling Education Programs in Michigan*, 3 RESOURCES, CONSERVATION AND RECYCLING 253 (1990); Joseph R. Hopper & Joyce M. Nielsen, *Recycling as Altruistic Behavior: Normative and Behavioral Strategies to Expand Participation in a Community Recycling Program*, 23 ENV'T & BEHAV. 195 (1991); Samuel Bowles & Sung-Ha Hwang, *Social Preferences and Public Economics: Mechanism Design When Social Preferences Depend on Incentives*, 92 J. PUB. ECON. 1811 (2008).

Actors	Financing/Funding[a]	Knowledge Generation and Dissemination/R&D[b]	Technical Assistance/Policy Advice[c]	Empowerment/Agency Enhancement[d]	Advocacy/Intermediary	Coordination/Agenda Setting/Consensus Building[e]	Norms/Standards[f]	Surveillance/Outbreak Response[g]	Health System Development/Sustainability[h]	Macro-Social Environment[i]	Evaluation and Monitoring
National/Subnational											
National Governments/MOH	***	***	***	***		***	***	***	***	***	***
National Research Institutes/MRCs		***	***	***		***	***	***	***	***	***
Local/Subnational Governments	***	***	***	***		***	***	***	***	***	***
Domestic NGOs/CSOs				**	***						
Academia		***	***	***		***	***		***	***	***
Domestic Foundations	**	***			***						
Regional											
UN/WHO Regional Office			***	**		***		***	**		
Regional Development Banks	**		***	**		***			**	**	
Regional NGOs/CSOs				**	***						
Regional Foundations	**				***						
Global/International											
WHO		***	***	***		***	***	***	**	**	***
Other UN organizations (e.g. UNICEF, UNFPA, UNDP)		***	***	***			***		**	**	
World Bank	**	***	***	***		***			**	***	
WTO							***			***	
Global Fund	**		**								
UNAIDS		**	**		**						
Global Health Research Initiatives		***	***			***	***	***	***	***	***

	a	b	c	d	e	f	g	h	i
International/Global NGOs/CSOs		**	***		**	***		**	**
Private Foundations	**	**	***	***	**	***		***	
Private Sector/Industry	**	**	***	**	**	***		***	***
PPPs (includes GAVI)	**	**	**	***	**	**		**	
U.S. Government/OECD Countries	**	**	***	**	***	***	***	**	***
European Union	**	**	***	**	***	***	***	**	***
G8, G2o	**	**	**	***	***	***	***	**	***
BRICs	**	**	***	**	**	**	**	***	***

*: Functions have both domestic and global/international dimensions; domestic functions served by national/subnational actors, who may also participate globally/internationally, and in Stages 1–2 by global actors (see Figure 2)

**: Stages 1–2

***: Stages 1–3

a: Indicates actors that originate and/or channel funding

b: Includes creation of new knowledge and technologies; transfer, application, adaptation of existing knowledge and technologies; knowledge and information management; development and maintenance of research and information capacity

c: Includes technical assistance and policy advice in equitable and efficient health financing, organization, delivery and regulation; training of medical and public health; professionals; management of health facilities standardized diagnostic categories

d: Includes reformation of state and local institutions to improve democratic governance; encouragement of political will for public action; assistance with improving public administration; provision of greater voice in national and international fora; assistance to ensure more effective citizen participation in decision-making; public health communication and education; enhancing individual and collective health agency

e: Coordination of donors/activities to reduce redundancy; leadership and increase effectiveness; global health policy development and planning

f: Includes proposal, negotiation, ratification of conventions, regulations, agreements, standards, and recommendations with respect to global health matters; development, establishment, promotion, and compliance with international standards concerning travel, global health citizenship (reciprocity in treatment by nations), food, biological, pharmaceutical, legal/illegal unsafe matter and similar products

g: Includes emergencies, transfer of pathogens/infectious agents (especially extremely resistant); public health surveillance systems at the national level (e.g. U.S. CDC) that feed into WHO's global surveillance system

h: Includes creation and maintenance of equitable and affordable health care and public health structures, financing, organization, delivery, regulation and stewardship of health system

i: Includes equitable growth facilitating growth in developing countries; promoting global financial stability; global good governance and public goods; debt relief and development assistance; fair trade and open markets; on the national/subnational level, this includes addressing the proximal determinants of health, such as safe food and water, basic sanitation, adequate living conditions, good governance, and literacy.

Abbreviations: MOH, Ministries of Health; MRC, Medical Research Council; NGO, non-governmental organizations; UN, United Nations; WHO, World Health Organization; UNICEF, United Nations Children's Fund; UNFPA, United Nations Population Fund; WTO, World Trade Organization; UNAIDS, Joint United Nations Programme on HIV/AIDS; PPP, public-private partnership; GAVI, Global Alliance for Vaccines and Immunization; BRICs, Brazil, Russia, India, China; US CDC: United States Centers for Disease Control and Prevention

FIGURE 21.2 Key Global Health Roles and Responsibilities*

TABLE 21.3

GHG as a temporal problem

	Progressive realization		
Stage I	Stage II		Stage III
Larger role for GH institutions around key functions	Smaller role for GH institutions around key functions		Homeostatically balanced equilibria
• Global health institutions to help states (where necessary) reach a point at which states can carry out specific health duties to ensure health capability of people living within their borders	• Policies and redistribution in Stage I enable states to meet health needs of their local population, and address health inequities, and externalities (disease surveillance and control at the domestic level)		• National health systems in connection with global health institutions have capacity to respond to external health shocks through internal regulation and adjustment, as sufficiently developed/ sophisticated: entails both the process of achieving balance and the balanced "end-state"
• When states are unjust or unable to carry out health duties, the global community helps states meet their obligations and works for health equity within the confines of those societies' self-determination and self-governance. The global community must provide assistance and oversight, but without using coercion; incentives and other forms of choice architecture may be useful	• States engage in resource distribution, oversight and regulation, and provision of health-related goods and services, based on some consensus notion of health equity reached through the political process and internalized in national health system		• Global health institutions and actors' specific duties defined by global health functions they perform. Global health actors and institutions held to account for effectively and efficiently fulfilling roles
• Force, power, coercion or sanctions might seem logical but such measures often cause more harm than good especially among populations suffering most (e.g., Iraq sanctions)	• Global health institutions continue to undertake tasks beyond national capacity, such as coordinating global efforts to limit and prevent externalities (e.g., disease outbreaks), supporting national/local		• When global health institutions are inadequate to their tasks, global health actors and states cooperate to reform or generate new consensus and multilateral mechanisms to deal with persistent or new challenges
• Global health institutions undertake tasks beyond national capacity, such as coordinating global efforts to limit and prevent externalities (e.g., disease outbreaks), supporting national/local health systems, creating and disseminating global public goods, norms and standards, addressing cross-border issues and continuing to build and maintain consensus on global health priorities and actions	health systems, creating and disseminating global public goods, norms and standards, addressing cross border issues and continuing to build and maintain consensus on global health priorities and actions		• Differentiation and integration among global health actors through consensus building process to achieve more complex, more comprehensive global health system to handle greater variety and greater complexity of tasks[1]

[1] Judith E. Innes & David E. Booher, Consensus Building and Complex Adaptive Systems: A Framework for Evaluating Collaborative Planning, 65 J. AM. PLANNING ASS'N 412–23 (1999); Kevin J. Dooley, A Complex Adaptive Systems Model of Organization Change, 1 NONLINEAR DYNAMICS, PSYCHOLOGY, AND LIFE SCIENCES 69–97 (1997).

It connects and aligns individuals and society. The assumption of duties should be based on moral grounds and should be voluntary, not coerced. Individuals who have internalized ethical commitments freely enter into them and create expectations for compliance. In other works, I have argued for "joint commitments" under plural subject theory as one mechanism for this. We accept our shared responsibility for health by jointly committing[48] to the global health enterprise. Collective global health action entails ethical commitments and public moral norm internalization as the glue holding the system together and making actors accountable.

Internalizing a public moral norm of health equity is important because effective health governance requires not just self- and national interest or even legal instruments, but individuals and groups willing to make choices to ensure health capabilities for all. This orientation in turn leads to domestic and global policies embracing health equity and measures to achieve it.

A paradigmatic change from rational actor to normative commitments in GHG also changes the framework for evaluating activities of global and domestic actors. Effectiveness in advancing the overarching goal of health equity must be the criterion. Thus, even though wealthy foundations and powerful developed countries have a legal right to shape expenditures by their own objectives, they have an ethical obligation to collaborate with other actors to enhance health equity. This one-goal, multiple-actors approach to GHG contrasts with the multiple-goals, multiple-actors approach of the current system.

C. SHARED GLOBAL HEALTH SOVEREIGNTY: A GLOBAL HEALTH CONSTITUTION

There is no world health government with global authority and enforcement powers. Thus, achieving effective global health policy and solving global health problems[49] will require alternative governance structures to coordinate independent yet interdependent actors. With no overarching institution, GHG as SHG entails a constitution of sorts to demarcate health governance globally. A "global health constitution" would delineate the actors (e.g., federal and state governments, global/international institutions, individuals) and specify their respective duties and obligations, thus allocating responsibility. The global health constitution would set a framework and procedures informed by authoritative standards and principles as presented elsewhere[50] as a foundation for assigning duties and obligations. Constitutional interpretation would then assess whether actors are meeting their obligations. To date, the different actors in the global health system have not known what their respective duties and obligations are. Holding them accountable for unspecified responsibilities is inappropriate. Under a global health constitution, obligations would be clear, and evading them would no longer be an option.

---

[48] Jennifer P. Ruger, *Shared Health Governance*, 11 Am. J. Bioethics 32 (2011).

[49] Dean T. Jamison et al., *International Collective Action in Health: Objectives, Functions, and Rationale*, 351 Lancet 514 (1998).

[50] Ruger, *supra* note 1.

The global health constitution need not be a legal constitution. It sets out a meta-level system of regulation (by self and others) through ethical commitments, but it neither replaces nor competes with the WHO constitution; rather, the two are complementary. The WHO's roles and responsibilities in GHG must be contextualized in an overall framework. The global health constitution arches above the WHO constitution; if the latter were able to serve this higher-order function, a global health constitution would become unnecessary. This higher-order charter is constitutional in prescribing institutional arrangements and procedures and in assigning responsibilities and authority to public and private actors. Accountability in the form of pressure from various groups may also be more possible under this regime, because it prescribes what duties individuals and institutions owe and to whom. The constitution must imbue public moral norms. Compliance, enforcement, and accountability of actors discharging global health duties most likely will occur at the country level; at the global level, the discharge of duties would be regulated by checks and balances among global actors in accordance with an overarching global health policy. An independent nongovernmental peer review organization such as a Global Institute of Health and Medicine (GIHM) is one possible institutional choice to serve these functions at the global level.

D. LEGITIMACY AND ACCOUNTABILITY IN GHG: EVIDENCE FROM MALAWI

Legitimate and reliable mechanisms are necessary to hold actors responsible for fulfilling their duties in the SHG framework. Unlike the rational actor model with its competing interests and contrasting goals, SHG's framework involves congruence among the goals and values of different actors and groups. It envisions full knowledge and mutual understanding of objectives and agreement on assessment indicators. Cost management and efficiency are integral parts of good SHG. Accountability (e.g., for resource use, implementation, and results) and mechanisms to ensure it are essential. Because primary duties and obligations occur at the state level, accountability and legitimacy mechanisms must start there. Under GHG as SHG, global health policy must also reflect health agency–enhancing processes.[51]

We have developed select indicators to assess these ideas empirically. These indicators measure: (1) goal alignment; (2) adequate levels of resources (human and financial); (3) mutual understanding of key outcomes and principle indicators for evaluating those outcomes (i.e., consensus about indicators and the statistics that measure them); (4) meaningful participation of key global, national, and subnational groups and institutions; (5) efforts to engage key vulnerable groups most affected by policy decisions (e.g., the poor, women, youths, persons with disabilities, and the elderly); and (6)

---

[51] The "health agency" concept has been discussed elsewhere. Ruger, *supra* note 1; Jennifer P. Ruger, *Rethinking Equal Access: Agency, Quality, and Norms*, 2 GLOBAL PUB. HEALTH 78 (2007); Jennifer P. Ruger, *Ethics in American Health 2: An Ethical Framework for Health System Reform*, 98 AM. J. PUB. HEALTH 1756 (2008).

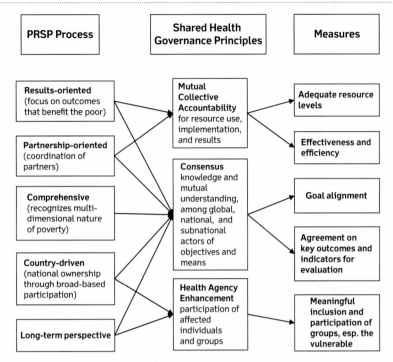

FIGURE 21.3 PRSP, poverty reductions strategy papers

effective, efficient resource use for priority areas. In 2005, we began developing a survey to examine these dimensions, and in 2007 applied it as a preliminary study of SHG in the Malawi Poverty Reduction Strategy Papers process.[52] Figure 21.3 illustrates how these concepts interrelate.

E. INTERNATIONAL HEALTH RELATIONS AT THE COUNTRY LEVEL:
THE MINISTRIES OF HEALTH IN KENYA AND MEXICO

In March 2006, the government of Kenya established the Office for International Health Relations in the Ministry of Health. The government explicitly noted that Kenya's health policy includes both domestic and foreign policy, and that bilateral and multilateral cooperation is a significant component of its health policy. The primary function of the Office is "coordinating activities with and keeping records of" entities including Global Organizations, the WHO, United Nations, The Common Wealth Secretariat, regional organizationsm and others.[53] Its mandate is to "ensure that the

---

52 Catherine Wachira & Jennifer P. Ruger, *National Poverty Reduction Strategies and HIV/AIDS Governance in Malawi: A Preliminary Study of Shared Health Governance*, 72 Soc. Sci. Med. 1956 (2011).

53 Kenya Office for Int'l Health Relations, International Health Relations (Ministry of Health 2006).

Ministry of Health fully participates in all activities and therefore enhance the benefits that Kenya accrues from these international organisations."[54] It focuses on Kenya's interrelationships with global health actors and how Kenya can most effectively fulfill domestic and international health obligations. The office of International Health Relations is also responsible for making sure that the Kenyan Ministry of Health's activities "are internally coherent and consistent with government-wide policies and...that Kenyan health policy and priorities are reflected in international activities."[55] Kenya is not the only example; the Mexican Ministry of Health has an Office of International Affairs,[56] which is aimed at health improvement of both Mexican and global citizens. It also focuses on partnerships with other countries, multilateral institutions, and NGOs in an effort to align domestic and global health policy with the global public health agenda. These are but two examples that, when considered alongside examples from other countries, offer insight regarding the interface between global and national health policy.

The Kenyan Office of International Health Relations and Mexican Office of International Affairs are consistent with GHG as SHG. They envision, at least on paper, a way for the state to manage up and across and coordinate its efforts in global health. SHG furthers managing up and across, along with managing down, because it enhances both the individual and collective health agency of the populations served and locates legitimacy and accountability with the nation-state, where primary responsibility rests. It therefore enables Kenyan and Mexican citizens, through their own representation, to share in governance, maintaining their own sovereignty and agency, in conjunction with the goals and objectives of the global health community. Countries may also band together to manage up or to manage across, as is the case with emerging countries in GHG.[57] Table 21.4 compares SHG components with those of the current global health regime.

IV. Conclusion

Global health actors should work together with state actors and institutions to correct and avert global health injustices through a framework of SHG resting on shared ethical commitments. GHG can be seen as a temporal problem, which first requires a large role for global health institutions to serve key functions until states are able to

---

54 *Id.*

55 *Id.*

56 Secretaria de Salud de Mexico, Estructura Orgánica Básica (2010), http://portal.salud.gob.mx/descargas/pdf/organigrama_salud.pdf (last visited June 2, 2011); Pan American Health Organization, U.S.-Mexico Diabetes Prevention and Control Project: Intervention Pilot Project for Phase 2 (2003), *available at* http://www.fep.paho.org/newdiabetes/spanish/Documents/INTERVENTION%20%20PHASE%20II.htm (last visited June 2, 2011).

57 Jennifer P. Ruger & Nora Ng, *Emerging and Transitioning Countries' Role in Global Health*, 3 St. Louis U.J. Health L. Pol'y 253 (2010).

TABLE 21.4

Shared health governance versus current global health regime

	Shared Health Governance	Current Global Health Regime
Values and Goals	• Joint commitments and mutual obligation, align common good and self interest • Consensus among global, national, and subnational actors on goals and measurable outcomes • Full knowledge and mutual understanding of objectives and means	• Pursuit of own interests and priorities that often conflict with those of other actors • Lack of agreement on strategies and outcomes • Ideology-driven rather than problem-driven
Coordination	• Actors are willing to be coordinated with or without communication or centralization	• Actors often do not coordinate and are often not willing to be coordinated
Evaluation	• Agreement on indicators for evaluation of common purpose	• Lack of agreement on outcomes and indicators for evaluation
Accountability	• Mutual collective accountability	• Limited accountability (esp. in bilateral aid, NGO implementation)
Agency/ participation	• Enhancement of individual and group health agency, special efforts to include marginalized and vulnerable groups; focus on enabling environments	• Intended beneficiaries often excluded from policy planning and program design; lack of knowledge and skills
Efficiency	• Cost management and efficiency are integral	• Competition between actors and the lack of participation by intended beneficiaries entail funding inefficiencies and cost escalation
Legitimacy	• Legitimacy through accountability and inclusive participation of stakeholders, through respect for self-determination, appeal to public reason and independent peer review	• Legitimacy of actors and initiatives not always clear due to inadequate representation of stakeholder interests and lack of effectiveness
Level of analysis	• Local and national actors as foci to perform the work of global health governance with global and national duties and institutions as a guide	• Top-down; country-driven efforts and reforms (e.g., CDF, PRSP) moderately successful; specific countries and local level collaboration programs highly successful (e.g., smallpox, OCP)

OCP, Onchocerciasis Control Programmes.

shoulder greater responsibilities. The eventual goal is a global health system in which national governments and global health institutions can work together as parts of a complex system to adjust to changing needs and environments (see Table 21.3). This chapter has put forth a few key features of GHG as SHG; further development of this framework is forthcoming.[58]

---

[58] Jennifer P. Ruger, Global Health Justice and Governance (Clarendon Press, forthcoming).

Health equity cannot be understood in terms of
the distribution of health care.

—Amartya Sen, *Why Health Equity*[1]

22

GLOBAL HEALTH CARE IS NOT GLOBAL HEALTH

Populations, Inequities, and Law as a Social Determinant of Health

Daniel S. Goldberg[*]

Engels, Virchow, and Global Health

This chapter argues that laws and policies are critical tools in the social and political processes that generate and sustain macrosocial structures that exert pronounced
effects on health and its distribution. If the processes that produce structures that
determine health and inequalities are fundamentally sociopolitical, it follows that
political actors are in some important sense responsible for shaping those structures.

The framework for these claims is historical, at least in part because historians of
public health have long argued that history is a vital analytic tool for thinking about
contemporary public health policies, practices, and priorities. Bashford and Strange
explain that "historically minded studies of public health confirm that past practices
inhere in current perceptions and policies, which, like their antecedents, unfold amidst
shifting amalgams of politics, culture, law, and economics, in addition to increasingly
sophisticated medical expertise."[2]

Thus, one key means of thinking about contemporary public health issues as they
manifest across the globe is by examination of their historical moorings. Moreover,
there is a meta-analytic advantage to thinking historically, as such a vantage point can

---

[*] Assistant Professor, Department of Bioethics & Interdisciplinary Studies, Brody School of Medicine,
East Carolina University. The author would like to acknowledge the assistance of Kenneth A. DeVille,
PhD, J.D., for reading and commenting on an early draft of this chapter.

[1] Amartya Sen, *Why Health Equity*, in PUBLIC HEALTH, ETHICS, AND EQUITY 24 (Sudhir Anand et al. eds.,
2002).

[2] Alison Bashford & Carolyn Strange, *Thinking Historically about Public Health*, 33 MED. HUMAN. 87, 88
(2007).

illuminate the political, economic, and social frameworks that govern global health discourse itself. Amid the general analytic power of a historical lens, one item stands out as particularly relevant for assessing the distinction between global health and global health care: the authorship, during the 1840s, of two of the most important publications in the modern history of public health.

In *On the Condition of the Working Class in England* (1845), Friedrich Engels accused British society of what he termed "social murder" by their toleration of socioeconomic structures that caused the destitution of the British urban poor.[3] In *Report on the Typhus Epidemic in Upper Silesia* (1848), Rudolf Virchow examined the causes and consequences of a typhus epidemic in an economically depressed Prussian province.[4] Although the authors of these two tracts had different purposes and intended the writings for different audiences, each of them laid critical groundwork for public health and social medicine in the modern West.

Situated in a Victorian milieu that emphasized sympathy and suffering, Engels wielded emotive language as a tool to galvanize public sentiment.[5] In contrast, Virchow's writing was not primarily intended to mobilize public action. Nevertheless, he stressed the necessity of conjoining moral and political sentiment with scientific investigation.[6] He argued that the virtuous healer could only proceed by understanding the sociopolitical realities in which the illness sufferers' experiences were situated.

Both Engels and Virchow adduced claims regarding the causes of the terrible outcomes they observed. Both insisted that acute medical intervention was insufficient to eradicate and prevent these shocking morbidities and mortalities; each focused on the need to ameliorate the deleterious social and economic conditions in which the populations they wrote about lived, worked, sickened, and died. And both identified the dramatic social changes in mid–nineteenth-century Europe as central factors in the destitution, disease, and death experienced by the British working poor and the Silesian people.

As to the British experience, Simon Szreter has painstakingly analyzed the demographic data in nineteenth-century Britain.[7] He developed his theory of the "four Ds," a

---

[3] FRIEDRICH ENGELS, ON THE CONDITION OF THE WORKING CLASS IN ENGLAND IN 1844 (Florence Kelley Wischnewetzky trans., Project Gutenberg e-books ed. 2005) (1845), *available at* http://www.gutenberg. org/ebooks/17306.

[4] Rudolf Virchow, *Report on the Typhus Epidemic in Upper Silesia*, *in* COLLECTED ESSAYS ON PUBLIC HEALTH AND EPIDEMIOLOGY 311 (L.J. Rather ed. & trans., Science History Publications ed. 1985) (1848). For modern commentary see, e.g., Howard Waitzkin, *One and a Half Centuries of Forgetting and Rediscovering: Virchow's Lasting Contributions to Social Medicine*, SOC. MED., February 2006, at 5, 5–10; Rex Taylor & Annelie Rieger, *Medicine as Social Science: Rudolf Virchow on the Typhus Epidemic in Upper Silesia*, 15 INT. J. HEALTH SERV. 547 (1985); George Rosen, *Approaches to a Concept of Social Medicine: An Historical Survey*, 26 MILBANK MEMORIAL FUND Q. 7 (1948).

[5] *See* Grace Kehler, *Gothic Pedagogy and Victorian Reform Treatises*, 50 VICTORIAN STUD. 437 (2008); ERIN O'CONNOR, RAW MATERIAL: PRODUCING PATHOLOGY IN VICTORIAN CULTURE (2000); Kristen Leaver, *Victorian Melodrama and the Performance of Poverty*, 27 VICTORIAN LANGUAGE AND CULTURE 443 (1999); STEVEN MARCUS, ENGELS, MANCHESTER, AND THE WORKING CLASS (1974).

[6] *See* Waitzkin, *supra* note 4, at 6–8; Taylor & Rieger, *supra* note 4, at 557.

[7] SIMON SZRETER, HEALTH AND WEALTH: STUDIES IN HISTORY AND POLICY (2004).

dialectic social process that typically attends rapid industrialization and urbanization: disruption, deprivation, disease, and death.[8] Szreter emphasizes that the links in the chain can be broken, but that unless remedial measures are undertaken, the outcomes remain likely to occur.[9] It is these "four *D*s" that were Engels and Virchow's central concern.

Another significant commonality is Engels and Virchow's emphasis on the distribution of disease. Indeed, the distribution of destitution—that it disproportionately affected the urban working poor—was obviously Engels's central point. Virchow too was not simply concerned with documenting an epidemic of gastrointestinal disease, which in mid–nineteenth-century Europe would have been all too common.[10] Rather, Virchow documented the relationship among class, occupation, and health, noting that typhus prevalence and outcomes were particularly severe among Silesian miners, an occupation that was heavily populated by members of the lowest classes.[11]

Engels was arguably more interested than Virchow in assigning culpability for these outcomes. He addressed not simply the causes of the devastation and misery he observed, but the social and political structures that he viewed as responsible. In this formulation, Engels presaged the modern British epidemiologist Sir Geoffrey Rose, who urged scientists and physicians to examine not just the causes of disease, but "the causes of the causes."[12] Engels deemed the collective morally responsible for erecting, sustaining, and fueling socioeconomic frameworks that to his mind caused the destruction he witnessed.

Similarly, Virchow pointed out that the harmful conditions in which Silesians lived and worked was the primary factor in determining their susceptibility to typhus.[13] Thus, like Engels, Virchow admonished against the tendency to assign the highest priority in helping the miners to the provision of acute medical care.[14] As a physician, Virchow understood the significance of caring for the sick, but he emphasized that the eradication and prevention of typhus could only be achieved by improving the socioeconomic conditions in which the Silesian miners worked and lived.[15]

It is these two commonalities—focus on socioeconomic conditions as causes of disease and attention to the unequal distribution of those outcomes—that arguably comprise Engels and Virchow's most critical contribution to modern public health. The thesis of this chapter draws on Engels and Virchow's observation regarding the role that laws and policies play in shaping and sustaining the sociolegal structures that

---

[8] *Id.* at 203–41.

[9] *Id.*

[10] *See* SZRETER, *supra* note 7, at 98–145; GERALD GROB, THE DEADLY TRUTH: A HISTORY OF DISEASE IN AMERICA 200–09 (2002).

[11] *See* Taylor & Rieger, *supra* note 4.

[12] GEOFFREY ROSE, THE STRATEGY OF PREVENTIVE MEDICINE (1992); Geoffrey Rose, *Sick Individuals and Sick Populations*, 14 INT. J. EPID. 32 (1985).

[13] Taylor & Rieger, *supra* note 4, at 550.

[14] *Id.* at 554 ("[Virchow] also insisted that medical intervention was insufficient ... real solutions required basic social change.").

[15] *Id.*

determine health and inequalities. In extending these issues to the globalization of health, there is ample evidence that myriad features of international political economies determine health both across the international political order as well as within different nations and regions. Thus, in Section I, I specifically analyze the extent to which laws and policies act as social determinants of global health. I argue that these structures shape health and its distribution both horizontally within individual polities and vertically across the international political order. However, although the sociolegal variables that determine health may be common to both the global North and the global South, I argue in Section II that the relative causal contributions are not equally distributed across the same axes. The idea that the developed world bears a much larger responsibility for laws, policies, and governance structures that create or intensify deleterious socioeconomic conditions has significant ethical implications, analysis of which is the subject of Section III. In Section III, I utilize Powers and Faden's model of social justice as an ethical framework for conceptualizing global health priorities.[16]

The normative claims developed in Section III embody the two central points emanating from Engels and Virchow's works: first, that a just social order must differentiate between health and health care and assess the relative significance of each; and second, that legal, political, and governance structures are primary factors in producing the socioeconomic conditions that substantially determine health and inequalities across the globe.

Before proceeding, it is important to note that time and space preclude extensive documentation here of the fact that social and economic conditions are the prime determinants of health and its distribution across the globe. Fortunately, this position enjoys virtually ubiquitous support, the most notable recent compilation of which exists in the 2008 Final Report of the World Health Organization's Commission on Social Determinants of Health (CSDH). The Report documented at length the ways in which social, economic, and political conditions powerfully determine health both in the global North and the global South.[17] Moreover, among the various conditions that shape the distribution of global health, there is similarly widespread if not uniform support for the idea that access to medical care is a *relatively minor* determinant. As the CSDH puts it:

> Traditionally, societies have looked to the health sector to deal with its concerns about health and disease. Certainly, maldistribution of health care ... is one of the social determinants of health. But the high burden of illness responsible for appalling premature loss of life arises in large part because of the conditions in

[16] MADISON POWERS & RUTH FADEN, SOCIAL JUSTICE: THE MORAL FOUNDATIONS OF PUBLIC HEALTH AND HEALTH POLICY (2006).

[17] World Health Organization Commission on the Social Determinants of Health, *Closing the Gap in a Generation: Health Equity through Action on the Social Determinants of Health* (2008), *available at* http://www.who.int/social_determinants/thecommission/finalreport/en/index.html.

which people are born, grow, live, work, and age—conditions that together provide the freedom people need to live lives they value.[18]

With this distinction between global health and global health care in mind, a population-level approach to global health requires stakeholders to direct their attention to the fundamental causes of disease,[19] the upstream conditions that determine health and its distribution in populations. They include factors such as:

- Socioeconomic status
- Education
- Occupation
- Housing
- Neighborhood
- Race/Ethnicity
- Gender
- Age
- Violence
- Stigmatization/Discrimination

And yet, there is one set of factors that acts as a critical mediator of these upstream determinants, one so significant that it has been recognized in its own right as a powerful social determinant of health (SDOH). This mediator is law, and Section I addresses the idea that law is itself a social determinant of global health.

I. Law as a Social Determinant of Global Health

There is a temptation to view laws and policies as mere channels through which upstream determinants of health flow.[20] This conception is flawed because of the increasing evidence that law and policy are not inert substrate, but are themselves determinants of a number of clinically relevant health outcomes. Global health law and policy therefore do not so much channel as create and institutionalize determinants of health.

Moreover, as I will argue, law and policy are a determinant of health that is common to both developing and developed world communities. This is not to assert that

---

[18] *Id.* at 26 (citations omitted); *see also* Steven H. Woolf et al., *Giving Everyone the Health of the Educated: An Examination of Whether Social Change Would Save More Lives Than Medical Advances*, 97 AM. J. PUB. HEALTH 679 (2007); Theodore Pincus et al., *Social Conditions and Self-Management Are More Powerful Determinants of Health Than Access to Care*, 129 ANNALS INT. MED. 406 (1998).

[19] Bruce G. Link & Jo C. Phelan, *Social Conditions as Fundamental Causes of Disease*, 35 J. HEALTH & SOC. BEHAV. (SPECIAL ISSUE) 80 (1995).

[20] *See* Scott Burris, *From Health Care Law to the Social Determinants of Health: A Public Health Research Perspective* (Temple University Legal Studies, Working Paper No. 2011–15, 2011), *available at* http://ssrn.com/abstract=1761425; Scott Burris et al., *Integrating Law and Social Epidemiology*, 30 J. L. MED. & ETHICS 510, 511 (2002).

identical laws and policies determine health in different cultural contexts, but rather that governance structures, law and policy per se determines health in both the developed and the developing world. Thus, my argument is that whatever matters to global health will be fundamentally shaped by prior, current, and contemplated laws and policies.

To understand the ways in which law and policy shapes health, an expansive conception is essential. As legal pragmatists have observed, "the law" is the name of a practice.[21] Because there are an enormous variety of actors and processes that shape laws and policies that are not captured by the cold record of positive law, the law is not reducible to such an entity. For example, private stakeholders play an immense role in shaping regulatory regimes, from priority setting to influencing specific rules and regulations.[22] This suggests that mere analysis of rules and regulations themselves is insufficient to generate a sophisticated comprehension of the many actors and processes that converge to shape regulatory policy.

Here are a few of a huge number of examples by which laws and policies determine health and its distribution: (1) There were over 30,000 fatal automobile accidents in the United States in 2009; laws and policies regulating access to public transit unquestionably have the power to raise or lower this number, both in absolute terms and in its relative distribution within populations.[23] (2) Occupational exposures are risk factors for a variety of injury and illness experiences; laws and policies regulating occupational health have significant power in determining the extent and distribution of such outcomes.[24] (3) Laws and policies governing the allocation of resources to early childhood development are likely to have a substantial impact on health and its distribution, given that such development's health effects are significant.[25] (4) Income levels are robustly correlated with health and its distribution, which implies that laws and

---

[21] *See* Richard Posner, *The Jurisprudence of Skepticism*, 86 MICH. L. REV. 827, 881 (1988) ("The law is not a thing [judges] discover. It is the name of their activity."); John Dewey, *Logical Method and Law*, 10 CORNELL L. Q. 17 (1914); WILLIAM JAMES, PRAGMATISM 92–93 (Dover Publications 1995) (1907); *accord* Daniel S. Goldberg, *It Does Not Mean What You Think It Means: How Kripke and Wittgenstein's Analysis on Rule Following Undermines Justice Scalia's Textualism and Originalism*, 54 CLEV. ST. L. REV. 273 (2006).

[22] *See, e.g.*, Michael P. Vandenbergh, *The Private Life of Public Law*, 105 COLUM. L. REV. 2029 (2005); Colin Scott, *Private Regulation of the Public Sector: A Neglected Facet of Contemporary Governance*, 29 J. L. & SOC. 56 (2002); Jody Freeman, *The Private Role in Public Governance*, 75 N.Y.U. L. REV. 543 (2000).

[23] Nat'l Highway Traffic Safety Admin., Fatality Analysis Reporting System (2009), http://www-fars. nhtsa.dot.gov/Main/index.aspx; Ana M. Novoa et al., *Road Safety in the Political Agenda: The Impact on Road Traffic Injuries*, 65 J. EPIDEMIOLOGY & CMTY. HEALTH 218 (2011); David S. Morrison et al., *Evaluation of the Health Effects of a Neighborhood Traffic Calming Scheme*, 58 J. EPIDEMIOLOGY & CMTY. HEALTH 837 (2004).

[24] *See, e.g.*, DAVID ROSNER & GERALD MARKOWITZ, DEADLY DUST: SILICOSIS AND THE ONGOING STRUGGLE TO PROTECT WORKERS' HEALTH (revised & expanded ed. 2006); ALAN DERICKSON, BLACK LUNG: ANATOMY OF A PUBLIC HEALTH DISASTER (1998).

[25] *See, e.g.*, Dennis Raphael, *Poverty in Childhood and Adverse Health Outcomes in Adulthood*, 69 MATURITAS 22 (2011); Lori G. Irwin et al., *Early Childhood Development: A Powerful Equalizer: Final Report for the World Health Organization's Commission on the Social Determinants of Health* (2007), *available at* http:// whqlibdoc.who.int/hq/2007/a91213.pdf.

policies that regulate (re)distribution of income could have powerful health effects. (5) Stigmatization and discrimination are independent SDOH; even after controlling for almost every conceivable confounder, the stress caused by living with daily stigma and discrimination seems to result in worse health.[26] Unsurprisingly, then, antidiscrimination laws in the arena of HIV/AIDS have had a documented effect in lessening the crushing and inequitable burdens of HIV/AIDS stigma.[27]

Indeed, the ways in which laws and policies determine health are so plentiful that this has given birth to what is known as the boundary problem in public health law (i.e., that virtually any conceivable law or policy can fairly be designated as within the ambit of public health).[28] Because the boundaries of public health law are correlated quite strongly with the boundaries of state power,[29] a broad conception of public health may result in a dangerously vast model of state power.[30] The key here is to recognize that the boundary problem in public health law exists precisely because the connections between law and policy and public/population health are extensive.[31]

In their 1840s tracts, both Engels and Virchow grasped the basic fact that law and policy and its absence structures health and its distribution in critical ways. But as noted above, Engels was particularly interested in *who* was responsible for the laws and policies he deemed so iniquitous. In this, Engels presaged the legal pragmatists' insistence on viewing the law as a social endeavor. If contemporary scholars take the pragmatists seriously in this regard, then we should follow Engels and reflect seriously on the agency behind the laws and policies that determine health and its highly inequitable distributions across and within the international political order.

Such an assignment pushes us to recognize that laws, policies, and governance structures do not simply exist in a vacuum. This is part of what it means to take seriously the connections between history and global health policy: global health problems look the way they do precisely because of past events, attitudes, practices, and

---

[26] *See* Nancy Krieger, *Does Racism Harm Health? Did Child Abuse Exist before 1962? On Explicit Questions, Critical Science, and Current Controversies: An Ecosocial Perspective*, 93 AM. J. PUB. HEALTH 194 (2003); Nancy Krieger & S. Sidney, *Racial Discrimination and Blood Pressure: The CARDIA Study of Young Black and White Adults*, 86 AM. J. PUB. HEALTH 1370 (1996).

[27] *See* U.S. Dept. Health & Human Services Health Resources & Services Admin., *Stigma and HIV/AIDS: A Review of the Literature* (Deborah L. Brimlow et al. eds., 2003), Gregory M. Herek et al., *HIV-Related Stigma and Knowledge in the United States: Prevalence and Trends 1991–1999*, 92 AM. J. PUB. HEALTH 371 (2002).

[28] *See* LAWRENCE O. GOSTIN, PUBLIC HEALTH LAW: POWER, DUTY, RESTRAINT 38–43 (2d ed. 2008); Mark A. Rothstein, *Rethinking the Meaning of Public Health*, 30 J.L. MED. & ETHICS 144 (2002).

[29] *See* GOSTIN, *supra* note 28; Rothstein, *supra* note 28.

[30] *See* GOSTIN, *supra* note 28.

[31] The similarities and differences between "public health" and "population health" is an important conceptual issue that is beyond the scope of this chapter. Nevertheless, I commit to Evans and Stoddart's definition of population health: "the health outcomes of a group of individuals, including the distribution of outcomes within the group." David Kindig & Greg Stoddart, *What Is Population Health?*, 93(3) AM. J. PUB. HEALTH 380, 381 (2003). This definition has the advantage of centering distributional concerns in the very idea of population health.

beliefs. Because Szreter has been at the vanguard of linking history and contemporary health policy, it is worth returning briefly to his theory of the four Ds.[32] Understanding this framework lays the groundwork for the question of agency that occupied Engels, which I submit is critical to thinking about global health.

II. Agency, Law, and Global Health

Szreter's work is critical insofar as it provides a window into understanding the relationship between rapid economic development, population health, and inequalities. Because this relationship is in turn critical to thinking about global health ethics and policy, the significance of Szreter's findings go far beyond nineteenth-century Britain. Szreter argues that the widely held conception that economic development inexorably leads to improved population health is vastly oversimplified.[33] Although it is likely accurate over the long-term, it is demonstrably untrue when such development is rapid.[34] Such development, Szreter argues, follows a pathway marked by the four Ds: disruption, deprivation, disease, and death.[35]

The important point in thinking about law and policy as determinants of global health is that the primary tool Szreter identifies as adequate to break the links between the four Ds is collective action in the form of social policy.[36] For example, a variety of factors converged to spark largely municipal action that resulted in the implementation of a number of public health policies and endeavors in mid–nineteenth-century Britain. Szreter emphasizes that the terrible morbidities and mortalities of the time were a function neither of insufficient understanding of disease causality nor of inadequate technical capacity, but rather reflected sociopolitical obstacles that impeded the enactment of sufficient responses:

> Although the germ theory of disease had not yet been developed, this society had adequate knowledge and practical capacity to protect itself against the worst hazards of dense and crowded urban living ... while the appropriate technology for water provision and for arterial sewering was well understood by the 1840s at the latest, it was the debilitating sociopolitical divisions, and their eventual resolution from the 1870s onward, that critically influenced the delay in provision of this vital public health resource.[37]

Szreter's work therefore emphasizes the social and human nature of laws and policies. If it is laws and policies that determine health, then it is social structures and organizations themselves that determine health and its distribution. Thus, Szreter's

---

[32] SZRETER, *supra* note 7, at 203–41.

[33] *Id.*

[34] *Id.*

[35] *Id.*

[36] *Id.*

[37] *Id.* at 220.

terminology is important in labeling this nineteenth-century British collective action: the polity, he says, "opted in."[38]

Furthermore, if the evidence that law and policy are critical determinants of health is overwhelming, so too is the evidence that the agency for such laws and policies is not distributed equally across the international political order. As Thomas Pogge puts it, "[g]lobal economic institutions reflect the highly uneven bargaining power of the participating countries and thus tend to reinforce and to aggravate economic inequality."[39]

Amartya Sen noted in *Poverty and Famines* that differing governance structures explained why closely neighboring regions in Sub-Saharan Africa sustained very different experiences in response to food insecurity and environmental pressures.[40] Similarly, Vicente Navarro observes that although the largest public health problem on the planet is famine, "[e]ven countries where the majority of people are hungry have enough productive land to feed their populations many times over."[41] This is true in one of the poorest countries in the world, Bangladesh, in which the wealthiest 16 percent of the population control almost 70 percent of the arable land—such control is obviously enabled and sustained by the legal, political, and class structures that are created, sustained, and enforced according to power relations.[42]

Paul Farmer's work on the role of international political economies in causing abject destitution in Haiti is compelling here.[43] In *Pathologies of Power*, Farmer relates the narrative of Acéphie Joseph, a Haitian woman who died of HIV/AIDS in 1991. Yet Farmer cautions that understanding the cause of her death as HIV is a cramped conception; her illness "was merely the latest in a string of tragedies that she and her parents readily linked together in a long lamentation."[44] Joseph's family had been farmers for generations near the village of Kay in the Artibonite River Valley.[45] In 1956, the Haitian government, with support and planning from the United States, erected the largest dam in Haiti near Kay.[46] After 1956, the Josephs' land lay buried at the bottom of the newly created lake, and Acéphie Joseph's parents "built a miserable lean-to on a knoll of high land jutting into the reservoir."[47] The extreme lack of opportunities and resources

---

[38] *Id.* at 356–59.

[39] Thomas Pogge, *Relational Conceptions of Justice: Responsibilities for Health Outcomes, in* PUBLIC HEALTH, ETHICS, AND EQUITY 139 (Sudhir Anand et al. eds., 2002).

[40] AMARTYA SEN, POVERTY AND FAMINES: AN ESSAY ON ENTITLEMENT AND DEPRIVATION 86–130 (1983); see also JEAN DRÈZE AND AMARTYA SEN, HUNGER AND PUBLIC ACTION (1989). In SRIDHAR VENKATAPURAM, HEALTH JUSTICE: AN ARGUMENT FROM THE CAPABILITIES APPROACH (2011), the author argues that Drèze and Sen's analysis on famine and entitlements is critical to a concept of health justice based on the capabilities approach.

[41] Vicente Navarro, *The World Health Situation, in* NEOLIBERALISM, GLOBALIZATION, AND INEQUALITIES 203 (Vicente Navarro ed., 2007).

[42] *Id.*

[43] PAUL FARMER, PATHOLOGIES OF POWER: HEALTH, HUMAN RIGHTS, AND THE NEW WAR ON THE POOR (2005).

[44] *Id.* at 32.

[45] *Id.*

[46] *Id.*

[47] *Id.* at 33.

prompted Joseph to flee to Port-Au-Prince, where she died, but not before giving birth to a HIV-positive daughter.[48] Shortly after she died, Joseph's father hanged himself.[49]

It is important to consider Joseph's illness narrative through Rose's formulation of the causes of the causes.[50] The destitution and misery that framed the range of options available to Acéphie Joseph were directly tied to the Josephs' struggle for subsistence. This struggle was driven much closer to the precipice by the intentional flooding of the Artibonite River Valley. Hence the devastating socioeconomic conditions the Josephs faced was in an important sense caused by the policy decision of the Haitian government, with support and backing from the United States, to build a dam and flood the village of Kay.

A similar narrative is evident in the experience of the Pima Indians, an Indian community centered in southern Arizona that features the highest prevalence of type II diabetes in the world, as well as high rates of substance abuse, suicide, and poverty.[51] Although scientific investigators have doggedly pursued genetic explanations,[52] the causes of the causes are almost certainly sociopolitical structures that disintegrated a way of life the Pima had cultivated for centuries. As documented in *Unnatural Causes*, the Pima depended in countless ways on the water of the Gila River and the fertile soil of the valley.[53] White settlers implemented a series of policies and programs that diverted the Gila River upstream to white communities.[54]

Given Szreter's framework, it is unsurprising that the disruption forced upon the Pima led to deprivation, and thence to disease, starvation, and death. The U.S. government began providing basic foodstuffs—white flour, lard, processed cheese, canned

---

[48] *Id.* at 35.

[49] *Id.*

[50] *See* ROSE, *supra* note 12.

[51] *See* National Institute of Diabetes and Digestive and Kidney Diseases, *The Pima Indians: Pathfinders for Health*, http://diabetes.niddk.nih.gov/dm/pubs/pima/index.htm (last visited Nov. 29, 2011); CAROLYN M. SMITH-MORRIS, DIABETES AMONG THE PIMA: STORIES OF SURVIVAL (2006); Carolyn M. Smith-Morris, *Diagnostic Controversy: Gestational Diabetes and the Meaning of Risk for Pima Indian Women*, 24 MED. ANTHRO. 145 (2005). The name of the tribe in the indigenous language is the Akimel O'odham. Spanish explorers gave the tribe the name "Pima," which has been reclaimed by the tribe itself. Fifty-two percent of the Gila River Indian Community lives below 100 percent of the federal poverty level, and 79.8 percent lives below 200 percent of the federal poverty level. *See* Arizona Department Health Services Bureau of Health Systems Development., *Gila River Indian Community Primary Care Area: Statistical Profile 2009* (2010), http://www.azdhs.gov/hsd/profiles/21121.pdf.

[52] *See, e.g.*, National Institute of Diabetes, *supra* note 51; William C. Knowler et al., *Diabetes Mellitus in the Pima Indians: Genetic and Evolutionary Considerations*, 62 AM. J. PHYS. ANTHRO. 107 (1983). For criticism of a molecular approach to understanding the prevalence of type II diabetes among historically marginalized ethnic/minority groups, see UNNATURAL CAUSES (California Newsreel Productions 2008); Yin Paradies et al., *Racialized Genetics and the Study of Complex Diseases: The Thrifty Genotype Revisited*, 50 PERSP. BIO. & MED. 203 (2007); *see also* Claudia Chaufan & Rose Weitz, *The Elephant in the Room: The Invisibility of Poverty in Research on Type 2 Diabetes*, 33 HUM. & SOC. 74 (2009); Daniel S. Goldberg, *Population Health, Ethics, & Genetic vs. Social Causes of Disease: Matters of Relative Priority in Public Health Policy*, EÄ, J. MED. HUMS. & SOC. STUD. SCI. & TECH., Aug. 2011, http://www.ea-journal.com/art3.1/Goldberg-Population-health.pdf.

[53] UNNATURAL CAUSES, *supra* note 52.

[54] *Id.*

foods, and oil—to the Pima.[55] However, these bore no resemblance to the traditional Pima diet of beans, vegetables, and wild game.[56] The connection between this diet and chronic illness is obvious, but its effects on Pima health go beyond fats and sugars. Given the powerful and important connections between food and a community's way of life, the destruction of the Pima's traditional diet contributed to the erosion of the Pima's social cohesion, a phenomenon that is robustly correlated with health and its distribution.[57] Lower social cohesion is also linked to substance abuse and violence,[58] two other problems that are highly prevalent among American Indian communities in the southwestern United States.[59]

One of the leading causes of death for Pima Indians is diabetic nephropathy.[60] But the cause of the cause is the disintegration of the Pima's way of life that centered on the Gila River. In turn, the diversion of the life-giving water was accomplished by legal and political mechanisms devised by white settlers in southern Arizona during the late nineteenth–early twentieth centuries. Ultimately, the laws and policies that destroyed the Pima's traditional diet and eroded their social cohesion is a significant determinant of the mortality rate for the Pima that is 1.9 times higher than the U.S. mortality rate across all races.[61]

Similarly, several scholars track Engels's focus on identifying the agents of the legal and political structures that determine health and its global distribution. Birn cites Engels's notion of social murder and argues that the CSDH Report fails to address "historical debates over the existence, tracking, meaning, and addressing of inequities in health ... In avoiding historical contextualization, [the report] misses the chance to trace the lines of accountability for the killing fields and the factories of social injustice."[62] Ultimately,

---

[55] *Id.*

[56] *Id.*

[57] *See, e.g.,* RICHARD G. WILKINSON & KATHERINE PICKETT, THE SPIRIT LEVEL: WHY GREATER EQUALITY MAKES SOCIETIES STRONGER (2009); ICHIRO KAWACHI & BRUCE KENNEDY, THE HEALTH OF NATIONS: WHY INEQUALITY IS HARMFUL TO YOUR HEALTH (2002); J. Lynch et al., *Social Capital—Is It a Good Investment Strategy for Public Health?* 54 J. EPIDEMIOLOGY & CMTY. HEALTH 404 (2000).

[58] *See, e.g.,* Sandro Galea et al., *The Social Epidemiology of Substance Use,* 26 EPIDEMIOLOGIC REVS. 36 (2004); Steven F. Messner, Eric P. Baumer & Richard Rosenfeld, *Dimensions of Social Capital and Rates of Criminal Homicide,* 69 AM. SOC. REV. 882 (2004); Sandro Galea et al., *Social Capital and Violence in the United States 1974–1993,* 55 SOC. SCI. & MED. 1373 (2002).

[59] *See* Daniel L. Dickerson & Carrie L. Johnson, *Mental Health and Substance Abuse Characteristics among a Clinical Sample of Urban American Indian/Alaska Native Youths in a Large California Metropolitan Area: a Descriptive Study,* 46 CMTY. MENTAL HEALTH J. (forthcoming 2012). The Indian Health Service reported that the 2003 age-adjusted alcohol-related death rate for American Indians/Alaska Natives is 43.7/100,000, which is over six times the U.S. All Races rate of 7.0. Indian Health Service, *Trends in Indian Health 2002–2003* 54, 61, 90 (2005), http://www.ihs.gov/nonmedicalprograms/ihs_stats/index. cfm?module=hqPubTrends03#p4. The same report noted that the rate of homicide among American Indians/Alaska Natives was 11.8/100,000, which is two times higher than the U.S. All Races rate of 6.0/100,000. *Id.* at 78.

[60] Maurice L. Sievers et al., *Impact of NIDDM on Mortality and Causes of Death in Pima Indians,* 15 DIABETES CARE 1541 (1992).

[61] *See* Indian Health Service, *supra* note 59.

[62] Anne-Emanuelle Birn, *Making It Politic(al): Closing the Gap in a Generation: Health Equity through Action on the Social Determinants of Health,* 4 SOC. MED. 166, 169 (2009).

Birn concludes, tne CSDH Report "calls for fairness, participation, and protection ... without naming who and what are the forces and institutions creating and perpetuating inequitable conditions in the first place."[63]

Navarro is even more explicit: "It is not inequalities that kill, but those who benefit from the inequalities that kill."[64] If international political economies shape the structures that in turn determine global health and its distribution across the globe, culpability cannot be denied. It is political actors, past and present, who constitute what Birn terms the "*causes* of the causes of the causes."[65]

However, it does not follow that culpability for these international political economies is equally distributed across the globe. Although Haiti won its independence from France in 1803, the fledgling nation faced serious risk of a French invasion and the restoration of slavery in 1825.[66] In exchange for French recognition, the Haitian government agreed to an indemnity of 150 million francs as well as a 50 percent reduction in excise taxes.[67] This staggering debt set Haiti on the path to penury and destitution, and debt "repayments" continued for 122 years, until 1947.[68] Such history is hardly the only reason for Haiti's struggles, but there is little doubt that it played an enormous role in determining the deprivation, disease, and death that the story of Acéphie Joseph typifies.[69]

If it is the case that international political economies are the primary determinants of global health, then the actors, agents, and institutions that constitute the primary engines of those economies bear collective responsibility for those determinants. As Pogge puts it: "By avoidably producing severe poverty, economic institutions substantially contribute to the incidence of many medical conditions. Persons materially involved in upholding such economic institutions are then materially involved in the causation of such medical conditions."[70] This is not to suggest that any individual actor bears the total quantum of such responsibility; by itself, such an argument perpetuates the fallacy of division. The assessment of responsibility is collective because the structures that determine population and ultimately global health are macrosocial.[71] Individual attitudes, practices, and beliefs constitute this collective in morally significant ways,[72] but the normative assessment cannot neatly move from the social to the individual without significant distortion. Engels accused British society of *social murder*.

---

[63] *Id.* at 172.

[64] Vicente Navarro, *What We Mean by the Social Determinants of Health*, 39 INT. J. HEALTH SERVS. 423, 440 (2009).

[65] Birn, *supra* note 62, at 172 (emphasis in original).

[66] *See* Paul Farmer, *Who Removed Aristide?*, LONDON REV. BOOKS 28 (Apr. 2004).

[67] *Id.*

[68] *Id.*

[69] *Id.*

[70] Pogge, *supra* note 39, at 137.

[71] *See* Sandro Galea & Sara Putnam, *The Role of Macrosocial Determinants in Shaping the Health of Populations*, in MACROSOCIAL DETERMINANTS OF POPULATION HEALTH 1, 3–14 (Sandro Galea ed., 2007).

[72] *See* Pogge, *supra* note 39, at 136.

The argument thus is first that international political economies shape the socio-political structures that constitute the prime determinants of global health and its distribution. Second, the developed and the developing world do not bear equal responsibility for these structures and the grievous inequities that result. This is not to deny responsibility to political actors in the global South. Even the terrible postcolonial legacies that the developed world has left the developing world do not excuse the transgressions of the Duvalier, Taylor, and Mugabe regimes, for example. As such, Navarro argues that the real issue is the ways in which power is concentrated in class structures within both the global North and the global South: "underdevelopment is rooted not only in international power relations but also in the power relations within the developing countries"[73] However, even these intranational power relations escape the significant influence of the developed world. In Pogge's words,

> [i]t is quite true ... that local economic institutions, and local factors more generally play an important role in the reproduction of extreme poverty in the developing world. But this fact does not show that social institutions we are materially involved in upholding play no substantial role. That the effects of flawed domestic institutions and policies are as bad as they are is often due to global institutions—to the institution of the territorial state, for instance, which allows affluent populations to prevent the poor from migrating to where their work could earn a decent living.[74]

As another example, Pogge cites the fact that global institutions grant authority in developing countries "to borrow in the name of its people and to confer legal ownership rights in the country's resources"[75] to those who obtain power in those countries. In so doing, "our global institutional order greatly encourages the undemocratic acquisition and exercise of political power especially in the resource-rich developing countries."[76]

In any event, whether one deems the global North as more or less culpable in creating and sustaining international political economies that determine health across the globe, the fact that the global North bears some nontrivial quantum of agency generates significant normative implications.

III. Social Justice and Relative Priority in Global Health Policy

In thinking about social justice and global health, it is imperative to chart the treacherous course between too little ethical theory and too much. The former is a danger because moving directly from descriptive epidemiologic evidence to normative

---

[73] Navarro, *supra* note 41, at 208; *see also* Navarro, *supra* note 64, at 427–28.
[74] Pogge, *supra* note 39, at 139.
[75] *Id.* at 140.
[76] *Id.*

conclusions perpetrates the naturalistic fallacy; the mere fact that the world is a certain way does not as such demonstrate the way the world ought to be. As staggering as they may be, the facts regarding global inequalities do not by themselves indicate which of those inequalities are unjust. Hence it becomes critical to differentiate between ethically tolerable and ethically intolerable global inequalities. Moreover, even if *all* global inequalities are deemed unjust, assessments of the relative priority of potential policy interventions—that is, which inequalities are most significant—do not automatically follow from the fact of global health inequalities. Illuminating directions for resolving these problems seems like a task for which rigorous ethical argument is well-suited.[77]

However, too much ethical theory is also a problem because, as necessary as clear thinking about social justice and health equity may be, intricate philosophical debates on whether modified versions of prioritarianism are preferable to strict egalitarianism are not and should not be a prerequisite to collective action. Larry Churchill's criticisms of American bioethics is relevant:

> Bioethical disputes ... often seem to be remote from the values of ordinary people and largely irrelevant to the decisions they encounter in health care. In this sense, philosophical theorizing might be considered harmless entertainment, which if taken too seriously would look ridiculous ....[78]

There is no particular reason for doubting that bioethical discourse on global health could track this general pattern.[79] There is sufficient agreement on the links between inequalities and global health to justify immediate action on a panoply of public policy interventions, even if philosophical questions of justice and equity remain open. Moreover, given that there is little evidence that intense scholarly debates in moral philosophy have influence on public policy, the writer concerned with the pragmatics of global health policy in the nonideal world has justification for avoiding dwelling completely in the house of such debates.

Thus, in this section, I chart a Goldilocks course between too little theory and too much. For a variety of reasons, Powers and Faden's account of social justice is important in making sense of the evidence discussed thus far and in generating public policy recommendations regarding global health and its determinants. First, Powers and Faden expressly link their model of social justice to public health policy, which may militate against the threat of too much theory.[80] Indeed, Powers and Faden argue that

---

[77] There is an abundance of excellent work on this topic; *see, e.g.*, VENKATAPURAM, *supra* note 40; JENNIFER PRAH RUGER, HEALTH AND SOCIAL JUSTICE (2010); NORMAN DANIELS, JUST HEALTH: MEETING HEALTH NEEDS FAIRLY (2008); PUBLIC HEALTH, ETHICS, AND EQUITY (Sudhir Anand et al. eds., 2002).

[78] Larry Churchill, *Are We Professionals? A Critical Look at the Social Role of Bioethicists*, DAEDALUS 253, 255 (Fall 1999).

[79] Indeed, even bioethics discourse in the developing world has come under fire for devoting too much attention to clinical and research ethics as opposed to public health ethics. *See* Jacquineau Azetsop, *New Directions in African Bioethics: Ways of Including Public Health Concerns in the Bioethics Agenda*, 11 DEV. WORLD BIOETHICS 4 (2011).

[80] POWERS & FADEN, *supra* note 16, at 7–10.

philosophical accounts of justice may underdetermine action guidance in terms of public policy.[81] Even after considerations of justice have been exhausted, they contend, multiple permutations of policies and priorities will remain possible.[82] Thus they characterize their model as a "nonideal theory that is concerned with the totality of the social structure having a profound and pervasive effect on the essential dimensions of well-being."[83]

This nonideal theory has particular relevance because resources are scarce, a fact that highlights the significance of relative priority in global health policy. Relative priority eschews the false choice fallacy and acknowledges that there are many ethically legitimate, noncontradictory goals of global health policy. That is, it is not the case that stakeholders must pursue policies regarding income equality and environmental exposures to the exclusion of policies regarding access to essential medicines and key medical infrastructure. All of these policies, and many others, are legitimate health priorities. But policy is inevitably contested space, and there is always an opportunity cost to expending any time and resources on any particular policy issue.[84]

Thus, a framework of relative priority requires moral agents to consider which of a bundle of policy options—all of which should be supported—ought to be prioritized relative to the other options. A similar idea seems central to Pogge's model of relational justice: "[T]here may be a competition among *judicanda*—one may have responsibilities with regard to achieving and maintaining the justice of several *judicanda* and may then have to decide how much of an effort one ought to make with regard to each."[85] Pogge further implies that the concept of relative priority is critical for pragmatic ends: "[I]ssues concerning responsibilities and their prioritization are crucial for giving justice a determinate role in the real world."[86]

Second, Powers and Faden's account of social justice is erected on the implications of the relevant social epidemiologic evidence base. Accordingly, the model is generally appreciative of the need to distinguish between health and health care. Powers and Faden expressly point out that "[a]lthough the limited role of medical care in explaining inequities in health status and life expectancy is widely recognized, this profound finding has received inadequate commentary in the bioethics literature."[87]

Third, Powers and Faden's account in conceptualizing global health provides a basis for distinguishing between just and unjust inequalities. They emphasize the fact that social disadvantage accumulates.[88] Because deleterious socioeconomic conditions tend

---

[81] *Id.* at 142–44.

[82] *Id.* at 143.

[83] *Id.* at 57.

[84] *See* Daniel S. Goldberg, *Universal Health Care, American Pragmatism, and the Ethics of Health Policy: Questioning Political Efficacy*, 7 Pierce L. Rev. 183 (2009); Deborah Stone, Policy Paradox: The Art of Political Decision-Making (rev. ed. 2002).

[85] Pogge, *supra* note 39, at 146.

[86] *Id.*

[87] Powers & Faden, *supra* note 16, at x.

[88] *Id.* at 7–9; *see also* Jonathan Wolff and Avner de-Shalit, Disadvantage (2007).

to beget other deleterious socioeconomic conditions,[89] those groups existing on the tail of the social gradient are more likely to stay in their current position or fall even lower on the social ladder:

> Some who fare worse than others, often in multiple respects, are members of groups who are socially situated within densely woven patterns of disadvantage … Inequalities of one kind beget inequalities of another, and over the course of a lifetime … the compounding of disadvantage makes avoidance or escape difficult without heroic effort or unexpected good luck.[90]

Moreover, disadvantage and its effects on health have intergenerational effects, which is one reason thinking about population health requires a life course perspective in which the effects of socioeconomic conditions are conceptualized across *multiple* life spans.[91] The critical facts that social disadvantages cluster and that health outcomes are robustly correlated with these disadvantages grounds Powers and Faden's answer for the critical questions of justice and inequalities highlighted in this section: "Which inequalities matter most? The answer we propose is that inequalities that contribute to systematic patterns of disadvantage are the ones that matter most."[92] Thus, under Powers and Faden's account, social inequalities that perpetuate the "densely woven patterns of disadvantage" are unjust, and even among other unjust inequalities, they are of highest ethical priority.[93]

Applying this framework to global health policy produces significant implications. A number of social inequalities contribute larger effects to expanding/contracting patterns of disadvantage than access to health care services. Indeed, there is a burgeoning litera-ture suggesting that novel health technologies can expand health inequalities even where they improve overall population health. Accordingly, Capewell and Graham argue that "whole population approaches," which utilize interventions intended to address upstream and macrosocial determinants of health across and within the whole population, are pref-erable to approaches that direct interventions to groups identified as high risk.[94]

Although it is true that access to health care services is a social determinant of health, the evidence supports Lantz PM, Lichtenstein RL, and Pollack's HA. warning against the medicalization of health policy: lack of access to health care services is sim-ply "not the fundamental cause of health vulnerability or social disparities in health."[95] Social inequalities are much more significant in structuring densely woven patterns

---

[89] POWERS & FADEN, *supra* note 16, 7–9.

[90] *Id.* at 193.

[91] *See, e.g.,* Neal Halfon & Miles Hochstein, *Life Course Health Development: An Integrated Framework for Developing Health, Policy, and Research,* 80 MILBANK MEMORIAL FUND Q. 433 (2002).

[92] POWERS & FADEN, *supra* note 16, at 193.

[93] *Id.*

[94] Simon Capewell & Hilary Graham, *Will Cardiovascular Disease Prevention Widen Health Inequalities?,* PLoS MED. e1000320 (Aug. 2010), http://www.plosmedicine.org/article/info:doi/10.1371/journal.pmed.1000320.

[95] Paula M. Lantz et al., *Health Policy Approaches to Population Health: The Limits of Medicalization,* 26 HEALTH AFF. 1253, 1256 (2007).

of disadvantage, the amelioration of which is therefore the highest ethical priority for global health. Moreover, because the developed world bears greater culpability for the international political economies that determine global health, it is the developed world's moral responsibility to spearhead policies and practices that prioritize amelioration of the structural determinants of global health.

What might such policies look like on the global scale? First, policies regarding access to "magic bullet" therapies would assume a lower priority relative to interventions that reflect whole population approaches. Navarro considers one of the acclaimed victories of the former—the eradication of smallpox—and argues that it is "a mixed achievement, since its success has inspired many other technical silver-bullet-type solutions that degrade rather than improve countries' public health situations."[96]

Second, approaches that target macrosocial determinants of health should be afforded higher priority than approaches that direct resources to high-risk populations. Examples of such policies are not difficult to find; notwithstanding the lacunae left in the CSDH Report, many of the policy recommendations there suggest good starting points. For example, there is little debate regarding the singular importance of very early childhood for health and inequalities across the life span. Accordingly, this is an obvious policy priority.[97] Other recommendations issued by the CSDH include policy interventions directed at housing, environment, occupation, taxation, and enfranchisement.[98] To a greater or lesser extent, there is generally evidence that laws and policies in each of these areas shape health and its distribution at the broad structural level.

Moreover, part of the argument for the relative priority of action on the social determinants is that many of these macrosocial determinants are common to both the developed and the developing world. Housing policies shape health in the United States and Europe, and in Sub-Saharan Africa.[99] The same is true for environmental exposures, occupation, and violence. Thus, the power of a whole population approach to global health is that it may have both horizontal and vertical effects, not merely across the international political order, but within regions and individual nation-states. Action on the social determinants is a global health priority because such action can improve population health, compress inequalities, and hence restructure the densely woven patterns of disadvantage that cause so much deprivation and human suffering in both the developed and developing world alike.

Conclusion

The thesis of this chapter is that Engels and Virchow were right in a number of ways. First, because the evidence strongly suggests that health care services are only a minor

---

[96] Navarro, *supra* note 41, at 207.
[97] World Health Organization Commission, *supra* note 17, at 50–59.
[98] *Id.* at 60–173.
[99] *Id.* at 60–71.

determinant of health and its distribution in human populations, health and health care must be distinguished. Second, socioeconomic conditions are far and away the most powerful determinants of health, whether in the global North or the global South. Social inequalities are robustly correlated with health inequalities; class structures and power relations are significant macrosocial determinants of health. Social disadvantage tends to accumulate, which means that so too do risk factors and poor health outcomes, with those located on the tail of the social gradient experiencing disproportionate burdens of disease and suffering.

Third, laws and policies are critical upstream factors that shape and determine health and its distribution. These laws and policies operate to affect health from the hyperlocal to the global; their influence is thus both vertical and horizontal across and within political economies. Fourth, laws and policies are caused by actors and entities past and present. Fifth, actors and entities in the developed world bear significant responsibility for creating and sustaining the international political economies that so strongly determine global health and its distribution. Sixth, relative priorities in global health policy can be arrayed according to Powers and Faden's account of social justice, which provides that inequalities that contribute to densely woven patterns of disadvantage are ethically paramount. Epidemiologic evidence suggests that addressing such inequalities via whole population approaches stands the best chance of improving overall population health and narrowing health inequalities. Seventh, it follows that the primary, albeit not exclusive, bundle of policies the developed world ought to follow are those tracking whole population approaches that emphasize action on macrosocial determinants of health.

Politics, Virchow famously noted, is nothing but medicine on a large scale. Understanding and acting on his admonition in the context of global health requires due attention to the critical distinction, one that likely would have been well-understood by Virchow and Engels, between global health and global health care.

23

GLOBAL RIGHTS AND THE SANCTITY OF LIFE

*Pavlos Eleftheriadis**

The Question

For the purposes of this chapter, I will assume that there is a moral right to health care. The right arises, let us say, from a number of philosophical arguments establishing the equal moral status and equal vulnerability of persons. But what follows from such statements? If there is a right to health care, it must help us specify duties of care or other means of health promotion, such as some public health policy. Further, the right must be universally applicable in the sense that it can specify duties in both domestic and international settings. This is true, for example, in the case of the right against torture or the right against religious discrimination, where the moral relation between right and duty is clearly visible. What is required by these rights follows from the manifest wrongness of torture and the manifest wrongness of intolerance. It is irrelevant whether the right holder is within or outside a particular jurisdiction, whether the right holder or the wrongdoer is a foreigner, or whether the violation takes place at home or abroad. This is what rights do: they determine categorical duties that everyone owes to everyone everywhere, without referring to the nationality or location or provenance of the beneficiary.

When we look at the documents establishing an international human right to health, such as the International Covenant on Economic, Social, and Cultural Rights of 1966, we find a different arrangement. There is no list of clear duties and no intimation of the manifest wrongness of the right's violation. Instead, we find obligations to achieve progressive realization of decent health levels, with those obligations contingent upon

* Fellow in Law, Mansfield College & University Lecturer in Law, University of Oxford. I am grateful to I. Glenn Cohen, Nir Eyal, Kevin Outterson, Jennifer Prah Ruger, and Dan Winkler for their comments and to Thana Campos for many discussions of these questions.

whether the necessary resources are available. This causes serious trouble for our conceptual framework. Are we still talking about rights? What theory can accommodate both categorical rights informed by manifest wrongness and non-categorical rights that aim at the "progressive realization" of a policy?

If both the right against torture and the right to health are moral rights, then there may be—surprisingly perhaps—two entirely different classes of rights: categorical and conditional. Categorical rights specify duties on the basis of a wrong, such as torture or religious discrimination. Conditional rights, by contrast, may specify duties that exist only when other political conditions apply, for example when government policy takes a particular direction to the benefit of some over others. But if the right to health is conditional, we cannot know whether rights violations have occurred without a precise view of economic and political conditions. The wrongness of the violation would dissolve into a general balancing of priorities and assessment of policy.

If such a distinction between categorical and conditional rights were to be accepted, then the simple proposition that there is a right to health would not tell us anything at all. We would need to know, in addition, which class of right the right to health involved. If it belonged to the categorical class, for example, then we would be guided in the clear way that the right against torture guides us. If, on the other hand, the right to health were classed as conditional, its duties would depend on satisfying the relevant social and economic conditions. We may also have something even more troubling: some aspects of health could fall under the first class and others under the second class.

This latter view, it seems to me, is the one that the international instruments implicitly take. The right to health is sometimes treated as a categorical right and at other times as a policy goal. The result is confusing indeed. Jennifer Prah Ruger summarizes these difficulties when she says that "one would be hard pressed to find a more controversial or nebulous human right than the right to health."[1] The difficulty is both philosophical and political, although the theoretical difficulty is more keenly felt. Human rights to health can be working political tools or rhetorical devices of persuasion, without being at the same time clear moral reasons.

The puzzle is not resolved when we look at legal rights. A legal right to health has a very specific context in a domestic case. No matter where, domestic rights to health operate against a thick background of law and policy. In the United Kingdom, for example, domestic rights to medical and social care were created by the National Health Service Act of 1977, the National Health Service and Community Care Act of 1990, the Health Act of 1999, and numerous other pieces of legislation and national and local government policy on social care.[2] In a recent case, the Supreme Court decided that a stroke victim did not on the facts of the case have a right to a night care provider, given the cost and the local authority's other policies. The Court issued its holding not on the basis of a general right to health, which is neither part of the constitutional law of the United Kingdom nor of the European Convention of Human Rights, but instead on

---

[1] JENNIFER PRAH RUGER, HEALTH AND SOCIAL JUSTICE 119 (2010).
[2] See CAROLINE BIELANSKA AND FIONA SCOLDING, HEALTH AND SOCIAL CARE HANDBOOK (2006).

the basis of various statutes on the provision of health care, for example the National Health Service and Community Care Act of 1990, and the National Assistance Act of 1948, the Chronically Sick and Disabled Persons Act of 1970, and on the basis of general principles of administrative law.[3]

There are many rights under English health and social care law, even though there is no single "right to health." In the international context, by contrast, there is no comparable backdrop of law and policy. Internationally, there is neither any legislature nor any public administration with responsibility to collect taxes and then spend the resources in social care for the whole world.

Given these peculiarities of the right to health, it may be tempting to conclude that there is no reason to speak of a single right to health that can operate in both domestic and international contexts. Yet accepting such a conclusion would be a loss to our moral thinking because it would deal a serious blow to our understanding of global inequality, because it would leave health disparities untouched. Still, how can we vindicate a global right to health in light of these complexities? In this chapter, I try to make a case for a right to health with global scope but narrow content.

I. The Challenge of Health Care Across Borders

It is difficult to establish the global perspective of a ubiquitous right to health because the human relations it captures are less frequent and less intense than those occurring within a single political community. I will start with two real examples of such relations.

A. THE SOUTH AFRICA AIDS LITIGATION

In the late 1990s, South Africa saw a very high rise in the number of HIV/AIDS infections. Most South Africans suffering from HIV/AIDS could not afford to pay for treatment with antiretroviral drugs. After much public disagreement with the local Pharmaceutical Manufacturer's Association, the South African government decided to enact legislation authorizing the parallel imports of patented pharmaceuticals. This became Section 15C of the South African Medicines and Related Substances Control Act. After the Act's passage, local manufacturers alleged that the law violated their intellectual property rights.

The issue was then taken up by the United States Pharmaceutical Research and Manufacturers of America, a powerful trade association, which brought civil proceedings before the South African High Court seeking to annul the change in the law. There followed a heated public debate in the world's media. Ralph Nader stated that Vice President Al Gore had engaged in "an astonishing array of bullying tactics to prevent

---

[3] R (on the application of McDonald) v. Royal Borough of Kensington and Chelsea, [2011] UKSC 33, *available at* http://www.supremecourt.gov.uk/docs/UKSC_2011_0005_Judgment.pdf.

South Africa from implementing policies, legal under international trade rules, that are designed to expand access to HIV/AIDS drugs."[4] The pharmaceutical companies obviously feared that the South African initiative would undermine their intellectual property rights in the developing world as a whole. The issue brought to the forefront the tension between intellectual property rights and health policy.[5]

After much criticism in the press, in April 2001 the companies dropped their action and section 15C remained the law. As a result of the controversy, the World Trade Organization (WTO) adopted the Declaration on the TRIPS Agreement and Public Health (Doha Declaration), which recognized the seriousness of the public health crisis *as well as* the legitimacy in principle of intellectual property protection for new medicines.[6]

B. OPERATION SMILE

Operation Smile is a British charity providing free surgery to repair cleft lips, cleft palates, and other facial deformities for children in developing countries. It regularly seeks donations by means of advertisements in newspapers. The advertisements show photographs of children before and after the surgical procedure. One does not need to see the photographs to understand that this is a highly effective campaign. The charity, according to their annual reports, received almost one million pounds in donations in 2009 and by all accounts has spent it very well.[7] One of their successful operations was on Rikta Ghosal, a young girl living in India. Her mother, Meehra Mondal Ghosal, is quoted on the charity's Web site:

> I am so extremely happy to see my daughter with a new face; it is a new life for her. God made her see the light of this world with a cleft lip and palate. But now Operation Smile has given back her smile, her life...My dream has come true today and I extend my most sincere regards and gratitude towards all those who have contributed towards realizing it. May God give you all long and happy lives. All the very best to all of you out there![8]

This heartfelt statement suggests that even a non-lifesaving operation can offer someone a new life. It is more than health care in the way that we tend to conceive of it.

---

[4] RALPH NADER, IN PURSUIT OF JUSTICE: COLLECTED WRITINGS 2000–2003 at 334 (2004).

[5] For an insightful analysis, see JOSEPH E. STIGLITZ, MAKING GLOBALIZATION WORK 103–32 (2006). *See also* Philippe Cullet, *Patents and Medicines: The Relationship between TRIPS and the Human Right to Health, in* PERSPECTIVES ON HEALTH AND HUMAN RIGHTS 179–202 (Sofia Gruskin, Michael A. Grodin, George J. Annas & Stephen P. Marks eds., 2005).

[6] One reason that the United States acquiesced to this declaration was that the United States and Canada had already expressed readiness to override patents on ciprofloxacine, held by the German company Bayer, given the drug's shortage during the anthrax scare of 2001, which killed five people and injured seventeen.

[7] OPERATION SMILE: UNITED KINGDOM, http://www.operationsmile.org.uk. (last visited Dec. 24, 2011).

[8] *See* Meera Mondal Ghosal, *Testimonals: Before and after Smiles*, OPERATION SMILE: UNITED KINGDOM, http://www.operationsmile.org.uk/testimonials/rikta/ (last visited Aug. 20, 2010).

C. THE MORAL CHALLENGE

How are we to understand the above examples of health and human relations? There is an immediate emotional reaction to the South Africa example, in that the pharmaceutical companies appear motivated by the basest of self-interests: they make money because people die. The fear of death is the best promotion of their products. Operation Smile, on the other hand, seems to run on the noblest of sentiments: pure benevolence. This initial reaction is perhaps too emotional. The pharmaceutical companies are motivated by self-interest, but they have put it to the best possible use. They risk billions of dollars on sophisticated biomedical research that would otherwise be unavailable. Their investment produces results that eventually benefit everyone, especially after their intellectual property rights expire, whereas they alone bear the risk of its failure. If these companies did not exist, their research units and their discoveries would not exist. Such an argument is very powerful. It was noticed by Adam Smith, who justified market relations by pointing out that he trusted not in his butcher's generosity of spirit but in his butcher's self-interest.[9] There is no wrong in the pursuit of profit through medical research.

Conversely, there is also a different side to Operation Smile. It is now well understood that pouring large amounts of aid dollars into developing countries ultimately harms the local economy, especially its exporters, because it changes the rate of currency exchange. By making the local currency more desirable, aid dollars make all exports more expensive and imports cheaper. Moreover, concentrating local resources in one well-paid area of medical care weakens all others, because professionals flock to the best-paid jobs. On a larger scale, public health must be the responsibility of governments; governments alone have the capacity to produce sustainable national systems of health and take responsibility for the appropriate ranking of priorities. External and ad hoc interference frustrates this long-term prioritizing.

Certainly, both examples raise important moral questions. Notice, however, the manner in which these questions change once we apply the idea that there is a global right to health. The argument about the long-term beneficial effects of a market in medicines becomes irrelevant. If there is a moral right to health, and if that right were categorical and not conditional, then the companies must be judged by a different standard. Their actions answer not to the test of the overall consequences but to claimable duties owed to specific individuals. Overall effects do not trump rights. We cannot justify the violation of rights on the basis of an increase in overall gain in productivity. So the introduction of the idea of rights transforms the moral debate. If the issue before us is not one of balancing but one of the violation of basic rights, then balancing is inappropriate. So we may have to argue, with Philippe Cullet, that "if compliance

---

[9] ADAM SMITH, WEALTH OF NATIONS 21 (Kathryn Sutherland ed., 2008): "It is not from the benevolence of the butcher, the brewer, or the baker, that we expect our dinner, but from their regard to their own interest. We address ourselves not to their humanity, but to their self-love, and never talk to them of our own necessities, but of their advantages. Nobody but a beggar chooses to depend chiefly upon the benevolence of his fellow-citizens."

with TRIPS leads to reduced access to drugs, this might imply a substantive violation of the ESCR Covenant."[10]

Notice that something similar happens in the Operation Smile example. If there is a human rights obligation of all states and all companies and all individuals to respect the human right to health, then Rikta Ghosal is actually the victim of a terrible injustice. Why did it take so long for the foreign surgeons to come to her rescue? What Operation Smile is doing cannot be seen to be giving charity. It is instead the long overdue remedy to an *injustice*. If anything, Rikta Ghosal's mother should be indignant that it took the surgeons so long. Being grateful instead of angry is thus a mark of her moral confusion, her ignorance of her rights—or at least this is where the human rights argument leads us. These concrete examples highlight the important implications of the debate on a moral right to health care.

II. Instrumental Theories

A popular philosophical view that is very influential in the human rights literature dissolves these dilemmas by means of an all-inclusive theory of rights. Under this view, rights serve *interests of well-being*. Such interests entail categorical duties sometimes and conditional duties at other times. The two classes of rights I have distinguished are, for this theory, really an expression of a single moral framework. What makes them rights is the connection between duties and a deeper layer of "interests."[11] Joseph Raz offers the most comprehensive defense of this view. He defines rights as "intermediate conclusions between statements of the right-holder's interests and another's duty."[12] The relationship between duty and interest is instrumental: the duty exists to promote the satisfaction of the interest.

This instrumental view defends a right to health on the basis of a distinct and sufficiently strong interest in health. Hessler and Buchanan have outlined precisely such a view of a right to health.[13] Hessler and Buchanan reject the view that the right to health is about "basic needs" because the idea of basic needs depends on social and cultural context and because of its implausible implications. For example, it is obvious that someone suffering from heart disease may need a heart transplant as a basic need in the sense that it would be essential to his or her survival. Yet, we cannot draw the conclusion that for this reason alone such a person has a right to a heart transplant.

---

[10] Cullet, *supra* note 5, at 194.

[11] *See* Neil MacCormick, *Rights in Legislation, in* Law, Morality and Society: Essays in Honour of H.L.A. Hart 189 (P.M. S. Hacker and J. Raz eds., 1977), Joseph Raz, The Morality of Freedom 165–92 (1986). For a qualified endorsement of Raz's view, see Amartya Sen, The Idea of Justice 376–79 (2009).

[12] Joseph Raz, Ethics in the Public Domain 259 (rev. ed., 1995).

[13] Kristen Hessler & Allen Buchanan, *Specifying the Content of the Human Right to Health Care, in* Medicine and Social Justice: Essays on the Distribution of Health Care 84–96 (Rosamond Rhodes, Margaret P. Battin & Anita Silvers eds., 2002). The essay is reprinted in Allen Buchanan, Justice and Health Care: Selected Essays 203 (2009).

Indeed, there *cannot* be such a right "[b]ecause donor hearts are scarce, and because a social guarantee of a heart transplant for everyone as needed would be prohibitively expensive, it would be impossible to guarantee heart transplants to all who need them to survive for a significant time."[14]

From this, Hessler and Buchanan conclude that the right to health care is not really the right to anything necessary to ensure anyone's survival. The key point here is in selecting an interest of well-being that is not simply of value to its holder but of paramount importance to all: "[T]he claim that health care is a human right is much stronger than the claim that health care is a good thing, or that it is desirable that all people have health care. One does not have a right to all those things that might increase one's well-being...Rather, human rights are moral entitlements..."[15] Not everything good is of paramount importance for all. So the interest that grounds the right is to be distinguished from the unspecified good or avoidance of harm that general benevolence may require of us.

The instrumental theory turns the dilemmas we faced in the South Africa example into a search for relevant moral "interests." Both sides may be seen to argue for the defense of such interests. The interests of the HIV/AIDS patients argue for the satisfaction of their immediate need for lifesaving treatment. The corporations can also argue in defense of the more long-term health interests of all people benefiting from medical research, which can only be served if intellectual property is respected. In such situations, Hessler and Buchanan conclude that all we can resort to is balancing. Thus, interests of well-being are not merely individual but are also collective, and some balance must be struck between the two. Raz also agrees with this approach when he states that rights are primarily about individual interests but can also, under certain conditions, be protections of the "common good."[16]

One question is: how do we strike this balance? A second question is: who ought to be the one to strike it? Hessler and Buchanan observe that in the case of the right to health, the balance should not be performed by international bodies, which may not be familiar with cultural characteristics that will be relevant to the specification of the right to health in a particular society. They candidly admit that "the fact that the human right to health care is grounded in the basic human interest in health does not imply anything about the specific content of the right to health care."[17] They admit the right's "vagueness." They argue that there can be no single, universal standard, and conclude that the answer lies in domestic democratic procedures, such as the lawmaking process of parliaments.[18] So in the end, for Hessler and Buchanan the right to health does not create any determinate duties, much less categorical ones. It creates only a requirement for a political procedure.

The Operation Smile example highlights a further problem. Let us say that the interests of the suffering children are found to be of paramount importance, compared with

---

[14] Hessler & Buchanan, *supra* note 13, at 89.

[15] *Id.* at 85.

[16] RAZ, *supra* note 12, at 44, 51.

[17] Hessler & Buchanan, *supra* note 13, at 92.

[18] *Id.* at 94.

the costs associated with the surgery. Does this tell us that the children have rights against: a) all foreign surgeons, b) all potential donors in the world or c) their own state's health system? I assume that most people would say c) and not a), or b). No surgeon can be bound by a moral duty to fly halfway around the world to help foreign patients to whom he or she is not already somehow connected. But how can we draw a distinction between a), b), and c), if rights are entailments of interests? The interest theory tells us that rights arise out of the interests of the intended beneficiary not out of personal or social relations. The recipient is the same in a), b), and c)—hence the problem. The interest theory cannot accommodate a distinction that most people consider natural.

III. Political Theories of Rights

I now wish to examine the South Africa and Operation Smile examples from the point of view of what I shall call "political theories" of rights. Such theories consider rights as primarily institutional arrangements. This institutional dimension is political in a straightforward sense: it arises out of the set of basic public rules that organize collective decision making in a community. This is what the classical political philosophers call the "civil condition." Political theories of rights distinguish between, on the one hand, moral rights that operate on agents universally and, on the other, political rights that bind officials when they act in the name of a political community by making use of its decision-making institutions. The argument is based on a fundamental commonality between moral rights and political rights. The right against torture—or the right against violation of one's bodily integrity such as the right against assault—is both a moral right enjoyed by everyone against everyone and a political right enjoyed against state institutions. The content is roughly the same in the two cases: the avoidance of intentional harm for the sake of breaking another person's will. The duty is violated in exactly the same way by a rogue policeman or a businessman's thug.

We cannot say the same about duties to provide for the poor. We are not certain how to alleviate poverty in the world, nor do we have in mind a particular action that would do so. Moreover, it is evident that no single person can provide for all the poor in the world. So there cannot be any such responsibility or any such universal right. Onora O'Neill explains this point as follows:

> Only failure to comply with universal obligations (owed to all others) or with special obligations (owed to others because of some special relationship) can violate rights. No agent or agency can have obligations to provide services, help and benefits for all others. Nobody can feed all the hungry, so the obligation to feed the hungry cannot be a universal obligation, and most of those who are hungry have no special relationship in virtue of which others should feed them, so special obligations will not be enough to remedy poverty and hunger.[19]

---

[19] Onora O'Neill, Faces of Hunger: An Essay on Poverty, Justice and Development 101 (1986).

Torture creates far more immediate duties. Its wrongness is a manifestation of a deeper principle that runs through our moral life and our law. This is the idea that the human body is inviolable and its integrity an end in itself. What animates this idea? Everyone understands that our vulnerability as agents largely is due to our bodily needs, the fact that we face hunger and feel pain or that we experience fear and stress in particularly debilitating ways. Without this bodily existence, of course, we are not agents at all. We know that our existence is tied to the continuing functions of this body. These are human fundamentals that inform the way we think about many categories of moral issues, from injuries and risk to health care and old-age pensions.

One way of expressing this thought it that of the sanctity of life, which is to be protected before any other aspect of physical integrity. The sanctity of life is a universal idea, as all cultures and peoples reject intentional killing as wrong in principle. Here is Ronald Dworkin's account, which in my view can work as a basis for any theory of the value of life:

> The life of a single human organism commands respect and protection...no matter in what form or shape, because of the complex creative investment it represents and because of our wonder at the divine or evolutionary processes that produce new lives from old ones, at the processes of nation and community and language through which a human being will come to absorb and continue hundreds of generations of cultures and forms of life and value, and finally, when mental life has begun and flourishes, at the process of internal personal creation and judgment by which a person will make and remake himself, a mysterious, inescapable process in which we each participate, and which is therefore the most powerful and inevitable source of empathy and communion we have with every other creature who faces the same frightening challenge. The horror we feel in the wilful destruction of a human life reflects our shared inarticulate sense of the intrinsic importance of each of these dimensions of investment."[20]

As all human cultures share these or similar ideas about the sanctity of life, this set of ideas can be seen as a fundamental presupposition of our moral codes and our laws, be they private, public, or criminal. To appreciate the significance of this argument, we do not need a theory of well-being or a theory of what else is good in life. The sanctity of life is presupposed by all prohibitions against violence and murder. It sets out a universal standard. The same attitude creates political rights and duties because it makes it essential that any common life set outs laws and procedures that make the prohibition public and effective. So we may say that the moral right to life leads to a political right to life, that is, to an effective system of civil and criminal justice.

We may now draw a further distinction between universal political rights and universal cosmopolitan rights. Such rights link political communities with the citizens

---

[20]   RONALD DWORKIN, LIFE'S DOMINION: AN ARGUMENT ABOUT ABORTION, EUTHANASIA AND INDIVIDUAL FREEDOM 84 (1993).

of other states. It is obvious that the right to life does create cosmopolitan rights and duties.[21] Governments cannot treat outsiders with indifference, as if their lives were irrelevant. This is precisely what the conventions for the protection of refugees have long established. Asylum seekers have immediate rights under these conventions to fair treatment and to asylum if their claims are justified. Universal cosmopolitan rights may also work indirectly. If we wish to respect the equal moral status of all other persons, we ought to recognize the duty and responsibility of all others to create a legitimate civil condition for themselves. We may thus say that the equal status of persons entails the equal standing of all states. So an aggressive foreign policy that sought the subjection of a neighboring people through force would be a violation of the political rights of that people to self-determination. This is a cosmopolitan right we all enjoy, because it is owed by all governments to all people.

We can now return to our examples. Do children suffering from facial disfigurement have moral or political rights against faraway surgeons? In the two examples, the sanctity of life and the integrity of the human body are at issue. Here, the distance between the parties matters. As O'Neill explained above, the duty to aid those to whom we are not in a special relationship is very weak. We may say that the duty to aid in such circumstances exists only when the benefit to them is high, the cost to us low, and we are linked by some other kind of proximity.[22] When distances are long and special relationships absent, a general moral duty of benevolence must remain imperfect and unspecified. So no such moral right is enjoyed by Rikta against the doctors. The suffering children do not have such an entitlement against them, and the foreign surgeons are not burdened by such a duty.

What about the pharmaceuticals example? Here the context is different. The disagreement is about private law entitlements and especially the protection of intellectual property rights. We have moved away from the domain of personal ethics to the domain of institutions. As we have seen, there are important differences. Private law, of which intellectual property law is a part, is a public set of institutions whereby private relations can be met with remedies through a complex scheme of civil justice. What is distinct in this domain is the jurisdiction of a court in determining legal relations in a conclusive way on the basis of public standards.

This kind of institutionally grounded jurisdiction is entirely absent from a private code of conduct. Morality has no remedies and no judges. Civil or criminal jurisdiction is, by contrast, a public matter. The move from the simple code of private conduct to private and criminal law requires, therefore, a new step: the setting up of appropriate institutions of law and justice and, in the end, government itself. Once these institutions are set up, they are to operate according to procedures of publicity, openness, and fair process. This makes the ideal of just rules different from that of unencumbered

---

[21] Cosmopolitan, Statist, and Intermediate theories of global justice are further discussed by I. Glenn Cohen in his chapter in this volume.

[22] Dworkin calls this proximity "confrontation" or "salience." See RONALD DWORKIN, JUSTICE FOR HEDGEHOGS 271–83 (2011).

moral introspection of agents about what action to choose. Institutional decision makers are not to act according to their own code of personal conduct.[23] It follows that political rights and duties will be something different from individual requirements to act in this or that way. They are institutional, not personal.

IV. Political Rights and Duties

Every state in the world and practically every culture has rules about assault, robbery, and murder. In such settings, moral intuitions call for restraining violence and exploitation for the sake of life itself and the bodily and personal integrity of individuals. It makes no difference whether or not a crime victim is a foreigner.

Given these universal moral imperatives, a fundamental human experience has been the collective establishment of institutions that, among other things, aim to protect everyone from wrongdoing. This pattern has strong theoretical roots: philosophers such as Kant, Rawls, and Waldron argue that there is a natural duty of justice, owed to all human beings, to act in such a way as to set up, or support and maintain legitimate public institutions of law and government that protect all of us from wrongs.[24] This natural duty of justice sits alongside the natural or basic duties we owe to others with regard to our conduct toward them. So the sanctity of life works on us twice: first by imposing a moral duty not to injure or endanger others and, second, to set up institutions that enforce this protection against wrongdoers. One might conclude, then, that the natural duty of justice is an interpersonal duty even though it gives effect to a new domain of social action: the political domain. The same personal duty requires that we do not kill and that the structures of law and government that we support make killing a crime.

Once the institutions of collective power are set up, they ought to be committed to principles that are publicly outlined and debated. These principles need to be general and abstract and suitable for interpretation by adjudicating bodies. In outlining public standards of conduct we ought to give them a new formality. Institutions are therefore supposed to work with abstraction about general responses to the problems before them. So in the end we must evaluate institutions as generalizations, in abstraction from the particular persons who happen to occupy them or the record of their decisions.

International law and institutions are part of the same institutional system and part of the same argument. If a civil condition is to survive, it will need the recognition and support of other civil conditions. If, for example, states do not recognize each others' registration of births and deaths and other states' passports, no stable system

---

[23] I have elaborated on this thought and its significance for the philosophy of law in Pavlos Eleftheriadis, Legal Rights 51–67 (2008).

[24] Immanuel Kant, *Metaphysics of Morals*, 6:306, *in* Kant, Practical Philosophy 450 (Mary J. Gregor trans., ed., 1996); John Rawls, A Theory of Justice 99 (rev. ed., 1999); Jeremy Waldron, *Special Ties and Natural Duties*, 22 Phil. & Pub. Aff. 3 (1993).

of private law or trade between states can be maintained (for, without this recognition, a person travelling to another state would have no recourse to legal rights). The same applies to the registration of companies. It follows that jurisdictions need to recognize the equal status of other jurisdictions. This is the genesis of a theory of legitimacy of international law. Just as there are constitutional essentials that determine the legitimacy of domestic institutions, there are moral essentials that determine the legitimacy of international institutions.

We can now return to the idea of a basic right to health and examine it as a political right. No one can live a moral life while ignoring the vulnerability of other human beings. Health is relevant to all three basic ideas that inform rights, namely life, liberty, and equality. We have duties not to injure others and duties not to exploit another's weakness for personal gain; on the contrary, we sometimes have a duty to affirmatively aid others, at least when we can do so without risk to ourselves. Such duties correspond to the most basic moral rights to health.

Yet it is obvious that it is not health itself that matters for these moral relations. What matters is the equal moral status of vulnerable human beings, whose life and liberty may be at stake when our political institutions have an impact on their lives. Those who are sick and their families are open to all sorts of exploitation and abuse by those who claim they can help. The urgent need for care creates an opportunity for exploitation and domination. Such forms of imposition and oppression are all wrong according to simple principles of conduct. They are wrong not because they prevent well-being, but because by being exploitative and humiliating they destroy our equal standing.[25] There is nothing special about health in this respect. It just happens that our mental and physical vulnerabilities are fertile grounds for injustice.

The setting up of a civil condition changes the mutual relations between those who are its members. Without the civil condition, their relations are informal. With the civil condition in place, its members become cocreators of political institutions and of a system of jurisdiction. If we are fellow citizens, then we are responsible for the benefits and burdens that result from our mutual cooperation. The creation of public institutions makes it possible for us to influence—and perhaps radically so—the lives of our fellow human beings. This creates a new moral responsibility for the results of our association. Rawls has called this the problem of social justice and argued that it is here that distributive justice become important. The members of a just civil condition must consider themselves responsible for the distribution of benefits and burdens among its members. And this must include health and health care. It follows that setting up a system of distribution of health care must be a duty for all. It arises as one of the conditions for satisfying the natural duty of justice. So the continuity between moral rights to life and political rights entails that there is a basic political right to live in a political community that is sensitive to human vulnerability and the need for equal access to health

---

[25] For some illuminating reflections on humiliation and poverty, see Avishai Margalit, The Decent Society 225–31 (Naomi Goldblum trans., 1996).

care. It does not follow that the system must be entirely publicly owned or entirely free. But it does follow that some such system ought to be in place.[26] It may also follow that such a system must provide what Jennifer Prah Ruger calls a "universal benefits package," namely a set of goods and services that addresses what she calls "central health capabilities."[27]

Are there any other rights with regard to health in addition to this basic political right? Our common legal experience is that there are. The British National Health Service, for example, creates a number of rights to health, as we saw above. These entitlements are not based on equal moral status or citizenship alone. They are derivative rights and duties whose authority is based on institutional action, for example, legislation and adjudication. Their authority is based on the political procedure that brought them about, not on their content or an account of manifest wrongness. In that sense, they are not morally basic. They are legislated entitlements that signal a choice, say, preferring one scheme of public distribution of resources over another. What makes them rights is their structure as bilateral sets of legal relations, that is, the fact that they organize claims and duties, liberties and no-rights, powers and liabilities, immunities and disabilities in meaningful grids of public reasoning. These are rights by analogy, not by way of their content. They are related to health, but do not outline a basic moral right to health. Alongside them we have publicly stated and endorsed goals that may entail "progressive realization" whenever appropriate conditions are in place.

Here, then, is a typology of rights and goals:

(i) *Basic moral rights and duties* outline basic standards of personal conduct with universal validity, focusing on the integrity of life, liberty, and equality.

(ii) *Basic political rights and duties* set out patterns of abstract and formal moral and legal relations in public relationships that can take the form of institutional rules and constitute preconditions of constitutional legitimacy; they are not entitlements to any particular aspect of well-being, but claims to respect life, autonomy, and equal citizenship whose effect is categorical and unconditional.

(iii) *Legislated political rights and duties* set out patterns of abstract and formal legal relations under a public system of collective decision making (involving parliaments, governments, and courts).

(iv) *Public political goals* set general standards of progressive realization, assuming certain conditions are satisfied, without specifying claimable duties.

---

[26] Some such view is carefully articulated and defended by Paul Hunt and Gunilla Backman, who argue for an effective health system as a "core institution" on a par with a "fair justice system and or democratic political system." *See* Paul Hunt & Gunilla Backman, *Health Systems and the Right to the Highest Attainable Standard of Health, in* REALISING THE HUMAN RIGHT TO HEALTH 40–59, 41 (Andrew Clapham & Mary Robinson eds., 2009).

[27] RUGER, *supra* note 1, at 184–87.

V. International Rights and Duties

What does this argument mean for international political rights? We have seen that if we are to live as equal members in a political community, then our institutions need to bring about processes by which we are protected from the risk of suffering and vulnerability that would make it impossible for us to live as equal members. But our institutions must also create processes and institutions that permit or at least do not impede the similar efforts of other peoples to set up legitimate institutions of law and government for themselves. It follows, I believe, that one of the conditions of legitimacy of international legal structures must be a duty binding all governments to protect and promote basic rights abroad. International relations cannot be legitimate on the basis that states can allow other states to violate the basic rights of their citizens.[28]

This produces a first category of international rights and duties as preconditions for the legitimacy of any international system. These are rights that states must assume to be true in any effort to engage in foreign relations with other states and in any effort to formulate standards of international law. They are constitutional essentials for international law:

(v) *Basic international political rights* are political rights that need to be respected by all states in their relations with other states for any legitimate processes of international law to be possible; they outline abstract and formal standards of conduct centered around respect for life, liberty, and equality that bind all states as subjects of international law.

This argument seeks to give expression to an idea offered by John Rawls, namely that a list of international human rights does not seek to replace the domestic list and apply it universally.

International rights are standards for the reciprocal relations of political societies. This is why Rawls's list of international human rights includes elementary rights that seem to offer less than the classic liberal canon. For Rawls, international rights include only the right to life (to the means of subsistence and security), to liberty (to freedom from slavery, serfdom, and forced occupation), and to a sufficient measure of liberty of conscience to ensure freedom of religion and thought; to property (personal property); and to formal equality as expressed by the rules of natural justice (which mandate that similar cases be treated similarly).[29] This list does not replace the list of basic rights that is defended in *Political Liberalism*.[30] It just applies to a different question: the question of legal relations among states that all could see as legitimate.[31]

---

[28] For this point, see Thomas W. Pogge, World Poverty and Human Rights: Cosmopolitan Responsibilities and Reforms 49 (2002).

[29] John Rawls, The Law of Peoples 65 (1999).

[30] John Rawls, Political Liberalism (1993).

[31] This does not mean that a state ought not to respect liberty and equality fully. It means that we cannot set up a mutually acceptable set of international legal institutions on the basis that all states adopt liberal ideals. We criticize decent but illiberal societies for their failure to fully respect liberty and equality, even if we welcome them into the society of peoples.

The legitimacy of international law opens the space, however, for a further category of rights and duties. Just as domestic institutions can create legislated rights, specifying claims and duties and other legal relations that are based on legitimate political decisions, so too may international decision making produce valid international standards for those subscribing to them. We thus have:

(vi) *Legislated international rights* that create clusters of legal relations that bind governments in their mutual relations, to treat their own populations in a certain way under some international system of supervision.

These are the rights created by the various documents of the human rights canon. We can thus read the international documents on the right to health not as affirmation of a basic moral right, but as legislated commitments that states make to each other.

And if this is true, then it must be equally possible to have the following:

(vii) *International policy goals* are those public policy aims collectively adopted by legitimate international decision making, even though such goals do not have the formality of clusters of legal relations (e.g., the goal of reducing global warming).

If this argument is correct, then not everything in the international human rights canon should be treated as a basic international right. There is room for both basic rights and for legislated rights or social goals. These three types of standards do not develop the same moral effects.

VI. Global Rights and Private Law

I wish now to return to the example of pharmaceutical companies working in South Africa and seeking to enforce their intellectual property rights. They must be taken to be arguing that the health needs of HIV/AIDS sufferers do not necessarily trump the legitimacy of the institutional structure of private law, which includes intellectual property law. In a way, what they seek is not incompatible with the idea of a basic health system. Without an effective system of intellectual property rights, no health system would be possible. An adequate solution would give effect to both moral imperatives: the need to promote research through intellectual property rights and the urgent needs of patients. Indeed, some such public standard of conduct is proposed by Joseph Stiglitz, who argues for several possible institutional solutions, from compulsory licenses to an "innovation fund."[32] A similar proposal has been put forward by

---

[32]   Joseph E. Stiglitz, Making Globalization Work 120–32 (2006).

Thomas Pogge along the lines of a "Health Impact Fund."[33] Such solutions are, in principle, open to political institutions with the power and authority to legislate.

Are there any moral limits to a system of intellectual property law imposed by a basic right to life? I think that an argument can be built along the lines mentioned above by O'Neill and the duty to rescue. Private law recognizes threats to life as an overriding reason in numerous ways. As Ernest J. Weinrib has put it: "[W]hen there is an emergency that the rescuer can alleviate with no inconvenience to himself, the general duty of beneficence that is suspended over society like a floating charge is temporarily revealed to identify a particular obligor and obligee, and to define obligations that are specific enough for judicial enforcement."[34] In such emergencies, private law recognizes a duty to rescue that goes beyond all other entitlements. So we may say that whatever the WTO agreements provide, all private law must recognize a basic moral limit at the point of respect for the sanctity of life. When access to medicines can be achieved without loss for the global pharmaceutical companies, then their private law rights must give way.

Kevin Outterson and Donald Light have argued on exactly such grounds that pharmaceutical companies are bound both in South Africa and elsewhere by the duty to contribute to the rescue of human lives when the importance of the rescue is high, their capacity is available, and the cost to them is low. Such a contribution may take the form, for example, of making available their intellectual property for free.[35] An additional test is that these companies must stand in a special proximity or special relationship with those suffering. Outterson and Light say that the test is satisfied when the companies have benefited from research and development funding out of the public purse.

The analysis offered above provides a clearer private law argument. When pharmaceutical companies operate in any given jurisdiction, they stand to benefit from the stability, such as it may be, of its institutions. They enter foreign markets when they judge that they can make profits on the basis of a system of effective contract and property. By entering a jurisdiction for profit, they become stakeholders in that jurisdiction. This is, to my mind, a relation of proximity that satisfies the moral test. It follows that companies hold duties to rescue toward other stakeholders operating in the same jurisdiction. By choosing to seek enforcement of their intellectual property rights in a state by mans of a system of civil justice, the companies submit themselves to the same system of private law rights that applies to everyone else. So the argument offered by Outterson and Light works in every jurisdiction. By the ordinary principles of private law, intellectual property rights are to be limited in any cases where an emergency creates a duty to rescue.

---

[33] Thomas Pogge, *The Health Impact Fund: How to Make New Medicines Accessible to All, in* GLOBAL HEALTH AND GLOBAL HEALTH ETHICS 241–50 (Solomon Benatar & Gillian Brock eds., 2011). The fund is further discussed in Outterson and Pogge's chapter in this volume.

[34] Ernest J. Weinrib, *The Case for a Duty to Rescue*, 90 YALE L.J. 247, 292 (1980).

[35] Kevin Outterson & Donald W. Light, *Global Pharmaceutical Markets, in* A COMPANION TO BIOETHICS 417 (Helga Kuhse & Peter Singer, eds., 2d ed. 2009).

Conclusion

What global rights to health care exist? I have argued that basic moral rights to health care exist in two cases. First, they exist when persons have a moral duty to respect the sanctity of life, by avoiding injury or risk to others, or to give aid to those in need. This also creates a right to be rescued by those with whom we are in some special relationship or in special proximity. Second, there is also a basic political right to health care against one's own government, whenever such a government exercises jurisdiction over persons and territory. The content of the right is the setting up of an effective health system—parallel, perhaps to a general system of civil and criminal justice— enabling individuals to live without fear of violence or exploitation. The source of this right includes a principle of equal citizenship, which ought to be a constitutional precondition of political legitimacy. Other rights and duties of the human rights canon are simply legislated rights or established policies. I conclude that it is a mistake to see the international human right to health as a single moral principle. Behind the slogan, there are several other principles at work. These complexities are clarified once we take rights to establish moral relations among persons, not entitlements of recipients under an instrumental view. What remains to be seen, however, is whether the ideas on which the political theory of rights is based—those of life, liberty, and equal citizenship—are robust enough to deliver the necessary content in global contexts. I briefly discussed the idea of the sanctity of life and suggested that Dworkin's formulation may work as a viable test. More work needs to be done to connect the theory of international human rights with such fundamental moral ideas. Such a task is important both for philosophy and law. In this domain, philosophical clarity and political effectiveness seem to me to go hand in hand.

Index

DATE DUE

JUL 1 6 2013		

GAYLORD   #3522PI   Printed in USA